THE LETTERS OF
A. E. HOUSMAN

THE LETTERS OF
A. E. HOUSMAN

VOLUME I

EDITED BY
ARCHIE BURNETT

CLARENDON PRESS · OXFORD

OXFORD
UNIVERSITY PRESS

Great Clarendon Street, Oxford OX2 6DP

Oxford University Press is a department of the University of Oxford.
It furthers the University's objective of excellence in research, scholarship,
and education by publishing worldwide in

Oxford New York

Auckland Cape Town Dar es Salaam Hong Kong Karachi
Kuala Lumpur Madrid Melbourne Mexico City Nairobi
New Delhi Shanghai Taipei Toronto

With offices in

Argentina Austria Brazil Chile Czech Republic France Greece
Guatemala Hungary Italy Japan Poland Portugal Singapore
South Korea Switzerland Thailand Turkey Ukraine Vietnam

Oxford is a registered trade mark of Oxford University Press
in the UK and in certain other countries

Published in the United States
by Oxford University Press Inc., New York

British Library Cataloguing in Publication Data

Data available

Library of Congress Cataloging in Publication Data

Data available

Typeset by Laserwords Private Limited, Chennai, India
Printed in Great Britain
on acid-free paper by
Antony Rowe Ltd, Chippenham, Wilts

ISBN 978-0-19-818496-6

1 3 5 7 9 10 8 6 4 2

ACKNOWLEDGEMENTS

I have great pleasure in recording with gratitude the names of those who have supplied that collaboration without which scholarship is not possible: the late Frederick B. Adams, Jr, and Mrs Adams; Vicky Aldus; Sue Campion; Tom Chandler; John and Janice Chesney; the late Alan Clodd; Professor Stefan Collini; Dr Justin Croft; Jeremy Crow of the Society of Authors; G. David, Bookseller, Cambridge (Neil Adams, David Asplin, B. Collings); Professor James Diggle; Professor Fraser Drew; Alex B. Effgen; Peter Fielden; Professor Benjamin Franklin Fisher IV; Professor L. E. Fraenkel; Jason Freeman; Adam Gitner (who translated two letters in Latin); Professor Wolfgang Haase; Dr Rinard Z. Hart; Professor Kenneth Haynes; Tim Pearce Higgins; Dr Leofranc Holford-Strevens (who cast an expert eye over letters dealing with classical subjects); Thomas Jones; Professor John Kelly; Paul Knobel; Peter Knottley; the Earl of Lytton; Dr John Maddicott; Jim McCue; Allyson McDermott; Janet Moore; the late Howard Moseley; Professor Joel Myerson; Jim Page; Marcus Perkins; Professor Rob Pope; E. W. M. Richardson; Professor Christopher Ricks; W. M. B. Ritchie; Elizabeth Robottom; Christine Rode; Crispin Rowe; the late Jeanne Sheehy; Professor Nicholas Shrimpton; Peter Sisley; Professor Alan Smith; Sotheby's (London); James R. Skypeck; Professor W. Keats Sparrow; Tony Thompson; Professor Robert B. Todd; Ulysses, Bookseller (London); Veronica Watts; Frances Whistler; Professor Henry Woudhuysen (who generously made available not only the Housman–Pollard letters but the notes of his privately published edition too); and Ellen O'Reilly Wrigley.

Special mention must be made of Paul Naiditch. By inviting me to Los Angeles to consult his files, by publishing his invaluable census of Housman's correspondence in the *Housman Society Journal*, and by communicating information from time to time about the rare book and manuscript trade, he greatly advanced the work towards completion. During the late stages, he answered numerous queries, read the script, and compiled the index. Hardly a page has not been improved by his published work. His scholarship and his friendship have been an inspiration for over twenty years.

I am very grateful to the Arts and Humanities Research Board in Britain for funding a Research Assistant for two and a half years. The appointment of Alison Waller in October 1999 breathed new life into the work. Following a move to Boston University in January 2001, I enjoyed the magical experience of expressing wishes by e-mail to her at Oxford Brookes University and then, within a week, finding they had come true. In the summer of 2005, thanks to funding from my colleague Christopher Ricks's Distinguished Achievement Award from the Andrew W. Mellon foundation, I enjoyed the privilege of research assistance from Daniel Harney, a graduate of the Editorial Institute at Boston University. Thanks to funding from Boston University, he was ably succeeded by another of the Institute's graduate students, James Sitar.

I have been greatly assisted by the staffs of various libraries and archives: Alfred University, New York (Laurie L. McFadden); Balliol College Library, Oxford (Anna Sander); the Bayerische Staatsbibliothek, Munich; Birmingham City Archives (Christine O'Brien); the Bodleian Library (Colin Harris); the John J. Burns Library, Boston College (John Attebury); Boston University Library (Sean D. Noel); Brigham Young University Library; the British Library (Lora Afric, Dr Arnold Hunt); the Mariam Coffin Canaday Library, Bryn Mawr College, Pennsylvania (Marianne Hansen, Kathy Whalen); the Bancroft Library, University of California, Berkeley; the William Andrews Clark Memorial Library, University of California, Los Angeles (Bruce Whiteman); the Charles E. Young Research Library, University of California, Los Angeles; California State University at East Bay, Hayward (Lucille Klovdahl); Cambridge University Library (Kathleen Cann); Christ's College Library, Cambridge (Candace J. E. Guite); the Dorset County Museum (Richard de Peyer); the University Library, University of Durham (Elizabeth Rainey); Emmanuel College Library, Cambridge (Dr H. Carron, Mrs Janet Morris, Gregory O'Malley, Professor Barry Windeatt); Eton College Library (Michael Meredith); Robert Manning Strozier Library, Florida State University Library (Deborah Rouse); Glasgow University Library (Simon Bennett); Gloucester Library (Graham Baker); Godalming Museum (Anne Collingridge, Alison Pattison); Guildford House Gallery (Tracey Mardles); the University of Illinois at Urbana-Champaign Library (Bruce Swann); the Lilly Library, Indiana University (Rebecca C. Cape, Elizabeth Powers, Saundra Taylor); the Milton S. Eisenhower Library, Johns Hopkins University (Joan Grattan); Kent State University Library (Jennifer Schrager); King Edward's School Library and Archive, Bath (Paul Davies, Dr F. R. Thorn); King's College Library, Cambridge (Jacqueline Cox, Dr Rosalind Moad); the King's

School Library, Canterbury (Peter Henderson, Paul Pollock); the Brotherton Library, Leeds University (Malcolm C. Davis, Jacqui Taylor); the Library of Congress; The Pepys Library, Magdalene College, Cambridge (Aude Fitzsimons); the John Rylands University Library, Manchester University (Peter McNiven); McGill University Library (Richard Virr); Merton College Library, Oxford (Fiona Wilkes); the University Library, University of Michigan (Kathryn L. Beam); the National Library of Scotland (Sally Harrower, Sheila Mackenzie); the National Library of Wales; the Newberry Library, Chicago; the Robinson Library, University of Newcastle (Dr Lesley Gordon); the Henry W. and Albert A. Berg Collection, New York Public Library (Stephen Crook); the Fales Library, New York University; Northwestern University Library (Sigrid P. Perry); Oxford Union Society Library (Dr David Johnson); Oxford University Press Archives (Dr Martin Maw, Melanie Pidd); Peterhouse College Library, Cambridge (Erica Macdonald); the Pierpont Morgan Library, New York (Christine Nelson, Robert Parks), Princeton University Library (Margaret Rich, AnnaLee Pauls); Reading University Library (Verity Andrews, Michael Bott); the Royal Academy of Arts Library (A. W. Potter); the Royal Archives, Windsor (Pamela Clark); the School of Oriental and African Studies Library, University of London (Alison Field); the Library, The Schools, Shrewsbury (James Lawson); the Morris Library, Southern Illinois University at Carbondale (Katharine Salzmann); the University Library, St Andrews (Mrs Rachel M. Hart, Meic Pierce Owen; Norman H. Reid); St John's College Library, Cambridge (Mrs Fiona Colbert, Jonathan Harrison, Ruth Ogden); St John's College Library, Oxford (Catherine Hilliard, the late Angela Williams); Somerville College Library, Oxford (Pauline Adams); The Harry Ransom Research Center, University of Texas at Austin (Molly Wheeler); the Wren Library, Trinity College, Cambridge (Diana Chardin, Adam C. Green, Dr David McKitterick, Jonathan Smith); Trinity College Library, Dublin (Estelle Gittins); the D. M. S. Watson Library, University College London (Julie Archer-Gosnay, Dr Matthew Clear, Rebekah Higgitt, Steven Wright); the National Art Library, Victoria and Albert Museum, London (Laura Try); University of Virginia Library (Eva M. Chandler, Margaret Downs Hrabe); the University of Wales Library, Aberystwyth (Chris Wilkins); Waseda University Library, Tokyo; Washington State University Library (Robert N. Matuozzi); Wellesley College Library, Massachusetts; West Sussex Record Office (Richard J. Childs); Winchester College Library (Suzanne Foster); Worcester College Library, Oxford (Dr Joanna Parker); the Beinecke Library, Yale University (Ngadi W. Kponou).

CONTENTS

ABBREVIATIONS

Ackerman (1974)	Robert Ackerman, 'Sir James G. Frazer and A. E. Housman: A Relationship in Letters', *Greek, Roman, and Byzantine Studies*, 15. 3 (1974), 339–64
AEH	Alfred Edward Housman (1859–1936)
AP	*Additional Poems* (1937; supplemented 1939)
Ashburner/Bell	*A. E. Housman. Fifteen Letters to Walter Ashburner*, ed. Alan Bell (1976)
ASL	*A Shropshire Lad* (1896)
Banfield (1985)	Stephen Banfield, *Sensibility and English Song: Critical Studies of the Early Twentieth Century* (1985)
Bancroft	The Bancroft Library, University of California, Berkeley
Berg	The Henry W. and Albert A. Berg Collection, New York Public Library
BL	The British Library, London
BMC	The Adelman Collection, Mariam Coffin Canaday Library, Bryn Mawr College, Bryn Mawr, Pennsylvania
Bodleian	The Bodleian Library, Oxford
Brotherton	The Brotherton Library, University of Leeds
Bynner/Haber	*Thirty Housman Letters to Witter Bynner*, ed. Tom Burns Haber (1957)
Classical Papers	*The Classical Papers of A. E. Housman*, ed. J. Diggle and F. R. D. Goodyear (1972)
Clemens (1936)	Cyril Clemens, ed., *The Mark Twain Quarterly*, A. E. Housman Memorial Number, 1. 2 (Winter 1936)
Clemens (1941)	Cyril Clemens, 'A. E. Housman and his Publisher: A Series of Unpublished Letters', *Mark Twain Quarterly*, 4 (Summer/Fall 1941), 11–15, 23
Clemens (1947)	Cyril Clemens, 'Some Unpublished Housman Letters', *Poet Lore: World Literature and the Drama*, 53. 3 (1947), 255–62
Columbia	Columbia University Library, New York
Critical Heritage	*A. E. Housman: The Critical Heritage*, ed. Philip Gardner (1992)
CUL	Cambridge University Library
CUP	Cambridge University Press
Eton	Eton College, Windsor, Berkshire
Fitzwilliam	The Fitzwilliam Museum, Cambridge
Gow	A. S. F. Gow, *A. E. Housman: A Sketch* (corrected impression, November 1936)
GR	Grant Richards (1872–1948), publisher

Graves	Richard Perceval Graves, *A. E. Housman: The Scholar-Poet* (1979; corrected impression, 1981)
Harvard	The Houghton Library, Harvard University
Hawkins (1958)	Maude M. Hawkins, *A. E. Housman: Man Behind A Mask* (1958)
Huntington	The Huntington Library, San Marino, California
HSJ	*Housman Society Journal*
Illinois	University Library, University of Illinois at Urbana-Champaign
KCC	King's College, Cambridge
KES	Katharine Elizabeth Symons (1862–1945), sister of A. E. Housman. Naiditch (2005), 155, notes that her first name was 'Katherine', but that she preferred the form 'Katharine'.
LC	The Library of Congress, Washington, D. C.
LH	Laurence Housman (1865–1959), brother of A. E. Housman
Lilly	The Lilly Library, Indiana University, Bloomington, Indiana
LP	*Last Poems* (1922)
Maas	*The Letters of A. E. Housman*, ed. Henry Maas (1971)
Manchester	The John Rylands University Library, University of Manchester
Martin (1937)	Houston Martin, 'With Letters from Housman', *The Yale Review*, (1937), 283–303
Memoir	Laurence Housman, *A. E. H.: Some Poems, Some Letters and a Personal Memoir* (1937); published in the United States as *My Brother, A. E. Housman: Personal Recollections, together with thirty hitherto unpublished poems* (1938)
Michigan	The University Library, University of Michigan, Ann Arbor, Michigan
MP	*More Poems* (1936)
Naiditch (1988)	P. G. Naiditch, *A. E. Housman at University College, London: The Election of 1892* (1988)
Naiditch (1995)	P. G. Naiditch, *Problems in the Life and Writings of A. E. Housman* (1995)
Naiditch (1996)	P. G. Naiditch, *The Centenary of "A Shropshire Lad": The Life & Writings of A. E. Housman*, Department of Special Collections, University Research Library, University of California, Los Angeles (1996)
Naiditch (2002)	P. G. Naiditch, 'The Extant Portion of the Library of A. E. Housman [Part I]. Greek Literature', *Housman Society Journal*, 28 (2002), 53–69
Naiditch (2003)	P. G. Naiditch, 'The Extant Portion of the Library of A. E. Housman [Part II]. Latin Literature', *Housman Society Journal*, 29 (2003), 108–51
Naiditch (2004)	P. G. Naiditch, 'The Extant Portion of the Library of A. E. Housman [Part III]. Classical Antiquity', *Housman Society Journal*, 30 (2004), 142–57

Naiditch (2005)	P. G. Naiditch, *Additional Problems in the Life and Writings of A. E. Housman* (2005)
N & Q	*Notes and Queries*
NLS	The National Library of Scotland, Edinburgh
NNAEH	[L. Dolenski and J. Dooley], *The Name and Nature of A. E. Housman* (1986)
NNP	*The Name and Nature of Poetry* by A. E. Housman. The Leslie Stephen Lecture, delivered at Cambridge, 9 May 1933 (1933)
OBR	*The Old Bromsgrovian Register, together with a brief history of the origin and growth of Bromsgrove School, Bromsgrove* (1908–10)
Page	Norman Page, *A. E. Housman: A Critical Biography* (1983; rev. edn., 1996)
p.c.	postcard
PM	The Pierpont Morgan Library, New York
Poems (1997)	*The Poems of A. E. Housman*, ed. Archie Burnett (corrected impression, 1997)
Princeton	Princeton University Library, Princeton, New Jersey
Pugh	John Pugh, *Bromsgrove and the Housmans* (1974)
Reading	The University Library, Reading
Recollections	*Alfred Edward Housman: Recollections* by Katharine E. Symons *et al.* (New York, 1937). This contained material supplementary to that in *Alfred Edward Housman: Recollections* (Bromsgrove, 1936), known as the '*Bromsgrove Memorial Supplement*'
Richards	Grant Richards, *Housman 1897–1936* (1941; corrected reprint, 1942)
Ricks (1988)	*A. E. Housman: Collected Poems and Selected Prose*, ed. Christopher Ricks (1988)
SCO	Somerville College Library, Oxford
Selected Prose	*A. E. Housman: Selected Prose*, ed. John Carter (1961; corrected impression, 1962)
SIU	The Morris Library, Southern Illinois University, Carbondale
SJCO	The Library, St John's College, Oxford
St Andrews	The University Library, St Andrews
TCC	The Wren Library, Trinity College, Cambridge
Texas	The Harry Ransom Humanities Research Center, University of Texas at Austin
TLS	*The Times Literary Supplement*
t.s.	typescript
UCL	University College London (in Housman's day, with a comma after 'College')
UCLA	The Department of Special Collections, Charles E. Young Research Library, University of California, Los Angeles
Virginia	University of Virginia Library
Waseda	The A. S. F. Gow Collection, Waseda University, Tokyo

Wellesley   Wellesley College Library, Wellesley, Massachusetts.
White (1950)   William White, 'Fifteen Unpublished Letters of A. E.
                       Housman', *The Dalhousie Review*, 29. 4 (Jan. 1950), 402–10
White (1959)   *A. E. Housman to Joseph Ishill: Five Unpublished Letters* by William
                       White (1959)
White (1978)   William White, 'A. E. Housman to John Masefield: An
                       Unpublished Letter', *The Journal of the Book Club of Detroit*, 3. 1
                       (1978)
Withers   Percy Withers, *A Buried Life: Personal Recollections of A. E.
                       Housman* (1940)
Yale   Beinecke Rare Book and Manuscript Library, Yale University
                       Library, New Haven, Connecticut

NOTE ON EDITORIAL PRINCIPLES

Editorial intervention has been kept to the minimum in order to preserve as much of the physiognomy of the letters as possible. Abbreviations, with and without the point (Co., Dr, Esq., Messrs, St., Oct, Nov.), superscript letters (M^r, 12th), ampersands, numerals written as words and as figures, single and double quotation marks, and non-indentation of paragraphs have been reproduced faithfully: Housman's practice was not consistent, but it causes no confusion, and regularizing it would sacrifice something of the informality of letters never intended for publication.

The only substantial intervention has been to standardize titles of works. Sometimes Housman underlined them; sometimes, and sometimes misleadingly, not; and at other times he placed them within single quotation marks. I have rendered all titles, whether of books, periodicals, or poems, in italic. Housman's references to classical texts have been left as they are, however: in these he followed different conventions from those for non-classical works, and changing them would have interfered drastically with the material substance of the text.

Usually, addresses and dates were placed top right by Housman; complimentary closes ('I am yours very truly', 'Yours sincerely') and his signature, bottom right. Sometimes complimentary closes were written at varying points to the left of the signature, but such fine gradations of spacing, many of them apparently dictated by nothing more than the size of the writing paper, are difficult to reproduce exactly, and I place them bottom right. Where Housman adopted a different format for addresses, dates, closes, and the signature, as for instance in postcards, the different format is followed. To economize on space, vertical rules have been inserted in addresses to indicate line-divisions: thus 'Trinity College | Cambridge' indicates that 'Cambridge' was written below 'Trinity College'. Addresses on headed writing paper are rendered in small capitals.

At the head of each letter the addressee is specified. At the end of each, details are given of the source of the text, the earliest printing, and, where applicable, the location of the letter in Maas's edition. Unless it is stated otherwise, it is to be assumed that the source for the text is an autograph letter or postcard, signed, in ink. Where possible, details of the address on the envelope or postcard are also supplied. When the text of a letter is from a typescript copy or a printed source that does not follow Housman's customary practice, the text has been silently modified. Usually this involves little more than changing the form of the address and date, or removing a comma after 'sincerely', 'truly', or 'faithfully' in complimentary closes. However, Housman's letters to newspapers and periodicals, none of which survives in manuscript, are presented as they were printed: he had to expect that the house style would be followed, and he never expressed any objection to it. In the unique case of the formal letter of application of 19 April 1892 accompanying testimonials, the printed text has also been followed: Housman would have had the letter and the testimonials printed, and would have seen proofs.

Evidence of drafting is represented by symbols used in my edition of Housman's poems (1997), though the reduction in their number reflects the less extensive and less complex drafting in the letters. Housman's cancellations are placed within angle brackets, < >; words written by him above or below the line, within slant brackets, \ /; cancelled words above or below the line within a combination of the two, \< >/. Everything else supplied editorially in the body of the text (missing letters or parts of words, necessary punctuation, addresses, or dates, for example) is placed within square brackets,[ ]; gaps in incomplete MSS are indicated by three dots [...]; illegible words by a question mark [?]. Uncertain readings are preceded by a question mark [?word]; words written to the left of the main body of the letter, by an arrow [←]. In a case such as the letter to Maurice Pollet of 5 February 1933, where there exists an extensive draft and a final version, both are presented in full, one after the other. A textual apparatus in such a case would confuse more than it would inform.

Casual slips and other minor blemishes are corrected silently or omitted. Corrections that represent revisions of wording have been included, however. Among them are those made during illness, even terminal illness. In these special cases I have additionally recorded all slips in order to represent Housman's heroic struggle to sustain his characteristic courtesy in answering letters. Throughout, his numerous inaccuracies are recorded in footnotes, not to get back at a man to whom accuracy was 'a duty and not a virtue',[1] but to reveal him as less rigorous when writing informally.

---

[1] *Manilius V* (1930), 105.

(It is a consideration too that unrecorded inaccuracies can be mistaken for misprints or the editor's errors.)

In the notes and in the List of Recipients, biographical information has been confined to Housman's lifetime (1859–1936), in order to give a true sense of relationship. When he writes to Gilbert Murray, for instance, he knows him not as the public figure Murray would later become but as a fellow classical scholar; and the only mention of John Rothenstein, who would later become eminent in the British art world, is when he is a boy of nine. It has not been possible to identify everyone or everything Housman refers to, however. Several composers—would-be composers?—who make applications to set Housman's poems to music do not appear in the most comprehensive reference work, *Musical Settings of Late Victorian and Modern British Literature: A Catalogue* by Bryan N. S. Gooch and David S. Thatcher (1976), or in specialist studies such as Banfield (1985), probably because no setting was subsequently published. And in the absence of documentary evidence, a few distant relations, admirers, or acquaintances, must go unidentified. (Some information can be gathered from addresses on envelopes or postcards, however, and that has been recorded.) It will be clear when it has not been possible to elucidate a reference, and I have chosen to remain silent rather than multiply notes saying 'Not identified' or 'Not traced': in such cases the footnote number does no more than divert with a false promise of enlightenment.

The letters are printed in chronological sequence by date. A stricter chronology cannot be established: the order in which letters were written on the same date is not known. Henry Maas's decision to interrupt the chronology and place the letters on classical subjects together at the end of the volume has not been followed, on the grounds that it sacrifices with very little gain a primary biographical function of an edition of the letters: to give a strong sense of the mix of Housman's activities from day to day, whether he writes as scholar, poet, citizen, colleague, relation, or friend.

Letters are printed from manuscripts wherever possible, or, failing that, from photographs or photocopies of manuscripts. This has resulted in a great many cases in a text that is more complete and more correct than any previously available. I have noted incompleteness in earlier published texts, but, with the exception of misdatings, I have on the whole refrained from recording inaccuracies. Maas's edition contained many errors of transcription,[2] as well as errors of other kinds, and the other printed sources are very far from immaculate, too. (Cyril Clemens's capacity for

---

[2] Naiditch (1995), 61–2, provides a substantial selection.

inaccuracy borders on the pathological.) Where Housman's poetry, and especially the poetry published posthumously, was concerned, a record of every error made by previous editors was a necessary complement to the establishment of the text; but, in the case of the letters, where there is less complexity and contentiousness, placing every error on record would probably be only a distraction (in more senses than one) to the reader. And distinctly unedifying to the editor, whose feeling in the matter is akin to W. H. Auden's feeling about repeatedly attacking bad books in reviews: that it's bad for the character.[3]

---

[3] 'Reading', *Selected Essays* (1964), 18.

INTRODUCTION

This edition aims to print all of A. E. Housman's letters, and it fails to do so: it is known, or it can be readily inferred, that he wrote more letters than those that are now accessible; and, no doubt, just as letters have come to light during the preparation of the edition, they will continue to turn up after publication. No letters have been found for entire years—1874, 1883, 1884, 1886, and 1888—and yet it is hard to imagine that Housman wrote no letters for such long periods. It is true, but small consolation, that most editions are incomplete. (And it is hard to imagine a publisher with the candour to announce a title beginning 'The Incomplete Letters of...', any more than 'Probably The Poems of...' where attributions are uncertain.) The attempt to be complete has been thought worthwhile, however, and chiefly for the reason that the degree of incompleteness of the standard edition by Henry Maas (1971) amounts to a deficiency. Paul Naiditch has noted that of some 1,500 letters Maas traced, he published 883, together with one fragment, and the facsimile of a letter whose text he did not transcribe. Naiditch has also shown that Maas did not discover all the letters he should have located, and that he did not print many he should have printed.[1] The shortcoming worsens once 2,327 letters and 4 fragments have been found.

The decision to print every letter found has not been taken lightly, however. The main justification has been to allow as full a revelation as possible of a man whose reserve was legendary. A remark by Philip Larkin in a review of the first volume of *The Collected Letters of Thomas Hardy*— 'one cannot read six or seven hundred letters by even as reticent a man as Hardy without learning something about him'[2]—applies in principle to Housman too. A partial representation would in Housman's case be unusually risky, as a comment by Andrew Gow, his colleague at Trinity College, suggests:

---

[1] Naiditch (1995), 157–61.
[2] *Further Requirements: Interviews, Broadcasts, Statements and Book Reviews 1952–85*, ed. Anthony Thwaite (2001), 272.

To many of those who met him casually at High Tables or on University committees he remained, as to the outside world, a figure alarming, remote, mysterious. To see Housman at his best, therefore, it was well to meet him in a small social circle, or at the fortnightly dinners of the Family, a dining club of a dozen members to which he belonged ... [He would] show himself as vivacious as any other member of the party ... and would greet the contributions of others with bursts of silvery laughter which retained to the end of his life something boyish and infectious.[3]

Not to print all the letters found would be rather like meeting Housman only on one of the kinds of occasion Gow describes. Even if the jigsaw is not complete, a better picture results from assembling all, rather than some, of the pieces available.

Incomplete representation can allow unwarranted hypotheses to flourish. Consider, for instance, the notion that Housman was an unsociable, even anti-social, man. Such a view cannot stand in the face of letters, usually functional and brief, in which he accepts or issues dining invitations, or makes arrangements to stay or visit; and their sheer number is important in establishing the truth. Similarly, Housman's misogyny needs to be heavily qualified in the light of affectionate letters to his sister Kate, early humorous letters to Elizabeth Wise, and many cordial letters to wives of colleagues and friends. Relationships sometimes need to be documented as fully as possible if they are not to be distorted. To print, as Maas did, only one letter from Housman to John Masefield, that of 11 May 1930 congratulating him on the Poet Laureateship, is in effect to suppress the fact that the correspondence between the two poets began twenty years previously, when Housman expressed friendly interest in Masefield's play *Pompey the Great*; and, worse, to render Housman's letter, on its own, seemingly presumptuous in attitude and obsequious in tone.

To include only letters that record Housman's opinions of literature, or that contain humour, bons mots, or scathing put-downs, would be to follow the agenda of an anthology. There is some legitimacy in doing this for particular purposes, though the risks of misrepresentation may still be too great. Consider, for instance, the extreme and astonishing case of E. V. Lucas's *William Cowper's Letters: A Selection* (1908):

In the following selection from the letters of William Cowper everything, or nearly everything, has been retained which shows him in the light of an agreeable philosophic correspondent; and nearly everything has been omitted which bears upon his own unhappy spiritual state or upon local,

[3] Gow, 50.

family, or literary matters that either are of no intrinsic interest or that involve repetition. The book, in short, has been arranged to display Cowper at his happiest: the charm and ease of his style, his domestic wit, his serene good sense, his winning playfulness.   (p. v)

It is rare to find perverseness so direct. But the candour with which Lucas declares that he has in effect removed all traces of Cowper's unignorable depression does not remove the gross distortion. It was Lucas who confessed later in life, 'I still want books to be cheerful and amusing';[4] and the blinkered indulgence of this predilection dictated his selection from Cowper's letters. Further, is it not for the reader to decide which matters, including literary matters, are of 'no intrinsic interest'? And does repetition disclose nothing? To Lucas's credit, he does point 'anyone requiring a fuller representation of the man' to the complete correspondence in Bohn's Library and other editions. But what he calls 'a fuller representation' is more than that: a truer representation.

Even a complete correspondence will not tell the whole truth, however. Tennyson's poignant reminder of this in *Old ghosts whose day was done ere mine began* applies tellingly to the case of A. E. Housman:

> Ye know that History is half-dream—ay
> even
> The man's life in the letters of the man.
> There lies the letter, but it is not he
> As he retires into himself and is:
> Sender and sent-to go to make up this,
> Their offspring of this union.
>
> … whatsoever knows us truly, knows
> That none can truly write his single day,
> And none can write it for him upon earth.

The best that can be expected—or hoped for—is the least distortion.

Another reason for aiming at completeness is to accommodate the variety of interests that readers will bring to the edition. I include, for instance, more than twice the number of letters on classical subjects in Maas, even though it is unlikely these days that an interest primarily in the minutiae of classical textual scholarship will be widely shared. Such letters are central to Housman's 'trade' (as he called it) of Professor of Latin, and to a form of intellectual activity in which he excelled and through which

---

[4] *Reading, Writing and Remembering: A Literary Record* (1932), 14.

he achieved international fame. Their exclusion would not only amount to an act of serious misrepresentation, but would deny classical scholars ready access to their content.

Last, a purely pragmatic consideration: to provide an adequate bibliographical record and summary of contents for letters of business (and business-like letters) would in many cases take up as much, if not more, space than the letters themselves. And, besides, letters of this type have something to tell too, especially those that provide a record of Housman's unusually close involvement as an author in all aspects of the publication process.

One category of exclusion should be noted: ceremonial public addresses that Housman composed, such as those in Latin to the Universities of Sydney, Melbourne, and Aberdeen, or in English to persons such as the Reverend Henry Montagu Butler (1913), Sir James Frazer (1921), and the King (1925, 1935).[5] In such cases, even when the address shares some characteristics with a letter, there is a distinction of genre to be drawn between letters composed by Housman and letters from him. I do, however, make an exception of the letter of 14 July 1919 to Henry Jackson, which Housman wrote to be signed by the Master and Fellows of Trinity College, including of course himself: first, it is indisputably a letter, not a public address; and, second, a personal warmth, a 'long and sure-set liking', glows throughout it, as Housman joins the 'affectionate friends' of Jackson in celebrating his eightieth birthday.

'Then again, he seems to have been a very nice man,'[6] Philip Larkin realized after reading Richard Perceval Graves's 1979 biography. How Housman comes across in his letters is for the reader, not the editor, to decide. But the editor is a reader too, and I will say only that I have found him to be an even gentler, more amiable, more sociable, more generous, more painstaking, and altogether more complex person than the biographies and the previous edition of the letters led me to believe; and that my admiration and liking for him have increased.

---

[5] These may be found in *Selected Prose*, 161–7. See also Naiditch (1988), 120.
[6] 'All Right when You Knew Him', *Required Writing. Miscellaneous Pieces 1955–1982* (1983), 263.

LIST OF RECIPIENTS

This is not an exhaustive list. Some recipients are identified in notes to letters. All recipients are listed in the Index.

ABBOTT, CLAUDE COLLEER (1889–1971). Poet, and translator of early medieval French lyrics. Lecturer in English Language and Literature, University of Aberdeen, 1921–32; Professor of English Language and Literature, University of Durham, 1932–54.

ABEEL, NEILSON (1902–49). Graduated from Princeton in 1925, managed the Brick Row Book Shop there, and acted as secretary to the American-Scandinavian Foundation for ten years. His favourite writers were Matthew Arnold, Rupert Brooke, and A. E. Housman, and he made pilgrimages to the places that they knew. He himself wrote poetry.

ABERCROMBIE, LASCELLES (1881–1938). Poet and critic. Professor of English Literature, University of Leeds, 1922–9; Hildred Carlile Professor of English Literature at Bedford College, University of London, 1929–35; Goldsmiths' Reader in English, University of Oxford, 1935–8. Publications include *Principles of English Prosody* (1924), *The Idea of Great Poetry* (1925), *Poems* (1930), and *Poetry, its Music and Meaning* (1932).

ADCOCK, ARTHUR ST JOHN (1864–1930). Poet, novelist, essayist, and editor of *The Bookman*. His *Collected Poems* was published in 1929.

ADELMAN, SEYMOUR (1907–85). Philadelphia bibliophile and art collector. His collection of AEH manuscripts and rare books is in the Mariam Coffin Canaday Library, BMC. He never visited England and thus never met AEH.

AGARD, WALTER RAYMOND (1894–1978). Classicist at the University of Wisconsin. Publications include: *The Glory that was Greece* (1930), *The Greek Tradition in Sculpture* (1930), *The New Architectural Sculpture* (1935), and *Medical Greek and Latin at a Glance* (1935).

ALINGTON, CYRIL ARGENTINE (1872–1955). Assistant Master at Marlborough, 1896–9, and at Eton, 1899–1908; Headmaster of Shrewsbury School, 1908–17, and of Eton, 1917–33; Chaplain to the King, 1921–33; Honorary Fellow of TCC, 1926; Dean of Durham, 1933–51.

ANDERSON, LADY JESSIE MINA [Innes] (b. 1861/2). Wife of physiologist and administrator Sir Hugh Kerr Anderson (1865–1928): FRS, 1907; Master of Gonville and Caius College, Cambridge, 1912–28; member of the Royal Commission on the Universities of Oxford and Cambridge, 1919, and of the Cambridge Commission, 1923; knighted, 1922.

ASHBURNER, WALTER (1864–1936). A Bostonian, educated in England. A bibliophile and gourmet, and a friend of Horatio Brown (q.v.). Assistant Reader in Equity to the Council of Legal Education; Professor of Jurisprudence at Oxford, 1926–9. He lived in England till 1903, thereafter mainly in Florence. His *The Rhodian Sea-Law* was published in 1909. See Naiditch (1988), 65–6, for further information.

BAKER, HETTIE GRAY (1881–1957). Pioneer woman in the film industry. Wrote scenario and story scripts for several silent films based on Jack London classics, including *Burning Daylight*, *The Valley of the Moon*, and *The Chechako*, all in 1914; edited John Ford's early film *The Iron Horse*, 1924. Later known for her knowledge of Siamese cats.

BANE, BLANCHE. Later Mrs William S. Kuder of Oakland, California. Housman collector and admirer, who published two poems on him: 'To A. E. Housman', *McClure's Magazine*, 28 (August 1907), 407; repr. in *April Weather* (1922); and 'The Shropshire Lad', *The Bromsgrovian*, 51 (Mar. 1938), 94, repr. in Joseph Henry Jackson's 'Bookman's Daily Notebook', *San Francisco Daily Chronicle*, 30 Apr. 1938.

BARNES, GEORGE [Reginald] (1904–60). Educated at Dartmouth and KCC; first class, Historical Tripos, Part II, 1925; Assistant Master at Dartmouth, 1927–30; Assistant Secretary, Cambridge University Press, 1930–5; joined the BBC in 1935.

BARRIE, J[ames] M[atthew] (1860–1937). Novelist and playwright, famous for the children's play *Peter Pan*, first performed in 1904. Novels include: *The Little Minister* (1891), *Sentimental Tommy* (1896), and *Tommy and Grizel* (1900). Dramas include: *What Every Woman Knows* (1906), *Dear Brutus* (1917), and *Mary Rose* (1920). Created baronet, 1913; OM, 1922.

BEERBOHM, MAX (1872–1956). Essayist and caricaturist. He admired AEH's poetry, but was not impressed by him in person: 'He was like an absconding cashier. We certainly wished he would abscond—sitting silent and then saying only "there is a bit of a nip in the air, don't you think?"' (D. Cecil, *Max: A Biography*, 1965, 262). See Naiditch (2005), 20, for further information.

BEESLY, EDWARD SPENCER (1831–1915). Positivist and historian. Professor of Ancient History (1881–4) and of Latin (1860–89) at Bedford College, London; Professor of Ancient and Modern History (1860–1915), and, from 1893, Emeritus Professor of History at UCL. He was a member of the committee that appointed AEH at UCL in 1892. See Naiditch (1988), 4, 9, 73–4, for further information.

BENIANS, E[rnest] A[lfred] (1880–1952). Historian. Fellow (1906), College Lecturer (1912), Tutor (1918), Senior Tutor (1926) and Master (1933–52) of St John's College, Cambridge. Author of *The British Empire and the War* (1915), and one of the editors of *The Cambridge History of the British Empire* (1929–).

BENNETT, ANDREW (1871–1958). Secretary to the Court, Senatus Academicus, and General Council of the University of St Andrews. He acted as Registrar and Law Agent to the University, 1903–41.

BENSON, A[rthur] C[hristopher] (1862–1925). Man of letters. Assistant Master at Eton, 1885; Fellow of Magdalene College, Cambridge, 1904; Master, 1915–25. Page, 105, notes that in Benson's diary 'his accounts of meetings with Housman between 1911 and 1925 lack objectivity to a remarkable degree: his judgments swing violently between approval and hostility, and ought not to be taken too seriously.'

BINYON, [Robert] LAURENCE (1869–1943). Poet, dramatist, and art historian. He worked at the British Museum, 1893–1933, first in the Department of Printed Books, later as Keeper of the Department of Oriental Prints and Drawings. Made Companion of Honour, 1932. Publications include: *Lyric Poems* (1894), *Winnowing Fan: Poems of the Great War* (1914); dramas *Attila* (1907) and *Arthur* (1923); *Painting in the Far East* (1908); and *Collected Poems* (1931), which included war poems such as his famous *For the Fallen*.

BLAKENEY, E[dward] H[enry] (1869–1955). Classical scholar and amateur printer. Headmaster at various schools: Sandwich Grammar School, 1895; Borlase School, Marlow, 1901; King Henry VIII's School, Ely, 1904–18. Assistant Master, Winchester College, 1918–30; Lecturer in English Literature, University College, Southampton, 1929–31; Lecturer in Latin at King Alfred's College, Winchester, 1933. Author of *Voices after Sunset* (1897), *War Poems* (1915), *New Poems* (1918), and *Alpine Poems* (1929); translator of Homer's *Iliad*, Horace's *De Arte Poetica*, Ausonius' *Mosella*, and Plato's *Apology*; and editor of Bacon's *Essays*, Milton's *Paradise Regained*, and *Everyman's Classical Dictionary*. See Naiditch (1995), 44, for further information.

BLUNT, WILFRID SCAWEN (1840–1922). Poet, diplomat, anti-imperialist, Arabist, and hedonist. Published *Sonnets and Songs by Proteus* (1875, etc.), in a copy of the 6th (1890) edn. of which AEH wrote: 'If boots were bonnets, | These might be sonnets. | But boots are not; | So don't talk rot': see *Poems* (1997), 250, 536. Blunt's other publications include: *The Wind and the Whirlwind* (1883), *Ideas about India* (1885), *In Vinculis* (1889), and *My Diaries* (2 vols., 1919–20).

BOWRA, [Cecil] MAURICE (1898–1971). Classical scholar and university administrator. Fellow of Wadham College, Oxford, 1922, Dean and Senior Tutor, 1930–1. In collaboration with H. T. Wade-Gery, he published a translation of *Pindar: Pythian Odes* (1928). Other publications include: *Tradition and Design in the Iliad* (1930), *Ancient Greek Literature* (1933), the Oxford edn. of *Pindari Carmina cum fragmentis* (1935), and *Greek Lyric Poetry from Alcman to Simonides* (1936).

BREUL, KARL HERMANN (1860–1932). Born at Hanover but later became a British citizen. Educated at the Universities of Tübingen, Strassburg, and Berlin; first University Lecturer in German at Cambridge, 1884; Hon. MA, 1886; Fellow of KCC, 1886; LittD, 1896; Schröder Professor of German, 1910; Professorial Fellow of KCC, 1926; President of the MLA, and founder and editor of *Modern Language Quarterly*. Publications include: critical editions of *Sir Gowther* (1883), *Le Dit De Robert*

Le Diable (1895), *The Cambridge Songs, A Goliard's Song Book of the XIIth Century* (1915), and *The Cambridge Reinaert Fragments* (1927).

BRIDGES, [Mary] MONICA, née Waterhouse (1863–1949). Daughter of the architect Alfred Waterhouse, RA (1830–1905) and Elizabeth Hodgkin (1834–1913). She married Robert Bridges on 3 Sept. 1884.

BRIDGES, ROBERT [Seymour] (1844–1930). Educated at Eton and Corpus Christi College, Oxford (1863–7), where he met Gerard M. Hopkins; MB, 1874, at St Bartholomew's Hospital; practised medicine until 1881; lived at Yattendon, Berkshire, 1882–1904, and from 1907 at Chilswell House, which he built on Boars Hill, Oxford; Poet Laureate, 1913; founder of the Society for Pure English, 1919; OM, 1929. Publications include: *Poems* (1873), *The Growth of Love* (1876), *Eros and Psyche* (1885), *Shorter Poems* (Books I–IV, 1890; Book V, 1894), *Collected Poems* (1912), *The Spirit of Man* (1916), *October and Other Poems* (1920), *New Verse* (1925), *The Testament of Beauty* (1929), and *Milton's Prosody* (1889; final edn., 1921).

BROCKINGTON, ALFRED ALLEN (1872–1938). Schoolmaster in Canada and England; vicar (ordained, 1898) in England, and Chaplain to the Forces on the French Front, 1915–17; writer of theological works, poetry, and criticism; Ph.D., University of London, 1931; Lecturer to the Cambridge Board of Extra-mural Studies, 1908; and contributor to various literary journals (*Athenaeum, Cornhill, Poetry Review*).

BROWN, B[ertram]. GOULDING. Cambridge resident who corresponded with AEH, 1931–6, and attended his lectures in 1933.

BROWN, HORATIO [Robert] F[orbes] (1854–1926). Educated at Clifton College, and New College, Oxford. An expert on Venice, where he lived from 1879. Publications include *Venetian Studies* (1888), *Venice, an Historical Sketch* (1893), and *Studies in the History of Venice* (2 vols., 1907). Literary executor of John Addington Symonds, author of *John Addington Symonds, a Biography* (1895), and editor of *Letters and Papers of John Addington Symonds* (1923).

BRUSSEL, I[sidore] R[osenbaum] (1895–1972). New York bibliophile and book scout. Contributed *Anglo-American First Editions, 1826–1900: East to West* (1935) and its counterpart *West to East* (1936) to Sadleir's Bibliographica series.

BULLETT, GERALD (1893–1958). Writer (principally of novels) and broadcaster. Graduated from Cambridge with first class honours in English, 1921.

BURKITT, AMY PERSIS. Daughter of William Parry, Rector of Fitz, Shropshire, and wife of Francis Crawford Burkitt.

BURKITT, FRANCIS CRAWFORD (1864–1935). Graduated high in the Mathematical Tripos at Cambridge, 1886, then in the first class in the Theological Tripos, 1888; University Lecturer in Palaeography, 1903, and Norrisian Professor of Divinity, 1905–35; FBA, 1905; Fellow of TCC, 1926. Publications include: 'Text and Versions' in *Encyclopaedia Biblica* (1903), an edn. of the old Syriac gospels (1904), *The*

Gospel History and its Transmission (1906), *The Earliest Sources for the Life of Jesus* (1910), *Jewish and Christian Apocalypses* (1914), and *Jesus Christ: An Historical Outline* (1932).

BUTLER, AGNATA [Frances] née Ramsay (1867–1931). Wife of H. M. Butler, whom she married in 1888. She was among the first women to take the Classical Tripos at Cambridge, and in 1887 she was placed in division one of the first class. Her edn. of the seventh book of Herodotus was published in 1889.

BUTLER, H[arold] E[dgeworth] (1878–1951). First class in *literae humaniores*, Oxford, 1900. Lecturer, 1901, and Fellow of New College, 1902–11; AEH's successor as Professor of Latin at UCL, 1911–42. Publications include: an edn. of *Propertii omnia opera* (1905, with commentary; 2nd edn., with translation, 1912), to the former of which AEH gave 'hardly what would be called a favourable review' (his words) in *CR* 19 (1905), 317–20; a translation of *Apuleius: Metamorphoses* (1910), and, with A. S. Owen, an edn. of *Apulei Apologia* (1914); an edn. of *The Sixth Book of the Aeneid* (1914); a Loeb edn. of *Institutes of Quintilian* (1920–2); and an edn., with E. A. Barber, of *Propertius: Elegies* (1933).

BUTLER, H[enry] M[ontagu] (1833–1918). Fellow of TCC, 1855; Headmaster of Harrow, 1860–85; Dean of Gloucester, 1885; Master of TCC, 1886–1918; Vice-Chancellor of Cambridge University, 1889–90; Publications include: *Ten Great and Good Men* (1909), *Lord Chatham as an Orator* (1912), and *Some Leisure Hours of a Long Life: Translations into Greek, Latin, and English Verse from 1850 to 1914* (1914).

BUTLER, J[ames] R[amsay] M[ontagu] (1889–1975). Son of H. M. Butler. Historian. Admitted to TCC from Harrow, 1907; first class, Part I, Classical Tripos, 1909, and Part II, Historical Tripos, 1910; Fellow, 1913–75, and tutor to Prince Albert (later George VI) and Prince Henry (later Duke of Gloucester); MVO, 1920; Senior Tutor, 1931–8. His *The Passing of the Great Reform Bill* was published in 1914.

BYNNER, [Harold] WITTER (1881–1968). American poet, translator, and playwright. Studied mainly English and philosophy at Harvard. Introduced to *ASL* by Richard Le Gallienne, he published in *McClure's Magazine*, in the period Dec. 1903–Sept. 1908, thirteen of the poems, thus introducing them to an American readership. (Richards, 55, describes the magazine's circulation at the time as 'huge and important'.) He lived with Robert Hunt for thirty-four years in Santa Fe, New Mexico. He knew D. H. and Frieda Lawrence from 1922 onwards, travelled with them on their first trip to Mexico the following year, and was the source for the minor character Owen Rhys in Lawrence's *The Plumed Serpent*. He was a pacifist and a strong supporter of equality for women and for blacks, and later for Indians and Spanish-speaking Americans. Though AEH and he exchanged correspondence for over thirty-two years, the two never met.

CAMPBELL, A[rchibald] Y[oung] (1885–1958). Classical scholar and poet. Fellow (1910–22) and Lecturer (1911–22) at St John's College, Cambridge; Gladstone Professor of Greek at Liverpool University (1922–50). Publications include: *Poems* (1912), *Horace. A New Interpretation* (1924), *Poems* (1926), and edns. of *Horati Carmina Viginti* (1935) and *The Agamemnon of Aeschylus* (1936).

CARTER, JOHN [Waynflete] (1905–75). Bibliographer and bibliophile. Educated at Eton and KCC; joined the London branch of the New York publishing house Charles Scribner's Sons, 1926–7, establishing the antiquarian bookselling side of the business, and becoming their London manager. Co-author with Graham Pollard of *An Enquiry into the Nature of Certain Nineteenth-Century Pamphlets* (1934).

CAVE, THE COUNTESS, née Anne Estella Penfold Matthews (d. 1938). Married George Cave (1856–1928) in 1885. He became Home Secretary (1916–19), Lord Chancellor (1922–8), and Chancellor of Oxford University (1925–8), and was created Viscount in 1918. On his death she was granted the title of Countess Cave of Richmond.

CHAMBERS, R[aymond] W[ilson] (1874–1942). Literary scholar. A member of AEH's Latin class at UCL (1892–4), he graduated with first class honours in English (1894). At UCL he became Quain Student (1899), Fellow (1900), Librarian (1901), Assistant Professor of English (1904) and, succeeding W. P. Ker, Quain Professor (1922–41). FBA, 1927. In 1904 he extracted *The Parallelogram* from AEH for anonymous publication in the *University College London Union Magazine*. Publications include: sympathetic reminiscences of AEH, particularly of the UCL years, in *Recollections*, 51–60, and in *Man's Unconquerable Mind* (1939), 365–86; *Widsith: a Study in Old English Heroic Legend* (1912), an edn. of *Beowulf* (1914), *Beowulf: an Introduction to the Study of the Poem* (1921), and *Thomas More* (1934). See Naiditch (2005), 18–19, for further information.

CLARK, ELLA E[lizabeth] (1896–1988). American writer and anthologist.

CLEMENS, CYRIL [Coniston] (1902–99). Cousin of Samuel Langhorne Clemens (Mark Twain). Founder the International Mark Twain Society in 1930, and editor of the *Mark Twain Quarterly* (later the *Mark Twain Journal*), 1936–82. Publications include numerous volumes and pamphlets on Twain, including *Mark Twain Anecdotes* (1929), *Mark Twain Wit and Wisdom* (1935), *Mark Twain and Mussolini* (1934), and *Mark Twain's Religion* (1935).

COCKERELL, SYDNEY [Carlyle] (1867–1962). Director of the Fitzwilliam Museum, Cambridge, 1908–37; Fellow of Jesus College, Cambridge, 1910–16, and of Downing College, 1932–7; hon. Litt.D., Cambridge, 1930; knighted, 1934. Secretary to, and literary executor of, Wilfrid Scawen Blunt, William Morris, and Thomas Hardy.

COOKE, GREVILLE (1894–1992). Studied History at Cambridge, *c.*1918. Rector of Crawsley near Kettering, Northants., 1921–56, during much of which time he was Professor of Piano at the Royal Academy of Music. See Norman Marlow in *HSJ* 4 (1978), 45.

COOPER, ALICE C[ecilia] (1878–1960). Editor of the American anthology *Poems of Today* (1924).

CORNFORD, FRANCIS MACDONALD (1874–1943). Classical scholar. Fellow of TCC, 1899; Lecturer in Classics, 1904; Laurence-Brereton Reader in Classics at Cambridge, 1927; first holder of the Laurence Chair of Ancient Philosophy, 1931–9. Husband of the poet Frances Cornford. Publications include: *Thucydides Mythistoricus* (1907), *Microcosmographia Academica* (1908), *The Origin of Attic Comedy* (1914), *The Laws of Motion in Ancient Thought* (1931), and *Before and After Socrates* (1932).

COULSON, C[harles] A[lfred] (1910–74). Educated at Clifton College, and admitted to TCC, 1928; took Part II of the Mathematical Tripos, 1931, and Part II of the Natural Sciences Tripos, 1932; Fellow of TCC, 1934–8.

COWELL, P[hilip] H[erbert] (1870–1949). Mathematician and astronomer. Educated at Eton and Cambridge; Fellow of TCC, 1894; FRS, 1906; Superintendent of HM Nautical Almanac Office, 1910. Recommended by H. H. Turner to Prof. Karl Pearson of UCL, and by Pearson to AEH, as an authority on calculating the position of planets (TCC MS, with Adv. c. 20. 26): Naiditch (1988), 93 n.

CROSS, WILBUR [Lucius] (1862–1948). BA (1885) and Ph.D. (1889), Yale University. Instructor (1894–7), Assistant Professor (1897–1902), Professor of English (1902–31), and Dean of the Graduate School (1902–30) at Yale, and editor of *The Yale Review* for thirty years. Publications include: *The Life and Times of Laurence Sterne* (1909), *The History of Henry Fielding* (1918), *Four Contemporary Novelists* (1930), and *The Development of the English Novel* (1933).

CUMONT, FRANZ [-VALÉRY MARIE] (1868–1947). Belgian orientalist and historian of religion. Publications include: *Catalogus codicum astrologum Graecorum* (1898) as joint editor, *Les Mystères de Mithra* (2nd edn., 1902), and *Les réligions orientales dans le paganisme romain* (1906, etc.).

DARWIN, LADY MAUD, née du Puy (1861–1947). Born in Philadelphia. Wife of Charles Darwin's son, the mathematician and geophysicist Sir George Howard Darwin (1845–1912).

DAVIDSON, A[lexander] MACKENZIE (1897–1979). Minor Scottish poet. Publications include *A Few Poems* (n.d.) and *Tinkler's Whussel* (n.d.).

DAVIS, [J. Irving] & ORIOLI, [Pino]. London dealers in manuscripts and rare books.

DE LA MARE, WALTER [John] (1873–1956). Poet, short-story writer, and anthologist. Publications include: poetry, *Songs of Childhood* (1902), *The Listeners* (1912), *Peacock Pie* (1913), *Motley* (1918); prose, *Henry Brocken* (1904), *The Return* (1910); and the anthology *Come Hither* (1923).

DIXON, W[illiam] MACNEILE (1866–1945). Professor of English at Glasgow, 1934. Publications include: the poetry anthology *The English Parnassus* with H. J. C. Grierson (1909), *English Epic and Heroic Poetry* (1912), and *Tragedy* (1924).

DRINKWATER, JOHN (1882–1937). Poet, dramatist and actor, and critic. Published *The Death of Leander and other Poems* (1906), *Poems, 1908–1914* (1917), *Tides* (1917), *Summer Harvest: Poems 1924–33* (1933), and two vols. of autobiography, *Inheritance* (1931) and *Discovery* (1932). Withers, 18, recalls AEH remarking that Drinkwater was 'not a poet'. AEH's meetings with Drinkwater were cordial, however: Withers, 38–9, 41–2.

Duff, James Duff (1860–1940). Admitted to TCC, 1874. Won the Porson Prize, 1874; fifth Classic, 1882; Fellow of TCC, 1883–1940, and Tutor, 1899–1909. Published edns. of Lucretius V (1889), Juvenal (1898), Lucretius III (1902), Pliny, Letters VI (1906), a selection of Cicero's correspondence (1911), three dialogues of Seneca (1915), Lucretius I (1923), Lucan (1928), and Silius Italicus (1934). He was a candidate for the chair of Latin at Cambridge in 1911 when AEH was appointed. See Naiditch (1995), 42–3, for further information.

Duff, J[ames] F[itzjames] (1898–1970). Son of J. D. Duff. Awarded a scholarship at TCC, 1914; commissioned in the Royal Flying Corps, and invalided out in 1917; first class in the Classical Tripos, Part I, and second in Economics, Part II; Assistant Lecturer in Classics, Manchester University, 1921; Lecturer in Education, Armstrong College, Newcastle upon Tyne, 1922; Senior Lecturer in Education, Manchester University, 1927, and Professor, 1932.

Edmonds, J[ohn] M[axwell] (1875–1958). Educated at Jesus College, Cambridge (1894–8), gaining first class in Part I of the Classical Tripos; taught classics at The King's School, Canterbury, and at Repton School, returning to Cambridge in 1908; University Lecturer in Classics, 1926; Fellow of Jesus College, 1914–20, and from 1946. Publications include: *An Introduction to Comparative Philology* (1906), and edns. with translations of *The Greek Bucolic Poets* (1912), *Longus: Daphnis and Chloe* (rev., 1916), *Lyra Graeca* (1922–7), and *The Characters of Theophrastus* (1929).

Ellis, Robinson (1834–1913). Fellow of Trinity College, Oxford, 1858–1913; Professor of Latin at UCL, 1870–6; Reader in Latin at Oxford, 1883–93; Corpus Christi Professor of Latin at Oxford and Fellow of Corpus Christi College, 1893–1913; FBA, 1902. Publications include: edns. of Catullus (1866), Ovid's *Ibis* (1881), and *Noctes Manilianae* (1891). AEH studied under him at Oxford, but did not greatly esteem his abilities. Under the pseudonym 'Tristram' he made fun of him (and others) in *The Eleventh Eclogue*, published on 22 June 1878, and in *Ibis' Reply to Ovid*: see *Poems* (1997), 230–5, 525–8; 289, 564. Of his corrections to Manilius AEH later wrote that 'one or two of them were very pretty, but his readers were in perpetual contact with the mind of an idiot child': Preface to *Manilius V* (1930); Ricks (1988), 387. For further information on AEH and Ellis, see Naiditch (1988), 32–4, 41–52.

Evans, [David] Emrys (1891–1936). Principal of University College of North Wales, 1927–58; Vice-Chancellor of the University of Wales, 1933–5.

Fenwick, John. Son-in-law of collector of books and manuscripts Sir Thomas Phillipps, baronet (1792–1872), whose library at Thirlestaine House, Cheltenham, contained a large collection of classical MSS. Fenwick later owned the collection.

Finberg, H[erbert] P[atrick] R[eginald] (1900–74). Educated at Merchant Taylors' School and SJCO. Founder in 1928 of the Alcuin Press at Chipping Campden, where in 1929 a limited edn. (325 copies, 300 for sale) of *ASL* and *LP* were printed. He was director of the Alcuin Press until 1936.

FLACCUS, KIMBALL (1911–72). A friend of Witter Bynner's. He published a volume of poems, *The Avalanche of April* (1934), sent AEH a copy, and visited him in Cambridge in 1935. Bynner to AEH, 17 July 1935 (BMC MS): 'Kimball Flaccus... has sent me a glowing report of you. I envy him.'

FLEET, C[harles?]. The BL catalogue lists two works: *Glimpses of our Ancestors in Sussex* (1878, 1882), and *Glimpses of our Ancestors in Sussex and Gleanings in East and West Sussex* (1883). He lived in Brighton.

FLETCHER, GEORGE (1848–1933) Educated at The Grammar School of King Edward VI, Bromsgrove, 1857–66 (*OBR*, 43), and at Clare College, Cambridge. MRCS, LSA, 1872; MA, MB, 1873. He worked as a surgeon at St Thomas's hospital, London, and lived in Highgate. His father Dr T. S. Fletcher had been the Housmans' family doctor, and his daughter for a time attended AEH's classes at UCL three or four days a week. See the textual note on the letter to him of 10 May 1928. See also Naiditch (1995), 23–4.

FOBES, F[rancis] H[oward] (1881–1957). Professor of Greek, Amherst College, Massachusetts, 1920–48. Editor of *Aristotelis Meteorologicorum libri quattuor* (1919).

FORSTER, E[dward] M[organ] (1879–1970). Eminent novelist and man of letters. Publications include: *The Longest Journey* (1907), *A Room with a View* (1908), *Howards End* (1910), *A Passage to India* (1924), and the homosexual novel *Maurice* (1914; published in 1971).

FOSTER, T[homas] GREGORY (1866–1931). Long associated with UCL: educated there, and taught in the English Department, 1894–1904; then, Secretary, 1900, Provost, 1904–29. Vice-Chancellor, London University, 1928–30; knighted, 1917; first baronet of Bloomsbury, 1930.

FOWLER, W[illiam] CARTER (b. 1856). Local and family historian. Publications include: *Collections for the History of Staffordshire* (1910); the introduction to *Abstracts of the Bailiffs' Accounts of Monastic and other Estates in the County of Warwick...* (1923); and *The Records of King Edward's School, Birmingham* (1924–).

FRAENKEL, EDUARD [David Mortier] (1888–1970). Studied in Berlin and Göttingen, where he received his doctorate in 1912; joined the staff of the *Thesaurus Linguae Latinae* in Munich, 1913; appointed Professor Extraordinarius in Berlin, 1917, Professor Ordinarius in Kiel, 1923, in Göttingen, 1928, and in Freiburg im Breisgau, 1931. As a Jew, forbidden by the Nazis to teach, 1933; Bevan Fellow of TCC, 1934; Corpus Professor of Latin at Oxford, 1935–53. Publications include *Plautinisches im Plautus* (1922), *Iktus und Akzent im lateinischen Sprechvers* (1928), and *Kolon und Satz: Beobachtungen zur Gliederung des antiken Satzes* (1932–3).

FRAZER, JAMES G[eorge] (1854–1941). Social anthropologist and classical scholar. Fellow of TCC, 1879. Publications include: *The Golden Bough* (1890, etc.) and many other works on anthropological subjects; a translation of Pausanius's *Description of Greece* (6 vols., 1898); and edns. of *Apollodorus: The Library* (2 vols., 1921), and *Publii Ovidii Nasonis Fastorum libri sex* (5 vols., 1929). FBA, 1902; first British Professor of Social Anthropology, at Liverpool, 1908–22; knighted, 1914; FRS, 1920; OM, 1925.

FRAZER, LADY, LILLY, née Elizabeth Johanna de Boys Adelsdorfer (1854/5–1941). Writer and translator. Married J. G. Frazer, 22 Apr. 1896. Translated *Adonis* (1921) and the one-vol. epitome of *The Golden Bough* (1923) into French.

GARDNER, RICHARD (1890–1972). Classical scholar (1910–12), Craven Student (1912–14), Junior Fellow (1919), Bursar (1919–60), and Senior Fellow (1923–60) of Emmanuel College, Cambridge.

GARROD, H[eathcote] W[illiam] (1878–1960). Literary and classical scholar. Fellow of Merton College, Oxford, since 1901, and tutor there, 1904–25. Published an edn. of *Manilius II*, 1911, which AEH declined to review, but which in 1930 he criticized roundly in the Preface to *Manilius V*: Ricks (1988), 388–91. Other publications include: an edn. of Statius (1906); several vols. of poetry (1912, 1919, 1925); studies of Wordsworth (1923), Keats (1926), and Collins (1928); *The Oxford Book of Latin Verse* (1912) and *The Profession of Poetry* (1912). CBE, 1918; Professor of Poetry at Oxford, 1923–8; FBA, 1931.

GARVIN, J[ames] L[ouis] (1868–1947). Influential journalist. Editor of *The Outlook* (1904–6), *The Pall Mall Gazette* (1912–15), and *The Observer* (1908–42).

GASELEE, STEPHEN (1882–1943). Librarian and scholar. Educated at Eton and KCC; Librarian of the Pepys Library, Magdalene College, Cambridge, 1908–19; Fellow, 1909–43; served in Foreign Office, 1916–19, where he was subsequently Librarian, 1920–43; Sandars Reader in Bibliography, Cambridge, 1935, specializing in the bibliography of Petronius; CBE, 1918; knighted, 1935. Publications include: the text of Petronius' *Satyricon* with William Burnaby's translation (1910); a revised edn. of William Adlington's 1566 translation of Apuleius (1915); translations of Parthenius (1916) and Achilles Tatius (1917); and *The Oxford Book of Medieval Latin Verse* (1928).

GIBSON, ELIZABETH (1869–1931). Daughter of the poet John Pattison Gibson. In 1911 she married the biblical scholar the Revd T[homas] K[elly] Cheyne (1841–1915).

GLOVER, T[errot] R[eaveley] (1869–1943). Classical scholar and religious historian. Fellow of St John's College, Cambridge, 1892–6; first Professor of Latin at Queen's University, Kingston, Ontario, 1896–1901; Classics Lecturer at St John's College, Cambridge, 1901–11, and University Lecturer in Ancient History, 1911–39; Wilde Lecturer in Natural and Comparative Religion, Oxford, 1918–21; Proctor, 1914–15, 1919–20, and Public Orator, Cambridge University, 1920–39; Deacon at St Andrew's Street Church, Cambridge, 1914–43. Publications include: *Studies in Virgil* (1904), *The Conflict of Religions in the Early Roman Empire* (1909), *The Jesus of*

History (1917), *Herodotus* (1924), *Democracy in the Ancient World* (1927), *The World of the New Testament* (1930), and *Greek Byways* (1932).

GOLDRING, DOUGLAS (1887–1960). Publications include: a collection of poems, *The Country Boy* (1910), which shows AEH's influence; a romance novel *The Permanent Uncle* (1912); and an autobiographical novel *The Fortune* (1923). He aired his anti-war, anti-imperialist views in the novels *The Black Curtain* (1920) and *Nobody Knows* (1923). In ch. 6 of *The Nineteen Twenties* (1945) he recounts a visit to AEH on 2 Jan. 1923: see *HSJ* 16 (1990), 50–3.

GOLLANCZ, ISRAEL (1863–1930). Quain English student and lecturer at UCL, 1892–5; Professor of English Language and Literature at King's College, London, 1903–30; a founder, original Fellow, and Secretary of the British Academy, 1902–30; knighted, 1919. His many publications concern works in the Old English, medieval, and Elizabethan periods.

GORECKI, THADDEUS (b. 1884). American composer. He was involved in composing music for *The Mummy Monarch. A Musical Comedy* (1907) and *When Congress Went To Princeton. Musical Comedy* (1908).

GOSSE, EDMUND [William] (1849–1928). Man of letters and minor poet. He married Ellen ('Nellie') Epps (1850–1929) in 1875. Clark Lecturer in English Literature, TCC, 1884–5; moved to Hanover Terrace, Regent's Park, London, in 1901, and there for many years entertained a large acquaintance on Sunday afternoons; friend of Asquith, who, as Prime Minister, sought his advice on many matters; Librarian of the House of Lords, 1904–14; knighted, 1925. Publications include the celebrated autobiography *Father and Son* (1907), *The Life of Algernon Charles Swinburne* (1917), and, with T. J. Wise, an edition of Swinburne's letters (1918).

GOSSE, Philip [Henry George] (1879–1959), naturalist, doctor, and author. Son of Edmund and Nellie Gosse. Author of *A History of Piracy* (1932).

Gow, A[ndrew] S[ydenham] F[arrar] (1886–1978). Classical scholar. Fellow of TCC, 1911; Assistant Master at Eton, 1914–25; Teaching Fellow at TCC, 1925–46, and Lecturer in the University, 1925–51. He compiled a list of AEH's writings and indexes to his classical papers, which was appended to his biographical study, *A. E. Housman: A Sketch* (1936).

GRAHAM, D[ouglas] L[eslie] (1909–91). Student at Trinity College, Dublin. BA, winter, 1931; MA, 5 Dec. 1934.

GURNEY, IVOR [Bertie] (1890–1937). English composer and poet. Born in Gloucester; entered the Royal College of Music, London, in 1911, and there studied under Sir Charles Stanford and later Ralph Vaughan Williams; served in the Gloucester Regiment as a private on the western front, 1915; wounded and gassed at Passchendaele, Sept. 1917, and sent to Bangour War Hospital near Edinburgh. Suffering from paranoid schizophrenia, he was admitted to Barnwood House Asylum, Gloucester, in 1922, and he died in the City of London Mental Hospital, Kent. He composed over 300 songs (including two Housman cycles, *Ludlow and Teme*, 1923, and *The*

Western Playland, 1925), and published two vols. of poetry, *Severn and Somme* (1917), and *War's Embers* (1919).

HACKFORTH, REGINALD (1887–1957). Fellow of Sidney Sussex College, Cambridge, 1912; University Lecturer in Classics, 1926; editor of *CQ*, 1927–34.

HALE, WILLIAM GARDNER (1849–1928). Held a fellowship at Harvard, 1870–1, and taught there till 1880, except for the year 1876–7, which was spent in study at Leipzig and Göttingen; Professor of Latin at Cornell, 1880, and Chicago, 1892–1919; editor of *CR*, 1906. Publications include: *The Art Of Reading Latin: How To Teach It* (1887); with Carl Buck, *Latin Grammar* (1903); and *A First Latin Book* (1907).

HALIFAX, VISCOUNT. See Wood, Edward Frederick Lindley.

HALL, F[rederick] W[illiam] (1868–1933). Fellow of SJCO, 1897, President, 1931; co-editor of *CQ*, 1911–30; co-editor of the Oxford edn. of Aristophanes (1900–1), and author of *A Companion to Classical Texts* (1913).

HAMILTON, GEORGE ROSTREVOR (1888–1967). Writer and civil servant. Educated at Exeter College, Oxford, 1909–11; worked for the Inland Revenue from 1912, becoming Assistant Secretary to the Board (1926) and Special Commissioner of Income Tax (1934). Publications (verse) include: *Escape and Fantasy* (1918), *Pieces of Eight* (1923), *The Making* (1926), *Epigrams* (1928), *Light in Six Moods* (1930), *John Lord Satirist* (1934) and *Unknown Lovers* (1934), and also the anthologies *The Soul of Wit* (1924), *The Latin Portrait* (1929), *The Greek Portrait* (1934), and *Wit's Looking Glass* (1934).

HAMILTON, WALTER (1908–88). Classical scholar. Entered TCC with major scholarship, 1926; won the Craven University Scholarship, 1927, the Chancellor's Classical Medal, 1928, and the Porson Prize; distinction in Part II of the Classical Tripos, 1929; Assistant Lecturer in Classics, University of Manchester, 1931–2; taught at Eton, 1931–46; limited-term Fellow of TCC, 1932.

HARDEN, D[onald] B[enjamin] (1901–94). Archaeologist. Entered TCC, 1922. Took part in excavations at Tunis (1923–4) and Carthage (1925, 1933), and in Egypt (1928–9). Professor of Latin at Aberdeen University, 1925; Assistant Keeper of the Ashmolean Museum, Oxford, 1929. Author of *The Glass of the Greeks and Romans* (1934) and *Roman Glass from Karanis* (1936).

HARDY, THOMAS (1840–1928). Eminent novelist and poet. He and AEH met on 18 June 1899, 'for the first time probably': Florence Emily Hardy, *The Life of Thomas Hardy 1840–1928*, rev. edn. (1972), 304. They held each other in esteem: see letters to Pollet and Martin, 5 Feb. and 28 Mar. 1933. AEH later contributed *Oh stay at home, my lad, and plough* (*LP* XXXVIII) to a MS vol. celebrating Hardy's 80th birthday (2 June 1919), and was a pall-bearer at his funeral. For further information on the relationship between the two writers, see Naiditch (2005), 15–18.

HARPER, GEORGE MCLEAN, the Elder (1863–1947). American essayist and Wordsworth scholar.

HARRISON, ERNEST (1877–1943). MA, Cambridge, LLD, Glasgow; Fellow of TCC, 1900, Lecturer, 1904–25, Tutor, 1914–25, and Senior Tutor, 1920–5; Registrar, Cambridge University, 1923; editor of *CR*, 1923.

HAYNES, E[dmund] S[idney] P[ollock] (1877–1949). Educated at Eton and Balliol College, Oxford (Brakenbury Scholar); articled to Hunter & Haynes of Lincoln's Inn, 1900; Knight Commander of the Holy Sepulchre, 1926. Publications include: *Standards of Taste in Art* (1904), *Religious Persecution, A Study In Political Psychology* (1904) *A Study of Bereavement: A Comedy in One Act* (1914), *Divorce as it Might Be* (1915), *The Decline of Liberty in England* (1916), *Lycurgus or the Future of Law* (1925), and *Much Ado About Women* (1927).

HIGGINS, [Alexander George MacLennan] PEARCE (d. 1983). Student at Christ's College Cambridge (BA, 1922, MA, 1926). He was the son of Alexander Pearce Higgins (on whom, see the letter of 28 Dec. 1924, n. 2). In 1924 his father took him as a dinner guest and introduced him to AEH.

HILL, G[eorge] F[rancis] (1867–1948). Numismatist. Educated at University College School, UCL, and Merton College, Oxford; double first in classics, 1889, 1891; with AEH, an applicant for the Chair of Latin or Greek at UCL, 1892; Assistant in the Department of Coins and Medals, British Museum, 1893; Deputy Keeper, 1911; Keeper, 1912; FBA, 1917; Director and Principal Librarian of the British Museum, 1931–6; knighted, 1933.

HINKSON, KATHARINE TYNAN (1859–1931), née Tynan. Prolific Irish poet and novelist. She married Henry Albert Hinkson in 1893.

HIRES, HARRISON S. (b. 1887). American writer. Author of *Invitation and Other Poems* (1938) and *For My Children* (1943).

HOLLAND, MICHAEL [James], MC (1870–1956). Son of the Revd Francis James Holland, Canon of Canterbury. Private Secretary to the Governor of the Gold Coast, 1896–7; served with Samory and Kazembe Expeditions, 1897, 1899, and during the First World War in France, 1915–16, and German East Africa, 1916–18.

HOLLOND, HENRY [Arthur] (1884–1974). Lawyer. Admitted to TCC, 1903; Fellow, 1909–74; Dean of the College, 1922–50. Co-author with H. D. Hazeltine of *Cambridge Studies in English Legal History* (1921).

HORSBURGH, JAMES MACDONALD (1854–1905). Assistant Master, Radley College, 1881–2; Librarian and Secretary of the London Institution, 1882–6; Secretary of UCL, 1886–1900. For further information, see Naiditch (1988), 95–6.

HOUSMAN, BASIL [Williams] (16 January 1864–1 Dec. 1932). AEH's younger brother; Foundation Scholar at The Grammar School of King Edward VI, Bromsgrove, 1875–82; won Sands-Cox scholarship to Queen's College, Birmingham, 1882, and went on to Queen's Hospital; FRCS, 1891, LRCP, London; on 24 July 1894, married Jane ('Jeannie'), daughter of the late Matthew Dixon of Tardebigge, Worcestershire; Assistant School Medical Officer, Worcestershire County Council,

1908; retired owing to ill health, 1929. A photograph appeared in the Housman Society's _Newsletter_, 19 (Feb. 2004), 10.

HOUSMAN, EDWARD (25 Jan. 1831–27 Nov. 1874). AEH's father; Bromsgrove solicitor; Conservative in politics. For information on his two marriages, see under Lucy Agnes Housman.

HOUSMAN, JEANNIE. See under Basil Housman.

HOUSMAN, KATHARINE [Elizabeth] (10 Dec. 1862–17 Nov. 1945), AEH's younger sister 'Kate'. On 13 Aug. 1887 she married Edward William Symons, (q.v.). Her publications include: _Unexplored Sources of Bath History_ (1921); _The Grammar School of King Edward VI, Bath, and its Ancient Foundations_ (1935), for research on which AEH made her a fully paid-up life member of the London Library (Pugh, Appendix E, lxiii); two reminiscences of AEH, reprinted from the school magazine _The Edwardian_ as _Memories of A. E. Housman_ and _More Memories of A. E. Housman_ (1936); and a chapter on AEH's boyhood in _Recollections_; and the Introduction to Richards (xi–xviii).

HOUSMAN, LAURENCE (18 July 1865–20 Feb. 1959), AEH's younger brother. Writer, dramatist, art critic, book illustrator, and pioneer pacifist, feminist, and socialist. Publications include: vols. of poems _Green Arras_ (1896), and _Spikenard_ (1898); the notorious and much parodied _An Englishwoman's Love-Letters_, published anonymously (1900); plays _Bethlehem_ (1902), _Angels and Ministers_ (1921), _Little Plays of St Francis_ (1922), and _Victoria Regina_ (1934); and novels _John of Jingalo_ (1912), _Sheepfold_ (1918), _Trimblerigg_ (1924), and _The Life of H. R. H. The Duke of Flamborough_ (1928),

HOUSMAN, LUCY AGNES (b. Freshford, Somerset, 9 Oct. 1823, d. Hereford, 12 Nov. 1907). AEH's stepmother. She married Edward Housman, her first cousin, in London on 26 June 1873. AEH's mother, Sarah Jane Housman (b. Stroud, Glos., 24 Aug. 1828, d. Bromsgrove, 26 Mar. 1871), had married Edward Housman on 17 June 1858, with Lucy as bridesmaid. Sarah Jane was the daughter of the Revd John Williams, who was Rector of Woodchester, Co. Gloucester, from 1833 till his death on 30 June 1857. She died of cancer on AEH's twelfth birthday when he was staying with the Wise family at Woodchester near Stroud.

HOWARD DE WALDEN, MARGHERITA ['Margot'] DOROTHY, LADY (1890–1974). Wife of Thomas Evelyn Scott-Ellis (1880–1946), 8th Baron Howard de Walden.

HUDSON-WILLIAMS, ALUN (1907–95). First class in Latin and in Greek, University of Wales at Bangor, followed by an M.Litt. at Cambridge University, 1928–30; Lecturer in the Department of Classics, University College of Wales, Aberystwyth, 1934–62, and Senior Lecturer 1962–72.

HUTCHISON, WILLIAM G[eorge] (1873–1907). Translator of _Tacitus and other Roman Studies_ by Gaston Boissier (1906), and author of _The Oxford Movement: being selections from tracts for the times_ (1906).

INNES, HUGH MCLEOD (1862–1944). First class in both parts of the Classical Tripos at Cambridge, 1882, 1884; Fellow of TCC, 1886; called to the Bar and began to practise, but returned to TCC and was re-elected Fellow in 1894; elected Junior Bursar, and, in 1898, Senior Bursar, a post he held for thirty years.

ISHILL, JOSEPH (1888–1966), American letterpress printer, typographer, and publisher of radical materials; owner of the Oriole Press, Berkeley Heights, New Jersey.

JACKSON, GERALD CHRISTOPHER ARDEN (b. 1900). Fourth son of Moses Jackson (q.v.), and AEH's godson. AEH's light verse, *Aids Towards Answering the First Question of the Catechism*, is addressed to him: *Poems* (1997), 271. Over the years AEH wrote more than thirty letters to him (of which only one has come to light); they sent each other a number of publications; and he attended AEH's funeral. See Naiditch (1995), 143, for further information.

JACKSON, HENRY (1839–1921). Fellow of TCC, 1864; Regius Professor of Greek at Cambridge, 1906–21; OM, 1908; Vice-Master of TCC, 1914; editor of *The Journal of Philology*, 1879–1921. Publications include *The Fifth Book of the Nicomathean Ethics of Aristotle* (1879) and *Texts to Illustrate a Course of Elementary Lectures on the History of Greek Philosophy from Thales to Aristotle* (1901). See Naiditch (1988), 165–71, for further information.

JACKSON, HENRY CHOLMONDELEY (1879–1972). Son of Henry Jackson. Educated at TCC; joined 1st Bedfordshire and Herefordshire Regiment, 1899; Major, 1915; Director of Military Training, Army HQ, India, 1926–30; Major-General, 1930; Lieutenant-General, 1935; Knight Commander of the Bath, 1936.

JACKSON, MARGARET ('Marg') ADELAIDE (alive, 1 Oct. 1936). Sister of Moses Jackson. Lived at Vales Court, Ramsgate, Kent: Naiditch (1995), 134 n.

JACKSON, MOSES [John] (14 Apr. 1858–14 Jan. 1923). 'Dear Mo', AEH's 'greatest friend' who 'had more influence on my life than anyone else' and who was 'largely responsible for my writing poetry'. At least two photographs of him hung in AEH's rooms in TCC, and he was the only person to whom AEH publicly dedicated a book, the edn. of Manilius, which contained the dedicatory poem *Sodali Meo M. I. Iackson*. AEH maintained a life-long devotion to him. It is extremely doubtful that AEH's feelings were reciprocated in like measure, and there is no evidence whatsoever that the relationship was, or could have been, at any time physical.

AEH and he met at St John's College, Oxford, where in the summer of 1877 they both won scholarships, Jackson in science, AEH in classics, prior to entry in Oct. 1877. From 1880 onwards they shared accommodation with A. W. Pollard. Jackson's interests included rowing and running. After graduating with first class honours, from 25 June 1881 onwards he worked in HM Patent Office, London, and shared accommodation with his brother Adalbert. AEH joined them for about two years. In 1883 Jackson received a doctorate in science from UCL, and at the end of 1884, Adalbert graduated from UCL and moved away to become a schoolmaster. In 1885, probably after an altercation, AEH and Jackson decided to live apart. Jackson left at the end of 1887 to become Principal of Sind College, Karachi. He returned on leave to England in 1889, and married the widow Mrs Rosa Julia Chambers on 9 Dec., but AEH was not invited to the wedding. At AEH's instigation, he was elected a fellow of UCL in Jan. 1894. He returned for a year-and-a-half of leave in 1897–8. He was not successful in his application for the Quain Chair of Physics at UCL, and AEH was not successful in having him appointed to the Headmastership of University College School. By 1898 AEH and Jackson seem to have become reconciled, and in 1900 Jackson asked AEH to stand as godfather for his fourth son, Gerald Christopher Arden Jackson. Jackson was again on leave in England in 1902, 1905, and 1908. After retiring in 1910, he lived on a farm ('Applegarth') in British Columbia. He died from stomach cancer on 14 Jan. 1923. For further information, see Naiditch (1995), 132–44 (the principal source); *Poems* (1997), 393–4, 454; and Robert B. Todd, 'M. J. Jackson in British Columbia: Some Supplementary Information', *HSJ* 26 (2000), 59–61.

Only AEH's last letter to Jackson (19 Oct. 1922) has come to light.

JACKSON, ROSA. See previous entry.

JAMES, M[ontague] R[hodes] (1862–1936). Biblical scholar, palaeographer, medievalist, and writer of ghost stories. King's Scholar at Eton, 1876; Fellow of KCC, 1887; Director of the Fitzwilliam Museum, Cambridge, 1893–1908; Provost of KCC, 1905–18; Vice-Chancellor of Cambridge University, 1913–15; Provost of Eton, 1918–36; FBA, 1913; OM, 1930.

JAMIN, GEORGES. French translator. Published an adaptation of Patrick Kearney's *A Man's Man* in 1934.

JENKINSON, F[rancis] J[ohn] H[enry] (1853–1923). Fellow of TCC, 1878, and College Lecturer in Classics, 1881–9; University Librarian, 1889–1923; Sandars Reader in Bibliography at Cambridge, 1907–8. Publications include an edn. of the seventh-century Hiberno-Latin poem *Hisperica Famina* (1908).

JONES, HENRY FESTING (1851–1928). Friend of the writer and artist Samuel Butler, with whom he collaborated on several musical compositions. Publications include various instalments of Butler's notebooks, 1912–21, and a biography, *Samuel Butler, Author of Erewhon (1835–1902)* (1919).

JONES, HENRY STUART (1867–1939). First class in *literae humaniores*, Oxford, 1890; Non-official Fellow of Trinity College, Oxford, 1890; Fellow, 1896; Camden Professor of Ancient History and Fellow of Brasenose College, 1919; Principal of the University College of Wales at Aberystwyth, 1927; Vice-Chancellor of the federal University of Wales, 1929–30; FBA, 1915; knighted, 1933. Publications include: an edn. of Thucydides' *Histories* (2 vols., 1898, 1900), *Companion to Roman History* (1912), and the revised and augmented *A Greek–English Lexicon*, by H. G. Liddell and R. Scott, 9th edn. (1928–40).

JUDGE, MAX. Founder in 1922 with A. J. A. Symons (1900–41) of the First Edition Club, a centre for bibliographical information and a dining club in Bloomsbury. Editor of the travel periodicals *The Sandgate Budget* (1897) and *The Bungalow*

(1899–1909), and author of *In the Days of Ancient Rome: being a Commentary on a series of etchings by W. Walcot* (1913).

KEARY, C[harles] F[rancis] (1848–1917). Numismatist and minor writer. Began work in the department of medals and coins of the British Museum, 1872; resigned, 1887.

KEYNES, GEOFFREY [Langdon] (1887–1982). Surgeon, bibliographer, and literary scholar. MD, 1918; FRCS, 1920. Publications include *Blood Transfusion* (1922); bibliographies of John Donne (1914), William Blake (1921), and Sir Thomas Browne (1924); and complete edns. of Blake and Browne (respectively, 3 vols., 1925, 6 vols., 1928–31).

KNOCHE, ULRICH (1902–68). German classical scholar. In 1926 he published 'Die Überlieferung Juvenals' in *Klassisch-philologische Studien*, 6. His edn. of Juvenal was published at Munich in 1950.

LANE, ALLEN (1902–70). Till 1919, Allen Lane Williams. He learned the book trade under his uncle John Lane (q.v.), and served on the board of directors of 'The Bodley Head' publishing house in 1925, chairing it in 1930. In 1936 he founded Penguin Books.

LANE, JOHN (1854–1925). Set up as bookseller and then publisher with Charles Elkin Mathews, 1887–94; published the first book under 'The Bodley Head' imprint, 1889; produced the *Yellow Book*, 1894–7, and works by several prominent writers of the *fin de siècle* (Davidson, Dowson, Le Gallienne, J. A. Symonds, Francis Thompson, William Watson, Wilde).

LAPSLEY, GAILLARD THOMAS (1871–1949). Fellow of TCC, 1904–49; Lecturer at TCC, 1904–32; Tutor, 1919–29; Reader in Constitutional History at Cambridge, 1931–7.

LAST, HUGH [Macilwain] (1894–1957). Open Scholar, Lincoln College, Oxford, 1914; first class in *literae humaniores*, 1918; Fellow of SJCO, 1919; University Lecturer in Roman History, 1927–36. He contributed to the *Cambridge Ancient History*: 6 chs. in vol. 9 (1932); 1 ch. in vol. 10 (1934); and 2 chs. in vol. 11 (1936).

LEE, G[eorge] M[ervyn] (1915–88). Entered TCC from Bedford School, 1934; first classes in both parts of the Classical Tripos, 1935, 1937; Bell's Exhibitioner, 1934; Davies Scholar, 1935.

LEIPPERT, JAMES GEORGE. Columbia University, 1929–33; Editor of *Lion and Crown*, 1932, corresponding with leading American poets of the day. Naiditch (1995), 41, identifies him as 'James George Leippert *alias* "Alfred Housman" Leippert *alias* "Edwin Robinson" Leippert *alias* J. Ronald Lane-Latimer, a young man who had invented an unusual method for obtaining letters from notable literary men'.

LEMPERLY, PAUL (1858–1939). American collector, based in Cleveland, Ohio.

xl   *List of Recipients*

LEONARD, WILLIAM ELLORY (1876–1944). American poet. Ph.D., Columbia, 1904; Assistant Professor of English, University of Wisconsin, 1906–44. Publications include: *Sonnets and Poems* (1906), *Two Lives* (1922), and a verse translation of Lucretius (1916).

LINDSAY, W[allace] M[artin] (1858–1937). First class in *literae humaniores*, Oxford, 1881; Fellow of Jesus College, Oxford, 1884–99; Professor of Humanity, University of St Andrews, 1899–1937. Publications include: *The Latin Language* (1894); *Introduction to Latin Textual Emendation* (1896), in which he argued that emendation should be limited to the correction of scribal errors; edns. of Martial (1903) and Plautus (1904–5); and *Early Irish Minuscule Script* (1910), *Early Welsh Script* (1912), and *Glossaria Latina* (1926–32). On AEH and Lindsay, see Naiditch (1995), 75–9.

LOGAN, R[obert] Y[oung] (b. 1905). Entrance Scholar at TCC, 1923; Senior Scholar, 1924; awarded 1: 2 in both parts of the Historical Tripos, 1925, 1926; BA, 1926.

LUCAS, E[dward] V[errall] (1868–1938). Prolific English man of letters. Publications encompass fiction, cricket, travel, art, and the works of Charles and Mary Lamb.

LULHAM, EDWIN PERCY HABBERTON (1865–1940). MRCS, LRCP. Educated at University School, Hastings and King's College, London, and worked at Sussex County Hospital and Guy's Hospital, London. Author of several vols. of poetry, including *Devices and Desires* (1904), *Songs from the Downs and Dunes* (1908), and *The Other Side of Silence* (1915).

MACCOLL, D[ugald] S[utherland] (1859–1948). Painter, poet, and journalist. Art critic of *The Spectator*, 1890–6, and of *The Saturday Review*, 1896–1906. Keeper, Tate Gallery, London, 1906–11; Trustee, 1917–24.

MACKAIL, J[ohn] W[illiam] (1859–1945). Classical scholar, translator, and poet. Fellow of Balliol College, Oxford, 1882–4; worked in the education department of the Privy Council (later the Board of Education), 1884–1919; Professor of Poetry at Oxford, 1906–11; FBA, 1914, and President, 1932–6; President of the Classical Association, 1922–3; President of the English Association, 1929–30. Classical publications include: a prose translation of the *Aeneid* (1885); *Select Epigrams from the Greek Anthology* (1890), *Latin Literature* (1895), *Virgil and his Meaning to the World of To-day* (1923); and an edn. of the *Aeneid* (1930). AEH and he held each other in esteem: he was one of the three advisers AEH consulted on the contents of *LP* (see the letters of 18 and 25 July 1922).

MACLAGAN, ERIC [Robert Dalrymple] (1879–1951). Read classics at Christ Church, Oxford; third class in honour moderations, 1900, and a fourth in *literae humaniores*, 1902; worked in the departments of textiles, 1905, and of architecture and sculpture, 1909, at the Victoria and Albert Museum and, following war service chiefly in the Foreign Office and the Ministry of Information, was appointed as the Museum's director, 1925. Produced *English Ecclesiastical Embroideries* (1907), the *Catalogue of Italian Plaquettes* (1924), and in collaboration with Margaret Longhurst, the *Catalogue of Italian*

Sculpture (1932). His Charles Eliot Norton lectures at Harvard were published as *Italian Sculpture of the Renaissance* (1935). CBE, 1919; knighted, 1933.

MacLaren, Malcolm [Shaw] (b. 1901). Poet and translator (into French). Publications include: *Poems* (1926); *Anthologie de la poésie française. Les modernes* (1929), *Douze Sonnets et Un Poème* (1929), and *Poèmes* (1930).

Macmillan, Frederick [Orridge] (1851–1936). Publisher: chairman of Messrs Macmillan and Company, 1896–1936. Knighted in 1909 for his work as chairman, from 1903, of the board of management of the National Hospital for the Paralysed and Epileptic in London.

Makin, W. Manager of the Richards Press.

Marie Louise Victoria, Princess (1872–1956). Youngest child of Prince Christian of Schleswig-Holstein (1831–1917) and Queen Victoria's third daughter Princess Helena (1846–1923). She wrote 2,000 letters in her own hand to secure contributions (including AEH's) to the elaborate doll's house that was presented to Queen Mary.

Markham, Edwin (1852–1940). American poet and anthologist. Author of *The Man with the Hoe and Other Poems*. AEH made fun of one of his literary echoes: *Poems* (1997), 271, 553.

Martin, Houston (1914–94). American bibliophile. Born in Wichita, Kansas; moved permanently to Philadelphia when 12; educated at the Friends' Central School, Pennsylvania, and at the University of Pennsylvania; served three years in the Air Force in the South Pacific, and then worked for thirty years as international advertising representative (among other things) for the *New York Times*. He and AEH never met. His collection of Housmaniana is incorporated in that of Seymour Adelman at BMC.

Marvin, F[rancis] S[ydney] (1863–1943). Historian. Publications include: *The Unity of Western Civilization: Essays* (1915), *Progress and History: Essays* (1919), and *Science and Civilization* (1923).

Masefield, John [Edward] (1878–1967). Poet, novelist, and playwright. Poetry includes *Salt-Water Ballads* (1902), *Ballads* (1903), *Ballads and Poems* (1910), *The Everlasting Mercy* (1911), and *Reynard the Fox* (1919). Prose includes *Dauber* (1913) and *Gallipoli* (1916) and the novels *Lost Endeavour* (1910) and *The Bird of Dawning* (1933). His most successful play was *The Tragedy of Nan* (1909). Moved to Boars Hill near Oxford, 1917, and set up a theatre in his house. Poet Laureate, 1930; OM, 1935.

Meakin, Annette Mary Budgett (1867–1959). Linguist, and author, 1901–32, of travel books, three of them on Russia; later FRGS. She attended AEH's Latin classes at UCL from 1897 till spring, 1900: Meakin to Grant Richards, 22 June 1943 (LC-GR1 MS). In *The Times*, 7 May 1936, she testified to the high opinion of AEH's scholarship held by Professor Ulrich von Wilamowitz-Moellendorff, whom she had visited in Charlottenburg in 1926: note reproduced in Richards, 84 n. AEH knew of her visit: see letter to Frazer, 22 Oct. 1927.

MERRILL W[illiam] A[ugustus] (1860–1930). Professor of Latin Language and Literature at the University of California, Berkeley, 1894–1927. Published works are mainly on Lucretius and include an edn., 1907, and *The Archetype of Lucretius* (1913).

MEYERSTEIN, E[dward] H[arry] W[illiam] (1889–1952). Writer. MA, FRSL. Only son of Sir Edward William Meyerstein. Assistant at the Department of Manuscripts, British Museum, 1913–18. Publications include: vols. of poetry *The Door* (1911), *Selected Poems* (1935); a translation, *The Elegies of Propertius done in English Verse* (1935); a novel, *Terence Duke* (1935); plays, *Heddon* (1921) and *The Monument* (1923); and a collection of short stories, *The Pageant and Other Stories* (1934).

MEYNELL, WILFRID [John] (1852–1948). Journalist, poet, editor, and biographer. Husband of poet Alice (1847–1922) from 1877.

MILLINGTON-DRAKE, EUGEN [John Henry Vanderstegen] (1889–1972). British diplomat. First Secretary and at times Chargé d'Affaires at Brussels, 1924–7, and Copenhagen, 1927–8; Counsellor of Embassy, Buenos Aires, 1929–33; Minister to Uruguay, 1934–41.

MONRO, HAROLD [Edward] (1879–1932). Poet, editor, and bookseller. Founded *Poetry Review* (1912), *Poetry and Drama* (1913–14), and *(Monthly) Chapbook* (1919–25). Published four vols. of his own poetry (1917–28), and a survey, *Some Contemporary Poets* (1920); and founded the Poetry Bookshop, Bloomsbury (1912–35), an important venue for publications, poetry readings, and meetings.

MONROE, HARRIET (1860–1936). American poet and anthologist, and editor of *Poetry* (Chicago), 1912. Compiled *The New Poetry: An Anthology of Twentieth-Century Verse in English* (1923).

MORING, MESSRS ALEXANDER. Publishing house to which Grant Richards's business was sold by the trustee, H. A. Moncrieff, after Richards's bankruptcy in 1904/5.

MORLEY, S[ylvanus] G[riswold] (1878–1970). Professor of Spanish at the University of California, Berkeley.

MOULT, THOMAS (1885–1974). Writer and anthologist. Edited *Georgian Poetry 1918–1919* (1920), and *The Best Poems of 1923* (1924), *The Best Poems of 1925* (1926), etc.

MUNSON, GORHAM [Bert] (1896–1969). American author and critic. Set up The New School, a pioneering creative writing programme, in New York's Greenwich Village, 1931; editor of various literary magazines (e.g. *Secession*, 1922–4); member of faculty of Middlebury College, Vermont, 1930–3, 1935.

MURRAY, [George] GILBERT [Aimé] (1866–1957). Classical scholar. Born in Sydney, Australia; educated at Merchant Taylors' School and SJCO; first class in *literae humaniores*, 1888; Fellow of New College, Oxford, 1888; Professor of Greek,

Glasgow University, 1889–99; returned to New College, Oxford, 1905; Regius Professor of Greek at Oxford, 1908–36; FBA, 1910. Publications include: *History of Greek Literature* (1897); an edn. of Euripides (1902–9); translations of Euripides and Aristophanes (1902 onwards); *The Rise of the Greek Epic* (1907); *Four Stages of Greek Religion* (1912), extended in 1925 to *Five Stages, Euripides and his Age* (1913); and *The Foreign Policy of Sir Edward Grey* (1915).

NEWALL, HUGH FRANK (1857–1944). Demonstrator in Experimental Physics, Cambridge University, 1886–90; FRS, 1902; Fellow of TCC, 1909; President of the Royal Astronomical Society, 1907–9; Professor of Astrophysics at Cambridge, 1909–28; first Director, Solar Physics Observatory at Cambridge, 1913–28. Publications include *The Spectroscope and its Work* (1910).

NOCK, A[rthur] D[arby] (1902–63). BA at TCC, 1922; Fellow of Clare College, Cambridge, 1923–30, and University Lecturer in Classics, 1926–30; Visiting Lecturer on the History of Religions at Harvard, 1929–30; Frothingham Professor of the History of Religions at Harvard, and editor of the *Harvard Theological Review*, 1930–63. Publications include an edn. of *Sallustius: Concerning the Gods and the Universe* (1926), and *Conversion: The Old and the New in Religion from Alexander the Great to Augustine of Hippo* (1933).

OLIVER, F[rancis] W[all] (1864–1951). Quain Professor and Emeritus Professor of Botany at UCL, 1888–1929, 1929–35; Professor of Botany, Cairo University, 1929–35. His recollections of AEH are included in Richards, 438–40.

OPPENHEIM, ELIZABETH [Alexandra], daughter of Lieutenant-Colonel Phineas Cowan. In 1902 she married Lassa [Francis Lawrence] Oppenheim, and they had one daughter, Mary. Oppenheim (1858–1919) studied law in Germany before moving to England in 1895. He was Lecturer in Law at the London School of Economics, 1898–1908, and Whewell Professor of International Law at Cambridge, 1908–19. His publications include *International Law: A Treatise*, 2 vols. (1905, 1906), and *Manual of Military Law* (1912).

OWLETT, F[rederick] C[harles]. Literary journalist. Author of *Kultur and Anarchy* (poems, 1917), *Chatterton's Apology*, with a short essay on Blake and a note on Cowper (1930), and *Francis Thompson* (1936).

PARRY, REGINALD ST JOHN (1858–1935). Fellow of TCC, 1881; Vice-Master, 1919.

PARTINGTON W[illiam] G[eorge] (b. 1888). English man of letters. Publications include *Smoke Rings and Roundelays: Blendings from Prose and Verse since Raleigh's Time* (1924) and *The Private Letter Books of Sir Walter Scott* (1930).

PAYNE, L[eonidas] W[arren], Jr (1873–1945). Professor of English in the University of Texas, 1919, author of textbooks, and compiler of anthologies.

PEARSON, A[lfred] C[hilton] (1861–1935). Gladstone Professor of Greek at Liverpool, 1919; Regius Professor of Greek at Cambridge, 1921–8, and Fellow of TCC. Publications include: *Fragments of Sophocles*, begun by Jebb and continued by

Headlam (1917); *Sophoclis fabulae* (1924), in a review of which AEH described him as 'an acute grammarian, a vigilant critic, and an honest man' (*Classical Papers*, 1093); and edns. of Euripides' *Helena* (1903), *Heraclidae* (1907), and *Phoenissae* (1909). FBA, 1924. He resigned at Cambridge owing to ill health.

PEASE, ARTHUR STANLEY (1881–1964). Ph.D., Harvard, 1905; Instructor in Classics, Harvard, 1906–9; Assistant Professor, University of Illinois, 1909–24; Professor of Latin, Amherst College, 1924–7, and President, 1927–32; Professor of Latin Language and Literature, Harvard, 1932–50. Publications include edns. of Cicero's *De Diuinatione* (1920) and of the fourth book of the *Aeneid* (1935).

PHILLIMORE, J[ohn] S[winnerton] (1873–1926). First class in *literae humaniores*, Oxford, 1895; Lecturer at Christ Church, Oxford, 1896; Tutor, 1898; Professor of Greek at Glasgow University, 1899; Professor of Humanity, 1906. Publications include: texts of Propertius (1901) and of Statius's *Silvae* (1905); an *Index verborum Propertianus* (1906); a translation of *Philostratus, in Honour of Apollonius of Tyana* (1912); and two vols. of poetry (1902, 1918).

PINKER, JAMES B., AND SON. London literary agents.

PLATT, [John] ARTHUR (11 July 1860–16 Mar. 1925). Fellow of TCC, 1884; married Mildred Barham Bond, 1885; tutor at Wren and Gurney's coaching establishment, Bayswater, 1886–94; Professor of Greek at UCL, 1894–1925. He was one of AEH's best friends, and AEH wrote an admiring and affectionate memoir of him as the preface to *Nine Essays* by Arthur Platt (1927): see *Selected Prose*, 154–60; Ricks (1988), 344–8.

PLATT, MILDRED. See the previous entry. Her father was Sir Edward Bond (1815–98), Principal Librarian of the British Museum, 1878–88; her grandfather, R. H. Barham of *Ingoldsby Legends* fame.

POLLARD A[rthur] W[illiam] (1859–1944). English bibliographer and editor. Met AEH and shared rooms with him and Moses Jackson during their time at SJCO; first class in *literae humaniores*, 1881; entered the printed books department of the British Museum, 1883; Keeper of Printed Books, 1919–24; Honorary Professor of Bibliography, University of London, 1919–32; Director of the Early English Texts Society, 1930–7. Publications include: *Chaucer* (1893); edns. of Sidney's *Astrophil and Stella* (1888), Herrick's poems (1891), Chaucer's *Canterbury Tales* (1894), *The Towneley Plays* with George England (1897), and *The Macro Plays* with F. J. Furnivall (1904); *Shakespeare Folios and Quartos: A Study in the Bibliography of Shakespeare's Plays, 1594–1685* (1909); *Fine Books* (1912); and *A Short-Title Catalogue of Books Printed in England, Scotland, & Ireland, and of English Books Printed Abroad, 1475–1640*, begun by Gilbert Richard Redgrave (1926).

POLLET, MAURICE. Professor of English at the Lycée d'Oran, Algeria.

POSTGATE, JOHN PERCIVAL (1853–1926). Fellow of TCC, 1878–1926; Professor of Comparative Philology at UCL, 1880–1910, and, for the last three years, at the University of London; 1884–1909, Lecturer, and, for the last six years, Senior

Lecturer in Classics at TCC; FBA, 1907; 1909–26, Professor, and, for the last six years, Emeritus Professor of Latin at Liverpool. Editor of the *Corpus Poetarum Latinorum* (2 vols., 1894, 1905), for which respectively AEH edited the texts of Ovid's *Ibis* and Juvenal. Editor of *CR*, 1898–1906, and of *CQ*, 1907–10. Other publications include: *Select Elegies of Propertius* (1881); edns. of Lucan, books 7 and 8 (1896, 1917); and a text and translation of Tibullus (1913). Naiditch (1988), 74–91, provides further information.

POWELL, J[ohn] ENOCH (1912–98). Attended King Edward VI School for Boys, Birmingham, 1926–30; won a Scholarship at TCC, 1930, and graduated in the first class of both parts of the Classical Tripos, 1931, 1933; awarded a Craven Scholarship, the Greek prose prize, the Porson Prize, and Sir William Browne medal; elected limited-term Fellow of TCC, 1934, following a thesis on *The Moral and Historical Principles of Thucydides*. Published *The Rendel Harris Papyri of Woodbrooke College, Birmingham* (1936).

PRIESTLEY, J[ohn] B[oynton] (1894–1984). Novelist, playwright, and broadcaster.

PULSIFER, HAROLD T[rowbridge] (1886–1948). American poet. Published vols. of poetry include *Mothers and Men* (1916), *Harvest of Time* (1933), and *First Symphony: A Sonnet Sequence* (1935).

PURVES, JOHN (1877–1961). MA, Edinburgh University, 1900; Lecturer in Italian at Edinburgh, 1920, and Reader, 1938–47; editor of anthologies *The South African Book of English Verse* (1915) and *A First Book of Italian Verse* (1930); and a collector of MSS and rare books.

PYM, THOMAS ('Tom') WENTWORTH (1885–1945). Admitted to TCC, 1905; BA, third class in the Classical Tripos, 1908; MA, 1912; as a student took part in amateur dramatic productions and was president of the Amateur Dramatic Club; ordained curate of Lytham, 1909; Chaplain of TCC, 1911–14; Chaplain to the Forces, 1914–19, and Assistant Chaplain-General, 1918; Head of Cambridge House, the university mission in Camberwell, 1919–25; Chaplain to the King from 1922; Warden of the College of St Saviour and Canon of Southwark, 1925–9; Canon of Bristol, 1929–32; Chaplain of Balliol College, Oxford, 1932–8. Publications include *Psychology and the Christian Life* (1921) and *A Parson's Dilemmas* (1930). His wife Dora, whom he married in 1918, wrote a reminiscence of AEH reading Horace, *Odes*, 4. 7, and his own version of it (*More Poems* V) in one of his lectures: see Richards, 289. She also wrote a memoir of her husband: *Tom Pym: A Portrait* (1952).

QUILLER-COUCH, ARTHUR (1863–1944). Editor of *The Oxford Book of English Verse* (1900, etc.) Knighted, 1910. Appointed King Edward Professor of English Literature at Cambridge, 1912. Fellow of Jesus College, 1912.

RACKHAM, HARRIS. (1868–1944). Fellow of Christ's College, Cambridge, 1894–1934; University Lecturer in Classics, 1926–34.

RAMSAY, A[llen] B[eville] (1872–1955), Assistant Master at Eton, 1895–1925; Master of Magdalene College, 1925–47. Nicknamed 'The Ram'.

RAMSAY, LADY MARGARET JOHNSTONE, née Buchanan (d. 1936). From 1881 wife of AEH's UCL colleague William Ramsay (1852–1916), Professor of Chemistry at UCL, 1887–1912, who was knighted in 1902 and won the Nobel Prize in 1904.

RICE, WALLACE DE GROOT CECIL (1859–1939). American author and lecturer.

RICHARDS, [Franklin Thomas] GRANT (21 Oct. 1872–24 Feb. 1948). Publisher and author. Son of Franklin Richards, who from 1894 was a Fellow of Trinity College, Oxford; left school at sixteen and served on the staff of *The Review of Reviews*, 1 May 1890–end of 1896; founded publishing firm, 1 Jan. 1897; published the 2nd edn. of *ASL*, 1898; following marriage that year, his first wife Elsina and he had three sons, Gerard, Geoffrey, and Charles, and a daughter, Gioia; 1897–9, published works of Maurice Materlinck, G. B. Shaw, Arnold Bennett, H. G. Wells, Grant Allen, Alice Meynell, and also the first works of John Masefield and G. K. Chesterton; went bankrupt, 1905, 1926; author of *Caviare* (1912), *Valentine* (1913), *Bittersweet* (1915), *Double Life* (1920), *Every Wife* (1924), *Fair Exchange* (1927), *The Coast of Pleasure* (1928), *The Hasty Marriage* (1928), *Vain Pursuits* (1931), and *Memories of a Misspent Youth* (1932); published *LP* (1922), and AEH's edns. of Manilius (1903–30) and Juvenal (1905); divorced, 1914; married Maria Magdalena Csanády (b. 1889/90), 2 July 1915; shared AEH's enjoyment of food, wine, and travel. His *Housman 1897–1936* (1941; corrected reprint, 1942) gives particulars of their business dealings and long friendship.

RICHMOND, O[liffe] L[egh] (1881–1977). Fellow of KCC, 1905, and College Lecturer, 1909; Professor of Humanity, Edinburgh University, 1919–48.

RIDLEY, M[aurice] R[oy] (1890–1969). Literary scholar. BA, Balliol College, Oxford, 1913; Ordained, 1919; Fellow and Tutor in English Literature at Balliol, 1920–45; Chaplain, 1920–32.

ROBBINS, FRANK E[gleston] (1884–1963). BA and MA, Wesleyan University, 1906, 1907; Ph.D., University of Chicago, 1911; Fellow in Greek, 1909–11, and Assistant in Greek, 1911–12, at Chicago; Instructor and Assistant Professor of Greek, University of Michigan, 1912–20; Assistant to the President, University of Michigan, 1921–53; Director of Michigan University Press, 1930–54.

ROBERTS, D[enys] K[ilham] (1903–76). Secretary to the Society of Authors, London, 1930–63.

ROBERTS, R[ichard] Ellis (1879–1953). At SJCO, 1897–1901, where he was vice-president of the Essay Society; Literary Editor of the *New Statesman*, 1928, of *Time and Tide*, 1933, and of *Life and Letters*, 1934–5, and also a writer, critic, and minor composer. Publications include: *Henrik Ibsen* (1912); a short story *The Other End* (1923); and *Reading for Pleasure, and Other Essays* (1928).

ROBERTS, S[ydney] C[astle] (1887–1966). Assistant Secretary, 1911, and Secretary to Cambridge University Press, 1922–48; Lecturer for the English Tripos, 1919–45;

President of the Johnson Society, 1929. Fellow, 1929, and Bursar, 1935–6, of Pembroke College, Cambridge. Publications include *A Picture Book of British History* (1914–32), *The Story of Doctor Johnson* (1919), and *A History of Cambridge University Press* (1921).

ROBERTSON, D[onald] S[truan] (1885–1961). Fellow of TCC, 1909; Regius Professor of Greek at Cambridge, 1928. Publications include *A Handbook of Greek and Roman Architecture* (1929) and *The Early Age of Greece* (vol. 2, from the notes of Sir William Ridgeway in collaboration with A. S. F. Gow, 1931).

ROBERSTON, PETICA [Coursolles] (1883–1941), daughter of Major Charles Jones of the Royal Artillery, and wife of D. S. Robertson, whom she married in 1909.

ROBINSON, OLIVER (1911–72). BA, DePauw University, 1933; Assistant Instructor of English at Vincennes University, 1934.

ROSS, [Edward] DENISON (1871–1940). Professor of Persian at UCL, 1896–1901; Principal of Calcutta Madrasa, 1901–11; Director of the School of Oriental Studies, and Professor of Persian, London University, 1916–37; knighted, 1918.

ROTHENSTEIN, ALICE [Mary] (1869–1955). Eldest child of artist Walter John Knewstub of Chelsea, who was a friend of Dante Gabriel Rossetti. Actress: stage name 'Alice Kingsley'. Married William Rothenstein on 11 June 1899.

ROTHENSTEIN, WILLIAM (1872–1945). English painter. Did three portrait drawings of AEH in 1906, and two more in 1915. Professor of Civic Art, Sheffield University, 1917–26; Principal of the Royal College of Art, 1920–35; Trustee of the Tate Gallery, 1927–33; Member of the Royal Fine Art Commission, 1931–3; knighted, 1931.

ROUSE, W[illiam] H[enry] D[enham] (1863–1950). Fellow of Christ's College, Cambridge, 1888–94; taught at Bedford Modern School, 1888–90, Cheltenham College, 1890–5, and Rugby School, 1895–1902, and was Headmaster of Perse Grammar School, Cambridge, 1902–28; Editor of *The Year's Work in Classical Studies*, 1906–10, and, with A. D. Godley, *CR*, 1911–20. Publications include: *Demonstrations in Greek Iambic Verse* (1899), *Demonstrations in Latin Elegiac Verse* (1899), *Greek Votive Offerings* (1902), and an edn. of Lucretius (1924).

RUDGE, WILLIAM E. (1876–1931). American printer and typographer.

RUTHERFORD, ERNEST (1871–1937). Physicist. Published *Radioactivity* (1904), and developed the nuclear theory of the atom, 1906–14; Cavendish Professor of Experimental Physics at Cambridge, 1919–37; FRS, 1903, and president, 1925–30; Nobel Prize for chemistry, 1908; knighted, 1914; OM, 1925; baron, 1931.

SAMPSON, JOHN (1862–1931). Literary editor (of William Blake) and philologist. Publications include *The Dialect of the Gypsies of Wales* (1926), *Romane Gilia: Poems in Romani with English Renderings* (1931), and *XXI Welsh Gypsy Folk Tales* (1933)

SASSOON, SIEGFRIED [Louvain] (1886–1967). Poet. Publications include: war poems in *The Old Hunstman* (1917) and *Counter-Attack* (1918); and semi-autobiographical vols. *Memoirs of a Fox-Hunting Man* (1928) and *Memoirs of an Infantry Officer* (1930).

SAVORY, GUNDRED [Helen]. Attended AEH's Latin lectures at UCL as an undergraduate, 1900–3.

SAYLE, CHARLES EDWARD (1864–1924). Poet and bibliographer. A member of the staff of the CUL, and Secretary to the club of Oxford men at Cambridge.

SCHOLFIELD, A[lwyn] F[aber] (1884–1969). Librarian of TCC, 1919–23; The Librarian, University Library, Cambridge, 1923–49; Professorial Fellow of KCC, 1923.

SCOTT-JAMES, R[olfe] A[rnold] (1878–1959). Journal editor and literary scholar. Worked on *The Daily News* (1902–13), founded *The New Weekly* (1914), wrote leading articles for *The Daily Chronicle* (1919–30), and *The Spectator* (1933–5), of which he was also assistant editor; and became editor of the *London Mercury* (1934–9), which strove to publish writers both new and established. Publications include *Modernism and Romance* (1908) and *Personality in Literature, 1913–1931* (1931).

SECKER, MARTIN (1882–1978). Till 12 July 1910, Percy Martin Secker Klingender. Publisher since 1910, and founder of London firm known as Martin Secker Ltd (1917–36).

SEMPLE, W[illiam] H[ugh] (25 Feb. 1900–10 Mar. 1981) Research student at St John's College, Cambridge, under AEH's supervision, 1925; Ph.D. thesis on *Quaestiones Exegeticae Sidonianae, being new interpretations of difficult passages in the works of Apollinaris Sidonius* approved, 27 June 1927, and published in *Transactions of the Cambridge Philological Society*, 1930; Lecturer in Classics, University of Reading, 1927; Reader, 1931; Hulme Professor of Classics, University of Manchester, 1937–67. See Ian Rogerson, 'W. H. Semple: A Research Student of A. E. Housman', *HSJ* 25 (1999), 70–2 (where, on p. 71, the date of AEH's testimonial and letter of 2 June 1927 are given wrongly as 27 Mar. 1927). Richards, 327, quotes a letter he received from Semple: 'I was Housman's pupil during the years 1925–7, and later I often consulted him about points of Latinity which puzzled me and, when in Cambridge, I always went to see him. To his direction and criticism and support I owe more than I could ever express.'

SETON, W[alter] W[arren] (1882–1927). Entered UCL in 1899, taking classes in various languages, including Latin with AEH, 1899–1902. Placed in the third class in English Language and Literature; MA, 1903; D.Litt., 1915; served as Assistant Secretary and then as Secretary on the executive and administrative staff of UCL, 1903–27, and as Lecturer in Scottish History, 1923–7. Publications include: *Two Fifteenth Century Franciscan Rules* (1914), *Some New Sources of the Life of Blessed Agnes of Bohemia* (1915), and *Blessed Giles of Assisi* (1918).

SHANKAR, BHAWANI. 'Lecturer in English at the University of Allahabad': Maas, 386 n.

SHEPPARD, JOHN [Tressider] (1881–1968). Fellow of KCC, 1906; University Lecturer in Classics, 1908–33; Vice-Provost of KCC, 1929–33, Provost, 1933–54; specialist in Greek tragedy, both in publications and in productions; Co-editor with R. W. Livingstone of *CR*, Feb. 1921–Feb. 1923; MBE, 1919.

SHEWRING, W[alter] H[ayward] [Francis] (1906–90). English classical scholar and poet, noted principally for translations. After taking a second class in *literae humaniores* at Corpus Christi College, Oxford, in 1928, he taught classics at Ampleforth.

SIMPSON, PERCY (1865–1962). Worked for the Clarendon Press, Oxford, 1913; first Librarian of the new English Faculty Library, 1914; Fellow of Oriel College, 1921–36; University Reader in Textual Criticism, 1927; Goldsmith's Reader in English Literature, 1930–5. Published *Shakespearian Punctuation* (1911) and *Proof-Reading in the Sixteenth, Seventeenth and Eighteenth Centuries* (1935), and, with his wife Evelyn, completed the edn., begun by C. H. Herford, of the works of Ben Jonson (11 vols., 1925–52).

SKUTSCH, OTTO (1906–90). Took his doctorate at the University of Göttingen in 1931 with a thesis entitled *Prosodische und metrische Gesetze der Iambenkürzung* (published, 1934). Received a government scholarship to work at the *Thesaurus Linguae Latinae* Institute at Munich, but his scholarship was not renewed under Nazi rule in 1934, whereupon he emigrated to Scotland.

SLATER, D[avid] A[nsell] (1866–1938). AEH's pupil at The Grammar School of King Edward VI, Bromsgrove, 1881–2. He found AEH a singularly inspiring sixth-form teacher: *Proceedings of the British Academy*, 25 (1939), 340. After a career as a schoolmaster, he became Lecturer in Latin, Glasgow University, 1900, and held Professorships of Latin at Cardiff (1903), Bedford College, London (1914) and Liverpool (1920). In 1911 he applied for AEH's chair at UCL: Naiditch (1988), 35 n., 228. Principal publication: *Towards a Text of the 'Metamorphoses'* (1927).

SOUTER, ALEXANDER (1873–1949). Lecturer in Latin at Aberdeen University, 1897–1903; Yates Professor of New Testament Greek and Exegesis at Oxford University, 1903–11; Regius Professor of Humanity, Aberdeen University, 1911–37; Editor of the *Oxford Latin Dictionary*, 1933–9. Other publications include: *A Study of Ambrosiaster* (1905), *Novum Testamentum Graece* (1910), *The Text and Canon of the New Testament* (1913), and *Pelagius's Expositions of Thirteen Epistles of St Paul* (1922, 1926, 1931).

SPARROW, JOHN [Hanbury Angus] (1906–92). Bibliophile, editor, and essayist. Educated at Winchester College, 1919–25, and New College, Oxford; first class in *literae humaniores*, 1929; Fellow of All Souls College, 1929–52; awarded the Chancellor's Prize for Latin Verse, 1929; called to the Bar, Middle Temple, 1931, and practised in Chancery Division, 1931–9. Publications include: edns. of John

Donne's *Devotions upon Emergent Occasions* (1923), *The Poems of Bishop Henry King* (1925), and selected poems by Abraham Cowley (1926); *Half-Lines and Repetitions in Virgil* (1931) and *Sense and Poetry: Essays on the Place of Meaning in Contemporary Verse* (1934). He wrote the pioneering study 'Echoes in the Poetry of A. E. Housman', *Nineteenth Century and After*, 115 (Feb. 1934), 243–56. His Housman collection is now at SJCO.

SPICER-SIMSON, THEODORE (1871–1929). American sculptor and portrait medallist. His medallions of English writers are reproduced in his *Men of Letters of the British Isles* (1924).

SQUIRE, J[ohn] C[ollings] (1884–1958). Poet, anthologist, essayist, and influential literary journalist. Literary editor of the *New Statesman*, 1913; founder and editor of the monthly literary periodical *The London Mercury*, 1919–34; chief literary critic of *The Observer*; knighted, 1933. Publications include: parodies *Imaginary Speeches* (1912) and *Steps to Parnassus* (1913); vols. of poetry *The Three Hills* (1913) and *The Survival of the Fittest* (1916); and anthologies *A Book of Women's Verse* (1921), *The Comic Muse* (1921), and *Selections from Modern Poets* (1921–34).

STAMFORDHAM, LORD (1849–1931). Arthur John Bigge. Assistant Private Secretary to Queen Victoria, 1880–95; Private Secretary, 1895–1901; Private Secretary to Prince George (later King George V), 1901–10, 1910–31; knighted, 1895; created baron, 1911.

STEVENS, P[aul] P[earman]. One of AEH's students at UCL, where he graduated in 1911: Maas, 206 n. 1.

STEWART, HUGH (1884–1934). Professor of Latin at Leeds University, 1926; Principal of University College, Nottingham, 1930.

STEWART, WILLIAM (1835–1919). Professor of Divinity, Glasgow University, 1873–1910; Clerk of the Senate of the University, 1876–1911.

SYMONS, [Arthur] DENIS (13 Sept. 1891–1951). MD, DPH. AEH's nephew, eldest son of Katharine (née Housman) and Edward Symons; married Phyllis Alexander (1892–1979), daughter of the Revd E. P. Alexander.

SYMONS, EDWARD [William] (1857–1932). BA (first class) in Mathematics, Oxford, 1879; Fereday Fellow, SJCO, 1880; Second Master, The Grammar School of King Edward VI, Bromsgrove (1886–7); Headmaster of Huddersfield College (1887–93), of Banbury Secondary School (1893–6), and of King Edward's School, Bath (1896–1921). He and AEH's sister Katharine married on 13 Aug. 1887.

SYMONS, KATHARINE ELIZABETH. See under Katharine Elizabeth Housman.

SYMONS, PHYLLIS. Wife of AEH's nephew Denis: see letter of 25 Feb. 1932.

THICKNESSE, LILY (d. 1952). Author of fictional works *Egeria* (1896), *Two Sinners* (1897), and *Stuff o' the Conscience* (1899), and of *Poems* (1901) and *Poems Old and New*

(1909). LH describes her as 'a friend whose suffrage sympathies he [AEH] did not share': *Memoir*, 203. Her husband, Ralph Thicknesse (1856–1923), was the author of two vols. on the Married Women's Property Acts (1882, 1884) and of *The Rights and Wrongs of Women: A Digest with Practical Illustrations and Notes on the Law in France* (1909, etc.). She told Richards on 7 Apr. 1940 that 'of the long talks I had with him [AEH], I chiefly remember the delicious humour of his descriptions of things and people': LC-GR MS.

THOMPSON, D'ARCY WENTWORTH (1860–1948). Scientist, classicist, mathematician, naturalist, and philosopher. Entered TCC, 1880; first class in Parts I and II of the Natural Sciences Tripos, 1882–3; Professor of Biology at University College, Dundee, 1884, and of Natural History, United College, St Andrews, 1917–48; CB, 1898, for his part in the International Fur Seals Commissions, 1896–7; FRS, 1916; Fellow of the Royal Society of London, 1916, Vice-president, 1931–3; President of the Classical Association (of Great Britain), 1928–9; Fellow of the Royal Society of Edinburgh, 1885, and President, 1934–9. Publications include: *A Glossary of Greek Birds* (1895), a translation of Aristotle's *Historia Animalium* (1910), and *On Growth and Form* (1917).

THOMPSON, EDWARD J[ohn] (1886–1946). Poet, playwright, anthologist, and expert on India.

THOMSON, J[oseph] J[ohn] (1856–1940). Physicist. Minor Scholar, Major Scholar, Fellow, and Master of TCC, 1876, 1878, 1881, 1918–40 respectively; Cavendish Professor of Experimental Physics at Cambridge, 1884–1919; FRS, 1884, and President, 1915–20; Nobel Prize, 1906; knighted, 1908; OM, 1912.

THRING, [George] HERBERT (1859–1941). Secretary to the Society of Authors, London, 1892–1930. A solicitor by training, he was the author of *The Marketing of Literary Property: Book and Serial Rights* (1933).

TILLOTSON, GEOFFREY (1905–69). Lecturer in English at UCL, 1931; Professor of English, Birkbeck College, London, 1944.

TONKS, HENRY (1862–1937). Surgeon, painter, and teacher of art. FRCS, 1888; assistant to Frederick Brown following Brown's appointment as Slade Professor of Fine Art at UCL, 1892; Slade Professor, 1918–30. A traditionalist, especially in draughtsmanship.

TORRENCE, [Frederick] RIDGELY (1875–1950). American writer. Author of *The House of a Hundred Lights* (1900) and *Hesperides* (1925).

TREVELYAN, G[eorge] M[acaulay] (1876–1962). Fellow of TCC, 1898; Regius Professor of Modern History at Cambridge, 1927–40; FBA, 1925; OM, 1930. Publications include: *History of England* (1926); *England under Queen Anne* (1930–4); and lives of John Bright (1913) and Sir George Otto Trevelyan (1932).

TROLLOPE, BLANCHE. Neighbour and close friend of AEH's friends the Wise family of Woodchester. Her name appears numerous times in their Visitors' Books.

UNTERMEYER, LOUIS (1885–1977). American scholar and anthologist. Publications include *American Poetry since 1900* (1923) and *American Poetry from the beginning to Whitman* (1931).

VAN DOREN, IRITA (1891–1966). Literary editor of the *New York Herald and Tribune*, 1926–63, and a leading light in New York literary society.

VAN DOREN, MARK (1894–1972). American poet and man of letters.

VOLLMER, FRIEDRICH KARL (1867–1923). German classical scholar; Professor at Munich. Publications include: an edn. of Statius, *Silvae* (1898); of Horace (1907), reviewed by AEH in *CR* 22 (May 1908), 88–9 (*Classical Papers*, 771–2); and of *Poetae Latini Minores* (1910–23), in the first vol. of which Vollmer thanks AEH (Naiditch, 1988, 138). AEH owned copies of some of Vollmer's publications: Naiditch (2003), 109, 147, 151; Naiditch (2004), 153, 154. His comments in their margins are sometimes scathing: Naiditch (2005), 130, 178, 180, 181.

WALSTON, CHARLES (1856–1927). Until 1918, Waldstein. Lecturer in Classical Archaeology, University of Cambridge, 1880–3; Director of the Fitzwilliam Museum, Cambridge, 1883–9; first Reader in Classical Archaeology, 1883–1907; Slade Professor of Fine Art at Cambridge, 1895–1901, 1904–11; knighted, 1912. He had rooms at TCC. Publications include: *Balance of Emotion and Intellect* (1878); *The Work of John Ruskin* (1894); *What May We Read?* (1912); *Patriotism, National and International* (1917); and *Harmonism and Conscious Evolution* (1922).

WALTERS, LETTICE D'OYLY (b. 1880). Poet and anthologist.

WARREN, [Thomas] HERBERT (1853–1930). Fellow, President, and Honorary Fellow, Magdalen College, 1877, 1885–1928, 1928; Vice-Chancellor of Oxford University, 1906–10; knighted, 1914. Warren's 1892 testimonial in support of AEH's application to UCL praised him as being 'one of the most interesting and attractive pupils I can remember. He had even then, as quite a young student, a combination of force, acumen and taste which I shall never forget': Naiditch (1988), 18. See ibid. 225–8, for further information.

WEBB, P[hilip] G[eorge] L[ancelot] (1856–1937). Educated at Westminster and Christ Church, Oxford; Clerk in the Patent Office, 1880; Private Secretary to Comptroller General of Patents, Designs & Trade Marks, 1883–8; Chief Clerk, 1898; Establishment Officer, Ministry of Munitions, 1915–16; Deputy Controller of Petrol, 1917–19; Assistant Comptroller of the Patent Office, 1920–1; CBE, 1918; CB, 1919. Publications include *Translations from Heine and Goethe* (1912), *More Translations from Heine* (1920), and *Poems* (1927).

WELLESLEY, KENNETH (1911–95). As a student at Peterhouse, Cambridge, took a first in the Classical Tripos (with a distinction in History) in 1934, and later taught Latin at Edinburgh University.

WEMYSS, LADY (1862–1937). Born Mary Constance Wyndham, daughter of the Hon. Percy Scawen Wyndham. In 1883 she married Hugo Richard Charteris, Lord Elcho (1857–1937), who in 1914 became ninth Earl of Wemyss.

WHARTON, EDITH (1862–1937). American novelist, famous for her depictions of New York society. Married Edward Robbins Wharton in 1885 and they settled in France in 1907. Publications include *The House of Mirth* (1905), *The Custom of the Country* (1913), and *The Age of Innocence* (1920).

WHEELOCK, JOHN HALL (1886–1978). American poet and writer on poetry. Published vols. of poetry include *Black Panther* (1922), *Bright Doom* (1927), and *Poems, 1911–1936* (1936).

WIGGINS, G. H. Publications Manager at the Richards Press.

WILKINSON, MARGUERITE [Ogden Bigelow] (1883–1928). American poet and anthologist. Compiled *New Voices: An Introduction to Contemporary Poetry* (1919, 1921, etc.) and *Contemporary Poetry* (1923).

WILLIAMS, CHARLES [Walter Stansby] (1886–1945). Poet, religious writer, and novelist. Reader for Oxford University Press, 1908–45.

WILSON, CHARLES (1891–1967). The 'Pitman Poet' of Willington, Co. Durham, where four small collections of poems were published: *'On Sick Leave'*, *'Warriors Three'*, *and other poems* (1915), *'When Duty Calls'*, *and other poems* (1915), *'The Unseen Guest'*, *and other poems* (1915), and *Time Will Tell* (1916). *The Poetical Works of Charles Wilson*, 159 pages, was published in 1916. Maas, 245 n.: 'In later years he dealt in books and autographs, and appears to have corresponded with Housman chiefly in order to acquire his answers.' Naiditch (1995), 162, notes that 'Some at least were sold by Wilson: see, e.g., *James F. Drake* cat. 196, 1928, no. 93'.

WILSON, EDMUND (1895–1972). American journalist and man of letters. Managing Editor, *Vanity Fair*, 1920; Associate Editor, *New Republic*, 1926–31. Publications include *The Undertaker's Garland* with John Peale Bishop (1922), and *Axel's Castle* (1931).

WINSTANLEY, D[enys] A[rthur] (1877–1947). Fellow of TCC, 1906; Tutor, 1919; Senior Tutor, 1925; Vice-Master, 1935.

WISE, EDITH. See next entry.

WISE, ELIZABETH [Mary] (1827–1911). Wife of Edward Wise (1809–74) of Woodchester near Stroud, and mother of Edward ('Ted') [Tuppen] Wise (1851–1934), Edith ('Edie') [Madeline] Wise (1854–1930), and Wilhelmina ('Minnie') [Harriet] Wise (1958–1931). She was AEH's godmother, his mother having been the daughter of the Rector of Woodchester. AEH was a lifelong friend of the family. The verses he wrote in, or for, their Visitors' Books are included in *Poems* (1997).

WITHERS, AUDREY (1905–2001). Younger daughter of Percy Withers, who recalls the spontaneous rapport between her and AEH at their first meeting: Withers, 70–1. Second class in Philosophy, Politics, and Economics at Somerville College, Oxford, 1927; worked on *Vogue* magazine, 1931–60. Her autobiography, *Lifespan* (1994), 181–6, contains an account of AEH.

WITHERS, MARY WOLLEY, née Summers (1870–1947). Wife of Percy Withers.

WITHERS, PERCY (1867–1945). Physician and writer. He made AEH's acquaintance after being transferred to war service in Cambridge in the early summer of 1917. After Withers's year on the National Service Board in Cambridge, a long friendship ensued: from 1921 onwards AEH was a regular visitor at his house, first Souldern Court, near Bicester, Oxon., and, from 1935, Epwell Mill near Banbury, Warwickshire. Withers occasionally visited AEH in Cambridge. He wrote a sympathetic but somewhat baffled memoir of AEH: *A Buried Life: Personal Recollections of A. E. Housman* (1940).

WOOD, EDWARD FREDERICK LINDLEY (1881–1959). Created Baron Irwin, 1926; third Viscount Halifax, 1934; Viceroy of India, 1926–31; President of the Board of Education, 1932–5; and Chancellor of Oxford University, 1933–59, in which capacity he wrote personally to ask AEH to accept an honorary degree.

WOODS, MARGARET L[ouisa Daisy], née Bradley (1855–1945). Novelist and poet. Daughter of G[eorge] G[ranville] Bradley, master at Rugby School and later Dean of Westminster. In 1879 she married the Revd Henry G[eorge] Woods (1842–1915), Fellow and later President of Trinity College, Oxford. Novels include *A Village Tragedy* (1887), *The Vagabonds* (1894), *Sons of the Sword* (1901), *The Invader* (1907), *A Poet's Youth* (1923), and *The Spanish Lady* (1927). She was also the author of several vols. of poetry: *Lyrics* (1888), *Lyrics & Ballads* (1889), *Aëromancy, and other poems* (1896), *Wild Justice. A Dramatic Poem* (1896), *Songs* (1896), *The Princess of Hanover* (1902), *Poems Old and New* (1907), and *The Return, and other Poems* (1921)

WOOLLRIGHT, ELIZABETH MARY (1803/4–79). The Wise family gravestone in the churchyard of St Mary the Virgin, Woodchester, states that Elizabeth Mary Woollright died on 24 Nov. 1879 aged 75. Naiditch (1995), 3 n., suggests that she was related to AEH's godfather John Woollright, and notes that various Woollrights appear in one of the Visitors' Books of the Wise family.

WRENCH, [John] EVELYN [Leslie] (1882–1966). Promoter of the British Empire, and author. Editor of *The Spectator*, 1925–32; knighted, 1932.

WRIGHT, [William] ALDIS (1831–1914). Literary and biblical scholar. Librarian, Fellow, and Vice-Master of TCC, 1863–70, 1878, 1888–1914; Joint Editor of *The Journal of Philology*, 1863–1913; Secretary to the Old Testament Revision Company, 1870–85. A wide range of publications includes: an edn. of Bacon's *Essays* (1862); the 2nd edn. of the Cambridge Shakespeare (1891–3); the Globe Shakespeare, with William George Clark (1864; rev. 1904); and edns. of Bacon's *The Advancement of Learning* (1869), of FitzGerald's *Letters and Literary Remains* (7 vols., 1902–3), of *Milton's Poems with Critical Notes* (1903), and of the Authorized Version of the Bible as printed in the original two issues (5 vols., 1909).

YOUNG, W[illiam] S[iddons]. Author of various vols. of Latin verses, such as *Senilia, 1891–1894* (1895), *Ruris Laudatio* (1899), and *Lamenta* (1900).

LETTERS
1872–1926

1872

[Perry Hall, Bromsgrove
c.1 Jan. 1872]

We the undersigned do hereby wish You, our Great Aunt Mary,[1] and our Cousin Agnes;—[2]

A happy New Year.[3]

(*Signed.*)

Alfred Edward Housman[4]

Robert Holden Housman

Clemence Annie Housman

Katherine E. Housman

Basil Williams Housman

Laurence Housman.

George Herbert **X** Housman[5]

BMC MS. AEH has written the greeting and his signature, and the others have signed for themselves, apart from George Herbert, who has written a cross and has had his name written for him.

[1] Aunt Mary would either be Mary Brettell Housman (1833–1917), also referred to in the verse letter of 22 Apr. 1875, or Felicia, wife of Joseph Brettell Housman (1842–1926), who was known in the family as 'Aunt Mary' (Pugh, 105); however, a great aunt would have to be the aunt of one of AEH's parents Edward and Sarah Jane Housman, and no such relative of that name is known.

[2] Possibly Helen Agnes (m. 1892). It is unlikely that it was her sister Lucy Agnes (1823–1907), whom Edward Housman married in 1873: LH recalled (*The Unexpected Years*, 57) that the children had met her only once, in 1872, before she became their stepmother, which would make a New Year greeting to her seem improbable.

[3] '1872' written on the MS by KES.

[4] Though he signs 'Alfred Edward Housman' here, 'Alfred Housman' [after late July 1873] 'Alfred E. Housman' (not before 9 Oct. 1873, 10 May 1880), 'A. E. Housman' (9 Jan. 1875, 23 Mar. 1880), 'Alfred' (29 Jan. 1875) 'Alfred Edouard Maisonhomme' (8 July 1877), and, again humorously, in verse epistles, 'A. E. H.' and 'A. Edward. *H*.' (22 Apr. 1875, 19 June 1878), his preferred form from 5 Apr. 1877 onwards is 'Alfred E. Housman'; until, on 4 Apr. 1881, he opts permanently for 'A. E. Housman', even in 'Your loving son | A. E. Housman' (29 Mar. and 10 June 1885). With the exception of the lighthearted letter to Pollard of 27 Mar. 1880, the notes on Silius Italicus sent to Duff on 11 July 1933, and the letter to KES of 27 Dec. 1935, which was written during illness, he reserved 'A. E. H.' for brief notes. He is also represented as 'A. E. H.' in letters to newspapers: 12 Mar. 1894, before 8 May 1924, and *c*.13 Dec. 1928.

[5] The ages of the children and the years of their births are entered on the MS by KES. In order, their ages are: 13, 12, 11, 10, 8, 7, and 4.

1873

TO LUCY HOUSMAN

[After late July 1873]

[…] three spires of Coventry, as well as of Harrow.

<I hope> Give my love to father, & all the others,

I remain my dearest mamma[1]
Your loving son
Alfred Housman

UCL MS Add. 126: a fragment. Edward Housman married his cousin Lucy on 26 June 1873, and LH, The Unexpected Years, *58, places the meeting with the family 'in late July', when AEH was 14.*

[1] LH notes that AEH's letters to his stepmother began with 'My dear Mamma': *Memoir*, 128. 'Mamma' was the title agreed between her and the children on the evening of their first meeting: *The Unexpected Years* (1937), 58. Though LH also states that as they grew up they called her 'Mater' and 'Mamma' fell into practical disuse, AEH still addresses her on 13 Sept. 1901 as 'My dear Mamma' and refers to her as 'mamma' on 7 Feb. 1907 and on 22 May 1913 (when he is respectively 42, 47, and 54).

1875

TO LUCY HOUSMAN

[London]
January 9th [1875]

My dear Mamma

I have now seen Oxford St, Regent St, Holborn, Cheapside, Cornhill, Piccadilly &c, but not much of the Strand. On Wednesday we went to Waterloo Place, Pall Mall & St James' park where I saw the band of the Grenadier Guards, & some of the 1st Life Guards. We went to the Chapel Royal for service,—the queen's present was given[1] by an attenuated person with gorgeous trimming, who<m> Cousin Mary[2] thinks is an earl, as there was one of those coronets on his carriage. Then we went to Trafalgar square, which is quite magical, & to Westminster. I explored the north transept where the statesmen are, I looked at Pitt's & Fox's monuments & went into Poet's[3] corner. Service was at 3, with an anthem by Greene[4] which was like a boa constrictor—very long & very ugly. We had a beautiful one by Goss[5] at the Chapel Royal in the morning.

On Thursday we went by Omnibus to Holborn Viaduct, got out & walked about the city, we saw the little boy in Panyer Alley,[6] & crossed Paternoster Row, which is not so narrow as you told me, after all; at St. Paul's I went up to the golden gallery, but Cousin Mary did not wish to repeat the experiment which she had tried before, [and] remained on terra firma. They would not allow me to go into the iron gallery inside. The day was so foggy that one could scarcely see the other side of the river, from the dome; & the mist had got into the cathedral.

---

[1] He means the queen's presence was represented.

[2] Maurice Greene (1696?–1755). Organist of St Paul's Cathedral, 1718, of Chapel Royal, 1727.

[3] John Goss (1800–80). Organist of St Paul's, 1838–72; knighted, 1872.

[4] Lucy Housman's sister, Mary Theophania (d. 4 Mar. 1905).   [5] For 'Poets''.

[6] The 'Panyer Stone', a statue, set into the wall of a house, of a nude boy sitting on a bread basket, commemorating the inn The Panyer Boy which was destroyed in the Great Fire of 1666. Beneath it is the inscription: 'When ye have sought | the citty round | yet still this is | the highest ground | August the 27 | 1688'. Panyer Alley in the vicinity of St Paul's Cathedral was not in fact the highest ground: there are higher spots in Cornhill and in Cannon Street.

We saw the Guildhall, Mansion House, Bank & Exchange, then the Monument, London Bridge & London stone. In the evening I went to the *Creation*[7] at the Albert Hall. Mme Lemens-Sherrington,[8] Vernon Rigby[9] & Lewis Thomas.[10] I think what charmed me most was *By thee with Bliss* [.] Mme Lemens-Sherrington has a most exquisite voice, so completely unaffected, but Mr Vernon Rigby's voice has not nearly power enough for that great building. I saw nothing more than the outline of the Albert Memorial. Though I was half an hour early, I could not get a seat in the shilling places, so I stood for the first part, & sat or lay on the floor for the rest. I was exactly opposie[11] the orchestra & heard very well.

Yesterday I went to the British Museum & spent most of my time among the Greeks & Romans.[12] I looked at your Venus—the Towneley Venus—in the alcove, but I do not admire her. What delighted me most was the Farnese Mercury. I examined some of the Ninivch[13] bulls & lions, & I went through the Zoological gallery. I met cousin Henry[14] there, but he had only ten minutes to spare,—& those were of course geological. I have come to the conclusion, which you may tell the readers of *The Centre of the Earth*,[15] that if the Mastodon and Megatherium were to fight, it would decidedly be a very bad job for the Megatherium.[16] I may also remark that the Ichthyosauri & Plesiosauri are by no means so large or terrific as those met by Professor Hardwigg & Co.[17]

To-day I am going to the Houses of Parliament, & to a ballad Concert in the afternoon. On Monday the Zoological gardens, & on Tuesday The south Kensington Museum.

---

[7] By Haydn.

[8] Helen Lemmens-Sherrington (1834–1906). First appeared at London concerts, 1856; leading English soprano from 1860, particularly in oratorio, and celebrated for her performances in Haydn's *The Creation*. AEH writes 'Lemens' for 'Lemmens'.

[9] [George] Vernon Rigby (b. 1840). Tenor.

[10] Lewis [William] Thomas (1826–96). Bass.   [11] For 'opposite'.

[12] In the Graeco-Roman Room at the British Museum. Cf. *ASL* LI 1–2 (written over twenty years later): 'Loitering with a vacant eye | Along the Grecian gallery'.

[13] For 'Nineveh'.

[14] Lucy Housman's brother, the Revd Henry Housman (1832–1914). Curate of All Saints', Notting Hill, London, at the time; Lecturer, Chichester College, 1879–1912; Rector of Bradley, Worcestershire, 1898–1912.

[15] Jules Verne's *Journey to the Centre of the Earth* (1864).

[16] In ch. 27 of Verne's novel, Professor Von Hardwigg, his nephew Henry, and the Icelander Hans Bjelke discover bones of these prehistoric creatures. In ch. 29, Henry dreams of seeing them when they were alive.

[17] In ch. 30, there is a fight between an ichthyosaurus (fish lizard) and a plesiosaurus (sea crocodile). The former is said to be not less than 100 feet long, and the neck of the latter to tower more than 30 feet above the waves.

I like the view from Westminster bridge, & Trafalgar square best of all the *places* I have seen, & I am afraid you will be horrified to hear that I like St. Paul's better than Westminster Abbey; The Quadrant[,] Regent St, & Pall Mall are the finest streets; but I think that of all I have seen, what has most impressed me is—the Guards. This may be barbarian, but it is true.

I hope your cold is getting better. I am serenaded every morning by some cocks, who crow as if their life depended upon it. If they were in my hands their life would depend upon it.

With love to my father & all
I remain
Your affectionate son
A E Housman

UCL MS Add. 126. Envelope addressed 'Mrs E. Housman | Fockbury House | Bromsgrove', and bearing a note in her hand: 'Alfreds first visit to London Jany 1875'. Memoir, 26 (excerpt); Maas, 5–6, with a facsimile of an excerpt after 202.

TO LUCY HOUSMAN

[The Grammar School of King Edward VI, Bromsgrove][1]
Friday. [29 Jan. 1875]

My dear Mamma

I am very much obliged to you for sending *Sir Walter Raleigh*[2] which I return, as you wished, now that I have copied it. I am also very much obliged for the *Standard* you sent me, though I am sorry to say that I did not go to that concert, for though I arrived there in plenty of time, all the shilling places were full, & I did not happen to have two shillings with me. However I went to Baker St & saw Mme Tussaud's,[3] which I should not otherwise have had time to see, though of course I should have preferred the concert. It was however, in a great measure, a repetition of the one which I heard on the Saturday after I went to London; Santley,[4] especially, sang exactly the same songs.

---

[1] Where AEH temporarily boarded: see Lucy Housman's note on the envelope (above).

[2] AEH's poem, which was awarded the Head Master's Prize for English Poem, Dec. 1873: Naiditch (1995), 5. AEH also won the prize with *The Death of Socrates* (1874) and *St Paul on Mars Hill* (1875): Naiditch (1995), 5; *Poems* (1997), 193–9, 504–8.

[3] Waxworks museum.

[4] Eminent baritone Charles Santley (1834–1922); knighted, 1907.

Please thank Clemence[5] for her letter & tell her that I am glad to hear that she has begun "H," & that I hope she progresses with it. I hope that the glandular swellings of your two patients are abating, and that Cook's appetite is reviving.

Yesterday I went into the churchyard, from which one can see Fockbury quite plainly, especially the window of your room.[6] I was there from 2 o' clock till 3. I wonder if you went into your room between those hours. One can see quite plainly the pine tree, the sycamore & the elm at the top of the field. The house looks much nearer than you would expect, & the distance between the sycamore & the beeches in the orchard seems very great, much longer than one thinks it when one is at Fockbury.

Give my love to my Father, & to my brothers & sisters & Believe me

Your affectionate son

Alfred.

Lilly MSS 1. 1. 2. Envelope addressed 'Mrs E. Housman | Fockbury House | Bromsgrove' and bearing a note in her hand: 'Alfred. When Scarlet Fever was in the house & he was at the Grammar School. Lines on Sir Walter Raleigh enclosed. Jany 1875'. Memoir, 27 (excerpt); Maas, 7.

TO LUCY HOUSMAN

[Fockbury House, Bromsgrove
22 April 1875][1]

My dear Mamma,
                    I cannot say
That much, since you have gone away,
Has happened to us, so of course
I must fall back on that resource,—
That great resource, which o'er the earth
Precedence holds, & which is worth
All other topics put together,
I mean, (I need not say) THE WEATHER.

[5] Clemence ('Clem') Housman (23 Nov. 1861–Dec. 1955). Younger sister of AEH. Later, militant suffragette, imprisoned for refusing to pay rates; talented embroiderer, dressmaker, and woodcut artist. She wrote *Were-Wolf* (1896) and the Arthurian romance *The Life of Sir Aglovale De Galis* (1905). Throughout her adult life she lived with LH.

[6] The family home was Fockbury House, previously known as 'The Clock House', in the hamlet of Fockbury, about two miles from Bromsgrove. Edward Housman had moved the family there from Perry Hall in 1873.

[1] Date on postmark.

The weather has been clear & bright
The sun has shed a vivid light
So hot & torrid, that my stout
Aunt Mary[2] has not ventured out,
Until the shades of evening fall
And gentle moonbeams silver all,
When lunatics are wont to prowl
As also are the bat & owl.[3]
Then to the shadowy garden fly
My relative,[4] & Clem, & I.
Clemence becomes a fancied knight
In visionary armour dight
And waves her lance extremely well
Terrific but invisible.
I turn into a dragon dire
Breathing imaginary fire,
Obscuring all the starry sky
With vapours seen by fancy's eye.
Aunt Mary is a hapless maid
Imprisoned in a dungeon's shade,
And spreading streams of golden hair
Impalpably upon the air.
Such is she 'neath the moon's pale ray
But during all the burning day
At open window she has heard
The notes of many a chattering bird,
Receiving quite an education
From all this feathered conversation.
"Look here! look here!" one of them cries,[5]

---

[2] See n. 1 on the single letter from 1872.

[3] John Fletcher (1579–1625), *Hence, all you vain delights*, 14–15: 'Moonlight walks, when all the fowls | Are warmly housed, save bats and owls!' AEH identified the anonymous author on p. 397 of his copy, now in the Bodleian Library, of *Fugitive Poetry 1600–1878*, ed. J. C. Hutchieson [?1878]. See also *At peep of day we rise from bed*, 19–20: *Poems* (1997), 270.

[4] Aunt Mary.

[5] Some of the bird calls are identifiable: "Look here! Look here!" (the song thrush starting a bout of song); "Peter" (the great tit); "Quick! quick! quick!" (the blackbird's semi-alarm cry, usually heard in the evening before roosting). (I owe this information to the late Dr Denis Owen of Oxford Brookes University.) In other cases AEH seems to be inventing his own verbal equivalents of the calls, as William Allingham did notably in *The Lover and Birds, Day and Night Songs* (1854), No. 21.

"Peter" another one replies.
(Perhaps a Roman Catholic bird,)
And scarcely has he said this word
When one of more ferocious mind
Screams out in fury "Whip behind!"
And scarcely has his clamour ceased
When shrieks arise of "You're a beast!"
Another, rest one moment brings
Saying in French pacific things,
Then one (piano) "Pretty Dick!"
One more (crescendo) "Quick! quick! quick!"
(Forte) "Look here! look here!" once more,
And so da capo, as before.

Far other sounds thine ears delight,
Far other shapes are in thy sight,
Where the pellucid Thames flows by
The towers of English liberty,[6]
Where he of Stoke[7] brays forth his din,
(That famous ass in lion's skin,)
Waves his umbrella high in vain
And shakes off dewdrops from his mane.
Or where, high rising over all
Stands the Cathedral of St. Paul
And [in] its shadow you may scan
Our late lamented ruler, Anne;
Or where the clouds of legend lower
Around the mediaeval Tower,[8]
And ghosts of every shape & size
With throttled throats & staring eyes
Come walking from their earthy beds
With pillow cases on their heads

[6] The Houses of Parliament.

[7] Edward Vaughan Hyde Kenealy, the Irish barrister (1819–80). He acted as junior counsel for the surgeon William Palmer, who was hanged in 1856 after poisoning his wife, his brother, and a friend for the purpose of obtaining money. Kenealy also acted as leading counsel for the Tichborne claimant, Arthur Orton, 1873, and was disbarred in 1874 for his violent conduct of the case. As MP for Stoke-on-Trent (Feb. 1875–80) he tried on 23 Apr. 1875, the day after AEH's verse letter, to instigate an inquiry into the case, but found no support.

[8] The Tower of London, the oldest part of which, the White Tower, was begun in 1078.

And various ornaments beside
Denoting why or how they died.
Or where all beasts that ever grew ⎫
All birds, all fish, all reptiles too ⎬
Are congregated at the Zoo. ⎭
Where singing turtles soothe the shade,
And mackarel[9] gambol through the glade,
Where prisoned oysters fain would try
Their wonted flight into the sky,
And the fierce lobster in its rage
Beats its broad wings against its cage.
Or where soft music's rise & fall
Re-echoes through St. James's hall,
Or where of paintings many a one
Adorn the House of Burlington,[10]
Or where the gilded chariots[11] ride
Resplendent through the Park of Hyde
Or where, when he's been doomed to feel
Death from Laertes' poisoned steel,
The lifeless corpse of Hamlet draws
Resuscitation from applause;
Or where—
　　You will perceive perhaps
These "wheres" have come to a collapse;
"The waxen wings that flew so high"[12]
Etcetera.
　　Mamma, goodbye.
You will be glad to hear it told
Father has almost lost his cold,
Miss Hudd is *healthy*, & all we
Are well as we could wish to be.
Our love for you we all declare

---

[9] For 'mackerel'.

[10] The Royal Academy of Arts mounted exhibitions in Burlington House, Piccadilly, from 1869 onwards.

[11] *gilded chariots*. Propertius, *Elegies*, 1. 16. 3: *inaurati … currus*. Also Pope, *The Rape of the Lock*, 1. 55; Gay, *Trivia*, 2. 525.

[12] Icarus escaped from exile in Crete with his father Daedalus by donning wings, but fell into the Aegean Sea when he flew too near the sun and the wax securing the feathers melted. Perhaps Marlowe's 'His waxen wings did mount above his reach' (*Dr Faustus*, 21) was in AEH's mind.

And our relations at Kildare,[13]
Hopes for your pleasure in Londòn,
And I remain your loving son.

A. E. H.

*UCL MS Add. 126. Envelope addressed 'Mrs E. Housman | 39 Kildare Terrace | Bayswater |
London W.', and bearing a note in her hand: 'Letter in rhyme from A. E. H. 1875'.* Recollections,
15 (excerpt); Maas, 7–10. Detailed notes on the MS are given in Poems *(1997), 509.*

[13] Not 'The house in Hereford belonging to Lucy Housman's family' (Maas, 10 n.), identified
in Pugh, Appendix E, lxix, as Kildare, Cantiloup Street, Hereford: see the address on the
envelope (above).

1876

TO MRS WOOLLRIGHT

M[rs] Woollright,

    with many and sincere congratulations on the manner in which (in spite of adverse circumstances & upset donkey-chairs) she has attained her present venerable age.[1]

Now thou'st passed the age the Psalmist
    Kindly has allowed to men,
When the pulse is (mostly) calmest,
    i.e. threescore years & ten.[2]

Now thou hast an honoured station,
    Children's children[3] round thee are,
And the rising generation
    Speaks of thee as "Grandmamma."

But thou art as warm as whiskey,
    Headstrong youth doth still survive,
And I think thou art as frisky
    As thou wast at twenty-five.

Hearken all & pay attention
    While a wondrous tale I tell
Almost past one's comprehension,—
    —What to Grandmamma befel!

Bad the road, & bad the weather,
    Yet that Grandmamma did dare

---

[1] The events of this poem are mentioned in AEH's poetic prophecy for 1877, *The world with its old velocity*, 49–50: *Poems* (1997), 208. This suggests a date of 1876, as Naiditch (1995), 3, notes.

[2] Ps. 90: 10: 'The days of our years are threescore years and ten', echoed also in *ASL* II 5.

[3] OT phraseology: Gen. 45: 10, Deut. 4: 25, 2 Kgs. 17: 41, etc.

To confront them both together
    Seated in a donkey-chair.

Plate-basket was put beside her,
    Sophie's[4] waterproof she wore,
Ted[5] walked on before to guide her,
    Donkey also walked before.

Darkness kept around her growing,
    Deep in mud the chair-wheels sank,
And the ass, the road not knowing,
    Wandered calmly up the bank.

Then that wondrous woman wondered,
    "Wonder where we're coming to,"
And moreover deeply pondered,
    "Wonder what I'd better do."

Through her aged constitution
    Pulsed again youth's hasty blood,
And she took her resolution,
    And she popped into the mud.

With a flutter, with a splutter,
    Like a soda-water cork,

[4] Sophie Becker (*c.*1844–1931) was the German governess-companion to the two daughters in the Wise family, Edith Madeline ('Edie'), 1854–1930, and Wilhelmina Harriet ('Minnie'), 1858–1931. She was AEH's senior by some fifteen years. Henry Maas established the year of her death by having her will examined: letter to John Carter, 20 Aug. 1971 (copy in Sparrow collection, SJCO). LH, *Memoir*, 24–5: 'When in late middle age she returned to Germany he [AEH] continued to correspond with her … I remember her coming to stay with us in 1874—a dark and rather plain woman, but sharp, shrewd, sensible, and brightly humorous.' KES to GR, 7 Dec. 1939: 'Alfred talked to Dr Withers about her soon after her death … I have a letter from him about it, telling me it was the *German governess* whom Alfred mentioned as one of his three chief friends' (LC MS). Withers, 129: 'He had loved and revered her from youth. In the earlier years companionship had been close and constant. Then distance and the exigencies of occupation had rendered meetings few and difficult, and of late years they had never met … as a consequence of her having returned to her homeland, Germany, to end her days.' AEH gave her address as 'Weissenburg Strasse 6^II| Wiesbaden' in a list, dated 19. 10. 22, of those who were to be sent complimentary copies of *LP*: SIU MS. No letters to her have been traced.
[5] Edward [Tuppen] Wise (1851–1934), only son of Edward (1809–74) and Elizabeth [Mary] Wise (1827–1911).

Down went she into the gutter,
  Down went carving-knife & fork.

Startled at this crash untimely
  Donkey said "Haw-he! Haw-he!"
But serenely & sublimely
  Down into the ditch went she.

Then, when lights at last appearing
  Glimmered down the lane so steep,
And when Grandma, reappearing,
  Rose like Venus from the deep,[6]

From galoshes unto bonnet,
  From her left hand to her right,
All her form, & all upon it,
  Was completely out of sight.

Not a flounce & not a gusset
  Not a button could you spy,
Everything was dirty russet,
  Everything except—her eye!

But the sight her eye presented
  Was the finest ever seen,
Every hue was represented,—
  Black & yellow, blue & green.

But it was no consolation
  For so horrible a mess,
All the eyes in all creation
  Cannot clean a blue silk dress.

And she had to change her clothing,
  And she had to go to bed,
And she had to take with loathing
  Nasty medicine, it is said.

---

[6] According to Hesiod, Aphrodite (Venus) rose from the foam of the sea.

So old people should be cautious
  How they skip, when past three-score,
Or the physic will be nauseous
  Which they down their throats must pour.

BMC MS. Above the prefatory note is written 'Alfred Housmans verses', apparently in the hand of Mrs Wise. I have changed a full-stop after 'Woollright' in the headnote to a comma. A reduced facsimile of the MS was published in NNAEH, *8–9.* Poems *(1997), 203–5.*

1877

TO ELIZABETH WISE

Bromsgrove
April 5th [1877]¹

My dear Mrs Wise

It is very kind of you to ask me to Woodchester for the holidays, & I am sure nothing could give me more pleasure, but I am afraid I shall be obliged to forego it on account of the pressure of work. I shall have a great deal to do in the holidays, as Mr Millington[2] has set his heart on some very wonderful achievements on the part of the school at next Midsummer, which can only be attained by constant working from now till then. Life is evidently becoming a very serious thing (!) & with the awful responsibility of breaking Mr Millington's heart (which is extremely liable to break on all possible occasions) hanging over me, I am chained to my books.

Apropos of your intended transit to Rome,[3] I will give you an anecdote about the Pope, which will show you that he is capable of defending

---

[1] Dated '*pre*-1875' in Sotheby's catalogue, London, 15 Dec. 1970, no. 811, and '1876' on the MS in what appears to be KES's hand. However, as Naiditch (1995), 12 n., argues, AEH's comments on prospective midsummer achievements for his school suggest the Oxford and Cambridge Schools Examinations for which he sat in 1877. He passed in elementary mathematics and in divinity, and with distinction in Latin, Greek, French, and History, an achievement which placed him in the top 1.66% in a field where over 47% of the candidates did not pass at all: Naiditch (1995), 7–8.

[2] Herbert Millington (1841–1922). Headmaster of The Grammar School of King Edward VI, Bromsgrove, 1873–91. A staunch admirer of AEH, he very probably arranged for him to teach the sixth form after his failure at Oxford in 1881. In his 1892 testimonial in support of AEH's application to UCL, he praised him as being 'a thorough and sympathetic teacher, warmly interested in his work and his pupils' who had 'left upon them and me a vivid impression of literary ability, ripe scholarship, and vigour and lucidity in communicating his knowledge of and enthusiasm for the Classics': Naiditch (1988), 21. In the preface to *Translations into Latin Verse* (1889), he acknowledged the 'valuable criticism' produced by the 'keen eye and sound learning' of his 'old pupil and distinguished friend', and sent AEH an inscribed copy of the volume (now in SJCO). AEH sent him copies of *ASL* and *LP* on publication. For further information, see Naiditch (1988), 232–4.

[3] See also AEH to Mrs Wise, 17 Feb. and 24 Nov. 1878. Naiditch (1995), 12, notes that in AEH's writings of the late 1870s 'appear anecdotes about Catholics, references to anti-Catholic sermons, and anti-Catholic sentiments'. AEH jokes about Mrs Wise converting to Roman Catholicism in *The world with its old velocity*, 59–60, written *c*. Jan. 1877 ('Yet still Mrs. Wise (to no one's surprise) | Will take and go over to Rome'): *Poems* (1997), 208, 513–14. He also makes fun of Catholic recruitment at Oxford in *Over to Rome*, 31–64, published in 1878: *Poems* (1997), 221–2, 523. In 1861 Mrs Wise had donated the land for a new parish church and graveyard in Woodchester, near Stroud, where the family lived. Woodchester had, however, been made a centre for Roman Catholicism by William Leigh, who bought Woodchester estate in 1846.

himself against howling Protestants. At one of his audiences there were two Protestant ladies, whose curiosity had brought them into the den of the Beast, but whose consciences operated like strychnine, & kept them sitting bolt upright, instead of kneeling to receive the pontifical benediction. Accordingly, the successor of Peter pauses in front of them, and turning round to his Cardinals remarks with an amiable smile "I perceive we have here some new additions to the gallery of statues in the Vatican!"

I should have liked to be a witness of the mingled emotions depicted on the faces of the Protestant Rocks!

Give my love to all who are at home & Believe me ever

very affectionately yours
Alfred E. Housman.

BMC MS.

TO ELIZABETH WISE

[Bromsgrove]
Lundi | 8me Juillet [1877]

Très chère Madame Guise

J'y suis; j'y reste. Je suis *revenu* chez moi; mais je ne suis pas un *Revenant*. Je suis *venu par* le chemin de fer; mais je ne suis pas un *Parvenu*. Nous sommes *venus*, nous deux, moi et ma mère; mais ni l'un ni l'autre de nous n'est pas *Vénus*. Qu'il est drôle, ce monde-ci! Nicht war? Et que je suis polyglotte! Et que je suis rempli de votre bonté; et que je vous donne mille reconnaissances; et que je hurlait de joie ce matin en regardant mes "collars" et en lisant la lettre de Mdlle Becker; et que j'ai pitié pour Henri Salle et pour Perry Salle;[1] et que je me trouve prochain <aux> au temps de poste! et que je suis tout à vous et à votre famille[.]

Alfred Edouard Maisonhomme

Mme Guise
   Maison de Chestre à bois
      Stroude
         Shire de Gloucestre
           Angleterre.

BMC MS. Reduced facsimile in NNAEH, *6.*

Woodchester became the principal house of the Dominican Order, and in 1860 a house of Franciscan nuns was opened. Some anxiety is indicated by the local feeling in 1863 that AEH's mother's memorial window in the new parish church was too Roman Catholic in manner. See *The Victoria History of the Counties of England, A History of the County of Gloucester*, 11. 296, 302–3; Pugh, Appendix C, xxxix–xliii.

[1] Perry Hall, Bromsgrove, where the Housman family moved in the summer of 1877.

TO LUCY HOUSMAN

St. John's Coll.
Sunday. [21 October 1877]

My dear Mamma,

The ceremony of matriculation, which you want to hear about, was as follows. At a quarter to five, on the Saturday afternoon all the freshmen of this college, twenty-two in number, were collected in M[r] Ewing's[1] rooms, & were there instructed how to write our names in Latin in the Vice-Chancellor's books. Alfred, he said, became Alfredus, Edward, Edvardus, & so on; the surnames of course remaining unchanged. Then he marched us off to New College, where we found the Vice Chancellor[2] seated in dim religious light[3] at the top of the hall. Another college was just concluding the ceremony, & when they had finished, we one by one inscribed our names in a large book, in this wise. "Alfredus Edvardus Housman, e Coll. Di. Joh. Bapt. Gen. Fil. natu max." which is being interpreted[4] "A. E. Housman, of the College of St. John the Baptist, eldest son of a gentleman." Sons of Clergymen write "Cler. Fil." & sons of officers write "arm. fil." Then I wrote my name in English in a smaller & less dignified book, & then <we sat down one> paid £2. 10. 0. to a man at the table, & then we sat down one by one in a row till all had written their names & paid their fee. Then an attendant brought in twenty-two copies of the Statutes of the University, bound in violet, & piled them on the table, hiding the Vice-Chancellor from the eye. Presently his head appeared <in> over the top, & we got up & stood in a sort of semicircle in front of him. Then he called up each of us by name & presented each with a copy of the Statutes, & with a paper on which was written in Latin, or what passes for Latin at Oxford:—

"At Oxford, in the Michaelmas term A.D. 1877, on the 13th day of the month of October: on which day Alfred Edward Housman of the College of St. John the Baptist, gentleman's son, appeared in my presence, & was admonished to <observe> keep the laws of this University, & was enrolled in the register (matricula) of the University.

J. E. Sewell
Vice-Chancellor"

---

[1] 'Robert Ewing (1847–1908), Tutor at St John's College, 1872; Rector of Winterslow, Wiltshire, 1889; Canon of Salisbury Cathedral, 1905': Maas, 11 n.
[2] James Edwards Sewell (1810–1903). Warden of New College, Oxford, 1860–1903; Vice-Chancellor of Oxford University, 1874–8.
[3] Milton, *Il Penseroso*, 160: 'a dim religious light'.
[4] Biblical phraseology: Matthew 1: 23, Mark 5: 41, etc.

Then he settled his gown over his shoulders & said, "Gentlemen of St. John's College, attend to me." We attended. He said, in Latin, "Allow me to inform you that you have this day been enrolled in the register of the University, & that you are bound to keep all the statutes contained in this book" (with the violet cover) "as far as they may concern you." Then we went. As to keeping the statutes contained in the violet cover, you may judge what a farce that is, when I tell you that you are forbidden to wear any coat save a black one, or to use fire-arms, or to trundle a hoop, among other things.

I went to M[r] Warren[5] at Magdalen yesterday. I am going to him three times a week. Then I have nine lectures a week in college besides. Two men have invited me to breakfast next week, & M[r] Ewing has asked me to tea today along with several others, apropos of some Sunday-Night Essays, which are read by him & others in his rooms & at which he invites us to attend. Reginald Horton[6] called on me the other day: he is a Commoner[7] at Worcester,[8] & lives in the vicinity, with his wife & children. He asked me to remember him kindly to my father.

I hear that the gale did dreadful damage at the School. I am very glad that we suffered so comparatively little. I was afraid those beeches in the orchard would go. With many thanks for your letter, which is dutifully burnt, & with love to my father & all

I remain

Your loving son

Alfred E. Housman, or, as the

Vice-Chancellor with superior scholarship writes,—

Al*u*redus Edvardus &c.

UCL MS Add. 126. Envelope addressed 'M[rs] E. Housman | Fockbury House | Bromsgrove'. I have changed the full stop after 'My dear Mamma' to a comma. Memoir, *40–2 (incomplete);* Maas, *11–12.*

[5] Thomas Herbert Warren: see List of Recipients.

[6] '1852–1914; son of a Bromsgrove doctor; educated at Bromsgrove School; assistant curate at St Barnabas, Oxford, 1880; Vicar of Dymock, 1883; Canon of Gloucester Cathedral, 1902': Maas, 12 n.

[7] A student who has not obtained a scholarship or other distinction.

[8] Worcester College, Oxford.

TO LUCY HOUSMAN

[Oxford Union Society]
Thursday [29 November 1877]

My dear Mamma

Thanks for the Bromsgrove papers. This letter is indited at the Union, pending the beginning of the debate; please therefore excuse its probable disjointedness. Nothing very remarkable has happened. I go to Ruskin's[1] lectures, which end on Saturday. I have received the great-coat, which is very nice: though the weather has not been such as to cause me to use it. It has been raining a little at unexpected times, but nothing much recently; about a fortnight ago a great deal of rain fell, & the Cherwell[2] & then the Isis[3] were flooded, as they still remain, altering the lanscape[4] to a great extent, & making Oxford look very picturesque from the Berkshire side. In times when the floods were more frequent than they are now, it must have been almost a moated fortress.

This afternoon Ruskin gave us a great outburst against modern times.[5] He had got a picture of Turners,[6] framed & glassed, representing Leicester & the Abbey in the distance at sunset,[7] over a river. He read the account of Wolsey's death out of *Henry VIII*.[8] Then he pointed to the picture as representing Leicester when Turner had drawn it. Then he said "You, if you like, may go to Leicester to see what it is like now. I never shall. But I can make a pretty good guess." Then he caught up a paintbrush. "These stepping-stones of course have been done away with, & are replaced by a be-au-ti-ful iron bridge." Then he dashed in the iron bridge on the glass of the picture. "The colour of the stream is supplied on one side by the indigo factory." Forthwith one side of the stream became indigo. "On the other by the soap factory." Soap dashed in. "They mix in the middle,—like curds" he said, working them together with a sort of malicious deliberation.

[1] John Ruskin (1819–1900) was the first Slade Professor of Fine Art at Oxford University, 1870–8, and held the position again, 1883–4.

[2] The river which meets the Thames at Oxford.

[3] The name for the Thames within Oxford's boundaries.   [4] For 'landscape'.

[5] Ruskin's habit of airing his 'own peculiar opinions' in his lectures alarmed the University authorities and partly led to his resignation in 1878.

[6] For 'Turner's'.

[7] 'Leicester Abbey, Leicestershire', *c*.1832, by J. M. W. Turner (1775–1851). The painting is untraced, but the provenance shows it to have been owned by Ruskin, who maintained a lifelong devotion to Turner after the two met in 1840. Ruskin's biographer Tim Hilton describes the painting as 'one of the Turners that were so close to his [Ruskin's] life and feelings': *John Ruskin: The Later Years* (2000). 560. Ruskin collected Turner's drawings eagerly and, as his executor, catalogued them.

[8] 4. 2. Wolsey died in Leicester Abbey.

"This field, over which you see the sun setting behind the abbey, is now occupied in a *proper* manner." Then there went a flame of scarlet across the picture, which developed itself into windows & roofs & red brick, & rushed up into a chimney. "The atmosphere is supplied—thus!" A puff & cloud of smoke all over Turner's sky: & then the brush thrown down, & Ruskin confronting modern civilisation amidst a tempest of applause, which he always elicits now,[9] as he has this term become immensely popular, his lectures being crowded, whereas of old he used to prophesy to empty benches.

How he confuted the geological survey,[10] & science in general, by the help of the college cook I have no time to tell you, but remain, with love to father & all

Your affectionate son
Alfred E. Housman.

UCL MS Add. 126. Envelope addressed 'Mrs E. Housman | Perry Hall | Bromsgrove'. Date as postmark. Memoir, *42–3 (incomplete); Maas, 12–13.*

[9] Cf. Edward Symons (see List of Recipients) to Lucy Housman, 27 May 1896 (UCL MS Add. 126), on a similar Ruskin performance: 'Ruskin greatly added to the dramatic effect by having the picture which was covered with a black cloth brought in by an attendant with great secrecy & solemnity just at the very moment when the interest of the audience was on tip-toe & he then fairly lifted it off its feet by cunningly adding a few touches with his head under the black cloth & his back to his listeners. When all was complete he kept everybody in roars of laughter by the unusual energy—not to say violence with which he rubbed in the colours for the factory chimney-smoke &c.'

[10] A typical Ruskin target. 'The labour of the whole Geological Society, for the last fifty years, has but now arrived at the ascertainment of those truths respecting mountain form which Turner saw and expressed with a few strokes of a camel's hair pencil fifty years ago, when he was a boy': *Stones of Venice* (1851–3), 3. 2.

1878

TO EDWARD HOUSMAN

[Oxford Union Society]
Tuesday. | February 12th [1878]

My dear Father

As this is likely to be a long letter, & as I have a good deal to tell you, I had better begin with a few little things that I may forget at the end. Please thank Mamma for the two *Bromsgrove Messengers*[1] which I got this morning.

I sent a copy of the *Round Table*[2] to Mrs Wise, & the other day I had a letter from her, inviting me to go to Woodchester in the Easter Vacation. The weather is now clearer, though rather cold, & the roads are dry at last: the mud here is quite à la Gloucestershire.

Last Thursday a motion was brought on at the Union,[3] to the following effect. That the Eastern policy of Lord Beaconsfield has been from the first, & remains[,] utterly unworthy of the confidence of the country.[4] This was moved by a Balliol Liberal. Mr Gladstone had been in Oxford a few days before, & a meeting was held at the Corn Exchange, where Mr Gladstone spoke,[5] &, I believe, moved some motion or other. A good many undergraduates in the hall held up their hands against this motion. Some of them were turned out, but I suppose Mr Gladstone was

---

[1] The local newspaper, *The Bromsgrove, Droitwich, & Redditch Weekly Messenger, County Journal, and General Advertiser.*

[2] *Ye Rounde Table: An Oxford and Cambridge Magazine*, Thos. Shrimpton & Son [and] J. Hall & Son: Oxford [and] Cambridge. It was first published on 2 Feb. 1878, and its sixth (and last) issue appeared on 22 June 1878. A complete unbound set is in the Sparrow Collection, SJCO. AEH served on the editorial board, and under the pseudonym 'Tristram' made contributions, in poetry or prose, to every issue. For his poetical contributions, see *Poems* (1997), 214–23, 230–5, and notes, 519–28.

[3] The Oxford Union Society, founded in 1823 as a debating society.

[4] The policy of the government led by Benjamin Disraeli, Lord Beaconsfield (1804–81), was to support Turkey in order to prevent Russian control of the Dardanelles. (War between Russia and Turkey had broken out in the Balkans in 1877.) Gladstone (1809–98) and the Liberal Party condemned the Turks for atrocities committed in Bulgaria in 1876.

[5] On 30 January, under the auspices of Thorold Rogers (see next note) and Oxford philosopher T. H. Green, Gladstone made a speech to the Oxford Liberal Association at the Corn Exchange. He announced that for the previous eighteen months he had been bent on unrelentingly counteracting the purpose of Lord Beaconsfield.

disconcerted, for thereupon uprose Thorold Rogers,[6] who holds, or rather has just vacated, the Professorship of Political Economy, & can therefore perhaps be scarcely held accountable for his actions,—he rose from Mr Gladstone's side, & bade the rt. hon. gentleman be of good cheer, & pay no attention to 'dissipated undergraduates'. Now undergraduate Oxford was rather riled at this, & Professor Thorold Rogers, who goes by the name of the Beaumont Street Gorilla, was considerably groaned for at the anti-Russian demonstration last Saturday, of which more anon,—and on Thursday this opprobrious epithet was rankling in our hearts, & most were disposed to do anything to spite W. E. G.[7] Owing to the excited state of the public mind, the attendance at the debate was tremendous: & then at the last moment before it began came those telegrams that the Russians were in Constantinople, & that Mr Forster had withdrawn his amendment.[8] The crush & the frantic excitement were such as the oldest inhabitant &c.

The debate began with most of the House perpendicular, & some floating off their legs. Private business was got through in speed & silence; & then the terms of the motion were read. Then ensued seven good minutes of storm & tempest, & the cheering & groaning were such that neither could roar down the other, & they ceased from pure exhaustion. Then the speech began. It was not violent, which was a mercy, & not rhetorical, which was a greater mercy still. The man was nothing of the orator, but he was fluent, & very cool & impudent. The speech lasted an hour, but the greater part of this time was occupied by the speaking of the House, & not of the honourable member. I should not say that his remarks took more than twenty minutes, but they only cropped up as islets in the oceanic demonstrations of opinion. About the middle of the speech, chairs were set on the dais usually reserved for speakers; then the back ranks made a rush forward, & more pressed in at the door: the poor new president[9] was always on his legs to maintain order,

[6] James Edwin Thorold Rogers (1823–90), Drummond Professor of Political Economy at Oxford, 1862–7, 1888–90; Lecturer in Political Economy, Worcester College, Oxford, 1883; MP for Southwark, 1880–5, and Bermondsey, 1885–6. Author of *History of Agriculture and Prices*, (6 vols., 1866–87).

[7] William Ewart Gladstone.

[8] William Edward Forster (1819–66), Liberal MP for Bradford and a former member of the Cabinet, on 7 Feb. withdrew his amendment to the Vote of Credit (which had been devised for military support of the British Empire in the East) at the news that the Turks had surrendered the defences of Constantinople.

[9] The Hon. William St John Freemantle Brodrick (1856–1942); educated at Eton and Balliol College, Oxford; President of the Union, 1878; Conservative MP, 1885–1906; Financial Secretary to the War Office, 1886–92; Under-secretary for War, 1895–8; Secretary of State for War, 1900–3, for India, 1903–5; Viscount Midleton, 1907, first Earl of Midleton, 1920.

& only the orator's head could be seen, which occasioned suggestions that
he should stand on the table:—rejected however, as savouring of stump
oratory. There came then three other speakers, one for the motion & two
against; the two were baldly bad, & the one was gaudily bad. Perhaps one
bye-cause of the great throng was the belief that Baumann,[10] who is the
best Union speaker, a Conservative, was going to speak. But he did not:
the crowd diminished a little after the third speech: then, after the fourth
speech, came the only glimmer of light in the darkness of debate: Burrows,[11]
the popular buffoon. He was better than I have heard him. It was rather
ludicrous to hear him say that this was not the first time it had been his duty
to vindicate Lord Beaconsfield's character, & that <it would> he hoped it
would not be the last. Not that he did, in reality, vindicate it at all. He merely stated that Lord Beaconsfield's fame was a thing that would come—&
come—& come, when the honourable mover was gone—& gone—&
gone. He then said that the honourable mover would rot. We must all rot.
He did not however anticipate any precipitate action in that direction on
the part of the honourable mover. Etc. etc.—sometimes slightly coarse, as
you see, & sometimes really slightly witty. Then there came a priest from
Keble, with an amendment which was precisely the same as the motion. He
was a liberal. Then a conservative priest from Christchurch,[12] in reply: then
vociferations for a division. But there were several more speakers all the
same. Then it was half past eleven. Then someone proposed the adjournment of the debate, & someone else seconded it. <Lord Lymington> The
President stated that twelve honourable members had informed him they
wished to speak on the question, & that some of them had left the House
in anticipation of the adjournment of the debate. This struck us as highly
insolent on their part, & we determined to serve them out by refusing to
adjourn, especially as we had our majority on the spot. The last straw was
laid on the camel's back by Lord Lymington[,][13] an ex-president, who
stated that he wanted to speak. His oratory is generally considered the one
thing worse than death, & so the adjournment was negatived by a vast
majority. The amendment was lost without a division. The division on

[10] Arthur Anthony Baumann (1856–1936). President of the Union, Easter 1877; MP,
1885–6; editor of *The Saturday Review*, 1917–21.

[11] Frank Robert Burrows (b. 1856). Treasurer of the Union, 1878; President, 1879; Assistant
Master at Blackheath School, 1883; author of a paper on the teaching of geography (1896) and
of *Geographical Gleanings* (1906).

[12] For 'Christ Church'.

[13] Newton Wallop, Viscount Lymington (1856–1917). BA (second class) in History, Balliol
College, 1879; President of the Union, 1877; MP, 1880–91; sixth Earl of Portsmouth, 1891;
Under-secretary for War, 1905–8.

the motion was—for the motion 68; against the motion 146,—majority against the motion—unheard in the transports of enthusiasm, & the general rush back to college; for you can only understand the patriotic state of excitement in which we were, when you consider that the division took place between ten & five minutes to twelve: & if you are not back in college at 12 the penalties, I believe, are something very fearful indeed.

I did not go to Gladstone: I did not discover he was in Oxford till the moment before. He was rather feeble, as he tried to be humorous, which was very unwise. I believe he was very fine at the Palmerston Club,[14] in the passage where he described his antagonism to Lord Beaconsfield.

On Saturday night an anti-Russian demonstration was held in the Corn Exchange. I went, because Sir Robert Peel[15] was coming: he did not come; but I heard Alfred Austin.[16] The hall was crammed. The orators were late. First *Rule Britannia*[17] was sung by the crowd; latent English Liberalism testifed by scattered hisses its decided objection to the marine rule of Britannia. Then we took up our parable & sang that we didn't want to fight, but by jingo, if we did, we'd got the ships, we'd got the men, we'd got the money too.[18] As a matter of fact we had not got the money yet, but that was immaterial; & growing impatience soon made it clear, by several ''mills'' in the body of the hall, that when we *did* want to fight we could perfectly well dispense with money, & ships too, for the matter of that, in the attainment of our desire. When it was getting towards eight, the orators came. Then there was great cheering, & the Mayor was unheard, & Mr Hall,[19] member for the city of Oxford, (along with Sir William Harcourt!)[20] began to speak. Then there was much cheering again, & much desultory ejection of malcontent Liberals, at intervals, between which the orator

[14] Inaugurated by Gladstone and Edward, Viscount Cardwell (1813–86), on 30 January.

[15] 1822–95. Eldest son of Sir Robert Peel, the former Prime Minister (1834–5, 1841–6); MP since 1850; a supporter of Disraeli's Eastern policy.

[16] 1835–1913. Leader writer to the *Standard*, 1866–96; Co-editor of the *National Review*, 1883–7; Editor, 1887–95; Poet Laureate, 1896–1913.

[17] Jingoistic song with words by James Thomson and music by Thomas Arne, first performed in 1740. Its refrain is 'Rule, Britannia, rule the waves; | Britons never will be slaves.'

[18] Music hall song *We Don't Want to Fight* by G. W. Hunt (1878), made popular by G. H. Macdermott: 'We don't want to fight, but, by jingo if we do, | We've got the ships, we've got the men, we've got the money too. | We've fought the Bear before, and while Britons shall be true, | The Russians shall not have Constantinople.'

[19] Alexander William Hall (1839–1919). Conservative MP for Oxford, 1874–80, 1885–92.

[20] William George Granville Venables Vernon Harcourt (1827–1904). President of the Union, 1849; Liberal MP for Oxford, 1868; Whewell Professor of International Law at Cambridge, 1869–87; knighted on appointment as Solicitor-General, 1873; denounced Turkey, 1876–8; following defeat at Oxford, MP for Derby, May 1880; Home Secretary, 1880–5; Chancellor of the Exchequer, 1886, 1892–5; Leader of the Liberal Party, 1896–8.

struggled on. I was close to the platform, so I heard well. He said nothing worth remark, except that the Christians of Turkey hated one another with a hatred passing the love of woman. This I relished very much, especially as his wife was sitting beside him. Then came Sir Henry Drummond Wolff,[21] weak; then Mr Hanbury,[22] frantic, but gentlemanly: then Alfred Austin, pointed & clever, but insufficiently audible. These speeches formed the interludes to about a dozen patriotic ejections,—one being that of an eminent liberal undergraduate who speaks much at the Union, & on this occasion attempted to scale the platform with an amendment. These ejections were vigorously prompted by a man on the platform with a long black beard. This I thought bad taste, so as I was close to the platform, I caught hold of Sir Drummond Wolff,—selecting his left hand, because he wore a large gold ring upon it, & was therefore likely to consider it the most valuable portion of his frame—and told him that I thought we should have scored off Gladstone, if we had abstained from following the ejective example set by his meeting, and I asked him whether he could not suppress the man with the black beard. But Sir Drummond Wolff was in a helpless state of imbecility, & could do nothing, & as Mr Hanbury looked as if he was going to faint after his oratorical exertions, & Alfred Austin was bent upon sitting immoveable & looking as much like Mr Disraeli as he could manage,—there was nothing to be done. But the result was a rather rowdy meeting. The motion <was>—Conservative and Turk—was of course carried with acclamation, & then the meeting fought itself out of doors & culminated in the combustion of an effigy of Mr Gladstone just outside our college.

On the Sunday before last, Canon King[23] of Christchurch[24] preached at St Mary's on 'binding & loosing'—a counterblast to Dean Stanley in the *Nineteenth Century*.[25] The sermon was unconscionably long, & considerably over our heads, brimming as it did with patristic learning, until, at the end of an hour & a quarter, he concluded with an apology to his younger brethren

[21] Henry Drummond Charles Wolff (1830–1908). Civil servant in the Foreign Office; knighted, 1862; Conservative MP for Christchurch, 1874–80, for Portsmouth, 1880–5; sent on mission to Constantinople to negotiate with Turkey over the future of Egypt, Aug. 1885; negotiated second convention with Turkey, May 1887, which was not ratified; subsequently envoy to Persia, Romania, and Spain.

[22] Robert William Hanbury (1845–1903). Conservative MP, 1872–80, 1885–1903; Financial Secretary of the Treasury, 1895–1900; President of the Board of Agriculture, 1900.

[23] The Revd Edward King (1829–1910). High Churchman and Tory; Professor of Pastoral Theology and Canon of Christ Church, Oxford, 1873–85; Bishop of Lincoln, 1885–1910.

[24] For 'Christ Church'.

[25] 'Absolution' by A[rthur] P[enrhyn] Stanley (1815–81), Dean of Westminster (1864–81), in *The Nineteenth Century*, 3 (Jan. 1878), 183–95.

for having bored them, & giving as his reason that Our Lord grieved Peter,[26]
which I did not quite see the force of. But I felt it was quite worth sitting still
for an hour & a quarter to watch such an interesting personality. He is tall,
but stoops; & haggard in the face but without grey hair; & his sermon was
most masterly here & there. The exquisitely deprecating way & affected
timidity with which he put his strongest points, & the mournful & apologetic
modulation of his voice where he was pulling Dean Stanley to pieces, were
really almost worthy of Disraeli, & not altogether unlike, were it not for
the deadly earnest, which was rather detrimental to the oratorical effect.
Last Sunday, Dean Church[27] in the morning. Dean Church, I regret to say
it, is dull. He is very nice to look at, & particularly ethereal in countenance,
& he speaks in earnest, & everything, but he is certainly tedious. I thought
so last term, & now I am confirmed. In the Afternoon, the Bishop of
Manchester,[28] who commenced operations by blowing his nose, which is
a rhetorical device he has apparently just found out, & which in the first
ecstasy of novelty he uses with injudicious profusion. In the bidding prayer
he prayed that this country might not be drawn into war. He took a text
to the effect that when we saw devils being cast out, the kingdom of God
would be at hand. As he went on it became apparent that the first devil
was the Turk. The second devil was the Pope, over whose death-bed the
Bishop uttered a wild whoop of triumph,[29] & then proceeded to inveigh
against the Romish Church, which inspired him with much despair, as it
did not seem inclined to die. This part of the sermon was garnished with
several quotations from Macaulay's essay on Von Ranke's history of the
Popes.[30] Now Canon Liddon[31] was present, & up to this point of course he
must have found himself in unexpected sympathy with the Bishop,—on
both the Turk & Rome. This was particularly kind on Dr Fraser's part, as,
in the morning, Canon Liddon, in getting into the pew at the end of which
the Bishop sat, had almost taken his seat on his Lordship's knees, for which
the Bishop had rewarded him with a smile of such Christian forgiveness
that Canon Liddon hastily made his way to the middle of the pew, &,

---

[26] John 21: 17: 'Peter was grieved because he said unto him the third time, Lovest thou me?'

[27] Richard William Church (1815–90). Select preacher at Oxford, 1868, 1876–8, 1881–2;
leading member of High-Church party; Dean of St Paul's, 1871–90.

[28] James Fraser (1818–85). Fellow and Tutor, Oriel College, Oxford, 1840–60; Bishop of
Manchester, 1870–85.

[29] Pope Pius IX died on 7 Feb. 1878, aged 85, after the longest pontificate in history
(1846–78).

[30] *Edinburgh Review* (Oct. 1840). Repr. in *Critical and Historical Essays*, 3 (1850).

[31] Henry Parry Liddon (1829–90). Vice-Principal, St Edmund Hall, Oxford, 1859; Canon
of St Paul's Cathedral, 1870, Chancellor, 1886; celebrated preacher.

taking up a prayer book, began to read it with an avidity & apparent sense of novelty which that interesting work does not often excite in the clergy of the Established Church of England. Well, the Bishop, having shown us a great deal of reason why the church of Rome was unlikely to go down quick into the pit, now began to give us a few slight crumbs of consolation, on which we might base a hope, though not a belief, that she would do so. And then he somehow got upon the subject of Ritualism & the Confessional in England. Poor Canon Liddon! He always sits with his hand over his face, so I could not see his emotions; but the revulsion of feeling must have been great, when the sermon[,] which began so promisingly, developed into this. But the Bishop was now far above canons & all the rest of the inferior clergy. He began to plunge into eloquence, in which he rather staggered. He even began a sentence with "Methinks,"—but got rather bewildered towards the end of it, & so found it time to conclude with a remark about freedom of conscience, which was calculated to bring down the house, & then blew his nose in the middle of the doxology or whatever you call it, to show how little trouble it had all cost him.

Here it is time to conclude these irrelevant recitals, which I hope will interest you a little. With love to Mamma & the rest, I remain

Your loving son
Alfred E. Housman.

P.S. The Union authorities decline to supply one with stamps up to more than a certain weight. Such is my wiliness that I intend to frustrate their parsimony by posting this letter in <*three*> *two* envelopes, <all> differently directed. I have numbered the sheets of this letter, that you may not be confused.

UCL MS Add. 126. Memoir, *44–51 (incomplete); Maas, 13–19.*

TO ELIZABETH WISE

[Oxford]
Sunday. [17 Feb. 1878]

My dear Mrs Wise

You were *going* to receive a Valentine from the Pope, but as the cantankerous old ruffian chose to shuffle off his mortal coil[1] at that inopportune moment, I was far too much overcome by the frustration of

---

[1] *Hamlet*, 3. 1. 69: 'When we have shuffled off this mortal coil'. On the death of the Pope, see previous letter, n. 29. See AEH to Mrs Wise, 5 Apr. 1877 and 24 Nov. 1878, about going 'over to Rome'.

my scheme to turn my poetic genius to any thing else. I enclose however some nonsense verses which will appear in the next number of the *Round Table*, composed by several members of the Editorial Staff together: the last verse is mine.[2] I am glad you liked the *Round Table*: the second number will be published next Saturday, & I will send it. I expect it will be considerably better than the first. It is selling here very well, & seems likely to become popular.

You are kind enough to ask me to come to Woodchester at Easter, if not better engaged. Setting aside the obvious absurdity of the notion that any engagement *could* be better, I shall be most delighted to come: only I must explain that the Easter Vacation does not begin at Easter, but just towards the end of March. It lasts about five weeks or a month; & if at any period starting from that date you can take me in, I shall like nothing better.

I hope you are better in health than when I saw you last. I also hope that Miss Becker has got over the preliminary horrors of her pupils.

I should be learning German myself this term, but for the great pressure of classical work for the time: I shall begin next term:[3] it is to some extent a necessity, as a great many of the most learned editions of Latins & Greeks are in German. I hope still more fervently that the cookery class enjoys itself: I was most edified when I heard who were its component parts. Have you heard of a physician in fragments being found anywhere in the neighbourhood as yet?

We have had Gladstone here, as you know: & about a week ago we had a counterblast, in the shape of a great anti-Russian meeting, to which I went: but it was rather a boisterous affair, though considerably more unanimous & enthusiastic than Gladstone's meeting. While that latter gentleman was describing the government as a *bag*, which he did in the course of his speech, some one called out "Why don't you put your head in it?" M[r] Gladstone happily did not hear the unfeeling remark.

I may remark, for the consolation of so noted a Papist as yourself, that the Bishop of Manchester[4] was here preaching last Sunday, & that even he considers that the Roman Candlestick Religion has still a long life before

---

[2] Attributed to 'King Arthur'. It is not known whether, or to what extent, AEH had a hand in verses 1–3. The third bears a resemblance to *The shades of night were falling fast*, 10, 12 ('desperate fellah… umberella'): *Poems* (1997), 210.

[3] Naiditch (1995), 67–9, presents evidence to suggest that AEH did not begin serious study of the German language until 1890.

[4] See the previous letter, n. 28.

it, & will continue to spread. After this ecstatic news I will send my best love to you & the rest and remain

Yours affectionately
Alfred E. Housman.

These are the Verses.[5]
1.

Oh, fair is the lovely peôny,
  Serene is the mildew of hate,
Most gay is the tail of the pony,
  All poets must yield unto fate.

2.

Oh, sour are the succulent juices
  That blow on the banks of the Cam:[6]
'Tis mustard the maiden induces
  To wallow in marmalade jam.

3.

Oh, fair was my new umberella
  Although its sweet handle was bent;
Oh, cursed be that desperate fellah
  To whom in my weakness 'twas lent.

4.

For it sank in a flatulent fluid
  And imbibed its auricomous[7] roar,
Till the deadly & dew-spangled Druid[8]
  Had dabbled his tendrils in gore.

BMC MS.

---

[5] Published in *Ye Rounde Table*, 1. 2 (23 Feb. 1878), 18. See *Poems* (1977), 214–15.

[6] Cambridge river.

[7] Of or pertaining to golden hair. *OED*'s first example is from 1864.

[8] Member of an order of priests in ancient Britain and Gaul, who appear in Welsh and Irish legends as prophets and mystics.

TO LUCY HOUSMAN

[Woodchester House | Woodchester | Stroud
3 March 1878]

My dear Mamma

It was very good of you to write, for I believe as a matter of fact I owed you a letter. The reason why I have been so remiss lately is that I have been in for the Hertford,[1] the result being that I am among the first six. Which is better than any one else thought I should do, and better than I myself fancied I had actually done. I enclose Kate's letter which I have copied out with scrupulous accuracy, reproducing even the erasures of the marvellous work.[2] If she chooses to compare it with my answer she will see how very closely & humbly I have trodden in her footsteps.

I am glad you are well enough to be about again. Lucky, considering youthful Louisas & unprotected dinner-plates. I expect I shall come back on Lady Day.[3] I have called on Mrs Sankey.[4] The Third *Round Table* will be out tomorrow.[5] There will be a considerably larger number of writers in it than heretofore.

With best love I remain

Your loving son
Alfred E. Housman.

UCL MS Add. 126. Envelope addressed 'Mrs Edward Housman | Perry Hall | Bromsgrove', and postmarked Stroud, 3 March 1878. Maas, 19, where it has the wrong date and address heading.

---

[1] The University Latin scholarship.

[2] KES's letter of 25 Feb. 1878 is copied out (UCL MS Add. 126) with errors of spelling and punctuation faithfully reproduced.

[3] 25 March.

[4] 'Mother of Housman's contemporary at Bromsgrove School, G. M. Sankey' is Maas's guess (19 n.); but AEH is in Woodchester, which would make this unlikely though not impossible.

[5] It did not appear until 16 March.

TO KATHARINE HOUSMAN

[Oxford Union Society
19 June 1878]
I began this tune
On the day of Wednesday,
The 19th of June,
And it wasn't a saint's day.[1]

My dearest Kate:
I need not state
That these words are hollow
And it doesn't follow
That I love you dearly
Or that you are really
My dearest Kate:
Oh dear me no!
Don't fancy so;
But I know quite well
Miss Milward Hell[2]
Would raise a yell
(And her voice *does* grate),
If I didn't *call* you
My dearest Kate:
And yet for all you
Can possibly tell
There may be thousands
Of dearest Kates
All hung on the boughs' ends
Or hid in the grates
(You notice, "boughs' ends"
Will rhyme with "thousands"
Quite well enoúgh for me
—As well as "cows' hands"
—Which is too great stúff for me<)>
For you'll surely allow

---

[1] '1879' is pencilled on the MS, apparently by KES. However, 19 June was a Thursday in 1879, but a Wednesday in 1878.
[2] Possibly a relative of Ensign (later Captain) Milward of Bromsgrove, mentioned in Pugh, 138, 172–3.

Hands don't grow on a cow)
And 'my dearest Kate'
Means nothing great,
It may mean loathing,
Or bitterest hate
It may mean nothing
—Or anything, Kate.

And now I'm aware
That in a short time
I shall want a rhyme
To rhyme with "sèche":[3]
Therefore prepare
Your Dictionaire
And look out "fraîches"[4]
And do they grow
At Fockbury,[5] oh?
They do. Just so.

Perhaps you consider
   That I'm a goose
To put a French word
   In constant use,
And as absurd
As the hopes of a spider
(Rhyme to "consider")
To catch a tench,
And you think I'm a nuis-
ance to ladies who blench
At the sound of French,
As perhaps you do:
(Sing tootle-tum-too!
One *must* force rhymes
In short lines, sometimes)
But ah-ha! oh-ho!
You do not know
That a rhyme will come

---

[3] *sèche*: dry.   [4] *fraîches*: fresh (for *fraises*, strawberries).
[5] *Fockbury*: AEH's birthplace.

(Sing tootle-too-tum)
—A rhyme to fraîches
As well as sèche—
At the very end.
Therefore attend.
Yes, yes, be sure
That you shall have
My "signiture"[6]
Ere I go to my grave.
Before I end
With honours rife
That "Shakespears life"
You so kindly portend.

One night, (you said)
You went to bed.
But *I*, oh no,
I didn't do so:
Such indolence scorning
I got up one morning!
(Êtes-vous donc sèche?[7])
I took my candle,
I was so quick!
I took my candle
(Oh, j'aime les fraîches[8])
I took by the handle
My candle-stick.
Though good health blessed me
Something 'oppresed' me:
A sort of preséntiment,
—The same thing you meant, I meant.
Oh dear, oh me!
What's that I see?
Coffee? or milk?
No, something better,
A sealèd letter
Containing blue silk.

---

6 On such errors, see the previous letter, n. 2.   7 'Are you dry, then?'
8 'Oh, I love strawberries' (*fraîches* for *fraises*).

I read it through
Boo-hoo! boo-hoo!
Alas, alas,
Can I endure
<[?Then]> When I write to her
To know what's certain
To come to pass?
By her bed-curtain
She reads my epistle
When she ought to be reading
A pious missal
Or some such proceeding
Or saying a prayer
Or combing her back-hair
<(Je suis tres>
(Aimes-tu les fraîches?⁹)
And first she catches
A box of matches
(La boite est sèche¹⁰)
And she smears these matches
All over the scratches
Made by my pen.
She does; and then
She makes quite sure
Of the 'signiture',—
She smears it over
With quite a cover
Of Lucifers¹¹
(Which are not hers)
And she lights a taper
With careful care
And she shoves the paper
Right bang in there
And when by dint of caressing
She's coaxed it into a blaze
She gives it a motherly blessing
And wanders forth on her ways.

⁹ 'Do you like strawberries?'   ¹⁰ 'The box is dry'.
¹¹ *Lucifers*: brand of matches, from *c.*1829.

And leaves it to burn to cinders
With a peaceful smile on her face
So innocent, nobody hinders
Her dawdling all over the place:
And she can't think of anything better
Than down the stairs to jump,
And hunt for her brother's letter—
—Where?—"In the kitchen pump." ! ! ! ! !

     *   *   *   *   *

Ah, cease, my passion;
Poem! refrain:
I think I'll fashion
Short lines again.
Good-bye. I'm screening
My wounded pride.
The late Miss Greening,—[12]
She took & died.
And if Miss Greenings
Can take & die
When they have leanings
That way, mayn't I?
Prepare the coffin,
The bier prepare.
To walk me off in—
No matter where!
I break my fetters,
Adieu, les fraîches!
Kate burns my letters,—
Elles sont trop sèches![13]

<Fond> When Greenings shuffle
Their mortal coil,[14]
Fond friends go 'snuffle!"[15]
—Their sorrows boil:—

---

[12] *Miss Greening*: possibly a relative of the late W. Greening of Bromsgrove mentioned in Pugh, 144, 146, 147.
[13] 'They are too dry'.   [14] *shuffle | Their mortal coil*: die (*Hamlet*, 3. 1. 69).
[15] AEH mixes single and double quotation marks.

With lavish purses
They make their heads
With plumy hearses
Like feather-beds[16]
With ringlets ghostly
Their heads they cram,—
Miss "Perins" mostly
Or "Bilingham".

But when this bosom
No more shall be,
And daisies blossom
Atop of me,
Will brows <gr[?ow]> be gloomy
Will gladness cease
Will heads grow plumy
At my decease?
When bells are tolling
And I interred
'Twould be consoling
Although absurd
To think they'd bought her
A funeral hat:—
My parents' daughter
Would look like that!
But no, 'tis fancy.
That hat, that grief
That graceful pansy
That handkerchief:—
No! when my mortal
Career is o'er,
She'll laugh & chortle
And simply roar!

Yet p'r'aps her wishes,
In midnight deep,

---

[16] Fiona Clark, *Hats* (1982), 36, remarks on 'the enormous popularity of birds' plumage as a trimming': 'This began in the 1860s with the use of a single feather or small wing ... By the late 1870s ... whole birds were frequently used.'

When beasts & fishes
Are gone to sleep,
May damp her spirits
And make her see
How many merits
Belonged to me:
In sorrow's fetters
She then may yearn
For other letters
To take & burn:
"Had I another"
She then may sigh,
"Another brother
To write to I!
But no! my candle
Must flare in vain:
He'll never handle
The pen again!"

Then come, I ask it,
When roses bloom
And put a basket
Upon my tomb:
<Yes, bring> And honey-suckle
And roses rare,
And do not chuckle
At putting it there,
Nor sit down on the daises[17]
To eat the wild *fraîches*
Unless the place is
Entirely *sèche*,
'Cause then you'd smother
Your doting brother
A. Edward. *H.*

P.S.   "That is a rhyme
           If you take it in time" Old Song.
P.P.S.   Address to this Letter

---

[17] For 'daisies'. (Perhaps another parody of KES's bad spelling.)

Fly forth O letter!
Though skies be damp,
Though even wetter
Your postage-stamp;
A hotter hand will
Soon seal your fate:—
—The tallow candle
Of Katherine Kate!

BMC MS. Stamped Oxford Union Society writing paper. Part of the MS, with AEH's drawing of KH wearing a funeral hat, is reproduced in Richards, 376 (and wrongly dated 17 June 1879). Graves, 46–7, prints ll. 110–16 and 223–30. For the full text, see Poems (1997), *223–30.*

TO ELIZABETH WISE

[Oxford Union Society]
Sunday. | November 24th [1878]

My dear Mrs Wise

This shamefully late answer to your long letter comes from an industrious youth who has a deal to do, which must be his excuse, if any. In a letter from Aunt Kate[1] I heard that you had returned from Bournemouth, & also, what I was very glad to hear, that Ted[2] had come back much better, & you yourself too. I had not the least idea that Bournemouth, or indeed any other sea side place in these days, was at all like what you describe it: pine-trees & sepulchres & the sea, & the greatness of the company of the preachers[3] engaged in damming a stream with spades instead of damning their fellow-creatures with the Commination Service[4] (one penny!) are certainly superior to parades & things: you must have enjoyed yourselves much, being a perfect colony, what with you & Mrs Joseph & the Cartwrights: rather a dissolute colony too, if two of the ladies corrupted their minds with novels all day.

It has come into my mind, can Bournemouth be the place described in the *World*[5] some time ago under a feigned name? The scenery was said to be lovely, especially the pine trees: but the atmosphere was said

[1] AEH's mother's sister-in-law, Mrs Basil Williams: P. G. Naiditch, *HSJ* 23 (1997), 38.
[2] See AEH to Mrs Woollright, 1876, n. 5.
[3] Ps. 68: 11: 'great was the company of the preachers' (Coverdale's *Book of Common Prayer* version).
[4] In the Anglican Liturgy for Ash Wednesday, the recital of divine threats against sinners.
[5] *The Pictorial World*, an illustrated weekly newspaper, 1874–92.

to be scented with Patchouli,[6] which was the title of the article. What is
Patchouli? Is it a kind of scent? And did you smell any? And what is the
force of saying that an atmosphere is scented with Patchouli? Is it a scent
particularly admired & used by the giddy votaries of fashion (this is not
meant for you), & do they throng Bournemouth when the season comes?
It is a conundrum which I have given up.

I heard from Miss Becker when she got to Siegen.[7] She prophesied that
she should make herself ill with eating cakes at tea. From Aunt Kate's letter
I gather that this prophecy has come true. Giddy young thing![8] Did she
cram them into her mouth at intervals to smother her emotion at meeting
Otto,[9] or what?

I wrote her a letter: but as they don't provide foreign paper at the Union,
I wrote it on this paper. It was one sheet & a half. They stamp the letter
here for you, if they are not over weight. It struck me afterwards that that
might be over weight. Do you suppose it was? & would she be let in for
ten shillings at the other end or something dreadful, owing to the morose
indignation of Bismark[10] at an Englishman not having put enough stamps
on his letter? He might suspect that the Bank of England was breaking,
& declare war on the spot:[11] what a shindy one might create: it would be
well worth trying.

I will now write down some intelligence for your Roman ear.[12] <About
a month ago> About the beginning of last vacation the authorities
announced to D[r] Pusey[13] that he would have two turns in the University
pulpit in October: who would he like to preach for him? They asked this
because he had not been able to preach himself for some time: but he sent
back & said "I'll preach myself." But when October came, D[r] Pusey had
the asthma, & they found it would be a moral impossibility to get him up
the pulpit stairs without machinery: and they didn't think he would look

---

[6] Asiatic tree with leaves yielding oil used in perfume manufacture; or, the perfume made
from it.

[7] Siegenburg, later in W. Germany.   [8] She was *c*.34.

[9] Possibly a reference to Bismarck, whose names were Otto Eduard Leopold.

[10] 1815–98. The 'Iron Chancellor' of Germany (1871–90).

[11] Bismarck had orchestrated wars with Denmark (1864), Austria (1866), and France (1870–1)
in order to effect the unification of Germany.

[12] See AEH to Mrs Wise, 5 Apr. 1877, and n. 3, and 17 Feb. 1878.

[13] Edward Bouverie Pusey (1800–82). Regius Professor of Hebrew at Oxford, 1828, and
Canon of Christ Church. He was suspended from the office of university preacher on a charge
of heresy in 1843, resuming in 1846. A leading figure in the Oxford Movement, he aimed at
restoring the High Church ideals of the seventeenth century. His efforts from 1865 to effect the
union of English and Roman churches were razed by the decisions of the Vatican Council in
1870.

well in machinery: so when the morning came, & the Church doors had been besieged a quarter of an hour before they opened, after all Canon Liddon made his appearance & preached Pusey's sermon for him. The sermon was the best I ever heard: I believe he has taken years in writing it, & it is the coping stone of the work of his life: it was about Religion & Natural Science. Canon Liddon of course preached it much better than Pusey could have done it himself, but still I was sorry to miss hearing the old man. On the next Sunday Dr Pusey was announced again, but again he had to depute some-one else; and this time the sermon was rather dull: perhaps it suffered in the delivery. You apparently have no chance of stagnation, with all the doings of your frisky Mutton. But what I wanted to say was, that here every one is going over to Rome like wildfire: the Pope's Chamberlain has taken up his abode here, though what becomes of the Pope & the Pope's Chamber in the mean time I'm sure I don't know: he asks men to breakfast<s>, & leads them into a private oratory where Mass is going on: & he says "Doesn't it look grateful, comforting?" and they say yes it does,—& then they think they should like to try how it feels, & then they go over to Rome. If you would only come & pay me a visit you might go over with great éclat & quite a string of young men at your heels, looking for all the world like Murillo's Madonna with her sky-full of Cherubs.[14] The Pope rushes out of the Vatican with "Are you my long lost daughter?"—you intimate that such is the case, & then you go into St. Peter's & get canonised quietly. In expectation of this glorious event, & with much love to yourself & all I remain

Yours most affectionately
Alfred E. Housman.

BMC MS. Stamped Oxford Union Society writing paper. Envelope addressed 'Mrs E. Wise | Woodchester House | Stroud'. Year as postmark.

[14] Bartolomé Esteban Murillo (1618–82), Spanish religious painter. AEH's reference is to his *Immaculate Conception of Soult.*

1879

TO ELIZABETH WISE

Sunday [Hilary Term: 14 Jan.–5 Apr. 1879]
Oxford.

My dear Mrs Wise

I hope your influenza is retreating by now, tho' I can't say the weather is likely to assist it: we have got the river frozen over again as it was at the end of last term, a most unusual thing: & though I have not got a cold or anything myself, a good many have, & as the poet[1] observes

> White is the wold, & ghostly
> The dank & leafless trees,
> And M's & N's are mostly
> Pronounced as B's & D's

something like this

> Dever bore bedeath the bood
> Shall byrtle boughs edtwide,
> Dever bore thy bellow voice
> Bake belody with bide

and I suppose it is much the same with you, & you go about the house saying "Where is Biddie?" and Minnie answers "Here I ab, Babba."

I was very much amused by your account of all your pets. I think Dachshunds[2] are dear creatures: there is one belonging to a fellow of our college who lives on the same staircase with me: sometimes it is shut out & sits howling on the stairs & then I entice it into my rooms & put it on an armchair in front of the fire & feed it on milk, by which means I am rapidly alienating its affections from its master.

Young England's appointment & Miss Billings's disappointment (or ought I to call her Old England?) at New Zealand is very interesting: England & New Zealand are said in the Geography books to be antipodes to one another: you should point out to Miss Becker that this is another

---

[1] Imaginary.   [2] The Wise family had a pet dachshund called Minka.

proof that the world is round. It is very curious too how the result of marriage always seems to be to "escape Australia." I have it on my mind to thank Miss Becker for my socks which are beautiful: I do not gather whether she is at Woodchester or not. You seem doomed to miscreants in the way of clergymen: I wonder you dont[3] start a waxwork collection of them as "the Woodchester chamber of Horrors." I am surprised to hear of the Searanckes[4] going to Italy: I thought M[r] Searancke had sworn by all the gods & goddesses that he would never set foot oversea again: however I suppose l'homme propose, la femme dispose.[5] With best love to all I remain

Always yours affectionately
Alfred E. Housman.

P.S. I just remember that I heard Hamilton was *not* to be married: Which has he chosen—Australia? or the Woodchester dramatic company?

BMC MS.

---

[3] For 'don't'.

[4] Mr Searancke was the second husband of AEH's mother's sister-in-law Mrs Basil Williams ('Aunt Kate'). Naiditch (2005), 5, makes the identification from the Housman family album. The name 'Alice E. Searancke' appears in the Visitors' Book of the Wise family on five separate occasions, 1883–6.

[5] A variant on Thomas à Kempis's saying 'Man proposes but God disposes' (*The Imitation of Christ*, 1. 19).

1880

TO A. W. POLLARD

Bromsgrove
Tuesday [23 Mar. 1880]

Dear Alurede G.[1]

Arnold's Thucydides[2] I shall very certainly bring up with me this term, but that I shall be able to lend it to you with any continuity I cannot expect. I may as well hereby give you fair notice that any questions as to what I have done in the Vac. will not evoke an answer. Heaven has always hitherto given me strength to tell such lies as might be from time to time generally necessary to my salvation, but supererogatory fiction I abhor & am not going to treat you to any of it, tho' I hope for a continuance of heaven's favours in the regular line, my first interview with <R>Bob[3] &c. That my birthday falls on <g>Good Friday or Good Friday on my birthday is tidings which fails to harrow me much. They nearly always have fallen on one another ever since I can remember,[4] & the sensation is growing insipid. The Millingtons[5] spent a week in London & as a consequence Bertie Millington[6] has come back with Lyceum[7] on the brain & must needs have a trial scene, which comes off next Saturday, the actors consisting chiefly of this family, & one or two other children, before an audience of parents. Rehearsals & manufacture of raiment are progressing with much fervour: Laurence is Shylock: apparently he will

---

[1] Aluredus Gulielmus is Latin for 'Alfred William', Alurede being the vocative. See the subscription to the letter of 21 Oct. 1877 to Lucy Housman.

[2] Thomas Arnold's three-volume edn. of Thucydides' *The History of the Peloponnesian War* (1830–5). Thucydides was a set author for Finals.

[3] Robert Ewing. See the letter to Lucy Housman, 21 Oct. 1877, n. 1. AEH seems to have held him in contempt as a scholar: Graves, 49; Page, 34.

[4] AEH's birthday (26 Mar.) fell on Good Friday in 1869, 1875, and 1880.

[5] Herbert Millington's family.

[6] The Millingtons' son Herbert Ashlin Millington (1868–1933). He was educated at King Edward VI Grammar School, Bromsgrove, until 1882: *OBR*, 90. He then attended Clifton College, 1882–6. He was appointed Town Clerk for Yarmouth in 1901 and Clerk of the Peace for Northamptonshire in 1904, and was awarded the OBE in 1918: *Clifton College Annals and Register 1862–1925*, ed. F. Borwick (1925), 179.

[7] *The Merchant of Venice*, with Henry Irving as a sympathetic Shylock and Ellen Terry as Portia, opened at the Lyceum Theatre on 1 November 1879 and ran for over 250 performances.

make up rather well: he conceived the character originally in a decidedly comic vein, but Mr Millington enforces Irving. Clemence is Portia: Herbert Antonio: the misery of his stage countenance suggests rather a ton than a pound of flesh as the forfeiture. I daresay Irving's conception is as you say wrong, but I rather fancy Shakespeare's is a good deal wronger: such slight acquaintance as I possess with the works of that fertile playwright enables me to see that several of his characters are superstitions, he learnt them in the nursery, they are traditions which he has not thought out. Richard III is one & Shylock is another; they are plausible guesses at what certain types might possibly be, by an outsider: they are admirable: they talk as men might be supposed to talk by a clever person unacquainted with the human race: but the things they say are not the things which human beings do say. I look forward to your essay:[8] especially the French clearness of style. Fast falls the eventide:[9] please remember me to M^r & M^{rs} & Misses Pollard: I hope he is still going on well.
I remain

several persons' very sincerely
A. E. Housman.

P.s. This is the new form of subscription which you require. On reading this letter over again, my remarks on Avon's bird[10] strike me as rather dishevelled. That I do not reconsider them is due to my disinterested haste that you should get this letter.

Private MS.

TO A. W. POLLARD

Easter Eve [27 Mar. 1880] | Bromsgrove

Dear Gulielme[1]

It was very kind of you to recollect me:[2] henceforth I hope I shall be less conspicuous for ignorance of Avon's bird. The book much interests my father who for some reason or other regards me as a devoted adherent of the accomplished author: he spends really much of his time at meals in

---

[8] Possibly an entry for the Chancellor's English Essay Prize, to be submitted at the end of March.

[9] 'Abide with me, fast falls the eventide': opening line of the hymn by H. F. Lyte.

[10] Shakespeare, called 'Sweet swan of Avon' by Ben Jonson in l. 71 of his commendatory poem in the First Folio (1623).

[1] The vocative form of the Latin.

[2] It looks as though Pollard had sent AEH a copy of A. C. Swinburne's *A Study of Shakespeare* (1880) as a birthday present.

making disparaging remarks on Mr Swinburne's versification at which he
expects me to inly writhe:[3] whether this refers to my Newdigate that should
have been,[4] or to what, I can't say: as a matter of fact he uses Swinburne
as an algebraical symbol for the Modern Spirit, concise, if inaccurate. I
am getting on decently at my compositions. Walter Sickart[5] is a bold man
to set foot in Birmingham at this crisistic hour: I expect his relations will
receive home some well-arranged ashes in urns of brass à la first chorus in
the *Agamemnon*.[6] I had seen in the papers that as I prophesied Oscuro Mild[7]
was to be the next attraction in *Time*:[8] also that that abandoned woman
Violet Fane was a contributor, to show how little she minded a touch of
additional infamy.[9] Laurence does not seem much wrecked by his illness:
Basil[10] is being confirmed to-day. The system of dating adopted at the head
of this letter is out of honour to Lord Beaconsfield.[11] Remember me please
to Mrs Pollard & your sisters & fervently congratulate Mr Pollard from me

[3] AEH admired Swinburne's early poetry, and his own translation of three Greek tragic
choruses, published in 1890 in Pollard's anthology *Odes from the Greek Dramatists*, he acknowledged
to be Swinburnian (letter of 22 Mar. 1933 to W. R. Agard). There were, however, signs of
disaffection towards Swinburne in his letter to LH of 31 Mar. 1895, and by 1909 or 1910,
when he gave his paper 'Swinburne' (Ricks, 1988, 277–95) he was openly critical. For further
information, see *Poems* (1997), 483.

[4] AEH's unsuccessful entry for the Newdigate Prize for English Verse at Oxford, *Iona*, was
written at an all-night sitting, *c*.30–31 Mar. 1879. The subject and the metre were not of his
choosing.

[5] Walter R[ichard] Sickert (1860–1942) had been a pupil and a friend at King's College
School in The Strand, London, which Pollard attended, 1870–7. From 1877 until he entered
the Slade School of Art in 1881, he played minor parts in Sir Henry Irving's company and those
of other well-known actors. He appeared under the name 'Mr Nemo', and often toured the
provinces. 'Sickart' seems to be a joke. He studied painting under J. A. M. Whistler, and was
also influenced by Pissarro among the French Impressionists. ARA, 1924; RA, 1934–5.

[6] Aeschylus, *Agamemnon*, 438–44: 'For Ares bartereth the bodies of men for gold; he holdeth
his balance in the contest of the spear; and back from Ilium to their loved ones he sendeth a
heavy dust passed through his burning, a dust bewept with plenteous tears, in place of men
freighting urns well bestowed with ashes' (trans. H. Weir Smyth and H. Lloyd-Jones). This is
from the second chorus: by 'chorus' AEH seems to mean specifically a stasimon.

[7] Oscar Wilde (1854–1900), at this time living in London and working as a secretary to the
actress Lillie Langtry (1853–1929). Writing on her behalf at the end of April, Wilde declined an
invitation to dinner from Violet Fane: *The Complete Letters of Oscar Wilde*, ed. Merlin Holland and
Rupert Hart-Davis (2000), 91–2.

[8] *Time: A Monthly Miscellany of Interesting & Amusing Literature*, edited at the time by Edmund
Hodgson Yates (1831–94). The issue for Mar. 1880 contained 'Songsters of the Day. No. 1 The
modern Sappho', signed 'Triolet Vane'. In the Apr. 1880 issue, the second Songster produced
'one of the first caricatures of "aesthetic Wilde"' (*The Complete Letters of Oscar Wilde*, 137 n. 3): a
parody of 'Oscuro Mild' as 'The Bard of Beauty'.

[9] Violet Fane—the name comes from Disraeli's first novel *Vivian Grey*, 1826–7—was the
pen-name of Mary Montgomerie Lamb (1843–1905). Her *Collected Verses* appeared in 1880, and
Time had begun the serialization of her novel *Her Sophy* in its issue of Apr. 1880.

[10] AEH's brother. See List of Recipients.

[11] Benjamin Disraeli (1804–81) was created Earl of Beaconsfield in 1876. He adopted pious
High Anglican practices in his 'Young England' novels of the 1840s.

on his turning to the bosom of our fold: there is more joy in heaven over one sinner that repenteth than over ninety & nine that don't.[12] Your ever sincerely

A. E. H.

Private MS.

TO LUCY HOUSMAN

Monday [10 May 1880] | Oxford

My dear Mamma

You have seen by now that the strife is o'er, the battle done, the triumph &c.[1] Last week of course has been a scene of great excitement: the campaign opened by the Vice-Chancellor announcing that any undergrad who should take part in any political meeting would be fined £5, which was gall & wormwood to a pretty large number of Liberals especially, who had been promising themselves the honour & glory of standing by Sir William Harcourt on the platform & spreading the wings of the University over him: Conservative undergraduates were less hard hit, as they none of them can speak decently. Hall himself however is an undergraduate, the senior undergraduate of Exeter;[2] whether they have fined him £5 I can't say. We had great fun with Mʳ Ewing who is one of the pro-Proctors[3] this year; we told him we knew of an undergraduate who had spoken at every Conservative meeting during the election, which wrought him up to wild excitement till we mentioned the name Alexander William Hall,[4] after which his ardour seemed to cool. All the nights there have been crowds of both parties promenading the streets & singing on the one hand *Rule Britannia* & on the other the following new & lovely lyric, composed I believe at the general election:—

"Hurrah! Hurrah!
Two Liberals there shall be!

---

[12] Luke 15: 7: 'joy shall be in heaven over one sinner that repenteth, more than over ninety and nine just persons, which need no repentance'.

[1] Francis Pott's hymn *Alleluia! Alleluia! Alleluia!*, 2–3: 'The strife is o'er, the battle done; | Now is the Victor's triumph won'. Pott is indebted to the Latin hymn *Finita jam sunt praelia*, which is of uncertain date and authorship.

[2] Exeter College, Oxford.

[3] Members of the university faculty assisting the two university proctors in executing their duties, which included keeping order, disciplining students, and punishing minor offences.

[4] In Mar.–Apr. 1880 the Liberals had won the General Election. Sir William Harcourt had held Oxford, and on his appointment as Home Secretary had submitted himself for re-election, only to be defeated by the Conservative candidate A. W. Hall.

Hurrah! Hurrah!
For Harcourt & Chit*ee!*"[5]

On Friday they were chairing Harcourt from the station to a mass-meeting at the Martyr's[6] Memorial, just outside college;[7] we kept shouting out of the front windows Hurrah for Hall, at which the crowd looked up & made the scathing rejoinder—"Yah! yer ain't got no votes!" which I daresay however was just as true for them as for us. On Saturday (election day) both the candidates were driving about all over the town: Hall had got his infant sons in an open carriage with him, by way of appealing to the feelings. About midday there came out a flaming poster in the Liberal colour (red) announcing that "Frank Hedges had been detected endeavouring to record his vote twice, & was now in custody." This I believe was true: but their[8] instantly came out a blue placard that "Frank Hedges had *not* recorded his vote twice & was now pursuing his ordinary avocations[,]" which was also true, as Frank Hedges, whoever he may be, had of course only *tried* to record his vote twice, & had since been bailed off. At about a quarter to seven the poll was declared with a Conservative majority of 54, & immediately afterwards the numerous spectators crowded round the front of the Roebuck,[9] Hall's headquarters, observed an exciting scene. This was Mr Hall at the centre window endeavouring to burst on to the balcony, & restrained by arm after arm thrown round his chest by his committee-men who dare not let him speak a word in that state of excitement. At intervals you saw him saying "I *will* speak to them!" & breaking from his keepers halfway out of the window, & then he would be overwhelmed again & disappear. Finally one of his committee came out instead: this gentleman's eloquence was confined to taking off his hat & whirling it round his head, & directing frightful grimaces of scorn & derision at the Randolph[10] where Sir William Harcourt was. That evening we we[re] forbidden to leave college after seven; but a good many got over that by leaving before seven: & we were also forbidden to look out of the windows or in any way attract the attention of the mob; however we blew horns out of the windows in great profusion, & on one of the dons coming

---

[5] Joseph William Chitty (1828–99). Fellow of New College, Oxford, 1852; called to the Bar, 1856; MP for Oxford, 1880; appointed justice of High Court, Chancery division, and knighted, 1881; Lord Justice of the Court of Appeal, 1897.

[6] For 'Martyrs".

[7] The monument erected in 1841 in St Giles outside St John's College to commemorate the martyrdom of Protestant prelates Hugh Latimer, Nicholas Ridley, and Thomas Cranmer, who were burned at the stake in 1555 and 1556.

[8] For 'there'.   [9] Public house in Market Street.   [10] Hotel.

round to demand the offending instrument he was presented with an aged & decrepit horn which had no inside & would not blow: so that in the morning he restored it with an apology, saying that he thought <th[?at]> he must have made a mistake, as he could not make it give out any sound at all. We heard Sir William Harcourt booming away from the Randolph opposite, & he drove off for the first train with a bodyguard of <ei[?ght]> six policemen but we could not make out what he said; he said however that he bore no ill-feeling &c &c, so I suppose there will not be a petition, though of course this morning everyone is talking about bribery, just as I believe they did after the last election. The Searanckes are in Oxford, they arrived in the thick of it on Saturday afternoon & were conveyed to the Randolph in a scarlet-streamered omnibus intended for voters: Mr Searancke contrived to make his way into Harcourt's committee room while he was making his speech at the window: he says he looked utterly upset & taken aback & was even on the verge of tears (taken aback by the poll, I mean, not by Mr Searancke's entrance). I am going to dine with them to-morrow: they stay here probably till Thursday. At the Randolph they have fallen in with a Mr Moss, member for Winchester,[11] who turns out to be an old friend of Mr Searancke's, & who says that the Provost of Eton[12] told him that Princess Christian[13] told him that "Mr Gladstone had forgotten that mamma was a lady, & had forgotten that she was his queen." They were in Italy about seven weeks & came home earlier than they intended for the elections. Have they made Mr Vernon[14] a baronet yet as the wages of sin?[15] I see by the papers you sent you have been having a fine exiting[16] fire, & Stillman[17] tells me Edith Sanders[18] is engaged to be married: so? As I don't see a letter-weight anywhere in sight & am not

---

[11] Richard Moss (1823–1905). Secretary (later Chairman) of the County Brewers' Society; MP for Winchester, 1850–85, 1888–92.

[12] The Revd Charles Old Goodford (1812–84). Headmaster of Eton, 1853–62; Provost, 1862–84.

[13] Princess Helena (1846–1923), daughter of Queen Victoria and wife of Prince Christian of Schleswig-Holstein.

[14] Harry Foley Vernon of Hanbury Hall, Droitwich (1834–1920). MP for East Worcestershire, 1861–8; created baronet, 1881, Maas, 22 n. 2, notes that he was a cousin of Lucy Housman.

[15] 'The wages of sin': Rom. 6: 23.   [16] For 'exciting'.

[17] William Beaufoy Stillman (1857–1903), formerly a contemporary of AEH's at school; at this time an undergraduate at Worcester College, Oxford; Rector of Downham Market, Norfolk, 1894 (Maas, 22 n. 1).

[18] Probably a member of a family with Bromsgrove connections. Several persons with the surname (but not Edith) are mentioned in Pugh (7, 148, 162, 168, 171; Appendix B, xxxviii), and in addition there is the son of the Revd Robert Sanders, Robert Coles Sanders (b. 1853), who left King Edward VI Grammar School, Bromsgrove, in 1868: *OBR*, 67.

clear about the weight of one of these sheets of paper, I shall employ two envelopes & put the Union Society to the expense of an extra penny. Give my love to my father & all & believe me ever

Your loving son
Alfred E. Housman.

UCL MS Add. 126. Envelope addressed 'Mrs E. Housman | Perry Hall | Bromsgrove'. Date as postmark. Memoir, *51–4 (incomplete); Maas, 19–22.*

1881

TO KATHARINE HOUSMAN

St. John's Coll. Oxford
April 4th [1881][1]

My dear Kate

"Sir", said the census-taker, "the first thing is to write your name in full."
I wrote down 'Albert Matilda Hopkins'[2] & waited for further instructions.
"We will now have" proceeded he, "your relation to the head of the
house".

"My relations with the President," replied I, "are, I regret to say, rather
strained. He makes me go to chapel every day now I am in college, & I
do not like it. No," I continued, taking out my handkerchief & howling, "I
can't abear it. I think I had better fill up that column with 'down-trodden
slave'." I did so.

"How old are you[?]" said he.

"303" responded I.

"You bear your great age well," he observed.

"I bear your great impudence well," I retorted. "What restrains me, I
wonder, from drawing my revolver from my breast-pocket & blowing out
your apology for a brain? What restrains me?"

He trembled & was silent: yet this was not a difficult question to answer.
What restrained me was the fact that there was no revolver in my
breast-pocket.

I then went on to tell him that I was married privately to the Queen,
but she didn't want it known just yet; so we agreed that I had better put
myself down as a widow, which I did.

"Where," said he, "were you born?"

"Where," said I, snatching up the poker, "will you die? in that corner or
in this? on, or under the table, or on the ground outside the window? Oh,
pray don't hurry," I continued, as he rushed in terror from the apartment,
"wouldn't you like to ask some more questions?—what my godfathers &

---

[1] The year of the census is pencilled on the MS by KES.
[2] The first of three sets of single quotation marks in a letter that otherwise favours double.

godmothers did then for me? or how, when, & where I like it? or why a miller wears a white hat? Pray don't go."

But he went: he told the porter that I was much more sublimer than a raging lion, & he hastily filled up the last column of my census-paper with the words "Imbecile, probably from birth".

I went down & corrected it into "Imbecile, probably from having been asked a string of impertinent questions". Finding that there was a good deal of room on the paper unoccupied, I filled it up by mentioning that my sister Kate was a woman of genius who had just written an affectionate & entertaining letter, & that though perhaps she spelt Napoleon with two a's instead of two o's & put a grave accent over the e, & deprived 'immensely' of an e and presented it to 'dancing',[3] yet still she was an ornament to her sex & I remained her affectionate brother

A. E. Housman.

Then I had to scratch this out & put Albert Matilda Hopkins instead.

Private MS. A copy in KES's hand, ending at 'impertinent questions' was inspected at Sotheby's, 14 Dec. 1998. Pugh, Appendix F, lxxiv–lxxv.

[3] AEH again makes fun of Kate's misspellings. See the letter to her of 19 June 1878.

1882

TO THE BURSAR, ST JOHN'S COLLEGE, OXFORD

15 Northumberland Place | Bayswater.
Dec. 4. 1882.

Dear Sir,

I beg to acknowledge with thanks the receipt of your cheque for £3. 19. 10, as balance of my scholarship.[1]

I am yours faithfully
A. E. Housman.

S JCO MS.

---

[1] The Open Scholarship he had been awarded by the College in the summer of 1877.

1885

TO LUCY HOUSMAN

82 Talbot Road | Bayswater W.
29 March '85

My dear Mamma

I was delighted to get your long letter <of> on the 26th: it was quite the best epistle I have ever seen, with the possible exception of the second of the apostle Paul to the Corinthians. The violets also were very sweet: I don't know whether St Paul used to enclose violets. Also please thank my father for his letter. Clemence and Laurence sent me a post card with a very lovely drawing on the back, representing Cherubim and Seraphim continually crying, and an inscription in Spanish or Portuguese, I think.

I saw the boat race yesterday, from the Thames boat house at Putney this time, so that I saw the start. It was a perfect day, beautiful sunshine but not too hot. There were many objects of interest on the river besides the crews: especially boats with brilliantly coloured sails displaying advertisements of various newspapers and theatres. There were much fewer people than usual, at least at Putney, and *very* little wearing of colours. Palm branches seemed to be the commonest decoration among the lower orders. The blue which they wore was a very artful shade, which could be made out to be either Oxford or Cambridge with equal plausibility, whichever might happen to win.[1]

Last Sunday morning there was a rather deep fall of snow here, but it soon melted. It is almost the only specimen of snow we have had all the winter.

The juvenile son of a friend of mine at the Office[2] has the loftiest ambition I ever heard tell of. When he goes to heaven, which he regards as a dead certainty, he wants to be *God*, and is keenly mortified to learn that it is not probable he will. However his aspirations are now turning into another channel: it has come to his knowledge, through the housemaid,

[1] Oxford won by two and a half lengths: Richard Burnell, *The Oxford and Cambridge Boat Race, 1829–1953* (1954), 154.
[2] Naiditch (1995), 19, conjectures that this was Henry Vize Maycock, son of John Maycock, AEH's colleague at HM Patent Office.

that the devil has horns and a tail; and in comparison with these decorations the glories of heaven have lost their attractiveness.

I will go and see Basil when he comes to town. I suppose he is going to stay with C. and L.[3] I should think his most convenient place to dine when at the College[4] would be the restaurant of the Inns of Court Hotel, just on the opposite side of Lincoln's Inn Fields. I daresay he will not be too much occupied to go to a theatre with me some evening.

An elaborate new Index of Trade Marks is being compiled at the Office. It goes on very remarkable principles which I do not quite understand. Under the head of "Biblical Subjects" is included a picture of an old monk drinking out of a tankard; and the Virgin Mary and St John the Baptist are put among "Mythical Figures".

I hope you and your household are well; and with love to my father and all I remain

Your loving son

A. E. Housman.

UCL MS Add. 126. Envelope addressed 'Mrs E. Housman | Perry Hall | Bromsgrove'. Memoir, 128–9 (incomplete); Maas, 23–4.

TO LUCY HOUSMAN

82 Talbot Road | Bayswater W.
10 June '85.

My dear Mamma,

You would never guess what I was doing on Tuesday week: serving on a Coroner's Jury. This comes of having one's name on the register of voters. Civil Servants I believe are exempt from serving on ordinary Juries, but not on Coroners'. Of course for once in a way it is rather amusing, and it is not likely to happen oftener than about once in four years. We sat on five bodies: one laundryman who tied a hundred-weight to his neck and tipped over into the water-butt; one butcher's man who cut his throat with a rusty knife and died a week after of erysipelas[1] (moral: use a clean knife on these occasions); one old lady who dropped down in a fit; one baby who died in convulsions; and one young woman who died of heart disease after eating spring onions for supper. I really do not know what is the good of a Jury or of witnesses either: the Coroner does it all: his mind seemingly is lighted by wisdom

---

[3] Clemence and Laurence Housman.
[4] The Royal College of Surgeons, on the S. side of Lincoln's Inn Fields.
[1] Inflammation of the skin caused by streptococcus.

from on high, so he tells the Jury what their verdict is and the witnesses what their evidence is: if they make mistakes he corrects them. The butcher's man had a brother-in-law: he looked radiantly happy: a member of his family had distinguished himself, and he was revelling in the reflected glory.

I think if there were an Inquest held on this Government of ours the verdict would have to be deliberate suicide: there does not seem to have been the least reason why they should have been beaten unless they wanted it.[2] I should say whether they go out or not the whole affair will do a lot of damage to the Conservatives,[3] because if they take office before the election they will have a fearful muddle to deal with, and if they do not, everyone will call them unpatriotic.

Who is the Mr Seymour who is your vicar elect?[4] I had not heard of the appointment.

There was a mild sort of scare at the Office the other day: a loud bang which collected quite a crowd. Civil Servants in these days of course live in hourly expectation of being blown up by dynamite for political reasons,[5] and the Patent Office has the further danger of the ingenious and vindictive inventor of explosives, who might try to lay the place in ruins if his patent did not go on smoothly. The room I sit in is considered the likeliest place, because it has a charming deep area outside which looks as if it was made to drop dynamite into; so when this explosion was heard, several people came trooping into the room in hopes of finding corpses weltering in their gore. However they had to go empty away: I believe the noise was really the firing of a charge of powder in a neighbouring chimney to bring the soot down.

I hope you have not been drowned in the last few days: the state of London you will have seen from the papers. Love to my father and the rest and believe me always

Your loving son
A. E. Housman.

UCL MS Add. 126. Envelope addressed 'Mrs E. Housman | Perry Hall | Bromsgrove'. Memoir, 130–1 (incomplete); Maas, 24–6.

[2] On 8 June 1885, Gladstone's Liberal government was forced to resign after defeat by 12 votes in the Budget division, 76 Liberals having failed to attend.

[3] The Conservatives under Lord Salisbury formed a caretaker government, but were defeated by the Liberals under Gladstone in the General Election of Nov.–Dec. 1885.

[4] 'The Revd Albert Eden Seymour became Vicar of Bromsgrove in 1885': Maas, 25 n.

[5] In 1884–5 advocates of Irish independence conducted what they called a 'Dynamite War' against the British. On Saturday, 24 Jan. 1885, there were two dynamite explosions in the House of Commons and one in the Tower of London. Property was damaged and a few police officers and civilians were injured.

TO MESSRS MACMILLAN AND CO

39 Northumberland Place | Bayswater W.
11 Dec. 1885.

Gentlemen,

I propose that you should, if you think fit, publish my recension of the text of Propertius, a specimen of which, consisting of the first book with its apparatus criticus, I send by the same post with this letter.[1] There are few authors for whose emendation and explanation so much remains to be done. The collation by Baehrens, in his edition of the text in 1880, of four important MSS previously overlooked has in a measure rendered obsolete all texts preceding or simultaneous with his own; while he himself was prevented, partly by haste and partly by a very natural bias of judgment, from making a really scientific use of his materials. No commentary possessing original value, with the exception of Mr Postgate's *Selections*,[2] has been published since Hertzberg's of 1845. Six years ago I formed the design of producing an edition and commentary which should meet the requirements of modern critical science, and have now completed the first of these two tasks:—the emended text accompanied by a register of such among the MS readings as are of import for constituting the words of the author or for classifying the MSS themselves.[3] The collection and arrangement of materials for the commentary will naturally demand further time and labour;[4] and I therefore judge it best that the text with its apparatus criticus should be issued separately, especially as I annually find not a

---

[1] Macmillan replied on 14 Dec. (BL Add. MS 55420, fo. 1458) that 'after due consideration' they could not offer to publish the book. Their reasons were that the sale would be very slow and the cost of publication might never be recouped, and they advised AEH to try the university presses of Oxford and Cambridge rather than a 'private publisher' like themselves. They were to reject *ASL* in 1895, allegedly on the advice of their reader John Morley, and, in 1924, AEH's edn. of Lucan. Charles Whibley (1859–1930) was one of Macmillan's chief readers. AEH did approach Oxford University Press: Naiditch (1988), 42.

[2] Published by Macmillan & Co, who issued a 2nd edn. in 1885: Naiditch (1995), 162.

[3] Gow, 12, comments that 'Propertius had been Housman's first love, and probably some of the emendations ... were produced in the hours which he refused to the curriculum of Greats'. He also notes that a complete transcript of the text, with apparatus, in careful handwriting, was found among his papers after his death. The MS does not survive: see Naiditch (1988), 41 n. 10–16.

[4] It seems certain that AEH never undertook the full commentary (Gow, 12–13). But see the next note.

few of my corrections anticipated by German scholars in philological periodicals.

I am, Gentlemen,

Yours faithfully
A. E. Housman.[5]

Messrs Macmillan & Co.

Macmillan MS. Copies in TCC Add. MS c. 112 and in BL Add. MS 55258, fos. 54–5.
Letters to Macmillan, *ed. Simon Nowell-Smith (1967), 241–2; Maas, 26.*

---

[5] AEH published 'Emendationes Propertianae', *JP* 16 (1887), 1–35; 'The Manuscripts of Propertius [I]', *JP* 21 (1892), 101–60; 'The Manuscripts of Propertius [II]', *JP* 21 (1892), 161–97; 'The Manuscripts of Propertius [III]', *JP* 22 (1893), 84–128. Naiditch (1995), 149, gives correct dates for the first, second, and fourth of these publications, and this implies the correct date of the third. See *Classical Papers*, 29–54, 232–76, 277–313, 314–47. Naiditch (1988), 27 n., notes that AEH appears to have abandoned his plans to publish an edition after an acrimonious controversy with Postgate over the relation between the MSS of Propertius late in 1894 and through the first four months of 1895. He outlines the controversy (80–3).

1887

TO KATHARINE HOUSMAN

Byron Cottage, North Road | Highgate N.
26 Feb. '87.

My dear Kate

I rather expected this. Well, as I do not agree with the stern parent in *Why They Eloped*[1] who said to his daughter "I do not wish you ever to marry", I am very glad to hear it and I should think you would have every prospect of being happy with Symons.[2] Being in love and engaged is the best thing that ever happens to any one in this world, and it makes them good as well as happy. The great thing is to make sure that one really is in love and not deceived by the pleasure one naturally feels at being paid the greatest compliment possible; but I have no doubt you are able to feel certain about your mind, so there is no advice to be given you, but only congratulation and good wishes. I suppose mamma is very happy, as she seemed to be in a wonderfully matrimonial frame of mind at Christmas. I remain your affectionate brother

A. E. Housman

Private MS. Pugh, Appendix F, lxxvi.

TO R. Y. TYRRELL

The phrase[1] plainly is one which a comic writer would hardly himself invent; and, if Aristophanes did employ it, the surmise would be natural that Aeschylus in the *Persae* had actually called Xerxes πόρις Δαρείου as a variation on πῶλος. I think perhaps he had.

The epode Pers. 677 *sqq.* Is handed down in this nonsensical form:—

ὦ πολύκλαυτε φίλοισι θανών,
τί τάδε δυνάτα δυνάτα

[1] A composition by their younger brother George Herbert Housman (1868–1901). There is a t.s. copy at BMC.
[2] Edward Symons: see List of Recipients.

[1] 'πόρι Δαρείου': Aristophanes, *Ranae*, 1028.

π ε ρ ì τ α̶ σ α̶ δίδυμα διαγόεν δι' ἁμάρτια
πάσᾳ γᾷ τᾷδε
ἐξέφθινται τρίσκαλμοι
νᾶες ἄναες ἄναες.

Blomfield suggested τί τάδε δυνατὰ δυνατὰ π α ι δ ì τ ῷ σ ῷ; perhaps Aeschylus wrote π ό ρ ε ι τ ῷ σ ῷ, which would explain the alteration τ α̶ σ α̶ by a scribe unfamiliar with πόρις masculine. The rest of the passage might possibly run thus: δίδυμα διὰ γοέδν' ἁμάρτια πάσᾳ γᾷ τᾷδε ἐξέφθινται τρίσκαλμοι νᾶες ἄναες, λαὸς ἄλαος, which would make sense of δίδυμα.

CR *1. 10 (Dec. 1887), 313. Tyrell (1844–1914), Fellow of Trinity College, Dublin, appended AEH's letter to his own paper. See Naiditch (1988), 216–20.*

TO W. ALDIS WRIGHT

Byron Cottage, North Road, | Highgate N.
28 December '87.

Dear Sir,

The authority of the best and oldest MSS both Greek and Latin is all in favour of the orthography Clytaemestra, Hypermestra &c., and most of the best Latin texts for some years past have spelt the names so.[1] In Greek the progress of reform is slower as usual, but Wecklein in his Aeschylus of 1885 always has Κλυταιμήστρα with the Medicean MS, and I believe there is a paper of his in the *Philologische Wochenschrift* for 1885 or 1886 stating the evidence on the point.

The detail however is a minute one, and if you think the spelling looks pedantic I shall have no vehement objection to the change.

I am

Yours very truly
A. E. Housman.

W. Aldis Wright Esq.

CUL Add. MS 4251/689. Maas, 397.

---

[1] Wright had questioned the spelling AEH used in his article 'The Agamemnon of Aeschylus', *JP* 16 (1888), 244–90 (*Classical Papers*, 55–90).

1889

TO A. W. POLLARD

Byron Cottage, North Road, | Highgate N.
28 Oct. '89.

My dear Pollard,

When I got your letter I was just off to Cambridge for the day,[1] and since then I do not seem to have had a minute to myself: last night I had just sat down to write when a man came in and walked me off to supper. I shall be very pleased to help your project[2] in any way, short of collaboration, that I can; but I do not think I should collabour nicely. I will begin with the selection of passages. In Jebb's article on Aristophanes in the *Encyclopedia Britannica*[3] he mentions what seem to be the prettiest bits, if I remember right, so I will leave that alone. In Euripides these are some of the best or most famous: Hipp. 525–564; Alc. 568–605; Hel. 1451–1511; Herc. fur. 637–700; Bacch. 370–431; Hec. 905–952: but none of his are at all equal to the best of the other two, and I suppose you will allot them more space than him. There are three of Sophocles' which seem to me very far his best: Oed. Col. 1211–1248;[4] Ant. 332–375, and 582–625; then Oed. Col. 668–719 has of course an immense reputation and could not be omitted; and then I suppose Oed. Tyr. 863–910, Ant. 781–800, Trach. 497–530 are some of the most generally admired. Out of Aeschylus it is hard to choose, they are all so good; but say Sept. 720–791; Agam. 104–257, 367–474, 681–781; Cho. 585–651; then in a different way Pers. 65–139 is very impressive. I don't know if you mean to include κομμοί &c., like Sept. 832–960, Agam. 1072–1177, Prom. 1040–fin.: these contain some of the very best poetry, but suffer more by detachment than the στάσιμα. The choruses I have been mentioning are mostly those that do not owe their merit mainly to their context, and so are suited for

---

[1] AEH was nominated by J. P. Postgate for membership of the Cambridge Philological Society on 24 Oct. 1889, and on that day 'read emendations of Ovid's Metamorphoses': *Proceedings of the Cambridge Philological Society*, 24 (1889), 8–9; Naiditch (1995), 73.

[2] An anthology of translations: *Odes from the Greek Dramatists. Translated into lyric metres by English poets and scholars*, ed. Alfred W. Pollard (1890).

[3] Richard Claverhouse Jebb (1841–1905) contributed the article to the 9th edn. (1875–9).

[4] AEH's translation of this chorus is in *Odes from the Greek Dramatists*, 84–7.

excerpting. But after all the original is not so much what matters as the translation: a good rendering of a second-rate chorus ought I should think to be preferred before an inadequate version of the best. I am afraid I don't know very many translations, but there is one which might escape your notice and which so far as I remember is good: Eur. Hec. 905–952 in a footnote in Coleridge's *Table-Talk*, done by his nephew Justice Coleridge (the *lawyer*,[5] not the present addle-head of the English Bench[6]). Have you seen Sir George Young's recent translation of Sophocles?[7] I only know it from reviews, and don't want to know any more as far as the dialogue is concerned: Sophocles doesn't run well into the style of Sheridan Knowles:[8] but there was a rather pretty version of εὐίππου ξένε.[9] I will look over Euripides, and if I see a chorus that looks translatable I will try to do it.[10] Jackson was at his old place, 26 Bloomfield St.,[11] but I believe he has now gone into the country for two or three weeks' stay.[12]

Allow me to wreathe with felicitations the cradle of your daughter.[13]

Yours sincerely
A. E. Housman.

Private MS.

---

[5] *Specimens of the Table Talk of the late Samuel Taylor Coleridge*, ed. H. N. Coleridge, (1835), 2. 208–10, under the initials J. T. C., for John Taylor Coleridge (1790–1876), Justice of the King's Bench, 1835–58. The translation was reprinted in *Odes*, 134–7.

[6] His son Sir John Duke Coleridge (1820–94), first Baron Coleridge, 1874, Chief Justice of the Queen's Bench, 1880–94.

[7] *The Dramas of Sophocles; Rendered in English Verse, Dramatic and Lyric*, by Sir George Young (1888), referred to in the Bibliography of Translations in *Odes*, 200.

[8] James Sheridan Knowles (1784–1862), verse dramatist.

[9] *Oedipus Coloneus*, 668–719. Joseph Anstice's translation is used in *Odes*, 78–83.

[10] AEH contributed a translation of *Alcestis*, 962–1005, to *Odes*, 108–11.

[11] More correctly, Blomfield Street, E.C. 2, in the City, and convenient for the Patent Office where Jackson worked. Moses' brother Adalbert had moved out in Dec. 1884.

[12] AEH's diary for 1889 records that three days previously, on the Friday evening, he 'Went to see him', but Jackson 'had just gone out to Camberwell'. On Saturday, 9 Nov., 'he started from Newport on a walking tour to Bletchley' and returned to London on 14 Nov.: LH, *A. E. Housman's "De Amicitia"*, annotated by John Carter, *Encounter*, 29. 4 (Oct. 1967), 38. Jackson had returned to England to marry the widow Rosa Chambers on 9 Dec. 1889, but seems not to have told AEH of this. AEH was not invited to the wedding. Jackson visited the Patent Office and had lunch with AEH and other colleagues on 22 Oct., and he visited AEH there a second time on 18 Nov. However, AEH records on 20 Nov. 'He meant to go home today'. And though the entry for 9 Dec. reads 'He was married', it is not until 7 Jan. 1890 that AEH records 'I heard he was married'.

[13] Joyce Kempthorne Pollard, the second of Pollard's three children, was born on 4 Oct. 1889.

1890

TO ELIZABETH WISE

Byron Cottage, North Rd, | Highgate N
30 July 1890.

My dear Mrs Wise,

Here I am (or, as our lively neighbour the Gaul would say, me voilà arrivé). I had a very good journey (bon voyage), as the weather improved and I found a through carriage to London (Londres) so that there was no need to change at Swindon (Swindres), after which the train stopped nowhere, not even at Reading (Lisant). My stay at Woodchester was "brief but delightful" like the lady in Byron who died young.[1] Please make my apologies to Sarah and Martha[2] for going away without saying goodbye: but I was told that Martha was upstairs, which from what I know of her character probably meant on the roof, whither I did not venture to follow her; while Sarah was said to be amongst her fowls,[3] where I sought her in vain. I enclose a cloak room ticket for Miss Becker and also a poem which I have written in her own beautiful language: please tell her this, because otherwise perhaps she may not know it: I assure her that it is the fact. Give my love to all, or at least to all to whom it may with propriety be given, and believe me

Yours affectionately
A. E. Housman.

Lilly MSS 1. 1. 3. [D. Randall,] A. E. Housman, An Exhibition, Lilly Library *(1961)*, *26; Maas, 27.*

---

[1] *Don Juan*, 4. 71. 5–6: 'Her days and pleasures were | Brief, but delightful'.

[2] Servants in the Wise household at Woodchester House. They are mentioned in an entry by Emily and Charles Ford in the first of the Wise family's Visitors' Books dated 11–19 Sept. 1889, and Martha is identified there as 'my own lady's maid'. AEH mentions them in his poem *The Rat*, and refers to Mrs Wise as 'Sarah's mistress': *Poems* (1997), 242–4.

[3] The Wise family kept poultry. See *At peep of day we rise from bed* and *Farewell, ye eighteen chicken: Poems* (1997), 270–1, 276.

TO THE REGISTRAR OF TRADE MARKS

Trade Marks Branch
9th October 1890.

Sir,

The Administrative Principal, Mr Webb,[1] has to-day taken up the comparison of Trade Mark applications. We beg most strongly to protest against his assumption of work in this Branch of the Office. We believe it is quite unusual that an officer should, without the most formal authorisation, take up a position in a Department other than that to which he belongs. In the present case such a course seems to us particularly objectionable because the position as Principal held by Mr Webb would give him a status not justified either by length of service or by acquaintance with the details of the work of this Branch. The present moment, moreover, seems peculiarly inopportune, since of late the amount of comparison work has not been sufficient to occupy the ordinary staff, one of whom has in consequence been filling up his time with other work. You are also aware that the question is now before the Comptroller whether one of the three present First Division men in the Trade Marks Department can be spared for transfer to another Office, and it therefore does not appear probable that the Department would be considered entitled to the services of a fourth.

We have the honour to be,
Sir,
Your obedient servants
F. W. H. Davies.
Francis Wm Hodges.
A. E. Housman.
H. C. A. Tarrant

To the Registrar.

CUL Add. MS 2594/15. In AEH's hand apart from the signatures of his colleagues.

---

[1] See List of Recipients.

TO A. W. POLLARD

Byron Cottage, North Rd. | Highgate N.
25 Oct. '90.

My dear Pollard,

I ought to have written earlier thanking you for the beautiful copy of the *Odes*,[1] and I hope I should have done so but for a beastly cold and Postgate demanding a paper for the Camb. Phil. Soc.[2] I believe you despise the get-up of David Stott's books in comparison with Kegan Paul's and others, but to my rash untutored taste it is very lovely. I think the prettiest thing in the book is Webb's translation from the *Alcestis*:[3] it does not quite give the feeling of the Greek, but it is a thing of beauty in itself: the metrical effect of the line "Still as the lute would play" is something quite uncommon. I should have thought this person ought to have been heard of on his own account in literature. When an insatiate public calls for a second edition, apply to me for corrigenda: this refers chiefly to the arrangement of verses in the English versions: e.g. when a woman does take the trouble to make strophe and antistrophe tally, like Miss Robinson in her ἔρως ἔρως, it is hard that the fact should be obscured by the printing.[4] I myself complain that in the second line of my *Alcestis* translation the printer has put "far-seeking" with a hyphen, which is quite contrary to my intention.[5] I had never before compared Swinburne's translation with the original: it is really wonderfully clever: indeed with the exception of the foolish "hell broad-burning" there is hardly a fault to be found.[6] The first of Browning's translations, which I had not seen before, is very impressive, though how

---

[1] No. 3 of 50 presentation copies of *Odes from the Greek Dramatists*, ed. Pollard (London: David Stott, 1890), printed on large paper and signed by the editor. AEH's copy is now at BMC.

[2] AEH joined the Cambridge Philological Society in 1889 and occasionally read papers to it. John Percival Postgate (1853–1926): see List of Recipients. He had a strong association with the Cambridge Philological Society, as Secretary, 1879–93, Vice-president, 1899 and 1905, President, 1894–5, and a member of the Council, 1896, 1901–4, 1908. On 30 Oct. 1890, AEH 'read … emendations of Euripides fragments': *Proceedings of the Cambridge Philological Society*, 25 (1890), 10.

[3] *Odes*, 107–9, *Alcestis*, 567–605, by Thomas Ebenezer Webb (1821–1903), Professor of Moral Philosophy and subsequently Professor of Laws at Trinity College, Dublin. It first appeared in the college magazine *Kottabos* in 1873.

[4] *Odes*, 103–5, the translation of Euripides, *Hippolytus*, 525–64, by A. Mary F. Robinson (Mme Darmesteter, Mme Duclaux), 1857–1944. Indentation of lines in the two sets of strophes and antistrophes is irregular. Her translation of *Hippolytus* was originally published in London in 1881.

[5] See the letters to Bynner, 4 Jan. 1928, and Agard, 22 Mar. 1933. For further information, see *Poems* (1997), 482.

[6] *Odes*, 155–9, Swinburne's translation of Aristophanes, *Aves*, 685–722. The phrase 'wings of darkness, in hell broad-burning' is in l. 14 (*Aves*, 698).

about the grammar of "whence … were wont to prance from"?[7] Miss Swanwick, I observe with horror, makes "stem" rhyme with "men".[8] Frere's translation from the *Alcestis* is very charming although a good deal of it is out of his own head.[9] Campbell apparently does me the honour to admire everything I write, and I will so far reciprocate as to say that the Aeschylus translations you give seem to me much better than what I have seen of his Sophocles, though I wish that both he and Morshead would not add so many beauties of their own to those of their author.[10] The second of Milman's pieces from the *Bacchae* is very good; I don't think I had read it before: isn't "rarest" at the end of the repetition of the refrain a misprint for "dearest"?[11] Oscar Wilde's piece is not at all bad.[12] I don't think I admire your fluent friend Anstice as much as you do.[13] I wonder whether our translations will seem as bad to the 20th century as those of the 18th century seem to us. ἀλλ' εὐφημεῖν χρή.[14]

I don't know why you should want to burn your Sallust. I remember thinking, if you will not disdain the suggestion, that perhaps "covetous of his neighbour's substance, spendthrift of his own" would better represent "alieni appetens" &c than your very condensed version.[15]

---

[7] *Odes*, 117–21, Robert Browning's translation of Euripides, *Hercules Furens*, 388–441. The awkward construction (117) is in fact 'Whence, having filled their hands with pine-tree plunder, | Horse-like was wont to prance from, and subdue | The land of Thessaly' (*Hercules Furens*, 372–4). The translation was first published in 1875 and reprinted in the *Poetical Works* (1888). Browning never changed the construction.

[8] *Odes*, 17: Anna Swanwick's translation of Aeschylus, *Persae*, 81–2.

[9] *Odes*, 105–7: *Alcestis*, 435–54, translated by John Hookham Frere.

[10] *Odes*, 9–13; 21; 43–51; 69–71; 95–7. Lewis Campbell (1830–1908) was Professor of Greek at St Andrews, 1863–1902. Campbell to Pollard, 14 Oct. 1890: 'M[r] Housman's rendering of [*Oedipus Coloneus*, 1211–48] strikes me as good, although the rhythms are obviously *Atlantaesque*, as I may say' (Private MS). Morshead is Edmund Doidge Anderson Morshead (1849–1912), schoolmaster, and translator of Aeschylus (1877, 1881, 1883) and Sophocles (1885). His translations appear in *Odes*, 35–43, 77–9, 91–3.

[11] *Odes*, 129–31. Henry Hart Milman (1791–1868), historian, and, from 1849, Dean of St Paul's, published his translation of Euripides in 1865. AEH is right about the misprint 'rarest' for 'dearest' on p. 131: the Greek is ὅ τι καλὸν φίλον ἀεί.

[12] *Odes*, 149–51: Wilde's translation of Aristophanes, *Nubes*, 275–90, 298–313. It had first appeared in the *Dublin University Magazine*, 86 (1875), 622, and was Wilde's first published verse, probably written during his first term at Oxford in 1874: see *The Complete Works of Oscar Wilde*, vol. 1, *Poems and Poems in Prose*, ed. Bobby Fong and Karl Beckson (2000), 3–4, 220, 330.

[13] Joseph Anstice's translations of Sophocles, *Oedipus Coloneus*, 668–719, and Euripides, *Iphigenia in Aulide*, 1036–97, appear in *Odes*, 79–83, 139–41. Anstice (1808–36) was Professor of Classical Literature at King's College, London, and author of *Selections from the Choric Poetry of the Greek Dramatic Writers, Translated into English Verse* (1832). Pollard included three of his translations.

[14] 'But one must keep a (religious) silence.' This was typically called for at the beginning of a prayer or ritual. See Aristophanes, *Peace*, 96; *Knights*, 1316; *Peace*, 1316; *Clouds*, 263.

[15] Pollard's translation of *The Catiline and Jugurtha of Sallust*, 2nd edn., revised (1891), *Catiline*, 5. 4: 'Covetous of his neighbour's substance, a spendthrift of his own, his desires knew no

My experience in textual criticism suggests to me that the apparition of
"Prestes the thief" in Swinburne's translation[16] is due to the resemblance
of O and P in your attractive handwriting.

Please remember me kindly to Mrs Pollard and believe me

Yours sincerely

A. E. Housman.

Private MS.

bounds.' No acknowledgement was made to AEH for the revised translation, which as originally
published in 1882 had been 'As covetous as prodigal, his desires knew no bounds'.

[16] *Odes*, 157.

1891

TO THE EDITOR OF *THE ACADEMY*

[17 North Road | Highgate N.]
7 March 1891

The fragment of the *Antiope* published by Prof. Mahaffy[1] in the last number of *Hermathena*[2] is emended in this month's *Classical Review* by two distinguished Grecians.[3] Their emendations are numerous and intrepid. Dr. Rutherford[4] "would restore" to Euripides the senarius σὺ μὲν χερῶν τὸ πνεῦμ' ἐκ πολεμίων λαβών which Euripides, I think, would restore to Dr. Rutherford. Prof. Campbell[5] proposes to enrich the tragic vocabulary by the importation of ἄχρι, in accordance with his opinion that it is not yet "time to cease from guessing and to begin the sober work of criticism."[6] When that time arrives it will occur to someone that l. 18 of fragment C, ὁλκοῖς γε ταυρείοισιν διαφερουμένη, is neither verse nor Greek, and should be amended ταυρείοισι διαφορουμένη: there is, of course, no such verb as διαφερῶ. It surprised me that the first editor did not correct this obvious blunder, and I looked to see it removed by the first critic who took the fragment in hand; but our scholars seem just now to be absorbed in

---

[1] John Pentland Mahaffy (1839–1919), first Professor of Ancient History at Trinity College, Dublin, 1869; Provost, 1914–19; knighted, 1918.

[2] 17 (Feb. 1891), 38–51. Mahaffy and A. H. Sayce had examined the Flinders Petrie papyri, and Mahaffy had recognized a fragment of a lost play by Euripides, the *Antiope*. For further information, see Naiditch (1988), 237.

[3] W. G. Rutherford and Lewis Campbell, 'Some Notes on the new *Antiope* Fragments', *CR* 5. 3 (Mar. 1891), 123–6.

[4] William Gunion Rutherford (1853–1907). Fellow and Tutor of University College, Oxford, 1883; Headmaster of Westminster School, 1883–1901. Publications include: *First Greek Grammar* (1878), *The New Phrynichus* (1881), an edn. of *Babrius* (1883), and edns. of Thucydides, Book IV (1889), the *Mimiambi* of Herodas (1892), and scholia to Aristophanes (3 vols., 1896–1905).

[5] See AEH to Pollard, 25 Oct. 1890, n. 10. Campbell's publications include: edns. of Plato's *Theætetus* (1861), and of Sophocles (2 vols., 1875–81); translations into English verse of Sophocles (1883) and Aeschylus (1890); completion of Jowett's edn. of Plato's *Republic* (3 vols., 1894). Campbell wrote strongly in favour of AEH's candidature for the Chair of Latin at UCL in 1892: Naiditch (1988), 17–18.

[6] Campbell in *CR* 5. 3 (Mar. 1891), 125: 'Professor Mahaffy's publication of this papyrus ... yields "delightful employment" ... to those who like the game of irresponsible guess-work. And when the guesses have been heaped together, and it is known where they jump, it will be time to cease from guessing and to begin the sober work of criticism.'

more exhilarating sport, so I will perform this menial office, at the risk of incurring Prof. Campbell's censure for premature sobriety.

A. E. Housman.

The Academy, *984 (14 March 1891), 259. Maas, 398.*

TO THE EDITOR OF *THE ACADEMY*

[17 North Road | Highgate N.]
22 March 1891

If Prof. Campbell will turn to v. 1100 of the *Aiax* of Sophocles, he will see what comes of assuming that any correction, however trivial, can be "too much a matter of course to be worth mentioning."[1] He will find that he and his brother-editors—Dindorf, Wunder, Schneidewin, Nauck, Jebb, Blaydes, Wecklein, Paley,[2] and, in short, the whole goodly fellowship—have printed in that verse the non-existent word λεῶν. They mean it for the gen. plur. of λεώς; but the gen. plur. of λεώς is λεών. And it looks as if another false accentuation were about to gain a foothold in our fragment of Euripides. The text is given in *Hermathena* without accents or breathings, but Frag. B has been twice invested with these perhaps superfluous ornaments—in the *Athenaeum* of January 31, and again by Prof. Campbell in the *Classical Review* for March; and in both places v. 4 begins with ἵκται. Now, ἵκται is the nom. plur. of ἵκτης, and makes no sense whatever: the word meant is ἵκται.[3] The reason why I do not descend so far as to correct the spelling of vv. 40 and 57 in Frag. C is that Nauck or Wecklein, whichever gets hold of the fragment first, can be trusted not to miss the chance of observing "ἄστεως scripsi" and "εὐνατήριον scripsi," and they derive more pleasure from these achievements than I do.

[1] Campbell's response to AEH's letter of 7 Mar.: *The Academy*, 39 (21 Mar. 1891), 283.

[2] W. Dindorf, various edns. (1825–67); E. Wunder, 2 vols. (1841); F. W. Schneidewin (1849–54); A. Nauck, revisions of Schneidewin (1867, 1886); R. C. Jebb, *Ajax* (1869), and works, 7 vols. (1884–96); F. H. M. Blaydes, many edns. (1859–1907); F. A. Paley, vol. 2 of one of Blaydes's edns. (1881), and his own edn. (1882); also a 2-vol. edn. by Blaydes and Paley in *Bibl. Classica* (1859–80); N. Wecklein, revision of Wunder's 1881 edn. (1875–90), and his own edn. (1884–1914). The German Nikolaus Wecklein (1843–1926) supported AEH's canditature for the Chair of Latin at UCL in 1892: Naiditch (1988), 25–6, 246–7. At this time he was Rector of the Maximilians-Gymnasium, Munich.

[3] Campbell concluded what he called 'this friendly correspondence' by stating that he was 'far from undervaluing' the minutiae to which AEH referred, but that he adhered to the principle that the emendation of classical texts was not an exact science: *The Academy*, 39 (4 Apr. 1891), 325. Naiditch (1988), 238, 239, points out that AEH had made no mention of the possible transformation of emendation into an exact science, but that he shared Campbell's view.

The further fragments of Prof. Campbell's *Antiope* (a drama which I much admire and hope to see completed), published in last week's *Academy*, have been slightly corrupted by the scribes, and I would venture to restore the poet's hand by the following emendations: for ποὖσθ' read ποῦ 'σθ', for στεγή read στέγη, for ἔνοντας read ἐνόντας and for ἰθαγένους read ἰθαγενοῦς.

A. E. Housman.

The Academy, *986 (28 Mar. 1891), 305. Maas, 398–9.*

TO ROBINSON ELLIS

Byron Cottage, North Road, | Highgate N.
30 October 1891.

Dear Mr Ellis,

I am glad to be able to make any sort of return for the information you have given me,[1] so I write to tell you that on examining the defloratio Brit. Mus. 18459 I find that your report of it is in error in one particular. It contains the verses 39 and 40 (quam mihi ... rupta tuis), and it does not contain the verses 35 and 36 (et noua ... ira pyra). This explains the absence of any statement in your app. crit. as to its reading *quem* or *quam* in 36.

Yours very truly
A. E. Housman.

It has *tibi sit* for *sit tibi* in 109, but this perhaps is not worth mentioning.

Bodleian MS Lat. misc. d. 43, fo. 86. Maas, 399.

---

[1] About MSS of the *Ibis* of Ovid. Naiditch (1988), 42–4, prints Ellis's letters. Ellis's edn. appeared in 1881, and AEH in his copy (TCC Adv. c. 20. 46) wrote many corrections and some scathing notes. AEH's edn. was published in Postgate's *Corpus Poetarum Latinorum* (1894).

1892

TO THE COUNCIL OF UNIVERSITY COLLEGE, LONDON.

H.M. PATENT OFFICE, LONDON,
19 *April*, 1892.

MY LORDS AND GENTLEMEN,

I have the honour to present myself as a candidate for the vacant Professorship of Latin in University College. If however the Latin Chair should be conferred on another I would ask to be considered as an applicant in that event for the Professorship of Greek.[1]

I am thirty-three years of age. I entered the University of Oxford as a scholar of St John's College in 1877; in 1879 I was placed in the first class in the Honour School of Classical Moderations; in 1881 I failed to obtain honours in the Final School of Litterae Humaniores. I have since passed the examinations required for the degree of B.A., and am of standing to take the degree of M.A. in the event of my appointment to a Professorship. In 1881 and 1882 I was for some time engaged in teaching the sixth form at Bromsgrove School, and in the latter year I obtained by open competition a Higher Division Clerkship in Her Majesty's Patent Office, which I now hold.

During the last ten years the study of the Classics has been the chief occupation of my leisure, and I have contributed to the learned journals many papers on ancient literature and critical science, of which the following are the more important.

Latin. In the Journal of Philology: *Horatiana*, vols. X., XVII., and XVIII.; *Emendationes Propertianae*, vol. XVI.; *On a Vatican Glossary*, vol. XX. In the Classical Review: *Notes on Latin Poets*, vols. III. and IV.; *Adversaria*

---

[1] The Chairs had been held jointly by Alfred Goodwin (1849–92), and the Council separated them at his death. AEH's application was supported by 17 testimonials, among them those from eminent classical scholars of the day such as Henry Nettleship, the Revd J. E. B. Mayor, R. Y. Tyrrell, Arthur Palmer, the Revd Lewis Campbell, T. H. Warren, Robinson Ellis, and the Revd J. B. Mayor, and, from overseas, B. L. Gildersleeve, and Dr Nikolaus Wecklein. AEH was informed in June of his appointment to the Chair of Latin: Naiditch (1988), 109. The Chair of Greek went to William Wyse (1860–1929), who resigned in 1894 to return to TCC. The election is treated comprehensively in Naiditch (1988).

Orthographica, vol. V. In the Transactions of the Cambridge Philological Society: *Emendations in Ovid's Metamorphoses,* vol. III.

Greek. In the Journal of Philology: *The Agamemnon of Aeschylus,* vol. XVI.; *Sophoclea,* vol. XX. In the American Journal of Philology: *On certain corruptions in the Persae of Aeschylus,* vol. IX. In the Classical Review: Σωφρόνη vol. II.; *Emendations in the Medea of Euripides,* vol. IV.

I have also published translations from the Attic tragedians into English verse in Mr A. W. Pollard's *Odes from the Greek Dramatists* (Stott, 1890).[2]

If I am honoured by your choice I shall give my best endeavours to the fulfilment of my duties and to the maintenance of accurate learning in University College.

I have the honour to be,
My Lords and Gentlemen,
Your obedient servant,
A. E. HOUSMAN.

Text as printed with Testimonials in Favour of Alfred Edward Housman *(Cambridge, 1892);* Memoir, *70 (brief excerpt);* Maas, *29–30.*

TO J. M. HORSBURGH

H. M. Patent Office | London W.C.
22 April 1892

Dear Sir,

I am sending to you this day by Parcel Post twenty printed copies of an application, with testimonials, for the vacant Professorship of Latin in University College, together with three sets of my principal writings, and a volume containing some translations of mine.

I am

Yours faithfully
A. E. Housman.

UCL MS: UCL Applications Classics 1892.

---

[2] The translations were of Aeschylus, *Septem Contra Thebas,* 848–60, Sophocles, *Oedipus Coloneus,* 1211–48, and Euripides, *Alcestis,* 962–1005, and were made specially for the volume.

TO THE EDITORS OF *THE PRIVATEER*[1]

[*c*.27 Oct. 1892]

The more closely the various elements of any institution are knit together, the better for the institution; and the scheme of a Union, which you have been good enough to bring to my notice, seems very well fitted to compass this end in University College. I should therefore be pleased to see it realised if it were found practicable. The only difficulty which occurs to me is this:—a man who now belongs only to one of the clubs or societies which it is proposed to unite, and who perhaps takes little or no interest in any other, may well object to pay the necessarily larger subscription to the Union for advantages which he does not want to enjoy and which therefore are not advantages to him. I hope, however, that the difficulty may not be found insuperable.

The Privateer: a Journal for the Students of University College and Hospital, *1. 5 (9 Nov. 1892), 2. Repr. in Naiditch (1995), 159.*

TO JOHN FENWICK

University College | London W. C.
27 Oct. 1892.

Dear Sir,

You would confer a favour on me if you could inform me of the whereabouts at the present time of two manuscripts of Ovid belonging to the library of Sir Thomas Phillipps[1] and numbered 1796 and 23620 respectively, which were employed by Mr Robinson Ellis in his edition of the *Ibis*. I have been told that they have now been sold.[2] Having chosen to edit the *Ibis* for a *Corpus Poetarum Latinorum* now in preparation at Cambridge, I am anxious to ascertain where these manuscripts at present are, and I hope you will accept this as my excuse for troubling you.

I am

Yours faithfully
A. E. Housman.

Bodleian MS Phillipps-Robinson e. 497, fos. 56–7.

[1] Written 'in response to a circular on the creation of a Union at UCL': Naiditch (1995), 159.

[1] Sir Thomas Phillipps (1792–1872), baronet, was an eminent collector of books and manuscripts. His collection, which John Fenwick had inherited, was kept at Thirlestaine House, Cheltenham. In 1885 the Fenwick family obtained judicial approval to disperse the collection, and many sales ensued, the last being in 1977.

[2] Robinson Ellis told AEH in a letter of 21 Mar. 1892 that he believed the best of the Phillipps MSS of the *Ibis* had been sold to Berlin, that many of the MSS had been sold, and that more would be: Naiditch (1988), 44, prints his letter, and provides further information. Whole groups of MSS in the Phillipps collection were sold, some to foreign governments. The Meerman collection, for instance, was bought by the German government.

1893

TO THE UNIVERSITY COLLEGE, LONDON, FELLOWSHIP COMMITTEE

[*c*.Nov./Dec. 1893]

I believe that if he[1] had been caught young and kept away from chemicals and electric batteries and such things, he might have been made into a classical scholar. Even now, in spite of his education, his knowledge of Liddell and Scott's Greek Lexicon has often filled me with admiring envy. He also, when his blood is up, employs the English language with a vigour and elegance which is much beyond the generality either of classical scholars or of men of science.[2]

UCL College Correspondence AM/D/15, fo. 8. No autograph MS found. Naiditch (1995), 141–2.

[1] Moses Jackson: see List of Recipients.
[2] Jackson was duly elected to a fellowship at UCL: Naiditch (1995), 142 n.

1894

TO THE EDITOR OF *THE STANDARD*

[17 North Road | Highgate N.
12 Mar. 1894]

Sir,—In August, 1886, Highgate Wood became the property of the Mayor and Commonalty and Citizens of the City of London. It was then in a very sad state. So thickly was it overgrown with brushwood, that if you stood in the centre you could not see the linen of the inhabitants of Archway-road hanging to dry in their back gardens. Nor could you see the advertisement of Juggins's stout and porter which surmounts the front of the public house at the south corner of the Wood. Therefore, the Mayor and Commonalty and Citizens cut down the intervening brushwood, and now when we stand in the centre we can divide our attention between Juggins's porter and our neighbours' washing. Scarlet flannel petticoats are much worn in Archway-road, and if anyone desires to feast his eyes on these very bright and picturesque objects, so seldom seen in the streets, let him repair to the centre of Highgate Wood.

Still we were not happy. The Wood is bounded on the north by the railway to Muswell-hill; and it was a common subject of complaint in Highgate that we could not see the railway from the Wood without going quite to the edge. At length, however, the Mayor and Commonalty and Citizens have begun to fell the trees on the north, so that people in the centre of the Wood will soon be able to look at the railway when they are tired of the porter and the petticoats. But there are a number of new red-brick houses on the east side of the Wood, and I regret to say that I observe no clearing of timber in that direction. Surely, Sir, a man who stands in the centre of the Wood, and knows that there are new red-brick houses to the east of him, will not be happy unless he sees them.

Sir, it is Spring: birds are pairing, and the County Council has begun to carve the mud-pie which it made last year at the bottom of Waterlow Park. I do not know how to address the Mayor and Commonalty; but the Citizens of the City of London all read *The Standard*, and surely they will respond to my appeal and will not continue to screen from my yearning gaze any one of those objects of interest which one naturally desires to see when one goes to the centre of a wood.

I am, Sir, your obedient servant.

A. E. H.

Highgate, March 12.

Text based on that in The Standard, *14 Mar. 1894. I have changed 'wood' in 'The wood is bounded' to 'Wood', in accordance with the other references to Highgate Wood.* Memoir, *73–4;* Maas, *30–1.*

TO WILLIAM SIDDONS YOUNG

University College, London | Gower Street, W. C.

19 April, 1894.

Dear Sir,

Allow me to thank you sincerely for your kindness in sending me your very graceful and entertaining *Halieutica.*[1] I wish I could flatter myself with the hope that I shall be as fortunate as Prof. Key[2] in having pupils capable of producing such verses, either forty-six years afterwards, or at any period of their lives.

I am, dear Sir,

Yours faithfully,
A. E. Housman.

Text from p. [iii] of a privately printed leaflet inserted in W. S. Young's Aridae Frondes *(Malvern, 1898): copy in Sparrow Collection, SJCO.*

---

[1] Latin verses in imitation of *Halieuticon* (on sea-fishing), or of *Halieutica* by Oppian of Cilicia. Paul Naiditch suggests to me that Siddons's verses may be an earlier version of his *Piscatus. Narratio vera* (in Latin verse), privately printed in 1900. Later, AEH cast doubt on Ovid's authorship of the *Halieuticon* on grounds that it contained false quantities: *CQ* 1 (1907), 275–8 (*Classical Papers*, 698–701).

[2] Thomas Hewitt Key (1799–1875), from 1832 joint headmaster of University College School, London, and sole headmaster and Professor of Comparative Grammar at UCL, 1842–75. He published *A Latin Grammar on the System of Crude Forms* (1845, etc.), but Latin and Greek verse composition were not taught at University College School.

TO LAURENCE HOUSMAN

I am sending the poems by parcel post.

Byron Cottage, North Road, Highgate
14 Dec. 1894.

My dear Laurence,

I have got your poems[1] into what seems to me a rough order of merit. *Love-bound Time* I think is the most original, and it is very well written and quite as lucid as one can expect; though I rather doubt if the English language will allow the stanza beginning 'Beauty may to beauty err' to mean anything in particular: however, it sounds nice. *Prisoner of Carisbrooke* ought certainly to be included, as it has more root in earth than most of its author's lays, and occupies the proud position of distinctly meaning something from beginning to end: also I think it good in itself, though 'well-watér' is rather neiges d'antan.[2] *The Three Kings* is very good verse, except the end of the 12th stanza and the 2nd line of the 13th; in the 14th too I don't like 'this tells', though I am afraid that cannot be altered without sacrificing 'Earth, Earth, Earth', on which you have probably set your young affections. Poems on pictures seem to me an illegitimate genre, but *Autumn Leaves* is a favourable specimen. Then I should include *The Fire-worshippers*, which has a deal of good diction, with a few alterations which I will come to presently, and *The Stolen Mermaid*, which has merit of the same sort and opens capitally, also with some alterations. *Loss and Gain* would be almost as good as any if it were at the same level throughout; but at the end of the third stanza I am stranded, and again in the fifth; might not the poem end where the stars are, after the fourth stanza? *The Tidal River* is pinned on to it and might keep it company, though Rossetti is very much to the fore in it: two other short pieces, *The Desire of Life* and *The Marred Face* are better I think. *A Dragon-fly* has some brilliancy of phrase and might well go in, but I should strike out the fourth stanza, where description lapses into catalogue; the third and fifth will be better together than apart. *Under the Rose* I admire to some extent, and others will admire it more, so put it in: the same may be said of *The Great Ride*. *Challengers* is perhaps better than either. *The Dead Face* I am not much smitten with, apart from the twang of Browning; but many might like it, and it would serve at any rate to vary the book. 'At the undarkening of days' might be made into something, but it would take a lot of making: at present it is

---

[1] The MS of LH's first volume of poems, *Green Arras*.

[2] Outmoded. Literally, 'snows of yesteryear', from the refrain of the ballade by François Villon (*c.*1461): 'Mais où sont les neiges d'antan?' ('But where are the snows of yesteryear?')

not only so obscure as to suggest that the poet does not quite know what
he would be at, but fearfully untidy into the bargain: for instance, one
cannot put an accent on the first syllable of 'interrogation'; and if 'hopen'
means 'holpen' it does not rhyme with 'open'. I doubt if *The Sleep of the Gods*
signifies much. *Blind Fortune* and *The King's Gifts* I should decidedly leave
out, and, for my own part, the remaining pieces: these shew[3] a certain
proficiency in a certain style, which shall wax old as doth a garment:[4]
still, I daresay some will admire them: your Scotch friend very likely, who
draws large cats.[5] I would die many deaths rather than use such words
as 'a-croon' and 'a-saw'; but that holy man St Jerome very truly observes
'nemo tam imperitus scriptor est qui lectorem non inveniat similem sui'
(the worst hand at writing in the world is sure to find some reader of his
own kidney).[6]

What makes many of your poems more obscure than they need be is that
you do not put yourself in the reader's place and consider how, and at
what stage, that man of sorrows[7] is to find out what it is all about. You
are behind the scenes and know all the data; but he knows only what you
tell him. It appears from the alternative titles *Heart's Bane* and *Little Death*
that in writing that precious croon you had in your head some meaning
of which you did not suffer a single drop to escape into what you wrote:
you treat us as Nebuchadnezzar did the Chaldaeans, and expect us to find
out the dream as well as the interpretation.[8] That is the worst instance;
but there are others where throughout the first half of a poem the hapless
reader is clawing the air for a clue and has not enough breath in his body
to admire anything you shew him. Take *The Stolen Mermaid*: I was some
time in discovering who was talking, whether it was the stolen mermaid
or the robbed merman. There matters might be made clearer by altering
the crabbed lines 'O, heart to captive be' etc. into something like 'This
land-bound heart of me Hears sound its mother-sea', only better expressed
I hope. In *The Great Ride*, to begin with, you had better add place as well as
date to the title, or the allusion may easily be missed. You start off "Where

[3] AEH used, or approved of, 'shew' and 'show' in the 1890s, but by 1904 he had abandoned 'shew' for show': Naiditch (1995), 91; Naiditch (2005), 110.
[4] Ps. 102: 26 (Coverdale's *Book of Common Prayer* version): 'they all shall wax old as doth a garment'.
[5] Louis Wain (1860–1939). He was born in London of N. Staffordshire stock, and he won fame through his affectionate and fanciful portraits of cats. Madness confined him to a mental hospital from around 1920. His paintings can be seen in the Guttman Maclay Collection in the Maudsley Hospital.
[6] The opening words of book 12 of Jerome's *Commentarium in Isaiam Prophetam Libri Duodeviginti*. AEH's 'nemo' should be 'nullus'.
[7] Isa. 53: 3.   [8] Daniel 2: 5–9.

the merciful waters *rolled*": the reader sees the past tense, and instead of thinking of the heavenly Jordan, as you want him to, he is off to Abana and Pharphar, rivers of Damascus,[9] and expects to hear you tell him about some historical crossing of a river where a lot of people were killed: all of which you would avoid by saying '*roll*'. Further: how soon do you imagine your victim will find out that you are talking about horses? Not till the thirteenth of these long lines, unless he is such a prodigy of intelligence and good will as I am: there you mention 'hoofs', and he has to read the thirteen lines over again. 'Flank' in line six is not enough: Swinburne's women have flanks.[10] And as line six is at present a foot too short I advise you to introduce hoofs into it; or tails?

Now I will go through some details. You will find here and there some marginal suggestions in pencil which may help to shew in what direction I think improvements might be made.

Love-bound Time. In the second line, should there be some stop after 'This'? a semi-colon or colon?

'Love's perfect *clime*': I first read this *chime*, which I think is better, because otherwise the dreams appear to 'rhyme' merely for rhyme's sake.

Prisoner of Carisbrooke. I don't much like the first line of the last stanza; especially 'track'.

The Fireworshippers is surely a very bad title and rather helps to confuse. 'Man, Truth, and Beauty' would be, not good I daresay, but better.

'Bowels': if terrific sublimity is what you are after, say 'guts';[11] which has the further advantage of being one syllable, and not two, like 'bowels', though I am aware that Aytoun rhymes the latter with 'howls'.[12] But nobody rent Prometheus' bowels that I know of, so I should say 'side', like an ordinary creature.

'*Speak the word* which spells' will suggest d-o-g, c-a-t etc. The first two <verses> lines of the fourth stanza I can't very well advise about, not knowing what they mean.

The Stolen Mermaid. 'To the bay's *caves*' is where the upward, not the downward tide would go.

'If, ah, but if' displays with almost cynical candour its mission to rhyme with 'cliff'. It might be 'hill' and 'if still, if still'.

---

[9] 2 Kgs. 5: 12.

[10] See, e.g., *Fragoletta*, 32: 'Thy strait soft flanks'; *Love and Sleep*, 12: 'The quivering flanks'.

[11] Cf. AEH, *Additional Poems* XVII 8: 'With flint in the bosom and guts in the head'.

[12] William Edmonstoune Aytoun (1818–65) rhymes 'howls' with 'powels' in *The Massacre of the Macpherson*, 46, 48. The poem was published in *Tait's Edinburgh Magazine*, 1844, and in *Bon Gaultier Ballads*, 1849.

A Tidal River. The last line seems to me weak, as being merely an epithetical addition to the noun 'star'. Perhaps 'And draws it home to his embrace'?

Under the Rose I call a bad title; because I suppose you don't mean it to signify *Clandestinely*, yet how can the reader think anything else? It strikes me too that, as you tell the tale, the hero gets his roses cheap, for we don't hear that he did give much mirth to earth: apparently he merely lay under the rose and chuckled, and earth said 'how that boy is enjoying himself!'

The Great Ride. "in *tragic* accord". I suspect Miss A. Mary F. Robinson began with *tragic*: then in the fulness of time she got to *insensate*:[13] be warned and pause.

What are 'gods of Mammon'? I thought Mammon was a god, since Spenser[14] and Milton:[15] in the other sense the newspapers have got it.

Challengers. 'Fire *for its use*' sounds poor.

The Sleep of the Gods.[16] Does one put one's head either to one's own heart or to another person's (for it is not clear which this god did) in order to hear the beat of feet?

The last stanza of this poem is one of your triumphs of obscurity. I have come to the conclusion, which may be wrong, that the two last lines are uttered by Deep to Deep,[17] and not sung by the gods, because the pronoun 'their' appears to require this interpretation; but if so, what black inhumanity on your part not to say 'whispered' or the like instead of 'trembled'.

Heart's Bane alias *Little Death* alias *White Rabbits*: if you print this, better *not* employ this last title, but keep your rabbits for an agreeable surprise in the last verse.

I daresay I have left out some things I meant to say, but here is the paper at an end.

> Your affectionate brother
> A. E. Housman.

BMC MS. Memoir, 156–60; Maas, 31–4 (both incomplete).

---

[13] A. Mary F. Robinson (1857–1944), 'The Conquest of Fairyland', 81: 'Cursed the insensate longing for life in the heart of a sick old man' (from *The New Arcadia*, 1884).

[14] *The Faerie Queene*, 2. 7. 3, 8, etc.   [15] *Paradise Lost*, 1. 678–9, etc.

[16] LH did not include the poem in *The Green Arras* (1896).

[17] Ps. 42: 7: 'Deep calleth unto deep at the noise of thy waterspouts: all thy waves and thy billows are gone over me.' LH did not include the poem in *The Green Arras* (1896).

1895

TO LAURENCE HOUSMAN

Byron Cottage, North Road, Highgate
31 March 1895.

My dear Laurence,

I think Le Gallienne[1] has picked out the four or five best. *The Blue Eyes of Margret* would be as good as any, if the words "while heart's memories met" conveyed any meaning, which to me they don't; and I think the poem would gain if they vanished. One does rather want to know *when* the b.e. of M. spake "Look" etc., whether in life or in fancy after death; and a clause beginning "while" seems as if it were going to tell us, but doesn't. If the first answer is the correct one, it might be given by "Once (or "Of old"), while gazes met", and in the last verse, "Then, when gazes met." *Lord Paramount* is superior in execution to anything I have seen of yours; though I think I said before that men were not created to write poems about pictures.[2] *The Keepsake*, with its beautiful moral lesson, is clever and striking; though your Muse is apt perhaps to preoccupy herself unduly with the phenomena of gestation. *The Queen's Bees* is about as good in another way; but on the last page the two lines about fashion and passion are evidently not meant literally: then how in the world are they meant? and their phraseology is precious cheap. I don't know if it wouldn't improve the poem to run on straight from "a poor man's way" to "Then would I give". Another point: do you really know what the Queen did to the poor man? If she bent him flat, as you said at first, that explains his resentment, though it sounds rather comic; but in the second version she gives him nothing to cry about. *The Cornkeeper* may go along with these. *The Christ Bride* and *To a Child Michael* are both successes I think, and so is *Failure* and *Holy Matrimony*. *The Stops of Love* is very melodious in parts. Here we begin to get towards the second class: *O Dearest Heart*; *The Dead Mistress*;

---

[1] Richard [Thomas] Le Gallienne (1866–1947). Poet and man of letters; original member of the Rhymers Club of young poets, founded by W. B. Yeats and Ernest Rhys, which flourished from early 1890 to 1894; reviewer for the *Star* and reader for Elkin Mathews and for LH's publisher, John Lane, in which capacities he encouraged many young writers.

[2] See the letter to LH of 14 Dec. 1894.

The Dead Comrade (not bad but rather affected in phrase); *Antaeus* (good in parts); *Spring Song* (pretty); *The House-builders* (rather overstrained perhaps); *The Gazing Faun* (a bit slipshod); *Love and Life* (begins well but tails off.) *A Song of the Road* (ditto)./ I don't care for any of the others I now see for the first time. I return the list you sent of Le Gallienne's rejections etc.: I have put a cipher to what I think should be left out and underlined what I think should be printed: where I have put no mark I have no definite opinion. As to *The Great Ride*, Le Gallienne truly says that it is in another key than the rest, but I don't know if that is altogether an objection: it may find its way to hearts from which *White Rabbits* run off like water from a duck's back. Its faults seem to me rather its length, and its theme, which I don't think really very well suited to poetry.

A few details.

The Keepsake. "she waits by the windowsill And whistles." Do you think so, Jim? The accomplishment is rare among women.

Holy Matrimony. "unfangled" could not mean what you want it to mean.

Spring Song. "A sense of want" is a trifle prosy: "a fluttering want" might do better. I would not alter the next line.

Fors Clavigera. "fortune" and "importune" is too cheap a rhyme to use even once, let alone three times.

The Bleeding Arras. This fails to impress, all the more because of the evident intention to impress. By the way, arras embarrass and harass are brazen effrontery.

Ursula. I don't like this myself, but I expect some would.

The House of Birth. This is less indecent than Rossetti and less comical than W. E. Henley, but that is all I can say for it.

The Two Debtors. I do not understand this, and perhaps that is why I think it perfectly odious.

King B's Daughter. Nor this; but that may be the fault of my ignorance in not knowing who this monarch was.

The Dedication is pretty, especially the end of the second verse. In some places it lumbers by reason of having heavy syllables where light ones ought to be: "Is each bird that *here* sings", "Where *dim* lights and *dark* shadows belong *Hangs* the arras of song". The beginning of the last verse I think is doggerel, especially the third line; and the third stanza is weak except at the end. But the chief objection is not merely the Swinburnian style of the whole[3] but the fact that Swinburne has twice used almost this

---

[3] AEH adopted the Swinburnian manner for his three translations of Greek tragic choruses in 1890, but changed his view. See *Poems* (1997), 165–8, 483.

same metre for a dedication. I should think you might break each stanza into two and add a fifth line rhyming with the fourth. The first half of what is now the last stanza might then disappear. By the way, the last line of the second stanza is a foot longer than the last lines of the rest.

I am going to Stockport for Easter. I see from the last number of the *Bromsgrove Messenger* that C. S. Boswell has published a translation of the *Vita Nuova;*[4] and they give a bit of verse-translation which is not bad, and much after Rossetti's fashion.

Your affectionate brother

A. E. Housman.

BMC MS. Memoir, *160–2; Maas, 34–5 (both incomplete).*

[4] Charles Stuart Boswell (b. 1861), son of Redditch solicitor Dr C. S. Boswell, was the author of *The Vita Nuova and its Author: being the Vita Nuova of Dante Alighieri, literally translated, with notes and an introduction* (1895). In 1908 he published *An Irish Precursor of Dante: A Study on the Vision of Heaven.* He joined the Grammar School of King Edward VI, Bromsgrove, in 1873 (*OBR*, 76), the same year as AEH's younger brother Robert Holden Housman (1860–1905).

1896

TO LAURENCE HOUSMAN

Byron Cottage, North Road | Highgate N.
20 March '96.

My dear Laurence,

Thanks for your letter. I told the publishers to send you a copy of the book,[1] and I should rather like to know if the one they sent you contained a "from the author": I ask because I also ordered one to be sent to Millington, who I hear had also ordered a copy himself, so that, if there is no indication, he won't know that I sent him the book.

Yes, the cover and title page are my own.[2] Blackett[3] was very amusing. He was particularly captivated with the military element; so much so that he wanted me at first to make the whole affair, with Herbert's[4] assistance, into a romance of enlistment:[5] I had to tell him that this would probably take me another thirty-six years. Then the next thing was, he thought it would be well to have a design on the cover representing a yokel in a smock frock with a bunch of recruiting-sergeant's ribbons in his hat:[6] this too I would not.

Everything has its drawbacks, and the binding seems to me so extraordinarily beautiful that I cannot bear to lose sight of it by opening the book:

[1] *ASL*, probably published in late Feb. The print run was at least 500, of which at least 150 bound copies were exported for publication in New York by John Lane.

[2] It had pale blue paper boards with a white false-parchment back, and a cream paper label lettered vertically in red. The title-page was printed in red and black. The book was published at AEH's expense.

[3] Identified by Maas, 36 n., as Spencer Blackett, Manager of Kegan Paul, Trench, Trübner, & Co Ltd, AEH's publishers.

[4] George Herbert Housman (1868–1901), AEH's youngest brother. He enlisted in the King's Royal Rifles in 1889 and ambitiously pursued a military career, reaching only the rank of sergeant, however. He was killed in the Boer War on 30 Oct. 1901. *LP* XVII and *MP* XL relate to his death.

[5] Naiditch (1995), 93, points out that, at an earlier stage in the Trinity MS, *ASL* began with *The Recruit* (*ASL* III) rather than with *1887*.

[6] Cf. *ASL* XXXIV 11, where the sergeant 'gives me beer and breakfast and a ribbon for my cap'.

when I take it down with the intention of reading it, the cover detains me in a stupor of admiration till it is time to go to bed.

Love to Clemence.

Your affectionate brother
A. E. Housman.

BMC MS. Memoir, *83, and Maas, 36–7 (both incomplete. Wrongly dated April 1896 by Maas.)*

TO LAURENCE HOUSMAN

Byron Cottage, North Road | Highgate N.
27 April '96.

My dear Laurence,

Why am I being reviewed in semi-religious papers like the *New Age*[1] and the *British Weekly*?[2] and how does that sort of literature find its way to Marloes Road?[3] and where do you suppose did the *British Weekly* learn my antecedents?[4]

There is rather a good notice in last week's *Sketch*.[5]

I thought the *New Age* review very nice, except the first paragraph disparaging the other chaps.[6]

Kate writes to say that she likes the verse better than the sentiments. The sentiments, she then goes on to say, appear to be taken from the book of *Ecclesiastes*. To prefer my versification to the sentiments of the Holy Ghost is decidedly flattering, but strikes me as a trifle impious.

Love to Clemence.

Your affectionate brother
A. E. Housman.

BMC MS. Memoir, *163; Maas, 37 (both nearly complete).*

[1] The issue of 16 Apr. contained an unsigned review by Hubert Bland (1855–1914), journalist, co-founder of the Fabian Society, and friend of George Bernard Shaw. Repr. in *Critical Heritage*, 58–61. See AEH to Martin, 22 Mar. 1936.

[2] The issue of 23 Apr. contained a review by 'Claudius Clear' (William Robertson Nicoll, 1851–1923), originally a minister in the Free Church of Scotland, but from 1885 a London journalist and man of letters. Repr. in *Critical Heritage*, 62–4.

[3] LH and Clemence Housman lived at 61 Marloes Road, Kensington.

[4] '… Mr Housman was at one time engaged in the Civil Service, and is now a Professor in University College, London'.

[5] The issue of 22 Apr. contained a review by 'O. O.', repr. in *Critical Heritage*, 61–2. Naiditch (2005), 95, notes the practice at the time of reviewers using different pseudonyms, and identifies him as William Robertson Nicoll.

[6] Without naming names, the reviewer berated other contemporary poets for being derivative and undistinguished.

TESTIMONIAL FOR R. W. CHAMBERS

UNIVERSITY COLLEGE, LONDON, | GOWER STREET. W.C.

16 June 1896

Mr R. W. Chambers was a member of my Senior Latin Class in this College from 1892 to 1894, and was placed first in the examinations at the end of each Session. I have no hesitation in saying that he possesses a knowledge of Latin which is not only adequate to the post of Assistant Librarian in the Gray's Inn Library, but probably much in excess of any requirements which will be made of him in that capacity. He is in fact a student of unusual accuracy. His methodical industry always struck me greatly, and appears to me a very valuable qualification for such an office as that which he seeks; and I sincerely wish that he may be successful in his application.[1]

A. E. Housman,
Professor of Latin.

UCL MS, Chambers Papers 1. Maas, 37–8.

TO P. G. L. WEBB

UNIVERSITY COLLEGE, LONDON, | GOWER STREET. W.C.

17 June 1896

My dear Webb,

Many thanks for your letter. I think that the Patent Office, having produced W. Dickson Morgan[1] and me, has shown itself quite worthy of being part of the Board of Trade, where most of our English poets are to be found.[2]

Yes, I am a great admirer of Heine: his is about the only German I can read with comfort.[3]

---

[1] Chambers worked in various libraries, the Guildhall Library among them, between graduation from UCL in 1894 and his return there as Quain Student in 1899.

[1] More correctly, J. Dickson Morgan, author of *The Jubilee Spectres* (1887) and *On a Visit to Ireland* (1887).

[2] P. G. L. Webb was one such poet: see List of Recipients.

[3] AEH's copies of *Neue Gedichte von Heinrich Heine* (1876), *Heinrich Heine's Sämtliche Werke* (1885), and *Buch der Lieder von Heinrich Heine* (1889) are at SJCO. He acknowledged Heine's influence on his poetry—see letter to Pollet, 5 Feb. 1933—and twelve specific instances of influence are noted in the commentary in *Poems* (1997), 338, 339, 340, 355, 363, 369, 390, 402, 405, 440, 442, 445. (P. G. Naiditch's Index to the commentary, published in 1998, is useful here.) AEH began seriously to study German *c*.1890: Naiditch (1995), 67–9.

The reviews are good, or at any rate well-meaning; only I wish they would not call me a *singer*.[4] One fellow actually says *minstrel*![5]

Don't look forward to my next book of poems; because most likely I shall never write one. Like Ennius, I only compose poetry when I am out of sorts.[6] This year I have not made a line yet.[7]

Yours very truly
A. E. Housman.

None of my friends have been hanged *yet*: such is the supineness of the police.

Princeton MS (Robert H. Taylor Collection).

TO LAURENCE HOUSMAN

Byron Cottage, North Road | Highgate N.
26 Sept. '96

My dear Laurence,

I have *Green Arras* and thank you very much for it. Of the poems I think I have seen all but one or two before. Of the illustrations I like *The Queen's Bees* the best, with its distant view and its kidney bean sticks: the scarecrow is full of life and is perhaps the best of your wind-blown pillow-cases to date; and the figure in the foreground wins upon one when one realises that what one at first took for his nose is really and truly his chin. *The Corn-keeper* looks much better than it did in *Atalanta*. The central or principal figure in *The House-builders* strikes me as very good indeed, if his right arm were a trifle shorter; but if I were the employer of those bricklayers I should take care to pay them by the piece and not by the day.

I am much disappointed to find no illustration to *White Rabbits*. I have attempted to supply this deficiency, and I enclose the result. You will see that I have had some difficulty with the young lady's arm; and the gentleman is not quite as tall as I could have wished. The moon (together

---

[4] Hubert Bland in *New Age*, 4. 81 (16 Apr. 1896), 37: 'the dominant note of all Mr. Housman's work as it was of Heine's alone among modern singers'; 'O. O.' in *Sketch*, 12 (22 Apr. 1896), 574: 'the singer's admirable talent of brevity'. For these reviews, see *Critical Heritage*, 59–62.

[5] No review has been found that contains the term.

[6] Ennius, *Satires*, 64 : *numquam poetor nisi si podager* ('I never write poetry unless I have the gout'), noted by Christoph Schäublin, *HSJ* 14 (1988), 42–5. Cf. 'I have seldom written poetry unless I was rather out of health': *NNP*, 49; Ricks (1988), 370. See also letters: to Gosse, 19 Jan. 1911; to de Rue, 12 May 1928; to Brussel. 15 Oct. 1931; to Pollet, 5 Feb. 1933. For further information and discussion, see Naiditch (1995), 86–9, Naiditch (2005), 189.

[7] Inconsistently, in 1922 AEH appears to have told Cockerell that *LP* IX (*The chestnut casts his flambeaux*) was 'Begun *c*.1900 (really Feb., 1896)'. The *Nbk* has fragments, Oct.–Dec. 1895, and a first draft, Dec. 1895–24 Feb. 1900.

with the weather-vanes and everything else which I could not draw) is behind the spectator, which accounts for the vivid illumination of the principal figures. You may remark that the rabbits are not running: true; but they have been running, and they are just going to begin again.

The other enclosure is not one of my finished works: I should hardly call it more than a sketch. It depicts the meeting at the end of *The Keepsake*.

I think I would have put either *The Keepsake* or else *The Queen's Bees* nearer the beginning of the volume, as these are the two pieces I should expect to attract most attention; and *The Comforters* does not strike me as a very ingratiating poem to put so early. Otherwise I think the arrangement is good.

There are some misprints besides those given in the Errata:—

p. 4, l. 15 *from of.*

p. 42, l. 1 and 3 *doors, shore.*

p. 65, l. 4: remove " at end.

p. 87, last line: add " at end.

I suppose too that on p. 3, line 6, *would* ought to be *wouldst*.

I think you will probably be able to congratulate yourself on having brought out this autumn at the Bodley Head a much better book than Davidson,[1] if the whole of his *New Ballads* are at all like those he has been publishing in the magazines. Not that this is a very lofty compliment.

Your affectionate brother
A. E. Housman.

BMC MS. Memoir, *163–4; Maas, 38 (both incomplete).*

TO PROFESSOR E. S. BEESLY

Byron Cottage, North Road | Highgate N.
3 Oct. 1896

Dear Professor Beesly,

I am in your debt for so many numbers of the *Positivist Review* and other writings that the least I can do is to ask you to accept a copy, which I have told the publishers to send you, of some verses of mine.[1] I don't know whether you, like Frederic Harrison[2] take any interest in our modern improvements on Shakespeare and Milton; but as one of the reviewers has

---

[1] John Davidson (1857–1909), Scottish poet, novelist, and playwright. Author of *Fleet Street Eclogues* (1st series, 1893), *Ballads and Songs* (1894), *Fleet Street Eclogues* (2nd series, 1896), *New Ballads* (1897).

[1] *ASL.*

[2] 1831–1923. Positivist, and author of many works on literary and historical subjects. Fellow of Wadham College, Oxford, 1854–6, where he was influenced by his colleague Richard

discovered from my poems that I have a deep tenderness for my fellow men, I hope they may appeal to you as a Comtist.[3]
I remain

Yours very truly
A. E. Housman.

Princeton MS (Robert H. Taylor Collection).

TO LAURENCE HOUSMAN

Byron Cottage, North Road | Highgate N.
5 Oct. 1896.

My dear Laurence,

I have forwarded the letter to Bob[1] for Basil,[2] and am sending £7. 9. 0 to Lee & Russell. As to the contribution to mamma's rent, my own feeling is that it would be best to send it through them: the expenses can only be a trifle. But I postpone sending it till some agreement is come to.

I was in Bridgnorth[3] for several hours. In the churchyard there I remembered having heard our mother describe it and the steps up to it, which I had absolutely forgotten for more than 25 years.

I ascertained by looking down from Wenlock Edge that Hughley Church could not have much of a steeple. But as I had already composed the poem[4] and could not invent another name that sounded so nice, I could only deplore that the church at Hughley should follow the bad example of the Church at Brou, which persists in standing on a plain after Matthew Arnold has said that it stands among mountains.[5] I thought of putting a note to say that Hughley was only a name, but then I thought that would merely disturb the reader. I did not apprehend that the faithful would be making pilgrimages to these holy places.

Congreve (1818–99), who in 1855 founded the positivist community in London; called to the bar, 1858. See Naiditch (1988), 73–4, for additional information.

[3] Disciple of the positivist and humanist founder of sociology, Auguste Comte (1798–1857).

[1] Their brother Robert Holden Housman (1860–1905).

[2] Their brother Basil: see List of Recipients.   [3] Shropshire town.

[4] *ASL* LXI, beginning 'The vane on Hughley steeple | Veers bright, a far-known sign', written Aug.–Dec. 1894. The church of St John Baptist at Hughley has no steeple as such, but a timber-framed belfry with brick infilling and pyramid roof. See AEH to an unnamed correspondent, 11 Feb. 1929. LH states that AEH's explanation of the change was that 'the place he really meant had an ugly name, so he substituted "Hughley" ': *Recollections*, 48. Robin Shaw, *Housman's Places* (1995), 115, and Carol Efrati, *HSJ* 22 (1996), 41–4, suggest that AEH had the steeple of St John's, Bromsgrove, in mind.

[5] *The Church of Brou* (1853).

Morris dead![6] now Swinburne will have something to write about. He wrote 12 epicediums on P. B. Marston,[7] so Morris ought to be good for at least 144.

Reading your poems in print I was a good deal struck by *Gammer Garu*, which I don't remember noticing much in manuscript. The last stanza is really quite beautiful.

A new firm of publishers[8] has written to me proposing to publish "the successor" of *A. S. L.* But as they don't also offer to write it, I have had to put them off.

I really quite forget what Housman lives at Lune Bank, so I don't know to whose care to address this.

Your affectionate brother
A. E. Housman.

BMC MS. Memoir, *82 (excerpt) and 165 (incomplete); Maas, 39 (incomplete).*

REFERENCE FOR KATHARINE M. MORTON[1]

24 November 1896.

UNIVERSITY COLLEGE, LONDON, | GOWER STREET. W.C.

Miss K. Morton attended my Senior Latin Class in this College during two Sessions, and from my acquaintance with her work I am able to say that she is fully competent to give elementary instruction in Latin. This indeed is sufficiently shown by her position in the London B.A. examination.

A. E. Housman
Professor of Latin.

BMC MS.

TO LAURENCE HOUSMAN

17 North Road, Highgate N.
4 Dec. 1896.

My dear Laurence,

I have an engagement on the 12th, but not on any other evening after the present. I should be very pleased to come to your affair.

---

[6] William Morris (b. 1834), poet, painter, designer, printer, and socialist, died on 3 Oct. 1896.

[7] Swinburne's twelve poems in memory of the poet Philip Bourke Marston (1850–77) were published in *Astrophel and Other Poems* (1894).

[8] Not GR, but as identified by Naiditch (2005), 14, John Lane's Bodley Head.

[1] Fuller version of name from Naiditch (1988), 126.

There has been no notice in the *Bookman* yet.[1] I feel sure you are wrong in thinking that A.M.[2] stands for Mrs Meynell;[3] partly because of the style, which is neither sufficiently correct nor sufficiently pretentious, and partly because the sub-editor's name is A. Macdonnell.

I have been reading your latest work,[4]—probably by this time it is not your latest work, but I can't read as fast as you write. What I chiefly admire in your stories, here as on previous occasions, is the ingenuity of the plan: this particularly applies to *The King's Evil*, which I thought a good deal the best of this set. The pieces of poetry interspersed seem to me better in point of diction than any in *Green Arras*. The sentiments are a bit lurid. *Long through the night, Amid this grave-strewn,* and *You the dear trouble* struck me as the best; but there are a number of good verses in the others. Love to C.[5]

Your affectionate brother
A. E. Housman.

BMC MS. Memoir, 166; Maas, 40 (both incomplete).

TO LAURENCE HOUSMAN

[17 North Road | Highgate N.]
24 Dec. 1896

[My dear Laurence,]

I am extremely anxious that you should spend a happy Christmas; and as I have it in my power,—here goes. Last night at dinner I was sitting next to Rendall, Principal of University College Liverpool and Professor of Greek there,[1] a very nice fellow and a great student of Marcus Aurelius and modern poetry. He was interested to hear that you were my brother: he said that he had got *Green Arras*, and then he proceeded, 'I think it is the best volume by him that I have seen: the *Shropshire Lad* had a pretty cover.'

I remain

---

[1] Of *Green Arras. The Bookman*, 10. 57 (June 1896), 83, published a favourable review of *ASL* (repr. in *Critical Heritage*, 65–6) and a biographical sketch of AEH in the August issue.

[2] The initials at the end of the review, very likely those of sub-editor Annie Macdonnell.

[3] Alice Meynell (1847–1922), poet, essayist and reviewer.

[4] *All-Fellows* (1896), a book of imaginary legends.

[5] Their sister Clemence, who lived with Laurence.

[1] The Revd Gerald Henry Rendall (1851–1945), Professor of Greek at Liverpool, 1880–97, and Headmaster of Charterhouse, 1897–1911. Author of *Marcus Aurelius Antoninus to Himself* (1926).

Your affectionate brother (what a thing is fraternal
affection, that it will stand these tests!)

A. E. Housman.

P.S. After all, it was I who designed that pretty cover; and he did not say
that the cover of *Green Arras* was pretty. (*Nor is it.*)

P.P.S. I was just licking the envelope, when I thought of the following
venomed dart: I had far, far rather that people should attribute my verses
to you than yours to me.

Memoir, 76–7, which has 'Rendal' for 'Rendall'; Maas, 40–1.

1897

TO LAURENCE HOUSMAN

A clever story is Mr Housman's *Gods and their Makers* (Lane);[1] it also has considerable humour. The Responsible Reader, to whom the book is dedicated, was, the author tells us, "cajoled into laughter" by it.[2] So was the Irresponsible one; but his mirth was tempered by the uneasy consciousness that there was an allegory lurking in the background of this *jeu d'esprit*, the hang of which he did not altogether catch. P. M. G.[3] 17. 4. 1897, which Romeike sends to me and wants to know if this be I.

A. E. H.

1 May '97.

Pray, on p. 61, did you write 'Katchywallah's inner god', and Lane alter it to 'man'?

BMC MS.

TO LAURENCE HOUSMAN

[17 North Road | Highgate N.]

12 May 1897

My dear Laurence,

There is a notice of *Gods and their Makers* in last week's *Athenaeum*:[1] I don't know if it is depreciatory enough to suit your taste.

George Darley[2] was the writer of the excellent sham 17th century song *It is not beauty I demand* which Palgrave printed as genuine in the 2nd part of the *Golden Treasury*.[3] Because it was so good I read another thing of his,

---

[1] LH's mythological novel, published in 1897.

[2] The preface is addressed to Agnes A. F. Pariss as LH's 'Responsible First Reader', to whom he says: 'its power of still cajoling you to laughter is chiefly responsible for its leap into publicity'.

[3] The *Pall Mall Gazette* commented: 'In a so-called preface Mr. Housman speaks of the "power" which the story possesses of "cajoling to laughter". We do not see any reason why the story, though carefully and often cleverly written, should cause laughter, for it possesses a very elementary sense of wit or humour. This fact, however, need not prevent the reader from recognizing the literary merits of the volume.'

[1] *The Athenaeum*, 3628 (8 May 1897), 614.   [2] Irish poet and critic (1796–1846).

[3] Where it was attributed to 'Anon.'

a sort of fairy drama whose name I forget,[4] and was disappointed with it
and read no more. But the piece you quote about the sea[5] is capital. He
was also the chief praiser of Beddoes' first play,[6] and a great detester of
Byron's versification when it was all the vogue.

The sea is a subject by no means exhausted. I have somewhere a poem
which directs attention to one of its most striking characteristics, which
hardly any of the poets seem to have observed. They call it salt and blue
and deep and dark and so on; but they never make such profoundly true
reflexions as the following:

> O billows bounding far,
> How wet, how wet ye are!
>
> When first my gaze ye met
> I said 'Those waves are wet'.
>
> I said it, and am quite
> Convinced that I was right.
>
> Who said those waves are dry?
> I give that man the lie.
>
> Thy wetness, O thou sea,
> Is wonderful to me.
>
> It agitates my heart,
> To think how wet thou art.
>
> No object I have met
> Is more profoundly wet.
>
> Methinks 'twere vain to try,
> O sea, to wipe thee dry.

---

[4] *Sylvia, or the May Queen: A Lyric Drama* (1927).
[5] Almost certainly from *Nepenthe: A Poem in Two Cantos* (1835; repr., 1897), canto 1 (p. 12):
'Hurry me, Nymphs, O, hurry me | Far above the grovelling sea, | Which, with blind weakness
and bass roar | Casting his white age on the shore, | Wallows along that slimy floor; | With his
wide-spread webbèd hands | Seeking to climb the level sands, | But rejected still to rave | Alive in
his uncovered grave.' AEH quoted the passage with approval in his paper on Swinburne, dated
1909 or 1910 in Naiditch (1988), 149: see Ricks (1988), 291.
[6] *The Bride's Tragedy* (1822), by Thomas Lovell Beddoes (1803–49).

I therefore will refrain.
Farewell, thou humid main.[7]

Farewell, thou irreligious writer.

Your affectionate brother
A. E. Housman.

Memoir, *166–8; Maas, 41–2.*

TO LUCY HOUSMAN

25 June 1897.
UNIVERSITY COLLEGE, LONDON. | GOWER STREET. W.C.

My dear Mamma,

I suppose that whether you went to Marloes Road or not you will now be at Chichester.[1] I came back to town yesterday. The time I had at Bromsgrove was not bad, as either the morning or afternoon of every day was sunny. The Valley is decent enough, though the cooking is not up to much. I saw both the Millingtons and the Kidds.[2]

On the evening of the 22nd[3] I started at eight in the evening for Clent, and got to the top of Walton hill about 9. 20. The sky was fairly clear, and so was the air to the north, but hazy southwards; Malvern had been invisible all day. (On Saturday when the rain was about I saw as good a view from Walton Hill as I ever saw, the Sugar Loaf and Black Mountain and Radnor Forest quite plain). One or two private bonfires started before the time, but most of them waited for 10 o'clock. Five minutes or so after the hour I easily counted 67. Some of these were small affairs in the near neighbourhood, which soon died down; but at half-past there were fifty-two burning merely on the south and west, from the Lickey on the left to the Wrekin on the right. Northward I did not attempt to count, as it was hard to tell the beacons from the ordinary illuminations of the Black Country. Of the distant fires Malvern was much the largest: the pile was sixty feet high and could be seen with the naked eye by daylight: through a

---

[7] *Poems* (1997), 255–6.

[1] Her brother, the Revd Henry Housman, was a lecturer at Chichester College.

[2] Hugh Cameron Kidd, MB London, FRCS Eng, was a Bromsgrove surgeon, medical officer of health to the urban district councils, and medical officer to the workhouse. He had two sons: Gerald Patrick (b. 1890) and Leonard Cameron (b. 1893), who later attended the Grammar School of King Edward VI, Bromsgrove: *OBR*, 136, 150.

[3] The day of the official celebration of Queen Victoria's Diamond Jubilee.

telescope it looked like the Eiffel tower, as it was much higher than its width and held together with iron. But it had been so saturated with paraffin that it burnt out in an hour. The Clent fire was on the further hill, and not on the top but on the south-western face. By midnight the number of fires had very much decreased, and only four, besides the Clent one, were visible at two o'clock: two distant ones somewhere by the Brown Clee, and two nearer,—one Droitwich way, and one on Kinver Edge which burnt till daylight brilliantly. It was a fine night, and at midnight the sky in the north had enough light for me to see the time by my watch. At two I heard a cuckoo, and immediately afterward the larks began to go up and make a deafening noise, and some person at Kingswinford, possibly wishing to stop the row, sent up a sky-rocket. (There had been a number of rockets at Birmingham before 10). About this time the first tinge that you could call blue came in the sky, which had turned buff and green soon after one: at 3 the clouds were red. I stayed to see the sun get above the mists and clouds, which was just 4 o'clock, and then I went back to bed at 5. 15. There was a fair crowd round the Clent fire, but a policeman, who told me at 3 that he had been on duty ever since 6 a.m. the day before, said that it was not near so large as in 1887.[4]

Bromsgrove was still as gay as I came through yesterday to the station, and had kept its Jubilee flags and festoons to enhance the splendour of the fair-day. The chief thing was a triumphal arch at the Strand.

Love to Cousin Henry and the family. I remain

Your loving son
A. E. Housman.

UCL MS Add. 126. Envelope addressed 'Mrs E. Housman | ᶜ/ The Rev. H. Housman | Chichester' and redirected to 61 Marloes Road, Kensington. Memoir, 131–3 (incomplete); Maas, 42–3. AEH writes both 'Walton hill' and 'Walton Hill'.

TO LUCY HOUSMAN

17 North Road | Highgate N.
22 Sept. 1897.

My dear Mamma,

I came home yesterday after having been just a month away, at Paris, Rome and Naples. I stayed in Paris a week, then went to Rome (two nights in the train) and stayed there three or four days, then to Naples, in order that my ticket might not expire. At Naples I stayed about ten days, and

[4] The year of Queen Victoria's Golden Jubilee, commemorated in *ASL* I.

then came back by the same route, stopping four or five days at Rome and one at Paris.

I think I saw most things that are to be seen at Paris in the week, and I also went to Versailles. I should have liked also to see St Germains[1] and Fontainebleau, but that week was rainy and not very propitious for distant excursions. What most strikes one in Paris is the countless number of handsome streets, any five of which would <be> constitute a fine town in England: imagine a place as well built as Edinburgh or Bath and practically about as large as London. Notre Dame is hardly equal to Westminster Abbey, and none of the modern churches are anything like St Paul's, but the number of such buildings, interesting or beautiful, is much greater than in London; and London has nothing at all equivalent to the Louvre. The Bois de Boulogne is wilder and more picturesque than any of our parks, and the garden of the Tuileries is more sumptuously laid out. They make a deal more of their river than we do of ours: it is all edged with handsome quays and crossed with handsome bridges.

When I got into Italy the weather was very hot, and remained so all the while I was there. The Neapolitans themselves were amazed at it; for though the first week of September is one of their hottest times, the heat generally ends on the 8th. The Scirocco was blowing part of the time: this is a very damp and enervating wind, which makes fish go bad six hours after they are caught. I went to Pompeii, which is more extensive than I thought, and to Vesuvius. You drive most of the way up; then you ride about a mile where the lava has buried the road; then you go up a cable-railway on the side of the cone, and then it is about ten minutes[2] walk to the top. The lower part of the hill is covered with vineyards and the like, with many houses among them: then you come to coppices of chestnut; then to the lava, which is various shades of grey and brown and has just the shape which is taken by melted lead when you drop it into cold water. When you get to the cone the lava is mostly buried under ashes: at the top the ground is streaked with sulphur, and steam issues from cracks and mingles with the smoke from the crater and the clouds which hang on the hill (it is about the height of Ben Nevis), so that it wants a guide to tell you which is which. Here you begin to hear an angry sound such as water will sometimes make in pipes, as if the mountain were gargling, or were trying to talk but had stones in its mouth; which indeed it has. This is the lava boiling inside. The volcano was unusually quiet, so that I was able to go quite to the edge of the crater, which is often impossible.

---

[1] For 'St Germain'.   [2] For 'minutes".

This is a great pit, sending out so much smoke that you hardly catch a glimpse of the other brim; the sides are ashes, with smears of sulphur and of an orange-coloured stuff which I believe is arsenic; in the centre there starts up at intervals a tall narrow fountain of red-hot stones, which then fall rattling back again into the funnel with a noise like a wave going down the beach. It is much the highest hill in the neighbourhood, so you see all the country, vineyards and olive yards and woods of young trees, dotted with white or pink houses; into this green carpet the lava runs out on every side in long grey tongues, as if you had spilt an inkpot. There had been an overflow about a month before I was there: part was still red-hot, and visible from Naples as smoke by day and a spot of fire by night. I went to the place: the surface had mostly turned grey, but the red hot part could be seen through cracks, and the heat in some parts was like a furnace. The guides fasten coins to the ends of long sticks, plunge them into these cracks, and withdraw them with the hot lava adhering to them; I have brought one of these home for you, as I believe such things amuse women and children. The best view near Naples is from the monastery of Camaldoli, on a hill behind the town: here you get not only the view of the bay to the south, which you see from Naples itself, but also the view to the north west, the bay of Baia, which I think more beautiful. I went to most of the places along the coast, and to the two islands of Capri and Ischia. Autumn is not the time for flowers in Italy any more than in England, but in one wood I found cyclamen blooming almost as thick as wood anemones in April. The chief ornament of gardens at this season is the oleander, which grows about the size of a lilac and is covered with trusses of rose-coloured flowers like carnations. The plumbago also grows and blooms very well, and so does the purple convolvulus. The town of Naples has a fine museum and a good palace, but not much else. Here I have said nothing about Rome, which I liked much best of the three; but I have to go into town this morning, so I will stop here for the present. Many thanks for your letter. Love to Cousin Mary.[3]

Your loving son
A. E. Housman.

UCL MS Add. 126. Envelope addressed 'Mrs E. Housman | 287 London Road South | Lowestoft'. Memoir, 134–5 (incomplete); Maas, 43–5.

[3] Mary Theophania Housman (d. 1905).

TO LUCY HOUSMAN

[17 North Road | Highgate N.
Oct.–15 Nov. 1897]

[…] I shall be interested to see the Devotional Poems.[1] Perhaps I myself may write a Hymn book for use in the Salvation Army:—[2]

> There is Hallelujah Hannah
>   Walking backwards down the lane,
> And I hear the loud Hosanna
>   Of regenerated Jane;
> And Lieutenant Isabella
>   In the centre of them comes,
> Dealing blows with her umbrella
>   On the trumpets and the drums.

Or again:—

> "Hallelujah!" was the only observation
>   That escaped Lieutenant-Colonel Mary-Jane,
> When she tumbled off the platform in the station
>   And was cut in little pieces by the train;
> Mary-Jane, the train is through ye,
>   Hallelujah! Hallelujah!
> We will gather up the fragments that remain.[3]

It seems to come quite easy.

I hope that Providence and Mr Sanders[4] will get your house for you on the 15th. I am all right, though it has not been a very nice October.

[1] LH's *Spikenard*, published in Feb. 1898.

[2] So named in 1878, organized on semi-military lines, and well known for its open-air meetings and brass bands.

[3] John 6: 12 (the feeding of the five thousand): 'Gather up the fragments that remain'. The two poems are included in *Poems* (1997), 256.

[4] The Sanderses seem to have been family friends: KES tells Lucy Housman in a letter of 25 June 1884 that they always send kind messages when she writes (Pugh, Appendix B, xxxviii). 'Sanders' is mentioned as attending the Speech Day at the Grammar School of King Edward VI in 1860 (Pugh, 148), and Mrs Sanders had a wholesale ironmongery business in Bromsgrove's High Street (Pugh, 7).

I remain

Your loving son
A. E. Housman.

California State University at East Bay, Hayward, MS (Henry H. Hart Collection). Photocopy at Bromsgrove School. The text in Memoir, *133, though also incomplete, supplies the opening words before 'myself', which are not represented in the MS.* Maas, *45. On the date, see* Poems *(1997), 542.*

TO THE EDITOR OF *THE ATHENAEUM*

University College, London
[*c.*12 Dec. 1897][1]

I shall be grateful if you can find room for these remarks on the text of Bacchylides.[2] My colleague Prof. Platt[3] allows me to quote several of his corrections, some of which coincide with my own.

i. 15 (p. 197). Εὐρωπίδα. 32. νόσων 34. ἶσον 42. λάχε τόνδε χρόνον.

ii. 4. θρασύχειρ ἄρ'.

iii. 22. παρ' ἄριστον. 48. τόθ' ἁβροβάταν ἐπέταν. 62. ἀνέπεμψε. 63. ὅσοι θέμιν. 64. μέγ' εὐαίνηθ'. 90. μινύνθει or μινυνθεῖ.

v. 48. ἴετ' ἀφνεόκροτον. 122. πλεῦνας. 151. μίνυνθεν or μινύνθει. 160. τοῖ' ἔφα. 184. ἦλθεν Φερένικος ἐς εὐπύργους. 189. ἀποσαμένους. 191. τᾷδε or τάνδε. 193. ἂν ἂν ἀθάνατοι τιμῶσι, τούτῳ καὶ βροτῶν φήμαν ἔπεσθαι.

vi. 3. προχοαῖς ἀέθλων.

ix. 10. φοινικάσπιδες. 13. ἄσαν γεύοντα. 35. βοάν τ' ὤρινε λαῶν οἳ 39. Ἀσωπόν. 41 should end with a colon, 44 with a comma. 45. πολυζήλωτε (so also Prof. Platt). 46. ἐγγόνου or ἐκγόνου. 55. τίς δ' οὐ χαριτώνυμον. 56. ἅ Διὸς πλαθεῖσα λέχει.

x. 51. γλῶσσαν ἰθείας.

xi. 8. μετ' εὐπλοκάμου κούρας. 24. δέ κ' ἐπί. 77. καμόντ' (Platt). 102 and 103 are spoken by Proteus. 110. ταί (so also Platt). 114. ἄνδρεσσι πρὸς ἱπποτρόφον ποίαν. 119. πρὸ γουνοῖ (Platt) ἔσσαν ἔμεν.

xiii. 29. παύροις βροτῶν αἰεί (Platt). 70. βοάσω. 117. παραί (so also Platt). 166. ἀμερσιεπής.

xiv. 1. δαίμονος (Platt). 3. ἐσθλόν κ' ἀμαλδύνειν. 5. θαητὸν ἰδ' ὑψιφανῆ τεύχοι. 9. μία δ' ἐξ ἀλλᾶν, 10. πᾶν χρεῖος κυβερνᾷ σύν. xv. 13. ἠϊθέοις.

---

[1] Date as indicated in *The Athenaeum*, 3660 (18 Dec. 1897), 856.
[2] The conjectures were elaborated upon in 'Notes on Bacchylides', *CR* 12 (1898), 68–74: *Classical Papers*, 442–54.
[3] See List of Recipients.

xvii. 7. πελεμαίγιδος. 17. μέλεον. 31. πλαθεῖσα. 35. μιγεῖσα. 38. κάλλυσμα. 43. ἐσιδεῖν. 49. θοῦρον. 62. Retain θράσει σῶμα. 68. Μίνῳ. 87. κῆρ.[4] 88. κατουρον. 90 σόεν νιν. 91. ἄητα. 100. μέγαρόν τε θεῶν ἔμολε.[5] 102. Retain ἔδεισε. 109. σεμνάν τε (so also Platt). 110. ἴδε βοῶπιν (ditto). 112. αἰόλαν πορφύραν. 118. Retain θέλωσιν.

xviii. 27. See Ovid, 'Ibis,' 407, "ut Sinis et Sciron et cum Polypemone natus." 35. μοῦνον συννοπαόνων. 51. κρατός θ᾽ ὕπο. 53. στέρνοις ἀμφί xix. 5. τέ ἐ καί (Platt). 19. τότ᾽ Ἄργον.

A. E. HOUSMAN.

The Athenaeum, *3661 (25 Dec. 1897), 887.*

TO H. J. MORTON

17 North Road | Highgate N.
29 Dec. 1897.

My dear Morton,

I hope the enclosed will do: I am sorry to have kept you waiting, but I have been travelling from place to place, and in the arduous festivities of the season it is hard to find leisure.

Of course I shall be very pleased to serve as a reference. I shall hardly recognise the College without you: we entered it together, and may be said to have rocked one another's cradles. Believe me, with all good wishes,

Yours very truly
A. E. Housman.

I was glad to see your place in the B.A.

[Enclosure]

University College, London
29 December 1897.

Mr H. J. Morton has attended my Latin classes in this College for the last five years, and I am therefore able to speak with knowledge of his attainments. I can say that both the width and the accuracy of his acquaintance with Latin are such as to enable him to teach the language to others, and that to these qualifications he adds a degree of literary taste and feeling which I do not often find in students.[1] I am sure too that

---

[4] See the letter of *c.*10 Jan. 1898.
[5] See the letter of *c.*10 Jan. 1898.

[1] At UCL Morton won first prize in the Junior Class of Latin in 1894: the prize volume, Thomas Crutwell's *A History of Roman Literature*, is now at BMC. In 1928 AEH agreed to sign a copy of one of his own books for Morton's sister: Naiditch (1988), 125.

the great amiability of his character will be appreciated by his pupils and colleagues.

A. E. Housman,
Professor of Latin.

BMC MS.

1898

TO THE EDITOR OF *THE ATHENAEUM*

University College, London.
[*c*.10 Jan. 1898]

I should like to add the following corrections to my former list:—[1]

i. 4. ὅν οὐδέ. 5. θῦνος (or θυνὸς) ἁδροῖο. 6. ζαχρεῖον ἂν θολοῖ. 7. ἐλαφρός. 8. ἀπόκλαρος καλῶν, τόσα.

iii. 27. Περσᾶν ἐπορθεῦντο. 87. εὐφρόσυνος. 96. λακών.

v. 12. should end with a full stop. 13. κεῖνος θεράπων ἐθέλει γᾶρυν 110. εἰσάνταν (Platt). 142. ἑλκύσασα.

vii. 9. ἐν or παρ' or πεδ'.

ix. 3. τό. 4. Retain εὔτυκος.

xi. 68. ἤρεικον. 79. Join κάλλιστον with τεῖχος.

xiii. 25. τᾳ δή. 27. ἀνδεθεῖσιν. 61. τεὸν γάμον (or γόνον). 62. παγξείνου χθονός. 153. εὐνομία σαοσίφρων (or τελεόφρων). 189. φοινικοκραδέμνοιο Μούσας ὕμνων τινὰ τάνδ' ἕκαθεν νᾶσον μολών.

xix. 12. σέ. 15. γέρας, εἴ τιν'.

In my former letter delete κῆρ at xi. 87, and correct ἔμολε to μόλεν at xi.101.

A. E. HOUSMAN.

The Athenaeum, *3664 (15 Jan. 1898), 87*

---

[1] See the letter of *c*.12 Dec. 1897 to the editor of *The Athenaeum*.

TO ELIZABETH WISE

17 North Road | Highgate N.
11 Jan. 1898.

My dear Mrs Wise,

This ought to have been a letter for New Year's Day, but that ancient person the poet Bacchylides has been taking up so much of my time[1] that many of my duties have been neglected and many tradesmen are wishing I would pay their bills. Today the College term has begun, so I am comparatively at leisure, and have written out the ballad of *Lucinda* which I promised to send you:[2] if it will deter Edie and Minnie[3] from climbing ladders or using the moon for culinary purposes, it will not have been written in vain;[4] and I suppose that is what you want it for. At Bath the weather was not bad, and I went a number of nice walks in various directions: the country is really very like Gloucestershire. Since I came back here nothing has happened, so I remain, with love to all,

Yours affectionately
A. E. Housman.

BMC MS.

TO GRANT RICHARDS

17 North Road, Highgate N.
21 Feb. 1898.

My dear Sir,

My brother Laurence has sent me a proposal from you to take over the remaining copies of *A Shropshire Lad* and publish a second edition at your own risk.

I suppose no author is averse to see his works in a second edition, or slow to take advantage of an infatuated publisher; and it is impossible not to be touched by the engaging form which your infatuation takes. But there are two points to consider at the outset.

---

[1] See his letter to the *Athenaeum*, *c*.12 Dec. 1897 and the previous letter. AEH's copies of edns. of Bacchylides from 1897 and 1898 survive in SJCO. Naiditch (2002), 59, describes them as, respectively, 'annotated' and 'heavily annotated'.

[2] AEH had visited the Wise family from 20 to 23 Dec. 1897. For *Lucinda*, see *Poems* (1997), 259–61, 544–5.

[3] See the entry on Elizabeth Wise in List of Recipients.

[4] In the poem, Lucinda climbs a ladder to the moon in order to make water boil; but the ladder falls, leaving her adhering to the moon.

I should not like the second edition to differ from the first in form,[1] nor to be sold at a higher price.[2] But, so far as I can judge from the finances of the first edition, unless it were produced cheaper or sold dearer, the sale of an entire edition of 500 copies[3] would not pay for the printing and binding and advertising; and so, apart from the royalty, which I do not care about, you would be out of pocket.

Also I should have to ask Kegan Paul[4] if their feelings would be lacerated by the transfer. I do not think very much of them as men of business, but their manager[5] has been nice to me and takes a sentimental interest in the book, like you.

At the present moment I can think of nothing else to damp your ardour.

I am yours very truly

A. E. Housman.

Grant Richards Esq.

Lilly MSS 1. 1. 3. Maas, 46.

TO LUCY HOUSMAN

17 North Road | Highgate N.

21 March '98

My dear Mamma,

The end of the term is now in sight, and I am quite ready for it; twelve weeks on end is not nice. I hope to see a good many of the hedges green by the time the holidays begin, as the spring is early in these parts. As I can't be sure of your address from your last letter, I send this to Marloes Road.

I am glad to gather from your silence that you have got rid of the traces of influenza. I have not looked out Cousin Henry's[1] new place on the map, but I have a sort of notion that I have walked through Bradley Green some time or other. I am glad it seems likely to suit.

The only poem that I can find is this.

I knew a Cappadocian
Who fell into the Ocean:

---

[1] AEH paid for the first edn. and corrected the proofs. Its text is correct: see *Poems* (1997), Introduction, xxiv–xxv, xxxi, and AEH to GR, 24 July 1898.

[2] Than 2s. 6d.

[3] The print run of the first edn., which took roughly a year and three quarters to sell out: Richards, 16 n. See AEH to Mrs Fairchild, 11 Apr. 1901, and notes.

[4] Kegan Paul, Trench, Trübner, & Co. Ltd., were the publishers of the first edn.

[5] See AEH to LH, 20 Mar. 1896, n. 3.

[1] The Revd Henry Housman (1832–1912) had become Rector of Bradley, Worcs.

His mother came and took him out
With tokens of emotion.

She also had a daughter
Who fell into the Water:
At any rate she would have fallen
If someone hadn't caught her.

The second son went frantic
And fell in the Atlantic:
His parent reached the spot too late
To check her offspring's antic.

Her grief was then terrific:
She fell in the Pacific,
Exclaiming with her latest breath
"I have been too prolific."[2]

I remain

Your loving son
A. E. Housman.

BMC MS. Memoir, 135–6; Maas, 46–7 (both incomplete).

TO LUCY HOUSMAN

17 North Road | Highgate N.
26 April 1898.

My dear Mamma,

This is the first day of term; so, as the holidays are over, I sit down to write a letter. I have to thank you for two, one on my birthday and one later. You will see that yours was not the only one I received on my birthday: I believe you collect the epistles of this amiable madman, so I enclose this one for you. He must have discovered th<at>e date from a publication called *Who's Who*.

I did go into Hampshire for five days at Easter; but it was not the south but the north, near Whitchurch. Since I came back I have been having good walks about the country to see things coming out in the sunshine, and I feel very well. I suppose Cousin Henry is settled in his rectory by this

[2] *Poems* (1997), 262.

time. I see from looking through your letters that Eva[1] is to be married to-morrow; so give her my benediction.

Marriage, and the necessity of filling this sheet of paper, remind me of one of my occasional poems, which I may or may not have told you of before:

> When Adam day by day
>   Woke up in Paradise
> He always used to say
>   'Oh, this is very nice.'
>
> But Eve from scenes of bliss
>   Transported him for life.
> The more I think of this
>   The more I beat my wife.[2]

I remain

Your loving son
A. E. Housman.

UCL MS Add. 126. Memoir, *136–7 (incomplete); Maas, 47–8.*

TO GRANT RICHARDS

Grosvenor Arms Hotel | Shaftesbury
20 July 1898

Dear Sir,

I am much obliged to you for your letter; but I have thought it proper to write to Kegan Paul & Co. before taking any immediate step. When I hear from them I will write to you again.

Yours very truly
A. E. Housman.

Grant Richards, Esq.

Illinois MS. Richards, 21 (summary and excerpt); Maas, 48.

---

[1] 'Lucy Housman's niece': Maas, 47 n.   [2] *Poems* (1997), 257.

TO GRANT RICHARDS

Grosvenor Arms Hotel | Shaftesbury
22 July 1898.

Dear Sir,

As Kegan Paul & Co say that their feelings would not be lacerated, and as I suppose Mr Archer's article[1] may create some sort of demand, I shall be very willing that you should bring out a second edition of my poems. I only stipulate for simplicity of get-up and moderateness of price. Your former proposals I have not by me at the moment, but I think you offered to pay me a royalty, or, in case I did not care for it, to hand the amount to a charity. I should prefer that it should go to reduce the price at which the book is to be sold.

I shall not be in town till August 3rd. I expect to be here till Wednesday, and then at the King's Arms, Dorchester.

I am

Yours very truly
A. E. Housman.

Illinois MS. Richards, 21; Maas, 48.

TO GRANT RICHARDS

Grosvenor Arms | Shaftesbury
24 July 1898.

Dear Sir,

I think it best not to make any alterations, even the slightest, after one has once printed a thing. It was Shelley's plan, and is much wiser than Wordsworth's perpetual tinkering, as it makes the public fancy one is inspired. But after the book is set up I should like to have the sheets to correct, as I don't trust printers or proof-readers in matters of punctuation.

3/6 is perhaps the largest sum which can be called moderate, but I suppose it does deserve the name. I am

Yours very truly
A. E. Housman.

Illinois MS. Richards, 22–3 (almost complete); Maas, 49.

---

[1] A favourable notice of *ASL* by the influential critic William Archer (1856–1924) which would appear in the *Fortnightly Review*, 64 (1 Aug. 1898), 263–8: *Critical Heritage*, 75–80.

TO JOHN LANE

17 North Road | Highgate N.
6 August '98

My dear Sir,

I am sorry that you should feel any disappointment; but you misapprehend the state of affairs when you speak of my 'offering' the book to any one. I have not lifted a finger in the matter: I have only yielded, after a long siege, to the repeated proposals of Mr Richards, whom I regard as an infatuated young man. It never occurred to me that any one else in the wide world would want to produce a second edition of a book whose first edition, I believe, is not yet sold out: but apparently I overestimate the prudence of publishers. Certainly I myself am quite willing that you should continue to sell the book in America. As to another volume, I have no reason to suppose that I shall ever write one. I am grateful for your good offices with Mr Archer.

I am

Yours very truly
A. E. Housman.

Alfred University MS.

TO AN UNKNOWN CORRESPONDENT

(Copy)   27 Oct. 1898.

UNIVERSITY COLLEGE, LONDON. | GOWER STREET. W.C.

Dear Sir,

You will remember that at our interview on Tuesday your attention was drawn to the fact that it was the wish of the Council that the school curriculum should in future give greater prominence than hitherto to the subjects now generally known as *modern*.

Bearing in mind that the majority of the boys go into commercial life, the Council desire, so far as is possible without lowering the standard of education aimed at, to make the work of these boys preparatory to the object they have in view.

I regret that my notes of your answers to the questions bearing on this point are not sufficient for the purpose of preparing a report such as the Council probably expect, and I should therefore be glad if you would inform me whether you consider it possible or advisable to differentiate the work of the boys in the school so as to make curricula suitable

(a) for those preparing to enter upon commercial life;

(b) for those preparing to enter a technical profession, such as that of an engineer or consulting chemist.

If so, could you, without entering into much detail, give me some idea of the way in which you would go to work; and would you also inform me whether you would be in sympathy with the objects at which the Council are aiming?

The next meeting of our Committee is on Tuesday next, Nov. 1st, and I should be glad to have your answer by the morning of that day.

I am

Yours faithfully
A. E. Housman.

UCL MS: College Correspondence AM/D/92.

TO R. ELLIS ROBERTS

University College, | London
31 Oct. 1898.

Dear Sir,

I am afraid I must make to you the reply which I always make to editors, that I have nothing written, that I cannot sit down and write things, and that I do not like writing in papers.

Papers have been known to prosper without contributions from me, so I daresay you will not be too resentful to accept my wishes for the success of your scheme.

I am yours truly
A. E. Housman.

MS inspected at Bonhams, 6 Dec. 1999. Envelope addressed 'R. Ellis Roberts Esq. | St John's College | Oxford'.

TO C. FLEET

University College | London
7 Nov. 1898.

Dear Sir,

I am much indebted to you for your two interesting and informing volumes. Certainly if I am ever at Brighton it will give me much pleasure to come and see you.

I am

Yours very truly
A. E. Housman.

C. Fleet Esq.
BMC MS.

TO WALTER ASHBURNER

17 North Road | Highgate N.
17 Nov. 1898.

Dear Mr Ashburner,

I am returning the edition of Martial you were good enough to lend me last midsummer. Markland's notes are many of them only the readings of manuscripts which he approves; and others are only the hasty jottings usual with him, based on a misunderstanding of the text: some of these he has himself cancelled.[1] There remain the following, which seem to me either true or at least worth considering, and which are new so far as I know: II. 66. 4 *genis* (I had hit on this myself), 71. 5 punctuation, III. 58. 41 *acto*, IV. 30. 8 *sua*, V. 38. 7 *sedebis*, VIII. 38. 9 *annuis*, 46. 4 *toto … Phryge*, IX. 51. 1 *hinc*, 60. 2 *uersat*, X. 21. 6 *set*, XI. 16. 3 *iam*, XIV. 42. 2 *quando*, 216. 2 *et capit*.

---

[1] AEH published a selection of annotations made by Jeremiah Markland in his copy of Schrevel's *Martial* in 'Corrections and Explanations of Martial', *JP* 30 (1907), 229–65. Among these, he praised *sedebis* at 5. 38. 7 as 'an emendation of the highest excellence', and noted that *sectis … genis* at 2. 66. 4 was 'a conjecture which I had made myself'. See *Classical Papers*, 738–9. In 1920 AEH expressed his high esteem of Markland: 'It is probable that Englishmen are right in counting Porson the second of English scholars, but many judges on the Continent would give that rank to Markland. He is the only one except Bentley who has been highly and equally eminent in Greek and Latin; and I believe that Bentley did him the honour, extravagant I admit, to be jealous of him' (*Classical Papers*, 1005).

I have thought of a motto to express the difference between Markland's and Vollmer's[2] editions of Statius' siluae: 'uix lumine fesso | explores quam longus in hunc despectus ab illo' (I. 1. 87).[3]

I am

Yours sincerely

A. E. Housman.

NLS MS 20369, fos. 168–9. Ashburner/Bell (1976), 9.

TO PROFESSOR WILLIAM GARDNER HALE

University College, | London

21 Nov. 1898.

My dear Professor Hale,

Two or three years ago, when I saw it announced that you had discovered a new MS of Catullus and were going to publish an account of it,[1] I wrote to my bookseller and told him to send it to me when it appeared. I have not yet received it (he is a bad bookseller and I have practically given him up), and as I have not been thinking much about Catullus for some time past, I only learn from your letter that it has been published. I suppose it cannot have been published very long,[2] or Ellis would have reviewed it already in at least two places. I have now written for it; but in the mean time I can do no more than acknowledge your letter and thank you for writing. Nor have I seen Schulze's paper:[3] in Chicago[4] no doubt you see all the periodicals as they appear: in London there is no place of the sort: this College takes in eight or nine, but *Hermes*[5] is not among them: the British Museum tries hard and with some success to withold[6] from readers

---

[2] AEH in 1908 cited Vollmer's edn. of Statius (1898) as one of two books in which 'the criticism of Latin poetry touched its nadir': *Classical Papers*, 771. AEH thought better of Vollmer's later work. On Vollmer, see List of Recipients.

[3] 'Scarce could your straining sight discover how far the downward view from this monarch to that'.

[1] In *CR* 10. 6 (July 1896), 314, Hale announced that he had found in the Vatican Library a Catullus MS, long misplaced and thus in effect lost, and announced the future publication of his collation and a facsimile. The MS, designated '*R*', he ranked alongside *O* (Oxford) and *G* (Paris) as a source for the reconstruction of the Verona archetype, from which our text of Catullus derives. The MS is Ottobonianus latinus 1829.

[2] Hale discussed the MS and Schulze's paper in 'The Codex Romanus of Catullus' in *CR* 12. 9 (Dec. 1898), 447–9.

[3] In *Hermes*, 33. 3.   [4] Where Hale was Professor of Latin.

[5] Schulze's article 'Der Codex Romanus des Catullus' appeared in *Hermes*, 34 (1899), 133–44.

[6] For 'withhold'.

everything less than a year old: I am not a millionaire, and even if I were,
Hermes would not be the first extravagance in which I should indulge.

I am

Yours very truly
A. E. Housman.

UCLA MS (William Andrews Clark Memorial Library).

TO GRANT RICHARDS

17 North Road | Highgate N.
11 Dec. 1898.

Dear Mr Richards,

I rather like the notion of a pocket edition. Large paper and illustrations
are things I have not much affection for. In any case I should like to correct
the proofs and to have them printed as I correct them. Last time some one
played games with the punctuation.[1]

It does you infinite credit that the sale should be so good: I wonder how
you manage it.

Yours very truly
A. E. Housman.

Illinois MS. Richards, 26 and 32 (excerpts, wrongly dated 17 Dec.); Maas, 49.

[1] The second edn. (1898) contained 40 alterations of the text of the first edn. in punctuation
alone. See *Poems* (1997), Introduction, xxv–xxvi.

1899

TO GRANT RICHARDS

17 North Road | Highgate N.
8 Feb. 1899.

Dear Mr Richards,

I do not want any profits.[1] They had better go towards paying that long bill which Mr G. B. Shaw sent in to you the other day.[2]

Yours very truly
A. E. Housman.

Illinois MS. Richards, 36; Maas, 49.

TO THE EDITOR OF *THE ATHENAEUM*

[17 North Road | Highgate N.
*c.*6 May 1899]

Juvenal, Sat. VI.—In the new fragment of Juvenal's Sixth Satire published in this month's *Classical Review*[1] the following emendations should be made.
Lines 1–3 should read:—

> In quacumque domo vivit luditque professus
> Obscenum, tremula promittit et omnia dextra,
> Invenies omnis turpes similesque cinædis.

Quacumque is relative, as usual.
Lines 12, 13:—

> Pars ultima ludi
> Accipit has animas aliusque in carcere nervos.

---

[1] AEH first agreed to accept royalties on *ASL* on 28 Dec. 1922: see his letter to GR.

[2] In presenting Shaw with a statement in respect of *Plays Pleasant and Unpleasant* (1898), GR had included an item for £10. 6s. for 'author's alterations and extra proofs'. Shaw's response, which was printed in *The Academy*, 1390 (24 Dec. 1898), 503, was a bill to GR for £281. 8. 9, for proof correction, design, and consultation, plus interest at 6 per cent for six months, less the £10. 6s. charged by GR. It is reproduced in *Bernard Shaw: Collected Letters*, ed. Dan H. Laurence (1976), 63.

[1] J. P. Postgate, 'On the New Fragments of Juvenal', *CR* 13. 4 (May 1899), 206–8.

Nervŏs is nominative singular.

    Line 27:—

<blockquote>Quem rides? aliis hunc mimum!</blockquote>

A. E. Housman.

The Athenaeum, *3733 (13 May 1899), 604. Maas, 399–400.*

TO P. G. L. WEBB

17 North Road | Highgate N.
7 Dec. 1899.

My dear Webb,

    I remember E. J. Wcbb's article on Postgate's Manilius:[1] I was particularly pleased to see that he knew astronomy, which modern scholars are often very ignorant of. It did not dawn upon me that he was your brother: there is another Webb going about, whose initials are C. C. J.,[2] and I had got it into my head that that was the one. I suppose Providence has not showered *two* classical brothers upon you?

    When I shall get to the end of Manilius I do not know. I have just been reading through the Latin translators of Aratus in order to throw light upon him; and I find that they also are in a shocking state and will want editing. For example, Germanicus prognostica II (III) 16 is believed to have written "*binos* Gradivus perficit orbes", i.e. Mars goes round the
earth } sun twice in one year. The editors don't know that Mars goes round the earth } sun about once in two years, and therefore don't see that it ought to be *bimos,* i.e. biennes.

Yours very truly
A. E. Housman.

Lilly MSS 1. 1. 3. Maas, 400.

---

[1] Edmund James Webb (1852–1945), classical scholar and astronomer, reviewed Postgate's *Silva Maniliana* in *CR* 11. 6 (July 1897), 303–13.

[2] Clement Charles Julian Webb (1865–1954). Theologian, philosopher, and historian; Fellow of Magdalen College, 1889–1922; Professor of the Philosophy of Religion, 1920; Fellow of Oriel College, Oxford, 1922–30; occasional contributor to *CR*.

TO PAUL LEMPERLY

University College | London
11 Dec. 1899.

Dear Sir,

The second edition of *A Shropshire Lad* contains nothing new except a few misprints. I have not published any other book.

I am much obliged by your letter and bookplate. I think yours is the only letter containing no nonsense that I have ever received from a stranger, and certainly it is the only letter containing an English stamp that I have ever received from an American. Your countrymen generally enclose the stamps of your great and free republic.

I am yours faithfully
A. E. Housman.

BMC MS. Envelope addressed 'Paul Lemperly Esq. | 16 Vestry Street | Cleveland | Ohio | U. S. A.'
A. Edward Newton, This Book-Collecting Game *(1928), 254; Maas, 50.*

1900

TO MILDRED PLATT

17 North Road | Highgate N.
12 March 1900.

Dear Mrs Platt,

I shall be very pleased to come to dinner on the 22nd.

The reason why you seldom see me is that when the weather is bad on Sundays I am afraid to come so far, and when the weather is good, the country, being both nearer and larger, drags me north. Platt, who knows everything, even Greek, will explain to you that every particle of matter in the universe attracts every other particle with a force directly as their masses and inversely as the square of the distance which separates them.

Moreover, at the last at-home I came to, you treated me very ill. I had hidden under the piano, or in it, I forget which; and you came and pulled me out.

I am

Yours sincerely
A. E. Housman.

UCL MS Add. 165. Maas, 50.

TESTIMONIAL FOR MISS A. M. B. MEAKIN

University College, London
26 March 1900.

Miss A. M. B. Meakin has during the last <four> \three/ years attended many of my Senior and Junior Latin classes in this College. She has displayed not only much intelligence but also an interest in and even an enthusiasm for her work such as I have seldom known. Her progress in general grasp of the subject has been steady and in some respects rapid. I have been particularly struck by the zeal with which she applied herself to Latin composition, not only in prose but in verse. It was at her own wish that she began the study of the latter art, which is not usually practised by students here; and she soon attained a fair degree of proficiency in more than one of the metres. If Miss Meakin should herself engage in the teaching of Latin, I have no doubt that she will be found both a careful and an effective teacher.

A. E. Housman,
Professor of Latin

Bodleian MS Eng. misc. d. 509, fo. 36. Maas, 51.

TO GRANT RICHARDS

17 North Road | Highgate N.
26 March 1900.

Dear Mr Richards,

I am much obliged by copies of the 3ʳᵈ edition[1] you have sent me, The new get-up is very pretty.

Yours very truly
A. E. Housman.

Illinois MS. Richards, 44 (excerpt); Maas, 50.

TO THOMAS HARDY

17 North Road | Highgate N.
29 March 1900.

Dear Mr Hardy,

I should be very happy to come at the end of July or thereabouts. That is the time of year at which I have been at Dorchester[1] before, and very pleasant it was.

I am yours sincerely
A. E. Housman.

Dorset County Museum MS.

[1] Of *ASL.*

[1] In Dorset. Hardy and his wife had lived nearby at Max Gate since 1885.

TO GRANT RICHARDS

17 North Rd, Highgate N.

I have just found your note of the 17th which I had overlooked. I am afraid there is no chance of another book from me yet awhile.

Yrs

A. E. Housman

30 March 1900.

Illinois MS: p.c. addressed 'Grant Richards Esq. | 9 Henrietta St. | Covent Garden | W. C.'
Richards, 46 (excerpt); Maas, 51.

TO GILBERT MURRAY

17 North Road, Highgate N.
23 April 1900.

Dear Murray,

I have put off thanking you for the *Andromache*[1] till I could send the Euripidea.[2] It is very interesting, very unlike anything one could have anticipated, and the end of it really moving. The piece of verse on p. 70 is so good that I wish you would write more. Ancient Greece, as you depict it, is rather more medieval than I thought it was, but I don't know how far this may be due to the notions I attach to words: the word 'lord' always carries me into the middle ages, and even 'castle', though I suppose it ought not. I rather doubt if man really has much to gain by substituting peace for strife, as you and Jesus Christ recommend. Sic notus Ulixes?[3] do you think you can outwit the resourceful malevolence of Nature? God is not mocked, as St Paul long ago warned the Galatians.[4] When man gets rid of a great trouble he is easier for a little while, but not for long: Nature instantly sets to work to weaken his power of sustaining trouble, and very soon seven pounds is as heavy as fourteen pounds used to be. Last Easter Monday a young woman threw herself into the Lea[5] because her dress looked so shabby amongst the holiday crowd: in other times and countries women have been ravished by half-a-dozen dragoons and taken it less to heart. It looks to me as if the state of

[1] Murray's three-act play, published in 1900.
[2] AEH's unpublished conjectures, which Murray used in his three-volume Oxford edn. of Euripides, 1902–9.
[3] Virgil, *Aeneid*, 2. 44 ('Is it thus that you know Ulysses?').
[4] Gal. 6: 7: 'Be not deceived; God is not mocked: for whatsoever a man soweth, that shall he also reap.'
[5] River that runs from Luton in Bedfordshire to the R. Thames in E. London.

mankind always had been and always would be a state of just tolerable discomfort.

The *Bacchae, Iph. Taur.*, and *Medea* are the only three plays I have really studied. I don't know if you are editing the fragments, so I don't send my conjectures on them. I enclose my own essay at an Andromache, only it is an Alcmaeon.[6]

When are we going to the music-hall?

Yours very truly
A. E. Housman.

Bodleian MSS Gilbert Murray, 7. 68–9. Maas, 51–2.

TO HORATIO F. BROWN

University College, London
3 June 1900.

Dear Sir,

I am much obliged by your kindness in sending me your poem. I may be in Venice this autumn, and I hope I may do myself the pleasure of calling on you.

I am yours faithfully
A. E. Housman.

William White, HSJ 12 (1986), 145. The original ALS was attached to the front flyleaf of a copy of ASL *(1898).*

TO LILY THICKNESSE

[17 North Road | Highgate N.]
11 June 1900

Dear Mrs Thicknesse,

I am sorry to hear Ray has been so ill, and I hope he continues to improve. I trust it was not the emotion of my farewell interview which gave a bad turn to his illness.

I ordered the *Londoner* some days ago,[1] but W. H. Smith and Sons[2] have not yet sent it: I don't know whether this is pure negligence on their part,

---

[6] *Fragment of a Greek Tragedy*, published in *The Bromsgrovian*, NS 2. 5 (8 June 1883), 107–9, and in *The University College Gazette*, 1. 13 (25 Nov. 1897), 100–1.

[1] The issue for 2 June 1900 contained her poem *Invocation*: Maas, 52 n. 5.

[2] Booksellers, whose policy was to sell no literature of questionable morality. Cf. ' "Look, look!" they cried; "this man has penned | Pictures of passion that appals;" | And Messrs Smith declined to vend | His writings at the railway stalls': *A Ballad of A Widower*, 29–32; *Poems* (1997), 252.

or whether they have detected in it anything which they think would be likely to demoralise me.

On Saturday Karl Pearson[3] and I are going for a walk in Buckinghamshire, to find a farmer who lays a particular kind of eggs, which tend to prove that there is no God.

Yours sincerely
A. E. Housman.

Memoir, 203–4; Maas, 52–3.

TO THOMAS HARDY

17 North Road | Highgate N.
11 July 1900.

Dear Mr Hardy,

I shall be very pleased to come, and the date you suggest will suit me excellently. The first Saturday in August is the 4th,[1] so if I am alive I hope you will see me then; but at present my tenure of existence is more than usually precarious, as I am learning the bicycle.[2]

I am yours very truly
A. E. Housman.

Dorset County Museum MS.

TO THOMAS HARDY

17 North Road | Highgate N.
30 July 1900.

Dear Mr Hardy,

Many thanks for your note: I will take the train you suggest, 12. 30 at Waterloo.

Yours very truly
A. E. Housman.

Dorset County Museum MS.

[3] 1857–1936. Professor of Applied Mathematics and Mechanics at UCL, 1884–1911; Galton Professor of Eugenics, 1911–33. See Naiditch (1988), esp. 92–3, for further information.

[1] The other guests were Hardy's friends Edward Clodd and Sir Frederick Pollock: Florence Emily Hardy, *The Life of Thomas Hardy 1940–1928*, rev. edn. (1972), 306. Clodd (1840–1930) was a banker, author, and free-thinker; Pollock (1845–1937) was Corpus Professor of Jurisprudence at Oxford.

[2] 'The Hardys were in the forefront of the dominant craze of the 1890s, bicycling': Robert Gittings, *The Older Hardy*, rev. edn. (1980), 120. Hardy and his wife Emma had each had nasty accidents: Martin Seymour-Smith, *Hardy* (1994), ch. 29.

TO LUCY HOUSMAN

17 North Road | Highgate N.
27 Sept. 1900.

My dear Mamma,

I got home on the evening of the 25th, and have just received your letter this morning.

The crossing to Calais was the windiest and rainiest I have ever had, and the rain or drizzle kept on right across France till nightfall. Artois, Picardy and Champagne are all very flat; large arable fields without hedges, only occasional groves and avenues of black poplar; and rain does not make them look cheerful. Just after sunset we came to Laon, which is built against a solitary ridge of hill, on the middle of which stood the cathedral, looking very fine with its five towers in the twilight; though not finer than the view of Canterbury from the Chatham line. Before we got to Rheims it was quite dark, so I saw nothing of the cathedral there. When the day broke we were in Switzerland approaching Basle, a country of very green meadows and bold but not very lofty hills with woods of the spruce fir. At Basle there is an hour's wait and a change of train: afterwards the same sort of country till you pass beside a small lake and then come to Lucerne, a biggish town with some picturesque bits of fortifications. The lake of Lucerne is in shape something like a clover leaf, only more so: it, and the neighbouring lake of Zug, keep the railway company for more than an hour, during which you are always coming across fresh bays of it and new views. The water is a strong opaque blue: the scenery, though it is not what I consider the best sort of scenery, must be quite the best of its sort: any number of cliffs falling straight to the water, pine trees and cottages adhering to them in impossible places, and narrow white waterfalls streaming all down them with a noise to be heard above the clatter of the train. After you quit the lake and draw near to the St Gothard the country is still interesting and in some respects beautiful: the valleys are often surprisingly soft and pretty, full of smooth meadows and orchard trees and foaming streams of yellowish water; but many of the mountains would be the better for having their tops taken off them. Some of their tops actually were taken off, so far as I was concerned, by the clouds and mist, and I saw no snow at all. The tunnel lasted seventeen minutes, and we came out into a sort of hazy sunshine. It is still Switzerland for two hours more, and the form of the landscape is much the same; but trees, especially firs, grow fewer and smaller, and the fig makes its appearance, and even once or twice the olive; and the towns and churches look Italian. The streams flow in the other direction, and have clearer water, and the waterfalls on the hills are more in number and less in volume; when I came back a month later they were most of them dry. The lake of Lugano, part Swiss and part Italian, is much like Lucerne in its broken outline; but its hills are less bold and less wooded, and its water a sort of burnished green. We pass the town of Como, but cannot see the lake; then the hills die into the plain of Lombardy, and you come to Monza, where the king was killed,[1] and then to Milan.

I suppose Milan is the least Italian town in Italy; it considers itself the intellectual capital of the country, and probably hopes to go to France when it dies. Much of it is new, with the ordinary fine wide streets, and its older parts are not very picturesque as wholes, though many of the single buildings are. There seem to be arches, some very old, at all the numerous gates. The castle, now a barracks <oer> overlooking a new park, is very huge and solid and medieval: two of the churches, St. Ambrogio and St. Eustorgio, are of the old Romanesque architecture from which our Norman is copied, and the former is a very fine example, with a square colonnaded court in front of it. In one street stand sixteen pillars of a Roman bath, with a tramway on each side. Next to the cathedral, the tramway seems to be the thing on which the Milanese chiefly pride themselves. The Cathedral, though one cannot call it good architecture if compared with French or English or even German or the best Italian Gothic, is certainly impressive from its mere size and magnificence and completeness, except the west front, which has a mean effect and actually looks small, thanks to the stupid Italian notion that the proper outline for a west front is the same as that for a dog-kennel, ⌂. From other points of view the building looks full its size, and indeed looks larger than St Peter's at Rome, though in fact it is much less. The ornament, the pinnacles and statues and finials at the top, and the niches at the side, looks rich at first, but it soon begins to look poor: the recesses are shallow, the usual Italian fault, the succession of upright lines is monotonous, and the buttresses and pinnacles, though marble, look almost like the ironwork of a drawing-room fender, owing to the thinness and stiffness of their ornament. The guide calls your attention to the fact that no two statues and no two flowers of the carving are alike; but they might just as well be alike; they could not produce a greater effect of sameness. The inside is very dark, a fault on the right side, and so the defects in details do not trouble one much, and the general effect is fine. The central aisle is half as high again as our highest, York and

---

[1] Umberto I of Italy (b. 1844), who ascended the throne on 8 Jan. 1878, was assassinated at Monza on 29 July 1900 by an anarchist, Gaetano Bresci.

Westminster, and is quite English in its breadth,—not the narrow French proportion: there are double aisles on each side, the lowest of which I calculate are as high as the nave of Winchester. The clerestory is small, and there is no triforium, so fully three quarters of the height of the nave is merely pillars and arches: the pillars are crowned, not by capitals, but by \octagonal/ stilts consisting of niches with statues in them, on the top of which the arches are perched: I suppose all this adds to the effect of height, but it is disproportioned and fatigues the eyes: if you look straight before you there is only column after column: you cannot help looking up, and then there is nothing to see except the arches and the roof at a distance where you lose their outlines. There is much stained glass, some of it old and fine: the three great east windows have good tracery and are very rich and gorgeous.

Here I must stop at present. I am sorry the festival has knocked you up. The enclosed is what the Venetians call the flower of the sea: it grows all over the salt marshes of the lagoon. Love to Cousin Agnes.[2]

Your loving son
A. E. Housman.

UCL MS Add. 126. Envelope addressed 'Mrs E. Housman | Kildare | Cantelupe Street | Hereford'. Memoir, 119 (excerpt) and 137–8 (incomplete); Maas, 53–5.

TO LUCY HOUSMAN

17 North Road, Highgate N.
2 October 1900.

My dear Mamma,

I was in Milan on the day of Bresci's trial:[1] at first I could not make out why the ends of all the streets round the Court of Justice were occupied by cavalry who let no wheeled traffic pass, but this accounted for it. I went to the top of the cathedral to see the view: the distance was not very clear, so that only the nearest Alps and Appennines were visible, not Mount Rosa. All round extends the plain of Lombardy as flat as a carpet, and very green with pollard trees and shrubs, red and white towns and towers here and there: the great Carthusian monastery and church of Pavia looks like a ship on the sea. Going from Milan to Venice at first you have merely this plain, cut up into small and narrow fields of Indian corn in all stages of growth (they make it into 'polenta' and a cheap sort of bread: they call it Turkish

---

[2] Lucy Housman's sister, Helen Agnes, who in 1892 married Sir William Smith (1823–93).

[1] 29 Sept. 1900. He was sentenced to life imprisonment.

corn, and to put matters straight they call a turkey an Indian fowl, poor
benighted Papists); these fields are separated not by hedges but by rows of
small trees, black poplar, willow, and especially mulberry: they also plant
the mulberry among the corn and in orchards by itself: they grow it for silk,
not fruit. You cross many rivers, and at this time of the year you can tell
by their condition where they come from: those which flow from the lakes
have plenty of water, but those which have to rely on their own springs
are merely brooks amidst broad white beds of sand and stones. When you
are getting towards Brescia the Alps come down from the north to keep
the railroad company: this part is very picturesque, the hills have towns
and churches and forts and convents perched here and there; but there is
a great lack of large trees: I believe there are not half a dozen large trees
in Italy except in gardens and parks. The Lombardy poplar does not seem
to be common in Lombardy: it grows badly, and they often lop it like a
Worcestershire elm. The railway runs close to the lake of Garda, the largest
and much the broadest of the lakes, and this is the most beautiful part of
the journey: the water is bright blue, and retreats into the mountains on
the north; on the south, where the shores are flatter, the landscape begins
to be ornamented with the cypress, the most telling of all trees. Now we
pass into the Venetian provinces, and between Verona and Vicenza the
Alps recede into the north again: the country is much like Lombardy, but
the fields <see[m]> are larger and farms and towns seem fewer; but every
town and village, even more than in Lombardy, seems to have built itself
a lofty brick bell-tower, which in Venetia generally has a short sort of spire
on the top (you know the great campanile of St Mark's at Venice): also
the poplar becomes more frequent: people who <lik[e]> live in very flat
countries (Lincolnshire for instance) must have tall towers and such things
to cheer them up. As the sun went down we came to what is called the
dead lagoon, where the sea and land begin to mix, but there is more land
than sea: the live lagoon, where there is more sea than land, is what Venice
stands in. The scene was very dreary at that hour: pools and canals, and
marshes all overgrown with that purple flower I sent you; and the last touch
of mystery and desolation was provided by three large staring red tramcars
about a quarter of a mile away which were being rapidly drawn, by one
very small horse apiece, into the Adriatic sea. (I found afterwards that they
go to a spot on the coast whence there is a steamer to Venice.) Then the
railway runs out on to the water to Venice over a bridge two miles and a
half long: Venice itself is not very well seen, and looks something like an
English manufacturing town with the chimneys transformed into towers.
Entering Venice itself, especially at nightfall, when most of the canals are

empty, the first impression is its stillness: you get a gondola at the landing place by the station, and are taken to the other end of the Grand Canal, where the hotels are, chiefly by short cuts through the lesser canals: the Grand Canal is ⟨sketch⟩ like an S. I hope your health is going on all right.

Your loving son

A. E. Housman

UCL MS Add. 126. Envelope addressed 'Mrs E. Housman | Kildare | Cantelupe St. | Hereford'.
Memoir, 138–40 (incomplete); Maas, 55–6.

TO LUCY HOUSMAN

17 North Road, Highgate N.
15 Oct. 1900.

My dear Mamma,

I suppose I had better take the contents of Venice in the order of date. The first is the best: the Byzantine architecture as represented by the cathedral of St. Mark, which I should think is the most beautiful, not the grandest, building in the world. It might be possible to erect in the Gothic style a more beautiful building, but I doubt if such a one exists. It is not lofty, and not large, except that it is broad for its length; but every square yard of it is worth looking at for an hour together. I used to go there nearly every day; but it would take years to exhaust it. It is all covered with coloured marble and alabaster, except where it has gold mosaics, or richly carved stone capitals to the pillars; and yet it does not look a bit like a piece of patch-work: everything helps towards the general effect. The preciousness of the material and the delicacy of the workmanship make it look almost more like jewellery than architecture, and one feels as if it ought not to be left out of doors at night. The inside is equally costly in material but not so good in general effect: the five domes with their gold mosaics are well enough, but the walls are of a brown alabaster which gives a rather dingy effect at a distance, though it is very beautiful to examine closely; and the building looks more like a cave hewn out of the solid than a building such as we are accustomed to, resting its weight on walls and pillars. The few remaining palaces of the same architecture I did not think much of, though Ruskin cries them up a great deal.[1] Of Gothic they had two sorts in Venice: one for the churches, very thin and poor, with naked red brick on the outside; another for their palaces, exceedingly rich and elegant, but rather timid and monotonous. Of this the Doge's palace is the

---

[1] In *Stones of Venice* (1851–3).

great example: you know its stupid general design, like a clothes-horse with a blanket on it: I am bound to say the reality is better than the pictures, because one can see that the flat and tame upper half of it is composed of <rea[l]> red and white marble, although the pattern is no better than you see on the cottages in the Stourbridge Road at Bromsgrove. The lower part, the two colonnades, are as beautiful and as full of fine carving as you could wish. There is a much smaller palace on the Grand Canal, called the Casa d'Oro, which is almost richer in effect. But the majority of the Gothic palaces are not satisfactory: they are all on the same pattern, part of the surface consisting of very rich arcades and windows, the rest of painfully flat wall, made worse by being painted. The earliest Renaissance work in Venice is very peculiar and very charming in detail, with much inlaying of coloured marbles, a device which they borrowed from the old Byzantine architecture: there was a family of architects called the Lombardi, who built the little church of St. Maria dei Miracoli and one or two palaces in this style, with beautiful foliated carving: in point of general design however they are not good or effective. Then comes the regular Renaissance, which we all know: the most imposing building of that date is the church of the Salute, with a large and a small dome, which always figures in pictures of the Grand Canal and is really very fine outside: inside, all the Renaissance churches are merely St Paul's on a smaller scale and with more ornament on the walls. The church of the Redentore, by Palladio, has a charmingly pretty and simple exterior to its east (or rather its south) end, which nobody except me seems to notice or admire.

The painter best represented in Venice is that lurid and theatrical Tintoret, whom I avoid, and Paul Veronese, whom one soon sees enough of. There are surprisingly few Titians, though two of them are very fine and famous. The best paintings to my thinking are those of Giovanni Bellini, who belongs to the previous generation, and his pupil Cima da Conegliano, mostly Madonnas and groups of saints; also two painters both called Bonifacio Veronese. The picture gallery really pleased me more than any I have seen, because of the beautiful glow of colour on all the walls, except of course where Tintoret was scowling Paul Veronese out of countenance in the large room which they have had given them to sprawl about in. Many of the best paintings are in the churches: there is a very interesting series by Carpaccio (scenes in the lives of St George and St Jerome) in St Giorgio dei Schiavoni, covering all the walls of the little building.

Often at sunset I used to go up the great bell-tower in St. Mark's Place. Venice looks like one large island (the canals cannot be seen): the lagoon lies all round, dotted with the stakes which mark out the navigable channels, and the water declares its depth or shallowness by its colour: as the sun goes down it turns partly a golden green and partly a pale vermilion.[2]

My gondolier[3] expressed a wish that he were your son. He wanted me to come to Venice next Christmas, and I explained that at Christmas I went to see you; and then he made this remark. The reason is, that if he were your son he would be well off and would have no family to provide for: so at least he says. At present he has to earn a living for one wife, two sisters, one mother, one mother-in-law, and half an uncle (who was once a champion oarsman and is now paralysed); which is pretty good for a young man of twenty-three who has had one eye kicked out by a horse.

On the other side of the island of Lido, which is the chief bulwark against the Adriatic, there is a great bathing place on the open sea with splendid sands, where I went several times. On this same island I also discovered a bit of real country; grass and a grove of trees round about the fort of St Nicolo,[4] where the Venetians have their great picnic in May. In addition to the usual English autumn wildflowers there was purple salvia and the evening primrose. There were also very attractive grasshoppers two inches long, which they call by the name 'salto-martino'. I went also to Mestre on the mainland, and saw for the first time in my life a swallow-tail butterfly on the wing: in England I believe it survives only in a few spots of the eastern counties.

Your loving son
A. E. Housman.

UCL MS Add. 126. Envelope addressed 'Mrs E. Housman | Kildare | Cantelupe St. | Hereford.' Memoir, *141–2 (incomplete); Maas, 56–8.*

---

[2] The 'green and sanguine shoals' commemorated in *MP* XLIV, written 10–30 Apr. 1922.

[3] Andrea, whom he employed on his visits to Venice. He is mentioned by name in *MP* XLIV 21 and in a letter to Brown, 6 Sept. 1901, but usually as 'my gondolier' or (when Andrea was very ill and just after his death) 'my poor gondolier': see Naiditch (1995), 58–9, where it is correctly noted that AEH never calls him a friend. Even marginalia in his copy (now at BMC) of Baedeker's *Italy: Handbook for Travellers,* First Part: Northern Italy (1899), 275, record 'my gondolier disagrees' and 'Pisani-Moretto says gondolier'. AEH's mode of reference may be compared to that of the narrator in Henry James's *The Aspern Papers* (1888), who refers to 'my gondolier' six times and 'my gardener' twice. *Pace* Graves, 150–3, there is no evidence that AEH had a 'love-affair' with the man: see Page, 122.

[4] For Nicolò.

1901

TO JOHN PURVES

2 January 1901
Hereford.

Dear Sir,

I am obliged by your letter, but I am sorry that I must make my usual reply,—that I have really nothing written, and also that I never think verses look well in a magazine, unless they deal with current events. If, for example, I had anything to say about the new century, you should be very welcome to it; but I have not.

I am

Yours very faithfully
A. E. Housman.

NLS MS Acc. 7175/1.

TO MRS FAIRCHILD

University College, London
11 April 1901.

Dear Mrs Fairchild,

(If I am so to address you). I am much obliged by your kindness in writing to me and in sending me your friend's poems. Some of them have a mixture of grace and simplicity which I admire very much: the four pieces XLII–XLV are good examples of it.

You need not alarm yourself by imagining that I am famous in England. The book[1] was very well reviewed, but the sale is only moderate,[2] and the third edition[3] is not yet exhausted.

---

[1] *ASL.*   [2] See *Critical Heritage* (1992), 58–93, and Benjamin F. Fisher, 'The Critical Reception of *A Shropshire Lad*', in *A. E. Housman: A Reassessment*, ed. Alan W. Holden and J. Roy Birch (2000), 20–36.

[3] The 1st edn. (published *c.* end of Feb. 1896) and 2nd edn. (Sept. 1898) were each of at least 500 copies. At the end of 1896, 445 copies of the first edn. were sold, with a further 16 and 36 in the two halves of 1897 (Richards, 16 n.). Of the 2nd edn., 397 copies were sold by the end of 1898, with a further 50 in 1899 (Richards, 26, 32).

[4] Of 1,000 copies, published at the end of Feb. 1900. 641 copies were sold in 1900, 263 in 1901 (Richards, 32).

I have relations in Canada and the States, but I do not much expect to cross the Atlantic. Italy is so much nearer, and so inexhaustible. So I am afraid we are not likely to meet; but let me renew my thanks for your letter, and add that I value it all the more because you describe yourself as an old woman. Old women and young men are the salt of the earth.

I am yours very truly
A. E. Housman.

BMC MS.

TO PROFESSOR DENISON ROSS

[University College, London]
11 May 1901.

Dear Ross,
I return the suit with many thanks. It was a pride to me and a joy to all beholders, and I hope it is not damaged by the cold sweat which broke out upon me when I found I was expected to sum up the debate.[1] The tie-clips are in the waist-coat pocket.

—Yours faithfully and obliged
A. E. H.

School of Oriental and African Studies, University of London, MS: PPMS 8 Ross Collection, Box 1 File 2. Published in Both Ends of the Candle: The Autobiography of Sir E. Denison Ross *(1943), 53, and by Maas in* HSJ, *2 (1975), 33.*

TO WALTER ASHBURNER

17 North Road | Highgate N.
31 May 1901

Dear Ashburner,
It will give me much pleasure to dine with you on Wednesday next.

Yours sincerely
A. E. Housman.

NLS MS 20369, fo. 192. Ashburner/Bell (1976), 10.

---

[1] 'On May 10, 1901, at a few hours' notice, Housman took the chair at the Annual Public Debate [of the UCL Debating Society] when Lord Avebury was unavoidably absent': Naiditch (1988), 142, citing UCL MS Add. 78/6 as his source. Naiditch also quotes Chambers, 379: 'When [AEH] took the chair at a debate on Democratic Government he summed up in favour of democracy, on the ground that it was difficult to betray a Government you had yourself chosen. He instanced cases where defeatists had welcomed the disasters of their own autocratic government, because such disasters must lead to revolution. "Democracy does save you from horrors like that", he said, and at the word "horrors" a shudder seemed to pass over him.' Naiditch (1988), 142: 'Arnold White had moved that Representative Government was a failure; Archdeacon Sinclair had opposed. The motion was lost by a sizeable majority.'

TO HORATIO F. BROWN

[HOTEL EUROPA | VENICE]
6 Sept. 1901

Dear Mr Brown,

I shall be very pleased to lunch with you and Mrs Brown on Sunday. Apparently I nearly encountered you both yesterday afternoon, for Andrea tells me you were on one side of the Lido while I was on the other.

Yours very truly
A. E. Housman.

White (1950), 403; Maas, 59.

TO LUCY HOUSMAN

[Castelfranco]
13 Sept. 1901

My dear Mamma,

This is written in pouring rain at the town of Castelfranco, which most likely you never heard of, and no more did I till four or five days ago. The pen and ink are too awful, so I must go on in pencil, which is all the better as there is no blotting paper. This is about twenty miles inland from Venice: it is celebrated as the birthplace of Giorgione, and as containing the only picture which is known with certainty to be his. It is a smallish place which once was smaller, for it stands partly within and partly without the fine old walls and moat: the walls are partly in ruins, and the space between them and the moat is now a sort of garden-bank, something like the castle at Hereford. I have been at Paris, Pisa, and Florence, and now lastly at Venice. Pisa is a rather handsome and very sleepy town, with all its chief buildings, the Cathedral, Baptistery, and leaning tower, packed in one corner on an open space of grass, surrounded on two sides by the ancient walls of the city, which still run right round it. The weather was very hot and bright, and by daytime one could hardly open one's eyes to look at things; for although the Cathedral etc. are about as old as any Norman architecture that we have got in England, they are chiefly built of Carrara marble, which in process of time does indeed become smeary and untidy, but never becomes mellow and venerable; and under an Italian sun it blazes like a dusty highroad. The cathedral is quite a failure, highshouldered and almost mean-looking outside, handsome and roomy inside, but not a bit religious: bands of black marble on white, looking painfully spic and span, in spite of its antiquity. The Baptistery, a large dome, is a beautiful building outside, much improved by the addition of some Gothic gables and pinnacles to the Romanesque original; the inside is quite uninteresting. By daylight the Baptistery is much the finest of the group of buildings, but in twilight and moonlight I think the leaning tower is superior, with its six rows of pillars picked out in light and shade. The country immediately around Pisa is flat, much of it having been deposited by the sea within human memory: the nearest hills are about five miles off, but the Appennine and other mountains are well in sight. I went out for a drive to the west to the park of the royal villa, which is a great game-preserve, planted with woods and avenues of the stone pine. The Arno at Pisa, being penned within embankments, is a respectable stream by moonlight, when you cannot see that it is liquid mud: however, after all it is not so bad as the Exe at Exeter: the Arno is like pea-soup, but the Exe is like tomato-soup. Between Pisa and Florence the Arno at present is merely a shallow brook meandering about a wide bed of pebbles: at Florence they try to make it look decent by a series of dams, but in this dry summer it does not succeed. I have only one candle, which is bothering to my eyes, and Florence would take up more space than I can fill before I go to bed, so here I will stop, and try to address the envelope legibly with the abandoned pen and ink.

Your loving son
A. E. Housman.

UCL MS Add. 126. Pencil from the 'g' in 'ago' in the first sentence onwards. Envelope addressed (in ink) 'Mrs E. Housman | Kildare | Cantilupe St. | Hereford | Inghilterra'. Maas, 59–60.

TO WALTER ASHBURNER

17 North Road | Highgate N.
13 September 1901.

Dear Ashburner,

Will you give me the pleasure of your company at dinner at Kettner's (Church St., Soho) on Friday Nov. 29th at 7 o' clock?

In order that you may not be lured into any horrors for which you are unprepared, I should explain that, as I do not belong to any club, after dinner we adjourn to a box in the adjacent Palace (the most proper of all the music-halls, not meet to be called a music-hall), and that when the Palace closes there is no refuge but Bow St. police station; which is the reason why I put the hour so early.

I met Horatio Brown in Venice in September,[1] just after he had left you in the Engadine.[2]

Yours very truly
A. E. Housman.

NLS MS 20369, fos. 194–5. Ashburner/Bell (1976), 11.

TO PROFESSOR W. M. LINDSAY

[17 North Road | Highgate N.
12 Dec. 1901]

Neither παριστορία nor any other noun in the nominative will make sense of the passage: *facta est* with a nominative can only mean 'became' or 'was rendered': if it means 'took place' or 'was done' it will admit no complement but an adverb or adverbial phrase. Is it proposed to take it as if it were *fuit*? Further, παριστορία means a story conflicting with fact, not a fact conflicting with story. I had half a mind to add to my note the words 'Now someone will conjecture παριστορία'; but I reflected that this would sound unamiable and could not be proved to be true, though I knew that it was.[1]

12 Dec. 1901

A.E.H.

St Andrews MS 36326, 202. ii: p.c. addressed 'Professor Lindsay | 3 Howard Place | St Andrews | N. B.' Peter Godman, 'Two Unpublished Letters of Housman', Proceedings of the Cambridge Philological Society, *204 (1978), 41.*

---

[1] See AEH to Brown, 6 Sept. 1901.   [2] Swiss portion of the upper Inn River valley.

[3] AEH is discussing the emendation of Martial, *De Spectaculis Liber*, 21. 8, from 'haec tamen res est facta ita pictoria' to 'haec tantum res est facta παρ' ἱστορίαν' ('this thing alone was done untold by history'), which he proposed in *CR* 15. 3 (Apr. 1901), 154–5 (*Classical Papers*, 536–7). Samuel Allen, *CR* 15. 4 (June 1901), 153–4, preferred παρ' ἱστορία. Lindsay's edn. of Martial appeared in 1902 (2nd edn., 1929). For further information, see Naiditch (1995), 169. Naiditch (2005), 148–52, provides examples of AEH withholding textual information on principle and anticipating false conjectures. See letters of 23 Mar. 1934 and 12 Apr. 1935.

1902

TO WALTER ASHBURNER

17 North Road | Highgate N.
8 July 1902.

Dear Ashburner,

I am very sorry I have an engagement on Thursday evening. Perhaps it is all the better for Brown,[1] who is dining with me on Friday (to meet a literary gent in whom he takes an interest),[2] and who might find me monotonous as an ingredient in the bill of fare two evenings in succession.

Yours very truly
A. E. Housman.

NLS MS 20369, fos. 197–8. Ashburner/Bell (1976), 12.

TO GRANT RICHARDS

17 North Road, Highgate N.
12 Oct. 1902.

Dear Richards,

If I may drop the Mr. I am sending simultaneously by parcel post the text and notes of the edition of Manilius I, and also a specimen of the Teubner classics[1] to show what sort of book I have in my mind's eye.[2] The notes should be printed at the foot of the text, and should run right across the page, not stand in two columns: the type of the notes should be smaller in proportion to that of the text than is the case in the German book: the

---

[1] Horatio F. Brown.

[2] Brown and he dined at the Café Royal, and were joined by GR, who was delayed by motoring mishaps. Richards, 38, is wrong about the date ('One day ... it may have been in the month of July, 1904') of what was the beginning of a long friendship with AEH. (AEH addresses him formally as 'My dear Sir', 'Dear Sir', and 'Dear Mr Richards'; then changes to 'Dear Richards' and 'My dear Richards', 12 Oct. and 8 Nov. 1902. The change indicates that the friendship had begun previously.)

[1] Inexpensive series of classical editions, containing only text and apparatus criticus, published at Leipzig since 1824.

[2] *Hamlet*, 1. 2. 184.

paper should be thicker, I think. As to my manuscript, the curved line
~~~~ under words \and figures/ and letters is meant to indicate Clarendon
type[3] (I am not sure if it is the correct sign); and the spaces which I have
left between sentences are meant to be preserved in printing. In the text,
I want the numbers in the *left*-hand margin, as I have put them: and the
letters 'j' and 'v', wherever they occur in the type-written copy, are to be
altered into 'i' and 'u' respectively:[4] I suppose this is a change which may
be left to the printer.

Before anything is done, I should be glad if you could let me have an
estimate of what the printing &c is likely to cost, as my resources are not
inexhaustible. In addition to what I am now sending, there will be a preface
of about 25 pages (as far as I can judge), and about an equal amount \(25
pages)/ of additional matter at the end.

When the next edition of the *Shropshire Lad* is being prepared, it would
save trouble to the compositor as well as to me if he were told that the
3rd edition is almost exactly correct,[5] and that he had better not put in
commas and notes of exclamation for me to strike out of the proof, as was
the case last time.

I think this is all I have to say. I remain

<div align="right">Yours sincerely
A. E. Housman.</div>

Illinois MS. Richards, 47–8; Maas, 60–1 (incomplete).

TO GRANT RICHARDS

<div align="right">17 North Rd., Highgate N.
8 Nov. 1902.</div>

My dear Richards,

4/6 is my notion of the proper price, for several reasons: firstly because I
want the book to be read abroad, and continental scholars are poorer than
English; secondly as a protest against the usual English prices—e.g. 12/6
for a single play of Sophocles by Jebb[1]—which I have always supposed

---

[3] A bold condensed fount.

[4] AEH consistently adopted this convention in prose. See letters of 28 Aug. 1911 to GR, 29
Apr. 1921 to Winstanley, and 20 Jan. 1928 to Gow. In poetry he followed a different convention.
See Naiditch (1995), 90; *Poems* (1997), 375; and Naiditch in *HSJ* 31 (2005), 102.

[5] The only likely errors in the 1900 edn. are 'wellnigh' (for 'well nigh') at XXXVII 10 and
'halfway' (for half way') at LXII 31: see *Poems* (1997), Introduction, xxviii.

[1]   Richard Claverhouse Jebb (1841–1905). Fellow of TCC, 1864–76; Professor of Greek at
Glasgow, 1875–89; Regius Professor of Greek at Cambridge and Professorial Fellow of TCC,

to be due to the cloth binding and gilt lettering; thirdly because I hardly like to ask more for a single book of a poem which contains five, when Lachmann's celebrated commentary on the whole of Lucretius[2] only costs 7/6. The Teubner book which I sent you as a specimen is priced at 4/-: true, it is a shocking bad book, but that makes no difference. Still, if 4/6 is one of those prices which publishers and booksellers for some mysterious reason dislike, and if your heart is set on 5/-, I have no strong objection; as I see that my notes in print are more voluminous than I imagined.[3]

The division of the notes in the proofs sent is satisfactory: the important thing is that the note on any verse should *begin* on the page which contains that verse. As to the Greek σ, I wish the letter to have this form at the end as well as in the body of words: fifty years hence all Greek books will be printed so.

I am hoping to receive from Rome in about a week's time some information about manuscripts in the Vatican which may involve additions or alterations in the notes on the first 80 lines.

Yours sincerely
A. E. Housman.

Illinois MS. Richards, 49–50; Maas, 61.

TO AN UNKNOWN CORRESPONDENT

UNIVERSITY COLLEGE, LONDON. | GOWER STREET. W.C.

19 Nov. 1902

Dear Sir,

The publisher is Mr Grant Richards, 48 Leicester Square.

Yours very faithfully
A. E. Housman

BMC MS.

1889–1905; knighted, 1900; OM, 1905. His chief work was an edn. of Sophocles (7 vols., Cambridge, 1883–96). Naiditch (1988), 178, 189, notes that Jebb acted as though AEH's chief articles on the text of Sophocles had never been published, and that the two 'held each other in mutual disesteem'.

[2] The commentary by leading German philologist and textual critic Karl [Konrad Friedrich Wilhelm] Lachmann (1793–1851) was published in 1850. In the preface to *Manilius I* (1903), AEH lamented that 'the Lachmanns and Madvigs are gone' (*Selected Prose*, 41), and in a review of Ellis's Catullus (1905), he spoke of his 'esteem for Lachmann' (ibid. 99; *Classical Papers*, 625). See also *Poems* (1997), 254, 540–1.

[3] Published at AEH's expense and sold at 4/6.

TO GRANT RICHARDS

17 North Road | Highgate N.
20 Nov. 1902.

Dear Richards,

I return the proofs,[1] in which I have made corrections on pages 18, 19, 21, 35, 52 and 92. What I want on pages 18 and 19 is to have the seventh line of each stanza[2] put level with the second and fourth: I don't know if I have expressed this desire in the correct form.

My attempt to get the readings of the Rome manuscripts through the British School there seems to have had no effect; but I am making another effort through another channel, the friend of a friend of mine, and I hope to succeed shortly.

Yours sincerely
A. E. Housman.

Illinois MS. LC-GR t.s. (misdated 20 March 1902); Richards, 50; Maas, 62.

TO GRANT RICHARDS

17 North Road | Highgate N.
30 Nov. 1902.

Dear Richards,

I have got the collation of the Vatican MSS, so I return the proof corrected. As I have not yet had my manuscript returned from the printers (except page 4) it is possible that slight further corrections will be necessary, but nothing to affect the arrangement of the printed matter on the pages, I hope.

The alterations to be made in the remaineder[1] of the first 80 verses (the part affected by the Vatican MSS) are not so formidable as in these first 37.

There is one general instruction which had better be given to the printers. When a colon or semicolon comes at the *end* of a quotation in italics, it ought to stand upright, not to slant (I have written 'rom.' in the margin, but I am not sure if that is the correct way to signify what I mean).

---

[1] Of the 4th edn. of *ASL* (1903). The publisher's file copy, bearing five corrections in AEH's hand, is at BMC: one is of wording ('seed' for 'seeds' at LIII 9), four are of punctuation.

[2] Of poem XI (*On your midnight pallet lying*).

[1] For 'remainder'.

With notes of interrogation, if they belong to the sense of the quotation, the case is different.

Yours sincerely
A. E. Housman.

Illinois MS. LC-GR t.s. Richards, 50 (excerpts); Maas, 62.

1903

TO GRANT RICHARDS

17 North Road | Highgate N.
5 Jan. 1903.

Dear Richards,

I return corrected the proofs which I have received.

As regards long notes, like those on 226 and 245, I see no objection to having a whole page, or two if necessary, filled with annotation, without any text at the top.

Either the type or else the printing of these slips is rather bad, and trying to the eyes to correct by lamplight.

I have made a good many changes in the title page, which ought to be as Latin as possible, I think; and I must confess that I don't know the Latin for Leicester Square.[1] I hope you will approve.

Yours sincerely
A. E. Housman.

Illinois MS. LC-GR t.s. Richards, 51 (excerpt); Maas, 62–3.

TO GRANT RICHARDS

17 North Road | Highgate N.
27 Jan. 1903.

Dear Richards,

I return the last portion of the text and notes corrected; and I enclose the manuscript of the matter which is to follow them at the end of the book. I have marked the two parts A and B to show their order.

As I was unwell in the Christmas holidays, the preface is still only partly written, and I do not get on with it very fast now that the work of the term has begun again.

Yours very truly
A. E. Housman.

Illinois MS. LC-GR t.s. Richards, 51 (excerpt); Maas, 63.

---

[1] GR's office was at 48 Leicester Square. The information was omitted from the title-page.

TO PROFESSOR W. M. LINDSAY

17 North Rd., Highgate N.
5 Feb. 1903.

My dear Sir,

I have waited to read your pamphlet on Martial[1] before thanking you for it, in order that I might be able to do so more intelligently. The collations, and the collection of variants between the three sources, will be very valuable, whether or not one adopts the theory to which you incline, that some of these latter go back to Martial himself. I don't myself take this view; for very similar phenomena occur in the texts of other much-read authors, such as Virgil and Lucan, and seem to be part of the penalty they pay. I think too that the purely palaeographical solution which you propose at II xx 2, III i 6–7, lxxii 3, is applicable to many other verses: IX lxi 9 'dominumq*ue ne*mus' = '-que mus' then 'que suum'; \X xiv 8 'arg*enti uenit*' = 'argenti', then 'missa' from above;/ I lviii 3 'de *me mea*' = 'de mea', then 'dolet hoc mea'; lxxvi 3 'cantus[*que* choros]*que*', then 'cantus citharamque'; (ciii 8 *terque* [qua*terque*] is an easy loss, but would hardly give rise to '*bis*que quaterque'); V xxii 7 'mulo*rum rum*pere' = 'mulorum pere'; then 'uincere'; VI xxxii 4 'pec*tora tota*' = 'pectora', then *nuda*; XII xvii 3 '*pariter pariter*que' (B) = 'pariterque' (C), then 'pariter tecumque' (A). Some of them are confusions I have met in all sorts of places: *pignus* and *munus*; *renouetur* and re*uocetur*; *lasso* and *fesso*; *umbras* and *undas*; *capiat* and *faciat*; and others belong to common types of corruption: *gemina* and *magni*; *mula* and *pluma*; *suillos* and *pusillos*. But certainly no one can say that you put forward your opinion with any undue confidence; and the details you give are most interesting.

I am yours very truly
A. E. Housman

St Andrews MS 36326, 202. i. The square brackets in the text are AEH's. Peter Godman, 'Two Unpublished Letters of Housman', Proceedings of the Cambridge Philological Society, 204 (1978), 41–2.

[1] *The Ancient Editions of Martial, with collations of the Berlin 38; Edinburgh MSS* (120 pp.), University of St Andrews Publications (1903).

TO H. E. BUTLER

University College, London
7 Feb. 1903.

Dear Sir,

I am very willing that you should include in your selection the poem you wish.[1] I do not know if it is necessary that you should also obtain the consent of the publisher (Grant Richards, 48 Leicester Square), but no doubt he would readily give it.

I am yours faithfully
A. E. Housman.

SJCO MS 305. Maas, 63.

TO GRANT RICHARDS

17 North Road | Highgate N.
12 Feb. 1903.

Dear Richards,

With regard to your note of today, I don't quite know the meaning of "the preliminary",[1] but I enclose the dedication[2] which is to follow the title-page. I suppose it had better be printed in italics. If it will not all go on one page, it should be broken at the point I have marked, and a catch-word should be added.

After this, and before the text and notes, there will come a long introduction, which, as I said, is not yet finished; but there is nothing else of the nature of a preliminary.

Many thanks for the copies of the *Shropshire Lad* which I received today. The colour attracts the eye, and the convolvulus-leaf[3] detains it in fascinated admiration.

Yours sincerely
A. E. Housman.

Illinois MS. LC-GR t.s. Richards, 51; Maas, 64.

[1] *1887 (ASL* I), for inclusion in *War Songs of Britain* (1903).

[1] 'The half-title, the title-page, the dedication page, the table of contents, &c., that precede the text of the book': Richards, 51 n.

[2] To *Manilius I*; a 28-line poem in Latin elegiacs inscribed to Moses Jackson. See *Poems* (1997), 289–91, 565–6. It had gone through two notebook drafts, one from Dec. 1895–24 Feb. 1900, the other from *c*.1900–7 June 1902.

[3] The 4th edn. had scarlet covers. As in the 1st (1896) and 2nd (1898) edns., but not the 3rd (1900), a convolvulus-leaf decoration was printed after each poem.

TO T. GREGORY FOSTER

University College
16 Feb. 1903.

Dear Foster,

The accounts of last year's Conversazione were duly audited last July by Professors Martin and Neill, but the audit sheet, together with all the other documents bearing on the Conversazioni which had been collected by the Secretary, is lost or mislaid. In these circumstances Starling, who was Chairman of the Committee, Travers, who was Secretary, and I, who was Treasurer, do not propose to prepare a fresh balances-sheet and call a meeting to present it, but we propose to spend the surplus, £2. 17. 3, for such public purposes as seem good to the three of us,—probably in augmenting the luxuries of the smoking-room: this intention we have signified verbally to many of the staff, and nobody has objected.

But as the Council was good enough to subscribe towards the Conversazione, it is proper that it should be informed how the money was spent; and I therefore enclose <two> \a/ document<s> which I beg you to lay before the Committee of Management. <The one> \It/ is a list drawn up by <me> \Travers/ of the subscriptions and items of expenditure, <; the other> classified under heads.

Yours very truly
A. E. Housman.

UCL Committee of Management 1/148.

TO GRANT RICHARDS

17 North Road | Highgate N.
15 March 1903.

Dear Richards,

In your announcement of my Manilius there are two misprints: *instruit* should be *instruxit* and *amendationes* should be *emendationes*. They do not cause me any piercing anguish, and I only write about it because I thought you might like to know.

The preface proceeds very slowly now that it is term-time. I hope I shall be able to send you an instalment of it in a fortnight or so.

Yours sincerely
A. E. Housman.

Illinois MS. LC-GR t.s. Richards, 52; Maas, 64.

TO G. F. HILL

University College, London
23 March 1903.

My dear Sir,

Your brother, my colleague,[1] encourages me to hope that you will let me trouble you with the following enquiries.

A. von Sallet, *beiträge z. gesch. u. numism. d. könige des Cimmer. Bosp.* (1866) pp. 69–70 mentions a coin of Pythodoris queen of Pontus, struck in 14 A.D., which has Tiberius' head on the obverse and the constellation Libra on the reverse: apparently it is also mentioned in a work which I have not seen, Ch. Giel, *kl. beiträge z. antiken Numismatik Süd-Russlands* (1886) pp. 12–18.

Since the constellation Capricornus, which often accompanies Augustus' head, is known to have been his natal star, it is natural to infer from this coin that Libra was the natal star of Tiberius; and I think that certain passages in Manilius point the same way. The points on which I want light are these.

1. Is the coin genuine? W. von Voigt in *Philologus* vol. 58 p. 176 speaks as if this were not certain.

2. Is the head certainly that of Tiberius, and the figure on the reverse certainly Libra?

3. Does Libra elsewhere appear in company with *either* Tiberius *or* Augustus? (for some think that this constellation also was connected with Augustus).

I beg that you will not trouble yourself seriously about a matter so unimportant: I only venture to apply to you because it is possible that a numismatist may be able to answer easily questions which a layman might fumble at for a long time without result.

I am

Yours very faithfully
A. E. Housman.

G. F. Hill Esq.

BL Add. MS 44919, fos. 163–4. Maas, 401–2.

---

[1] Micaiah John Muller Hill (1856–1929), Professor of Pure Mathematics at UCL, 1884–1907; Astor Professor of Mathematics, University of London, 1907–23; Vice-Chancellor, 1909–11. For further information, see Naiditch (1988), 67–70.

TO G. F. HILL

University College, London
25 March 1903.

My dear Sir,

I am very much obliged by your kind reply to my letter, which tells me just what I wanted to know.[1]

If I find I cannot get Reinach's work[2] in the Reading Room[3] I shall be glad to avail myself of your offer to use the departmental library.

Yours very truly
A. E. Housman.

BL Add. MS 44919, fos. 165–6. Maas, 402.

TO W. G. HUTCHISON

University College, London
25 March 1903.

Dear Sir,

I shall be very willing that you should print the poem you wish in your collection.[1] I do not know if it is necessary that you should also get the consent of the publisher (Grant Richards, 48 Leicester Square), but no doubt he would readily give it.

I am yours very faithfully
A. E. Housman.

W. G. Hutchison Esq.

SJCO MS, Sparrow Collection.

---

[1] For the coin, see *Manilius I*, p. lxxi.
[2] *L'Histoire par les Monnaies: Essais de Numismatique Ancienne*, by Théodore Reinach (Paris, 1902).
[3] Of the British Museum.

[1] *Songs of the Vine: with a Medley for Malt-worms*, ed. Hutchison (1904), a selection of verse in praise of alcoholic drinks. It contained *ASL* LXII (*Terence, this is stupid stuff*).

TO WITTER BYNNER

University College, London
8 April 1903.

My dear Sir,

I am much obliged by your letter and the poem[1] which you have been good enough to send me, and by the kindness which they express.

I am yours very faithfully
A. E. Housman.

Harvard MS Eng 1071/1. Envelope addressed 'Witter Bynner Esq. | McClure's Magazine | 141–155 East Twenty-Fifth St. | New York | U. S. A.' Bynner/Haber (1957), 3.

TO HENRY JACKSON

17 North Road | Highgate N.
4 May 1903.

My dear Jackson,

I write to inform you of the safe arrival of Platt: my own you will probably infer by some logical process derived from the study of Aristotle, so I need not explicitly record it.

I think, in spite of the weather, I have enjoyed this visit to Cambridge more than any other.

Yours very truly
A. E. Housman.

TCC Add. MS c. 32⁴⁹, Maas, 64–5.

TO WITTER BYNNER

University College, London
3 June 1903.

My dear Sir,

You seem to admire my poems even more than I admire them myself, which is very noble of you, but will most likely be difficult to keep up for any great length of time. However, it is not for me to find fault with you; and naturally there is a pleasure in receiving such ardent letters as yours.

---

[1] *With a Copy of 'A Shropshire Lad':* He whistles of the lasting sleep | A melody to hear and keep, | Beguiling you the little while | You've need to sigh and chance to smile, || And whistles next of happy things | That each unhappy waking brings. | Until you've half forgotten why | You've need to smile and chance to sigh.

Bynner published other poems about AEH: *To A. E. Housman* (see AEH to Bynner, 6 Aug. 1924, n. 1); *Housman* in *Against The Cold* (1940); and *A. E. Housman* in *Take Away The Darkness* (1947).

As to your enquiries: I wrote the book when I was 35,[1] and I expect to write another when I am 70, by which time your enthusiasm will have had time to cool. My trade[2] is that of professor of Latin in this college: I suppose that my classical training has been of some use to me in furnishing good models, and making me fastidious, and telling me what to leave out. My chief object in publishing my verses was to give pleasure to a few young men here and there, and I am glad if they have given pleasure to you.

I am yours very truly
A. E. Housman.

Harvard MS Eng 1071/2. Envelope addressed 'Witter Bynner Esq. | Mc Clure's Magazine | 141 East Twenty-Fifth St. | New York. | U. S. A.' Bynner/Haber (1957), 4; Maas, 65.

TO GRANT RICHARDS

17 North Road | Highgate N.
5 June 1903.

My dear Richards,

There is no American publication which regularly reviews classical books, but the *American Journal of Philology* (Johns'[1] Hopkins University, Baltimore) reviews a certain number, and I have no objection to your sending them a copy.[2] But I doubt if they would review it: American scholars are mere grammarians and collectors of statistics, and what we call critical scholarship hardly exists there.

Yours sincerely
A. E. Housman.

The *Classical Review* circulates in America and has American sub-editors.

Illinois MS. Richards, 52; Maas, 65.

---

[1] Not accurate, as is noted in Bynner/Haber, 4. At least 7 and at most 15 poems were done before AEH was 35, and 36 of the 63 poems in *ASL* were completed after his thirty-sixth birthday. See *Poems* (1997), Introduction, lvi–lvii.

[2] 'Formerly used very widely, including professions': *OED* (*sb.* 5.a.). Dr Johnson remarks of Cibber's work as a playwright, 'that was his trade': *Boswell's Life of Johnson*, ed. George Birkbeck Hill (1891), 3. 83. (not cited in *OED*). AEH uses the word on grounds of deriving a livelihood: see AEH to Bynner, 14 Dec. 1903, n. 1.

[1] For 'Johns'.

[2] *AJP* did not review *Manilius I* as such, but W. A. Merrill inserted a brief note on AEH's polemical style at 27 (1906), 487.

TO WALTER ASHBURNER

17 North Road | Highgate N.
21 June 1903.

My dear Ashburner,

Will you come and dine at the Café Royal on Tuesday July 7th, at 7. 30?

I hope everything went well at Wiesbaden. It is a place I am often incited to go and see, as a lady lives there who is one of my oldest friends;[1] but Germany does not attract me so much as other places, and I hate the thought of having to learn up phrases of conversation and the names for common objects in a third continental language.

The Committee of Management, on being deserted by us, has become the scene of various excitements: Stephen Coleridge[2] having accused our vivisectors of torturing dogs so loud that the Slade School cannot paint (and perhaps that explains it), and Lord Kelvin[3] having said in *our* Botanical Theatre (to the horror of Karl Pearson[4] and doubtless of our eminent founders)[5] that the vegetable kingdom requires a God, though the mineral could do without him.

Yours very truly
A. E. Housman.

NLS MS 20369, fos. 203–4. Ashburner/Bell (1976), 13.

---

[1] Sophie Becker.

[2] Stephen [William Buchanan] Coleridge (1854–1936). Educated at TCC. Barrister, author, Director of the National Anti-Vivisection Society, and founder of the NSPCC.

[3] William Thomson, Baron Kelvin (1824–1907), scientist and inventor. Fellow of Peterhouse, Cambridge, 1846–52, 1872–1907; Professor of Natural Philosophy, Glasgow, 1846–99; FRS, 1851, and President, 1890–4; OM, 1902. He retained a strong religious faith throughout his life.

[4] Professor of Applied Mathematics and Mechanics at UCL. See the note on the letter to Lily Thicknesse, 11 June 1900.

[5] UCL, which first admitted students in 1828, was committed to higher education free from religious tests, and became known as the 'godless institution of Gower Street'. Chief founders, and influences on its secular, rational, and utilitarian principles, were Henry Peter Brougham, first Baron Brougham and Vaux (1778–1868) and Jeremy Bentham (1748–1832).

TO GRANT RICHARDS

17 North Road | Highgate N.
22 June 1903.

Dear Richards,

I have no objection to Mr Ettrick[1] setting the verses to music; but I have not exacted fees from other people who have set other pieces, so I don't want to begin now. Vanity, not avarice, is my ruling passion; and so long as young men write to me from America saying that they would rather part with their hair than with their copy of my book, I do not feel the need of food and drink.

Yours sincerely
A. E. Housman.

Illinois MS. LC-GR t.s. Richards, 54 (nearly complete); Maas, 66.

TO GRANT RICHARDS

17 North Road | Highgate N.
24 June 1903.

My dear Richards,

As I started with the vague notion that the book would cost about £100, I regard anything short of that as clear gain. Also my classes have been unusually large this year, and the extra fees may possibly balance this extra expenditure; which tempts one to believe in the existence of Providence. I rather think that the difference between the printers' estimate and the actual cost is caused not merely by my additions and alterations but also by an initial miscalculation on their part as to the amount of matter contained in the manuscript.

Would you add to the list of people to whom copies are to be sent—
J. W. Mackail Esq.
    6 Pembroke Gardens
      Kensington
        W

Yours sincerely
A. E. Housman.

Illinois MS. Richards, 55 (nearly complete); Maas, 66.

---

[1] Henry Havelock Ettrick, who published some song settings, 1903–4, though a setting of a Housman poem is not among them.

TO GRANT RICHARDS

17 North Road | Highgate N.
18 July 1903.

My dear Richards,

1. I enclose a cheque for £83. 9. 0.

2. Is there any press-cutting agency which can be trusted to collect notices from the learned journals of the Continent?

3. There is still one more person to whom I want a copy to be sent,— M. Louis Brandin[1]

62 Faubourg S. Antoine
Paris

Yours sincerely
A. E. Housman.

Illinois MS. Richards, 56 (excerpt).

TO GRANT RICHARDS

17 North Road | Highgate N.
24 July 1903

My dear Richards,

I can only give the *full* address of two of the enclosed; but I suppose the names of the towns where they are published will be enough.

Mackail congratulates me on my publisher 'who has produced quite an elegant book'; and he is quite an authority.

I rather gather, from some letters which I have received, that the copies sent to my friends were not accompanied by an indication that they were sent by me.

Yours sincerely
A. E. Housman.

Illinois MS. Richards, 56 (excerpts); Maas, 66–7.

---

[1] Louis Maurice Brandin (1874–1940), who consulted MSS of Juvenal in Paris for AEH: edn. of Juvenal (1905), viii–ix; Naiditch (1988), 240 n. 78–2. AEH also sent him a signed copy of the edn. (now in the Rare Book and Manuscript Library, Columbia University). Brandin was later elected Fielden Professor of French and of Romance Philology in the University of London.

TO GRANT RICHARDS

17 North Road | Highgate N.
26 July 1903.

My dear Richards,

I should like the two morocco-bound copies to have the edges cut all round and gilt all round.[1] No gilt should be put on the edges of the interleaved copy, which is merely for me to scribble in.

I am obliged to you for Ellis's letter, which I return.

I should be glad if you would take such steps as may seem good to you for collecting press-cuttings from the learned journals of the Continent.

Yours sincerely
A. E. Housman.

Illinois MS. LC-GR t.s. Richards, 56 (excerpts); Maas, 67.

TO J. W. MACKAIL

17 North Road, Highgate N.
31 July 1903.

Dear Mackail,

Many thanks for your notes,[1] which I will perpend (odious word). I put down here some remarks on some of them.

34 I meant the words "notitiae congruenter" to forestall your objection: the names were not revealed by Mercury directly, but they owe their existence to his revelation of the properties which they indicate. 30 and 31 were placed after 37 by Stoeber;[2] but the three lines 35–37 cannot belong to the sentence "quis foret ... conatus?"; they evidently describe the purpose of the gods in unfolding astronomy to men.

[1] One of these copies of the *Manilius I* went to its dedicatee, Moses Jackson: AEH to GR, 11 Aug. 1903. AEH inscribed it 'M. J. Jackson | from A. E. Housman.' The volume was sold at Sotheby's on 6 Nov. 2001. Maas, 67 n., conjectures plausibly that the other copy was for Lucy Housman.

[1] On AEH's edn. of *Manilius I*. On 24 June AEH had arranged for a copy to be sent to Mackail.

[2] Elias Stoeber in the commentary added to the 1767 reprint of the edn. of 1739 by Richard Bentley. AEH's copy survives, and bears his annotations: Naiditch (2003), 126. AEH held Bentley in the highest esteem, but not Stoeber: 'Stoeber's mind, though that is no name to call it by, was one which turned as unswervingly to the false, the meaningless, the unmetrical, and the ungrammatical, as the needle to the pole': Preface to *Manilius I*; Ricks (1988), 375.

88 I don't think there is any Latin word in which *inter* is prefixed to another preposition. The first ship might naturally be supposed to be a *linter*, a hollowed trunk.

214 was ejected by Bentley; but first we want to know in what form the interpolator wrote it for at present it will not construe. You say that "259, 261 seem to go better after 260"; but then 260 will refer to the zodiac and be foolish: and you go on "the *signa* of 255 includes both the fixed stars *omnia quae caelo possis numerare*:—but in your order of verses, as I say, these words refer to the zodiac only—"and the planets"—but Manilius never elsewhere calls the planets *signa*.

288 *diuerso cardine* means the two opposite poles, and answers to Arat. 24. καί μιν πειραίνουσι δύω πόλοι ἀμφοτέρωθεν.

340 But did Leda ride on Jupiter's back? Europa did.

355 I think Germanicus 199 shows that *relictam* must be kept and referred to Andromeda.

407–9 "An ample guarantee that she possesses these powers is the colour and motion of the star that glitters at her mouth. It is hardly less than the sun himself, only it is placed far off and darts with its blue-green countenance a light that conveys no heat."

417 Is there any objection to *una*? Coruus and Crater are closely connected by the fact that they are both perched on the poor long-suffering Anguis, and by the story told in Ovid fast. II 243–266.

571 "Why *medio*?" because only at midsummer does the sun touch the tropic of Cancer.

588 may not be a pretty line, but Manilius cannot have mentioned the distance between all the other circles and omitted the distance between these two; especially if he was going to add up the numbers and give the total as 30 in 594. I don't think he would be likely to write *per ter denas* when he might have written *per tricenas*. Why do you say that the objection that the *fines tempora signantes* are 3, not 5, applies equally to 598? That verse means that the circles keep pace with one another in their diurnal revolution and that they rise in the east as fast as they set in the west.

680 "The zodiac is not the *culmen*"; no, nor is the milky way at 714: the *culmen* is the sky overhead, which these circles decorate. *caelare* takes two sorts of accusatives: the material on which the *caelatura* is imposed (caelare argentum), and the figure which the *caelatura* imposes (caelare centauros). *caelatum culmen* answers to the first of these, and *caelatus*

Delphinus to the second, but *caelatum lumen* to neither. The *lumen* is neither the material chiselled (that is *tenebrae* rather) nor the form created by chiselling: it is the touch of the chisel itself.

766 The society in the milky way was much too select to admit either *castra* or *Troia*.

788 Yes, *prior palma*. Marcellus was the third winner (Virgil "tertia palma Diores") of the *spolia opima*, Cossus was *prior palma*, and Romulus *prima*.

825 If you want a participle to agree with *fine* I think it will have to be masculine in Manilius. I am very much pleased and flattered that you should have read the commentary through. So little did I venture to hope that you would, that originally I did not think of sending you a copy of the book: it was your sending me your *Odyssey*[3] shortly before that brought it down on your devoted head.

> Yours very truly
> A. E. Housman.

Lilly MSS 1. 1. 3. Maas, 402–4.

TO LAURENCE HOUSMAN

> 17 North Road | Highgate N.
> 9 August 1903.

My dear Laurence,

To write a paper on Patmore would be an awful job, especially in the holidays, so I send you two poems, of which you can print whichever you think the least imperfect.[1] I hope you won't succeed in getting anything from Meredith,[2] as I am a respectable character and do not care to be seen in the company of galvanised corpses. By this time he stinketh: for he hath been dead twenty years.[3]

> Your affectionate brother
> A. E. Housman.

BMC MS. Memoir, 168; Maas, 67.

---

[3] Translated into English, 3 vols. (1903–10).

[1] LH had asked AEH to contribute an essay on Coventry Patmore to *The Venture: An Annual of Art and Literature*, which he edited with Somerset Maugham. AEH sent him *Atys* (*AP* I) and *The Oracles* (*LP* XXV), and LH printed the latter, its earliest publication: *Memoir*, 168, 212.

[2] George Meredith (1828–1909), novelist, poet, and man of letters. He made no contribution to *The Venture*.

[3] John 11: 39: 'by this time he stinketh: for he hath been dead four days'. Meredith's reputation was high at this time.

TO THE DUCHESS OF SUTHERLAND

17 North Road | Highgate N.
11 Aug. 1903.

Dear Duchess of Sutherland,

I send with much pleasure a short piece of verse for inclusion in your book,[1] if you think it worthy of the eminent company which you have gathered together.

I am,

dear Duchess of Sutherland,

yours very faithfully
A. E. Housman.

Princeton MS (Robert H. Taylor Collection).

TO GRANT RICHARDS

17 North Road | Highgate N.
11 Aug. 1903.

My dear Richards,

I don't want to appear impatient, but I shall leave for the continent in about a week's time, and I particularly desire to have one of the morocco-bound copies of the Manilius before then, in order to send it to India to the friend to whom the book is dedicated.[1] I suppose it must be nearly ready now.

The Duchess of Sutherland is under the impression that I not only gave her my consent to print some verses of mine in a novel of hers, but also wrote her a kind letter about it; neither of which things did I ever do. I have no doubt that you gave her my consent, as you have given it to other people; and I have no particular objection: but when it comes to writing kind letters to Duchesses I think it is time to protest.

Yours sincerely
A. E. Housman.

Illinois MS. LC-GR t.s. Richards, 56; Maas, 68.

---

[1] *Astronomy (LP* XVII), for *Wayfarer's Love: Contributions from Living Poets* (1904), ed. the Duchess of Sutherland. It was the first printing of the poem. The anthology was published in aid of the Potteries and Newcastle Cripples' Guild.

[1] See AEH to GR, 26 July 1903, and note.

TO GRANT RICHARDS'S PUBLISHING MANAGER

17 North Road | Highgate N.
14 Aug. 1903

Dear Sir,

I have received the interleaved copy of the Manilius, for which I am obliged.

I am leaving England on Friday the 21st inst., and I hope it may be possible to send me one of the morocco copies before then.[1] If not, my address *until the 26th* will be

Hotel Normandy
Rue de l'Echelle[2]
Paris.

After the 26th I shall have no permanent address.

I will try to find out the exact address of the *Revue Critique*.

I am yours faithfully
A. E. Housman.

Illinois MS. LC-GR t.s. Richards, 57 (excerpt).

TO GRANT RICHARDS

[Venice
10 Sept. 1903]

If I can find sufficient industry I hope to go on with the Manilius; but not immediately, because at this moment I am rather sick of writing and want to read; moreover book II is the most serious job of the whole lot. I am sure your father's annotations[1] would be valuable.

Either you or I or the Duchess of Sutherland seems to have a treacherous memory: let us hope it is the Duchess.

Yrs
A. E. Housman.

*Illinois MS: p.c. addressed 'Grant Richards Esq. | 48 Leicester Square W. C. | London |
(Inghilterra)'. LC-GR t.s. Richards, 57, where the date and place are supplied; Maas, 68.*

---

[1] See AEH to GR, 26 July 1903, and note.   [2] For 'l'Échelle'.

[1] GR had offered AEH his father's copy of Manilius bearing his manuscript annotations: Richards, 57 n.

TO GILBERT MURRAY

17 North Road, Highgate N.
22 Sept. 1903.

Dear Murray,

I have just come back from Italy and found your letter here, and as regards the Music Hall I hasten to observe that it is your own fault if I have not taken you there already: the last time I saw you in London you had armed yourself with tickets for Duse's *Magda*[1] and were not amenable. If you will let me know a little beforehand when you think of being next in town, and what evening or evenings you will be free, I will get you to come and dine somewhere with me, and try to find some other educated person to keep us company. Next month? I am bound to say however that on the last three occasions of going to a Music Hall I found the entertainment of the most harrowing dulness: I don't know whether it is that the Halls are deteriorating or that I am improving.

Radicalism in textual criticism is just as bad as conservativism; but it is not now rampant, and conservati \vi/sm is. Radicalism was rampant 30 or 40 years ago, and it was then rebuked by Madvig[2] and Haupt:[3] now it is conservativism that wants rebuking. Similarly, in social morality, puritanism is a pest; but if I were writing an Epistle to the Parisians I should not dwell on this truth, because it is not a truth which the Parisians need to consider: the pest they suffer from is quite different.

Some time ago I saw somewhere an extract from a prelude of yours to a tale of chivalry, in heroic couplets, which struck me as very rich and fine: I should be glad to hear any more news of it.

Yours very truly
A. E. Housman.

Bodleian MSS Gilbert Murray, 9. 98–9. Maas, 68–9.

---

[1] Eleonora Duse (1858–1924), the celebrated Italian actress, appeared in London, 1893–1923, to enthusiastic receptions. She was famous for playing leading roles in plays by Gabriele D'Annunzio and Henrik Ibsen. *Magda* was the English translation of the play *Heimat* (performed in 1893) by the leading German naturalist writer Hermann Sudermann (1857–1928). It was first produced in London in 1896.

[2] Johan Nicolai Madvig (1804–86) was the Danish classical scholar who helped lay the foundations of modern textual scholarship of Latin and Greek. He was Professor of Latin Language and Literature at the University of Copenhagen, 1829–80. For evidence of AEH's esteem of Madvig, see the letter of 30 Nov. 1919 to Phillimore, and the *Cambridge Inaugural Lecture* (1911), Ricks (1988), 299: 'Half a century later the English learnt Latin from the continent, ... from ... Lachmann and Madvig and Ritschl'. See also *Poems* (1997), 254–5, 540–1.

[3] Moriz Haupt (1808–74). German classical scholar, and pupil of Karl Lachmann.

TO WITTER BYNNER

17 North Road | Highgate N.
13 Oct. 1903.

Dear Mr Bynner,

With reference to your kind letter of Sept. 10, there is no 'next book of verses' in existence, nor do I know that there ever will be; but if there ever is, I will bear in mind what you say.[1]

Yours very truly
A. E. Housman.

Harvard MS Eng 1071/3. Bynner/Haber (1957), 5.

TO GILBERT MURRAY

17 North Road | Highgate N.
13 Oct. 1903.

Dear Murray,

Many thanks for the Introduction. I have also been reading your translations from Euripides.[1] With your command of language and metre you are really a noble example of ἐγκράτεια,[2] in that you don't produce volumes of original poetry.

I don't think I have anything on the plays you mention.

Yours very truly
A. E. Housman.

Bodleian MSS Gilbert Murray, 9. 107–8. Maas, 69.

---

[1] 'Bynner had asked him to let McClure, Phillips & Company publish his next book': Bynner/Haber (1957), 5 n.

[1] *Hippolytus* and *The Bacchae*, in *Euripides* (1902).   [2] Self-control.

TO WITTER BYNNER

University College, London
14 Dec. 1903.

Dear Mr Bynner,

I have never taken money for any of my verses,[1] and accordingly I return you, with many thanks, the draft which you have kindly sent me.[2]

I have no copy of the piece called *The Olive*,[3] which is not particularly good: it was published on the conclusion of peace[4] in June 1902, in the *Outlook*.[5] I enclose however a poem[6] which I have contributed to a collection which the Duchess of Sutherland is bringing out for charitable purposes;[7] only, as the book is not yet published, you must not go printing it in America.

I am much obliged for the copies of the magazine, an[d] remain

Yours very truly
A. E. Housman.

Harvard MS Eng 1071/4, torn at 'and'. Envelope addressed 'Witter Bynner Esq. | c/ McClure's Magazine | Fourth Avenue & 23ʳᵈ Street | New York | U. S. A'. Bynner/Haber (1957), 6; Maas, 70.

[1] Richards, 24, reports AEH saying in one of their earliest conversations: 'I am not a poet by trade; I am a professor of Latin. I do not wish to make profit out of my poetry. It is not my business.' After the publication of *LP* in 1922, AEH agreed to accept a royalty of fifteen per cent on the book (Richards, 200). See AEH to GR, 28 Dec. 1922.

[2] Richards, 24, reports AEH also telling him about returning the cheque sent to him every time a poem of his appeared in McClure's magazine.

[3] Two drafts appear pp. 230 and 231 respectively of *Nbk B*, and the second contains corrections to the version printed in *The Outlook*.

[4] The peace of Vereeniging ended the second Boer War on 31 May 1902.

[5] 9. 227 (7 June 1902), signed 'A. E. Housman', at the end of the second of the Boer Wars (1899–1902).

[6] *Astronomy*, later *LP* XVII.

[7] See AEH to The Duchess of Sutherland, 11 Aug. 1903, and note. The poem appeared, signed, on p. 65 of the volume.

1904

TO DR P. HABBERTON LULHAM

17 North Road | Highgate N.
28 June 1904.

Dear Sir,

I have received your kind gift[1] and have been reading it with much pleasure. The pieces *Red Dawn, Now, Forbid, A Sorrow in Spring, Birds,* and *Stricken,* particularly took my fancy, as well as many passages in the other poems, such as the opening of *Between the Tides.* If I may make one criticism, it is that although I knew that *morn* and *dawn* rhymed in London, I cherished the hope that it was not so in Kent, at least in Thanet.

With sincere thanks I remain

Yours very truly
A. E. Housman.

Hove Central Library MS Autograph Collection, 34. Maas, 70.

TO GRANT RICHARDS

17 North Road | Highgate N.
27 July 1904.

My dear Richards

Thanks to your treatment last night I am quite restored to health this morning.

I enclose a copy of our joint work.[1] The results of your collaboration are noted on pages 4, 22, 45, 55, 71, 77, 78, 92, 116 (this last occurred also in the previous edition, where I overlooked it). I don't mark details of punctuation.

I am bound to say however that the leather binding[2] makes a very pretty book.

Yours sincerely
A. E. Housman.

Illinois MS. Richards, 58; Maas, 70–1.

[1] Lulham's vol. of verse *Devices and Desires* (1904).

[1] The 5th edn. of *ASL,* in GR's 'Smaller Classics' series. The text contained numerous errors: see *Poems* (1997), Introduction, xxv, xxvi–xxvii.

[2] Sold at 1*s.* (the cloth-bound version being 6*d.*).

TO GRANT RICHARDS

17 North Road | Highgate N.
10 August 1904

My dear Richards,
    You can do what you like about the enclosed.

Yours sincerely
A. E. Housman.

Illinois MS. LC-GR t.s.

TO GRANT RICHARDS

17 North Road | Highgate N.
18 Aug. 1904

My dear Richards,
    The text and notes of the Juvenal[1] which you are burning to publish are now finished, and I think the printers had better have them to play with while I am writing the introduction; so as I expect to go abroad on the 27th I propose to send you the manuscript some time next week.
    My notion is that the book should be identical in form and print with the Manilius, which is so much admired by people who are connoisseurs in these matters. The text is about four times as long as the Manilius, but the notes are on a very much smaller scale, and the introduction will be much shorter too; so that the whole volume would probably be rather slimmer.

Yours sincerely
A. E. Housman.

Grant Richards Esq.

Illinois MS. LC-GR t.s. Richards, 58 (excerpts); Maas, 71.

TO GRANT RICHARDS

17 North Road | Highgate N.
26 August 1904

My dear Richards,
    As I am just going abroad for a month, I send you by Parcel Post, registered, the type-written text and manuscript notes of the Juvenal. Will you acknowledge receipt to me at 'Hotel Normandy, Rue de l'Échelle, Paris', where I expect to be till Wednesday.

---

[1] *D. Iunii Iuuenalis saturae editorum in usum*, published by Richards in 1905. The text was based on that prepared by AEH for the *Corpus Poetarum Latinorum*, ed. J. P. Postgate, vol. II, part V (1905).

To what I said in my former letter I add that perhaps it would be best for text and notes to be printed at first separately in slip, as this (I suppose) increases the ease and decreases the expense of corrections.

On the opposite page are some directions for the printers.

Yours sincerely

A. E. Housman

Grant Richards Esq.

Illinois MS. LC-GR t.s.

TO GRANT RICHARDS

PÉRA-PALACE

CONSTANTINOPLE le 5me *SEPTEMBRE* 1904

My dear Richards,

I have not received an acknowledgement of the priceless manuscript I sent you when I left England ten days ago. Anxiety is preying on my health, and if the Sultan next Friday observes my haggard countenance in the crowd, he will certainly suppose me to be a conspirator and order me to be thrown into the Bosphorus: then you will have to intervene, as John Lane did in the case of William Watson;[1] and that will cost you much more than a postage stamp. If my money holds out I shall be here long enough to hear from you.

Yours sincerely

A. E. Housman.

Illinois MS. Richards, 59; Maas, 71.

TO GRANT RICHARDS

PÉRA-PALACE

CONSTANTINOPLE, le 9 Sept 1904

My dear Richards,

Your letter addressed to Highgate has just reached me here. I advised you not to produce the book at your own expense, and now you recognise my superior wisdom. I will pay for it. Will you get from the printers an

---

[1] In Max Beerbohm's *The Poet's Corner* (1904), the caricature of Watson carries the caption: 'Mr William Watson, secretly ceded by the British Government to Abdul Hamid, but, in the nick of time, saved from the trap-door to the Bosphorus by the passionate intercession of Mr John Lane.' In *The Purple East: a Series of Sonnets on England's Desertion of Armenia* (1896), Watson attacked the Turkish despot Abdul Hamid for his purging of the Armenians, and the British Government for turning a blind eye on the situation. Most of the sonnets had been published in the *Westminster Gazette* in 1895–6.

estimate of the cost? In addition to what I have sent there will be an introduction of some 30 pages or more. It will not be anything like £84, as that amount was reached in the case of the Manilius largely because of unforseen[1] alterations.

Yours sincerely
A. E. Housman.

I shall be home in about 10 days.

Illinois MS. LC-GR t.s. Maas, 72.

TO LUCY HOUSMAN

[17 North Road | Highgate N.
Sept. 1904]

The ruins are not nearly so lofty as some of our English castles, but what strikes one is their immense extent and the loneliness around. Inside, the skirts of the city are thinly peopled, more market gardens than houses; outside, the country is rolling downs and graveyards, with cultivation only here and there. A Turkish graveyard is a forest of cypresses with an undergrowth of tombstones, which dies much sooner than the trees; for a Turkish tombstone is no thicker and no broader than a plank, and is ill fixed in the ground, so that they soon begin to lean in all directions, and finally lie down flat upon the earth. The Jews bury their dead on the bare hillside under slabs: the great cemetery is west of Pera, above the Golden Horn, and makes the downs look as if they were sprinkled with large hailstones or coarse-grained salt.

Constantinople is famous for its sunsets, and I used to watch them from the western edge of the hill that Pera stands on, looking over the cypresses of what was once a graveyard but now contains only dust and dogs and is beginning to be built over. From here you look across the Golden Horn and see the western half of Stambul, and the downs still further west, where the sun goes under. The sky would be orange and the hillside of the city would be dark with a few lights coming out, and the Golden Horn would reflect the blue or grey of the upper sky; and as there was a new moon, the crescent used to come and hang itself appropriately over the mosque of Muhammad the Conqueror.

It was a great comfort to me not to have you with me in Constantinople: it would have been 'poor doggie!' every step of the way, and we should never have got a hundred yards from the hotel. They lie all about the

---

[1] For 'unforeseen'.

streets and the pavement, mostly asleep, and almost all have got something the matter with them. They are extremely meek and inoffensive: Turkey is a country where dogs and women are kept in their proper place, and consequently are quite unlike the pampered and obstreperous animals we know under those names in England. The Turkish dog spends his life much like the English cat: he sleeps by day, and at night he grows melodious. He does not bark over his quarrels so much as English dogs do, and when he does bark it is sometimes rather like the quacking of a soprano duck; but he wails: whether he is winning or losing seems to make no difference, so dejected are his spirits. I soon got used to the noise however, and it did not spoil my sleep. The people are very good in not treading on them, and so are the beasts of burden; but wheeled vehicles, which have got much commoner of late years, are <not> \less/ good to them, and the trams are not good to them at all. One night in the dark I trod on a dog lying exactly in the middle of the road: he squealed in a bitterly reproachful tone for a certain time; when he had finished, the next dog barked in an expostulatory manner for the same period, and then the incident was closed. Carts drawn by white oxen or by black buffaloes are pretty frequent in the streets; and once my carriage was stopped by a train of camels, but these are not common. The sheep, many of which are horned, have the whitest and prettiest wool I have ever seen. The Turks keep fighting rams as pets, and make matches between them: these lively creatures may sometimes be met in the streets, invading the green-grocers' shops, and butting at the boys, who catch them by the horns.

The population is very mixed, and largely descended from kidnapped Christians. Pure Turks are rather rare, Greeks and Armenians common: a man is an Armenian when his nose is like this ͨ. I have come across the handsomest faces I ever saw: their figures are not so good. Some of the Greeks make you rub your eyes; the features and complexions are more like pictures than realities: though the women unfortunately bleach themselves by keeping out of the sun. The Turks, when they are good looking, I like even better; there is an aquiline type like the English aristocracy very much improved: if I could send you the photograph of a young man who rowed me to the Sweet Waters of Asia, and asked you to guess his name, you would instantly reply 'Aubrey de Vere Plantagenet'. But unless they take to outdoor work they get fat at an early age. What colour there is in the clothes of the people at Constantinople is chiefly centred in the red fez; but at Brusa in Asia, the old Turkish capital, where I spent two nights, the streets are very picturesque with the various hues [...] last centuries of the Byzantine empire, and helped the Turks to take Stamboul. It is the great place to see the view from, as it commands the whole city, and shows you parts of the Bosphorus and Golden Horn and Sea of Marmora and the coast of Asia opposite. It is now used as a watch tower for fires, which are common and dangerous in a city mostly built of wood. <That> The watchmen pace round and look out of the eight windows continually for smoke or fire: then they signal <with> by hanging out a flag by day or a lamp by night from the window which looks towards the fire, and this sign is seen by all the fire-stations. The fire-engines then go to the spot indicated and gaze at the conflagration: if the owner of the property likes to hire them, they will put out the fire for him, but not otherwise.

I went to see the Sultan go to […] and stuffs of the shirts and sashes and knickerbockers.

Well, I must stop somewhere.

Your loving son
A. E. Housman.

On my journey to Brusa I was accosted by a fellow-traveller who turned out to be the Recorder of Hereford, an amiable gentleman, though rather egotistical.

BMC MS (incomplete). Memoir, 142–5 and Maas, 72–4 (both with passages missing from the already incomplete MS). Maas, 72 n., follows LH in giving the address as Constantinople, despite deducing that the letter was written after AEH's return to England. He also follows him in thinking that the passage beginning 'It is the great place to see the view from' is a fragment of a subsequent letter. I think it is probably part of the same long letter: its subject-matter and tone are the same; at the end AEH is conscious of the considerable length; and it would seem tedious for him to have written two long letters to the same person dealing with a trip to the same place abroad.

TO GRANT RICHARDS

17 North Road | Highgate N.
23 Sept. 1904

My dear Richards,

The printers' estimate for the Juvenal seems absurd, and they don't appear to understand the facts.

They say that 'the extent of both books is nearly the same'. That is true if they are talking about the amount of paper, but false if they are talking about the amount of print. The chief expense of the Manilius must have been the voluminous notes: the notes in the Juvenal, I should think, are not one quarter of what the Manilius notes were. The *text* of the Juvenal is about four times the text of the Manilius; but the text, though it fills a lot of paper, cannot be expensive to set up;—it is merely 4000 lines or so. The only thing that I can think of to explain their estimate is that the

Juvenal notes will require a much larger proportion of clarendon type, which perhaps is expensive.

Moreover the final cost of the Manilius was largely due, I had supposed, to the rather numerous alterations which I made in proof. Their original estimate for the Manilius was nothing like £84: it was something less than £50. (True, this was when I thought the introduction would be only 25 pages, and it afterwards ran to 75 pages; but they now say that introductions are cheap to print, so this won't explain the difference.) Possibly you have the original estimate for the Manilius in your archives: if so, it would be useful and instructive to compare it.

You understand what my point is: a page of the Manilius consisted on the average of less than 12 lines of text (large print) and more than 35 lines of notes (small print). In the Juvenal the proportion, I should think, will be more like 25 lines of text to 15 lines of notes, or often less: I remember one place (at the end of the 5th satire) where there are 30 lines of text without a single note.

I *can* pay the sum they ask, but I very much object to, as Constantinople and the Orient Express are both pretty expensive, and I want to go to Italy next spring.

Yours sincerely
A. E. Housman.
P T. O.

If they are now printing the text and notes, as I understand they are, it ought to be quite easy to ascertain the proportion they bear to one another.

Illinois MS. LC-GR t.s. (incomplete); Richards, 59–60; Maas, 74–5.

TO GRANT RICHARDS

17 North Road | Highgate N.
28 Sept. 1904

My dear Richards,

I shall make no objection to the price of £70. 17. 11 now asked by the printers. It is probably exorbitant (they were most likely encouraged by the tameness and promptitude with which I paid £84 for the Manilius), but never mind.

Yours sincerely
A. E. Housman.

Grant Richards Esq.

LC-GR3 t.s.

TO GILBERT MURRAY

13 Oct. 1904

UNIVERSITY COLLEGE, LONDON. | GOWER STREET, W.C.

Dear Murray,

If you would send me two tickets[1] for the 21st or 28th I should be pleased to make use of them.

You cannot deny that you are now in London, therefore your long-impending music-hall can no further be delayed. When is it to be? I am engaged to morrow[2] and on Saturday, but not later, except that Tuesdays and Wednesdays are less convenient than other evenings.

I received some weeks ago a letter from South Africa whose contents may interest you. The writer, whose name I forget, divides poetry into two classes: that which is tainted with the spirit of Le Gallienne, and that which is not. The latter class is small, and indeed appears to comprise only the following examples. First, and seemingly foremost, *A Shropshire Lad*. Secondly, Shakespeare's songs (not, it appears, anything else of his). Thirdly, a few early English poems. Fourthly, Goethe's *Ueber allen Gipfeln*.[3] Fifthly a translation from a fragment of Euripides, about woods,[4] which he once heard read by Professor Murray of Glasgow.

Yours very truly
A. E. Housman.

Bodleian MSS Gilbert Murray, 10. 124–5. Maas, 75.

TO GILBERT MURRAY

17 North Road | Highgate N.
25 Oct. 1904

Dear Murray,

I went to the Court on Friday with your two tickets and with a good deal of apprehension, as I find it generally a trial to hear actors and actresses reciting verse. But though I can't say that witnessing the play gave me as much pleasure as reading it, it did give me pleasure and indeed excitement. I thought Theseus[1] on the whole the best. Phaedra is one of the parts

---

[1] For Euripides' *Hippolytus*, in Murray's translation, which opened at the Court Theatre on 16 Oct. 1904 after a short run at the Lyric Theatre.

[2] No hyphen.

[3] The opening words of the second *Wandrers Nachtlied*, written in 1780.

[4] The first speech of the Messenger: *Bacchae*, 1043–1152.

[1] 'Alfred Brydone (1864–1920)': Maas, 76 n.

which I used to plan out in detail a long while ago, and Miss Olive's[2] plan, though it may be as good, is rather different from mine, and so I was not quite happy with it. Ben Webster[3] is not Hippolytus, but who is? The most effective and unexpected thing to me was the statue of Cypris standing quiet there all the time.

Your lyrics, which are the most alluring part to read, were of course only imperfectly audible when sung: on the other hand some of the rhetoric in the dialogue came out very well indeed, especially the close of the messenger's speech. I hear that although you have not quite repeated Aeschylus' triumph with the *Eumenides*,[4] you have caused members of the audience to be removed in a fainting condition.

Yours very truly
A. E. Housman.

Bodleian MSS Gilbert Murray, 10. 137–8. Maas, 75–6.

TO GILBERT MURRAY

17 North Road | Highgate N.
4 Nov. 1904.

Dear Murray,

Many thanks for your Euripides,[1] which came just in time to prevent me from buying a copy. It is much the pleasantest edition and clearest apparatus to use; and I have been looking through the earlier part of the *Heracles* in general agreement with your selection of readings. Turning over the pages at random, it strikes me that Verrall[2] has exerted a baleful influence: e.g. <τί> at suppl. 149 is what I should call a perfectly impossible reading. Why didn't Porson[3] make the conjecture? Not from any lack of fondness for palaeographical neatness: he had that taste, and it sometimes led him too far (as when he proposed κριταί <τε> at Aesch.

---

[2] 'Edyth Olive (d. 1956) began on the stage in 1892 in F. R. Benson's company. She later appeared in two other of Murray's translations': Maas, 76 n. She was born in 1872.

[3] '1864–1947, acting since 1887': Maas 76 n.

[4] According to the ancient life of Aeschylus which accompanied his plays, pregnant women miscarried and children died because the Furies in *Eumenides* were so frightening.

[1] Vol. 2 of Murray's Oxford edn.

[2] A[rthur] W[oollgar] Verrall (1851–1912), Fellow of TCC, 1874–1912 and Professor of English at Cambridge, 1911–12. He read proofs of Murray's edn., and Murray thanks him in the preface for communicating to him copious material throughout the entire book. AEH is among those acknowledged for various notes. For further information on AEH and Verrall, see Naiditch (1988), 211–15.

[3] Richard Porson (1759–1808). Regius Professor of Greek at Cambridge from 1792. AEH wondered whether Porson or Jeremiah Markland stood second to Richard Bentley in textual scholarship: *Classical Papers*, 1005.

cho. 37), but not so far as this. In fact Attic tragedy has been studied so long and so minutely by such great men that all the corrections which consist in iteration of syllables, or separation of letters or the like, must almost necessarily have been made already; and when one at this date makes a conjecture of this sort one ought to do it with one's hair standing on end and one's knees giving way beneath one; because the odds are a hundred to one that it is a conjecture which our betters were witheld[4] from making by their superior tact. Such chances as remain for us are practically confined to cases like Horace serm. I 9 39, where I thoroughly believe in Verrall's *sta re*; cases where there was some special obscuring cause, such as ignorance of the form *ste = iste*, which was first brought to light by Lachmann in 1850.

One detail which has just caught my eye: at Her. 1351 the order of the names "Wilamowitz et Wecklein" is neither alphabetical nor chronological. But *suum cuique*[5] is a precept which it is hardly any use trying to keep: e.g. I observe that the Duchess of Sutherland thinks that you are a professor and I only a gentleman. Your poem and mine, by the way, according to Horatio Brown, are the gems of the volume: I think I preferred Mackail and the Irishman who has my initials.[6]

Yours very truly

A. E. Housman.

On p. 27 of the collection there is an easy emendation to be made, quite devoid of palaeographical or neographical probability, but certain none the less.

Bodleian MSS Gilbert Murray, 10. 153–6. Maas, 404–5. The two angle brackets are AEH's, and mean 'insert' (not 'cancelled').

TO GRANT RICHARDS

17 North Road | Highgate N.

17 Nov. 1904.

My dear Richards,

As you sent my Juvenal to the printers early in September, it seems to me that they ought to have done something to it by this time.

Yours sincerely

A. E. Housman.

PM MS. LC-GR t.s. Richards, 61 (excerpts).

---

[4] For 'withheld'.   [5] 'To each his own'.

[6] G[eorge] W[illiam] Russell (1867–1935), poet, dramatist, and journalist, who used the pseudonym 'Æ'.

TO GRANT RICHARDS

17 North Road | Highgate N.
24 Nov. 1904.

My dear Richards,

Almost immediately after I wrote to you last week, I heard, and was very sorry to hear, that there is a crisis in your affairs.[1] I hope that this will come out straight, and in the meantime I do not want to worry you with correspondence: I only write just to let you know, as is proper, that I propose to try to find someone else to undertake the publishing of the Juvenal, though I shall not find anyone who will do it for nothing, as you were good enough to say you would. I suppose I may assume that you have no objection, and I will take silence to mean consent.

I don't know if you would have leisure or inclination to come and dine with me somewhere next week, but I should be very pleased if you would: say Friday Dec. 2nd. Perhaps I could get my brother to come.[2]

Yours sincerely
A. E. Housman.

PM MS. LC-GR t.s. Richards, 61; Maas, 76.

TO GRANT RICHARDS

17 North Road | Highgate N.
28 Nov. 1904

My dear Richards,

Café Royal, 7. 30, Friday next. My brother will come.

I have not done anything about the Juvenal beyond asking the printers whether they had begun to print it. The *Shropshire Lad* I don't at all want to interfere with.

Yours sincerely
A. E. Housman.

PM MS. LC-GR t.s. Richards, 61–2.

---

[1] Richards was declared bankrupt in 1905 and his firm was sold. He resumed business, initially under his wife's name, 'E. Grant Richards', and officially acting as manager. See AEH to Elsina Richards, 8 June 1905.

[2] They dined at the Café Royal, and afterwards, perhaps following a visit to a music-hall, went to the Criterion Bar: Richards, 62 ('I had never before, and have never since, seen him in a bar').

1905

TO LAURENCE BINYON

University College, London
3 Feb. 1905

Dear Sir,

I am much obliged by your letter, and may perhaps write to you later on the subject; but just at present I am not taking any steps with regard to the *Shropshire Lad.*

I am yours truly
A. E. Housman.

BL Loan 29 (papers of Laurence Binyon, placed on deposit by Nicolete Gray).

TO WALLACE RICE

University College, London
15 Feb. 1905.

My dear Sir,

You are very welcome to include in your selection[1] the piece *To An Athlete Dying Young*; but I object to the inclusion of the other two extracts, because one is only a fragment[2] and the other merely mentions football and cricket as palliations of misery.[3] If I may offer advice, I should recommend you not to insert poems containing mere casual allusions to athletics.

I am obliged by the kindness of your letter, and also by the graceful book of poems which you have been good enough to send me.

I am yours very truly
A. E. Housman.

Newberry Library (Chicago) MS Ri. Maas, 77.

---

[1] *The Athlete's Garland* (1905).
[2] Probably *ASL* XXVII 9–16: 'Is football playing... the keeper | Stands up to keep the goal'.
[3] *ASL* XVII 3–4, 7–8: 'Football then was fighting sorrow | For the young man's soul', 'See the son of grief at cricket | Trying to be glad'.

TO WILLIAM STEWART

University College, London
17 February 1905.

Dear Sir,

I gratefully acknowledge the flattering offer of the Honorary Degree of Doctor of Laws which in your letter of yesterday's date you have kindly communicated to me from the Senate of the University of Glasgow. But, for reasons which it would be tedious and perhaps difficult to enumerate, though they seem to me sufficient and decisive, I long ago resolved to decline all such honours, if they should ever be offered me. I have already, with feelings of equal embarrassment, excused myself from accepting a similar title at the hands of another University;[1] and if I ever in the future receive the same compliment I shall return the same reply. I can only beg to express my high appreciation of the kindness which has prompted the Senate of your University to offer me this valued distinction, and my great regret that I am not able to accept it.

I am your obedient servant
A. E. Housman.

W. Stewart Esq.

Glasgow University MS GUA 22369. Maas, 77.

TO GRANT RICHARDS

17 North Road | Highgate N.
1 March 1905.

My dear Richards,

The applicant may publish the songs so far as I am concerned, but I had rather that you should tell her so, as I do not want to write letters to a lady whose name is Birdie.[1]

---

[1] Naiditch (1988), 219, suggests that sometime between 1899 and 1904, and perhaps after the publication of the *Manilius I* in 1903, R. Y. Tyrrell tried to have AEH accept an honorary doctorate from Trinity College, Dublin. AEH subsequently declined at least eight honorary doctorates, as well as election to the British Academy: P. G. Naiditch in *Classical Scholarship: A Biographical Encyclopedia*, ed. Ward W. Briggs and William M. Calder III (1990), 201. The only public honour he ever accepted was an honorary fellowship of his old Oxford college, St John's. LH, *Memoir*, 99, notes that AEH wrote 'This is me' against a passage in a review of T. E. Lawrence's *Seven Pillars of Wisdom* that included 'There was a craving to be famous; and a horror of being known to like being known. Contempt for my passion for distinction made me refuse every offered honour.'

[1] Identified as Birdie (Bywater or Bywaters) Bennett in Naiditch (1995), 162.

I told my solicitors to tell your Trustee the state of things about *A Shropshire Lad*.[2] As to the Manilius, they advised me to take possession of the copies, and offered to store them for me temporarily; and I believe this is now being done.[3] Thank you for the statement of accounts which you sent me the other day.

Yours sincerely
A. E. Housman.

Illinois MS. LC-GR t.s. Richards, 63 (excerpt); Maas, 78.

TO WITTER BYNNER

17 North Road | Highgate N.
3 March 1905.

Dear Mr Bynner,

As you are so good as to offer to send me some books from your catalogue, I should be very glad to have

> *Ivan Ilyitch*, by Tolstoy
> *Letters from a Chinese Official*[1]
> *The Man with the Hoe.*[2]

The new volume of poems in which you take such an affectionate interest seems to be as far off as ever.

I am yours very truly
A. E. Housman.

Harvard MS Eng 1071/5. Bynner/Haber (1957), 8.

---

[2] As there was no contract for *ASL*, rights in it could be sold as Richards's assets. The book remained with Richards's trustee, and in 1906 Richards issued as a 6th edn. the remaining sheets of the 1903 printing.

[3] Richards, 63: 'the stock of the Manilius was his property'.

[1] *Letters from A Chinese Official: Being An Eastern View Of Western Civilization* by G. Lowes Dickinson (1903).

[2] *The Man with The Hoe and Other Poems* by Edwin Markham (1902). See *Poems* (1997), 271, 553, for a short satire prompted by his reading the volume.

TO GRANT RICHARDS

17 North Road | Highgate N.
16 March 1905

My dear Richards,

Many thanks for your father's translation of Heliodorus.[1] I have never read that author, so my mind will be much improved.[2]

The surviving stock of Manilius I am allowing to remain in its present lodgings at Messrs Leighton, where it seems to be eating its head off, for they want about £8 before they will consent to part with it. I ought to finish writing the Juvenal preface in ten days, and the greater part of it went to the printers a fortnight ago, but I have not received the proofs yet. I hope you are as flourishing as can be expected.

Yours sincerely
A. E. Housman.

Illinois MS. LC-GR t.s.; Richards, 63 (excerpt).

TO WITTER BYNNER

17 North Rd., Highgate N. | London
28 March 1905

Dear Sir,

I am much obliged to you for the three books which I have just received, and also for your letter of the 14th. Your office seems to be the spot on earth where I am most esteemed.

I am yours very truly
A. E. Housman.

Harvard MS Eng 1071/6. Bynner/Haber (1957), viii (excerpt), 9.

---

[1] *Heliodorus Aethiopica: or The Adventures of Theagenes and Chariclea,* translated afresh from the Greek by Franklin T. Richards, with short notes and essays. Book I (printed for private circulation, 1905).

[2] In the preface, 4, Richards noted that although Heliodorus is 'generally classed among the *Scriptores Erotici*' his language is 'remarkably free from offence'.

TO GRANT RICHARDS

17 North Road | Highgate N.
11 April 1905.

My dear Richards,

I had better let you know that the Juvenal is now all printed except the index, and is all made up into pages except the preface, so that the question of publication is close at hand.

Yours sincerely
A. E. Housman.

PM MS. LC-GR t.s. Richards, 63 (nearly complete).

TO GRANT RICHARDS

17 North Road | Highgate N.
17 April 1905

My dear Richards,

I am very sorry to see your father's death in to-day's paper;[1] both for the loss to scholarship of his simple and disinterested love of learning, and also that this grief should come upon you now in addition to your other troubles.

I am yours sincerely
A. E. Housman.

PM MS. LC-GR t.s. Richards, 63–4; Maas, 78.

TO GRANT RICHARDS

17 North Road | Highgate N.
19 April 1905

My dear Richards,

I have a letter from R. & R. Clark[1] this morning in which they state the present stage of affairs thus:

'We shall make up the preliminary leaving the publishers' imprint blank, and you can instruct us regarding this when you return proofs.'

I had written to tell them that the paper was to be the same as was used for the Manilius; and on this they say:

---

[1] *The Standard.* He must have missed the obituary in *The Times* on 15 Apr.

[1] Printers.

'Some considerable time ago Mr Richards requested us to write to him when paper was required and give him the opportunity of supplying it. If you wish it supplied by Mr Richards please write to him accordingly, otherwise please let us know and we shall attend to the matter'.

Yours sincerely
A. E. Housman.

Illinois MS. LC-GR t.s.

TO ELIZABETH WISE

17 North Road | Highgate N.
25 April 1905

My dear Mrs Wise,

Here you see the effects of Woodchester air. I am not yet, perhaps, so great an artist as Laurence, but it seems to me that the enclosed sketch[1] (for it is little more) has a simple beauty of its own, and that the likenesses are lifelike.

Yours affectionately
A. E. Housman.

Lilly MSS 1. 1. 3. Maas, 78.

TO GRANT RICHARDS

17 North Road | Highgate N.
4 May 1905

My dear Richards,

The last proofs of the Juvenal have arrived to-day; so is it to be *Grant Richards* or *E. Grant Richards*?[1] Saturday morning will be soon enough for the answer.

Yours sincerely
A. E. Housman.

Illinois MS. LC-GR t.s. Richards, 64 (excerpt).

---

[1] Depicting three adults between the Wise's dachshund Minka and a cockerel. It has 'THIS SIDE UP' at the top and 'DEFENCE OF MINKA' at the bottom. AEH stayed with the Wise family from 20 to 25 Apr. 1905.

[1] See AEH to GR, 24 Nov. 1904, n. 1.

TO GRANT RICHARDS

17 North Road | Highgate N.
7 May 1905.

My dear Richards,
   The only address I added was London,[1] which I suppose is right.
                                        Yours sincerely
                                        A. E. Housman.

Illinois MS.

TO GRANT RICHARDS

17 North Road | Highgate N.
28 May 1905

My dear Richards,
   R. & R. Clark are binding the Juvenal themselves, as they say the style
is quite in their line. They think they will be able to get it done by the
middle of June, and they want to be told where to *deliver* the copies.
                                        Yours sincerely
                                        A. E. Housman.

Illinois MS. LC-GR t.s.

TO GRANT RICHARDS

17 North Road | Highgate N.
5 June 1905

My dear Richards,
   R. & R. Clark have sent me six copies of the Juvenal, of which I send
you one; and they say that the rest of the 100 are finished and ready to be
forwarded.
                                        Yours very truly
                                        A. E. Housman.

Illinois MS. LC-GR t.s.

---

[1] The title-page of the edn. of Juvenal specified 'Londinii'.

TO ELSINA RICHARDS

17 North Road | Highgate N.
8 June 1905.

Dear Mrs Grant Richards,

Many thanks for your letter: I am proud to be your first author.[1] I have told the printers to send you the 94 bound copies which remain of the 100, six having been sent to me. I will send in a few days a list of the individuals and the reviews to which I want to have copies forwarded.

I am yours sincerely
A. E. Housman.

I am sending, to your address, a letter to G. R. which I want him to receive as soon as possible.

Illinois MS. Richards, 64 (excerpt, wrongly dated 1 June); Maas, 79.

TO GRANT RICHARDS

17 North Road | Highgate N.
8 June 1905.

My dear Richards,

As I hear that you want to see me soon, it occurs to me to send you the enclosed,[1] in case you may be willing and able to use it. If you go, I shall be there about 9 o' clock, just drunk enough to be pleasant, but not so incapable as a publisher would like an author to be. If you don't go, you will probably escape a very tiresome entertainment.

Yours sincerely
A. E. Housman.

Illinois MS. Richards, 64 (nearly complete); Maas, 79.

TO GRANT RICHARDS

13. 6. 05
30, ALBEMARLE STREET [LONDON]

Your flamboyant production is not on any account to be printed. The following might serve:

---

[1] See AEH to GR, 24 Nov. 1904.

[1] 'A card for some unspecified entertainment': Richards, 64.

"A critical edition of Juvenal by Mr A. E. Housman, intended to make good some of the principal defects in existing editions, and especially to supply a better knowledge of the manuscripts, will be published by ... "
(No nonsense about Shropshire Lads),

Yrs.
A. E. Housman.

Illinois MS. Pencil. Richards, 64–5 (nearly complete); Maas, 79. In the draft in ink (University of Illinois MS) on headed UCL writing paper, AEH corrected 'in particular' to 'especially', and explicitly stated that the edn. would be 'published by E. Grant Richards'.

TO GRANT RICHARDS

17 North Road | Highgate N.
27 June 1905

My dear Richards,

I suppose the delay is more annoying to you than to me, so I will not declaim about it.

Yours sincerely
A. E. Housman.

Illinois MS. Richards, 65; Maas, 80.

TO KATHARINE TYNAN HINKSON

University College, London
4 July 1905

Dear Mrs Hinkson,

You have my permission to use the verses you require, and I daresay my brother will not be disagreeable.[1]

I am yours sincerely
A. E. Housman.

Texas MS. Maas, 80.

---

[1] In *A Book of Memory: The Birthday Book of the Blessed Dead* (1906) she included four short extracts from *ASL* (stanza 2 of LIV, stanza 3 of XIX, the last two stanzas of XXIII, and the first and last two stanzas of LII), and one short extract from a poem by LH. The extracts from *ASL* were all printed slightly inaccurately.

TO GRANT RICHARDS

17 North Road | Highgate N.
6 July 1905

My dear Richards,

Many thanks.[1] I don't think any advertisement is required: books of this sort are best advertised by reviews and the lists of 'books received' in the learned journals.

Yours sincerely
A. E. Housman.

Illinois MS. Richards, 65.

TO WALTER ASHBURNER

17 North Road | Highgate N.
6 July 1905

Dear Ashburner,

I have told them to send you a copy of an edition of Juvenal which I have just brought out. I wish you to regard it not so much as a monument of genius and erudition as of amiability and forbearance. Though I have the honour of your acquaintance, though you are a palaeographer, and though you reside in Florence, I nevertheless did not ask you to examine for me codex Laurentianus plut. XXXIV 42;[1] and the Commercial History of the Italian Republics[2] has suffered no interruption from me.

Sir John Rotton[3] has brought word that you are not coming to England this summer any more than last. If you were here, your valuable advice would be sought on an important question, for I hear that Ellis[4] is asking undergraduates and other persons whether they think that he had better marry. I have not seen him for some time, and I fear I am rather in disgrace at present through having reviewed his last edition of Catullus in

---

[1] 'I asked him whether he wanted the book advertised anywhere': Richards, 65.

[1] Not one of the most important Juvenal MSS.

[2] Ashburner's next publication was in fact an edn. of *The Rhodian Sea-Law* (1909).

[3] 1837–1926. Legal Assistant to the Medical Department of the Local Government Board, 1869–76, and Legal Adviser, 1883; member of the Council of UCL, 1869–1906, and Vice-president of the Senate, 1878 and 1882; knighted, 1899. He left his library of some 14,000 vols. to UCL.

[4] Professor Robinson Ellis.

a manner which inspires deep indignation among the correspondents of the *Oxford Magazine.*[5]

I saw Horatio Brown twice this time last year: I suppose he is in England now, but I have not come across him. The bill to incorporate the College in the University has passed the Lords and been read once in the Commons. I expect to be in Italy in September, but not near Florence.

Yours sincerely
A. E. Housman.

NLS MS 20369, fos. 217–18. Ashburner/Bell (1976), 14.

TO J. D. DUFF

17 North Road | Highgate N.
15 July 1905

Dear Mr Duff,

I am glad you have had Munro's book[1] reprinted and am much obliged to you for the copy you have sent me. I think though that his recantation of the remarks on 68 68[2] should have been among the matter added.

I do not suppose that you overlooked anything of importance in T;[3] but I mean, as I say, that we have all the variants of certain MSS registered and not all the variants of T. For example, if it anywhere has a *quotiens* in agreement with P,[4] I do not feel sure that this would necessarily appear in your notes.

The *tituli* were the very first thing I threw overboard. Are they any use? In Martial they are, no doubt.

I have been pleased to see that you expel from your text most of the things which I had crossed out in Lindsay's.[5] As you do not accept your

[5] AEH's review appeared in *CR* 19 (1905), 121–3 (*Classical Papers*, 623–7). On 24 May 1905 the *Oxford Magazine* contrasted the 'great dignity of tone and signal generosity' of Ellis's review of *Manilius I* in *Hermathena* with AEH's review in a journal 'which will not get wider support in Oxford so long as it prints reviews such as that of which we speak'.

[1] *Criticisms and Elucidations of Catullus* by H. A. J. Munro (1819–85), originally published in 1878. The 2nd edn. (1905) contained, along with a prefatory note by Duff, three additional papers, and further illustrations from Munro's manuscript notes.

[2] In the *Journal of Philology*, 8 (1879), 333–5.

[3] T is the florilegium Thuaneum, Paris, Bibliothèque nationale de France, MS latin 8071. In his recension of Martial in vol. 2 of J. P. Postgate's *Corpus Poetarum Latinorum* (1905) AEH contributed emendations of Duff's text. He also edited Juvenal for the vol.

[4] P is Biblioteca Apostolica Vaticana, Palatinus 1696.   [5] Published in 1900.

own emendation of IX 3 14[6] I suppose I shall be driven to edit Martial myself, much against my will, in order that it may come to its rights.

I am yours very truly
A. E. Housman.

Text based on that in Maas, 405–6, which was based on the autograph MS once in the possession of R. Shaw-Smith and now missing.

TO GRANT RICHARDS

17 North Road | Highgate N.
3 Aug. 1905

My dear Richards,

My competent or incompetent hand is quite innocent of any intention to edit Catullus; but Nonconformist ministers will say anything.[1] They believe in justification by faith, and act accordingly.

Yours sincerely
A. E. Housman.

Thanks for the German review (very hostile) of the Manilius. It is written by a young man who makes false quantities.

Illinois MS. Richards, 65; Maas, 80.

TO WITTER BYNNER

17 North Road | Highgate N.
26 Aug. 1905

My dear Mr Bynner,

If you will send me, as you kindly offer, these volumes out of your catalogue:—

> Woodberry's *Swinburne*[1]
> W. S. Cather's *Troll Garden*[2]
> W. B. Smith's *Color Line*[3]

I shall be very much obliged.

---

[6] *Quo* for *quod.*

[1] Richards, 65, thinks that the Revd W. Robertson Nicoll, editor of *The British Weekly*, may have made an announcement, but nothing has been traced.

[1] George Edward Woodberry, *Swinburne* (McClure, Phillips, & Co., 1905).

[2] *The Troll Garden* (1905), a collection of seven short stories by Willa Cather, who had visited AEH in London in 1903.

[3] William Benjamin Smith, *Color Line* (1905).

It is amiable of you to wish to inscribe your poems[4] to me, and I cannot exactly refuse my permission; only I would rather that neither you nor anyone else should do so.

> I am yours very truly
> A. E. Housman.

Harvard MS Eng 1071/7. Bynner/Haber (1957), 10.

TO GRANT RICHARDS

> 21 Sept. 1905
> 7, RUE L'ÉCHELLE

NORMANDY HOTEL | PARIS
My dear Richards,

I have been moving about in Italy and have only just received your letter of the 5th. I shall be back on Monday, and shall be pleased to look at the translation if you desire it.

> Yours sincerely
> A. E. Housman.

Illinois MS. LC-GR t.s. Richards, 65 (excerpt)

TO GRANT RICHARDS

> 17 North Road | Highgate N.
> 25 Sept. 1905.

My dear Richards,

You can send a copy for review to Mr Waltzing.

If you will let me take you to dine somewhere, I will let you take me to a music hall or theatre afterwards, on Wednesday or any later evening of the week. As I am just back from France and Italy, I am feeling British, and unless you protest I will take you to the Holborn and order the one good dinner which I know how to order there (there is only one): it is very simple and straightforward and distinctly British; so if you don't think you can stand it, say so. I leave you to fix the day, and also the hour.

> Yours sincerely
> A. E. Housman.

PM MS. LC-GR t.s. Richards, 65; Maas, 81 (both almost complete, and in Maas dated as c.23 September).

---

[4] *An Ode to Harvard and Other Poems* (1907). Bynner to T. B. Haber, 13 Nov. 1956, quoted in Bynner/Haber (1957), 10: 'I almost wish now I had done so in spite of him'.

TO GRANT RICHARDS

17 North Road | Highgate N.
5 Oct. 1905.

My dear Richards,

Don't send a copy of the Juvenal to the *Oxford Magazine*. The request merely means that Owen[1] would like to write a second anonymous review.

Yours sincerely
A. E. Housman.

Illinois MS. LC-GR t.s. Richards, 66 (almost complete); Maas, 81.

TO J. L. GARVIN

University College, London
11 Oct. 1905.

Dear Sir,

I am much obliged by your letter of the 9th; but, as you anticipate, I am not able to compose a poem on Trafalgar.[1] I am afraid too that I admire Napoleon more even than Nelson.

I am yours sincerely
A. E. Housman.

Texas MS.

TO WITTER BYNNER

1 Yarborough Villas, | Pinner | Middlesex
21 Oct. 1905

My dear Mr Bynner,

I have received the four books you have been good enough to send me, and I return my best thanks to you and your firm.

[1] S[idney] G[eorge] Owen (1858–1940), Student of Christ Church, Oxford, since 1891, and editor of the Oxford text of Persius and Juvenal (1903). AEH made scathing remarks on the Juvenal in *CR* in Nov. that year (*Classical Papers*, 602–10), ignored it in his own edn. (1905), came back to it in his Lucan (xvii n. †), and further exposed Owen's shortcomings as a scholar in *CR* 18 (1904), 227–8 (*Selected Prose*, 95–7; *Classical Papers*, 617–18). See Naiditch (1995), 26–7, for further information.

[1] Garvin was editor of *Outlook* at the time, and seems to have asked AEH for a poem to mark the centenary of the British victory under Nelson at the battle of Trafalgar on 21 Oct. 1805.

You will see that I have a new address.[1]

> I am yours very truly
> A. E. Housman.

Harvard MS Eng 1071/8. Bynner/Haber (1957), 11.

TO GRANT RICHARDS

> 17 North Road | Highgate N.
> 31 Oct. 1905

My dear Richards,

After our failure to meet last week I am afraid that I forgot, together with many other things, that you wanted to see me; my excuse is the bother and discomfort of a change of house which is now going on. On Thursday after 2 o'clock I can meet you where you like.

> Yours sincerely
> A. E. Housman.

Illinois MS. LC-GR t.s. Richards, 67; Maas, 81.

TO W. W. SETON

> 10 Nov. 1905
> UNIVERSITY COLLEGE, | LONDON. | GOWER STREET, W.C.

Dear Seton,

I will compose a Latin epistle to the University of Melbourne,[1] if I cannot induce my assistant[2] to do it for me. These functions however belong properly, in a properly constituted academic body, not to the Professor of Latin but to the Public Orator; which reminds me that I have never seen any provision made for that officer in any of the schemes for completing the equipment of the College. Perhaps the Council will take the matter into consideration.

> Yours very truly
> A. E. Housman.

UCL MS (Council file 1/43b).

---

[1] When his landlady Mrs Hunter moved to Pinner from Byron Cottage, 17 North Road, Highgate, where he had lived from 1886, he moved with her.

[1] This was done, but the text is missing. AEH also composed celebratory public addresses to the universities of Sydney and Aberdeen, and another for the Charles Darwin centennial: see Naiditch (1988), 120, for further information.

[2] Lawrence Solomon, appointed in 1904: Naiditch (1988), 120 n.

TO GRANT RICHARDS

1 Yarborough Villas | Pinner
14 Nov. 1905

My dear Richards,

It afflicts me very much that I cannot come to your lunch and meet your attractive company of guests, but I have got much too bad a cold and cough. I have been in the country, and reached here only last night, when I found your note.

Yours sincerely
A. E. Housman.

Illinois MS. Richards, 67 (incomplete); Maas, 82.

TO GRANT RICHARDS

15 Nov. 1905

UNIVERSITY COLLEGE, LONDON. | GOWER STREET, W.C.

My dear Richards,

I have come up to the College to do what is necessary, but I am not fit for company. My colds are always bad ones. I am very much annoyed on your account as well as my own. I send you my best wishes.

Yours sincerely
A. E. Housman.

My books are in confusion at present, but I will look out a copy of the *Shropshire Lad*.

Illinois MS. LC-GR t.s. Richards, 68 (incomplete); Maas, 82.

TO GRANT RICHARDS

1 Yarborough Villas | Pinner
15 Nov. 1905.

My dear Richards,

Here is a copy of the first edition; but if you are going to publish a new one, let me see the final proofs. There is no other way to ensure accuracy.

Yours sincerely
A. E. Housman.

The Clarks tell me that they have sent you 100 bound copies of Juvenal.

Illinois MS. Richards, 68 (incomplete); Maas, 82.

TO J. W. MACKAIL

1 Yarborough Villas | Pinner
23 Nov. 1905

Dear Mackail,

I am glad to have the *Hundred Poems*,[1] both on their own account and because it was I who suggested to the publishers that they should ask you to edit them: I forget exactly what I said, but probably I described you as the least barbarous Scotchman of my acquaintance. They were so much pleased with the result that they wrote to thank me.

You seem to admit elegiacs from almost anyone except the three regular practitioners.[2] What they produce is not of course lyrical poetry in the strict ancient sense, but it is sometimes poetry, which is more than I could say of Horace's sapless political odes or the talk-talk of Boethius. I think I should have included the Copa.[3] I am glad to see No. 79.[4] *stabilis per aeuom terminus*[5] and *vepris inhorruit ad ventum*[6] will earn you the fool's reproach; which, says Blake, is a kingly title.[7]

Yours very truly
A. E. Housman.

BMC MS.

TO GRANT RICHARDS

1 Yarborough Villas | Woodridings | Pinner
20 Dec. 1905.

My dear Richards,

John Lane wrote to me about a week ago, asking if I could give him the publication of *A Shropshire Lad* in England and America, or in America only. I replied that I had given the publication in England to E. Grant Richards and that I could not do anything about America without consulting that

---

[1] An advance copy of *The Hundred Best Poems (Lyrical) in the Latin Language*, selected by J. W. Mackail, repr. with corrections (Gowans & Gray, 1906).

[2] Catullus, Tibullus, and Propertius.

[3] Short poem in elegiacs, wrongly attributed to Virgil, describing a tavern girl who dances to castanets to entertain her customers.

[4] Seneca, *Troades*, 361–80 (on death having no terror).

[5] In Horace, *Carmen Saeculare*, 26, where the usual reading would be *stabilisque rerum*.

[6] In Horace, *Odes*, 1. 23. 5, where Bentley and Keller proposed the reading Mackail adopted (instead of *veris inhorruit adventus*).

[7] *The Marriage of Heaven and Hell*, plate 9, l. 8: 'Listen to the fool's reproach: it is a kingly title'.

firm.[1] Then he writes me the enclosed, on which I should like to have your views. Please return the letter.

Thanks for Drummond's *Cypress Grove*,[2] which is new to me. The cover, if you want my opinion, is both ugly and silly;[3] but you probably have a just contempt for my artistic taste and will not allow this remark to embitter your Christmas.

Yours sincerely
A. E. Housman.

Illinois MS. Richards, 68; Maas, 83.

[1] 'John Lane evidently and not unnaturally thought that my difficulties left Housman open to offers': Richards, 68. Though John Lane had bought for distribution in the United States 162 copies in sheets of the first edn. of *ASL* (1896) from Kegan Paul, Trench, Trübner, & Co. Ltd., and 300 copies of the third edn. from Richards in 1900, the book was not copyright there and Lane held no rights in it.

[2] Prose work by William Drummond of Hawthornden (1623). GR reprinted it as 'the first of the Venetian Series, a collection of sixpenny books on which I vainly embarked': Richards, 68.

[3] 'The cover... was made of a patterned paper specially brought from Varese. I was proud of it': Richards, 68.

1906

TO GRANT RICHARDS

1 Yarborough Villas | Woodridings | Pinner
17 Jan. '06

My dear Richards,

Lane is pressing for a reply: how about McClure's?[1]

Thanks for Hyde's illustration,[2] which I think very nice. I have read the Parisian part of *The Sands of Pleasure*:[3] it is interesting and well written.

Yours sincerely
A. E. Housman.

P.S. The above remark about the novel is not to be regarded as an entry for your prize competition.

Illinois MS. LC-GR t.s. Richards, 69 (excerpts); Maas, 83.

TO BLANCHE BANE

University College, London
20 Jan. 1906

The publisher is E. Grant Richards, 7 Carlton Street, London W. There is to be a new edition soon, but I think that the last is not yet exhausted.

A. E. Housman.

William White, 'More Housman Letters', Mark Twain Quarterly, 5. 4 (Spring 1943), 13.
The MS is a card written in answer to his correspondent's enquiring where she could secure a copy of ASL.

---

[1] McClure, Phillips and Company. At the instigation of Witter Bynner, *McClure's Magazine* had introduced many American readers to poems from *ASL*.

[2] GR had sent AEH a specimen topographical illustration of *ASL* by William Hyde with the idea of interesting AEH in an illustrated edn., which GR would eventually publish in 1908. William Hyde (1859–1925) studied at the Slade School of Art and specialized in printmaking techniques of etching, engraving, and mezzotint to produce illustrations. He illustrated Milton, Shelley, and Belloc, among others. He burnt much of his work, however, judging it to be not good enough.

[3] Novel by [Alexander Bell] Filson Young (1876–1938), published by GR.

TO GRANT RICHARDS

1 Yarborough Villas | Woodridings | Pinner
24 Jan. 1906.

My dear Richards,

I ought to tell you at once, as it may affect your plans, what I hear from John Lane this morning:—that John Lane Company of New York have informed him that they intend to make plates and reprint *A Shropshire Lad* in America. The history of the matter is this. Lane, as I told you, wrote to me on Dec. 12, asking to be given the publication of the book, or its publication in America, and adding that of course there was nothing to prevent him from reprinting the book there, but that he would not 'commit this act of piracy'. I replied that I must consult E. Grant Richards, but that if, on second thoughts, he could bring himself to turn pirate, it would inflict no injury on me personally, as I should not in any case accept royalties. John Lane Company say that they regard my kind letter as tantamount to permission to do what they intend to do.

It may interest my publisher to learn that she has broken all the traditions of the trade by making arrangements with another publisher in New York[1] without giving John Lane Company the opportunity of taking the new edition: that company is reluctantly, in self-defence, compelled to issue an edition of its own. There is etiquette, I daresay, even in Pandemonium.[2]

Yours sincerely
A. E. Housman.

Illinois MS. Richards, 69–70 (wrongly dated as 20 January); Maas, 84.

---

[1] Mitchell Kennerley, whose edn. appeared in 1907: Naiditch (2005), 95–6. It was one of several unauthorized American edns.: see William White, 'A. E. Housman, An Annotated Check-list', *The Library*, 4th series, no. 23 (1943), 33; *A Shropshire Lad by A. E. Housman*, Jubilee edn., with notes and a bibliography by Carl J. Weber (1946), 93. See AEH to GR, 8 Feb. 1919, n. 1. See also Naiditch (2005), 95–6, for further information.

[2] The palace in hell built by the fallen angels in *Paradise Lost*.

TO GRANT RICHARDS

[1 Yarborough Villas | Woodridings | Pinner]
I prefer McClure's; though they are under a delusion when they think I have promised them anything.[1] I particularly do not want to have anything to do with the other worthy.[2]

Yrs
A. E. Housman.

28 Jan. 1906.

Illinois MS: p.c. addressed 'Grant Richards Esq. | 7 Carlton Street | Regent Street S. W.' Richards, 70 (excerpt).

TO PROFESSOR HENRY JACKSON

1 Yarborough Villas | Woodridings | Pinner
30 Jan. 1906.

My dear Jackson,

I wished that you should get the Greek professorship,[1] in order that you might cease to sit up till 4 in the morning preparing lectures and looking over essays; but as your most intimate friends assure me th[at] you do this because you like it, I do not see any particular reason why I should congratulate you. In any case, do not take any notice of this letter, as your mass of correspondence must be only second to that of your friend Chamberlain when he got in for West Birmingham.[2]

Yours sincerely
A. E. Housman.

TCC Add. MS c. 32⁵⁰. Piece torn off at 'that'. Maas, 84.

---

[1] Witter Bynner, who worked on McClure's staff, had asked AEH to let McClure, Phillips and Company publish his next book. See AEH to Bynner, 13 Oct. 1903.

[2] John Lane.

[1] Jackson had been elected to succeed Sir Richard Jebb as Regius Professor of Greek at Cambridge.

[2] Joseph Chamberlain (1836–1914), Mayor of Birmingham, 1873–5, Liberal MP for Birmingham, 1876, and president of the Board of Trade, 1880–5, was elected MP for West Birmingham in Dec. 1885 following a campaign on what George Joachim Goschen famously dubbed the 'Unauthorised Programme' of the Liberal Party.

TO GRANT RICHARDS

1 Yarborough Villas | Woodridings | Pinner
10 Feb. 1906.

My dear Richards,

Thanks for cheque for £3. 2. 3.

As to the Manilius, I have no objection to incurring any publicity which may be entailed by your suing the binders as you propose. I will neither pay anything nor risk paying anything (because enough copies have been sold to make known what I wanted made known, and my spare money I prefer to spend on producing other works). But when you say that it is of course understood that you pay the bill, I do not see why you should want to pay it, and I do not see what particular advantage you would gain by the rescue of my property from Leighton.[1]

Yours sincerely
A. E. Housman.

Illinois MS. Richards, 71 (incomplete); Maas, 85.

TO GRANT RICHARDS

1 Yarborough Villas | Woodridings | Pinner
17 Feb. 1905.[1]

My dear Richards,

I am not a member of the Authors' Society.[2]

I enclose your receipt of July 20th 1903 for £83. 9. 0.

Yours sincerely
A. E. Housman.

Illinois MS.

[1] Richards, 71, removes the last two words. Leighton was probably the binder who held stock of the Manilius. See AEH to GR, 1 Mar. 1905, n. 3, and 16 Mar. 1905.

[1] AEH wrote '1905', corrected on the MS to 1906 in another hand: Richards, 71, is sure it should be 1906.

[2] The Society of Authors, founded in 1884 to promote the business interests of authors and protect their rights.

TO WILLIAM ROTHENSTEIN

1 Yarborough Villas | Woodridings | Pinner
26 Feb. 1906.

Dear Rothenstein,

I shall be very pleased to dine with you on Friday at 7. 15.

I am yours sincerely
A. E. Housman.

Harvard bMS Eng. 1148 (740) 1.

TO GRANT RICHARDS

1 Yarborough Villas | Woodridings | Pinner
11 March 1906.

My dear Richards,

When I found your letter on the breakfast-table this morning, it reminded me that I had been dreaming about the subject in the night. I suppose that your amiable interest had been acting on me by telepathy. Anyhow I dreamt that I met the friend who introduced me to the wine, and asked him for its name, and he told me, and it was right; but alas, that is just the part of the dream that I have forgotten. It was a longer name than Corvo or Syracuse.

Yours sincerely
A. E. Housman.

I have been looking at the map of Sicily and I think it was *Camastra*.[1]

PM MS. LC-GR t.s. Richards, 71; Maas, 85.

TO GRANT RICHARDS

1 Yarborough Villas | Pinner
17 March 1906.

My dear Richards,

Please let me know when you are in possession of the Manilius, in order that I may close accounts with the lawyers I employed.

Yours sincerely
A. E. Housman.

Illinois MS. Maas, 85.

[1] Confirmed by AEH to GR, 29 Mar. 1906.

TO ELIZABETH GIBSON

University College, London
20 March 1906.

Dear Madam,

I thank you for your kindness in sending me your poems, which I have read with pleasure, especially perhaps the pieces on pp. 15 and 16 of *From a Cloister.*[1]

I am yours faithfully
A. E. Housman.

BMC MS.

TO GRANT RICHARDS

1 Yarborough Villas | Woodridings | Pinner
29 March 1906

My dear Richards,

Thanks for your news about Manilius and for your efforts in the matter, now crowned with success.

I have ascertained that the name of the wine *is* Camastra, for the other day I was turning out a pocket and came upon the note I had made at the time. It appears that this benighted metropolis, full as it is of execrable Capri, contains none; but mind you order it if you find yourself at the Cavour in Milan.

I am afraid there is no chance of my being in Paris, at any rate so early as Easter Tuesday.

Yours sincerely
A. E. Housman.

Illinois MS. Richards, 71 (nearly complete); Maas, 86.

---

[1] Vigo Cabinet Series, no. 22 (Elkin Mathews, 1904). The poem on p. 15 is *Mad*: O Maidens, would ye learn my pride and glee, | Why garlanded adown the wind I flee— | At Mary Mother's shrine to bend the knee? ... | *For three long days my lover cherished me.* || Nay, Ask not whither fled my kingly guest. | I rear upon my happy field a nest, | Heedless if he be gone, north, south, east, west ... | *For three nights long I lay upon his breast.*

The poem on p. 16 is *The Bridge*: I built a bridge across the severing stream; | And, though you never come, | The waters erewhile dumb | Beset the piers with happy singing-dream. || When I have fallen asleep to their sweet sound | You may pass, longing, by, | And your heart, waking, cry, | "Could but the builder of the bridge be found!"

TO GRANT RICHARDS

1 Yarborough Villas | Woodridings | Pinner
7 April 1906

My dear Richards,

Thanks for the copies of *A Shropshire Lad*. I suppose it is the edition of 1903 put into a white cover instead of a red,[1] as it seems to have only the few misprints which distinguish that issue.[2] The get-up, to my untutored eye, is nice.

If I am in Paris at all, it will be, roughly speaking, from the 19th to the 24th.

Yours sincerely
A. E. Housman.

Illinois MS. Richards, 72 (incomplete); Maas, 86.

TO PROFESSOR HENRY JACKSON

1 Yarborough Villas | Woodridings | Pinner
29 April 1906

My dear Jackson,

I enclose a paper for the *Journal of Philology*.[1]

I hope I am doing correctly and acceptably in still directing to you as "Dr".[2] I have been told by some authority that it is the higher title.

I may be in Cambridge this day week, and if so I will come and look you up.

Yours sincerely
A. E. Housman.

TCC Add. MS c. 32^{51}. Maas, 86.

[1] It was.   [2] See AEH to GR, 20 Nov. 1902, n. 1.

[1] 'Corrections and Explanations of Martial', published in *JP* 30 (1907), 229–65 (*Classical Papers*, 711–39).
[2] Since Jackson's appointment as Regius Professor of Greek at Cambridge.

TO GRANT RICHARDS

1 Yarborough Villas | Woodridings | Pinner
7 May 1906

My dear Richards,

I have just been away at Cambridge for the week-end.

I shall be free on Thursday, (Friday I am not quite sure of), and I will look after the dinner if you will see about some dramatic entertainment that does not begin too early. I must warn you that I will *not* go to *Nero*.[1]

I came back from Paris on April 26. The weather was only just decent.

Yours sincerely
A. E. Housman.

Illinois MS. Richards, 72 (incomplete).

TO PROFESSOR HENRY JACKSON

1 Yarborough Villas | Woodridings | Pinner
18 May 1906

My dear Jackson,

In Mart. XI 99 5–6 I quite agree with you about *nimias*, and I think *Minyas* absurd as well as ungrammatical; but I never have been able to stomach *magni*, because *culus* is πρωκτός,[1] not πυγή,[2] and there seems to be no point in accusing the lady of εὐρυπρωκτία.[3] I think she was what Squire Western calls Lady Belleston in *Tom Jones* book XVII chap. 3,[4] nothing more.

At X 68 9–10 I have been accustomed to content myself with this interpretation: 'Shall I tell you how you talk; respectable married woman that you are? Just as lasciviously as if you were abed with your man',—the question *numquid* being equivalent to a negation. You make the distich cohere much better with what follows, but you have to pour into *scire cupis* more meaning than it can easily hold.

At XI 68 2 on the other hand I think the next line follows less naturally after your interpretation of the parenthesis. Certainly III 26 5 is a striking parallel, but I am not at ease about that verse itself: Madvig says '*puta* non potest ironice dici pro eo quod est *putasne*'.[5]

---

[1] '*Nero* was a Beerbohm Tree production at His Majesty's. Stephen Phillips wrote it': Richards, 72.

[1] The anus.   [2] The buttocks.

[3] Having a wide anus (through being often sodomized).   [4] 'That fat a—se b—'.

[5] *Adversaria critica ad scriptores Graecos et Latinos*, 2 (1871–84), 163.

I have not read any of De Quincey since I was at school, so I do not know what he says about Suet. Dom. 10,[6] a chapter which contains a good deal.

The passages I quoted at XII praef. seem to me to show that *candor* and *candidus* often lie well on the sunny side of their English derivatives, and signify something very like generosity or indulgence. At XII 69 it is true that Friedlaender's[7] words do not actually exclude the possibility that he understands the epigram as I do; but I think that if he did he would have taken occasion to say that he disagreed with the earlier commentators.

I suppose you see that Grenfell and Hunt[8] have found a lot of the *Phaedrus* and *Symposium* in Egypt. The *Symposium* is the one dialogue of Plato that I have properly read, so I am interested.

Yours sincerely
A. E. Housman.

Princeton MS (Robert H. Taylor Collection).

TO GRANT RICHARDS

1 Yarborough Villas | Woodridings | Pinner
23 June 1906.

My dear Richards,

I enclose the lawyers' exciting narrative of the rescue of Manilius, which they have sent to me.

I have been reading the *Athenaeum*: you seem to me to have the advantage in argument and especially in temper.[1]

Yours sincerely
A. E. Housman.

Illinois MS. Richards, 72 (nearly complete).

[6] De Quincey argued that in ch. 10 of Suetonius's Domitian the retort 'laudanti vocem suam dixerat, *Heu taceo*' of Aelius Lamia was a corruption of 'Suauem dixisti? Quam uellem et Orpheutaceam' ('Sweet is it? Ah, would to heaven it might prove to be *so* sweet as to be even Orpheutic'). De Quincey attributed the corruption to the gnawing of a rat or to the spilling of obliterating fluid on a unique manuscript: *The Collected Writings of Thomas De Quincey*, ed. David Masson, 6 (1890), 421–8.

[7] The standard edn. of Martial by L. Friedländer (Leipzig, 1886).

[8] Papyrologists B[ernard] P[yne] Grenfell (1869–1926) and A[rthur] S[turridge] Hunt (1871–1934) who had carried out excavations in the Fayum in Egypt.

[1] GR was attacked in *The Athenaeum*, 4101 (2 June 1906), 671, and 4103 (16 June 1906), 732–3, by E. V. Lucas (1886–1938), for whom he was publisher before the failure of his publishing house in 1904. Lucas claimed that GR's new publication of W. G. Waters's *Travellers' Joy* was derivative, in idea, format, illustration and binding, of his own anthology *The Open Road: A Little Book for Wayfarers* (1899), and argued that since GR still owed him royalties for the anthology, which had been subsequently reissued by Routledge, Waters's similar text was 'the one kind of book which neither Mrs. nor Mr. Grant Richards was entitled to put forth'. GR

TO J. D. DUFF

1 Yarborough Villas | Woodridings | Pinner
26 June 1906

Dear Mr Duff,

I agree that at Plin. ep. VI 8 6 the text seems to give no coherent sense. What one expects is something like 'quid autem, quam reparare non posse quod amiseris, grauius est?' but I cannot think of any plausible correction.

In 22 7 I suppose *satis* means 'fully': it pretty often inclines to this sense: thus *sat scio* regularly means 'I know right well', and in *scitago* it is very prominent. I think *nimis* would fall short of the sense required, as the moral of the anecdote is that one cannot trust even one's most intimate friends; and *omnibus satis* would be rather beside the question.

In 11 4 *quam me* is legitimate for *quam ego sum* since the case in the other member of the comparison is accusative also: Madvig § 303.b.[1]

I am yours sincerely
A. E. Housman.

TCC Add. MS a. 225[58(3)].

TO J. D. DUFF

1 Yarborough Villas | Woodridings | Pinner
30 June 1906

Dear Mr Duff,

At VI 22 7 I think your insertion of *plus quam* is very pretty and very likely right.

VI 11 4 I should construe like this: 'I pray those same gods (listen you to my words) that it may be their good pleasure that everyone who thinks it worth while to imitate me may excel me'. He is showing us what a noble nature he has.

Yours sincerely
A. E. Housman.

TCC Add. MS a. 225[58(4)].

replied in *The Athenaeum*, 4102 (9 June 1906), 701, and 4104 (23 June 1906), 765–6, to the effect that Lucas's case was 'based on misapprehension, or on ignorance of all the facts'. By 23 June, GR had been provoked by Lucas's repeated references to the failure of 1904: 'If I sold matches in the street I should certainly please some people, but under the most favourable circumstances I could not hope to earn enough … to wipe out the bankruptcy proceedings … By and by I hope my creditors may realise that in being connected with the starting of a new publishing house I am selling what talents I have for their advantage.'

[1] Of his *Latin Grammar* (1857, etc.).

TO MR LOWE

1 Yarborough Villas | Woodridings | Pinner
4 July 1906

Dear Mr Lowe,

Many thanks for the Blake tickets.[1] Your offer about Heine is very handsome, but I beg you to dismiss from your mind the notion that I shall ever translate either him or anyone else. I should want about £20,000, and I should stipulate for anonymity.

Yours very truly
A. E. Housman.

CUL Add. MS 8534.

TO WITTER BYNNER

1 Yarborough Villas | Woodridings | Pinner | England
23 July 1906

Dear Mr Bynner,

I have received Woodberry's *Swinburne* (this is the second copy you have been good enough to send me) and also Lowes Dickinson's *Greek View of Life*.[1] This I am very glad to have: his writing is always worth reading; and I am pleased to see that he is appreciated in America, for in this country he is hardly so well known as he ought to be.

I am yours sincerely
A. E. Housman.

Harvard MS Eng 1071/9. Bynner/Haber (1957), 12.

TO MESSRS ALEXANDER MORING

1 Yarborough Villas | Woodridings | Pinner
17 Aug. 1906

Dear Sirs,

Mr Grant Richards included my book *A Shropshire Lad* in his series of *The Smaller Classics*[1] without consulting me, and to my annoyance. I contented myself with remonstrating, and did not demand its withdrawal; but now

---

[1] For the Carfax (London) exhibition of *Frescoes, Prints and Drawings by William Blake* (1906).

[1] *The Greek View of Life* (originally 1896) by historian and philosophical writer G[oldsworthy] Lowes Dickinson (1862–1932), Fellow of KCC, 1887, and Lecturer in Political Science, 1896–1920.

[1] The 5th edn. (1904).

that I have the chance, I take it, and I refuse to allow the book to be any longer included in the series. I hope that you will not be very much aggrieved; but I think it unbecoming that the work of a living writer should appear under such a title.

I am yours faithfully
A. E. Housman.

Lilly MSS 1. 1. 3 (t.s. in LC-GR). Published in Grant Richards, Author Hunting, by an Old Literary Sportsman: Memories of Years Spent Mainly in Publishing *(1934), 99; Maas, 87.*

TO GRANT RICHARDS

1 Yarborough Villas | Woodridings | Pinner
17 Aug. 1906

My dear Richards,

Alexander Moring Ld. have written to me asking to be allowed to continue to include *A Shropshire Lad* in *The Smaller Classics*. I have refused, and have told them how atrociously you behaved in ever including the book in the series, and how glad I am to have the chance of stopping the scandal.

I suppose you won't be in Paris between next Tuesday and Saturday. I shall be at the Normandy.

Yours sincerely
A. E. Housman.

18 Aug. Mr Balfour Gardiner[1] may publish *The Recruit* with music if he wants to. I always give my consent to all composers, in the hope of becoming immortal somehow.

Illinois MS. Richards, 72–3 (nearly complete); Maas, 87.

---

[1] English composer [Henry] Balfour Gardiner (1877–1950). His setting was performed on 3 July 1906, and subsequently published. He also did settings of *When the lad for longing sighs* (1906), and *When I was one-and-twenty* (1908): Banfield (1985), 449.

TO WITTER BYNNER

1 Yarborough Villas | Woodridings | Pinner | England
21 Sept. 1906

Dear Mr Bynner,

I have been travelling about Europe, and your letter of a month ago has only just reached me. You have already been good enough to send me copies of all the works of Mr Lowes Dickinson which you mention, except that on *Religion*.[1]

I am yours sincerely
A. E. Housman.

Harvard MS Eng 1071/10. Envelope addressed 'Witter Bynner Esq. | c/ McClure, Phillips & Co. | 44 East Twenty-Third St. | New York | U. S. A.' and redirected to The Players Club. Bynner/Haber (1957), 13.

TO GRANT RICHARDS

1 Yarborough Villas | Woodridings, Pinner
30 Sept. 1906

My dear Richards,

I make no objection to their printing the verses, though the translation is stupid.

Yours sincerely
A. E. Housman.

Illinois MS. LC-GR t.s.

TO ALICE ROTHENSTEIN

1 Yarborough Villas | Woodridings | Pinner
17 Oct. 1906

Dear Mrs Rothenstein,

It will give me great pleasure to come to supper on Monday.

I am yours sincerely
A. E. Housman.

Harvard bMS Eng 1148 (740) 2.

[1] *Religion: A Criticism and a Forecast* (1905).

TO GRANT RICHARDS

1 Yarborough Villas | Woodridings | Pinner
31 Dec. 1906

My dear Richards,

I am now back from the country and can see you any time on the 3rd Jan.

I am not anxious to accede to Lane's proposal: quite the reverse.

Yours sincerely
A. E. Housman.

Illinois MS. Richards, 73 (incomplete).

1907

TO WILLIAM ROTHENSTEIN

1 Yarborough Villas | Woodridings | Pinner
14 Jan. 1907

Dear Rothenstein,

Will you dine with me at the Café Royal on Friday, February 1ˢᵗ, at 7. 30? The form which these orgies take is that after dinner we go to a music-hall, and when the music-hall closes, as I have no club, we are thrown on the streets and the pothouses: so you know what to expect.

On the evening when I last saw you, you were stricken with illness, and I afterwards heard that you had gone to Brighton to recruit. I hope you are well now. My kind regards to Mrs Rothenstein.

Yours very truly
A. E. Housman.

Harvard bMS Eng 1148 (740) 3. Maas, 87–8.

TO WILLIAM ROTHENSTEIN

1 Yarborough Villas | Woodridings, Pinner
23 Jan. 1907

My dear Rothenstein,

I had asked two other people, but you will meet them both to-night, I believe, if you go to Trench's[1] affair. I am sorry you cannot come; but I will make another effort on some future day, when perhaps we may contrive to defeat the counterplots of Mrs Rothenstein.

I am yours sincerely
A. E. Housman.

Harvard bMS Eng 1148 (740) 4.

---

[1] Frederic Herbert Trench (1865–1923), poet and playwright. His *New Poems: Apollo and the Seaman, The Queen of Gothland, Stanzas to Tolstoy and Other Lyrics* was published in 1907, though possibly later in the year (the Bodleian copy is stamped 16.11.07).

TO ALICE ROTHENSTEIN

1 Yarborough Villas | Woodridings | Pinner
26 Jan. 1907

Dear Mrs Rothenstein,

I shall be very pleased to come to supper on Wednesday. I am suffering much more from sorrow than from anger.

I am yours sincerely
A. E. Housman.

Harvard bMS Eng 1148 (740) 5.

TO LAURENCE HOUSMAN

1 Yarborough Villas | Pinner
7 Feb. 1907

My dear Laurence,

I have induced Dr Morris[1] to tell me, on condition that mamma does not hear that he told, the amount of his bill for last year. It is about £70. 0. 0; and I want to find out, if possible, what this will mean to mamma. I have no clear notion of what her income is and what margin it generally leaves her; and perhaps you or Clemence can give me some notion. I am anxious to prevent her from feeling any severe pinch from the bill, but on the other hand I don't want to be extravagant or ostentatious; so if you can help me to judge what I should give her in order to effect these two ends I should be much obliged.

Your bad behaviour in the theatre[2] I first heard of from your letters which were read to me at Hereford; I had seen nothing in the papers. I see the play is now taken off, but I suppose it will go into the provinces. I hope at any rate you made something out of it.

[1] Dr Edgar Freeman Morris, LSA, London, of 134 St Owen Street, Hereford, the town in which Lucy Housman was now living.

[2] LH had collaborated with Harley Granville Barker on the libretto for Liza Lehmann's light opera *The Vicar of Wakefield*, and had withdrawn his name from the production when substantial alterations were made during rehearsal. At the première on 12 Dec. 1906 he nearly got into a fight with the manager of the Prince of Wales's Theatre, Mr Curzon, whose untruthful account of events was reported in the newspapers. LH's account is in *The Unexpected Years* (1937), 234–8.

Rothenstein has made me a present of one of his three portraits of me.[3] Perhaps when the weather is warmer and the spring more advanced you and Clemence will come out here and look at it.

> Your affectionate brother
> A. E. Housman.

BMC MS. Memoir, 168–9; Maas, 88 (both slightly incomplete; the latter with the wrong date).

TO C. F. KEARY

> 1 Yarborough Villas | Woodridings | Pinner
> 9 Feb. 1907

Dear Keary,

I shall be very pleased to dine with you on Wednesday, 7. 45.

I saw Ker[1] the other day and told him you were in town, and he expressed the intention of finding you out.

> Yours very truly
> A. E. Housman.

Private MS.

TO W. W. SETON

> 5 March 1907
> UNIVERSITY OF LONDON. | UNIVERSITY COLLEGE.
> GOWER STREET, LONDON, W.C.

Dear Seton,

In reply to your note of the 2nd, which I find here this morning, I do desire that Mr Solomon[1] should be re-appointed as my Assistant.

> Yours faithfully
> A. E. Housman

The Secretary.

UCL Council Correspondence 1/158.

---

[3] Drawings, done in 1906.

[1] W[illiam] P[aton] Ker (1855–1923). Quain Professor of English Language and Literature at UCL, 1889–1922. Assistant to W. Y. Sellar, Professor of Humanity, Edinburgh University, 1879–80; Fellow of All Souls College, Oxford, 1879–1923; Professor of English Literature and History, University College of South Wales, Cardiff, 1883–9; and Professor of Poetry at Oxford, 1920–3. Publications include: *Epic and Romance* (1897), *The Dark Ages* 1904), *English Literature: Medieval* (1912), and edns. of Dryden's *Essays* (1900) and of Lord Berners's translation of Froissart's *Chronicles* (1901–3). For further information, see Naiditch (1988), esp. pp. 57–64.

[1] See AEH to Seton, 10 Nov. 1905, n. 2.

TO GRANT RICHARDS

NORMANDY HOTEL | 7, RUE DE L'ÉCHELLE | PARIS
Wednesday, 17 April 1907

My dear Richards,

On receiving your letter this morning I have sent you off a telegram, asking you, or rather commanding you (as is the manner of telegrams) to come and dine on Friday or lunch on Saturday. Perhaps it is impossible for you, however obedient, to get here on Friday; but, if you can, name your own dinner-hour, no matter how late.

I may be still here on Sunday, but it is uncertain.

Yours
A. E. Housman.

Illinois MS. LC-GR t.s. Richards, 73–4; Maas, 89.

TO WILLIAM ROTHENSTEIN

1 Yarborough Villas | Woodridings | Pinner
23 April 1907

My dear Rothenstein,

I am returning to you by Parcel Post Hudson's *El Ombú*,[1] which I have kept longer than I ought. I have read it with respect rather than admiration: the last story, the supernatural one, I thought the best. A piece like *El Ombù* itself, hateful characters and harrowing events, showing man and God at their worst, is good to some extent if it is true, because then it is a weighty indictment of the nature of things.

I also send a copy of my poems which I promised you a long while ago. I think it is practically free from misprints, except one in the last piece, which I have corrected.[2] The copy now in your possession I beg you to throw in the fire[3] while there is a fire, before Mrs Rothenstein has had her spring cleaning and put Brunswick black[4] on the grate.

---

[1] *El Ombú and Other Tales* by W[illiam] H[enry] Hudson (1841–1922) was published in 1902.
[2] In *ASL* LXIII 9, 'seeds' corrected to 'seed'. See AEH to GR, 20 Nov. 1902, n. 1.
[3] Probably the 5th edn. (1904), possibly the 2nd edn. (1898), of *ASL*, both of which were inaccurately printed: see *Poems* (1997), Introduction, xxv.
[4] Black varnish made from turpentine and asphalt or lamp black.

Would you come and dine with me at the Café Royal on Friday May 10th at 7. 30?

Yours sincerely
A. E. Housman.

Harvard bMS Eng 1148 (740) 6. Maas, 89.

TO LAURENCE HOUSMAN

1 Yarborough Villas | Pinner
30 April 1907

My dear Laurence,

I don't at all want to contribute to Mrs Bland's[1] publication.[2] I contributed to the *Venture* only because you were the editor.[3] I suppose she already knows that I am morose and unamiable, and will not experience any sudden or agonising shock.

Your affectionate brother
A. E. Housman.

Now all day the hornèd herds
Dance to the piping of the birds;
Now the bumble-bee is rife,
And other forms of insect life;
The skylark in the sky so blue
Now makes noise enough for two,
And lovers on the grass so green
—Muse, oh Muse, eschew th'obscene

BMC MS. Memoir, 169, but the verse is misleadingly appended to letter of 16 Feb. 1929 (Memoir, 182); as also in Maas, 276.

---

[1]   E[dith] Nesbit (1858–1924), writer of children's literature and wife of Hubert Bland, founder member of the Fabian Society. She was a friend of LH.

[2]   The magazine *The Neolith*, first issued in Nov. 1907, combined literary and pictorial art. LH contributed to the second issue. It foundered after the fourth.

[3]   See AEH to LH, 9 Aug. 1903.

TO PROFESSOR ROBINSON ELLIS

1 May 1907.
UNIVERSITY OF LONDON. | UNIVERSITY COLLEGE.
GOWER STREET, LONDON, W.C.

Dear Mr[1] Ellis,

Loewe's edition of the cod. Matr. M 31 of Manilius has been sent over from Goettingen and is now in the library of this college, where it will remain till midsummer. I send you word of this in case you may wish to consult it; or I should be very pleased to give you any information about it.

I am yours very truly
A. E. Housman.

UCLA MS S/C 100/45. Removed from M. Manilii astronomicon liber primus, *ed. Housman (1903) (UCLA S/C 84563 v. 1). Naiditch (1996), item 35.*

TO WALTER ASHBURNER

1 Yarborough Villas | Woodridings | Pinner
2 May 1907

My dear Ashburner,

I have not heard anything of you since two Septembers ago, when we met in Milan and you introduced me to Camastra, an acquaintance which has materially alleviated the sorrows of the Italian table d'hôte. If you are coming to England this summer I hope you will dine with me some evening; I might almost say any evening outside the last fortnight of June, which is filled and embittered with examination papers.

I spent about three weeks in Italy last autumn, chiefly in Rome and Capri, which latter was new to me, and gave me my first real contact with the South-Italian character, which is interesting, but rather vile.

I have not been doing much in the way of writing, but I hope that the Commercial History of the Italian States[1] is going forward. The College prospers passably: it is now incorporated in the University, but one does not discover any difference, except that the Senate is now called the Professorial Board.

I am yours very truly
A. E. Housman.

NLS MS 20369. Ashburner/Bell (1976), 16.

[1] Instead of the more friendly 'Dear Ellis'.
[1] See AEH to Ashburner, 6 July 1905, n. 2.

TO GRANT RICHARDS

1 Yarborough Villas | Woodridings | Pinner
7 May 1907

My dear Richards,

Thanks for cheque for £1. 10. 5.

Wednesday is my best day for lunch, or else Friday.

The *Athenaeum* had previously reviewed both the Manilius and the Juvenal some time ago: to the Manilius they gave quite a long review in large print.[1]

Thanks for *The Triumph of Mammon*,[2] which is much more interesting to read than *The Theatrocrat*;[3] but as for his knowledge which is going to change the world, it is just like the doctrine of the Trinity: probably false, and quite unimportant if true. The five lines at the top of p. 17 are the sort of thing he does really well.[4]

Yours sincerely
A. E. Housman.

Illinois MS. LC-GR t.s. Richards, 74 (nearly complete); Maas, 89–90.

TO GRANT RICHARDS

1 Yarborough Villas | Woodridings | Pinner
23 May 1907.

My dear Richards,

On pages 1, 8, 13, 24, 46, 72, 73, 83, I have marked for correction, if possible, certain ugly over-running of words from one line to another. Since these over-runnings existed in neither the 1896 nor the 1900 edition, it seems absurd that they should be necessary in this, which has smaller print than the former and a larger page than the latter. Moreover, on general grounds, a person like me, who habitually writes in metres which have short lines, ought not to be deprived by printers of the neatness which it is easy, in such metres, to preserve.

[1] *The Athenaeum*, 4148 (27 Apr. 1907), 504, a review of both the Juvenal and the Manilius. AEH was praised as 'one of the most trenchant and skilful Latin scholars of the day', whose 'brilliant and uncompromising expositions of textual matters' were a pleasure to read; but the reviewer remarked also that 'a little modesty would improve his case'.

[2] *God and Mammon: A Trilogy*, vol. 1, *The Triumph of Mammon*, by John Davidson (E. Grant Richards, 1907).

[3] Published in 1905.

[4] [beauty breaks] In blossoms and the sweet sex of the rose | Perfumes the way, or when the crescent moon, | Recut anew in pallid gold, adorns | The saffron sunset, like an odour changed | To purest chrysolite and hung in heaven …

The further over-runnings which I have marked on pages 68, 82, 101, occurred in one or other of the two other editions, and therefore I do not so much object to them; but I suspect that they are really unnecessary. The over-runnings on p. 48, on the other hand, may be necessary, as they occurred in the 1st edition and were only avoided in 1900 by not indenting the lines; but I am disposed to think that non-indentation would be preferable.

I feel that I did not earn my lunch the other day by the amount of information I was able to afford.

Yours sincerely
A. E. Housman.

Illinois MS. Richards, 74–5; Maas, 90.

TO GRANT RICHARDS

1 Yarborough Villas | Pinner
26 May 1907

My dear Richards,

I shall be very pleased to call for you at 4. 30 on Tuesday, though you have not told me anything about your friend or his pictures[1] before.

Yours sincerely
A. E. Housman.

Illinois MS.

TO GRANT RICHARDS

1 Yarborough Villas | Pinner
4 June 1907.

My dear Richards,

I enclose, as you asked me, some suggestions for Shropshire views.

I have just received some press-cuttings from America, from which it appears that in addition to John Lane's edition[1] there is one by Mosher.[2] If you have facilities for getting hold of these, I should be rather interested to see them.

Yours sincerely
A. E. Housman.

Illinois MS. Richards, 75.

[1] The artist William Hyde. See AEH to GR, 17 Jan. 1906.

[1] First in 1897, from plates of the first edn. (1896), then in 1906.

[2] T[homas] B[ird] Mosher's unauthorized edn. first appeared in 1906.

TO GRANT RICHARDS

1 Yarborough Villas, Pinner, 12 June 1907.
I have just noticed a \trifling/ misprint which I think I did not mark in the proofs of the new *Shropshire Lad*. In the poem XXIV, p. [36], 1st stanza, 2nd line, the stop after the word 'prime' should be a full stop, not a comma.

I am much obliged for the Mosher edition, which is nicely got up, except for the stupid practice of breaking stanzas in two at the foot of a page. It has misprints too.

Yrs.
A. E. Housman.

Illinois MS: p.c. addressed 'Grant Richards Esq. | 7 Carlton Street | Regent Street | S. W.' The square brackets in the text are AEH's. Richards, 76.

TO GRANT RICHARDS

[1 Yarborough Villas, Pinner]
15. 6. 07.

Oh no, it is not worth while inserting an erratum.

A. E. Housman.

Illinois MS: p.c. addressed 'Grant Richards Esq. | 7 Carlton St | Regent St | S. W.' Richards, 77 (nearly complete).

TO JOHN LANE

1 Yarborough Villas | Woodridings | Pinner
29 June 1907.

Dear Mr Lane,

Many thanks for the two copies of your American edition: I am no judge of book-production, but they seem to me quite nice. I am sorry that I am not free next Friday and cannot have the pleasure of meeting you and Mrs Lane and your impressive list of guests.

I am yours very truly
A. E. Housman.

BMC MS.

TO GRANT RICHARDS

1 Yarborough Villas | Pinner
29 June 1907

My dear Richards,

Pray who gave Mr E. Thomas leave to print two of my inspired lays in his and your *Pocket Book of Poems and Songs?*[1] I didn't, though he thanks me in the preface. Just the same thing happened in the case of Lucas' *Open Road,*[2] issued by the same nefarious publisher. You must not treat my immortal works as quarries to be used at will by the various hacks whom you may employ to compile anthologies. It is a matter which affects my moral reputation: for six years back I have been refusing to allow the inclusion of my verses in the books of a number of anthologists who, unlike Mr Thomas, wrote to ask my permission; and I have excused myself by saying that I had an inflexible rule which I could not transgress in one case rather than another. Now these gentlemen, from Quiller-Couch[3] downward, will think I am a liar.

Mr Thomas thanks me for 'a poem', and prints two: which is the one he doesn't thank me for?

My temper, as you are well aware, is perfectly angelic, so I remain yours sincerely

A. E. Housman.

Illinois MS. Richards, 77–8; Maas, 91.

TO GRANT RICHARDS

1 Yarborough Villas | Pinner
2 July 1907.

My dear Richards,

Thanks for your letter. What you have got in your head is the fact that I allow composers to set my words to music without any restriction. I never hear the music, so I do not suffer; but that is a very different thing from being included in an anthology with W. E. Henley or Walter de la Mare.

---

[1] GR's *Pocket Book of Poems and Songs for the Open Air* (1907), edited by the nature writer and (later) poet Edward Thomas (1878–1917), contained *ASL* IV and XLII (*Reveille, The Merry Guide*).
[2] GR published the anthology *The Open Road* by his literary adviser the journalist and essayist E. V. Lucas (1868–1938) in 1899.
[3] Essayist and critic Arthur Quiller-Couch (1863–1944) was editor of *The Oxford Book of English Verse* (1900). He was knighted in 1910 and appointed Professor of English at Cambridge in 1912.

I did not remonstrate about the *Open Road*: I was speechless with surprise and indignation.

Yours sincerely
A. E. Housman.

Illinois MS. Richards, 78; Maas, 91.

TO WITTER BYNNER

1 Yarborough Villas | Woodridings | Pinner | England
20 August 1907

Dear Mr Bynner,

I thank you for your kindness in sending me your book of poems[1] with its very varied contents. The passage on p. 34, 'And there, as though the night …' [,][2] is really beautiful poetry. Among the lighter pieces I like *The Hypocrite*[3] best.

When you wrote to me last you were embarking on some new line in life, which you did not specify;[4] I hope that you are prospering.

I am yours sincerely
A. E. Housman.

Harvard MS Eng 1071/11. Envelope addressed 'Witter Bynner Esq. | c/ Messrs Small, Maynard & Co. | Publishers | Boston, Mass. | U. S. A.' and redirected to 'Lidge Lodge | Chesham | N. H.' Bynner/Haber (1957), 14.

[1] *An Ode to Harvard and Other Poems* (1907).

[2] And there, as though the night were their especial hour, | None others using it so well as they, | I heard the bell, that rings at dusk beside the balconied tower, | Send gently with its iron tongue | All those that wake away.

[3] When Celia said that for her sake | I must not take of wine, | My habit or her heart must break, | I straightway drew the line— | Yet not so much for Celia's sake | As secretly for mine. || By grace of her I'm full of wit,— | (Or think I am—what matters it?) || I gave it up because I won | A wine thereby so rare | That out of all the vineyards none | Has yielded to compare!— | I left it off because I won | The sparkling of her hair! || By grace of her I feel my worth | Immortal on a mortal earth. || And Celia meantime loves to laud | My exodus from vice, | And does not guess me by the fraud | Intoxicated thrice, | Watches in fact a little awed | The seeming sacrifice. || I wonder would she take amiss | Confession of my wickedness?

[4] In 1906 Bynner left *McClure's* and the publishers McClure, Phillips & Co., for Small, Maynard & Co. and freelance writing.

TO THE EDITOR OF *COUNTRY LIFE*

[UNIVERSITY OF LONDON | UNIVERSITY COLLEGE
GOWER STREET, LONDON, W.C.]
7 Nov. 1907

Dear Sir,

I am obliged by your proposal, but several causes, of which bar-renness is the chief, prevent me from contributing verses to periodical publications.

I am yours faithfully
A. E. Housman.

White (1950), 404; Maas, 92.

TO GRANT RICHARDS

1 Yarborough Villas | Woodridings, Pinner
31 Dec. 1907.

My dear Richards,

I am here, and not likely to go away. I believe I have not thanked you for sending me certain books published by you, or rather by Mrs Richards. A happy new year to both of you.

Yours sincerely
A. E. Housman.

Illinois MS. Richards, 79 (incomplete).

1908

TO GRANT RICHARDS

1 Yarborough Villas | Pinner
3 Jan. 1908

My dear Richards,

I am not disposed to give Mr Levey the permission he asks for. For several years back I have refused to have my verses printed in *collections*.

Yours sincerely
A. E. Housman.

Illinois MS. Richards, 80 (almost complete).

TO ALICE ROTHENSTEIN

1 Yarborough Villas | Woodridings | Pinner
9 Feb. 1908.

Dear Mrs Rothenstein,

I am sorry for the misunderstanding and shall be very pleased to come on the 19th.

When Rothenstein gave me his portrait of me[1] he also lent me (not *gave*) a portfolio to carry it away in. This ought long ago to have returned to him, but it has been swallowed by the man who framed the portrait, or otherwise vanished; so I have sent another, which I hope has now reached the artist and will occasionally remind him of me when he uses it.

Yours sincerely
A. E. Housman.

Harvard bMS Eng 1148 (740) 7. Maas, 92.

[1] One of three done in 1906.

TO LAURENCE HOUSMAN

1 Yarborough Villas | Woodridings | Pinner
17 Feb. 1908

My dear Laurence,

I am not in any hurry for the money advanced towards Miss Lake, and I should be grieved to hear that you had poisoned Cousin Mary and Cousin Agnes on my account.

I should be very glad to look through your selections.[1] Did I ever say anything abusive about *Spikenard*?[2] I think on the whole it is about the cleverest of your poetry books.

Could you give me the exact reference to a paper by Phillimore on the *Greek Anthology* which you once showed me, I think, in the *Monthly Review*?[3]

Your affectionate brother
A. E. Housman.

So overpowering is your celebrity that I have just received an official letter from my own college addressed to 'Professor L. Housman'.

BMC MS. Memoir, *169–70; Maas, 92 (both incomplete).*

TO GRANT RICHARDS

1 Yarborough Villas | Woodridings | Pinner
17 Feb. 1908

My dear Richards,

I am told that a young lady[1] whom I have met once or twice in Gloucestershire, and who "wants to take up black and white drawing" \(having done watercolours hitherto, I think)/ and who "has lately been studying under Cameron,[2] and he says that her architectural drawings are wonderful", wants an introduction to my publisher. (I rather gather that she is under the deplorable impression that my publisher is Macmillan, but

[1] For LH's *Selected Poems* (1908).
[2] Published in Feb. 1898. 'He had described it as "nonsense verse" ': LH, *Memoir*, 169 n. See the letter dated Oct.–15 Nov. 1897.
[3] No such article appeared in *The Monthly Review*.

[1] Hester Frood, later Mrs Gwynne Evans. 'Unfortunately, I could at the time find no serious work for the lady': Richards, 80. Born in 1882, she exhibited at the Royal Academy and held several one-woman shows. Richards records that she did a painting of his small office at 7 Carlton Street for him: *Author Hunting*, 225. She first met AEH at Woodchester in the summer of 1906 when he was visiting the Wise family (Richards, 325).
[2] David Young Cameron (1865–1945). Painter and etcher. Elected Royal Academician, 1920; knighted, 1924. Richards (81 n.) avers that though Cameron praised her work she was not in any sense his pupil.

let that pass.) As you were talking the other day about some architectural book, I wondered if you would care to see her. She is tall and beauteous, but let that pass too.

And pray what is the exact process of introducing people to one's publisher? Does one provide them with a letter, which they present at the door of the spider's parlour?

Yours sincerely
A. E. Housman.

Illinois MS. Richards, 80; Maas, 93.

TO GRANT RICHARDS

1 Yarborough Villas | Woodridings | Pinner
20 Feb. 1908

My dear Richards,

I showed your picture to our professor of Archeology,[1] who says that it is mostly fanciful, and the rowing arrangements impracticable. Representations of triremes exist at Pompeii and have been reproduced in several books, the best of which is probably Baumeister's *Denkmaler*.[2]

Thanks for your reply about Miss Frood, for such is her name, and also for Filson Young's book,[3] which is pretty.

Yours sincerely
A. E. Housman.

Illinois MS. Richards, 81 (slightly inaccurate); Maas, 93.

[1] Ernest Arthur Gardner (1862–1939). Professor of Archaeology at London University, 1896–1929. AEH's spelling 'Archeology' is non-standard.

[2] A. Baumeister (ed.), *Denkmäler des klassischen Altertums zur Erläuterung des Lebens der Griechen und Römer in Religion, Kunst und Sitte*. 3 vols. (München and Leipzig, 1884–8). AEH writes 'Denkmaler'.

[3] *The Lover's Hours*, published in 1907 by Richards (Richards, 81 n.). Maas's error in identifying the volume, corrected in Naiditch (1995), 162, may have been caused by Richards's transcription error of 'new book' for 'book', though Maas does not repeat this particular error.

TO J. P. POSTGATE

1 Yarborough Villas | Woodridings, Pinner
22 Feb. 1908

Dear Postgate,

I return Headlam's pamphlet,[1] for which I am much obliged, and hope I have not kept it an unconscionable time. He has the comic vocabulary and phraseology at his fingers' ends, and keeps a sharper eye on the metre than Wilamowitz;[2] but he does not see so far as he ought into the situations and the action, and this has led him into some strange mistakes.

Yours sincerely
A. E. Housman.

Newcastle MS. Maas, 94.

TO ALICE ROTHENSTEIN

1 Yarborough Villas | Woodridings | Pinner
26 Feb. 1908.

Dear Mrs Rothenstein,

During the last week I have been engaged on a special piece of work which interested me and caused me to postpone as much of my ordinary work as could be postponed; so that now I have arrears which must be got rid of, and will not allow me to be with you to-night. I am very sorry.

Yours sincerely
A. E. Housman.

Harvard bMS Eng 1148 (740) 8. Maas, 94.

---

[1] The posthumously published 'Restorations of Menander' (1908) by Walter [George] Headlam (1866–1908), Fellow of KCC, 1890–1908. AEH's copy of the pamphlet survives (SJCO, b 4): Naiditch (1995), 22 n. Headlam's publications include: *Fifty Poems of Meleager, with a Translation* (1890), *On Editing Aeschylus: A Criticism* (1891), and *A Book of Greek Verse* (1907). AEH inscribed *Here are the skies, the planets seven (AP* V) in the copy of the *Manilius I* (1903) he presented to Headlam. On AEH and Headlam, see Naiditch (1995), 22–3.

[2] Ulrich von Wilamowitz-Moellendorff (1848–1931), eminent German classical scholar. Professor of Greek Studies at Berlin, 1897; editor of series *Philologische Untersuchungen*, 1880–1925; editorial director of *Inscriptiones Graecae*, 1902. He published 'Der Menander von Kairo' in *Neue Jahrbücher für das klassische Altertum* (1908), 34–62.

TO LAURENCE HOUSMAN

1 Yarborough Villas | Woodridings, Pinner
1 March 1908.

My dear Laurence,

With your inclusions[1] from *Spikenard* I agree, except that I have very decidedly struck out one. In the other books I have actually not struck out anything \(except once)/, and have even made one or two additions, which I think quite as good as the average of the inclusions. The pieces which I think your best, apart from *Spikenard*, are, in *Rue, Long through the night, Amid this grave-strewn, What know ye of,* and *Dark to its nest*; in *Mendicant Rhymes The Settlers*; and in *The Little Land The Elphin Bride*: so I think these should in any case go in. *Mendicant Rhymes* itself, though rather obscure and untidy, is decidedly pretty, but the stanza where 'Chloe' rhymes with 'Evoe' would have to be altered, because Evoe is a word of two syllables, εὐοῖ, and the *oe* is a diphthong, and you might put two million dots on the top of it instead of two without changing its length! Speaking generally, I think the inclusions at present too many and too monotonous: I should not put in all the sonnets of *The Little Land* (sonnets stodge up a book more than anything, even blank verse), nor so much of *Rue.* The strong point of your poetry seems to me to be a lively fancy: you seem rather to value the pieces on account of thoughts or emotions which suggested them, without enough considering whether these are really reproduced in the words. Thus *Across these barren clods* is much more attractive and intelligible to a reader than a great deal of its surroundings, which you prefer; and similarly *A Garden Enclosed* is more successful than *The Man in Possession*, though I don't understand 'life's a fault' in the last verse. *The New Orpheus* I should call too long, and by no means so good in its way as *Advocatus Diaboli*, though this wants making clearer and neater in parts. I should be glad to look over the text when the selections are made, especially as you have a way of treating words like 'Messiah' and 'royal' as if they were a syllable shorter than they are,—possibly in the vain hope of making amends for 'Evoë'.

Your affectionate brother
A. E. Housman.

BMC MS. Memoir, *170–1; Maas, 94–5.*

---

[1] See AEH to LH, 17 Feb. 1908.

TO GRANT RICHARDS

1 Yarborough Villas | Pinner
27 March 1908

Dear Sir,

Messrs Goodwin & Tabb[1] may have the permission they desire to publish a setting of *When I was one-and-twenty*.

Yours faithfully
A. E. Housman.

Illinois MS.

TO GRANT RICHARDS

1 Yarborough Villas | Woodridings, Pinner
8 May 1908

My dear Richards,

I could look in about 3. 30 next Thursday, if that would suit you.

Yours sincerely
A. E. Housman.

Illinois MS.

TO GRANT RICHARDS

1 Yarborough Villas | Woodridings | Pinner
16 May 1908

My dear Richards,

Mr I. B. Gurney[1] (who resides in Gloucester Cathedral along with St. Peter and Almighty God)[2] must not print the words of my poems in full on concert-programmes (a course which I am sure his fellow-lodgers would disapprove of); but he is quite welcome to set them to music, and to have them sung, and to print their titles on programmes when they are sung.

If you can lunch with me on Wednesday I will come down about 1 o' clock.

Yours sincerely
A. E. Housman.

Illinois MS. Richards, 81; Maas, 95.

---

[1] London orchestral librarians and music publishers.

[1] See List of Recipients.

[2] He was an unofficial assistant organist there: Banfield (1985), 234.

TO LAURENCE HOUSMAN

1 Yarborough Villas | Pinner
26 May 1908

My dear Laurence,

I enclose cheque for five guineas which Kate has asked me to send you towards the sundial in Bathwick cemetery.[1] I was down there last Saturday: the stone looks well enough, but the dial is conspicuously marked with an advertisement of the Birmingham Art Company, or whatever it is, which will have to be erased. The sign of our redemption, which has also been added, is less obnoxious, except that its addition is due to a lying priest.[2]
[…]

Text, slightly corrected, from that in Hawkins (1958), 165.

TO GRANT RICHARDS

1 Yarborough Villas | Pinner
27 May 1908.

My dear Richards,

I have written to R. & R. Clark.[1]

The fates seem to be against our meeting, but after all I don't know that it is necessary we should meet about Hyde's drawings.[2] I did not know that they were to be in colour, and should have preferred black and white; but the colour has a good effect in the autumnal scene on Wenlock Edge. As to the four I saw, I liked three of them; but the one entitled *On The Teme* had nothing distinctive about it and might have been anywhere: the crescent moon, for instance, is a cosmopolitan embellishment, and I have seen it in France. He might have got a much more striking and characteristic view of the Teme under Whitecliff just opposite Ludlow. But the three views of Clee Hill and Ludlow and Wenlock Edge are quite the sort of thing required.

Yours sincerely
A. E. Housman.

Illinois MS. Richards, 81–2 (nearly complete); Maas, 96.

[1] The churchyard of St Mary the Virgin, Smallcombe, on the outskirts of Bath, where Robert Housman died in 1905. The sundial is a family memorial, encircled by plates commemorating the members.
[2] The vicar thought the monument pagan, but agreed to it provided it was surmounted by a cross, which was eventually carved on the sundial's side. There is a photograph in *HSJ* 25 (1999), between pp. 56 and 57.

[1] Edinburgh printers responsible for AEH's *M. Manilii astronomicon liber I* (1903).
[2] For the illustrated *ASL* (1908).

TO GRANT RICHARDS

1 Yarborough Villas | Pinner
5 June 1908

My dear Richards,

Gowans and Gray[1] have written to me and I have told them that for eight years I have been refusing permission to others and cannot make an exception for them.

Yours sincerely
A. E. Housman.

Illinois MS.

TO GRANT RICHARDS

1 Yarborough Villas | Pinner
6 June 1908

My dear Richards,

1. I do not in the least want the crescent moon *removed* from the drawing *On The Teme*, as Mr Hyde seems to think.

2. I suppose it was you who sent him on his wild goose chase to Hughley.[1] I carefully abstained from suggesting that subject.

3. A view of the Wrekin from the neighbourhood of Much Wenlock, as he suggests, would do quite well.

4. I have no objection to his proposal about the frontispiece.

5. Long years ago I warned Laurence that if ever I wrote a book I would never let him decorate it.

Yours sincerely
A. E. Housman.

Illinois MS. Richards, 82; Maas, 96–7.

[1] Publishers.

[1] To discover that the church in *Hughley Steeple* (*ASL* LXI) in fact had no steeple. See AEH to LH, 5 Oct. 1896, and to an unknown correspondent, 11 Feb. 1929. 'I had not sent Hyde to Hughley': Richards, 82.

TO PROFESSOR HENRY JACKSON

1 Yarborough Villas | Woodridings | Pinner
26 June 1908.

My dear Jackson,

No doubt you are snowed up with congratulations:[1] do not take any notice of this. There is something to be said for a Liberal government after all.[2]

If you experienced a sudden access of salubrity about 1. 45 to-day, that was caused by Rothenstein and me drinking your health.

Yours sincerely
A. E. Housman.

TCC Add. MS c. 32[52]. *Maas, 97.*

TO LAURENCE HOUSMAN

1 Yarborough Villas | Woodridings, Pinner
27 June 1908

My dear Laurence,

I enjoyed parts of your play[1] very much, especially the first transformation of the picture, which was so effective that I think the act ought to have ended there. Olangtsi is very good and very well acted, and Mee-Mee too is quite nice, and the Jews, especially the opulent one, are amusing. The acting of the students on the other hand, especially their voices and intonation, I thought almost the worst I had ever come across; and the words they have to say \and sing/ seem to me to contain a good \deal/ of your wet wit. And then there is the infernal music.[2] Theatres are beginning to exhibit notices asking ladies to remove their hats: my patronage shall be bestowed on the theatre which goes a step further and requests the orchestra to be silent. The sleep-walking scene ought to have been good; but it left me faint and weak from the effort of straining to hear the human voice through the uproar of pussy's bowels.

Rothenstein asked me to express to you his great pleasure and admiration. He also explained to me the moral; which is that if one wants to be a

---

[1]   On his appointment to the Order of Merit.
[2]   The Liberals, led by Sir Henry Campbell-Bannerman, won a landslide victory in the 1906 general election, and in government would have recommended Jackson for the OM.

[1]   *The Chinese Lantern*, which opened at the Haymarket Theatre on 16 June 1908.
[2]   By Joseph S. Moorat (1864–1938), chiefly known as a songwriter.

great artist one must be *absorbed* in a work of art. He very politely assumed that I saw it myself; but alas, I did not.

Both Millington and George Fletcher[3] want to see me at the Bromsgrove dinner on the 8th, so I am going; but I have announced to Bunting[4] that I shall not make a speech.

I read an article on your work by a most affected writer in a magazine whose name I forget,[5] though I have got it in the next room; and I have sufficient artistic taste to be aware that the drawing of a lady and a tortoise is good. About the *Night* I should not have felt sure; not that I have anything against it.

Your affectionate brother
A. E. Housman.

BMC MS. Memoir, *171–2; Maas, 97–8.*

TO GRANT RICHARDS

1 Yarborough Villas | Woodridings | Pinner
27 June 1908

My dear Richards,

On the title page the three words *A Shropshire Lad* should be in one line, as in all the editions except the atrocious production of 1904. I have also marked small details on pp. vii and 13. The repetition of p. 3 as p. 11 is one of those sacred mysteries with which I don't interfere.[1]

The corrections apply also to the American edition; but I am retaining the proofs of that unless you want them back.

Bywater[2] is resigning the Greek chair at Oxford, and Herbert Richards[3] ought to succeed him. Whether he will is quite another question.[4] It is a

---

[3] See List of Recipients.

[4] William Louis Bunting (b. 1873), who taught at The Grammar School of King Edward VI, Bromsgrove, 1897–1904, and was now secretary of the Old Bromsgrovian Club: Maas, 98 n.

[5] 'The Work of Laurence Housman' by Charles Kains-Jackson, in *The Book Lover's Magazine: Books and Book-Plates*, 7. 6 (1908), 227–35.

[1] Richards, 83, supposes that AEH's corrections are to the proofs of the illustrated edn. of *ASL* (1908).

[2] Ingram Bywater (1840–1914), Fellow of Exeter College, Oxford, 1863–84; Reader in Greek at Oxford, 1884, and Regius Professor, 1893–1908.

[3] Herbert [Paul] Richards (1848–1916). Fellow of Wadham College, Oxford, 1873. He was GR's uncle, and also one of the examiners who had failed AEH in Greats in 1881 (Richards, xx, 125, 144). The others were Bywater, T. H. Grose, H. J. Bidder, and R. W. Macan. Richards, 144, notes that AEH respected Herbert Richards as a scholar and got on well with him. All mentions of him in AEH's letters confirm this.

[4] Gilbert Murray was appointed.

Regius professorship, and the King generally asks the advice of one or two persons whom he supposes to be good judges. He has not applied to me: possibly because we have not been introduced.

Yours sincerely
A. E. Housman.

Have I changed my publisher? What has become of E. Grant Richards?[5]

Illinois MS. Richards, 83 (nearly complete); Maas, 98.

TO GRANT RICHARDS

1 Yarborough Villas | Woodridings | Pinner
4 July 1908

My dear Richards,

The manuscript is numbered M 31 in the Biblioteca Nacional at Madrid. It contains Manilius and the *Silvae* of Statius. What I really want is to have photographs of the first 107 pages, on which the Manilius is written.[1] The cheapest process is called (I think) *rotary-bromine*, in which no negative is used: whether this is practised in Madrid I can't be sure. The sums one is charged for photographs of MSS vary greatly in different towns and countries: I am prepared to go to £20, though it ought to be less, and in Rome at any rate would be very much less, probably about £5.

Yours sincerely
A. E. Housman.

Illinois MS. Richards, 84; Maas, 99.

TO ALICE ROTHENSTEIN

1 Yarborough Villas | Woodridings, Pinner
15 Aug. 1908.

Dear Mrs Rothenstein,

This is annoying: now that you are in Gloucestershire[1] I am back in Middlesex, and expect to be before long in Italy. The place where I was staying was Woodchester, on the opposite side of Stroud to you. I have never been nearer Thougham than Bisley, where there used to be seven springs and five curates.

---

[5] GR was again publishing under his own name (rather than that of his wife).

[1] AEH was now working on his edn. of *Manilius II*, published by GR in 1912.

[1] The Rothensteins had bought Iles Farm, Far Oakridge, Gloucestershire, in the summer of 1908.

I saw an impressive and mysterious work of Rothenstein's, *The Doll's House*[2] at the Franco-British Exhibition.[3]

Some parts of Gloucestershire are horribly infested with harvest-bugs at this time of year: I hope you are not devoured by them, or otherwise prevented from enjoying yourself.

Yours sincerely
A. E. Housman.

Harvard bMS Eng 1148 (740) 9.

TO GRANT RICHARDS

1 Yarborough Villas | Woodridings, Pinner
26 Aug. 1908.

I am going abroad on the 30th for about a month, and expect to be in Paris in the third week of September, probably at the Normandy.

Yrs.
A. E. Housman.

Illinois MS: p.c. addressed 'Grant Richards Esq. | 7 Carlton Street | Regent Street | S. W.'
Richards, 84 (nearly complete).

TO WALTER ASHBURNER

1 Yarborough Villas | Pinner
27 Aug. 1908.

Dear Ashburner,

I expect I shall pass through Lausanne early on <Monday> \Tuesday/ morning. I shall not stop, but shall scrutinise earth, water and sky in order to decide whether it is a fit place for me to stop some other time.

I am afraid I am hardly likely to be in Venice as late as the 18th, unless Brown or Andrea or the weather is quite extraordinarily fascinating, or unless Garda detains me on my way there longer than I expect. But no doubt the glories of your new hotel will be all-sufficing and deprive you of any wish for my company or anyone else's.

Yours very truly
A. E. Housman.

NLS MS 20369, fos. 226–7. Ashburner/Bell (1976), 17.

---

[2] Reproduced in Rothenstein's *Men and Memories*, 1. 346 f.

[3] An exhibition of French and British manufacturing and art held May–October 1908 in Shepherd's Bush, London, to promote *entente cordiale*.

TO PROFESSOR FRIEDRICH VOLLMER

22 Sept. 1908

Dear Sir,

I am much obliged by your postcard and by your offer to send me your photographs of MSS; but I do not purpose to write any more on the *Culex*,[1] and I have no doubt that your edition, when it appears, will provide information as full and accurate as could be wished. I have read with interest your paper on the 'kleineren Gedichte' in the *Kgl. Bayer. Akad.*, and I am very glad that you are also preparing an edition to supersede the disorderly and untrustworthy production of Ellis.[2] Your power of work is admirable and amazing: I see that you also have on hand an edition of *Phaedrus* and the fabulists.

I am yours faithfully
A. E. Housman.

Bayerische Staatsbibliothek MS: p.c. addressed 'Herrn Dr. Fr. Vollmer | Professor Kgl. Bayr. Universität | München | Königstr. 69' | Germany'.

TO PROFESSOR GILBERT MURRAY

1 Yarborough Villas | Woodridings | Pinner
17 Oct. 1908

Dear Murray,

I see in the paper the confirmation of what has been common rumour for some time past, and I congratulate you on having survived a Scotch professorship long enough to obtain what I hope will be consolation even for that.[1]

I think you are now well on your way to take that place in the public eye which used to be occupied by Jowett[2] and then by Jebb; and as you are a much better scholar than the one and a much better man of letters

[1] 'AEH had just published 'The Apparatus Criticus of the *Culex*', *Transactions of the Classical Philological Society*, 6 (1908), 3–22 (*Classical Papers*, 773–86), mentioning his photographs of MSS Vat. lat. 2759 and Corsinianus 43 F 5.

[2] Robinson Ellis's edn. of the *Appendix Vergiliana* appeared in 1907.

[1] Murray was Professor of Greek at Glasgow, 1889–99, and had just been appointed Regius Professor of Greek at Oxford.

[2] Benjamin Jowett (1817–93). Regius Professor of Greek at Oxford, 1855–93; Master of Balliol College, 1870–93. He published translations of Plato (4 vols., 1871), Thucydides (2 vols., 1881), and Aristotle's *Politics* (1885). AEH held his scholarship in low esteem: see Naiditch (1988), 175–6.

than the other, the public will be a gainer without knowing it, and good judges (by which I mean myself) will be less at variance with the public.

I am yours sincerely
A. E. Housman.

You will be buried under letters of congratulation, so take no notice of this.

Bodleian MSS Gilbert Murray, 14. 90–1; I. Henderson, Gilbert Murray: An Unfinished Biography *(1960), 143; Maas, 99.*

TO LAURENCE HOUSMAN

1 Yarborough Villas | Woodridings | Pinner
3 Nov. 1908

My dear Laurence,

On page 11[1] 'when first knighted' sounds very prosy,[2] though I don't think my suggestion much better, as it is ambiguous. I have not found much else to note. The pieces on pp. 18 and 28[3] are really quite nice: I dont[4] remember noticing them much before.

I was at Cambridge a week or two ago, and met a lady who asked if I were the author of *Gods and their Makers*.[5] Always honest, I owned that I was not: I said I was his brother. 'Oh, well,' said she, 'that's the next best thing'. It appears that the work is a household word with them: they have a dog or a cat called after one of your divinities.

I thought your selections were to be published by Grant Richards, but I see another name on the proofs.[6]

Love to Clemence and Cousin Mary.

Your affectionate brother
A. E. Housman.

BMC MS. Memoir, *172–3; Maas, 100 (both slightly incomplete).*

---

[1] Of the page proofs of LH's *Selected Poems* (1908).

[2] Printed as 'a good knight newly knighted'

[3] *Two Songs: I:* Sleep lies in every cup | Of land or flower: | Look how the earth drains up | Her evening hour! || Each face, that once so laughed, | Now fain would lift | Lips to Life's sleeping-draught, | The goodlier gift. || Oh, whence this overflow, | This flood of rest? | What vale of healing so | Unlocks her breast? || What land, to give us right | Of refuge, yields | To the sharp scythes of light | Her poppied fields? || Nay, wait! Our turn to make | Amends grows due: | Another day will break, | We must give too!
and *The Fellow Travellers*: Fellow-travellers here with me, | Loose for good each other's loads! | Here we come to the cross-roads: | Here must parting be. || Where will you five be to-night? | Where shall I? We little know. | Loosed from you, I let you go | Utterly from sight. || Far away go taste, and touch, | Far go sight, and sound, and smell! | Fellow-travellers, fare you well, — | You I loved so much!

[4] For 'don't'.

[5] Published in 1897.

[6] Sidgwick & Jackson were the publishers.

TO LAURENCE HOUSMAN

1 Yarborough Villas | Woodridings | Pinner
8 Nov. 1908

My dear Laurence,

The changes in *Advocatus Diaboli* are very judicious.

The line on p. 52 is as bad as ever. I think you should try what you can do with *default* or *assault*;[1] for I am afraid that salt and malt and cobalt are no good. There is however a kind of stiff clay called gault, in which I daresay sepulchres are sometimes dug.

On p. 71, last line but one, I should restore the old reading, because it is not good to have two lines with their last halves so much on the same model as *the pangs he bore* and *the wound he wore*.[2]

On p. 86 there is a foot missing from line 7.

The misprint on p. 101 is eloquent of the printer's cockney pronunciation.

Your affectionate brother
A. E. Housman.

'Time's assault' is perhaps a thing towards which you might take up some attitude or other in your ancestral vault.

BMC MS. Memoir, *173; Maas, 100 (both incomplete).*

TO GRANT RICHARDS

1 Yarborough Villas | Pinner
8 Nov. 1908.

My dear Richards,

I do not care for the new edition;[1] but as it was brought out simply to please you and not me, that does not matter. Coloured plates always strike me as vulgar (though I understand that they are the fashion at present), and these drawings of Hyde's do not seem to me nearly so good as those in his London book.[2] The end papers, on the other hand, I rather like; though the horses seem to be letting the man do all the ploughing. It lies, I find, on drawing-room tables, so all is well.

---

[1] As printed: Or, open to the skies, a vault | Where basking sunnily I lie, | And, negligent to Time's assault, | With foot in earth prepare to die.

[2] As printed: Little ye know the pangs He bore, | Ye friends whom Love forgave: | There was a bitterer wound He wore | For souls he could not save.

[1] The illustrated edn. (2000 copies) of *ASL.*

[2] *London Impressions: Etchings and Pictures in Photogravure* (1898).

.To the fate of the widows and orphans whom it appears that you have been introducing to outside brokers[3] I am totally indifferent, having no spirit in my body.[4]

Yours sincerely
A. E. Housman.

Illinois MS. Richards, 85; Maas, 101.

TO MARGARET WOODS

1 Yarborough Villas | Woodridings | Pinner
17 Nov. 1908

Dear Mrs Woods,

Naturally I do not like refusing a request of yours; but still I feel a sort of repugnance to signing copies for sale. I have never signed any except for personal acquaintances, and, on one occasion, for American ladies who declared that they had crossed the Atlantic on my account. Bazaars, too, are often held for objects which I disapprove, though I daresay yours is quite respectable.

The notion of coming to lunch some day is much more attractive; but perhaps that is only conditional, and held out as an inducement.

I am yours sincerely
A. E. Housman.

BMC MS.

TO GRANT RICHARDS

25 Nov. 1908

UNIVERSITY OF LONDON. | UNIVERSITY COLLEGE.

Permission may be given to Miss R. C. Smyth to set the three poems Nos. 13, 15 and 18 as she wishes.

A. E. Housman.

Illinois MS.

[3] 'The *Academy*, through, I believe, the pen of T. W. H. Crosland, had just then attacked me for allowing (for payment) a book-mark advertising the business of an outside broker to be placed for a while in the books I published': GR, 85. *The Academy*, 66 (24 Oct. 1908), 392–3, brought to notice the fact that GR had placed in all his publications a bookmark advertising the *Financial Review of Reviews*, the publication of The Investment Registry Ltd. *The Academy* acknowledged GR's need, but questioned this method, to pay off his creditors. Speculating on the high probability of GR's publications being read largely by 'widows and orphans', it asked: 'Would Mr. Grant Richards or Mr. A. E. Housman ... advise a widow or an orphan possessed of securities to entrust the management of them to an outside broker?' (393).

[4] Daniel 7: 15: 'my spirit in the midst of my body'; James 2: 26: 'the body without the spirit is dead'.

TO KATHARINE SYMONS

1 Yarborough Villas | Woodridings, Pinner
26 Nov. 1908

My dear Kate,

When I got your letter I intended to answer it almost immediately, but the news about Aunt Mary checked me by causing me to expect something new each morning, and so now the days have gone by, and I have neither sent back your enclosures nor answered your invitation. As to this, I could not have got away last week end, nor can I this, as I am going to Wimbledon; and the week after I have an engagement which would force me to curtail the visit, and meanwhile I am afraid the leaves are rapidly coming off the trees, and the weather (affected, my dear Kate, by the streams of meteors, which at this season intersect the earth's orbit) will be growing nasty; so I think I had better wait. The two letters I return, and I also enclose the family tree sent me by Colonel Chippindall.[1] I think you had better keep this as you are the only one of us to continue the race;[2] only remember that it is my property, and if I want it back when they make me a peer you are not to say I gave it to you nor pretend that you have lost it. Colonel Chippindall says that he has portraits of our great-grandfather's mother and sister, and invites me to go to Bedford to lunch some day and look at them. He also said (in September) that Lune Bank was for sale, and seemed anxious that one of us should buy it.

I went abroad at the end of August for about three weeks, which I spent chiefly at Venice and on the Lake of Garda, where I was five years ago. This time however I stayed at some of the less frequented places, such as Garda itself, which on the former occasion struck me as the prettiest part of the lake, when viewed from the steamboat in which I was coming away. On land it is not so satisfactory, as the cypresses and olives which ornament the hills are mostly in private grounds, and there is the usual Italian lack of real open country. Also the food and cooking did not suit me, and when I got to Venice, as sitting all day in a gondola is not the best thing in the world for restoring one's digestion, I was more uncomfortable, for about five days, than I have been for a long time. The campanile has

---

[1] Richards, 460–1, provides a facsimile of a 'family chart written out by A. E. Housman in 1908 for Colonel Harold Chippindall, a relative who was preparing a much more extensive chart'. W[illiam] Harold Chippindall (b. 1850) was an expert on parish and family history.

[2] The rest of the Housman family was childless.

now risen to half of its old height and the work is going on more briskly,[3] so that they expect to finish it […]

LC-GR2 t.s.: copy of part of a letter. Richards, 378 (brief excerpt). I have corrected 'May' to 'Mary' and 'Lime' to 'Lune' (Lune Bank being ancestor Robert Housman's home).

TO PROFESSOR FRIEDRICH VOLLMER

[30 Nov. 1908]

My dear Sir,

I have examined with great pleasure the cod. Harl. 2745,[1] which contains 'flora <V>uirgilii' on pp. 84[vers.]–86[rect.]; but among these I find nothing from the append. Verg. except Culex 79 sqq. on p. 85[vers.] written thus: […] This is preceded by 'stimulas dedit aemula uirtus' (= Luc. 1. 120) <which> and followed by Verg. Aen. <VI> X 467 sq. <breue et> *breue* etc.

But on p. 97[rect.], preceded by excerpts from Juvenal and followed by excerpts from [?Bretlin], are the following 'flores uirginalis': […]

SJCO MS, draft in pencil corrected in pencil on torn foolscap sheet, with P. Ouidi Nasonis Metamorphosen Libri XV, *ed. Otto Korn (Berlin, 1880). The MS is accompanied by another torn foolscap sheet bearing references in AEH's handwriting to passages in the cod. Harl. 2745.*

TO LAURENCE HOUSMAN

1 Yarborough Villas | Woodridings, Pinner
16 Dec. 1908

My dear Laurence,

Thanks for your poems.[1] I suppose if I say anything in praise of the cover and get-up you will detect insinuations as to the contents, so I had better not.

Your affectionate brother
A. E. Housman.

BMC MS. Memoir, *173.*

---

[3] The Campanile of S. Marco, some 99 m. high, was first built 888–912, and completed 1156–73. On 14 July 1902, it collapsed. An exact reproduction was immediately begun, and opened on 25 Apr. 1912. See *MP* XLIV 23 ('The tower that stood and fell'), and notes in *Poems* (1997), 456.

[1] In a letter of 24 Nov. 1908, Vollmer had asked AEH to examine the British Museum MS for him: with AEH's copy of Vollmer's *Poetae Latini Minores*, 5 (1914), SJCO b 1.

[1] *Selected Poems* (1908).

TO ALICE ROTHENSTEIN

1 Yarborough Villas | Woodridings, Pinner
16 Dec. 1908

Dear Mrs Rothenstein,

Alas, your letter, which I suppose came by the second post, did not get into my hands till I came back from College this afternoon, and so I cannot make time to escape to Hampstead out of the press of work of this last week of term.

I am very sorry, but I hope you will have a happy Christmas.

Yours sincerely
A. E. Housman.

Harvard bMS Eng 1148 (740) 10.

TO ROSA JACKSON

1 Yarborough Villas | Woodridings, Pinner
17 Dec. 1908

Dear Mrs Jackson,

I am sending you a copy of the latest edition of my poems, illustrated. I do not admire the illustrations so much as I admire the poems, but it was done chiefly to please the publisher.[1]

I was glad to have your information about Mo.[2] How did Rupert[3] fare at Cambridge? A merry Christmas to all of you.[4]

Yours sincerely
A. E. Housman.

Private MS, inspected at Sotheby's, 4 Nov. 2001. Tipped-in on front fixed end-paper of copy of ASL *(1908). Copy in Lilly MSS, 3. 1. 6. Excerpt quoted in Sotheby's catalogue,* The Library of Frederick B. Adams, Jr, Part 1: English & American Literature *(6 Nov. 2001), 31.*

[1] See AEH to GR, 8 Nov. 1908.
[2] Moses Jackson. See List of Recipients.
[3] Rupert W. P. Jackson (b. 2 Oct. 1890), eldest son of Moses and Rosa. He received a doctorate, and, during the First World War, won both the Military Cross and the Croix de Guerre: Naiditch (1995), 143.
[4] In a letter of 5 May 1936 to LH (BMC), Rosa Jackson wrote of AEH: 'I have been honoured with his friendship for over 40 years & my late husband (who was at Oxford with him) & my sons all loved him dearly.'

1909

TO GRANT RICHARDS

[1 Yarborough Villas | Woodridings, Pinner]

No, I never go abroad in the winter; and also I am going on a visit in Surrey.

Yrs

A. E. Housman

7 Jan. 1909.

Illinois MS: p.c. addressed 'Grant Richards Esq. | 7 Carlton Street | Regent Street | S. W.'
Richards, 85.

TO WILLIAM ROTHENSTEIN

1 Yarborough Villas | Woodridings, Pinner

15 Jan. 1909

My dear Rothenstein,

Will you dine with me at the Café Royal on Friday Feb. 5th at 7. 45?

I am anxious to know what it is that you think British Art requires in order to regenerate it: whether it is ribald laughter going up to heaven, or a river of laughter coming down from heaven; for the papers are not agreed.[1]

Remember me to Mrs Rothenstein.

Yours very truly

A. E. Housman.

Harvard bMS Eng 1148 (740) 11. Maas, 101.

---

[1] In his lecture at the London Institution Rothenstein had argued that art would remain second-rate 'until a great river of laughter comes down from Heaven at ... the pictures which are daily shown as works of serious importance'.

TO GRANT RICHARDS

1 Yarborough Villas | Woodridings, Pinner
15 Jan. 1909

My dear Richards,

Miss or Mrs Jewell[1] may be told that she can set and publish to her heart's content. If you like to add that she displays an honourable scrupulousness which is doubly remarkable inasmuch as it makes its appearance in a woman and an American; or if you like to quote the opinion of a doctor which I see in today's paper, that there are more people with unbalanced minds in Boston than anywhere else, do so; but don't say that I put you up to it.

Will you dine with me at the Café Royal on Friday Feb. 5th at 7. 45? I am also asking Rothenstein.

Yours sincerely
A. E. Housman.

I will remember about the Cheshire Cheese.[2]

Illinois MS. Richards, 86; Maas, 101–2.

TO GRANT RICHARDS

1 Yarborough Villas | Woodridings, Pinner
23 Jan. 1909

My dear Richards,

I have received your noble present of Montaigne,[1] and I only wish the rest of my library were fit to keep it company. I have never read him yet in Florio's translation: as a boy I used to study Cotton's,[2] which is good, but less good, I suppose. Thank you also for the guide to Paris.[3] The question whether I ever go to Vienna depends on the question whether you produce a similar guide to it.[4]

---

[1]   American composer Lucina Jewell (b. 1874). She did not publish any settings of AEH.

[2]   Ancient eating-house in Fleet Street, London, associated with Dr Johnson and also with the Rhymers' Club, which met there, 1891–4: see W. B. Yeats's account in *The Trembling of the Veil* (1922).

[1]   Translation by John Florio (1553?–1625), first published in 1603, of Montaigne's *Essais*, repr. by GR in his Elizabethan Classics series. LH was responsible for the decoration on the spine (Richards, 86).

[2]   The translation by Charles Cotton (1630–87), first published in 1685.

[3]   *Paris* (1908) by Leonard Williams, the first in a projected series of Grant Richards's Waistcoat-Pocket Guides.

[4]   GR produced no such guide, and AEH never did visit Vienna.

The pudding[5] was not only palatable but digestible.

Yours sincerely
A. E. Housman.

PM MS. LC-GR t.s. Richards, 86; Maas, 102.

TO MR THOMPSON

University College, London
16 March 1909

Dear Mr Thompson,

I expect to suffer much from the Bazaar,[1] especially in purse; but my reputation, such as it is, I will preserve intact, and not injure it by writing verse to order. I have never done so for anyone, even when offered bribes, literature not being my trade. And I certainly shall not molest my poor brother, who ought not to suffer for mere consanguinity, which is no crime.

I hope you will be more successful in capturing other prey, and will bear me no ill-will for my ungraciousness.

I am yours truly
A. E. Housman.

Photocopy of ALS in LC AEH Collection.

TO PROFESSOR FRIEDRICH VOLLMER

University College, London
1 May 1909.

Dear Sir,

I am much obliged by the gift of your treatise on the *Appendix Vergiliana*, which is full of information and interest.[1]

Your opinion that the *Zanclaea* of Vat. 2759 at cul. 332 comes from Ouid. fast. IV 499 may gain some support from the fact, which I pointed out in the *Journal of Philology* XXV p. 244, that the *sua pagina dicit* of the same MS at cul. 402 comes from the same poem, III 791 'itur ad Argeos: qui sint, *sua pagina dicet*'.[2]

I am yours faithfully
A. E. Housman.

Bayerische Staatsbibliothek MS.

---

[5] 'The beef-steak, lark, kidney and oyster pudding of the Cheshire Cheese': Richards, 86

[1] A fund-raising event arranged by one of the colleges of London University.

[1] *P. Vergilii Maronis iuvenalis ludi libellus von Fridericus Vollmer* (München 1909): Naiditch (2003), 151.

[2] In 'Lucretiana', *Journal of Philology*, 25 (1897), 226–49; *Classical Papers*, 423–41, and specifically 437.

TO GRANT RICHARDS

[1 Yarborough Villas | Woodridings, Pinner]
12 May 1909

Thanks. Manilius Book II may perhaps be ready next year.

Yrs

A. E. Housman.

Illinois MS: p.c. addressed 'Grant Richards Esq. | 7 Carlton Street | Regent Street | S. W.'
Richards, 87 (nearly complete).

TO ALICE ROTHENSTEIN

1 Yarborough Villas | Woodridings, Pinner
28 May 1909

Dear Mrs Rothenstein,

I hope that my conversation through the telephone yesterday did not sound brusque. I am very little accustomed to using that instrument. I was very sorry not to be able to come to the theatre with you, but I had an engagement out of town for the evening, and I was just leaving the college to catch my train when the beadle told me that someone had been enquiring for me.

Please tell Rothenstein that all my Jewish students are absenting themselves from my lectures from Wednesday to Friday this week on the plea that these are Jewish holidays. I have been looking up the Old Testament, but I can find no mention there of either the Derby or the Oaks.[1]

Yours sincerely
A. E. Housman.

Harvard bMS Eng 1148 (740) 12. Maas, 102–3.

TO ALICE ROTHENSTEIN

1 Yarborough Villas | Woodridings, Pinner
29 May 1909

Dear Mrs Rothenstein,

It is an attractive proposal, and if it is decently fine on Monday I will come over some time in the day. If you go out, perhaps you would leave

---

[1] Horse races run at Epsom on 26 and 28 May 1909. In 1909 the Jewish Feast of Weeks (Shavuot) fell on 26 and 27 May.

word behind you as to what part of the heath[1] you are likely to be found on at some hour or other.

Yours sincerely
A. E. Housman.

Harvard bMS Eng 1148 (740) 13.

TO GRANT RICHARDS

1 Yarborough Villas | Woodridings, Pinner
6 July 1909

My dear Richards,

I am very much indebted to you for sending me Royall Tyler's *Spain*,[1] which is a capital straightforward business-like book, exactly the sort of thing I like and find *exciting*. How the public will bear the absence of the usual twaddle I don't know.

My only objection is to the title, as I think Spain is a neuter noun.[2]

Yours sincerely
A. E. Housman.

Illinois MS. Richards, 87; Maas, 103.

TO GRANT RICHARDS

1 Yarborough Villas | Woodridings, Pinner
18 July 1909

My dear Richards,

I must thank you for *Antonio*,[1] though I have no time at present to do more than glance at it, and also for your cheque, of which I send no formal receipt, because you told me last year it was unnecessary.

Yours sincerely
A. E. Housman.

Illinois MS. Richards, 87.

---

[1] Hampstead Heath in London.

[1] *Spain: A Study of Her Life and Arts* (1909), published by GR.

[2] It is nevertheless conventional to make countries feminine.

[1] Novel (1909) by Ernest [James] Oldmeadow (1867–1949), published by GR. It deals with Portugal and the wine trade.

TO ALICE ROTHENSTEIN

1 Yarborough Villas | Woodridings | Pinner
11 Aug. 1909

Dear Mrs Rothenstein,

I am glad you have found such a pleasant spot and are enjoying yourselves. I have been rather industrious and have only been away for short visits. I may perhaps be going for another to Swanage, where my married sister and her family are, or *were*; for I hear nothing from them, and they have probably perished in the water-famine which you just escaped.

I don't expect to come to France much before September, and then I shall not stay very long; and all the time that I can spare from the vices of Paris (as to which, consult William) I expect to spend in visiting cathedral towns which I have not yet seen. The life you sketch at Vaucottes-sur-mer,[1] and kindly invite me to join you in, is very attractive, but when it is gone it is gone, and has not stored one's mind (except of course with the instructive conversation of the Rothenstein family, including John's[2] views on the soul and our future life) and one cannot boast about it afterwards. Though, after all, that is equally true of the vices of Paris.

Remember me to all who remember me, and believe me yours sincerely
A. E. Housman.

Harvard bMS Eng 1148 (740) 14. Maas, 104.

TO LILY THICKNESSE

[1 Yarborough Villas | Woodridings, Pinner]
11 Aug. 1909

Dear Mrs Thicknesse,

My blood boils. This is not due to the recent commencement of summer, but to the Wrongs of Woman,[1] with which I have been making myself acquainted. 'She cannot serve on any Jury'; and yet she bravely lives on. 'She cannot serve in the army or navy'—oh cruel, cruel!—'except'—this adds insult to injury—'as a nurse'. They do not even employ a Running

---

[1] Where the Rothensteins often spent the summer.
[2] John [Knewstub Maurice] (1901–92) the Rothensteins' eldest son.

[1] *The Rights and Wrongs of Women: A Digest, with Practical Illustrations and Notes on the Law in France*, by Ralph Thicknesse (1909), a practical guide for those who wished to see the law changed in favour of women.

Woman instead of a Running Man for practising marksmanship. I have been making marginal additions. 'She cannot be ordained a Priest or Deacon': add *nor become a Freemason.* 'She cannot be a member of the Royal Society';[2] add *nor of the Amateur Boxing Association.* In short, your unhappy sex seem to have nothing to look forward to, excepting contracting a valid marriage as soon as they are 12 years old; and that must soon pall.

Thanks for the picture card. I did not know, or had forgotten, that you were at Woodbridge.[3] If you can find an old hat of Edward FitzGerald's they will let you write three columns about it in the *Athenaeum.* But some literary people are so proud that they despise these avenues to fame.

Yours sincerely
A. E. Housman.

Memoir, *204; Maas, 103–4.*

TO GRANT RICHARDS'S PUBLISHING MANAGER

1 Yarborough Villas | Woodridings, Pinner
17 Aug. 1909.

Dear Sir,

The applicant may be given *permission* to publish settings of the four poems, but must be told that this permission conveys no exclusive *rights* of any kind.[1]

I am yours faithfully
A. E. Housman.

I should be obliged if the enclosed envelope could be forwarded to Mr Richards.

Illinois MS. Richards, 87 (incomplete).

[2] The quotations are from pp. 13, 15, and 14.
[3] In Suffolk, home for the last twenty-three years of his life of Edward Fitzgerald (1809–83), best known for his translation of *The Rubáiyát of Omar Khayyám* (1859, etc.).

[1] 'Somebody must have been warning Housman of the possibility that one or other of the composers to whom the poet so readily granted permission might be under the impression that he was the only one so favoured': Richards, 87.

TO GRANT RICHARDS

1 Yarborough Villas | Woodridings, Pinner
24 Aug. 1909

My dear Richards,
    I shall be very pleased to dine with you on Thursday, if you are not then dead of ptomaine poisoning,[1] in which case please appear as a ghost and cancel the engagement.

Yours sincerely
A. E. Housman.

PM MS. LC-GR t.s. Richards, 88.

TO GRANT RICHARDS'S PUBLISHING MANAGER

1 Yarborough Villas | Woodridings | Pinner
14 Sept. 1909

Dear Sir,
    The enclosed request must be refused.

Your[s] faithfully
A. E. Housman.

Illinois MS. The final 's' in 'Yours' is inadvertently omitted by AEH.

TO ALICE ROTHENSTEIN

5 Oct. 1909

UNIVERSITY OF LONDON. | UNIVERSITY COLLEGE,
GOWER STREET, LONDON, W.C.

Dear Mrs Rothenstein,
    I shall be very pleased to come to tea to-morrow, full of good advice. This is our first week of term, and I am writing this note in the intervals of giving good advice to students; so I am in full practice.

Yours sincerely
A. E. Housman.

Harvard bMS Eng 1148 (740) 15.

---

[1] Food poisoning. Ptomaine is the generic name of certain alkaloid bodies found in putrefying animal or vegetable matter. 'I have no idea why the possibility of poisoning entered his head': Richards, 88.

TO GRANT RICHARDS

8 Oct. 1909
UNIVERSITY OF LONDON. | UNIVERSITY COLLEGE,
GOWER STREET, LONDON, W.C.

My dear Richards,

I have noted the day and hour at which I am to go and have my teeth taken out by Lamb,[1] but I find that I have not got his address.

I like Masefield[2] very much. Who was the other young man, who reads Manilius?[3]

Yours sincerely
A. E. Housman.

Illinois MS. Richards, 88; Maas, 104–5.

TO PROFESSOR GILBERT MURRAY

1 Yarborough Villas | Woodridings | Pinner
12 Oct. 1909

Dear Murray,

I shall be very pleased to stay with you the night of Nov. 26. I have work at the College in the morning, and will come down in the afternoon.

I have chosen a dry subject for my paper,[1] as I have no doubt that scholarship at Oxford is taking on an excessively literary tinge under the influence of the new professor of Greek.[2]

I am yours sincerely
A. E. Housman.

Bodleian MSS Gilbert Murray, 16. 85–6. Maas, 105.

[1] Henry [Taylor] Lamb (1883–1960), who studied painting in London and Paris and was a founder-member of Camden Town and London groups. He qualified at Guy's Hospital, 1916, and served as medical officer, being awarded the MC in 1918. Later he did portraits of other writers, including Lytton Strachey, Evelyn Waugh, and Lord David Cecil.

[2] The poet John Masefield: see List of Recipients.

[3] Eric Maclagan.

[1] 'Greek Nouns in Latin Poetry', read to the Oxford Philological Society in New College on 26 Nov. It was later published as 'Greek Nouns in Latin Poetry from Lucretius to Juvenal' in the *Journal of Philology*, 31 (1910), 236–66 (*Classical Papers*, 817–39).

[2] Murray.

TO ALICE ROTHENSTEIN

14 Oct. 1909.

UNIVERSITY OF LONDON. | UNIVERSITY COLLEGE,
GOWER STREET, LONDON, W.C.

Dear Mrs Rothenstein,

I shall be very pleased to come to tea to-morrow.

This afternoon I am to have my portrait done, again;[1] not at my own desire, needless to say. Three hours sitting, which I have already gone through for Rothenstein, ought to be quite enough for one mortal life.

Yours sincerely
A. E. Housman.

Harvard bMS Eng 1148 (740) 16.

TO GRANT RICHARDS

1 Yarborough Villas | Woodridings, Pinner
16 Oct. 1909

My dear Richards,

I can sit to Lamb again next Thursday at the same hour, if that will suit him. Why was I ever born? This question is addressed to the universe, not to you personally.

Yours sincerely
A. E. Housman.

Illinois MS. Richards, 89; Maas, 105.

TO GRANT RICHARDS'S PUBLISHING MANAGER

[1 Yarborough Villas | Woodridings, Pinner]
7 Nov. 1909

Permission must not be given to Mr Williams[1] to print the poems in his programme.

A. E. Housman.

Illinois MS.

---

[1] See AEH to GR, 8 Oct. 1909, n. 1.

[1] Vaughan Williams: see next letter.

TO GRANT RICHARDS

1 Yarborough Villas | Woodridings, Pinner
11 Nov. 1909

My dear Richards,

'The terms' on which Mr Lambert[1] may print my words with his music are that he should spell my name right.

As to Mr Vaughan Williams, about whom your secretary wrote: he came to see me, and made representations and entreaties, so that I said he might print the verses he wanted on his programmes.[2] I mention this lest his action should come to your ears and cause you to set the police after him.

Yours sincerely
A. E. Housman.

Illinois MS. LC-GR t.s. Richards, 90; Maas, 105–6.

TO GRANT RICHARDS

1 Yarborough Villas | Woodridings, Pinner
27 Nov. 1909

My dear Richards,

Well, I will go to Lamb next Thursday if he likes, and I have written to tell him so: I have addressed the letter to 8 Fitzroy Street, though I am not quite sure if that is the number: if not, let me know.

I hope you will relate this incident to Mrs Richards, in order that she may see what a false notion of my temper she has, and how angelic it really is.

I met your uncle[1] in Oxford yesterday, and returning here I find his last book,[2] for which I am much obliged to the author or publisher, whichever is the donor: the enclosed slip says that it is sent for review and will not be published till the 29th of last month.

Yours sincerely
A. E. Housman.

Illinois MS. Richards, 90 (nearly complete); Maas, 106.

---

[1] E. Frank Lambert's setting of *ASL* XXII (*The street sounds to the soldiers' tread*) was published in 1914.

[2] *On Wenlock Edge*, a song cycle for tenor voice, piano, and string quartet, by Ralph Vaughan Williams (1872–1958), was completed in 1909. It consisted of settings of *ASL* XXXI (*On Wenlock edge the wood's in trouble*), XXXII (*From far, from eve and morning*), XXVII (*Is my team ploughing*), XVIII (*Oh, when I was in love with you*), XXI (*Bredon Hill*), and L (*In valleys of springs of rivers*).

[1] Herbert Richards.

[2] *Aristophanes and Others* (1909), published by GR. Herbert Richards was also the author of *Notes on Xenophon and Others* (1907), *Platonica* (1911), and *Aristotelica* (1915).

TO PROFESSOR GILBERT MURRAY

1 Yarborough Villas | Woodridings, Pinner
9 Dec. 1909.

Dear Murray,

I have read Mrs Taylor's poems,[1] that you were kind enough to give me, with a good deal of pleasure and interest. There are phrases and lines that are quite beautiful, and she has not only technical skill but impulse; and yet there is a curious indistinctness about the general impression, and hardly a poem that rings clear. She is rather like the second Lord Lytton;[2] susceptible to the beauty of other people's poetry, and giving out an answering note, beautiful in its way; and she is not so terribly fluent as he was, nor such a bare-faced thief. The appeal to the optic nerve is almost shameless, and becomes monotonous. I like best some of the short pieces, like *The Young Martyrs*.[3] The poem on the Magi,[4] as you said, is also good.

Will it ever be possible to break female poets of using such words as "passional"[5] and feeling proud of it?

Yours sincerely
A. E. Housman.

Bodleian MSS Gilbert Murray, 16. 125–6. Maas, 106–7.

TO ALICE ROTHENSTEIN

1 Yarborough Villas | Woodridings | Pinner
30 Dec. 1909

Dear Mrs Rothenstein,

I shall be very pleased to dine with you on Wednesday, and in the mean time I wish you all a happy new year.

Yours sincerely
A. E. Housman.

Harvard bMS Eng 1148 (740) 17.

[1] *Rose and Vine* (1909) by Rachel Annand Taylor (1876–1960).
[2] Edward Robert Bulwer Lytton ('Owen Meredith'), first Earl of Lytton (1831–91), and son of the novelist Edward George Earle [Bulwer-] Lytton (1803–73). His published verse includes *Clytemnestra, The Earl's Return, The Artist and Other Poems* (1855), *The Wanderer* (1859), *Fables in Song* (1874), and *King Poppy* (1892).
[3] 'They wore their wounds like roses | Who died at morningtide. | From Youth's enchanted closes, | From loves that did adore them, | With perfumes broken o'er them, | As bridegroom goes to bride, | They rode the Flaming Ride. | They wore their wounds like roses | Who in their morning died.'
[4] *The Magi.*
[5] Mrs Taylor has 'The passional Porch-verse' (in *The Race*) and 'passional pomegranates' (in *The Tree of Life*).

1910

TO ALICE ROTHENSTEIN

1 Yarborough Villas | Woodridings, Pinner
4 Jan. 1910

Dear Mrs Rothenstein,

I am quite happy and content with the new arrangement, and will come in some time before 9.

Yours sincerely
A. E. Housman.

Harvard bMS Eng 1148 (740) 18.

TO AN UNKNOWN CORRESPONDENT

University College, London
10 Feb. 1910

Dear Sir,

For some years past I have refused to anthologists permission to print poems of mine, because these requests were becoming frequent and the poems are few. I am afraid therefore that I cannot in fairness make an exception in your case.

I am yours faithfully
A. E. Housman.

BMC MS.

TO GRANT RICHARDS

1 Yarborough Villas | Woodridings, Pinner
11 Feb. 1910

My dear Richards,

I should be very glad to come on the 27th, or, as you suggest, on the night of the 26th. Only don't ask your friend Crosland[1] to meet me.

Yours sincerely
A. E. Housman.

Illinois MS. LC-GR t.s. Richards, 90 (nearly complete).

---

[1] 'I did not. I had no thought of doing so. I do not know whether Housman ever read much of T. W. H. Crosland's work, but he certainly thought poorly of him as a man .... My

TO ALICE ROTHENSTEIN

15 Feb. 1910
UNIVERSITY OF LONDON. | UNIVERSITY COLLEGE.
GOWER STREET, LONDON, W.C.

Dear Mrs Rothenstein,

It is a nuisance, but I am going away at the end of the week, and am consequently obliged to pack into the middle of it work which I should otherwise postpone, and so I really am not able to come. I am very sorry, but your gatherings are always such galaxies of intellect that you will not miss me severely.

I saw a whole row of portraits by W.[1] at Dr Herringham's[2] the other night.

Yours sincerely
A. E. Housman.

Harvard bMS Eng 1148 (740) 19.

TO GRANT RICHARDS

1 Yarborough Villas | Woodridings, Pinner
15 Feb. 1910.

My dear Richards,

As you are so good, I could come down on the 26th by the 5. 50 from Paddington (I am writing with only a rather obsolete Bradshaw[1] at hand), and I should be very glad to stay till the Monday morning. Let me know the name of your house, unless your own celebrity in the neighbourhood is sufficient.[2]

In Venice I almost always go to the Europa, which has absolutely the best possible situation and is not too large. In dignity, according to my gondolier,[3] it ranks next to Danieli's, where the food and drink are better,

own connexion with Crosland, whether as a man or as a writer, had ceased years before': Richards, 90–1. T[homas] W[illiam] H[odgson] Crosland (1865–1924) was a poet, anthologist, and miscellaneous author. GR had published two works by him in 1903: *The Five Nations*, and a reprint of his 1902 anthology *English Songs and Ballads*.

[1] William Rothenstein.
[2] Wilmot Parker Herringham (1855–1936), physician. Vice-chancellor of London University, 1912–15; knighted, 1914. His wife Christiana (1852–1929), an accomplished artist in tempera and watercolour, and the translator of the *Book of the Art of Cennino Cennini* (1899), was a friend of Rothenstein.

[1] Railway guide, published 1842–1961.
[2] He had been invited to GR's house Bigfrith, at Cookham Dean in Berkshire: Richards, 91 n.
[3] Andrea.

but which is noisy, and not central enough, and dearer. A cheaper hotel, which I hear well spoken of, is the Luna, close to the royal palace: I have been inside it, and it struck me as well managed. The Grand should be avoided, they say.

The best restaurant to my thinking is the Vapore, and my gondolier tells me that all foreigners say the same. From the Piazza you go under the clock and along the Merceria till you come to a high bridge over a canal: there, instead of crossing it, you turn sharp to the left. Much greater simplicity is to be had at either of the two Giorgiones, one near San Silvestro and one near the Santi Apostoli; but the food is not very appetising, except the *Baccalà pizzicato* (salt cod mashed up with milk and pepper) which they have on Fridays.

At Milan I always stay at the Cavour, which I believe is really the best hotel, and certainly the most pleasantly situated. It is rather far from the cathedral, but fairly near to the picture gallery. The Hôtel de la Ville, in the centre of the city, is, according to Horatio Brown, the best in Italy, but Ashburner dislikes it: you have met them both, so you can choose which to believe. The Cavour is not cheap, but nothing outrageous. The restaurants of Milan I know nothing about. I suppose I have been in one or two, but if so I have forgotten them.

Yours sincerely
A. E. Housman.

PM MS. LC-GR t.s. Richards, 91–2; Maas, 107 (both nearly complete).

TO GRANT RICHARDS

1 Yarborough Villas | Woodridings, Pinner.
28 Feb. 1910

My dear Richards,

We were prematurely separated at Praed Street and I could not take a proper farewell of you, so I must write to say how much I enjoyed myself, and to congratulate you on the combined excellencies of your neighbourhood, your house, and your family.

Yours sincerely
A. E. Housman.

PM MS. LC-GR t.s.; Richards, 92.

TO WITTER BYNNER

1 Yarborough Villas | Woodridings, Pinner
28 Feb. 1910

Dear Mr Bynner,

I was glad to hear from you and to learn that you are well and active; but as to your enquiry, I have not published any poem since the last that you have seen. The other day I had the curiosity to reckon up the complete pieces, printed and unprinted, which I have written since 1896, and they only come to 300 lines, so the next volume appears to be some way off. In barrenness, at any rate, I hold a high place among English poets, excelling even Gray.[1]

I am yours sincerely
A. E. Housman.

Harvard MS Eng 1071/12. Bynner/Haber (1957), 16; Maas, 108.

TO MILDRED PLATT

1 Yarborough Villas | Woodridings, Pinner
2 March 1910

Dear Mrs Platt,

I shall be very pleased to come on Monday. Gin is defined in the dictionary as "a trap or snare", but it is quite unnecessary in this case.

Yours sincerely
A. E. Housman.

UCL MS Add. 165. Maas, 108.

TO ALICE ROTHENSTEIN

1 Yarborough Villas | Woodridings, Pinner
4 March 1910

Dear Mrs Rothenstein,

People are asking me out a great deal too often, and you are one of the chief offenders. I am not a social butterfly like you: nature meant me for solitude and meditation \(which frequently takes the form of going to sleep)/: talking to human beings, whether "lovely ladies" or not, for

---

[1] Thomas Gray (1716–71) wrote over 3000 lines of poetry. As *ASL* contained 1331 lines, and the classical translations published in 1890, 119 lines, an additional 300 would bring the total to 1750. The verse published in AEH's lifetime, including light verse, amounts almost exactly to the same corpus as Gray's.

any length of time leaves me in a state of prostration, and will finally undermine my health unless I take care. By declining your invitation for next Wednesday I calculate that I shall make you very indignant, and then you will leave me severely alone for a long time, which may save me from premature decease,—at least, if other people do the same, as I will try to make them.

Yes, I had a very fine and pleasant Sunday at Marlow, or rather Cookham Dean.[1]

I am, though you may not think so, yours sincerely

A. E. Housman.

Harvard bMS Eng 1148 (740) 20. Maas, 108.

TO WILLIAM ROTHENSTEIN

1 Yarborough Villas | Woodridings, Pinner
22 March 1910.

Dear Rothenstein,

I am much obliged to you for sending me Mrs(?) Cornford's poems.[1] I do not call them exactly good, except in phrases here and there; but they are really interesting and I am glad to have them. The verses about the horse and donkey are quite capital,[2] and the triolet about the unhappy lady in gloves has moved me to the imitation on the opposite page.[3]

I hope Mrs Rothenstein does not languish.

Yours sincerely
A. E. Housman.

O why do you walk through the fields in boots,
    Missing so much and so much?
O fat white woman whom nobody shoots,
Why do you walk through the fields in boots,

---

[1] With the Richards family.

[1] Frances [Crofts] Cornford (1886–1960), Charles Darwin's granddaughter. Rothenstein persuaded her father Francis Darwin to print privately her first book, *Poems* (1910), and it met with some critical acclaim, e.g. in Roger Fry's review in the *TLS*: 'Frances Cornford Writes', *Poetry Book Society Bulletin*, 3 (Sept. 1954), 1. She published nine vols. of poetry in all. She married F. M. Cornford in 1909: see notes on AEH's letter of 1 May 1934.

[2] The light verse *A Short Prayer*.

[3] In Frances Cornford's *To a Fat Lady seen from the Train*, AEH replaces 'gloves', 'loves', and 'doves', with 'boots', 'shoots', and 'coots', and cuts out the repetition of the first two lines at the end. See AEH to Rothenstein, 4 May 1932. For a discussion of AEH's version and of his fondness for making such alterations, see Archie Burnett, 'Poetical Emendations and Improvisations by A. E. Housman', *Victorian Poetry*, 36. 3 (Fall, 1998), 289–97.

When the grass is \<as\> soft as the brea\<th\>st of coots
   And shivering-sweet to the touch?
O why etc.

Harvard bMS Eng 1148 (740) 21. Maas, 109.

TO GRANT RICHARDS

1 Yarborough Villas | Woodridings, Pinner
12 April 1910.

My dear Richards,

   Whatever the result may be, I am very much obliged both to Maclagan and you for your warfare against the Spanish character.[1]

   I also have to thank you for Masefield's two novels, of which I have read *Captain Margaret*.[2] Quite readable, and containing a number of interesting details; but bad.

Yours sincerely
A. E. Housman.

Illinois MS. LC-GR t.s. Richards, 93; Maas, 109.

TO ALICE ROTHENSTEIN

1 Yarborough Villas | Woodridings, Pinner
17 May 1910

Dear Mrs Rothenstein,

   Many thanks for the card,[1] which I shall probably utilise on the 27th rather than the 26th, as I shall have more time at my disposal.

   I hope to find some of the works which Rothenstein executed last August, with you holding his chair to save him from being blown over the cliff; and I shall be interested in trying to discover if the strokes of the artist's brush show any traces of the struggle between Love and Death which was raging around him.

Yours sincerely
A. E. Housman.

Harvard bMS Eng 1148 (740) 22. Maas, 110.

[1] GR and Eric Maclagan had been trying to procure photographs of the Madrid MS of Manilius. See AEH to GR, 15 July 1910. AEH had previously failed to obtain photographs: See *CQ* 1 (1907), 291 (*Classical Papers*, 704).
[2] Published by GR in 1908. The other was *Multitude and Solitude* (1909), also published by GR.

[1] For admission to the private view of an exhibition of Rothenstein's paintings and drawings (including one of AEH) at the Goupil Gallery. See AEH to Alice Rothenstein, 18 July 1910.

TO GRANT RICHARDS

1 Yarborough Villas | Woodridings | Pinner
4 June 1910

My dear Richards,

I am sorry I cannot come to your desolate home, but I am engaged here tomorrow. I have telegraphed, which I don't know whether I ought to have done, as I daresay you are charged a lot for delivery.

Yours sincerely
A. E. Housman.

LC-GR MS. LC-GR t.s. Richards, 93 (nearly complete)

TO LAURENCE HOUSMAN

1 Yarborough Villas | Woodridings, Pinner
9 June 1910.

My dear Laurence,

I would rather not sign your memorial;[1] chiefly because I don't think that writers as a class are particularly qualified to give advice on the question; and moreover it is certain to be signed by Galsworthy[2] and Hewlett[3] and everyone I cannot abide. Also I cannot say that 'the solution of this question appears to me to be urgent'. Even if I were actually in favour of women's suffrage in the abstract I think I should like to see some other and less precious country try it first: America for instance, where the solution ought to be just as urgent as here.

Thanks for the pamphlet. I see you have another just published;[4] but as that costs 6[d] I recognise that it is my duty to buy it; which indeed I am quite able to do, as your literary activity has fallen off of late, and my finances are recovering from the strain it used to put on them.

Love to Clemence: I hope she has read, or will read, *Ann Veronica*[5] (the prison scenes).[6]

Your affectionate brother
A. E. Housman.

McGill MS. Memoir, 174–5, where it is printed out of chronological sequence; Maas, 110.

[1] 'A declaration by authors in favour of Woman Suffrage': *Memoir*, 174 n.
[2] John Galsworthy (1867–1933), novelist and dramatist. Many of his plays deal with social injustice.
[3] Maurice [Henry] Hewlett (1861–1923), novelist and poet.
[4] *Articles of Faith in the Freedom of Women.*
[5] By H. G. Wells, 1909. The heroine is an emancipated 'new woman' and a suffragist.
[6] Clemence was imprisoned in Holloway Gaol, 30 Sept.–6 Oct. 1911, for non-payment of taxes. She was protesting against taxation without representation. See K. L. Mix in *HSJ* 2 (1975), 47.

TO GRANT RICHARDS

1 Yarborough Villas | Woodridings, Pinner
19 June 1910

My dear Richards,

I shall be very pleased to come the Saturday after next and stay till the Monday.

Yours sincerely
A. E. Housman.

LC-GR MS. LC-GR t.s.

TO GRANT RICHARDS

1 Yarborough Villas | Woodridings, Pinner
30 June 1910.

My dear Richards,

The train on Saturday which would suit me best if it suits you is the 4. 50 from Paddington. I can stay till the Monday morning.

Yours sincerely
A. E. Housman.

LC-GR MS. LC-GR t.s.

TO GRANT RICHARDS

1 Yarborough Villas | Woodridings, Pinner
15 July 1910

My dear Richards,

I have received the photographs, which are quite satisfactory, and I am very grateful to you as well as to Maclagan and his hidalgo,[1] for I should never have got them without your assistance.

Also I must thank you for Masefield's plays,[2] which are well worth reading and contain a lot that is very good; only he has got the Elizabethan notion that in order to have tragedy you must have villains, and villains of disgusting wickedness or vileness.

Yours sincerely
A. E. Housman.

LC-GR t.s. Richards, 94; Maas, 111.

[1] The Spanish gentleman was Don Guillermo de Osma (1853–1922), identified by Maclagan in a letter to GR of 31 Jan. 1937 (LC-GR1 MS) and in a note in Richards, 94. Maas, 111 n., notes that he was an Oxford-educated Spanish diplomatist and founder of the Instituto de Valencia de Don Juan in Madrid.

[2] *The Tragedy of Nan, and Other Plays* (1909).

TO ERIC MACLAGAN

1 Yarborough Villas | Woodridings, Pinner
15 July 1910

Dear Mr Maclagan,

I have received and examined the photographs, and find them complete and quite satisfactorily clear; and I assure you that it is a great comfort to possess them, and that as I shall constantly be using them I shall constantly be feeling gratitude to you for your trouble and your success. I must also thank you for the rather surprisingly low price at which you have managed to secure them.

I will write as you suggest to Don G. de Osma. I enclose cheque for £2. 15. 0, and am yours sincerely and gratefully.

A. E. Housman.

Private MS. Richards, 94; Maas, 111.

TO ALICE ROTHENSTEIN

1 Yarborough Villas | Woodridings, Pinner
18 July 1910

Dear Mrs Rothenstein,

It is a pleasure to hear that anyone is so happy as you appear to be, and when you say that no one can possibly be so happy in England I am not in a position to contradict you. I am engaged in composing an erudite work, which you will refuse to read, and my feelings do not rise much above tranquil satisfaction and the consciousness of virtue. I am afraid there is no chance of my sharing your raptures, as I shall not get away till the end of August, and then shall most likely go to Belgium.

I went to Rothenstein's show with the ticket,[1] and admired particularly the farmyard and the quarry, which I had seen before, and the piece called *Spring*, which I had not; but particularly and extremely the picture *Night*, though I fear that the subject may have something to do with this, and that a dark tree with the moon rising behind it might produce much the same effect on me even if it were painted by Mr B. W. Leader.[2] The *Standard* called it a great picture; and I suppose that a picture which is praised by the *Standard* and admired by me must have something wrong

[1] See AEH to Alice Rothenstein, 17 May 1910.
[2] Benjamin Williams Leader (1831–1923), painter of landscapes in England and Wales. His paintings include *'In the Evening there shall be Light'* (1882), a depiction of a sunset beyond a deserted graveyard, which secured his election to the Royal Academy in 1883.

with it, and that Rothenstein will reel under this double blow. I find on looking at my catalogue that I have supplied alternative titles to some of the pictures: opposite *57. A Study* I have written 'Mrs Rothenstein detected in a prevarication', and opposite 42 the elucidation 'Lady, watching her 1st husband die of poison administered by herself, reflects, with melancholy, that her 2nd may be no better'. Tell Rothenstein that while standing before the portrait of the artist I heard another visitor say, with just an instant's pause between the utterances, 'Very unkind,—very like'.

At the end of this month I am going for a few days to Swanage, which reminds me that I have never seen a picture of what I think one of the most wonderful views I know, Egdon Heath, seen from the hills south of it, with the heather in bloom and Poole Harbour reaching its arms into the midst of it. But this is such a summerless year that I doubt if the heather will be properly out when I get there. It may be better in France: if so I congratulate both of you.

I am yours sincerely
A. E. Housman.

Harvard bMS Eng 1148 (740) 23. Maas, 111–12.

TO PROFESSOR D'ARCY THOMPSON

1 Yarborough Villas | Woodridings, Pinner
22 July 1910

My dear Sir,

I am much obliged for your interesting paper on the Crab.[1] I do not know if you have observed, what was new to me when I read it in Boll's *Sphaera* (Teubner 1903) pp. 304–5 and tab. IV, that Cancer appears in Egyptian zodiacs sometimes as a beetle.

I am yours sincerely
A. E. Housman.

St Andrews MS 23587.

---

[1] 'The Emblem of the Crab in relation to the sign Cancer', *Transactions of the Royal Society of Edinburgh*, 39 (1899), 603–12.

TO GRANT RICHARDS

NORMANDY HOTEL | 7 RUE DE L' ÉCHELLE | PARIS
5 Sept. 1910

My dear Richards,

I am going home on Wednesday, so we have accurately timed our visits so as to miss one another, which is annoying, but cannot be helped. The first thing I was told of when I got here was the recent departure of my friend M. Gran' Reesharr.

Yours sincerely
A. E. Housman.

LC-GR MS. LC-GR t.s. Richards, 94–5 (nearly complete); Maas, 112.

TO MESSRS GRANT RICHARDS

19 Oct. 1910
UNIVERSITY OF LONDON, | UNIVERSITY COLLEGE.
GOWER STREET, LONDON, W.C.

Dear Sirs,

You are right in assuming that I object to the printing of my poems in concert programmes.

I am yours faithfully
A. E. Housman

Illinois MS. LC-GR t.s. Richards, 95 (nearly complete).

TO AN UNKNOWN CORRESPONDENT

1 Yarborough Villas | Woodridings | Pinner
24 Oct. 1910

Sir,

I shall be obliged if you can send me 15 of the volumes enumerated over the page.

Yours faithfully
A. E. Housman.

[Overleaf]

Müller (C. O.) *History of the Doric Race*, trans. by Tufnell & Lewis.
James (Montague Rhodes). *Ghost-Stories of an Antiquary*
Tabb (John B.). *Lyrics.*
 ,,   ,,   *Poems.*
Butler (Samuel, St. John's Coll. Camb.), *The Way of All Flesh.*
Benson (A. C.). *Life of E. W. Benson.*

Benson (E. F.). *The Babe B.A.*
Coleridge (Sara), *Phantasmion.*
Bierce (Ambrose), *In the Midst of Life*
Beyle (M. H.). *The Chartreuse of Parma*, tr. by Lady Mary Loyd.
Proctor (R. A.). *Watched by the Dead.*
Benson (A. C.). *Walter Pater.*
Bennett (Enoch Arnold). *Anna of the Five Towns.*
Cory (W.) *Extracts from Letters Etc. by F. W. Cornish*
Ellis (H. Havelock). *Man and Woman.*
Vizetelly (H.). *Port and Madeira.*

BMC MS.

TO GRANT RICHARDS

1 Yarborough Villas | Woodridings, Pinner
15 Nov. 1910

My dear Richards,

Mr Hemsley may print the verses he wants in his Latin book.[1] As to the Manilius, tell the enquirer that you have no information.

I have just been lunching with Frank Harris,[2] who came down on me at the College like a wolf on the fold.

Yours sincerely
A. E. Housman.

Illinois MS. LC-GR t.s. Richards, 95 (nearly complete); Maas, 113.

TO JOHN MASEFIELD

University College, London
25 Nov. 1910

Dear Mr Masefield,

If you have a spare ticket for *Pompey*[1] I am sure I should be interested to see it.

I am very glad you can come on the 9th.

I am yours very truly
A. E. Housman.

Texas MS.

[1] *Latin Elegiac Verse-Writing. Modelled upon Ovid*, by W. J. Hemsley and John Aston (1911). It contains *ASL* XX (*Oh fair enough are sky and plain*) under the title *Reflections* for translation into Latin.
[2] Controversial author, journalist, and editor (1856–1931). See his *Latest Contemporary Portraits* (1927), 272–83 ('A Talk with A. E. Housman'), for his (inaccurate) account of the interview.
[1] Masefield's play *Pompey the Great* (1910).

TO D. A. SLATER

University College, London
21 Dec. 1910

Dear Slater,

Many thanks for your book of verses.[1] 'Other men on other manors rob the hen-roosts of to-day'[2] might have appeared in the third part of *Locksley Hall* if Tennyson had lived to write it.[3]

I am yours very truly
A. E. Housman.

BMC MS.

---

[1] *Aeneas, and other verses and versions* (1910).
[2] The line appears in poem XIII, *To A Clerk of Oxenforde (H. W. G.)*.
[3] Tennyson's *Locksley Hall* (1842) and *Locksley Hall Sixty years After* (1886) are written in the metre of the line quoted.

1911

TO GRANT RICHARDS

1 Yarborough Villas | Woodridings, Pinner
17 Jan. 1911

My dear Richards,

Will you dine with me at the Café Royal on Friday Feb. \3ʳᵈ/ <10ᵗʰ> at 7. 45? I am asking Platt, whom you have already met under other circumstances.[1]

Yours sincerely
A. E. Housman.

LC-GR MS. Richards, 97 (nearly complete); Maas, 114.

TO GRANT RICHARDS

[19 Jan. 1911]

No certainly not[1]

HOUSMAN.

LC-GR t.s. Telegram dated Jan. 19, 1911 addressed to 'Richards | Capitol Hotel | London'. Richards, 99.

TO MILDRED PLATT

Pinner, 19 Jan. 1911

Dear Mrs Platt,

Yours was the first letter,[1] so I will answer it first and thank you for your congratulations, which show a very Christian and forgiving spirit, considering my remissness in attending your at homes. The prospect of exchanging you for Mrs Frazer[2] is one of the clouds on my horizon; but please do not repeat this remark at all to your Cambridge acquaintances.

[1] At AEH's instigation, Platt had visited GR to see if he would publish *The Agamemnon of Aeschylus*: Richards, 96.

[1] AEH is refusing to be interviewed by a London daily newspaper: Richards, 99.

[1] Congratulating AEH on his appointment as Professor of Latin at Cambridge.

[2] See List of Recipients.

I should be very pleased to dine with you any day next week but Tuesday.

Yours sincerely
A. E. Housman.

UCL MS Add. 165. Maas, 114.

TO PROFESSOR F. C. BURKITT

University College, London
19 Jan. 1911

Dear Professor Burkitt,

I have to thank you both for a kind letter and for interesting material from MSS. Often, when I look into the Vienna Corpus,[1] and see the many excellent spellings, frequently relegated to the foot of the page by the editors, I am almost persuaded to be a Christian.[2]

I am yours sincerely
A. E. Housman.

CUL Add. MS 7568 B.461.

TO EDMUND GOSSE

University College, London
19 Jan. 1911

My dear Gosse,

Many thanks for your kind letter. In most respects, though not quite in all, I think the change is matter for congratulation. If the exhalations of the Granta[1] give me a relaxed sore throat, more poems may be expected.[2]

Yours sincerely
A. E. Housman.

Brotherton MS (Gosse Correspondence). Maas, 114.

---

[1] *Corpus scriptorum ecclesiasticorum latinorum*, an edition of early Christian writings begun in Vienna in 1866.

[2] Acts 26: 28: 'Then Agrippa said unto Paul, Almost thou persuadest me to be a Christian.'

[1] Cambridge river.

[2] AEH associated his writing poetry with ill-health. See the letter to Webb, 17 June 1896, n. 6.

TO GRANT RICHARDS

1 Yarborough Villas | Woodridings, Pinner
20 Jan. 1911

My dear Richards,

First, many thanks for your congratulations. Then, as to the dinner, Platt is an easy-going character and will not mind having the date shifted if you cannot come on the 3ʳᵈ. Next week will be quite time enough to let me know. Thirdly, I am afraid there is no safe immediate prospect of my finding my way to your French cook, as next Sunday I lunch in town, and expect to be at Godalming on the next after that. Thank you all the same.

I suppose the mysterious "six" in the enclosed telegram is really an official emendation of ("sic"), and has no reference to a six o' clock tram.

Yours sincerely
A. E. Housman.

LC-GR MS. LC-GR t.s. Richards, 97; Maas, 115 (both incomplete).

TO H. MCLEOD INNES

1 Yarborough Villas | Woodridings | Pinner
21 Jan. 1911

My dear Innes,

I beg you to inform the Master and the College Council that I accept their offer of a fellowship with great gratitude and a high sense of the honour done me. Macaulay[1] used to rank a Fellow of Trinity somewhere in the neighbourhood of the Pope and the Holy Roman Emperor: I forget the exact order of the three, but I know that the King of Rome was lower down, and His Most Christian Majesty of France quite out of sight. Platt will no longer be able to despise me.

Also I thank you for your own kind congratulations.

I am yours sincerely
A. E. Housman.

TCC Add. MS Letters c. 1¹⁹².

[1] The historian Thomas Babington Macaulay, first Baron Macaulay (1800–59), who entered TCC in 1818 and was elected to a Fellowship in 1824.

TO ALICE ROTHENSTEIN

1 Yarborough Villas | Woodridings, Pinner
22 Jan. 1911

Dear Mrs Rothenstein,

I thank you sincerely for your very kind letter. I expect I shall see you and Rothenstein sometimes in Cambridge, as I know you have friends there. Besides, the Cambridge terms are agreeably short, and I shall most likely spend some part of each year in London.

To have less work and more pay is always agreeable, and that will be the case with me. The drawback is that I shall be obliged to be less unsociable.

I am glad to hear your news from Benares.[1]

I am yours sincerely
A. E. Housman.

Harvard bMS Eng 1148 (740) 24. Maas, 115.

TO THOMAS HERBERT WARREN

1 Yarborough Villas, | Woodridings, Pinner
25 Jan. 1911.

Dear Mr President,

Many thanks for your kind letter of congratulation. There were at any rate two members of the College [1] in my time whose teaching I remember with gratitude, and both are still living: Mr Snow[2] and Mr Bidder.[3]

I am yours sincerely
A. E. Housman.

MS inspected at Bloomsbury Book Auctions, 24 Jan. 2006.

[1] Nowadays known as Varanasi, on the L. bank of the Ganges in N. India, one of the seven sacred cities of the Hindus. It was made a new state by the British in 1910. Rothenstein was painting in India, 1910–11.

[1] SJCO.

[2] T[homas] C[ollins] Snow (1852–1926). At SJCO, Fellow, 1875–82, Librarian, 1877–82; Lecturer in Classics, 1883–1903, and in English Language and Literature, 1895–1903; Lecturer in English Language and Literature, Jesus College, Oxford, 1906–17. Hugh Last described him as the 'only serious classical scholar among the Fellows of St John's in 1877': *The Oxford Magazine*, 56 (1937), 189. Gilbert Murray regarded him and Ulrich von Wilamowitz-Moellendorff as the two teachers of whose influence he was especially conscious: *Ancient Greek Literature* (1897), xi. He taught AEH, 1877–9, and wrote a warmly supportive testimonial when AEH applied for the professorship at UCL in 1892: Naiditch (1988), 20. AEH sent him copies of his edn. of Juvenal (1905) and of *LP* (1922), and perhaps of other publications. For further information, see Naiditch (1988), 239–41.

[3] The Revd H[enry] J[ardine] Bidder (1847–1923). Fellow of SJCO, 1871–1923, and in his time also Bursar and Keeper of the Groves. He regarded AEH as 'a man on whom he had done

TO MARGARET, LADY RAMSAY

1 Yarborough Villas | Woodridings, Pinner

26 Jan. 1911

Dear Lady Ramsay,

Many thanks for your kind congratulations. Joy does predominate over sorrow, as I am fond of money and fond of leisure; but as I am also fond of solitude, and shall not have it at Cambridge, there is some sorrow mingled with the joy; apart from leaving friends and the College.

I am yours very truly

A. E. Housman.

UCL MS: Sir William Ramsay: Letters and Papers, *15. 155. Maas, 115.*

TO LAURENCE HOUSMAN

1 Yarborough Villas | Woodridings, Pinner

30 Jan. 1911

My dear Laurence,

Although you are very conceited and Clemence, I fear, very rowdy, I thank you both for your congratulations. It is not by any means certain that I could have secured the Oxford chair by waiting for it; and on the whole I think I prefer Cambridge.

I spent one of my hard-earned half-crowns on the *English Review* containing the trial-scene of your play:[1] it interested me, but I did not think it would interest most people, without the Censor's assistance.

Disraeli visited the villa where your heroine resided in Italy,[2] soon after the trial. Its decorations, he says, were of such a character that it was

his best to make an impression—and failed' because he 'refused to consider Plato's meaning except so far as it was relevant to the settlement of the text': Hugh Last to A. S. F. Gow, 1 Nov. 1937 (TCC Add. MS a. 71[162]). Last also reports that Bidder found that 'his efforts to commend the argument of the *Republic* to Housman's consideration were apt to be parried by a monologue in the varied display of scholarship to be found in the work of Bekker, K. E. C. Schneider, Stallbaum, and K. F. Hermann': *The Oxford Magazine*, 56 (1937), 69. Bidder was one of the five examiners who had no option but to fail AEH in Greats, though he was forbidden by examination statute to discuss or pass judgement on a member of his college.

[1] Act 3 of LH's *Pains and Penalties*, which was concerned with George IV's attempt to divorce Queen Caroline, appeared in the issue of Nov. 1910. Though refused a licence by the Lord Chamberlain, the play was published in 1911.

[2] The Villa d'Este on Lake Como, which Disraeli visited in 1826.

painful to view them in company with a lady.[3] The local Italians regarded the tumult in London as a great joke.[4]

Your affectionate brother

A. E. Housman.

There may be material for another loyal and Hanoverian drama in the trial which begins on Wednesday.[5]

BMC MS. Memoir, *174; Maas, 116 (both incomplete).*

TO WALTER ASHBURNER

1 Yarborough Villas | Woodridings, Pinner

30 Jan. 1911.

My dear Ashburner,

Many thanks for your congratulations. Ker and I were talking about you the day before your letter came, and he gave me your new address. I attribute my election to the fact that I was personally unknown to the majority of the electors, and the other candidates were not. I hope next year to come and see Italy in the spring for the first time,[1] and Florence earning its name. If by any chance you ever go to Cesena, tell me beforehand, and I will annoy you by providing you with an hour's job.[2]

Yours sincerely

A. E. Housman.

NLS MS 20369, fos. 251–2. Ashburner/Bell (1976), 18.

---

[3] 'It is a villa of the first grade—and splendidly adorned, but the ornaments are with[ou]t an exception so universally indelicate that it was painful to view them in the presence of a Lady and only the drawing rooms and the saloons are exhibited for the upper apartments are of a nature beyond all imagin[at]ion. We were refused admittance ... ': to his father, 2 Sept. 1826; letter 52/75 in *Benjamin Disraeli Letters: 1815–1834,* ed. J. A. W. Gunn (1982).

[4] 'Here if they possessed any interest might you obtain thousands of stories of her late Majesty—but the time is passed thank God for them. Our riots in her favour are the laughing stock of all Italy' (Disraeli in the same letter).

[5] The King *vs.* Edward Frederick Mylius, who was charged with publishing a libel of and concerning the King, specifically attacking the royal marriage. (Mylius was found guilty and sentenced to twelve months' imprisonment.)

[1] He visited Sicily. See AEH to Webb, 19 Apr. 1912.

[2] To consult MS S 25. 5, written in 1457. It contains Manilius and Q. Serenus Sammonicus: see *Codici e libri a stampa della Biblioteca Malatestiana di Cesena: ricerche ed indagini di Raimondo Zazzeri* (Cesena 1887), 462, and Mucciolo's *Catalogus* (Cesena 1780–4), 2. 164–5. By 1930, AEH had seen it for himself: *Manilius V,* xvii n. †.

TO AGNATA BUTLER

1 Yarborough Villas | Woodridings, Pinner
3 Feb. 1911

Dear Mrs Butler,

I have been solacing my journey home with your son's[1] excellent verses which the Master[2] was good enough to give me.

Oxford men, following Dryden, sometimes refer to Cambridge as Thebes.[3] Trinity Lodge, at any rate, seems to me a happy combination of Athens and Sybaris.[4]

I am yours sincerely
A. E. Housman.

TCC MS (J. R. M. Butler papers).

TO PROFESSOR HENRY JACKSON

1 Yarborough Villas | Woodridings, Pinner
12 Feb. 1911

My dear Jackson,

I have to thank you for your detective treatise,[1] which I have been reading with great interest and with the result that I am more uncertain than ever. I do now see more clearly the objections to Datchley being Edwin; but on the other hand the experimental title *Edwin Drood In Hiding* which you quote on p. 86 most strongly suggests that he was not killed. And I feel in the marrow of my bones (though I do not pretend that that is the seat of intellect) that Datchley is no woman. Moreover, unless Dickens was a great knave, his account in c. xviii of how Datchley 'became bewildered', 'with a general impression on his *mind* that Mrs Tope's was' etc., shows that Datchley, though familiar with the events, knew Cloisterham only from hearsay. I am rather coming round to my first impression that Datchley was Bazzard. It is true that they are not a bit alike, except in the colour of their eyebrows; and in God's world that would be against the identification; but Dickens's world is less like God's than is Shakespeare's or even Balzac's.

---

[1] See List of Recipients. He is not known to have published any verses.

[2] H. M. Butler: see List of Recipients.

[3] In *Prologue to the University of Oxford* (*Tho' Actors cannot much of Learning boast*), 37: '*Thebes* did His Green, unknowing Youth ingage'.

[4] i.e., of intellectual and cultural pre-eminence and wealth.

[1] *About Edwin Drood*, published by Cambridge University Press (1911).

The Special Board for Classics ask me to say, *not later than the 17th*, what lectures I propose to give in the next academic year. As this depends on the question whether I am to lecture in this academic year, I should be grateful if I could be informed what decision the General Board comes to as soon as possible after their meeting on the 15th. I know of course that the final decision lies with the Senate.

Yours sincerely
A. E. Housman.

TCC Add. MS c. 32^{54(a)}.

TO ALICE ROTHENSTEIN

1 Yarborough Villas | Woodridings, Pinner
15 Feb. 1911

Dear Mrs Rothenstein,

If the Thursday you speak of is next week, I should be very pleased to come; but if, as past experience leads me to fear, your Thursday means to-morrow, I am sorry I have got an engagement already.

Yours sincerely
A. E. Housman.

Are you in the New Machiavelli?[1] and if so, who are you?

Harvard bMS Eng 1148 (740) 25.

TO GRANT RICHARDS

1 Yarborough Villas | Woodridings, Pinner
7 March 1911

My dear Richards,

The Wolsey Hall[1] people do not know what they are talking about: my Juvenal would be no use to students whatever. The proper Juvenal for English students is Duff's, Cambridge Press.[2]

---

[1] H. G. Wells's *The New Machiavelli* (1911) concerned a politician involved in a sexual scandal.

[1] Oxford correspondence college, founded in 1894.

[2] Published in 1898, 1900, and 1914.

When Blackwell[3] says "Eriphyle" he means the *Fragment of a Greek Tragedy* which appeared in *Cornhill* about ten years ago.[4]

Yours sincerely
A. E. Housman.

Illinois MS. LC-GR t.s. Richards, 100–1; Maas, 116.

TO LAURENCE HOUSMAN

32 Panton Street | Cambridge
27 April 1911

My dear Laurence,

This is to say that I am not coming to hear your seditious play,[1] and I shall not make any attempt to see you, as your time will probably be taken up with more whole-hearted admirers. For the same reason I suppose you will not be coming to see me, though I shall be glad to see you if you do.

Your affectionate brother
A. E. Housman.

BMC MS. Memoir, *175; Maas, 117.*

TO GRANT RICHARDS

32 Panton Street | Cambridge
27 April 1911

My dear Richards,

Mr Butterworth may have permission.[1] I shall go to Paris on Thursday May 11th and come back the following Tuesday.

Yours sincerely
A. E. Housman.

Illinois MS. LC-GR t.s. Richards, 101 (nearly complete).

---

[3] Oxford bookseller Benjamin Henry Blackwell (1849–1924).

[4] *The Cornhill Magazine*, NS 10 (Apr. 1901), 443–5, the third printing of the parody AEH wrote in 1883.

[1] In defiance of the Lord Chamberlain, LH gave a public reading from *Pains and Penalties*.

[1] See AEH to GR, 21 Nov. 1911.

TO F. M. CORNFORD

32 Panton Street | Cambridge
17 May 1911

Dear Cornford,

Thanks for your letter, which I found when I came back last night.

I caught sight of your face at one point of the lecture,[1] and was gratified by the expression it wore.

Yours sincerely
A. E. Housman.

BL Add. MS 58427, fos. 94–5.

TO WITTER BYNNER

Trinity College, Cambridge
17 May 1911

Dear Mr Bynner,

It is true that I am now Professor of Latin here, and I thank you for your congratulations. Of course it is nonsense when they talk about my 'steadily refusing to write any more poetry': poetry does not even *steadily* refuse to be written by me; but there is not yet enough to make even a small book.

I am glad to hear of you and your projects.

Yours very truly
A. E. Housman.

Harvard MS Eng 1071/13. Bynner/Haber (1957), 17; Maas, 117.

TO SYDNEY COCKERELL

21 Panton St., Cambridge
26 May 1911

Dear Mr Cockerell,

It is very good of you to offer to show me over the Museum,[1] and I should be glad to avail myself of your kindness some morning between 10 and 1. I think I had better leave you to fix the day, as your time is

[1] AEH's inaugural lecture at Cambridge, 9 May 1911.

[1] See the textual note on the next letter.

probably much more occupied than mine: the only professorial function I am discharging this term is that of residing.

> I am yours very truly
> A. E. Housman.

Princeton MS (Gen. MSS. Misc.). Maas, 117.

TO SYDNEY COCKERELL

27 May 1911

Many thanks: I will come at 11 o' clock on Monday.

> A. E. Housman.

BL Add. MSS 54316–17, fo. 619: p.c. addressed 'The Director | Fitzwilliam Museum' and marked 'Local' by AEH.

TO PROFESSOR ISRAEL GOLLANCZ

Trinity College, Cambridge
9 June 1911

Dear Sir,

I am greatly obliged by your letter and by the kind and flattering proposal of the Council of the British Academy, but I beg that I may not be nominated for election as a Fellow. The honour is one which I should not find congenial nor feel to be appropriate.[1]

I am, dear Sir,

> Yours faithfully
> A. E. Housman

The Secretary of the British Academy

BMC MS. Memoir, 112 (excerpt).

TO LAURENCE HOUSMAN

1 Yarborough Villas | Woodridings, Pinner
11 June 1911

My dear Laurence,

Although I had very few official duties during the Cambridge term I was much occupied with social duties, which are a deal worse, and either from the climate or the heat was generally tired when I was not occupied, so that

---

[1] This is consistent with AEH's usual practice of refusing public honours. See AEH to Stewart, 11 Feb. 1905, and note.

I have not thanked you for the proofs of your play.[1] It interested me, but I should not have thought it would interest most people, nor be effective on the stage. However, everyone who heard you was loud in praise of your reading,[2] and apparently swallowed Caroline whole.

An undergraduate came to me to get your address, which I gave him, after exacting assurances that he was not bent on avenging the glorious house of Hanover.[3]

I shall now be here, off and on, till October probably.

> Your affectionate brother
> A. E. Housman.

BMC MS. Memoir, 175; Maas, 118; both slightly incomplete, and the latter with the wrong address.

TO H. E. BUTLER

> 1 Yarborough Villas | Woodridings, Pinner
> 28 June 1911

Dear Butler,

I did not see at the time the announcement, which I understand has been made, of your appointment as my successor, so that I am rather belated in sending my best wishes for your success and happiness. I think you will find at University College pleasant colleagues and tractable pupils.

If there is any information about the work that you think I could supply I should be very pleased to do so; but you will very likely be able to get all you want from Platt, whose classes are in many respects parallel to the Latin.

> I am yours very truly
> A. E. Housman.

SJCO MS 305. Maas, 118.

---

[1] *Pains and Penalties.* See AEH to LH, 30 Jan. 1911, n. 1.

[2] See AEH to LH, 27 Apr. 1911, n. 1.

[3] LH's play dealt incidentally with 'the marital relations of King George IV and his wife Queen Caroline', and the Lord Chamberlain's office banned it on grounds that 'the author had dared to pass unfavourable comments on the character of King George IV; and hostile reference upon the stage to the great-grand-uncle of our reigning Sovereign was ... incompatible with respect for the institution of monarchy': LH, *The Unexpected Years* (1937), 245.

TO EDITH WISE

1 Yarborough Villas | Woodridings, Pinner
11 July 1911

My dear Edie,

I suppose you have now been back some time from your Coronation jaunt.[1] I can hardly imagine <you at> Woodchester without you at Woodchester House;[2] but this is the very remark my mother made to the William Housmans[3] in a letter which she wrote when Mr and Mrs Wise had just taken up their abode there. I always thought the Arthur Dunn's house and garden very eligible, though I never yet have been inside either of them.

About my coming to see you for a week end: I shall be going on a short visit to Kate in her cottage at Swanage about the first week in August: would it suit you if I came either just before or just after that?

I was in residence at Cambridge during the May term, though with no definite work to do. I shall go there permanently at the end of September, and be living in Trinity College.

I went away to Godalming to avoid the Coronation, and had a very wet day there, but a fine bonfire in the evening.

Laurence came to Cambridge while I was there, and read to an admiring audience his censored play about Queen Caroline;[4] but I lent no countenance to sedition.

Love to all.

Yours affectionately
A. E. Housman.

BMC MS.

TO ALICE ROTHENSTEIN

Woodchester, Glo'ster
4 Aug. 1911

Dear Mrs Rothenstein,

It unfortunately happens that I am away, and paying a series of visits. This is about six miles from Bisley, near which you once spent a summer holiday.

---

[1] George V was proclaimed king on 6 May 1910, and his coronation took place in Westminster Abbey on 22 June 1911, with celebrations in London.

[2] Following the death of Edith's mother on 13 Feb. 1911, the Wise family moved from Woodchester House to Oakley House, Woodchester, near Stroud.

[3] William Housman, solicitor at Bromsgrove and then Bath, was AEH's father's uncle, and father of AEH's stepmother Lucy. Pugh, 28–33, provides further information.

[4] *Pains and Penalties.*

I had not heard about New York,[1] but I suppose it is natural revulsion after India. I hope Rothenstein will find subjects equally inspiring. I may be going to Belgium and making the acquaintance of the van Eycks,[2] who were, when I last received information on the subject, *the* painters.

Yours sincerely
A. E. Housman.

Harvard bMS Eng 1148 (740) 26. Maas, 118–19.

TO GRANT RICHARDS

1 Yarborough Villas | Woodridings, Pinner
15 Aug. 1911.

My dear Richards,

This is rather a miscellaneous letter.

1. The Second Book of Manilius is nearly finished, and a large portion of it will be ready for the printers by the end of this month, so I want them to start upon it while I am abroad in September. It had better be published on the same arrangement as the First, if you have no objection.

2. I expect to be in Paris in the first week of September and again in the third: about the 24th I shall take up my abode permanently in Cambridge, of which I will send you due notice when the time comes.

3. Can you tell me anything definite of the Hôtel de Crillon as to expense? e.g. whether one would get a bedroom and bathroom for 20 francs or so. I shall most likely go either there or to the Continental.

Yours sincerely
A. E. Housman.

Illinois MS. LC-GR t.s. Richards, 101; Maas, 119.

TO GRANT RICHARDS

1 Yarborough Villas | Woodridings, Pinner
17 Aug. 1911

My dear Richards,

I did not receive the letter you wrote to Cambridge. Did you address it to Trinity College or to 32 Panton St.?

---

[1] Rothenstein spent four months of 1911 involved in exhibitions of his drawings and paintings in New York, Boston, and Chicago.

[2] Flemish painter Jan Van Eyck (1390?–1441), who perfected oil painting, and Hubert (d. 1426), supposed by some to be his brother.

You may make the announcement[1] in the *Athenaeum* if you will let me see it first.

The arrangement I prefer is to deal with the printers through you, as they will pay you more attention than me.

Thanks about the Crillon.

Yours sincerely
A. E. Housman.

Illinois MS. LC-GR t.s. Richards, 101 (excerpts).

TO GRANT RICHARDS

[1 Yarborough Villas | Woodridings, Pinner]
Yes, I received the *Gourmet's Guide*,[1] for which of course I ought to have thanked you before, as also for several other books of yours; but the fact is you spoil me.

A.E.H.

20 Aug. 1911.

Illinois MS p.c. addressed 'Grant Richards Esq. | 7 Carlton Street | Regent Street | S. W.' LC-GR t.s. Richards, 101–2.

TO GRANT RICHARDS

1 Yarborough Villas | Woodridings, Pinner
28 August 1911

My dear Richards,

1. I have just despatched to you by Parcel Post the text and notes of the Manilius. If you will be good enough to acknowledge receipt of them, I can go abroad with a mind at ease.

2. This second book is to be printed in just the same form as the first, of which the printers had better have a copy to guide them.

3. It will be convenient to me if at first, in slip, the text and notes are printed separately, not together as on the former occasion.

---

[1] Of vol. II of the *Manilius*, published in 1912.

[1] Lieut.-Col. N. Newnham-Davis's *The Gourmet's Guide to Europe*, of which GR published the 3rd edn. in 1911: Richards, 101–2 n.

4. The type-written text contains the letters

J (cap.)   j (l.c.)   v (l.c.)

These are everywhere to be changed to

I   i   u.[1]

The compositor's simplest way to avoid error will be to put lids on the receptacles containing the types of the forbidden forms, so that his hand cannot get into them; but no doubt he is too proud to take advice from me.

5. As to errors of the press and corrections. On former occasions the proofs have come to me full of the usual blunders,—numerals wrong, letters upside-down, stops missing, and so on. I have then, at the cost of much labour, removed all these errors. Then, when the last proof has left my hands, the corrector for the press has been turned on to it, and has found nothing to correct; whereupon, for fear his employers should think he is not earning his pay, he has set to work meddling with what I have written,—altering my English spelling into Webster's American spelling, my use of capitals into his own misuse of capitals, my scientific punctuation into the punctuation he learnt from his grandmother. What ought to be done is the reverse of this. The errors which are introduced by the printer should be removed by the press corrector, who will do it more easily and rapidly, though not more efficiently, than I; then and not till then the proofs should come to me, and after that no corrections should be made except by me.

> I am yours sincerely
> A. E. Housman.

P.S. Because my hand is particularly good and clear, printers misread it wherever they can; but there is only one letter which they can misread, and that is the letter *r*. At the end of a word they pretend they think it is *s*, and in other positions they pretend they think it is *v*. If they would just notice how I write it, and not expect to find *ʐ*, it would save trouble.

Illinois MS. Lined foolscap sheets. LC-GR t.s. Richards, 102–3; Maas, 119–20.

---

[1] See AEH to GR, 12 Oct. 1902, n. 4.

TO GRANT RICHARDS

1 Yarborough Villas | Woodridings, Pinner
30 Aug. 1911

My dear Richards,

It is a sine qua non that Book II of the Manilius should be identical with Book I in type, arrangement, paper, and get-up generally. If this can be secured, I have no *decisive* objection to changing the printers.

But still I should prefer Clark,[1] unless you have some decided reason on the other side. They are more accurate than Maclehose[2] or any one who has ever printed the *Classical Review*; and when the Juvenal was finished they wrote to me to say that they hoped I would employ them for any similar work in future: though I don't suppose this was due to any sentimental affection for me. Moreover I am a conservative, and do not like changing anything without due reason, not even a printer,—nay, not even a publisher.

Your *Athenaeum* notice is quite chaste in style. I have put in a word or two.[3]

I am off to Paris to-morrow, and shall be at the Continental for a week. Any letter after that had better be addressed here.

Yours sincerely
A. E. Housman.

Princeton MS (J. Harlin O'Connell Collection 3 E-M, Housman folder). LC-GR t.s. Richards, 103 (nearly complete); Maas, 120.

TO GRANT RICHARDS

2 Sept. 1911

Yes, this lady can have what she wants.

A. E. Housman.

LC-GR t.s.

---

[1] R. & R. Clark of Edinburgh.
[2] For 'MacLehose' (the printers of vols. II–V of the Manilius).
[3] The notice in *The Athenaeum*, 4376 (9 Sept. 1911), 302, read: 'Prof. A. E. Housman has nearly ready for the press a second book of his critical and explanatory edition of Manilius. It will be published, as was the first, by Mr. Grant Richards.'

TO GRANT RICHARDS

[Hatch End
22 Sept. 1911]

I don't know if you have given my old address to the printers; but if so, please tell them also of the change.

BMC MS. LC-GR t.s., which supplies the address and date from the postmark. On printed card announcing 'Mr A. E. HOUSMAN| has moved to | TRINITY COLLEGE, | CAMBRIDGE.' Richards, 103.

TO GRANT RICHARDS

<UNIVERSITY ARMS HOTEL> \Trin. Coll./, | CAMBRIDGE.
1 Oct. 1911

My dear Richards,

The account for Manilius I is not where I thought it was, and to look for it through my heaps of old bills and letters would take more time than I can spare; so unless I come across it by accident I cannot send it you. But I find from my bank book that I paid you a cheque for £83. 9. 0, and a month later another for £3. 1. 0, which I suppose was for binding. I have told you already that I think this second book must cost more. The Juvenal, including binding of 200 copies, was £69. 7. 0; but that is irrelevant.

I am horrified at your bringing back a Tauchnitz[1] and sending it to a respectable person like me. I gave it to you because otherwise I should have left it in France.

There is a lovely portrait of my disreputable relatives[2] in yesterday's *Standard*.

Yours sincerely
A. E. Housman.

Lilly MSS 1. 1. 3. LC-GR t.s. Richards, 104 (nearly complete).

---

[1] A volume from the Leipzig publisher, Bernhard Tauchnitz, probably from the 'Library of British and American Authors', of which there were more than 4000 volumes in 1908. The volumes were intended exclusively for Continental distribution.

[2] LH and Clemence, on the occasion of the latter's imprisonment for non-payment of taxes. See AEH to LH, 9 June 1910, n. 7. 'On 30 September 1911 she was arrested by the bailiff's official from Somerset House, sentenced, and taken to Holloway Gaol in a taxi, Laurence riding with her, and press photographers following. That night the *Evening Standard* printed the picture of Clemence and Laurence in front of the Gaol ... ': K. L. Mix, *HSJ* 2 (1975), 47. The picture is reproduced in *HSJ* 18 (1992), opposite p. 42.

TO GRANT RICHARDS

<UNIVERSTY ARMS HOTEL,> \Trin. Coll./ | CAMBRIDGE.
5 Oct. 1911

My dear Richards,

Your letter of July 27 has at last turned up, and I return its enclosure.

Thanks for your cheerful information about the price of the Manilius; but we don't know what the author's corrections will run to.

Yours sincerely
A. E. Housman.

BMC MS. LC-GR t.s. Richards, 104 (nearly complete).

TO GRANT RICHARDS

Trinity College, Cambridge
18 Oct. 1911

My dear Richards,

I am grateful for the cuttings you send me and for your note about Filson Young, and also to him; but it is too soon at present, <and> as I shall not have spare money for indulging my passions in that direction for some time to come.[1]

I should like to know when you are going to America, and for how long, on account of the Manilius. The printing seems very creditably correct, but I have little time to revise the proofs just at present; and in any case I mean to revise the *notes* en masse, and not piece-meal as the instalments come.

Yours sincerely
A. E. Housman.

Princeton MS (J. Harlan O'Connell Collection). LC-GR t.s. Richards, 104.

---

[1] 'For some time Housman had been talking of setting up a car of his own, but since that, to be useful, would also have necessitated the hiring or setting up of a chauffeur, the project came to nothing. Filson Young, just then, was an authority on motoring, and had volunteered, through me, to take Housman over the Olympia show and to see that he had the opportunity of examining those cars which would be most suitable. Housman, when he came to see me in Berkshire, would often take a car from Cambridge for the journey, and he seemed when touring in France always to travel by car rather than by train': Richards, 104–5.

TO GRANT RICHARDS

Trinity College, Cambridge
24 Oct. 1911

My dear Richards,

I enclose the whole *text* of Manilius II corrected. The notes will occupy me longer.

Yours sincerely
A. E. Housman.

BMC MS. LC-GR t.s. Richards, 105 (nearly complete).

TO H. W. GARROD

Trinity College, Cambridge
24 Oct. 1911

My dear Sir,

I have no wish to prevent other scholars from editing Manilius, but rather the reverse; and I think the world is probably wide enough for both our books,[1] as each contains a good deal which the other does not. I congratulate you on your addition to our knowledge of the cod. Venetus.[2]

I am yours very truly
A. E. Housman.

SJCO MS, Sparrow Collection. Maas, 121.

TO WILFRID SCAWEN BLUNT

Trinity College, Cambridge
6 Nov. 1911

My dear Sir,

It is very kind of you to ask me to pay you a visit,[1] and it would give me great pleasure to do so; but as I am a new comer to Cambridge I am at present much tied by invitations, and it is not possible for me to get away

---

[1] Garrod's translation of, and commentary on, Book II of Manilius was published in 1911. AEH declined to review it on its publication, but attacked it unrelentingly in the preface to *Manilius V* (1930): 'His conjectures were singularly cheap and shallow ... The apparatus criticus is neither skilful nor careful, often defective and sometimes visibly so ... The commentary ... contains so much error that the only readers who can use it with safety are those whose knowledge extends beyond Mr Garrod's': *Selected Prose*, 47: Ricks (1988), 388–9.

[2] AEH in the Preface to *Manilius V*: 'The most valuable part of its contents was the new and enlarged knowledge of the cod. Venetus provided by his discovery of Gronouius' collation in the margin of a book of Bentley's': *Selected Prose*, 47; Ricks (1988), 388.

[1] See AEH to Blunt, 19 Nov. 1911.

next Saturday. The earliest date at which I am free is a fortnight later, and as you are good enough to ask me to name a time I will suggest Saturday the 25th to Monday the 27th, if that is convenient to you.

I am yours very truly
A. E. Housman.

West Sussex Record Office MS: Blunt MSS, Box 29.

TO MESSRS GRANT RICHARDS & CO

Trinity College, Cambridge
9 Nov. 1911

Dear Sirs,

   I have been very agreeably surprised by the accuracy of Messrs MacLehose's printing.

I am yours faithfully
A. E. Housman.

BMC MS. LC-GR t.s. Richards, 105 (nearly complete).

TO MESSRS GRANT RICHARDS & CO

Trinity College, Cambridge
11 Nov. 1911

I should be obliged if you would send me one copy of the 2/6 edition (I think that is the price) of *A Shropshire Lad*.

A. E. Housman.

SIU MS VFM 1082: p.c. addressed 'Messrs Grant Richards & Co. | 7 Carlton Street | Regent Street | S. W.' LC-GR 3 contains a t.s. copy. White (1950), 404.

TO WILFRID SCAWEN BLUNT

Trinity College, Cambridge
19 Nov. 1911

Dear Mr Blunt,

   There appears to be a suitable train which will bring me to Southwater at 5. 48 on the 25th, and another which will take me away at 10. 34 on the Monday morning, so I propose to use these.[1]

I am yours very truly
A. E. Housman.

West Sussex Record Office MS: Blunt MSS, Box 29.

---

[1] AEH and the author and editor Wilfrid Meynell (1852–1948) were Blunt's guests for the weekend. See letter to Blunt, 6 Nov. 1911. In *My Diaries: being a personal narrative of events,*

TO GRANT RICHARDS

[Trinity College | Cambridge
21 November 1911

My dear Richards,]

The composer Butterworth is said to say that he has your express permission to print my words on concert programmes. What is the truth of the matter?[1]

I know you are in America and shall not expect an answer till you return.

[Yours sincerely
A. E. Housman.]

Richards, 105.

TO GRANT RICHARDS

Trinity College, Cambridge
10 Dec. 1911

My dear Richards,

I hope you are back safe from among the Americans.

I enclose, corrected, the first 4 slips of the Manilius notes. These can now be printed in pages, in combination with the text, which I returned corrected more than a month ago. Care should be taken that at any rate the *beginning* of a note on a line \of the text/ should be on the same page as the line itself. This is not *absolutely* necessary where the two pages are both presented to the eye at once; but it is absolutely necessary where turning the leaf would be involved.

Now that the term is over I shall be progressing quickly with the corrections and the preface. I mean to stay here for the vacation.

Yours sincerely
A. E. Housman.

BMC MS. LC-GR t.s. Richards, 106.

1888–1914, ii, *1900–1914* (published 1919–20), 387, Blunt recorded of AEH: 'He does not smoke, drinks little, and would, I think, be quite silent if he were allowed to be.' Gow, 47: 'Housman said the description was perfectly accurate (except that so far as he could remember there was little to drink)'.

[1] Butterworth was at fault in that he 'had failed ... to distinguish between permission to set to music and permission to print in concert programmes': Richards, 105. See AEH to GR, 27 Apr. 1911.

TO GRANT RICHARDS

Trinity College, Cambridge
13 Dec. 1911

My dear Richards,

I enclose slips 5–12 of the Manilius notes.

I also have over-eaten myself this term (being asked to so many College feasts) and drunk too much of that noble but deleterious wine Madeira.[1]

Yours sincerely
A. E. Housman.

LC-GR MS. LC-GR t.s. Richards, 106–7.

TO GRANT RICHARDS

Trinity College, Cambridge
19 Dec. 1911.

My dear Richards,

I now enclose about half of the preface to Manilius, with figures *a* to *g* for insertion. Over the page I give some directions for the printers.

Yours sincerely
A. E. Housman.

[Overleaf]
Preface.

The type, both large and small, should be the same as in the preface to book I.

The figures must be neatly and clearly executed. They should on no account be larger than I have drawn them; indeed I should like them to be considerably smaller, provided that clearness is not sacrificed.

BMC MS. LC-GR t.s. Richards, 107 (nearly complete).

TO GRANT RICHARDS

Trinity College, Cambridge
28 Dec. 1911

My dear Richards,

I enclose:—

The second half of the preface to Manilius, (13 pages), with 3 figures.

The remainder of the notes (slips 23–54) corrected.

---

[1] 'Housman had a great liking for Madeira, drinking it now and again instead of Port': Richards, 107 n., where it is also noted that AEH once paid the excess cost of a madeira above TCC's Wine Committee's limit in order to secure the wine for the college.

I should have thought I ought to have received by this time the combination of text and notes (slips 1–22). A fortnight hence I shall begin to be busy again, and have little time for this job. But I suppose all Scotland will be drunk.[1]

Yours sincerely
A. E. Housman.

BMC MS. LC-GR t.s. Richards, 107 (incomplete).

TO GRANT RICHARDS

Trinity College, Cambridge
29 Dec. 1911

My dear Richards,

I return corrected the pages 1–16 of Manilius, which are satisfactory in most respects. But I must call attention to the transpositions of letters on pp. 6, 8, 9. These errors are *new*; and the printers ought to take care not to introduce new errors.

Yours sincerely
A. E. Housman.

BMC MS. LC-GR t.s.

TO KATHARINE SYMONS

Trinity College, Cambridge
30 Dec. 1911.

My dear Kate,

I am staying here through the vacation as I am seeing a book through the press and found that I could not do much at it during the term. Being conscientious, I took a good deal of time to prepare my lectures; and being a new-comer, I was much asked out to dinner. People here are very hospitable and friendly. The attendance at my lectures was from 20 to 30 (which, though not large, is from 20 to 30 times greater than the attendance at my predecessor's),[1] several of whom were lecturers themselves. I believe the lectures are considered good (as indeed they are).

I don't know that the climate exactly suits me, and probably I have drunk too much port at College Feasts; but I am not feeling stupid, which is the great thing.

---

[1] Following New Year celebrations, which AEH surmises will affect MacLehose the printers.

[1] J. E. B. Mayor (1825–1910), who had been Professor of Latin since 1872.

The twins of Mrs Martin of Hereford called on me the other day, when they were up for scholarships. They were as fluent and self-possessed as ever, and conversed affably on subjects which they thought likely to interest me. I see that each got a scholarship or exhibition, though only for £40,[2] Cambridge being less munificent than Oxford and they less intellectual than Gadd.[3]

I was glad to have your letter at Christmas: I also heard from Jeannie. Love to all.

Your affectionate brother
A. E. Housman.

TCC Add. MS c. 50[1]. Memoir, 146 (incomplete); Maas, 121.

TO GRANT RICHARDS

Trinity College, Cambridge
31 Dec. 1911.

My dear Richards,

1. I have returned under another cover the seven diagrams executed by the printers, with directions.

2. I enclose herewith a diagram (Z) and letter-press, both of which are to stand on the page facing the first page of text and notes: their size must therefore be regulated accordingly. This is the last diagram which I shall require: they are eleven in all, I think.

3. I also enclose a short paragraph to stand at the beginning of the preface.

4. Will you lunch with me at the Café Royal on Wednesday Jan. 3; and, if you can, will you name your own time?

Yours sincerely
A. E. Housman.

5. I have to thank you for a note and a novel.

BMC MS. LC-GR t.s. Richards, 107–8 (nearly complete).

---

[2] Stephen Staffurth Martin of St Paul's School, London, was admitted to KCC on 8 Oct. 1912 as a 'Fielder Exhibitioner'. He was killed in action on 13 Aug. 1917 while serving as a corporal in the Middlesex Regiment. Thomas Lyttle Martin (1893–1982), also of St Paul's School (1906–12), was elected to a scholarship worth £40 p.a., at Emmanuel College, Cambridge, to which he was admitted on 7 Oct. 1912. He graduated BA, 1918, and MA, 1921, and went on to teach at St Paul's School.

[3] Cyril John Gadd (1893–1969), a pupil at King Edward's School, Bath (where KES's husband Edward was headmaster) won a scholarship to Brasenose College, Oxford. A classical scholar, he later became the leading British Sumerologist of his time.

TO GRANT RICHARDS

[Trinity College | Cambridge]

As regards the Manilius diagrams, it occurs to me that perhaps I ought to remark that I drew them as they are to appear in print, without allowing for the reversal of right and left which takes place in printing.

A. E. Housman.

31. 12. 11.

BMC MS: p.c. addressed to 'Grant Richards Esq. | 7 Carlton St | Regent St | S. W.' LC-GR t.s. Richards, 108 (nearly complete).

TO MESSRS GRANT RICHARDS LTD

Trinity College | Cambridge
31 Dec. 1911

Dear Sirs,

I return the seven drawings of diagrams for the Manilius, and I return also my own original drawings, *which must also be returned to the printers.*

The work is very nicely executed, and the only fault I find with it is that the artist has imitated too closely my own imperfect draughtsmanship. I have failed in several cases to put Π and Ω on the same level, and in the diagram c (hexagona) the inequality is unpleasant to the eye and should be corrected somewhat as I have pencilled on the tissue paper.

As to the size of the blocks, the chief matter to be considered is the following. It is important that the diagrams should be inserted exactly at those points in the letterpress which I have indicated in my MS. But when the preface is put into pages, it may happen that the end of a page will cut a diagram in two; and the greater the perpendicular height of the diagram, the oftener this is likely to happen, and the more difficult it will be to remedy.

The printers must remember to place under the diagrams the titles shown in my drawings.

I am yours faithfully
A. E. Housman.

Messrs Grant Richards Ld.

LC-GR t.s. Richards, 108 (nearly complete); Maas, 122.

1912

TO GRANT RICHARDS

Trinity College, Cambridge
4 Jan. 1912

My dear Richards,

I return pp. 17–48 of the Manilius notes corrected. The printers have introduced two new errors, *aque* for *quae* on p. 25 and II for I on p. 33: this last is a perfectly atrocious action, and I cannot imagine how such a thing could come to pass. I wonder where they will stop if they once begin altering numerals: it will be impossible for me to detect them except by chance.

I want to have pp. 1–16 again, as I overlooked some things which were wrong.

Yours sincerely
A. E. Housman.

BMC MS. LC-GR t.s. Richards, 109; Maas, 122.

TO MESSRS GRANT RICHARDS & CO

Trinity College, Cambridge
7 Jan. 1912

Dear Sirs,

I return the three redrawings of diagrams, together with the originals, which should also be returned to the printers.

The only error is that in the diagram M the small loop of the sign of Leo is not rightly executed. I have now drawn it more clearly in pencil on the original.

Yours faithfully
A. E. Housman.

Messrs Grant Richards.

BMC MS. LC-GR t.s. Richards, 109 (nearly complete).

TO MESSRS GRANT RICHARDS LTD

Trinity College, Cambridge
9 Jan. 1912

(*Manilius*)

I am obliged by your note of yesterday; but I certainly do wish to see pp. 17–48 again at some time before they are printed.

A. E. Housman.

BMC MS: p.c. addressed to 'Messrs Grant Richards Ld | 7 Carlton St. | Regent St. | S.W.' LC-GR t.s. Richards, 109 (nearly complete).

TO GRANT RICHARDS

Trinity College, Cambridge
12 Jan. 1912

My dear Richards,

   I hope that the Manilius may appear before the end of February, and it occurs to me that it might avoid delay if they already began to prepare the cover: they know the number of pages (text and notes and preface combined) well enough to be able to judge of the size: the only addition will be about 3 pages of index, which I cannot complete till the preface is paged. I therefore enclose a rough pattern: the type and colour to be just the same as vol. I. The label on the back to be

MANILII II. HOVSMAN

Yours sincerely
A. E. Housman.

BMC MS. LC-GR t.s. Richards, 109–10; Maas, 122.

TO GRANT RICHARDS

Trinity College, Cambridge
1 Feb. 1912

My dear Richards,

   I enclose the only parts of the Manilius in which there are still corrections to be made, and I also send the Index (to be printed in double columns just as in the other volume), and corrigenda to Book I, to face p. 118. This completes the book.

Yours sincerely
A. E. Housman.

BMC MS. LC-GR t.s. Richards, 110.

TO THOMAS PYM

Trinity College
2 Feb. 1912

Dear Pym,

I am very grateful indeed for the tragic drama.[1] I will not enquire which of you invented the bedmaker arriving on the bicycle; but that is the supreme stroke.

I am yours sincerely
A. E. Housman.

Text based on that in Dora Pym, Tom Pym: A Portrait *(1952), 39.*

TO GRANT RICHARDS

Trinity College, Cambridge.
11 Feb. 1912

My dear Richards,

I enclose the last corrections of proofs. I do not want to see them again, and so far as I am concerned all is now ready for publication. I suppose I can trust them to make the binding the same colour as Book I.

Yours sincerely
A. E. Housman.

BMC MS. LC-GR t.s. Richards, 110; Maas, 123.

TO SYDNEY COCKERELL

Trinity College
14 Feb. 1912

Dear Cockerell,

Will you come to the Combination Room[1] a little before 7. 45 tomorrow?

Yours very truly
A. E. Housman.

Private MS.

---

[1] *Fellow or Felon?* or *The Master and the Miscreant,* a tragic melodrama in two acts by 'Thomas Wentworth' and 'William Brown' [alias Pym and Denys Winstanley]. It was first performed in the A.D.C. Theatre, Cambridge, at a Smoking Concert on 22 Feb. 1909, and first revived, with Pym in his original part, in the Lent term Smoking Concert of 1912.

[1] The Fellows' common room at TCC.

TO GRANT RICHARDS

Trinity College | Cambridge
18 Feb. 1912

My dear Richards,

I enclose a list of copies to be sent 'from the author', and also for review.

Yours sincerely
A. E. Housman.

BMC MS. LC-GR t.s. Richards, 110 (nearly complete).

TO GRANT RICHARDS

Trinity College | Cambridge
29 Feb. 1912.

My dear Richards,

I enclose cheque for £75. 8. 10.

When will the precious work be published? The Cambridge term ends on March 15, the coal-strike begins to-morrow,[1] and the destruction of the national wealth is a question of days.

Yours sincerely
A. E. Housman.

BMC MS. LC-GR t.s. Richards, 110; Maas, 123 (both nearly complete).

TO GRANT RICHARDS

[4 March 1912]

I expressly said no corrections required Housman.[1]

LC-GR t.s. Telegram dated March 4, 1912, addressed to 'Richards | 7 Carlton Street | London | S. W.' Richards, 110; Maas, 123.

[1] The national strike of miners, in support of their demand for a minimum wage for every man and boy working underground, continued until 11 April.

[1] 'The printers ... must have raised some fresh query about the proofs': Richards, 110.

TO P. G. L. WEBB

Trinity College, Cambridge
19 April 1912

Dear Webb,

I have just come back from abroad and found here the translations from Heine you have been kind enough to send me.[1] I have been dipping into them, and was very much pleased with the piece on p. 33.[2] The conclusion of *Faust* I don't like any better than the original. I am very glad to have the book.

I have been in Sicily, where the weather and wild flowers were all that could be desired.

Yours sincerely
A. E. Housman.

Lilly MSS 1. 1. 3. Maas, 123.

TO GRANT RICHARDS

[Trinity College | Cambridge]

When Manilius II is published, if it ever is, will you send a copy 'from the author' to

Monsieur G. Saenger[1]
Wasili-Ostrow, 16ème ligne, N 9
St Petersburg

in addition to the list of names you have already.

A. E. Housman.

Cambridge, 23 April 1912

Princeton MS (J. Harlan O'Connell Collection): p.c. addressed 'Grant Richards Esq. | 7 Carlton Street | Regent Street | S. W.'

---

[1] *Translations from Heine and Goethe*, by Philip G. L. Webb (1912).
[2] 'from Die Heimkehr': The moon is up and cresting | The waves with silver rays, | My love in mine arms is resting, | Her head on my heart she lays. ‖ The lovely child is clinging, | As I lie by the lone sea-strand; | 'What song is the wild wind singing? | Why trembles thy snow-white hand?' ‖ 'Those are no winds go sighing, | But mermaids' songs they be; | And it is my sisters crying | Who were drowned long since in the sea.'

[1] Gregory E. Saenger was the author of six classical papers in Russian, 1910–12, and he had sent copies to AEH: see Naiditch (2004), 155.

TO GRANT RICHARDS

Trinity College, Cambridge
28 April 1912

My dear Richards,

A month ago you wrote to say that you were informed that Manilius II was on the sea. Where are you now informed that it is? at the bottom? or is the vessel approaching London via Yokohama?

Yours sincerely
A. E. Housman

BMC MS. LC-GR t.s. Richards, 110; Maas, 124.

TO GRANT RICHARDS

Trinity College, Cambridge
1 May 1912

My dear Richards,

Mr Butterworth can have what he wants.[1]

Two months ago I sent you a list of the persons and newspapers to which I wished copies of the Manilius to be sent. Probably you have lost it, in which case please let me know at once and I will draw up a new one: don't keep the poor wretches waiting another couple of months.

Whether I can lunch with a person who is so far from being what he should be is a question which I will consider between now and my next visit to London.

Yours sincerely
A. E. Housman.

BMC MS. LC-GR t.s. Richards, 110–11; Maas, 124 (both nearly complete).

---

[1] Composer George Butterworth (1885–1916) was almost certainly seeking permission to publish *'Bredon Hill' and Other Songs from 'A Shropshire Lad'* (1912), which included settings of XXI (*Bredon Hill*), XX (*Oh fair enough are sky and plain*), VI (*When the lad for longing sighs*), XXXV (*On the idle hill of summer*), and LIV (*With rue my heart is laden*). His settings of six different songs from *ASL* had been published in 1911.

TO F. J. H. JENKINSON

Trinity College
3 May 1912

Dear Jenkinson,

I shall not need to consult further the Holkham MS of Manilius, and so far as I am concerned it may be returned. I am very grateful to you for procuring it.

Yours very truly
A. E. Housman.

CUL Add. MS 6463 (E) 7386.

TO WITTER BYNNER

Trinity College | Cambridge
17 May 1912

Dear Mr Bynner,

It is very good of you to have sent me your poem,[1] which I return as you request. It has a number of fine lines, as

That homeless politics have split apart
The common country of the human heart.

The only criticism I have to make, if it is a criticism, is that my personal ear is not pleased by verses of more than 10 syllables in this mixed metre, though I know that Patmore[2] and others have used them.

I am yours sincerely
A. E. Housman.

Harvard MS Eng 1071/14. Bynner/Haber (1957), 18.

[1] *An Immigrant*, the Phi Beta Kappa poem read at Harvard in June 1911 and enlarged and published in 1915 as *The New World*.

[2] Coventry Patmore (1823–96), who used such metres (iambics with irregular numbers of feet per line) in *The Unknown Eros, Amelia*, and *Tamerton Church-Tower*.

TO J. W. MACKAIL

Trinity College, Cambridge
22 May 1912

Dear Mackail,

You well describe as extraordinary the pleasure with which you are kind enough to say you read my commentary.[1] I don't believe any one in Cambridge will read it, whether with pleasure or with agony: the Latinists here are very well disposed towards me but terribly afraid of Manilius.

I return your notes, which I am obliged to you for sending me, and I add remarks on some of them.

3. <23> I don't think it admits of dispute that *sub* with the abl. in Manilius can mean 'in the person of'. There is another example at IV 766, about which I wrote on p. lxxi of the 1st volume; and in IV 25 no other interpretation is possible, for Troy, except as embodied in Aeneas, was overthrown. That *non euersa* means the opposite of *uicta* is a circumstance which does not affect the question. Of course *tutam sub Hectore* is also quite good in itself: I only prefer *uictam* because I think it more appropriate.

23. The nymphs in Stat. Theb. IV 684 are *fluuiorum numina* because they belong to the rivers, but the rivers do not belong to them. *ustic* is not very like *at*.

55. *durato ore* = beak[.]

90. *haec seditio* 'ces deux mouvemens opposés de l'océan' Pingré. Stat. Theb. IX.141–2 *Siculi… seditione maris*, the tides of the straits of Messina.

193. If you came across *superest, quaeritur alterum*, it would surprise you a good deal more than *superest et quaeritur unum*.

246. You understand the phrase much as I do; my only difficulty is the lack of an exact parallel.

324. *sequentum* surely would not make sense, for the *partem summam* belongs only to the 4th sign. *sequentis* is wanting in precision, but so is *prioris*; and the defence, as I say in my note, is that only the signs where the angles come are taken into consideration.

328. I don't think there is any ellipsis of the subject of *duplicat*: its subject is the nearest preceding substantive.

337. The angle in question is 90°, not 60°.

419–21 (and 718 and 774–81). If you are going to rid Manilius of redundant ornament, you have your work cut out for you: even his

[1] On *Manilius II.*

admirer Scaliger confesses that he does not know when to leave off. Here you will have to remove 422 as well, because *sic* etc. will have nothing proper to refer to; and if you eject the description of summer and winter you ought not to spare its pendant, the description of spring and autumn which follows.

521. The four tropical signs are the leaders of the four triangles, and the opposition of triangle to triangle is effected by the two diameters which join those signs. The other four diameters, joining the subsidiary signs (e.g. Taurus and Scorpius), can only say ditto.

534. (*quid*) *mirer*, I agree, is not Manilius' usual way of talking, but it is inoffensive in itself and can hardly be got rid of without great expense. In your conjecture I think *neu* should be *ne*, as no conjunction is in place.

574. *que* unites the participle *defixa* and the clause *quod ... feruntur*, both of which are causal. So in Ouid. met. V 367 *que* unites *postquam exploratum satis est* and *deposito metu*, both of which are temporal.

544. *dant* would certainly have the advantage of making the construction of *Pisces* clear, and *Scorpius acer* would quite account for the change to *dat*[.]

552. The Centaur is called *geminus* (IV 784) as being *bimembris*.

566. *fugata* seems to me not only more violent but less suitable than the *fugiens* I conjectured in 1903. With a passive participle one would expect *uirtute* or *a uirtute* rather than *sub*.

615. If you like *uellere* better than *corpore* I think you ought to like *tergore* better still.

644–5. It is desirable to procure a *stellarum* for *uagarum*, but what *parte* wants is the genitive *mundi*, and I don't think the sense of your supplement is admissible.

699. Of course *ecce* much oftenest stands at the beginning of a verse, but it has no native repugnance to the end, and stands there in Verg. Aen. III 219.

745. (Lucr. VI 85). *quōque* does not seem to be found except in *quoqueuersus*.

826. If *quae* is right, *at caeli* is probably as good as anything else; but *qui* is supported by the parallels I quoted.

860. The future participle of *nascor*, so far as it exists at all, is *nasciturus*; and the sense which you procure is not germane to the matter in hand.

891. *que* is not attached to words ending in *c* by poets earlier than the 4th century (Madvig Cic. de fin. V 40, Haupt opusc. III pp. 508–10): the exception, Ouid. fast. IV 848, is one of those which prove rules. *huice* is not used in the classical period at all.

917. If we had *thea* here I should have expected *theos* in 909–10.

Yours very truly
A. E. Housman.

Lilly MSS 1. 1. 3. Maas, 406–7.

TO PROFESSOR D'ARCY THOMPSON

Trinity College, Cambridge.
15 June 1912

I have been away for a week, and find here your two papers, for which many thanks. I am reading *Bird and Beast*[1] with great interest.

Yours very truly
A. E. Housman.

St Andrews MS 23590: p.c. addressed 'Professor D'Arcy Thompson C.B. | University College | Dundee'.

TO GRANT RICHARDS

Trinity College, Cambridge
2 July 1912

My dear Richards,

I shall be staying in London during the first few days of next week; so that if you are there, and still cherish your benevolent intention of asking me to lunch, you will have your chance.

I see that you are coming out as a novelist: *Huîtres* or *Crevettes roses* or some such title.[1]

Yours sincerely
A. E. Housman.

LC-GR MS. LC-GR t.s. Richards, 111.

---

[1] 'On Bird and Beast in Ancient Symbolism', *Transactions of the Royal Society of Edinburgh*, 38 (1897), 179–92.

[1] *Caviare*, Richards's first novel, published in 1912.

TO GRANT RICHARDS

Trinity College, Cambridge
5 July 1912

My dear Richards,

I shall be delighted to lunch with you on Tuesday. I expect to sleep Saturday night at Liverpool St., Sunday at G. Vize,[1] 15 Spencer Rd, Putney, Monday at Charing Cross Hotel.

You can send Manilius to this infatuated philosopher, since he seems to want him.

Yours sincerely
A. E. Housman.

BMC MS. LC-GR t.s. Richards, 111 (nearly complete).

TO MESSRS GRANT RICHARDS & CO

Trinity College, Cambridge
2<2>3 July 1912.

Dear Sirs,

I suppose that what Mr Byrne really wants to do is to print one poem out of *A Shropshire Lad* with a Greek translation. This he may do: of course he must not print the whole book; nor more than one poem, unless he makes separate application for each.

Yours faithfully
A. E. Housman.

SIU MS VFM 1082. LC-GR t.s. Richards, 111.

TO GRANT RICHARDS

Trinity College | Cambridge
30 July 1912

My dear Richards,

I remember the name of Graham Peel[1] as a composer to whom I gave some permission. If he mentions the name of the author I don't think he is

---

[1] George Henry Vize (*c*.1845–1914). 'Collector of antiquities and china, once champion heavy-weight boxer &c.': AEH to GR, 6 June 1912. George and Kitty Vize were friends of AEH's colleague at the Patent Office, John Maycock: see Naiditch (1995), 19–20. AEH kept a cutting of Vize's poem *London Wall* from the *Putney Weekly Press and South-Western Post*, 24 June 1904: SJCO, Higham Collection. Vize was one of the best known all-round athletes of his time, winner of numerous swimming and rowing races, and once holder of the Queensberry heavyweight boxing championship.

[1] In 1911 Gerald Graham Peel (1877–1937) published a setting of *Bredon Hill* (*ASL* XXI) under the title *In Summertime on Bredon*.

bound to mention the name of the book; and he probably altered the title because *Bredon Hill* has been set to music by so many composers[2] and he wanted to differentiate, which I think is harmless.

It was not Bourg but Bourges that I went to.

I saw your case in the papers and wondered what exactly it was about. I don't think any of my letters are very incriminating.[3]

Yours sincerely
A. E. Housman.

LC-GR t.s. Richards, 111–12; Maas, 124.

TO ALICE ROTHENSTEIN

Trinity College, Cambridge
11 Aug. 1912

Dear Mrs Rothenstein,

It is a great pleasure to hear from you, and possibly I may soon have the still greater pleasure of seeing you. I know where Oakridge Lynch is, and this week I shall be staying at Woodchester, two miles on the other side of Stroud. If you could tell me the exact position of your abode, from Chelford station, or from the mouth of the tunnel, I could easily walk over on Thursday or Friday,—that is to say, unless my hosts have made other arrangements for me. My address will be

    c/ E. T. Wise Esq.

        Oakleigh

        Woodchester.

I go there on Tuesday and return on Saturday.

Yours sincerely
A. E. Housman.

Harvard bMS Eng 1148 (740) 27.

[2] 'Yet Peel's "Bredon Hill" is only the fourth or fifth of those traceable, a number hardly warranting the "so many"': Banfield (1985), 236.

[3] GR's first publishing business had been sold by the Trustee H. A. Moncrieff to Alexander Moring of the De La More Press, who in due course came into possession of the firm's correspondence. It included letters from a number of well-known authors, AEH among them, which Moring sold commercially to a bookseller. GR, alerted to this by Clement Shorter in the *Sphere*, began legal action against the bookseller, which came to nothing. However, he later recovered a number of letters, including letters from AEH, from the bookseller's son: Richards, 112–13.

TO ALICE ROTHENSTEIN

Oakleigh, Woodchester.

Wednesday [13 Aug. 1912]

I shall be delighted to come over to lunch on Friday. I will try to arrive a little before 1. I must be back here about 7, so unfortunately I cannot stay for the night.

Yrs.

A. E. H.

Harvard bMS Eng 1148 (740) 28.

TO GRANT RICHARDS

7 Sept. 1912

HÔTEL DE L'EUROPE | VENISE

My dear Richards,

Your gift[1] came just as I was starting, and prevented me from paying W. H. Smith & Son six shillings for some much less entertaining work to read on the journey. I read with great interest all through, though the Monte Carlo parts perhaps are not equal to the Parisian and American. These last seem to me particularly good. I have just seen a favourable review in the *Telegraph*.

I hope you will not now take to writing poetry or editing Manilius.

I am now going to Paris and shall be at the Continental probably till the 16th.

Yours sincerely

A. E. Housman.

BMC MS. Richards, 113; Maas, 125.

TO GRANT RICHARDS

Hôtel Continental, Paris

12 Sept. 1912

My dear Richards,

The date at which I expect to be back is 3. 25 at Charing Cross on Wednesday the 18th. If you carry your kindness so far as to ask me to Cookham Dean that night, I should be very pleased to come; if not, I can easily go on to Cambridge and see my anointed sovereign.[1]

[1] Of Richards's novel *Caviare*, which was just appearing.

[1] King George V, who interrupted a Scottish holiday to watch large-scale military manoeuvres around Cambridge. He arrived on 17 Sept. and stayed for a few days at TCC: *The Cambridge Review*, 34. 838 (17 Oct. 1912), 4–5.

I don't advise you to go any more to the Tour d'Argent.[2]

Yours sincerely
A. E. Housman.

LC-GR MS. LC-GR t.s. Richards, 113 (nearly complete).

TO EDWARD MARSH

Trinity College, Cambridge
1 Oct. 1912

Dear Mr Marsh,

I well remember meeting you at Gosse's, though I did not then connect you with the Master of Downing.[1] The lady who sat next me at supper, on hearing your name, wondered if you were the author of *The Beetle:*[2] I had not then read that book, so I did not know what a fearful suspicion this was. I now have a suspicion, less fearful though perhaps equally erroneous, that you may be the author of a little book[3] Bowes and Bowes[4] have just sent me, containing a beautiful poem on Good Friday; if so, I thank you for the gift.

If you want to get poetry out of me,[5] you must be either a relative or a duchess;[6] and you are neither. As a brother and as a snob I am accessible from two quarters, but from no others. Besides, I do not really belong to your 'new era'; and none even of my few unpublished poems have been written within the last two years.

I shall be very much interested in your book. One of the names you mention is new to me, and there are others of whom I have only read a little. You do not mention Chesterton: his *Ballad of the White*

[2] Eminent Parisian restaurant, 'of which we were both fond' (Richards, 113).

[1] Howard Marsh (1839–1915), father of polymath Edward Marsh (1872–1953), was Professor of Surgery at Cambridge and Master of Downing College.

[2] Mystery novel (1897) by Richard Marsh (1857–1915).

[3] *XAPITEΣΣI*, by Elizabeth Bridges, published anonymously in 1911.

[4] Cambridge booksellers and publishers, who published the book again in 1912. *Good Friday* was on p. 28: Where angel flowers up-torn | Lonely to die, | By angel hands are planted | The cooling love-enchanted | Streams anigh; || Where pure-joyed woodland creatures | Lustfully slain | To squandering slaughter driven, | Their fair strength meekly given | Receive again; || Thy delicate love rejected | Shall drink the dew, | Thy wistful comfort wasted | Shall there its power untested | Revive anew.

[5] For the annual collection *Georgian Poetry* which Marsh edited, 1912–21.

[6] See AEH to LH, 9 Aug. 1903, and to the Duchess of Sutherland, 11 Aug. 1903. AEH subsequently contributed poems (*LP* II, XXXVII, XXXVIII) to *The Blunderbuss* (3 Mar. 1917), *The Times* (31 Oct. 1917), and *A Tribute to Thomas Hardy O.M.* (2 June 1919): see *Poems* (1997), 37, 410, 412.

Horse[7] is absurd in its plan and its conception and often cheap and brassy in its ornament, but it contains quite a lot of really magnificent verses, which impressed me more than anything I have read for a long time.

However, literary criticism is not what you were asking me for.

I am yours truly
A. E. Housman.

Berg MS. Edward Marsh, Patron of the Arts: A Biography, *by Christopher Hassall (1959), 194 (excerpt); Maas, 125–6.*

TO MILDRED PLATT

Trinity College, Cambridge
10 Oct. 1912

Dear Mrs Platt,

I shall be coming to town on the 17th to attend a meeting at University College, so I give you notice, as you kindly told me to do, in order that you may ask me to dinner if you feel inclined.

The last winter was so mild that I had no excuse for drinking the sloe gin: it is therefore still maturing, and no doubt will become specially excellent. I gave some to a fellow of the College who has gout, and is consequently a connoisseur, and he admired it very much.

I am yours sincerely
A. E. Housman.

UCL MS Add. 165. Maas, 126.

TO OLIVE BENSON

Trinity College, Cambridge
15 Oct. 1912

Dear Miss Benson,

You have my permission to publish your settings of the poems you speak of.

I am yours sincerely
A. E. Housman.

Miss Olive Benson.

Lilly MSS 1. 1. 3. Envelope addressed 'Miss Olive Benson | North Augusta | S. C. | U. S. A.', and postmarked 16 Oct. 1912.

---

[7] G. K. Chesterton (1874–1936) contributed an extract from the poem.

TO EDWARD MARSH

[Trinity College | Cambridge]

Yes

<No>

I have done as much for less deserving persons.

A. E. H.
12. 11. 12.

Berg MS: p.c. self-addressed 'E. Marsh Esq. | 5. Raymond Buildings | Gray's Inn | London W C'.
The card bears Marsh's instruction 'Please scratch out the alternative rejected', and AEH has
cancelled 'No'.

TO GRANT RICHARDS

Trinity College, Cambridge
14 Nov. 1912

My dear Richards,

Miss Fox may set the poem to music.

The female novel which you gave me when I saw you last was very readable. I forget its name, but it contained an indiscreet portrait of Somerset Maugham.[1]

Yours sincerely
A. E. Housman.

SIU MS VFM 1082. LC-GR t.s. Richards, 113–14 (nearly complete).

TO THOMAS HARDY

Trinity College | Cambridge
28 Nov. 1912

Dear Mr Hardy,

Let me say how sorry I am to see to-day the news of your bereavement.[1] Several times since I was at Dorchester in 1900 I had met Mrs Hardy at the Gosses' when she was visiting London, and though the last of these occasions was some years ago,[2] I had not heard of any

[1] Ada Leverson's *The Limit*, published by GR in 1912: Richards, 114. GR takes the view that her character Hereford Vaughan had 'very little likeness' to Maugham.

[1] Emma Lavinia, Hardy's wife, had died the previous day, aged 72. They had been married over 38 years.

[2] On 6 May 1909: *The Book of Gosse*, 263 sq. (CUL Add. MS 7034), as P. G. Naiditch testifies in *HSJ* 26 (2000), 107.

failure of her health. I beg you to accept my sympathy and believe me always

Yours very truly
A. E. Housman.

Dorset County Museum MS. Maas, 127.

TO A. S. F. GOW

Trinity College
28 Nov. 1912

Dear Gow,

I have taken tickets for *Milestones*[1] for Tuesday Dec. 3. They are in the front row of the circle, which I hope suits you: it is my favourite part of a theatre.

Yours sincerely
A. E. Housman.

TCC Add. MS c. 112[1]. Maas, 126.

TO MESSRS GRANT RICHARDS LTD

Trinity College | Cambridge
11 Dec. 1912

Dear Sirs,

The permission asked by the Rev. H. S. Allen to print the lines from *A Shropshire Lad* must be refused.[1] I return his letter.

Yours faithfully
A. E. Housman

Messrs Grant Richards Ltd.

LC-GR t.s. Richards, 114.

---

[1] Arnold Bennett's most successful play, written in collaboration with Edward Knoblock (author of *Kismet*), which was being performed at the New Theatre, Cambridge. It was first produced at the Royalty Theatre on 5 Mar. 1912.

[1] 'I have forgotten the reason, but it may well have been anticlericalism': Richards, 114.

TO MILDRED PLATT

Trinity College, Cambridge
26 Dec. 1912

Dear Mrs Platt,

I received yesterday your kind and beautiful present of the Dogana,[1] in its sumptuous frame, which I suppose I must not admire unless I want to be suspected of not having taste enough to admire the picture properly, which I think I do. I am very grateful, and hope that heaven will reward you with a happy new year.

I was much in need of something to divert my mind from the horrors of my situation, for Trinity College is a besieged city. A week ago there came a telegram to say that one of the junior Fellows, Pearse,[2] whom Platt will know by name, had left his home, mad and armed, and would probably make his way here. All entrances to the College have therefore been closed, except the Great Gate, which is guarded by a double force of Porters. Cambridge was perplexed at first, but has now invented the explanation that it is the Master[3] who has gone mad, and has made these arrangements in order that he may shoot at the Fellows from the Lodge as they come through the Great Gate. The Provost of King's[4] gives imitations of the Master thus engaged: "Ah, there is dear Dr Jackson!" bang!!

What makes matters worse is that the College evidently sets no value on my life or even on that of the Archdeacon of Ely;[5] for Whewell's Court is left quite unprotected, and I have to look under the bed every night.

My remembrances therefore to your husband and family: to-morrow I may be no more than a remembrance myself.

Yours sincerely
A. E. Housman.

UCL MS Add. 165. Maas, 127–8.

[1] The often-portrayed Venetian counting-house.

[2] Percy James Pearse (b. 1884). Subsizar at TCC, 1903; Major Scholar, 1904; firsts in both parts of the Classical Tripos, 1906, 1907; BA, 1907; Fellow of TCC, 1909–15.

[3] H. M. Butler. See List of Recipients.   [4] M. R. James. See List of Recipients.

[5] The Revd William Cunningham (1849–1919), clergyman and economic historian. BA, TCC, 1872, Chaplain, 1880–91, Fellow, 1891; vicar of Great St Mary's, Cambridge, 1887–1908; Professor of Economics, King's College, London, 1891–7; Archdeacon of Ely, 1907–19; FBA, 1903. Author of *The Growth of English Industry and Commerce* (7 edns., 1882–1910).

1913

TO GRANT RICHARDS

Trinity College, Cambridge
4 Jan. 1913

My dear Richards,

If the *Dly*[1] *Sketch* is an English paper, will you ask it what business it has to do this? I am assuming that copyright covers such cases.[2]

Yours sincerely
A. E. Housman.

SIU MS VFM 1082. LC-GR t.s. Richards, 119 (nearly complete).

TO GRANT RICHARDS

Trinity College | Cambridge
17 Jan. 1913

My dear Richards,

I am exceedingly sorry to hear of your illness. I remember your having some similar trouble, which you bore with great fortitude, once when we were in Paris together.[1] One of my chief objections to the management of the universe is that we suffer so much more from our gentler and more amiable vices than from our darkest crimes.

If the *Daily Sketch* will publish an expression of regret, that is all I want:[2] no fee, on any account. What I object to is that when some people have asked leave to print my poems, and I have refused it, other people go and print them without asking.

Yours sincerely
A. E. Housman.

---

[1] i.e. '*Daily*'.

[2] AEH had discovered through his press-cutting agency that the newspaper had published *ASL* XVIII (*Oh, when I was in love with you*) on 2 Jan. 1913 without permission. 'His assumption was correct, but nevertheless nothing much could be done ... except to remonstrate with the editor and warn him not to do it again': Richards, 119.

[1] In 1907, when GR went to France 'to convalesce after a sharp attack of influenza followed by a worse bout of shingles' (Richards, 116).

[2] It printed a brief apology on 25 January.

I shall be in London for a few hours on Tuesday, but only to keep a dinner engagement. I don't know when I am likely to be up for any time.

SIU MS VFM 1082. LC-GR t.s. Richards, 119–20 (nearly complete); Maas, 128.

TO A. S. F. GOW

Trinity College
29 Jan. 1913

Dear Gow,

I think this may answer your purpose, though the part about the planets is slovenly.

The fisherman's book, I find, is not much good as an exposition of astronomy.

I especially warn you against spending 2^s on a much-advertised work called *Celestial Motions*.[1]

Yours
A. E. H.

TCC. Add. MS c. 112².

TO STEPHEN GASELEE

[Trinity College | Cambridge]

What I should have said and thought I was saying is that the hiatus of monosyllables occurs only in the 2$^{nd.}$ syllable of the dactyl and *in that place* the hiatus of words rather than monosyllables does not occur,—the only exception being in proper names, *Panopeaĕ et, Ennĭ imaginis.* <Elisions> Hiatus like *etesiaĕ esse* occurs even when there is no Greek word, *ualĕ inquit*, and probably Lucr. 6. 743 *remigĭ oblitae.*

Yrs
A. E. Housman.

12 Feb. 1913

UCLA MS S/C 100/72: p.c. addressed 'S. Gaselee Esq. | Magdalene College' and marked 'Local' by AEH. Naiditch (1996), item 36.

[1] By William Thynne Lynn (1884, etc.).

TO ALICE ROTHENSTEIN

Trinity College | Cambridge
14 Feb. 1913

Dear Mrs Rothenstein,

Bertrand Russell[1] said to me yesterday 'Have you seen anything of the Rothensteins lately', and it went through my heart like a spear of ice that neither had I seen them *nor had they heard from me*, though you wrote to me at the beginning of the year. But if you ever have to examine for University Scholarships you will find as I do that all one's leisure is fully occupied by wishing that one was dead; and I am only just at the end of this tribulation.

I suppose I am right in directing this letter to your town mansion and not to your place in Gloucestershire. *Iles*[2] is a regular Gloucestershire name. I have not been down there since I saw you last. I was telling Russell that I can remember when his father and mother used to live on the hill just opposite Woodchester. You and William ought to be in the country now to observe the progress of this extraordinary spring, or winter as it calls itself.

I suppose you have seen Mrs Cornford's new book.[3] Her portrait in the frontispiece is pleasing and recognisable, but Cornford's is almost a caricature.[4]

Best wishes to all of you.

Yours sincerely
A. E. Housman

Harvard bMS Eng 1148 (740) 29. Maas, 128–9.

TO LILY THICKNESSE

[Trinity College | Cambridge]
8 March 1913

Dear Mrs Thicknesse,

The chief excitements of the term here have been an agitation, by a highly undistinguished set of persons, to introduce conscription for undergraduates, as a last effort to frighten the Germans; and an exhibition

---

[1] Bertrand [Arthur William] Russell (1872–1970). Mathematician, philosopher, and social reformer. Second son of Viscount Amberley and grandson of the first Earl Russell, whom he succeeded as Earl in 1931. Fellow of TCC, 1895; lecturer, 1910. Published *The Problems of Philosophy*, 1912, and the third and final vol. of his *Principia Mathematica*, 1913.

[2] See AEH to Alice Rothenstein, 15 Aug. 1908.

[3] Frances Cornford's *Death and the Princess* (1912).

[4] Mrs Bernard Darwin's frontispiece illustration depicts the Princess with a large, horned, cloven-footed woodland god.

of post-impressionist undergraduate art, which is calculated to frighten the Germans a good deal more.

My respects to both of you.

Yours sincerely
A. E. Housman.

Memoir, *204–5; Maas, 129.*

TO GRANT RICHARDS

Trinity College, Cambridge
20 April 1913

My dear Richards,

I return with thanks Frank Harris's story,[1] which I am glad to have read, though I think the conception is better than the execution. Thanks also for the book about wine.

I forgot, when you were going off to Paris, to tell you to eat *morilles*,[2] which are in season now. But perhaps you did so, or had done so already.

Yours sincerely
A. E. Housman.

LC-GR MS. LC-GR t.s. Richards, 120.

TO MESSRS GRANT RICHARDS & CO

Trinity College, Cambridge
22 April 1913.

Dear Sirs,

Mr Cripper[1] may print the five poems with his music.

Yours faithfully
A. E. Housman.

SIU MS VFM 1082. LC-GR t.s. White (1950), 404.

---

[1] *The Irony of Chance* in *Unpath'd Waters*, which GR had sent in proof: Richards, 120.
[2] 'A sort of corrugated mushroom, and very, very good': Richards, 120.

[1] An error for [A. Redgrave] Cripps, whose *'A Shropshire Lad' Cycle of Five Songs* was published in 1914. The settings were of XXIX, XV, XXII, XIII, and LVII. Cripps's settings of a further nine poems were published in 1932.

TO A. S. F. GOW

Trinity College
22 April 1913

Dear Gow,

Will you dine with me in my rooms on May 10th at 8 o' clock? I hope very much you may be able to come.

Yours sincerely
A. E. Housman.

TCC Add. MS c. 112³.

TO PERCY W. AMES

13 May 1913.

I am very grateful to those who have nominated me for a seat on your Academic Committee, among so many eminent men; and to yourself for your proposal to bring forward my name for election as Honorary Fellow of the Royal Society of Literature; but I must nevertheless beg leave to decline both favours, which, however gratifying and honourable, are remote from my tastes and pursuits.

BMC MS. Draft of reply written on t.s. letter from Percy W. Ames, Secretary to the Academic Committee of the Royal Society of Literature of the United Kingdom. Lilly MSS 3. 1. 10 (t.s. copy).

TO A. C. BENSON

[Trinity College]
16 May 1913

[Dear Benson,]

You write me a very kind letter, but your suasions fall upon the deaf ear of an egoistic hedonist. I suffer a good deal from life, and do not want to suffer more; and to join the Academic Committee or any similar body would be an addition to my discomforts, not overwhelming, but still appreciable. To analyse my feelings, which may be morbid, would only be a matter of curiosity; what concerns me is the feelings themselves, and there they are … For any practical purpose it would find me quite useless, and it can very well dispense with any lustre which might be shed upon it by my exiguous (though eximious) output.

[Yours sincerely]
A. E. Housman.

TCC Adv. c. 20. 25: copy in E. F. Benson's hand. Graves (1981), 170 (excerpt).

TO JAMES G. FRAZER

In 1906 I was in the island of Capri on Sept. 8, the feast of the Nativity of the Virgin. The anniversary was duly solemnised by fireworks at nine or ten in the evening, which I suppose were municipal; but just after sundown the boys outside the villages were making small bonfires of brushwood on waste bits of ground by the wayside. Very pretty it looked, with the flames blowing about in the twilight; what took my attention was the listlessness of the boys and their lack of interest in the proceeding. A single lad, the youngest, would be raking the fire together and keeping it alight, but the rest stood lounging about and looking in every other direction, with the air of discharging mechanically a traditional office from which all zest had evaporated.

A. E. H.

Here it is: not much, you see; but I cannot spin it out to more.

17 May 1913

TCC Add. MS b. 36$^{82(2)}$ *(t.s copy). Ackerman (1974), 357.*

TO JAMES G. FRAZER

Trinity College
21 May 1913

Dear Frazer,

The pious orgy at Naples on Sept. 8 went through the following stages when I witnessed it in 1897. It began at 8 in the evening with illumination of the façade of St Maria Piedigrotta and with the whole population walking about blowing penny trumpets. After four hours of this I went to bed at midnight, and was lulled to sleep by the barrel-organs, which supersede the trumpets about that hour. At four in the morning I was waked by detonations as if the British fleet was bombarding the city, caused, I was afterwards told, by dynamite rockets. The only step possible beyond this is assassination, which accordingly takes place about peep of day. I forget now the number of the slain, but I think the average is eight or ten, and I know that in honour of my presence they murdered a few more than usual.

I enclose the extract from the *Standard* about Satan in Scotland.

Yours sincerely
A. E. Housman

Text based on TCC Add. MS b. 36$^{82(1)}$ *(t.s. copy). Ackerman (1974), 358.*

TO WILFRID MEYNELL

Trinity College, Cambridge
22 May 1913

Dear Mr Meynell,

I must not altogether, as you suggest, put off thanking you for the three books you have been kind enough to send me; but it would be rather impertinent to do more than thank you.

I am yours sincerely
A. E. Housman.

You may have heard that I had the pleasure of meeting your son[1] the other day.

BMC MS. Envelope addressed 'Wilfrid Meynell Esq. | 2ᴬ Granville Place | Portman Square | W.'

TO KATHARINE SYMONS

Trinity College, Cambridge
22 May 1913

My dear Kate,

I must return you your chart,[1] which is a monument of industry and ingenuity, and I cannot add anything to it. My edition of Prince's *Worthies*[2] is 1810, the same as yours. The marginal note you speak of must mean 'Sir W. Pole's *Description of Devon*, chapter on Exmouth'. This book was in manuscript when Prince wrote, but has since been published.[3] Neither this College nor the University Library has a copy, but I may be able to find one somewhere in Cambridge. I don't know anything of the Clevedon lady,[4] except that I have heard mamma speak of her.

Your affectionate brother
A. E. Housman.

Lilly MSS 2. Maas, 129–30.

---

[1] Francis Meredith Wilfrid Meynell (1891–1975); later book designer, publisher, and founder of the Nonesuch Press (1923).

[1] Of the Housman family tree.

[2] *Danmonii orientales illustres: or, the worthies of Devon ...* by John Prince, first published 1701.

[3] In 1791, as *Collections towards a description of the county of Devon Now first pr. From the autograph in the possession of Sir J.-W. De la Pole.*

[4] Mrs Gathorne-Hill (identified in KES's note pencilled on the MS).

TO ALICE ROTHENSTEIN

Trinity College | Cambridge
4 June 1913

Dear Mrs Rothenstein,

Alas, no, I cannot come to London on the 10th; though I ought not to say alas, as the obstacle consists in my having been asked to dine at Jesus to meet Thomas Hardy, who is receiving an honorary degree.[1]

If my friends ask me to Woodchester, and you are in your country mansion at the time, I certainly will come and see you. Remember me to Wm.

Yours sincerely
A. E. Housman.

Harvard bMS Eng 1148 (740) 30. Maas, 130.

TO WILFRID MEYNELL

Trinity College, Cambridge
10 June 1913.

Dear Mr Meynell,

This is indeed rather overwhelming, but I manage to gasp out my thanks.

I am particularly glad to have the whole of *Orison-tryst*,[1] whose first lines you repeated to me.

I am sorry to hear from Cockerell this evening that you are not well.

Yours sincerely and gratefully
A. E. Housman.

BMC MS. Envelope addressed 'W. Meynell Esq. | 2ᴬ Granville Place | Portman Square | W.'

---

[1] D.Litt. Hardy dined at Jesus College on the evening of 10 June, and Sydney Cockerell invited AEH along to meet him: P. G. Naiditch, 'Thomas Hardy and A. E. Housman', *HSJ* 26 (2000), 107.

[1] Poem by Francis Thompson (1859–1907). Wilfrid Meynell, as his literary executor, in 1913 published *The Collected Poetry of Francis Thompson* in two limited edns., of 500 and 2,500 copies respectively.

TO PROFESSOR HENRY JACKSON

Trinity College
10 June 1913

My dear Jackson,

I cannot express in words how little store I set by the enclosed composition,[1] and how impossible it will be for you to injure my amour propre by any criticisms and corrections. I apprehend that it may be both too short and too stiff, apart from other demerits and defects; but now it is your turn.

I am going abroad on Saturday, and expect to be away rather more than a week.

Yours sincerely
A. E. Housman,

TCC Add. MS c. 32[53]. Maas, 130.

TO GRANT RICHARDS

Trin. Coll. Camb.
11 June 1913

I am going to Paris on Sunday for about a week, most likely to the Hotel Majestic, Avenue Kléber.

Yrs
A. E. Housman.

LC-GR MS. LC-GR t.s. P.c. addressed 'Grant Richards Esq. | 7 Carlton St. | Regent St. | S. W.'
Richards, 120 (nearly complete).

TO A. V. HOUGHTON

Trinity College | Cambridge
11 June 1913

Dear Sir,

For twelve years or so I have been refusing to allow my poems to appear in anthologies, so I am afraid I must return a refusal to your request also.

I am yours faithfully
A. E. Housman

A. V. Houghton Esq.

Bodleian MS Sidgwick & Jackson 285, fo. 24.

---

[1] The draft of an address from the Fellows of Trinity College to congratulate the Master, the Revd H. M. Butler, on his eightieth birthday. See *Selected Prose*, 161–2, 200.

TO ALICE ROTHENSTEIN

Trinity College | Cambridge
3 Aug. 1913

Dear Mrs Rothenstein,

You were kind enough some months ago to ask me to come and stay with you either before or after I went to Woodchester, and I had been intending to try to manage things so; but I am going to Woodchester on the 13th for a week, and I have got other engagements both before and afterwards, so that I am afraid I shall have to confine myself to coming over to see you one day when I am there, if you will let me. Is *Iles Farm* still the correct address?

I have not been away yet for any long time, though I spent a week in Paris in June. I expect at the end of the month to be going to the cathedral towns in Normandy which are not easily accessible from Paris,—Coutances, Bayeux, and so on. I sometimes meet friends of yours here,—the other day McEvoy the painter,[1] who is depicting Prof. James Ward.[2]

My best respects to both of you.

Yours sincerely
A. E. Housman.

Harvard bMS Eng 1148 (740) 31.

TO PROFESSOR D. A. SLATER

GRAND HÔTEL TERMINUS | RUE S^T LAZARE | PARIS
le 17 Sept. *1913*

Dear Slater,

I have been travelling about in Normandy beyond the reach of letters, and yours is one of a batch which has been forwarded here.

So far as I remember, all I did at the British Museum MSS of the *Metamorphoses* was to consult them in the 15th book and the destitute parts of the 14th, at those places where Korn's apparatus[1] gave variants. My only reason for consulting them was that Postgate had sent me in proof his article on book XV,[2] and I have no recollection of examining them in

---

[1] Arthur Ambrose McEvoy (1878–1927). Entered Slade School of Fine Art, 1893. Later in his career, turned from landscapes and interiors to portrait painting, for which he became famous.

[2] 1843–1925. Philosopher and psychologist. Fellow of TCC, 1875; Professor of Mental Philosophy and Logic at Cambridge, 1897–1925; FBA, 1902.

[1] The edn. of the *Metamorphoses* (1880) by [Carl Paul] O[tto] Korn (1858–1935).

[2] 'On Book XV of Ovid's *Metamorphoses*', *JP* 43 (1894), 144–56.

the earlier books; nor do I know that anyone else has done so. As they are none of them eminent even among the poor MSS containing book XV, I should not expect them to be of any use beside the better MSS in the earlier books; but of course one never can tell.

If you do as you suggest about the Tours MS of the *Ibis* I shall be very grateful for a sight of the photographs.

It so happens that next term I am lecturing on book I of the *Metamorphoses*; so it would be no trouble to me to look through that part at any rate of your text and apparatus.[3]

Your proposal at XIV 671[4] does not seem to me better than some others (I have seen *tam digna* somewhere, perhaps only in my own margin) nor very likely on general grounds. I am not at all sure that *audacis* wants changing: Ulysses was *audax* (though he had other characteristics more prominent and more often mentioned) and I believe I have noted down another place where he is called so. Further, a reading like *timidi aut audacis*, giving correct metre and grammar and a clear though foolish sense, suggests to me interpolation rather than a confusion of letters.

I am returning to Cambridge at the end of the week.

Yours sincerely
A. E. Housman.

Lilly MSS 1. 1. 3. Maas, 408.

TO GRANT RICHARDS

Trinity College, Cambridge
23 Sept. 1913

My dear Richards,

Your new encroachment on literature reached me just as I was going abroad, and I found it excellently suited for reading while travelling. I am only just back, or I would have thanked you before. I have seen a review which says it is better than *Caviar*,[1] and I hope the public will take that view, though I found *Caviar* the more continuously entertaining.

I was chiefly in the west of Normandy, riding about in a motor car which I hired very cheap in Paris.

Yours sincerely
A. E. Housman,

SIU MS VFM 1082. Richards, 120–1; Maas, 131.

[3] Slater's Oxford edn. of the *Metamorphoses* was never completed.
[4] Slater excluded this from his article 'On three Passages of Ovid', *CR* 27. 8 (Dec. 1913), 257–8, and later abandoned *tam digna* in his book *Towards a Text of the Metamorphoses of Ovid* (1927).
[1] For '*Caviare*'.

TO GRANT RICHARDS

Trinity College, Cambridge
24 Sept. 1913

My dear Richards,

Thanks for the cheque, for which I enclose receipt. It is rather a weight off my mind, as I thought you might have been betting on horses whose names began with JE.[1]

Rothenstein told me that he had given permission to reproduce one of his drawings of me.[2] There are two, one of which is much more repulsive than the other, because the artist touched it up with a lot of imaginary black strokes; and no doubt this is the one selected. It is no good my minding, so I do not mind: if I did mind, I daresay I should mind the letterpress even more.

You will have had a note from me about *Valentine* which crossed yours.

Yours sincerely
A. E. Housman.

BMC MS. LC-GR t.s. Richards, 121; Maas, 131–2.

TO GRANT RICHARDS

Trinity College, Cambridge
27 Sept. 1913

My dear Richards,

Mrs Marillier may publish her settings without paying a fee.[1]

If I remember right I have met H. C. Marillier[2] at Laurence's.

Yours sincerely
A. E. Housman.

No, I shall not be in Paris. I am now staying at home and being good.

LC-GR t.s. Richards, 121 (excerpt).

[1] Much of the plot of *Caviare* hinges on the fact that two horses have names that begin with these letters: Richards, 121.

[2] In Holbrook Jackson's *The Eighteen-Nineties: A Review of art and Ideas at the Close of the Nineteenth Century*, published by GR in 1913.

[1] Settings of *ASL* II (*Loveliest of trees*) and XXXIV (*The New Mistress*) by Christabel Marillier (1883–1976) were published in 1920 and 1923 respectively.

[2] Writer and tapestry expert Henry Currie Marillier (1865–1951).

TO WILLIAM ROTHENSTEIN

Trinity College | Cambridge
8 Oct. 1913

My dear Rothenstein,

Full term begins on Friday, and this is to remind you that when you come here on your mission to our dusky brethren[1] you are going to stay with me. I should like to know as far ahead as possible when you are coming, how long you can stay, and what your engagements are.

I hired a motor in Paris and went for a tour in western Normandy in very good weather.

I suppose you are now back in London having your children educated. My kind regards to Mrs Rothenstein.

Yours sincerely
A. E. Housman.

Harvard bMS Eng 1148 (740) 32. Maas, 132.

TO LAURENCE HOUSMAN

[Trinity College | Cambridge]
10 Oct. 1913

My dear Laurence,

An American ecclesiastic was here the other day, who asked to be presented to me, and from whom I gathered that his favourite work would be *A Shropshire Lad*, but for the existence of that fascinating story, *The Were Wolf*,[1] which, again, would be his favourite work, but for the existence of the most brilliant political satire ever written, *King John of Jingalo*.[2]

Your affectionate brother
A. E. Housman.

Memoir, *176; Maas, 132.*

[1] In 1910 Rothenstein proposed and co-founded the India Society, for the promotion and understanding of Indian art and literature.

[1] By Clemence Housman. It originally appeared in *Atalanta* (Dec. 1890), 132–56, and was published in volume form by John Lane in 1896: Benjamin Franklin Fisher IV, *HSJ* 10 (1984), 39.
[2] By LH (1912).

TO WITTER BYNNER

Trinity College | Cambridge
12 Oct. 1913

My dear Mr Bynner,

I was particularly glad to get your letter, because what delayed my acknowledgment of your book[1] was the fact that I had not your address, except an old one at McClure's. I thought the drama very vivid and telling, and I can praise it the more impartially because I am quite out of sympathy with its propaganda.[2]

I remember my promise, and when new poems are published you shall have them. Perhaps you are even entitled to have one which I wrote more than a year ago in an album,[3] so I copy it here.

I am yours sincerely
A. E. Housman.

The sigh that heaves the grasses
 Whence thou wilt never rise
Is of the air that passes
 And knows not if it sighs.

The diamond tears adorning
 Thy low mound on the lea,
Those are the tears of morning,
 That weeps, but not for thee.[4]

Harvard MS Eng 1071/15. Envelope addressed 'Witter Bynner Esq. | Windsor | Vermont | U. S. A.' Bynner/Haber (1957), 19.

---

[1] *Tiger* (1913), repr. in *A Book of Plays* (1922).

[2] It is concerned with the 'white slavery' of prostitution. The patron of a brothel discovers one of the prostitutes to be his daughter and saves her from a life of vice.

[3] Documentary evidence is lacking for this. In AEH's *Nbks*, the first draft dates from Dec. 1895–7 June 1902, probably after 30 Oct. 1901; the second draft, *c*.1900–Sept. 1917, possibly *c*.1900–5, but not Oct. 1910–Oct. 1912. AEH gave the date 'soon after 1900' to Sydney Cockerell (*TLS*, 7 Nov. 1936; Richards, 437). AEH forgot that he had sent this unpublished poem to Bynner: see AEH to Harriet Monroe, 30 Nov. 1921.

[4] First published as *LP* XXVII (1922).

TO PROFESSOR D. A. SLATER

Trinity College, Cambridge
23 Oct. 1913

Dear Slater,

Ar. Thesm. 1070 τί ποτ' Ἀνδρομέδα περίαλλα κακῶν | μέροσ ἐξέλαχον. In Latin I think the only piece of direct evidence is Germ. phaen. 201, where the variants -*e*, -*ae*, -*a*, -*am*, in a context which requires the nominative, certainly point to *Andromeda*; but the indirect evidence of the accusative *Andromedan*, attested by metre in Ouid. her. XVIII 151 and met. IV 757, is better.

I am glad you will stay here.

Yours sincerely
A. E. Housman

Lilly MSS 1. 1. 3. Maas, 409.

TO THOMAS HARDY

Trinity College | Cambridge
4 Nov. 1913

Dear Mr Hardy,

I send you the first set of our Vice-Chancellor's ghost stories,[1] about which I was speaking.[2] They are not much like any others that I know, and they are very satisfactorily appalling; and there is a lot of curious detail which yet is relevant to the main purpose. The most ingenious and inventive is perhaps *Oh Whistle and I'll Come to You My Lad*, *Count Magnus* the most blood-curdling. I hope you may find some pleasure in them, if read in broad daylight.[3]

I am yours sincerely
A. E. Housman.

Dorset County Museum MS.

---

[1] *Ghost stories of an Antiquary* (1904; repr. 1913) by M. R. James (1862–1936), Vice-Chancellor of Cambridge University, 1913–15. Naiditch (1995), 35 n., notes that the 1913 reprint contained both stories mentioned by AEH, and that, contrary to the supposition made in *The Collected Letters of Thomas Hardy*, ed. Richard Little Purdy and Michael Millgate, 4 (1984), 321, AEH need not also have sent *More Ghost Stories of an Antiquary* (1911). For AEH's interest in acquiring *Ghost Stories of an Antiquary*, see the letter to an unknown correspondent, 24 Oct. 1910.

[2] During Hardy's recent visit to Cambridge to receive an honorary fellowship of Magdalene College. AEH was among Hardy's friends who attended the celebratory dinner: Florence Emily Hardy, *The Life of Thomas Hardy 1840–1928* (rev. edn., 1972), 363.

[3] Hardy to AEH, 15 Nov. 1913: 'Two or three of them have been read aloud in this house [Max Gate], beginning with those you suggested, & I was agreeably sensible of their eeriness, even though the precaution was taken of reading them at a safe distance from bed-time. There is much invention shown in their construction, especially in those you mention' (BMC MS; Purdy and Millgate, 4. 320).

TO EDMUND GOSSE

Trinity College, Cambridge
20 Nov. 1913

My dear Gosse,

My Oxford troubles are to be over on the morning of Dec. 10, and it will give me great pleasure to come to your dinner in the evening.

I do not indulge the passion of hatred, and certainly none of your guests have ever tempted me to.

Yours sincerely
A. E. Housman.

BL Add. MS 70949, fo. 553. Envelope (fo. 554) addressed 'Edmund Gosse Esq. C.B. |
17 Hanover Terrace | Regent's Park | N. W.'

TO EDMUND GOSSE

Trinity College | Cambridge
11 Dec. 1913

My dear Gosse,

I must just write to say how much I enjoyed your dinner and the august and agreeable society which you had got together.

Never before have I seen, and never do I expect to see again, a Prime Minister and a Poet Laureate composing a Missive to a Monarch.[1]

Yours sincerely
A. E. Housman.

Brotherton MS (Gosse Correspondence). Maas, 133.

[1] Herbert Asquith and Robert Bridges were guests at Gosse's dinner party. Their letter to the king was probably on the subject of home rule for Ireland. Asquith (1852–1928) had been MP, 1886–1918, 1920–4; Home Secretary, 1892–5; Chancellor of the Exchequer, 1905–8. He was Prime Minister, 1908–16. For Bridges, see List of Recipients.

1914

TO AN UNKNOWN CORRESPONDENT

Trinity College, Cambridge
15 Jan. 1914.

Dear Sir,

When the meaning of a poem is obscure, it is due to one of three causes. Either the author, through lack of skill, has failed to express his meaning; or he has concealed it intentionally; or he had no meaning either to conceal or to express. In none of these three cases does he like to be asked about it. In the first case it makes him feel humiliated; in the second it makes him feel embarrassed; in the third it makes him feel found out. The real meaning of a poem is what it means to the reader.

I am yours very faithfully
A. E. Housman.

BMC MS.

TO GRANT RICHARDS

Trinity College, Cambridge
24 Jan. 1914

My dear Richards,

Mrs Kington David may have what she wants.

Our special Guest Nights this term are Thursday Feb. 19 and Wednesday March 4. Will you come and stay the night here at either date?

Yours sincerely
A. E. Housman.

SIU MS VFM 1082. LC-GR t.s. Richards, 121 (nearly complete).

TO A. S. F. GOW

Trinity College, Cambridge
11 Feb. 1914

Dear Gow,

In the cod. Lemouicensis[1] and some other MSS, which have Seruius'
commentary without Seruius' name, there is a quantity of additional
matter, largely antiquarian and mythological, sometimes called *scholia
Danielis*, because first edited by P. Daniel in 1600, sometimes *Seruius auctus*
or *plenior* or the like. It is not by Seruius, but is at least as old, and more
valuable. This is what Thilo prints in italics.[2]

Yours sincerely
A. E. Housman.

TCC Add. MS c. 112⁴. Maas, 409.

TO W. A. MERRILL

Trinity College, Cambridge
12 Feb. 1914

Dear Sir,

The subject of *armaret* in Germ. frag. V 9 is the same as that of *procederet*,
i.e. Eurus and Zephyrus.[1] The sense is 'and from what quarter Eurus and
Zephyrus go forth over the waters and arm their brethren right and left
to make war upon the sea'. The *fratres circumpositi* are those of the twelve
winds which are immediately adjacent to Eurus and Zephyrus respectively;
ἀπηλιώτησ and εὐρόνοτοσ to Eurus, ἀργέστησ and λίψ to Zephyrus. The
great winds are figured as furnishing arms to their subordinates: see Sen.
n. q. V 16 3 'quattuor … caeli partes in ternas diuidunt et singulis uentis
binos subpraefectos dant.'

I have to thank you for sending me your paper on the archetype of
Lucretius, in which the tabulated pagination is very serviceable.

I am yours faithfully
A. E. Housman.

Bancroft MS.

[1] Leiden, Vissianus Latinus O 80, called Lemouicensis by Pierre Daniel, implying that it came from Saint-Martial de Limoges.
[2] Georg Thilo (1831–93) in *Seruii grammatici qui feruntur in Vergilii carmina*, rec. Georgius Thilo et Hermannus Hagen, 3 vols. (1878–87). AEH owned a copy: Naiditch (2003), 146.

[1] In a letter of 25 Jan. 1914 (SJCO Higham MS) Merrill had asked AEH the grammatical subject of *armaret* and how he would translate the whole line *et circumpositos armaret in aequora fratres* in Germanicus.

TO MESSRS GRANT RICHARDS LTD

Trinity College, Cambridge
24 Feb. 1914

Dear Sirs,

Mr Robertson may have permission to set the poem *Bredon Hill* as he
wishes.

Yours faithfully
A. E. Housman.

LC-GR t.s.

TO GRANT RICHARDS

Trinity College, Cambridge
26 Feb. 1914

My dear Richards,

Dinner is at 7. 45. By all means come by the train you speak of if you
cannot come earlier. I suppose you could not come for lunch? because I
have some rather particular hock.

Drive to Whewell's Court, Trinity, Sidney Street entrance.[1] My rooms
are over that gate.[2]

Yours sincerely
A. E. Housman.

LC-GR MS. LC-GR t.s. Richards, 121–2.

TO GRANT RICHARDS

Trinity College, Cambridge
1 March 1914

My dear Richards,

It is very good of you to arrange to come earlier, so much so that I could
not possibly ask you to come earlier still; but how matters stand is this.

Your 12. 20 St. Pancras train gets to Cambridge at 1. 31, not 1. 21 as
you say, and lunch could hardly begin before 1. 45. I have asked A. C.
Benson[1] to meet you, and he is obliged to leave us at 2. 40, which is rather
short time. If you could come by the 12 o' clock, \reaching Cambridge

---

[1] 'Apparently my first visit to him at Cambridge': Richards, 121.
[2] On staircase K, up 44 stairs.

[1] See List of Recipients.

at 1. 18,/ we could sit down \nearly/ at 1. 30 and be more comfortable. But that train is not only earlier but starts from Liverpool Street; and I can't expect \or wish/ you to sacrifice serious business for such a small difference. In any case, when you get to the station, take a taxi. They are not allowed \to stand/ in the station-yard, but a porter will call one, or you can walk across the yard to the rank in the road. My address, I forget if I told you, is Whewell's Court, Trinity, Sidney Street entrance.

Yours sincerely
A. E. Housman.

LC-GR MS. LC-GR t.s Richards, 122.

TO A. S. F. GOW

Trinity College, Cambridge
8 March 1914.

Dear Gow,

I am sorry for your affliction, and that you could not come to *The Alchemist*,[1] which however would have aggravated the symptoms, as laughing is bad for the mumps. Stuart[2] went in your stead. It was very long, and there was a certain amount of repetition, but a great deal that was very amusing,—more amusing now than it can have been in Ben Jonson's day. The acting too was very good on the whole. I did not think Dennis Robertson[3] really satisfactory as Subtle, and both Birch[4] as Face and Burnaby[5] as Ananias (who was very comic) overacted now and then, and Abel Drugger's voice, which was excellent, was better than his acting: the representative of Sir Epicure Mammon[6] seemed to me to act most evenly

---

[1] By Ben Jonson. Performed at Cambridge by the Marlowe Society, 5, 6, 7, 9, and 10 Mar. 1914.

[2] Charles Erskine Stuart. Classical scholar. Admitted to TCC with a Major Scholarship, 1901; BA, 1905; MA, 1908; Fellow of TCC, 1907–17.

[3] Dennis Holme Robertson (1890–1963). First class in Classical Tripos and Economics Tripos, Cambridge, 1910, 1912; Fellow of TCC, 1914–38; MC, 1917; University Lecturer, 1924; Girdlers' Lecturer, 1928; Reader in Economics at Cambridge, 1930.

[4] Francis Lyall Birch (1889–1956). Double first in History, Cambridge, 1912; Fellow of KCC, 1916–38; recruited as intelligence officer, 1916; Lecturer in History, Cambridge, 1921–8, resigning to become theatre producer and actor.

[5] John Burnaby (1891–1971). First class in Classical Tripos; Craven scholarship, 1912. Fellow of TCC, 1915; Junior Dean, 1919; Steward and Praelector, 1921–30; Junior Bursar, 1921–31; Tutor, 1931–8.

[6] Identified by Maas (133 n.) as C. E. Harman: Quiller-Couch's review of the production in *The Cambridge Review*, 35. 878 (11 Mar. 1914), 367–8, notes the silence of the programme on the real names of the actors. Charles Eustace Harman (1894–1970) won a classical scholarship at KCC, 1913. Returning to Cambridge after the war, he gave a famous performance for the

and to be most like a real person. The widow is a weak and silly element in the play, and was acted by a young man who succeeded in looking like an underbred young woman.

I heard several ladies in the audience declaring that now they must read the drama, and I daresay I shall.

Fletcher[7] is leaving us and going to London <the> to help Lloyd George[8] manage the panel doctors.

I hope you will soon be well; but you see the results of going to live among contagious boys.

Yours sincerely
A. E. Housman.

TCC Add. MS c. 112⁵. Maas, 133–4.

TO F. J. H. JENKINSON

Trinity College
8 Mar. 1914

Dear Jenkinson,

The MS[1] called l by this collator is pretty clearly Vat. 5951, one of the two best; none of his MSS correspond to the other, Med. plut. 83, but seem to belong to the inferior class.

His date, I should think, cannot be much earlier than 1800, as he seems not to use the long *s* except when *t* follows. He therefore is not, as I thought for the moment he might be, the collator and editor Targa (1769); and moreover he designates his MS by a different set of signs.

I return the book with many thanks.

Yours very truly
A. E. Housman.

CUL Add. MS 4251 (B) 690. Maas, 409–10.

Marlowe Society as Falstaff in *Henry IV, Part 1*. He achieved first class in the Classical Tripos in 1920, and took silk in 1935.

[7] Walter Morley Fletcher (1873–1933). Fellow of TCC, 1897; Tutor, 1905; MD, 1908; Sc.D., 1914; FRS, 1915; Secretary to the Medical Research Committee under the National Insurance Act, 1914; KBE, 1918; CB, 1929.

[8] David Lloyd George (1863–1945). MP, 1890. As Chancellor of the Exchequer he introduced a contributory health insurance scheme in 1911, which met with opposition from doctors who saw the creation of a public health service as a threat to private practice.

[1] Of Celsus' *De Medicina*.

TO GRANT RICHARDS

Trinity College | Cambridge
1 April 1914

My dear Richards,

I have no particular objection to your doing as you propose about the Riccardi Press.[1]

I have to thank you for the article you sent me on Carcassonne,[2] which was very well written. I am going to Paris on Sunday and thence to Marseilles on Tuesday: what next I don't exactly know. I expect to be back here about the 27th.

Yours sincerely
A. E. Housman.

LC-GR t.s. Richards, 122 (excerpt).

TO SYDNEY COCKERELL

Trinity College
9 May 1914

Dear Cockerell,

I am very much obliged for the two narratives,[1] which I return. Both are delightfully entertaining, and Blunt's very charming as well.

Yours sincerely
A. E. Housman.

Princeton MS (Gen. MSS. Misc.). Maas, 135.

---

[1] GR proposed to give Philip Lee Warner and the Riccardi Press permission to print a special, limited edn. of *ASL*, the kind of book to which AEH would normally have objected (Richards, 122). An edn. of 1000 paper copies and 12 vellum copies (10 for sale) was produced in 1914. Paper copies with board covers cost 7*s*. 6*d*., those with parchment 15*s*.; and the vellum copies cost £12 12*s*.

[2] Capital nowadays of the Aude *département* of the Languedoc-Roussillon region in SW France. The Cité part of the town has famous medieval fortifications.

[1] Accounts by Wilfrid Scawen Blunt (1840–1922) and Lord Osborne Beauclerk (1877–1953), of a visit paid by six poets, including W. B. Yeats and Ezra Pound, to Blunt's house, Newbuildings Place, Sussex, on 18 Jan. 1914. AEH visited Blunt on 25–6 Nov. 1911, when Blunt described him in his diary as having 'no trace ... of anything romantic, being a typical Cambridge Don, prim in his manner, silent and rather shy, conventional in dress and manner, learned, accurate, and well-informed': *My Diaries, being a Personal Narrative of Events 1888–1914*, part 2, 1900–1914 (1920). On 3 Dec. 1911, Blunt wrote to Cockerell: 'We all liked Housman when he was here a week ago, though anything less like a Shropshire Lad it would be impossible to conceive': Maas, 135 n.

TO GRANT RICHARDS

Trinity College | Cambridge
9 May 1914

My dear Richards,

I ought to write and give you some account of my doings in the south, about which you gave yourself so much trouble. I took the walk you mapped out from Cassis to La Ciotat on a very beautiful day, and followed your lines I think pretty well. I did not go to Ste Baume however, as it did not happen to square with my other plans. I ate much bouillabaisse, the best at Isnard's, the next best in the suburb of L'Estaque; but in several places it was not so good as at Foyot's in Paris. Brandade I did not think much of, and Aioli at Pascal's was rather nasty, perhaps because lukewarm. The *Gourmet's Guide* on Marseilles is full of blunders: the errors are as bloody as the Dwarf.[1]

I hired a motor with an amiable meridional chauffeur who knew the country, and went to Aix, Arles, Aigues-mortes, Montmajour (which is probably what you meant when you wrote Fontveille), Les Baux, St Remy, Beaucaire, Nimes, Pont du Gard, Avignon,[2] Villeneuve les Avignon, Vauclure, Carpentras (where I did not see Dreyfus,[3] nor much else), Vaison, Orange, and I think that is all. Weather good, with a few days of mistral; judas trees in very magnificent bloom. I was in Paris with the King,[4] but he did me no harm except once keeping me waiting half-an-hour to cross the street.

The College library wants as many editions as it can get of the *Shropshire Lad*, so will you send me one specimen of each of those you now have on sale.

Yrs. sincerely
A. E. Housman

LC-GR t.s. Richards, 123 (wrongly dated 2 May). I have corrected 'doing' to 'doings' and 'county' to 'country'. Other errors are corrected in ink on the MS in an unidentified hand.

---

[1] On the *Guide*, see AEH to GR, 20 Aug. 1911. Its author was known as 'The Dwarf of Blood' of the *Sporting Times*: Richards, 101–2 n.

[2] For 'Saint-Rémy', 'Nîmes', and 'Villeneuve-lès-Avignon'.

[3] Captain Alfred Dreyfus (1859–1935), wrongfully convicted of treason in 1894, was Jewish, and lived at Carpentiers, a centre for French Judaism, for a time *c*.1900.

[4] George V, on his first State visit to Europe.

TO L. J. DOWNING

Trinity College, Cambridge
18 May 1914

My dear Sir,

You have my permission to publish your setting of my poem *Think no more, lad*. Pray accept my thanks for the songs you have been kind enough to send me.

Yours very faithfully
A. E. Housman.

L. J. Downing Esq.

Berg MS. Tipped-in in copy of ASL *(1896) which bears the signature 'W. A. Sim' and, on the verso of the fly leaf, the inscription 'A. E. Housman. | 17 July 1924'.*

TO GRANT RICHARDS

Trinity College | Cambridge
31 May 1914

My dear Richards,

The errors in the Marseilles pages of the *Gourmet's Guide* are not such as to lead anyone seriously astray in practice (except the statement that you get Bouillabaisse in perfection at La Reserve)[1], and some of them are only misprints. The really outrageous thing is the fairy-tale on p. 104 about a wine called Pouilly Suisse after the proprietor of a vineyard, both non-existent. The wine is Pouilly-Fuissé, i.e. Pouilly blent with Fuissé, or Fuissey as they sometimes spell it.

You ought not to reprint my immortal poems, as you appear to have done in 1912, without asking me about corrections. The consequence is that two mistakes in punctuation have been carried on.

I observe that the illustrated edition is now bound in black instead of white. It strikes me as ugly, but I don't set up to be a judge, and I am indifferent to the fate of that edition, which was only printed to amuse you. I daresay black is appropriate to the funereal nature of the contents.

Yours sincerely
A. E. Housman.

SIU VFM 1082. LC-GR t.s. Richards, 124; Maas, 135.

---

[1] For 'Réserve'.

TO DR BARNES

Trinity College
5 June 1914

Dear Dr Barnes,

I am obliged to you for sending me your petition, but I am returning it without signature. I confess I am attached to the current forms of words, and <I> also I am what you have often heard of but perhaps not often seen, a real conservative, who thinks change an evil in itself.

I am yours very truly
A. E. Housman.

BMC MS.

TO GRANT RICHARDS

Trinity College | Cambridge
6 June 1914

My dear Richards,

I shall be paying one of my rare visits to London next Tuesday and lunching with a friend (G. H. Vize, collector of antiquities and china, once champion heavy-weight boxer etc.) at the Café Royal at 1. 30, and should be very pleased if you could join us. If you can, will you let me know by the first post on Tuesday: if you do not reply I will not expect you.

Yours sincerely
A. E. Housman.

LC-GR MS. LC-GR t.s. Richards, 124.

TO GRANT RICHARDS

Trinity College, Cambridge
12 June 1914

My dear Richards,

Mr Shortland may set *Bredon Hill* to music. I return both letters. Newnham Davis[1] has got himself, or you have got him, into a great muddle.

Yours sincerely
A. E. Housman.

LC-GR t.s. Richards, 124–5 (excerpt).

[1] See the note on AEH to GR, 20 Aug. 1911.

TO F. B. SUGDEN AND R. G. MARTIN

Trinity College | Cambridge
13 June 1914

My dear Sirs,

For many years past I have been refusing to English anthologists permission to print poems of mine; but they are not copyright in America, so that I have no power over them and no right to object if they are printed there.

I am yours very truly
A. E. Housman.

F. B. Sugden and
R. G. Martin, Esquires.

BMC MS.

TO GRANT RICHARDS

Woodchester, 28 June 1914

My dear Richards,

These Riccardi people[1] must needs annoy me when I am away on a week's holiday. I have made in pencil corrections of all the errors I have found, some of which seem to be deliberate. I go back to Cambridge on Tuesday.

Yours sincerely
A. E. Housman.

SIU MS VFM 1082. LC-GR t.s. Richards, 125; Maas, 135–6.

TO GRANT RICHARDS

Trin. Coll. Camb.
10 July 1914

My dear Richards,
These[1] seem to be right.

Yours
A. E. Housman.

LC-GR t.s. Richards, 125.

[1] Philip Lee Warner and the Riccardi Press produced a limited edn. of *ASL* in 1914.

[1] Proofs sent by Philip Lee Warner.

TO KATHARINE SYMONS

Trinity College | Cambridge
24 July 1914

My dear Kate,

I return the two interesting letters of this extraordinary enthusiast Mr Carter. I am prepared to finance the impecunious clergyman to the extent of five pounds, which at his rates ought to cover a sufficient number of wills.

I have been reading Laurence's new novel,[1] which I think is his best, though there is a lot of unnecessary disaster at the end.

Your affectionate brother
A. E. Housman.

Private MS.

TO GRANT RICHARDS

Trinity College, Cambridge
5 Sept. 1914

My dear Richards,

I have corrected two misprints in the poem, and I have no objection to its being printed, as it was printed, I believe, in a similar connexion by Ross[1] in a bibliography.

Do not disturb Frank Harris in his beliefs, which are sincere and characteristic, that I am a professor of Greek and that there are 200 pages in *A Shropshire Lad.*

Yours sincerely
A. E. Housman

LC-GR t.s. Richards, 125 (wrongly dated 6 Sept.); Maas, 136.

[1] *The Royal Runaway and Jingalo in Revolution* (1914).
[1] Probably the writer Robert Ross (1869–1918), Oscar Wilde's friend and literary executor.

TO MESSRS GRANT RICHARDS LTD

Trinity College, Cambridge.
10 Sept. 1914

Dear Sirs,

Permission must not be given: it has already been refused in a precisely similar case; and for 10 or 12 years I have adhered to the rule of not allowing my verses to appear in anthologies.

Yours faithfully
A. E. Housman.

Messrs Grant Richards Ld.

LC-GR t.s. Richards, 125 (incomplete).

TO A. S. F. GOW

Trinity College | Cambridge
15 Sept. 1914

Dear Gow,

I thought that *aireur arathis* looked like an Irish gloss (*arathus* being Irish for a plough), so I wrote to Quiggin,[1] and here is his reply.

If you are in a hurry you had better write to him direct.

Yours sincerely
A. E. Housman.

TCC MS, Gow E 2/4.

TO MESSRS GRANT RICHARDS LTD

20 Belmont | Bath
18 Sept. 1914

Dear Sirs,

Mrs Phipps may have permission to set to music the poem she mentions.

Yours faithfully
A. E. Housman.

Messrs Grant Richards Ld.

LC-GR t.s.

---

[1] Edmund Crosby Quiggin (1875–1920). Celtic and linguistic scholar, and Fellow of Gonville and Caius College, Cambridge. First teacher of Gaelic at Cambridge. Author of *A Dialect of Donegal* (1906) and *Prolegomena to the Study of the Latter Irish Bards, 1200–1500.*

TO GRANT RICHARDS

20 Belmont | Bath
2 Oct. 1914.

My dear Richards,

You say the weekend of the 16, which is a Friday: if you mean the 18, I should be very pleased to come from the Saturday to Monday. I go back to Cambridge next Wednesday. Please remember me kindly to your uncle,[1] who was good enough to call on me in Cambridge last June, when unfortunately I was out.

Yours sincerely
A. E. Housman.

LC-GR MS. LC-GR t.s. Richards, 125 (excerpt).

TO PROFESSOR GILBERT MURRAY

Trinity College | Cambridge
14 Oct. 1914

My dear Murray,

I suppose I ought to have written, and I am sorry I gave you the trouble of telegraphing.

My chief objection was not to the terms of the manifesto but to signing any manifesto at all.[1]

Yours sincerely
A. E. Housman.

Bodleian MSS Gilbert Murray, 25. 68–9.

[1] See AEH to GR, 27 June 1908, n. 3.

[1] There are two possible manifestos. The first is *The Writers' Manifesto*, published by Murray as a letter in the *Times*, 18 Sept. 1914, and signed by writers in support of the war. Signatories included Granville Barker, Barrie, Bridges, Chesterton, Conan Doyle, Galsworthy, Hardy, Kipling, Masefield, Trevelyan, and Wells, though Yeats and Shaw did not sign: Duncan Wilson, *Gilbert Murray OM 1866–1967* (1987), 219–20. The second was a manifesto addressed to Russian intellectuals. Murray elaborated on this in a pamphlet, *Thoughts on the War*, published in Oct., in which he wrote of the 'presence in Russia, above all nations, of a vast untapped reservoir of spiritual power, of idealism, of striving for a nobler life' (Wilson, 220). Kipling and Walter Raleigh refused to sign it, though Henry James did sign.

TO EDMUND GOSSE

Trinity College, Cambridge
2 Nov. 1914

My dear Gosse,

Pyrenen is Milton's reprehensible way of spelling *Pirenen*,[1] the fountain at Corinth where Pegasus was drinking when Bellerophon caught him, and which some of the poets (Persius, prologue v. 4, Statius, *Silvae* 2. 7. 3 and *Thebais* 4. 60–1) confused with Hippocrene on Helicon, which sprang up under Pegasus' hoof, and treated as a source of poetic inspiration.

'Mr Chaucer was a great man,' says Artemus Ward, 'but he could not spell'.[2]

Yours sincerely
A. E. Housman.

BMC MS.

TO LILY THICKNESSE

[Trinity College | Cambridge]
24 Nov. 1914

Dear Mrs Thicknesse,

The thirst for blood is raging among the youth of England. More than half the undergraduates are away, but mostly not at the front, because they all want to be officers. I am going out when they make me a Field Marshal. Meanwhile I have three nephews[1] being inoculated for typhoid and catching pneumonia on Salisbury Plain and performing other acts of war calculated to make the German Emperor realise that he is a very misguided man.

Yours sincerely
A. E. Housman.

Memoir, 205; Maas, 136.

---

[1] Milton, *Elegia quinta: in adventum veris*, 10: 'Et mihi Pyrenen somnia nocte ferunt' ('and at night my dreams bring Pirene to me').
[2] 'Some kind person has sent me Chawcer's *poems*. Mr. C had talent, but he couldn't spel': 'At the Tomb of Shakespeare' in *Artemus Ward in London; comprising the Letters to 'Punch', and other humorous papers*, ed. E. P. Hingston (1870), 44.

[1] Arthur Denis Symons (b. 1891), Clement Aubrey Symons (b. 1893), and Noel Victor Housman Symons (b. 1894).

TO THOMAS HARDY

Trinity College | Cambridge
27 Nov. 1914

My dear Mr Hardy,

I am very grateful for the gift of your poems,[1] which are, as always, fuller of matter and sincerity than anyone else's. Some of them naturally I saw when they first appeared. If you care to know my favourites, they are *In Death Divided* (the second stanza of which is quite perfectly beautiful), *At Castle Boterel*, *Regret Not Me*, and *Seen by the Waits*.

I am yours sincerely
A. E. Housman.

Dorset County Museum MS.

TO MESSRS GRANT RICHARDS LTD

Trinity College, Cambridge.
1 Dec. 1914

Dear Sirs,

Miss Hacking may publish the two settings and give them the titles which she suggests.

Yours faithfully
A. E. Housman.

LC-GR t.s.

---

[1] *Satires of Circumstance* (1914).

1915

TO STEPHEN GASELEE

Trinity College
8 Jan. 1915

Dear Gaselee,

We were enjoying ourselves so much that Amaryllis was left weeping on the doorstep. I think your second interpretation is right,—that what she now loves is something more valuable than any nuts, chestnuts or otherwise;[1] but I think the right punctuation is that of Heinsius and Burman,[2] who put no stop in the pentameter. If we had scholia on the poem they would say '*castaneas nuces ἀπὸ κοινοῦ*'. By writing 'aut castaneas nuces, quas Amaryllis amabat' Ovid would have affronted his most intelligent readers; by writing 'aut \nuces/quas Amaryllis amabat (sed nunc eas non amat)' he might have left his least intelligent readers in the dark: by mentioning the species casually in the second clause he avoids both.

I hope you did not lose much at bridge.

Yours very truly
A. E. Housman.

Birkbeck College MS, of which TCC Add. MS Letters c. 1[188] is a photocopy. Maas, 410.

TO EDMUND GOSSE

Trinity College, Cambridge
27 Jan. 1915

My dear Gosse,

You don't realise the situation. It is not your hand that the Censor does not find clear; it is your vocabulary.[1] One man of letters writing to

---

[1] Ovid, *Ars Amatoria*, 2. 267–8: 'aut quas Amaryllis amabat— | At nunc castaneas non amat illa nuces' ('or the nuts that Amaryllis loved—but she doesn't love chestnuts now'), an allusion to Virgil, *Eclogues*, 2. 52: 'castaneasque nuces mea quas Amaryllis amabat' ('chestnuts which my Amaryllis loved').

[2] Burman's variorum edn. (Amsterdam, 1727) included notes by Heinsius, whose edn. had originally appeared in 1661.

[1] A letter from Gosse to Compton Mackenzie in Capri was delayed by the Censor for a week before being sent on with a note telling Mackenzie to advise his correspondent to write 'shortly and clearly'. Gosse's letter of protest appeared in *The Times*, 27 Jan. 1915.

another naturally writes in English, an ancient and a copious tongue. But nobody in the Censor's office knows 500 words of English: 450 words of English, with 550 of slang, are amply sufficient to express all the ideas which circulate in that studious cloister's pale.[2] And if the Censor finds your letters long, it is not that they are long by measurement, but that they take a long time to read when most of the words have to be looked out in the dictionary. For instance, you may have used the word *tendency*. That is a word which nobody in the Censor's office ever utters, ever hears, or ever sees: when they mean *tendency* they always say *trend*, and so do all the writers whom they have ever read. (What they say when they really mean *trend* I don't know: perhaps they never do mean it). Again, writing to a novelist, you may possibly have made some allusion to 'my uncle Toby'.[3] Imagine the scene in the Censor's office: the perusal of your letter suspended, and piles of other correspondence accumulating, while the Postal Directory is searched for Tobias Gosse, who is not to be found: then the Censor has to knit his brows over the problem whether perchance you have a maternal uncle christened Tobias or whether this is a code-word by which you and Compton Mackenzie[4] have agreed to designate the German Emperor. And considering that one of you writes from Hanover Terrace,[5] while the other resides in Capri, a place of which the Censor never heard except in connexion with Krupp,[6] I think he treats you very handsomely in taking the more lenient and less probable view and allowing your letter to pass.

To add that I wish to be remembered to Mrs Gosse is irrelevant, but sincere; and I am yours ever

A. E. Housman.

BL MS Ashley B. 903, fos. 39–40. Maas, 136–7.

---

[2] Milton, *Il Penseroso*, 156: 'the studious cloister's pale'.

[3] As in Laurence Sterne's *The Life and Opinions of Tristram Shandy*.

[4] Prolific novelist (1883–1972).

[5] Gosse had lived at 17 Hanover Terrace in Regents Park, London, since 1901.

[6] Friedrich Alfred Krupp (1854–1902), head of the large German corporation manufacturing steel and armaments. In 1902 he was accused by a Naples newspaper and the German Socialist paper *Vörworts* of homosexual practices in Capri. He did not try to clear his name, and died of a stroke soon afterwards.

TO CHARLES GALLUP

30 Jan. 1915.

My dear Sir,

If you will accept my signature without a quotation, here it is.

Yours faithfully
A. E. Housman.

Charles Gallup Esq.

BMC MS.

TO MESSRS GRANT RICHARDS LTD

Trinity College, Cambridge
11 Feb. 1915.

Dear Sirs,

I should be pleased to oblige Mr Thomas,[1] whose book on Swinburne[2] I thought very good; but I have been saying no to all anthologists for more than 12 years, and it is impossible to make an exception now.

Yours faithfully
A. E. Housman.

LC-GR t.s. Richards, 126.

TO GRANT RICHARDS

Trinity College, Cambridge
14 Feb. 1915

My dear Richards,

1. I have just had a bill from R. & C.[1] Clark for binding 50 copies of Juvenal on 3 Dec. 1914. I daresay it is all right, but I had the impression that these items generally appeared as sets-off in your accounts with me.

2. My holidays begin on March 13, and I am beginning to consider what to do with them. What are your present ideas about the Riviera? My own notion is to spend about 3 weeks abroad, and it would suit me best if those 3 weeks were either at the beginning or the end of the vacation: i.e. roughly March 13 to April 3, or else April 5 to April 26; but these limits I

---

[1] Edward Thomas. See AEH to GR, 29 June 1907.
[2] *Algernon Charles Swinburne: A Critical Study* (1912).

[1] For 'R. & R.'

mention as the extremes of earliness, lateness, and narrowness: I need not necessarily go so early nor so late, nor be abroad so short a time.

You probably know that passports will be necessary, and that all old passports ceased to be valid on the 1st of this month.

Would you come and spend a night here some time before the end of term? All our feasts and also our usual guest-nights are suppressed, and our meals are somewhat simplified; but on Tuesdays and Thursdays we have rather better dinners than on other days. I don't ask you for a Sunday, because we have a Sabbatarian kitchen and I could not give you a proper lunch. The only Tuesday or Thursday ahead which would not suit me is the 25th inst. If you can select a date to come, come for lunch, and I will try to invite a kindred spirit. I have lately invested in some rather good Corton 1898.

You seem to have changed your business address.

Yours sincerely
A. E. Housman.

LC-GR MS. LC-GR t.s. Richards, 126 (incomplete); Maas, 137–8.

TO GRANT RICHARDS

Trinity College, Cambridge
17 Feb. 1915

My dear Richards,

I have not received the second letter which I understood you to say you had written; but I take it that you will be here to lunch at 2 o' clock on Tuesday March 2. Come straight to my rooms, Whewell's Court, Sidney Street Gate, and do not be surprised if a sentry tries to keep you out with a bayonet, as this is now a barracks, sparsely inhabited by four Fellows of Trinity.

We do not dress for dinner.

I enclose the bill from Clarks'.

Yours sincerely
A. E. Housman.

LC-GR MS. LC-GR t.s. Richards, 126–7 (incomplete).

TO MRS PERKINS

Trinity College
1 March 1915

Dear Mrs Perkins,

I am very sorry to be prevented from accepting your kind invitation to dine on Wednesday, but I have to attend a club-meeting that evening.

I am yours sincerely
A. E. Housman.

BMC MS.

TO SIR JAMES G. FRAZER

Trinity College | Cambridge
7 March 1915

My dear Frazer,

I have had for some time your two volumes of Addison without acknowledging the gift as I ought to have done, for it has made me read some parts which I had not read before of an English Classic, and also a paper which I had no chance of reading before: though I do not believe it is by Steele or Budgell,[1] nor Tickell[2] neither.

I am not brought round to any hearty liking for Addison, apart from the Coverley[3] pages: he is a terribly industrious humourist, like Charles Lamb,[4] and Fielding in the introductory chapter to the various books of *Tom Jones*;[5] and his admired English has nothing like the vernacular raciness of the best of Cowper's[6] earlier letters, for instance. Indeed I really think the vogue of the *Spectator* impoverished the language of prose. But it is a comfort to have Addison alone, and to be rid of Steele.

I am going in a few days to the Riviera, which Providence, for my benefit, has cleared of Germans. In its normal state I always refused to visit it. Whewell's Court is now a barracks, and soldiers above my ceiling

---

[1] Eustace Budgell (1686–1737), cousin of Joseph Addison (1672–1719), and contributor to *The Spectator* (1711–12) by Addison and Richard Steele (1672–1729).

[2] Thomas Tickell (1685–1740), minor poet, and friend of Addison.

[3] Sir Roger de Coverley, 'a gentleman of Worcestershire, of ancient descent, a baronet', who figures in a number of papers in *The Spectator*.

[4] 1775–1834, author of *The Essays of Elia* (1823).

[5] Novel, published in 1749, by Henry Fielding (1707–54).

[6] The poet William Cowper (1731–1800). His letters, published posthumously, have been much admired.

practise step-dancing with a vigour which ought to be prophylactic against frost-bite.

I hope you and Lady Frazer are still contented with your metropolitan hermitage. With kindest regards and thanks,

> I am yours sincerely
> A. E. Housman.

TCC Add. MS b. 36⁸³: t.s. copy, with 'Budyell' for 'Budgell' and 'practice' for 'practise'. Ackerman (1974), 358–9.

TO J. CAMERON C. TAYLOR

> Trinity College | Cambridge
> 7 March 1915

Dear Sir,

You have my permission to publish your settings of Nos. 13, 49, and 63 of *A Shropshire Lad*. In the 1904 edition there were several misprints, and one of them, if I remember right, was *seeds* (which ought to be *seed*) in 63.

> I am yours faithfully
> A. E. Housman.

BMC MS. Envelope addressed 'J. Cameron C. Taylor Esq. | Bromleigh | 47 Blythe Hill | Catford | S. E.'

TO LILY THICKNESSE

> [Trinity College | Cambridge]
> 7 March 1915

Dear Mrs Thicknesse,

On the 16ᵗʰ I shall be beyond the Channel or beneath it: more probably the former, for steamers seem to ram submarines better than submarines torpedo steamers. Hitherto I have always refused to go to the Riviera, but now is my chance, when the worst classes who infest it are away.

Here we have 1000 undergraduates and 20,000 soldiers, 500 of them billeted in the building in which I write these lines, and one of them doing a quick-step overhead.

> Yours sincerely
> A. E. Housman.

Memoir, 205; Maas, 138.

TO WITTER BYNNER

Trinity College, Cambridge | England
7 March 1915.

Dear Mr Bynner,

Please receive my best thanks for the royalist play[1] from your republican pen which you have kindly sent me and I have read with pleasure and interest.

Yours very truly
A. E. Housman.

Harvard MS Eng 1071/16. Bynner/Haber (1957), 21.

TO GRANT RICHARDS

Trinity College | Cambridge
7 April 1915

My dear Richards,

I found here your gift of Dreiser's book,[1] which I have been skimming, and I am glad to see that he recognises some of your many virtues.

The mathematician[2] whom you sat next to at our high table, upon hearing that I had been to the Riviera with you, said that he hoped you had not been running after women all the time. Whether this was an inference from your conversation or a generalisation from his own experience of travelling-companions I do not know.

You crowned all your good actions by sending me that note about the permit from the Prefecture, as to which you were right when both Cook[3] and the Consulate were wrong.

Yours sincerely
A. E. Housman.

Pages 71–86 are missing in my copy. I am not starving for them, but you may like to drop on your binder.

LC-GR t.s. Richards, 137; Maas, 138–9 (both incomplete).

---

[1] *The Little King* (1914), repr. in *A Book of Plays* (1922).

[1] *A Traveller at Forty* (1913) by Theodore Dreiser (1871–1945). The book describes Dreiser's first visit to Europe and contains a friendly account of GR, his family, and his friends. 'Barfleur' (as Dreiser calls him) is said to be 'one of the most delightful persons in the world... a sort of modern Beau Brummel with literary, artistic and gormandizing tendencies'.

[2] James Whitbread Lee Glaisher (1848–1928), Fellow of TCC, lecturer and assistant tutor, 1871–1928; FRS, 1875; President, London Mathematical Society, 1884–6; President, Royal Astronomical Society, 1886–8, 1901–3.

[3] Thomas Cook & Sons, tour operators.

TO GRANT RICHARDS

Trinity College | Cambridge
14 April 1915

My dear Richards,

You should not let what the mathematician said worry you. When his mind is not occupied by mathematics or pottery[1] it is apt to run on the relations of the sexes, and I seldom sit next him without that topic arising. He possesses all the editions of *Fanny Hill*,[2] a book with which I daresay you never polluted your mind. The question he asked would probably have been asked about anyone else who had been travelling with me. You told me that Belfort Bax[3] made some such enquiry about me.[4]

Yours sincerely
A. E. Housman

LC-GR t.s. Richards, 137–8; Maas, 139.

TO CHARLES SAYLE

[Trinity College
23 Apr. 1915]

Martial 1. 21. 8.

A. E. H.

Lilly MSS 1. 1. 3: p.c. addressed 'C. Sayle Esq | 8 Trumpington Street' and marked 'Local' by AEH. Date as postmark.

[1]   Glaisher was a notable collector of ceramics.

[2]   *Fanny Hill: Memoirs of a Woman of Pleasure* (first published in 1748–9) by John Cleland (1709–89).

[3]   [Ernest] Belfort Bax (1854–1926), barrister, author, and journalist. GR and AEH met him and his wife at the Café de Paris, Monte Carlo (Richards, 135). 'Bax's persistent curiosity, his old-fashioned scholarship and ponderous humour gave Housman pleasure; his wife's Germanic domesticities and her fussy preoccupations with her lord's comforts and dignities amused him' (Richards, 130).

[4]   He had asked GR about AEH's attitude to women: Richards, 138.

TO MESSRS GRANT RICHARDS LTD

Trinity College | Cambridge
17 May 1915

Dear Sirs,

Mr H. S. Goodhart-Rendel has my permission to publish, without payment of any fee, his settings of the three poems he mentions.

Yours faithfully
A. E. Housman.

LC-GR t.s.

TO D. S. MACCOLL

Trinity College | Cambridge
7 July 1915

Dear MacColl,

Many thanks indeed. It is, as you say, merry. We have here an American, a very British one, as one of our fellows,[1] and he has a pince-nez on his nose; so I have sent it across to him, and await results. He may criticise the punctuation: I do not, because I surmise it to be artistic, as the illustrations certainly are.

Yours very truly
A. E. Housman.

Glasgow University MS (MacColl Collection H385).

TO J. P. POSTGATE

Trinity College, Cambridge
13 July 1915

Dear Postgate,

I think Luc. VIII 152 only means that they saw her every day, just as if she belonged to the place. In 308 there is not much difference between *fata* and *dei*: compare Ouid, trist. II 174 with Claud. III cons. Hon. 89.

I don't think you have asked me before about works on Latin prosody since L. Mueller:[1] anyhow I know of none, and have not seen Plessis' book.[2]

---

[1] Gaillard Thomas Lapsley, who had a Ph.D. from Harvard: see List of Recipients.

[1] Lucian Mueller, *De re metrica poetarum Latinorum praeter Plautum et Terentium libri septem* (1894). AEH owned a copy: Naiditch (2004), 154.

[2] The edn. of Horace by Frédéric Edouard Plessis (b. 1851), published in various forms from 1911 onwards, which contained an account of metrics and prosody in the *Odes* and *Epodes*.

The Alcaic stanza[3] is one of the worst puzzles, and even Schroeder,[4] who usually talks like the Pythia on her tripod,[5] is evidently uncomfortable about it. We have not even a full and consistent theory, however stupid, from antiquity; for Hephaestion,[6] who gives his view of the 4th verse, gives two incompatible views of the 1st and 2nd, and none of the third. I have no clear notion of the extent to which the Aeolic lyrists thought they might depart from homogeneity. The only point on which I have anything worth saying to say is that <the> synaphea[7] between the 3rd and 4th verses, which we already suspected to be the true rule from Horace's occasional employment of it and from the absence of hiatus at that point in Alcaeus' fragments, is now found in Oxyrh. papyr. X p. 74 last line.

You will have read Innes in to-day's *Times*.[8] Colonel Dauber's son was fined for having no light on his bicycle; so he has a quarrel with the town. The housebreaking, with its noise and dust, is opposite his lodgings; so he has a quarrel with the college. Add to this the opinion, much held by non-combatants in khaki, that working men should be allowed no choice except between enlistment and starvation, and you have the genesis of Colonel Dauber's letter.[9]

Yours sincerely
A. E. Housman.

With you and Duff both ill, I wonder how your examinations came off. I hope you will both soon be all right again.

BMC MS.

[3] One of the forms used by Horace.

[4] Otto Schröder (1851–1937), Direktor des Kais.-Augusta-Gymnasiums, Berlin.

[5] i.e. in the oracular manner of the priestess of Apollo at Delphi.

[6] Of Alexandria, Greek metrist of the second century AD.

[7] The linking of two verses into one: by prohibiting hiatus between them and permitting elision, by prohibiting *brevis in longo* at the last position in the first and allowing a single word to carry over into the next.

[8] H. McLeod Innes of TCC wrote to the newspaper to defend the college's rebuilding of two houses in Trinity-street.

[9] Lieutenant-Colonel J. H. Dauber, of 20 Trinity-street, wrote a letter published in *The Times* on 9 July 1915, 9, in which he complained about TCC demolishing two large four-storeyed buildings opposite his rooms. He argued that such work, which he characterized as 'thoughtless dissipation of strength', should be postponed so that men returning home after the war could be given employment; that the government should prohibit undertakings that were not essential to military success; and that men of military age and capacity should not be employed in such work. (He also objected to the addition of a new wing to the public library.) In reply, Innes maintained that the college had made an irreversible commitment to the work during a time of high unemployment, and pointed out that three-fourths of the workmen were over 40 and only two of them under the age of 36.

TO GRANT RICHARDS

Trinity College | Cambridge
15 July 1915

My dear Richards,

I am sorry I cannot avail myself of your kind and attractive invitation, as early in August I am going to stay with my sister and brother-in-law at Dulverton, and must first finish the text and notes of my 3rd book of Manilius, which, though it will not sell so well as your novel,[1] is really a much more classy work. The printers, if they have not all gone to the wars, may just as well be printing this while I am on my holiday, and I should be grateful if you would begin to make arrangements. The preface is already written in the rough, and will be ready for them when they are ready for it.

Yours sincerely
A. E. Housman.

LC-GR t.s. Richards, 138; Maas, 139.

TO MESSRS GRANT RICHARDS LTD

Trinity College, Cambridge
17 July 1915

Dear Sirs,

Mr Leslie Brooke[1] must be informed that for 12 years back I have adhered to the rule of not allowing poems of mine to be printed in selections.

Yours faithfully
A. E. Housman.

LC-GR t.s.

TO GRANT RICHARDS

Trinity College | Cambridge
28 July 1915

My dear Richards,

Many thanks for the novel.[1] I remember exactly where I left off, and can start from that point, so you see that the pen and ink of genius have burnt themselves into my brain.

---

[1] His third, *Bittersweet* (1915).

[1] [Leonard] Leslie Brooke (1862–1940), children's author and anthologist.

[1] See AEH to GR, 15 July 1915.

About the Manilius, it is not the preface but the text and notes that I shall have ready first. I will send them to your office, as you tell me, in about 10 days, with directions to the printers. But who are the printers? If Maclehose,[2] as last time, don't trouble to reply, but enjoy your holiday.

Yours sincerely
A. E. Housman.

LC-GR t.s.

TO MESSRS GRANT RICHARDS LTD

Trinity College | Cambridge
5 Aug. 1915

Dear Sirs,

In accordance with the directions of Mr Grant Richards I am sending you to-day by Parcel Post, Registered, the manuscript of the Text and Notes of my edition of Manilius, Book III, and I shall be obliged if you will acknowledge its receipt.

I understand from Mr Richards that the printing is to be put in hand at once. A copy of the edition of Book II should be sent to the printers as a model; and I shall also be obliged if you will convey to them the directions which I enclose on a separate sheet.

Yours faithfully
A. E. Housman.

Messrs Grant Richards Ltd.
LC-GR t.s.

TO GRANT RICHARDS

Trinity College | Cambridge
12 Sept. 1915

My dear Richards,

I have now been back nearly a week, and you probably longer. I am writing now because Walter Raleigh[1] has asked if he may print some poems

---

[2] For 'MacLehose'.

[1] 1861–1922. First Professor of English Literature at Oxford, 1904–22, after holding chairs at Liverpool and Glasgow.

from *A Shropshire Lad* in one of the *Times Broadsheets* for the trenches,[2] and I have said he may; so don't immediately send him a lawyer's letter when you see them.

There is someone in your office who sends me proofs addressed to S. E. Homeman. I don't mind opprobrious names,[3] but I am apprehensive that the missives may go astray.

Yours sincerely
A. E. Housman.

Lilly MSS 1. 1. 3. LC-GR t.s. Richards, 138; Maas, 140.

TO GRANT RICHARDS

Trinity College | Cambridge
Sept. 20, 1915

My dear Richards,

I have just sent you in a separate cover, registered, the Preface to Manilius III, which perhaps you will acknowledge receipt of, if it arrives. This completes the book, except the index and a few trifles which cannot be added till the rest is in print.

The three figures to be inserted in the preface are to be executed just in the same way as those in Book II. I have drawn them exactly to scale.

Yours sincerely
A. E. Housman.

BMC MS. LC-GR t.s. Richards, 138–9 (nearly complete).

TO GRANT RICHARDS

Trinity College | Cambridge
3 Oct. 1915

My dear Richards,

I congratulate you very heartily and send you every wish for your happiness;[1] and perhaps you will also convey my respects to Mrs Richards and, I am inclined to add, my congratulations too because, whatever

---

[2] Broadsheet No. 38 printed *ASL* IV (*Reveille*), XXII (*The street sounds to the soldiers' tread*), XXXI (*On Wenlock Edge*), XXXV (*On the idle hill of summer*), LIX (*The Isle of Portland*), and LXII (*Terence, this is stupid stuff*). There is a copy in Lilly.

[3] 'Mr Pecksniff called him opprobrious names': Dickens, *Martin Chuzzlewit*, ch. 9.

[1] On 2 July 1915, GR had married for the second time, but had just told AEH about it: Richards, 139. His new wife was Maria Magdalena Csanády, a Hungarian widow eighteen years younger than he with a daughter.

your other faults may be, there can be few ladies who have a more good-tempered husband.

It would give me great pleasure to come and see you on the last week-end of the month.

The third volume of Manilius will probably not be more than $\frac{3}{4}$ of the second in size. I enclose a cheque for £50, which ought to keep the printer quiet.

I see in the paper that you are having some bother over Hugh Lane's will,[2] which certainly seems to be ungrammatical.[3]

Yours sincerely

A. E. Housman.

LC-GR t.s. Richards, 139; Maas, 140 (both incomplete).

TO KATHARINE SYMONS

Trinity College | Cambridge

5 Oct. 1915

My dear Kate,

I have been scanning the casualty lists in these last days, and when I saw your card this morning I feared what the news must be.[1] Well, my dear, it is little I or anyone else can do to comfort you, or think of anything to say that you will not have thought of. But I remember your telling me at the beginning of the war that he had almost a hope and expectation of dying in battle, and we must be glad that it was a victorious battle in which he died. I do not know that I can do better than send you some verses that I wrote many years ago;[2] because the essential business of poetry, as it has

---

[2] Sir Hugh Percy Lane (1875–1915) went down in the *Lusitania*, leaving Richards as one of his two executors. In 1913 he bequeathed his collection of modern paintings to the National Gallery, London, but in Feb. 1915, three months before his death, he added a codicil to his will, unfortunately unwitnessed, leaving the paintings to the City of Dublin. The pictures were later shared between the two cities.

[3] AEH seems to be referring to the syntax of 'My Sargent portrait, the modern pictures now being shown in Belfast, and any modern pictures of merit (John's drawings, etc.) that I possess to the Dublin Gallery of modern Art, other than the group of pictures lent by me to the London National Gallery, which I bequeath to found a collection of modern Continental art in London.' Lane's public bequests were printed in *The Times*, 3 Oct. 1915, 12.

[1] KES's third son, Lieut. Clement Aubrey Symons (b. 3 Sept. 1893), 10th Battalion Gloucestershire Regiment, was killed in action near the village of Hulluch in France on 25 Sept. 1915.

[2] *Illic Jacet* (later *LP* IV). Two drafts had been written between Dec. 1895 and its first publication on 24 Feb. 1900 in *The Academy*. KES had it reprinted in the 1915 issue of the magazine of her son's school, *The Edwardian*, King Edward's School, Bath, under the heading 'Illic Jacet. | IN MEMORIAM. | C. A. S.' For full bibliographical information, see *Poems* (1997), 374–5.

been said,[3] is to harmonise the sadness of the universe, and it is somehow more sustaining and more healing than prose. Do assure Edward[4] of my feeling for you all, and also, though I do not know her, the poor young girl.[5]

Your affectionate brother
A. E. Housman.

I send back the copy of his letter, because others will want to see it. I do not know where Jerry[6] is, but never mind that at present.

Lilly MSS 1. 1. 3. Envelope addressed 'Mrs Symons | 20 Belmont | Bath'. Richards, 37 (excerpt); Maas, 140–1.

TO GRANT RICHARDS

Trinity College | Cambridge
16 Oct. 1915

My dear Richards,

I do rather think that the birthday etc. might go off better if no irrelevant visitor were there to spoil the fun; and so, in spite of my affection for children, I should like to postpone my visit. Probably any week-end in November that suited you would suit me.

As to the blind people, they may have what they want.

Yours sincerely
A. E. Housman.

LC-GR t.s. Richards, 139–40; Maas, 141.

---

[3] Sir Leslie Stephen, *A History of English Thought in the Eighteenth Century* (1876), 2. 352: 'Nothing is less poetical than optimism; for the essence of a poet's function is to harmonise the sadness of the universe'. The passage appears on p. 44 of AEH's 'Nbk X' (BMC).

[4] KES's husband.   [5] Clement's fiancée.

[6] Her youngest son Noel Victor Housman Symons (1894–1986), known as 'Jerry'. He enlisted in Aug. 1914 in the 1st Wessex Field Corps of the Royal Engineers, saw active service in France by Dec., and was awarded the Mons Medal for bravery. He was transferred to the Worcestershires, fought at Ypres, and was awarded the Military Cross. For further information, see the tribute by Jo Hunt in *HSJ* 12 (1986), 1–8.

TO MESSRS GRANT RICHARDS LTD

Trinity College | Cambridge
22 Oct. 1915

Dear Sirs,
   Permission must be refused[1] in this case.

Yours faithfully
A. E. Housman.

LC-GR t.s. Richards, 140.

TO GRANT RICHARDS

Trinity College, Cambridge
26 Oct. 1915

My dear Richards,
   The 5. 50 train at Paddington on Nov. 5 will suit me quite well. I shall be glad to meet your uncle[1] again.

Yours sincerely
A. E. Housman.

LC-GR MS. LC-GR t.s. Richards, 140 (excerpt).

TO GRANT RICHARDS

Trinity College | Cambridge
27 Oct. 1915.

My dear Richards,
   I enclose, corrected, the proofs of the text and notes of Manilius III. They may now be combined and put into pages; and I enclose some directions to the printers about carrying this out. Please acknowledge receipt.

Yours sincerely
A. E. Housman.

LC-GR t.s. Richards, 140.

---

[1] 'Some permission to use *A Shropshire Lad* must have been asked by the Women's Employment Publishing Company': Richards, 140.

[1] Herbert Richards.

TO GRANT RICHARDS

Trinity College | Cambridge
21 Nov. 1915

My dear Richards,

I enclose the following portions of Manilius III.

1. Corrected proof of Preface, which can now be put into pages.

2. Revise of text and notes, which only requires two corrections.

3. MS page to face p. 1.

4. MS page to face p. 68.

All that I shall have to add is the Index, which will be two or three pages.

As the bulk of the volume can now be precisely ascertained, they had better begin making the cover, which will be just the same as that of Book II (price and all), except that SECVNDVS will be TERTIVS, and the date MDCCCCXVI, and that the label on the back will have III instead of II.

Yours sincerely
A. E. Housman.

LC-GR t.s. Richards, 140–1.

TO GRANT RICHARDS

Trinity College | Cambridge
11 Dec. 1915

My dear Richards,

I enclose the MS of the Index to Manilius III, which completes the book, and I also return the paged proofs with some further corrections. By the way, in the process of putting into pages, two errors were introduced which were not in the slips, on pp. 25 and 57. I hope that these are the only two, and that the future will not produce others.

What has your friend Tod Sloan[1] been up to?

Yours sincerely
A. E. Housman.

LC-GR t.s. Richards, 141.

---

[1] 'An amusing, rather vainglorious chap, he was a friend of mine on the principle that an author should always be the friend of his publisher. I had encouraged, and assisted, him to write his reminiscences. No one questions that he was a great jockey': Richards, 141.

TO GRANT RICHARDS

Trinity College | Cambridge
14 Dec. 1915

My dear Richards,

It will not be necessary for me to see again the proofs of Manilius III down to p. 64; but the printers and their proof-readers must not make any alteration, even the slightest, on their own responsibility without asking me.

Yours sincerely
A. E. Housman.

LC-GR t.s.

TO W. FOWLER CARTER

Trinity College | Cambridge
17 Dec. 1915.

Dear Sir,

I have received safely and read with great interest your researches into the history of the Holden family,[1] and I have much pleasure in enclosing a cheque for £5. I very much admire the industry and ingenuity with which these obscure individuals have bee[n] tracked out. I am [a]fraid I do not myself take so much interest in my ancestors as some of my family do, and as to the printing which you are good enough to propose I must consult my sister, who just at present is immersed in other things.

With many thanks for your labours and their result I remain

Yours very truly
A. E. Housman.

Birmingham City Archives MS. The missing letters in 'been' and 'afraid' are the result of holes being punched in the MS.

[1] Ancestors of AEH's father Edward. See Jo Hunt's chart in Pugh, Appendix I.

TO GRANT RICHARDS

Trinity College | Cambridge
22 Dec. 1915

My dear Richards,

I enclose the last pages of Manilius III with two corrections, and the book may now be printed and published without any more tinkering from me.

Yours sincerely
A. E. Housman.

The compliments of the season.

LC-GR t.s. Richards, 141; Maas, 141.

1916

TO GRANT RICHARDS

Trinity College | Cambridge
8 Jan. 1916

My dear Richards,

I write about Manilius III, and shall probably write again, not out of impatience, but because, when book II was publishing, you and the printers went to sleep in each other's arms for a whole month[1] and then wrote to ask me for corrections though I had said there would be none.

I sent all that I had to send before Christmas. I hope that, as I suggested, the binding is being got ready, so that the rest of the book will not have to wait for it.

Yours sincerely
A. E. Housman.

LC-GR t.s. Richards, 142; Maas, 142.

TO MESSRS GRANT RICHARDS LTD

Trinity College | Cambridge
1 Feb. 1916

Dear Sirs,

The cover and label, which I return, are correct, and I have corrected the two errors queried in the proofs, which I also return.

Yours faithfully
A. E. Housman.

Messrs Grant Richards Ltd

LC-GR t.s. Richards, 142 (excerpt).

---

[1] Richards, 142, comments: 'no printer has a great number of compositors and readers competent both to handle efficiently and expeditiously such a manuscript'.

TO GRANT RICHARDS

Trinity College | Cambridge
3 Feb. 1916

My dear Richards,

When you say you '*would* like to' go to France with me, is that a mere sigh or a serious wish? Because I should be both agreeable to it and desirous of it; only I understood that the difficulties now put in the way of getting a passport were almost insuperable. In any case I should not make the venture without a courier such as you to protect me.

Can I induce you to come and stay with me a night or two some time this term? Oldmeadow[1] is going to be dining in hall on Sunday the 20th with the Roman Catholic Monsignore,[2] if that will attract you, and possibly, though I am not sure, I might get him to dine with me on the Saturday. But any date that would suit you would probably suit me.

I have not been able to see the *Studio*[3] yet.

Yours sincerely
A. E. Housman

LC-GR t.s. Richards, 142–3; Maas, 142.

TO GRANT RICHARDS

Trinity College | Cambridge
10 Feb. 1916

My dear Richards,

I am writing to tell you, directly on hearing it myself, that cerebro-spinal meningitis exists among the soldiers quartered in this college, who are supposed to have brought it with them from Ashford. I am not going to stir, and I believe that infection is conveyed only by close association; but consider whether this will make you change your mind about coming here on the 19th, and let me know as soon as is convenient to you.

---

[1] See the notes on the letter of 8 July 1909.

[2] Identified by Maas (142) as The Revd Christopher Scott, Provost of Northampton and Rector of the Church of the English Martyrs, Cambridge, since 1890.

[3] *The Studio: An Illustrated Magazine of Fine & Applied Art*, 66. 274 (15 Jan. 1916), 277, contained a review of the New English Art Club exhibition in which Hester Frood's *Countess Weir* was praised as 'an admirable water-colour' worthy of being 'specially mentioned'.

Mrs Richards is exceedingly kind, but I should not think of going abroad with the two of you, even if dates suited. I hope it will set both of you up.

Your sincerely
A. E. Housman.

LC-GR t.s. Richards, 143 (incomplete); Maas, 142 (incomplete and dated c.10 February).

TO GRANT RICHARDS

Trinity College | Cambridge
14 Feb. 1916

My dear Richards,

You must come in May, when the soldiers may be gone and in any case the place will be looking better.

I ought to be in London for business this next Thursday, and I may as well try to combine pleasure with it; so will you assist me by coming to lunch at the Café Royal at 1. 15? I hope to be there by that time, though trains are not punctual.

Yours sincerely
A. E. Housman.

PM MS. LC-GR t.s. Richards, 143.

TO GRANT RICHARDS

Trin. Coll. Camb.
15. 2. 16

My dear Richards,

Yes, Mr Farrar may have what he wants.

Yours
A. E. Housman.

LC-GR t.s.

TO MESSRS GRANT RICHARDS LTD

Trinity College | Cambridge
15 Feb. 1916

Dear Sirs,

I return the printers' query, with the answer added.

Yours faithfully
A. E. Housman.

Messrs Grant Richards Ltd
LC-GR3 t.s.

TO GRANT RICHARDS

Trinity College | Cambridge
19 Feb. 1916

My dear Richards,

I am very sorry indeed to see in the paper to-day the sudden death of your uncle,[1]—though I suppose it was not altogether sudden, as it took place in the Acland Home. When I saw him last, at your house, he seemed full of sturdiness. There are too few severe and thorough scholars of his sort.

Yours sincerely
A. E. Housman.

LC-GR MS. Richards, 143 (wrongly dated as 18 February); Maas, 143.

TO A. S. F. GOW

Trinity College | Cambridge
25 Feb. 1916.

Dear Gow,

The *-it* of the perf. was originally long in the 4th as in the other conjugations, and remains so in Plautus; but by Virgil's time it had become short in the regular verbs, as is shown by *audiĭt* and *ambiĭt* in the 5th foot at Aen. VII 516 and X 243[1]: its lengthening is artificial in Ouid. met. XII 392.[2] On the other hand in *eo* and *peto* it is never shown by the metre to be short and often shown to be long, for it occurs where artificial lengthening is not allowed, as in Ouid. met. II 567.[3] The source of all wisdom on this subject is Lachmann's note on Lucr. III 1042:[4] the only material addition that I find in my margin is Stat. Theb. XII 396 *to cupiĭt unam* (so the best MS is now reported: *cupiens* cett.),[5] which may seem to show natural

---

[1] *The Times*, 10: 'Mr. Herbert Paul Richards, Senior Fellow, Sub-Warden, and Librarian of Wadham College, died suddenly yesterday at the Acland Home, Oxford. He had been much affected by the fate of a nephew, a pupil of his own at Wadham, who had won a high place in the Civil Service, but volunteered early in the war and fell fighting in Flanders.'

[1] Draft: 'foot of the hexamater at A. 7. 516 and 10. 243' (TCC MS with Adv. c. 20. 15).

[2] Gow had enquired about the length of the last syllable of the third person singular perfect indicative ending in -iit for -ivit: Gow to AEH, 23 Feb. 1916 .

[3] Draft: '<On the other hand in <*peto* and> *eo* and *peto* it is never short.> its lengthening is artificial in Ou. met. 12 392. On the other hand in *eo* and *peto* it is never short, and it is long <in places> where artificial lengthening is not allowed, as in Ou. met. II 567.' Gow: 'My impression was that it was naturally short except in eo and peto'.

[4] In his edn. of 1850.   [5] Draft: '(best MS *cupiens* cett.)'.

length, as Statius does not elsewhere allow artificial lengthening except at the caesura[6] in the 3rd foot.

Yours sincerely
A. E. Housman.

TCC Add. MS c. 112[6]. Maas, 410–11 (wrongly dated).

TO GRANT RICHARDS

Trinity College, Cambridge
2 March 1916.

My dear Richards,

W. A. Merrill published in 1907 an edition of Lucretius, containing nothing original, but collecting the work of others with that bibliographical fulness in which Americans excel. He has since changed his opinions on the text and developed originality as a reactionary, and his obtuseness enables him to stick to the reading of the manuscripts in many places where the critics whom he formerly followed abandoned them. I have a very low opinion of his intelligence, and he is bumptious into the bargain.

I hope, if you do succeed in getting abroad with Mrs Richards, I shall hear of your success.

I return Merrill's letter.

Yours sincerely
A. E. Housman.

Probably you will have seen a notice of your uncle in last week's *Oxford Magazine*,[1] written I suppose by the Warden[2] or someone else at Wadham.

LC-GR t.s. Richards, 146; Maas, 143 (both nearly complete).

---

[6] Draft: 'the regular caesura'.

[1] *The Oxford Magazine*, 34. 13 (25 Feb. 1916): 'The late Mr. H. P. Richards will be missed in many places, but in no place more than his favourite haunt of an afternoon—the Coffee Room at the Union Society. He arrived almost always at the same hour, and would then read *The Times* methodically through from cover to cover, always folding the page into double columns. He was there as usual on the afternoon before his death ... The Union has lost in him a constant and generous friend.'

[2] The Warden from 1913 to 1927 was Joseph Wells (1855–1929), previously Fellow of Wadham.

TO GRANT RICHARDS

Trinity College, Cambridge
18 March 1916

My dear Richards,

The verses are the last lines of *The Choice*, by John Pomfret, b. 1667, d. 1702;[1] which is said both by Johnson[2] and by Southey[3] to be the most popular poem in the language. Perhaps in your uncle's youth it was not yet quite forgotten.[4]

Your uncle or his source has left out the fatal verses which interfered with the author's advancement in the Church and incidentally led to his catching smallpox and dying.[5] And, after all, the poor man *had* a wife.[6]

I take occasion to remark that on Lady Day[7] it will be three months since I sent the final corrections of Manilius III.

Yours sincerely
A. E. Housman.

PM MS. LC-GR t.s. Richards, 147 (incomplete). The letter is accompanied by a sheet on which AEH supplies four lines missing from Herbert Richards's quotation from Pomfret: 'And as I near approached the verge of life, | Some kind relation (for I'd have no wife) | Should take upon him all my worldly care, | Whilst I did for a better state prepare. | Then I'd not be etc.'

[1] 'Whate'er Assistance I had Pow'r to bring ... All Men would wish to live and die like me', quoted in Richards, 146–7. It dates from 1700 and is modelled on Horace, *Satires*, 2. 6, which describes the pleasures of a quiet country estate.

[2] 'Perhaps no composition in our language has been oftener perused': 'John Pomfret', *The Lives of the English Poets*.

[3] 'Why is Pomfret the most popular of the English Poets? The fact is certain, and the solution would be useful': *Specimens of the Later English Poets, with preliminary notices* by Robert Southey (1807), 1. 91.

[4] The unattributed passage of verse was found among Herbert Richards's papers, and the Revd John Richards, who had been AEH's contemporary and acquaintance at Oxford, had sent it to GR in order that he might find out its author. AEH replied immediately: Richards, 146–7.

[5] Pomfret 'might have risen in the Church', but his application to Dr Compton, Bishop of London, for institution to a valuable living, was obstructed by 'a malicious interpretation of some passage in his *Choice*; from which it was inferred, that he considered happiness as more likely to be found in the company of a mistress than of a wife.' The delay 'constrained his attendance in London, where he caught the smallpox, and died' (Johnson).

[6] Pomfret was indeed a married man. In *The Choice*, however, he chooses to have no wife, but rather 'Near some obliging modest fair to live' so that her 'conversation' can 'impart | Fresh vital heat to the transported heart' and 'new joys inspire'.

[7] 25 March.

TO GRANT RICHARDS

Trinity College | Cambridge
28 March 1916

My dear Richards,

I am assuming that you either were not on the *Sussex*, or are one of the rescued.[1]

I enclose a list of the papers and persons to whom I wish copies of Manilius III to be sent.

Yours sincerely
A. E. Housman.

LC-GR t.s. Richards, 147.

TO GRANT RICHARDS

Trinity College | Cambridge
29 March 1916

My dear Richards,

There are corrections to be made on pp. 18, 27, 35, 49, 95.

The sinking of the *Sussex* is no deterrent to me; quite the reverse. I argue thus: only a certain number of steamers are destined to sink; one of that number has sunk already without me on board; and that diminishes by one the number of my chances of destruction. But women cannot reason, so I suppose your designs are knocked on the head.[1]

I have pretty well made up my mind to go at least as far as Paris, probably about April 20th.

Yours sincerely
A. E. Housman

LC-GR t.s. Richards, 148; Maas, 143 (both incomplete, and in Maas dated c.30 March).

[1] The SS *Sussex* was torpedoed by a German submarine off the French coast on 24 Mar. 1916. 'There had been talk of my wife and myself crossing at about that time': Richards, 147.

[1] By Mrs Richards.

TO PROFESSOR ARTHUR PLATT

Trinity College | Cambridge
6 April 1916.

Dear Platt,[1]

If you prefer Aeschylus to Manilius you are no true scholar; you must be deeply tainted with literature, as indeed I always suspected that you were.

The Bible is supposed to be full of types, and perhaps St Paul—ce type là—prefigures Don Quixote.[2] The resemblances you mention had not struck me, but they will bear thinking on. I wonder if St Paul's experiences in the third heaven[3] are susceptible of the same explanation as Don Quixote's in the moon.[4]

Yours sincerely
A. E. Housman.

BMC MS. Memoir, *207; Maas, 144.*

TO GRANT RICHARDS

Trinity College | Cambridge
6 April 1916

My dear Richards,

Many thanks for your letter and your wish to preserve my life; but I have just applied for leave to go through Folkestone and Dieppe by the 7. 0 p.m. from Charing Cross on Wednesday the 19th. After all, a quick death is better than a slow journey; and as I am only an author and not a publisher I am comparatively well prepared to meet my God. But I shall be sorry if my choice of the shorter route spoils any chance I may have had of crossing in your company. I shall pretty certainly be in London the Monday before I go, and may perhaps see you then.

I shall be interested to read my new volume of poems, but you don't tell me who the publisher is.[1] By the way, when are you going to bring out

---

[1] On grounds that they were 'too Rabelaisian', Mrs Platt destroyed all other letters from AEH to Platt after her husband's death.

[2] Platt read a paper on Cervantes to the University College Literary Society in 1916; repr. in *Nine Essays by Arthur Platt*, with a preface by A. E. Housman (1927), 116–38.

[3] 2 Corinthians 12: 2–4: 'I knew a man in Christ ... caught up to the third heaven. ... And I knew such a man, (whether in the body, or out of the body, I cannot tell: God knoweth;) How that he was caught up into paradise, and heard unspeakable words, which it is not lawful for a man to utter.'

[4] Don Quixote was blindfolded whilst supposedly riding the famous horse Clavileño through the heavens: *Don Quixote*, part 2, ch. 41.

[1] GR had passed on a fresh rumour that there was to be a successor to *ASL*: Richards, 148.

my edition of Catullus? Clement Shorter announced it on your behalf ten years ago.[2]

Yours sincerely
A. E. Housman.

PM MS. LC-GR t.s. Richards, 148; Maas, 144.

TO GRANT RICHARDS

Trinity College | Cambridge
9 April 1916

My dear Richards,

Last year you proved so much better informed than Cooks and Consulates that I am prepared to accept whatever you say; but the Military Permit Office has just written to me: 'I am unable to state definitely by which route you will be allowed to proceed, as alterations are at present taking place'.

Many thanks for your invitation to Bigfrith, but I think I had better hold myself free from engagements, as I have several things to do before I go.

I don't know if you sent copies of Manilius III to the list of persons and papers I gave you; but, if so, some of them at any rate have not reached their destination.

Yours sincerely
A. E. Housman.

LC-GR t.s. Richards, 148–9.

TO GRANT RICHARDS

Trinity College | Cambridge
15 April 1916

My dear Richards,

Not on account of mines or torpedoes, which I despise as much as ever, but because the Folkestone route is closed and the voyage by Southampton–Havre, without the solace and protection of your company, is a long and weary subtraction from the short holiday I meant to take, I am not going to France.

---

[2] According to Richards, 148 n., AEH mistakes Shorter for W. Robertson Nicoll, editor of *The British Weekly*: see the letter to GR of 3 Aug. 1905. Clement K. Shorter (1857–1926) was author of various biographical works, and editor of *English Illustrated Magazine*, 1890, the *Illustrated London News*, 1891, the *Sphere*, 1900, and the *Tatler*, 1901.

Many thanks for the present of Valpy's Manilius[1] from you and your relatives.[2] I had the edition already, but not so neat a copy.

Yours sincerely
A. E. Housman

LC-GR t.s. (with 'torpedos' corrected to 'torpedoes'). Richards, 149; Maas, 145.

TO J. W. MACKAIL

Trinity College | Cambridge
4 May 1916

Dear Mackail,

Many thanks for your notes.[1] What I say at 113 is that political oratory (*rostris*) has no business in the middle of forensic matters. As to *numerosis* in 172, although I think *pro spatio magna* can mean 'of a length proportioned to the distance', I do not think that *magnus* could mean 'great or small' without help, nor *numerosus* 'many or few'; and if it could, what a thing to think of saying! *longa dies* in 482 is the long day of midsummer. At 325 as a parallel to *gradus* perhaps you would prefer Soph. Ai. 7–8 εὖ δέ σ' ἐκφέρει ... βάσις. It is not for equality but for sense that I adopt the future in 361, as in 333.

Yours sincerely
A. E. Housman.

TCC MS R.1.92.1. Hawkins (1958), 187; Maas, 411.

TO GRANT RICHARDS

Trinity College | Cambridge
15 May 1916

My dear Richards,

Will you come here for some week-end this term, which ends June 12? As I have to lecture on Mondays, I shall not be absent any week-end, and all would suit me alike.

Yours sincerely
A. E. Housman.

LC-GR MS. LC-GR t.s. Richards, 149.

---

[1] 1819. [2] From the library of Herbert Richards: Richards, 149.

[1] On AEH's edn. of *Manilius III*, of which AEH had sent him a copy.

TO GRANT RICHARDS

Trinity College | Cambridge
12 June 1916

My dear Richards,

The first observation I have to make is that you have not answered my last letter. Your secretary wrote to me on May 17 that she had sent it after you to the continent, and added 'it will be some days before you can hear from him'. And so it was.

I asked you to come here for a week-end during the May term. The term is now over, but there will still be a certain number of people here, and if you like to come I shall be pleased to have you.

I don't know when you go to Cornwall, but I don't think you will carry me off there before the end of July, because this is my chief time for work.

I shall be interested to hear of your experiences of travel, because toward the end of August I think of trying to get to France, if not Italy.

Yours sincerely
A. E. Housman.

LC-GR MS. LC-GR t.s. Richards, 149–50; Maas, 145.

TO MILDRED PLATT

Trinity College | Cambridge
14 June 1916

Dear Mrs Platt,

It is very good of you to ask me to the rites of Bona Dea[1] (as you have married a walking dictionary you can soon find out all about her); and, to be strictly honest, it would be possible for me to come to London on the 19th. But it would not be convenient, and also I should have to cut a meeting and deprive the Vice-Chancellor of my valuable advice; so laziness and conscientiousness combined enable me to master my passion for tea and ladies, and I hope you will not be vindictively wrathful if I say no.

[1] Roman fertility goddess whom AEH is identifying with Minerva. Annual rites in her honour held on 19 June at her temple on the Aventine were attended exclusively by women.

Ladies in Cambridge are getting into closer touch with war: they are to be allowed to paint shells. I greatly fear that patriotism together with feminine unscrupulousness will lead them to poison the paint.

Yours sincerely
A. E. Housman.

UCL MS Add. 165. Maas, 145–6.

TO GRANT RICHARDS

Trinity College | Cambridge
26 June 1916

My dear Richards,

I ought of course to have answered your letter before now. Your invitation[1] is very attractive, and I should like to come, so far as I can judge at present. I have never been into Cornwall except just across the Tamar.

From what I hear, it seems as if the advance on our front were to begin to-morrow. Civilians are not to cross to France for the next three weeks or so, and all vessels crossing for some time back have been filled with big guns, even to the exclusion, except at fixed dates, of officers on leave.

Yours sincerely,
A. E. Housman.

LC-GR t.s. Richards, 150; Maas, 146.

TO WILLIAM ROTHENSTEIN

29 June 1916

I shall be glad to see you any time next month if you will let me have a couple of days' notice.

Yrs.
A. E. H.

Trin. Coll. Camb.

Harvard bMS 1148 (740) 33: p.c. addressed 'W. Rothenstein Esq. | Far Oakridge | Stroud' and redirected to c/o Prof Turner, Huntercombe Road, Blackhall, Oxford.

---

[1] To spend a week or two at the Richards' cottage at Ruan Minor, a village near The Lizard in Cornwall: Richards, 150.

TO WILLIAM ROTHENSTEIN

'An evening train' is reprehensibly vague: shall you be in time for dinner in Hall at 7. 45? I hope so. We don't dress, as you probably remember.

Yours

A. E. Housman.

2 July 1916
Trinity College, Cambridge

Harvard bMS Eng 1148 (740) 34: p.c. addressed 'W. Rothenstein Esq. | Far Oakridge | Stroud'.

TO GRANT RICHARDS

Trinity College | Cambridge
6 July 1916

My dear Richards,

I should think the 4th would be better than the 5th of August for travelling, with the double Bank Holiday looming ahead; so if you will make arrangements on that hypothesis it will be very nice of you.

As to how long I should stay, which we have not fixed, the first and great point of course is that my stay falls entirely within your own, and I am not going to be left unprotected among your huge family in a remote corner of England.[1]

Thanks for the newspaper extracts.

Yours sincerely
A. E. Housman.

LC-GR MS. Richards, 150; Maas, 146.

TO ALICE ROTHENSTEIN

Trinity College | Cambridge
10 July 1916

Dear Mrs Rothenstein,

It is extremely kind of you to ask me to Oakridge, and of course it is attractive; but after Cornwall I shall probably be going to my sister in Somerset, and not long after, if possible, to France, so my holidays will be pretty well filled up.

---

[1] 'My wife, my aunt Mrs. Grant Allen, and five children, a nurse and maids, all, with the exception of my aunt, crowded into a small and ancient cottage, which, however, had many rooms': Richards, 151.

Your William has behaved quite nicely here, and I have just sent him off all safe and sound, so any breakages will have been caused by the journey and I shall not be responsible.

Yours sincerely
A. E. Housman.

Harvard bMS Eng 1148 (740) 35. Maas, 147.

TO THE REVD HENRY MONTAGU BUTLER

Trinity College
23 July 1916

My dear Master,

I have just heard with great sorrow of your son Gordon's death. His ability I knew from what I had seen of his work, and his modesty and amiable nature from what I had seen of himself. I beg that you and Mrs Butler will accept my sincere sympathy: consolation I do not offer, for you will find that in the life he lived and the cause for which he died. οὐ γὰρ ἀθανάτους σφῶν παῖδας ηὔχεσθον γενέσθαι, ἀλλ' ἀγαθοὺς καὶ εὐκλεεῖς.[1]
I am my dear Master

Yours sincerely
A. E. Housman.

TCC MS (JRMB M3/1/544).

TO GRANT RICHARDS

Trinity College | Cambridge
23 July 1916

My dear Richards,

Many thanks for your letter and its directions, which I will follow on Aug. 4. My idea is to stay about a week, if that will suit you.

I am glad to see, from a fly leaf I received the other day, that they are getting up a memorial to your uncle at Wadham.[1]

Yours sincerely
A. E. Housman.

LC-GR t.s. Richards, 150.

---

[1] A modified version of Plato, *Menexenus*, 247d5: 'For you two prayed not that your children become immortal but brave and glorious'.

[1] Herbert Richards, formerly Fellow of Wadham College, Oxford. The memorial was a small drawing: Richards, 150.

TO MARGARET, LADY RAMSAY

Trinity College | Cambridge
27 July 1916

Dear Lady Ramsay,

I have heard with great regret of the death of your husband,[1] from whom I always received the utmost kindness and friendliness throughout the many years which we passed as colleagues in London and during which I had the pleasure of watching the growth of his reputation and influence. I had been told indeed of his serious illness, but the loss to science and to his friends, though not unexpected, is none the less grievous; and I beg you to accept my sincere sympathy with you and your family in your bereavement.

I am yours sincerely
A. E. Housman.

UCL MS: Sir William Ramsay: Letters and Papers, *16. 213. Maas, 147.*

TO GRANT RICHARDS

What is the address to which my letters should be forwarded when I am with you? I hope you are both enjoying Dartmoor.

A. E. H.

Trin. Coll. Camb.   28 July 1916

LC-GR MS: p.c. addressed 'Grant Richards Esq. | The Duchy Hotel | Princetown | Devon'.
LC-GR t.s.

TO GRANT RICHARDS

Trinity College | Cambridge
13 Sept. 1916

My dear Richards,

I was very much distressed, and not on your account only, to see poor Gerard's death in the *Times*.[1] He was a nice boy, and it was sad that he had not the health and strength of other boys.[2] I hope you and

---

[1] See Lady Ramsay in List of Recipients.

[1] The Richards' eldest son was killed at the age of sixteen by the collapse of a sand-cave on the beach at Poldu: Richards, 151, 153. His death was announced in *The Times*, 13 Sept. 1916, 1.

[2] 'Housman was under some misapprehension in thinking that the boy lacked health and strength': Richards, 154.

Mrs Richards are well, and not more overcome by sorrow for his loss than must needs be.

Yours sincerely
A. E. Housman.

PM MS. LC-GR t.s. Richards, 153, 324 (excerpt); Maas, 147.

TO GRANT RICHARDS

Trinity College | Cambridge
4 Oct. 1916

My dear Richards,

My young friend who was at Oundle[1] is now lost to my sight in the R.A.M.C.[2] and I have not heard from him for six months; and as he left school six or seven years ago, his information might not be up to date.

Thanks for the copy of *A Shropshire Lad*; but I wonder why the printer, when directed to remove a comma from the end of a verse on p. 49, turned it upside down and added it at the beginning.

Yours sincerely
A. E. Housman.

LC-GR t.s. Richards, 154 (excerpt).

TO GRANT RICHARDS

Trinity College | Cambridge
16 Oct. 1916

My dear Richards,

I shall be delighted to see you both at lunch on the 31st.[1] Let me know whether it shall be 1. 45 or 2 o' clock.

Thanks for the note from the printers. If they are guiltless, their predecessors seem to have been extraordinarily wicked.

Yours sincerely
A. E. Housman.

LC-GR t.s. Richards, 154.

---

[1] Oundle School, Northamptonshire, founded in 1556.   [2] Royal Army Medical Corps.

[1] GR and his wife were to be in Cambridge at the start of a bookselling tour through England and Scotland: Richards, 154.

TO GRANT RICHARDS

Trinity College | Cambridge
23 Oct. 1916

My dear Richards,

I am grateful though ashamed to receive your present of a new stick. The old one perished nobly in the destruction of a venomous serpent,[1] and I only hope the new one may make as good an end.

1. 45 on Tuesday the 31st let it be. My kind regards to Mrs Richards and the family.

Yours sincerely
A. E. Housman.

LC-GR MS. LC-GR t.s. Richards, 154; Maas, 148.

TO A. S. F. GOW

Trinity College, Cambridge
30 Oct. 1916.

Dear Gow,

1. For *-cque* see Madvig Cic. de fin. V 40[1] and Haupt opusc. III p. 508[2] = Herm. V p. 38. The only classical example is Ouid fast. IV 848 '*sic*' *que*, where *sic* is said by one person and *que* by another. Where *tuncque* occurs, as at Manil. III 481, it should be *tumque*; *hancque* etc. don't occur except in inferior MSS.

2. Adjectives are allowed, though rarely, at the end of pentameters, as in her. X 138 *grauis*, amor. II 6 58 *pias*, trist. IV 3 42 *piae*, and I don't think it makes any difference whether they are predicates. In fast. I and II, omitting numerals, 2 are predicates (I 168, 230), 4 are not (I 222, II 56, 114, 546).

3. In Ibis 223 I suppose *in aduerso culmine* means 'on a house-top (or other eminence) opposite'. Ibis was born out of doors, as you see from what follows.

4. *uirides campos* or the like is quite common, *niueos campos* or the like very rare, but not unexampled, e.g. amor. I. 9. 19 *graues urbes*, art. II 594 *insidias illas*, fast. II 300 *graues imbres*, ex Pont. I 4 56 *dis ueris*. But an exception is

---

[1] On a walk with Richards and his children in Cornwall, AEH had broken his stick in killing an adder: Richards, 153.

[1] 1839.   [2] 1875–6.

made for possessive pronouns, and *nostris oculis, suos annos* etc. are pretty frequent.

Yours sincerely
A. E. Housman.

TCC Add. MS c. 112⁷. Maas, 411–12.

TO GRANT RICHARDS

[Trinity College | Cambridge
6 November 1916

My dear Richards,]
They can make their record if they like:[1] all I want is not to have to write letters.

[Yours sincerely
A. E. Housman.]

Richards, 154.

TO J. P. POSTGATE

Trinity College | Cambridge
6 Nov. 1916

Dear Postgate,
The paper, as you will see, deals more with method than with prosody.[1]
About *conubium* I agree with L. Mueller and Munro at Lucr. III 776. I should not read *conubia* in Verg. Aen. VII 555, as it has very weak authority and, being the commoner word in Virgil, might come to the pen of the scribe when it should not.

---

[1] GR had received a request from a music publisher to make 'a gramophone record of a song' with words from *ASL*: Richards, 154. 'In March 1917 Gervase Elwes made a recording of *On Wenlock Edge* ... though "song" in the singular could indicate Graham Peel's "In summertime on Bredon", which was also recorded by Elwes': Banfield (1985), 236.

[1] See Naiditch (2005), 50–1 ('A. E. Housman's "Prosody and Method"'). Naiditch comments that identifying the paper AEH mentions to Postgate is 'surprisingly difficult: it may be the lost lecture on Stat. silu. II 773 sq. (*Proceedings of the Cambridge Philological Society* 115, Oct. 26, 1916, p. 16 = *Cl.Pap.* p. 1264)' or 'The Thyestes of Varius, published *CQ* 11. 1, Jan. 1917, pp. 42–48 (*Cl. Pap.* pp. 941–949)' (51 n. 1).

Thanks for the reference to Sommer's works.[2] I have not yet gone through the process which since August is required for getting books from Germany.

Yours sincerely
A. E. Housman.

BMC MS.

TO GRANT RICHARDS

Trinity College, Cambridge
7 Nov. 1916

My dear Richards,

I hope you and Mrs Richards enjoyed your tour,—or are enjoying it, as I don't know if you are back yet.

But what I am writing about is this. A friend of mine (and acquaintance of yours) went to Bowes and Bowes to-day and asked for a 6d. copy of *A Shropshire Lad*. They brought it, but charged him 1/- for it, saying that it had gone up to this owing to the war. I said I thought probably they were out of 6d. copies and offered him a 1/- one instead, but he sticks to his story.[1]

Yours sincerely
A. E. Housman.

LC-GR t.s. Richards, 154–5; Maas, 148.

TO GRANT RICHARDS

Trinity College | Cambridge
5 Dec. 1916

My dear Richards,

It would have given me great pleasure to come and see you and Mrs Richards, but I am engaged to spend the week-end in London, if the Government allows me to travel at all.[1]

---

[2] Ferdinand Sommer's *Handbuch der lateinischen Laut- und Formenlehre: eine Einführung in das Sprachwissenschaftliche Studium des Lateins* (Heidelberg 1914). AEH acquired a copy: Naiditch (2004), 152.

[1] Without consulting AEH, GR had doubled the price to meet rising costs: Richards, 155.

[1] There were no travel restrictions in force, probably a reflection of the uncertainty following the government reconstruction announced in the previous day's *Times*. Asquith resigned as Prime Minister on 5 Dec. and Lloyd George succeeded him on 6 Dec. and formed a coalition government.

Your Hunhunter at Clare,[2] from your account, must have troubles enough without adding me; and I for the last three weeks have been having a series of three colds on the top of one another. But if you like to let me know his name and rank, perhaps I may try to make his acquaintance when I am better.

I do not make any particular complaint about your doubling the price of my book, but of course it diminishes the sale and therefore diminishes my chances of the advertisement to which I am always looking forward: a soldier is to receive a bullet in the breast, and it is to be turned aside from his heart by a copy of *A Shropshire Lad* which he is carrying there. Hitherto it is only the Bible that has performed this trick.

Yours sincerely
A. E. Housman.

LC-GR t.s. Richards, 155; Maas, 148–9.

---

[2] Captain Desmond Young, author (with Justin McKenna) of *The Hun Hunters*, recently published by GR.

1917

TO GRANT RICHARDS

Trinity College | Cambridge
11 Jan. 1917

My dear Richards,

Will you tell the lady that I do not give permission to print my poems in anthologies, but remind her that in America I neither possess nor claim any control in the matter.

Yours sincerely
A. E. Housman.

LC-GR t.s. Richards, 156.

TO MESSRS CONSTABLE & CO

Trinity College | Cambridge
13 Jan. 1917

Dear Sirs,

I make no objection to the quotation of my poem in *L. of C.*,[1] if you will have the enclosed corrections made.

I am yours faithfully
A. E. Housman.

Messrs Constable & Co.
BMC MS.

TO GRANT RICHARDS

Trinity College | Cambridge
14 Jan. 1917

My dear Richards,

Thanks for cheque, for which I enclose receipt.

There must also be some account to be regulated between us about Manilius III. I sent you £50 on account, but the production probably cost

---

[1] *L[ines] of C[ommunication]* (1917). See AEH to GR, 21 Aug. 1920, and n. 1.

more. But I see you say you have only got out accounts to the end of 1915.

When I last saw you, you made a light and easily-forgotten promise to let me know the average sale of *A Shropshire Lad* of late years.

When I was in London on New Year's Day, I was not my own master. I was discharging an important mission, testing wines in company with other members of the Wine Committee of this College.

Yours sincerely
A. E. Housman.

LC-GR t.s. Richards, 156.

TO MESSRS GRANT RICHARDS & CO

Trinity College, Cambridge
24 Jan. 1917

Dear Sirs,

1. Mr A. Marleyn may have permission to publish his setting of *Bredon Hill*.

2. Mr Goodhart-Rendel may have permission to publish his setting of *The Recruit*.

Yours faithfully
A. E. Housman.

Messrs Grant Richards & Co.

LC-GR t.s.

TO LAURENCE HOUSMAN

Trinity College | Cambridge
10 Feb. 1917

My dear Laurence,

Thanks for your *Return of Alcestis*,[1] which as a whole I do not very much admire, in spite of a good many good lines. On the other hand the last work of yours that I read, *The Royal Runaway*,[2] I thought even better than *John of Jingalo*,[3] at least till the revolution came, which I did not much believe in.

---

[1] First published in LH's trilogy *The Wheel* (1919).
[2] *The Royal Runaway and Jingalo in Revolution: A Sequel to John of Jingalo* (1914).
[3] *John of Jingalo: The Story of a Monarch in Difficulties* (1912).

I was at Eton last Sunday and came across two boys, the sons of suffragists named Harben living somewhere near, to whom on one occasion in a closed carriage you recited reams of poetry which they supposed to be your own; but the only fragment which they could repeat was mine. It says a great deal for your conversational ascendancy that the incident took place, for in any other company those two boys would do the talking and not the listening.

Your affectionate brother
A. E. Housman.

BMC MS. Memoir, *176; Maas, 149.*

TO GRANT RICHARDS

Trinity College | Cambridge
25 Feb. 1917

My dear Richards,

It is one of several proofs that I am suffering from confinement in these islands mentally as well as physically, that though I have turned over a good many pages and thought about the matter from time to time, I have not got hold of any sentence that will hit off your uncle.[1]

Many thanks for the Nevinson,[2] though I will not pretend that I am sufficiently educated to appreciate it properly.

Yours sincerely
A. E. Housman.

PM MS. LC-GR t.s.; Richards, 156–7.

TO GRANT RICHARDS

Trinity College | Cambridge
4 March 1917

My dear Richards,

Yes, I have read Haynes' book,[1] and thought it very well written and full of good sense.

---

[1] 'I asked Housman if he could think of some phrase from a Greek or Latin author to put on Herbert Richards's tombstone, a few words which would indicate something of his character': Richards, 156.

[2] 'The large coloured plate, "Reliefs at Dawn", by C. R. W. Nevinson which ... I had reproduced': Richards, 157.

[1] E. S. P. Haynes, *The Decline of Liberty in England* (1917), published by GR.

I forget if I ever thanked you for sending me the Nevinson; if not, I do so now.

Yours sincerely
A. E. Housman.

LC-GR t.s.; Richards, 157 (excerpt).

TO GRANT RICHARDS

Trinity College | Cambridge
18 March 1917

My dear Richards,

I should be very pleased to come to you for this next week-end, Friday the 23rd.

Yours sincerely
A. E. Housman.

LC-GR MS. LC-GR t.s. (with 'shall' for 'should').

TO EDMUND GOSSE

Trinity College, Cambridge
9 April 1917

My dear Gosse,

Naturally I have been reading your life of Swinburne,[1] and naturally also I have been enjoying it. It is a great comfort to have it done by some one who knows chalk from cheese: only I am surprised that you think so much of the second series of *Poems and Ballads*,[2] apart from *Ave atque Vale*. And by the by it rejoices me to find that the only two things I ever admired in his later volumes,—*Ave atque Vale* itself and the prologue to *Tristram*,—are both of them early. I offer you the following as a heading for chapter VIII:[3]

---

[1] *The Life of Algernon Charles Swinburne* (1917).

[2] Published in 1878, and praised by Gosse (239–40) as a 'serene volume' that 'exhibits his purely lyrical genius in its most amiable and melodious form'.

[3] 'Gosse's chapter deals with the rehabilitation of Swinburne by Watts, relating specifically how under Watts's influence Swinburne became "little more than the beautiful ghost of what he had been in earlier years" (p. 268); and the chapter ends with Swinburne's death on April 10, 1909. Hence Housman's fantasy of Watts as Coleridge's LIFE-IN-DEATH winning Swinburne as the mariner from DEATH in the game of dice. A further prompt may have been a quotation from Swinburne on p. 227 of Gosse's biography: "I am still engaged on the period where the influence of rhyme and the influence of Marlowe were fighting, or throwing dice, for the (dramatic) soul of Shakespeare" ': Archie Burnett, 'Poetical Emendations and Improvisations by A. E. Housman', *Victorian Poetry*, 36. 3 (Fall 1998), 291.

The naked hulk alongside came,
And the twain were casting dice;
'The game is done! I've won, I've won!'
Quoth Watts, and whistles thrice.[4]

It is above my usual standard; and I have composed part of another stanza, equally fine:

Is that a Death, and are there two?
Is Death that Dunton's mate?[5]

Now, in prospect of a second edition, I make these remarks.

Pp. 45–7. Swinburne put it out of the power of the judges to award him the Newdigate, by breaking the rules of the competition. In his time, and for years afterwards, the prescribed metre was the heroic couplet.[6]

P. 79. Not *A Winter's Tale* but *The Merry Wives*, revived by Phelps at the Gaiety; and the date would be 1874, for I heard it[7] sung in January 1875.

P. 100. His pocket was either metaphorical or very large, for *Atalanta* was written in a ledger, now in the Fitzwilliam Museum.[8]

P. 155. I have seen *Cleopatra* in a magazine of the sixties, *Cornhill* I think, with an illustration.[9]

P. 168. *Ave atque Vale* had been published, I think, in the *Fortnightly* in 1875.[10]

P. 200. Whose is the verse in inverted commas, slightly reminiscent of Wordsworth?[11]

---

[4] *The Rime of the Ancient Mariner* (1834 text), 195–8, with 'she' replaced by 'Watts'. 'Whistles' refers discreetly to the attack which Swinburne, influenced by Watts, made on his former friend, the painter James McNeill Whistler (1834–1903) in *The Fortnightly Review* (June 1888).

[5] With 'Dunton's' for the source's 'woman's'. Watts changed his name to Watts-Dunton in 1896.

[6] Swinburne's entry for the Newdigate Prize Poem at Oxford in Mar. 1858 on the subject 'The Discovery of the North-West Passage' was written in a more adventurous metre. Gosse (45) thought it had been denied the prize because it dealt exclusively with the fate of Franklin and his companions. The prize was won by Francis Law Latham of Brasenose College.

[7] Swinburne's song *Love laid his sleepless head*, later published in *Poems and Ballads: Second Series* (1878). Gosse (79) thought it had been written 'about 1876'.

[8] Gosse: 'Swinburne proceeded, with the beginning of *Atalanta* in his pocket, to ... the Isle of Wight.'

[9] Gosse (98): 'Swinburne wrote some verses called *Cleopatra* to a drawing by Frederick Sandys which appeared as a wood-cut in the *Cornhill Magazine* in September 1866'. Gosse (155): 'He published, in a very small edition, in paper covers, *Cleopatra*, which was new'.

[10] 'A Vision of Spring in Winter', *The Fortnightly Review*, 100 (1 Apr. 1875), 505–7.

[11] Gosse has 'The "marvellous boy, that perished in his prime"' for Wordsworth's 'the marvellous Boy, | The sleepless Soul that perished in his pride' (*Resolution and Independence*, 7. 1–2).

P. 229. What you say about the *Persae* is quite wickedly false:[12] 'here lies our good Edmund' in fact.[13]

But what ought to turn the pudic snows of your countenance to scarlet is the bottom of p. 125, where you have taken Swinburne's heavy-handed irony for seriousness. That view of Mary is the view he imputes to his enemies her defenders.[14]

Perhaps we should both blush if you unfolded the awful inner meaning of 'a way which those who knew him will easily imagine for themselves' on p. 82.[15]

You may possibly be able to say, from your own knowledge or Mr T. J. Wise's,[16] whether Swinburne is the author of two poems signed *Etonensis*[17] in a volume entitled *The Whippingham Papers*,[18] sold in Paris to Anglo-Saxons.

Lord Redesdale misdates Swinburne's death on p. 317.[19]

My kind regards to Mrs Gosse.

Yours sincerely
A. E. Housman.

BL MS Ashley B. 903, fos. 41–3. Maas, 149–51.

TO EDMUND GOSSE

Trinity College, Cambridge
13 April 1917

My dear Gosse,

If you are going to indulge in depression of spirits because I manage to find half a dozen mistakes in 350 pages, you will cut yourself off from my valued corrections in the future. As for my finding 'little to like', you

---

[12] Gosse makes reference to 'the odes in praise of Athenian liberty which break up the scenes of the *Persae*'. See AEH to Gosse, 13 Apr. 1917.

[13] An application to Edmund Gosse of Goldsmith's mock-epitaph on Edmund Burke: 'Here lies our good Edmund, whose genius was such, | We scarcely can praise it or blame it too much': *Retaliation*, 29–30.

[14] ' ... the qualities [in Mary Stuart] which he [Swinburne] summed up at last (in 1882) as her "easiness, gullibility, incurable innocence and invincible ignorance of evil, incapacity to suspect or resent anything, readiness to believe and forgive all things" ': Gosse, 125–6.

[15] A jocular reference to Swinburne's passion for flagellation.

[16] Thomas James Wise (1859–1937), book-collector, bibliographer, and forger; formed the Ashley Library, which was sold to the British Museum after his death.

[17] *Arthur's Flogging* and *Reginald's Flogging* by 'Etonensis', attributed to Swinburne.

[18] *The Whippingham Papers: A Collection of Contributions in Prose and Verse, chiefly by the author of the 'Romance of Chastisement'* (1888).

[19] A letter from Redesdale, printed as an appendix, has 1910 instead of 1909.

know perfectly well that you write delightfully and that your taste and knowledge made you just the man for the work; and you do not need to hear it from me, especially when all the world is saying it. For my own part I always feel impertinent and embarrassed when I praise people: this is a defect of character, I know; and I suffer for it, like Cordelia.[1] The chief fault of your book is one which I did not mention, that there is too little of it.

There are not, and could not be, any odes in praise of Athenian liberty in the *Persae*, for all the odes are sung by Persian elders. You probably had in your mind a celebrated passage of dialogue, where Atossa enquires who is lord and governor of the Athenians, and is answered that they are no man's servants or subjects.[2] There is an ode in praise of Athens (though not of its liberty) in Euripides' *Medea*,[3] but I suppose Swinburne would not deign to recite him.

I am sending *The Whippingham Papers* by parcel post. The two poems have some affinity to passages in *Love's Cross Currents* and *The Sisters*;[4] the verse seems to me good enough for Swinburne, and in the second poem the stanza is like him; and the names *Reggie* and *Algernon* are observable.[5] You will see that on p. iii the poet is said to be the author of another work, *The Romance of Chastisement*,[6] which I have not come across: my library is sadly incomplete, and not at all worth leaving to the British Museum when I die.

Yours sincerely
A. E. Housman.

BL MS Ashley B. 4395, fos. 55–6. Maas, 151–2.

---

[1] Who in *King Lear* was dispossessed and banished by Lear when she could not bring herself first to declare and then to overstate her love for him.

[2] *The Persae*, 241–2.   [3] Lines 843–7.

[4] Respectively an epistolary novel (1905) of thirty letters with a prologue of five chapters, serialized pseudonymously under the name 'Mrs Horace Manners' in *The Tatler* between 25 Aug. and 29 Dec. 1877 as *A Year's Letters*, and a tragedy (1892) by Swinburne. *A Year's Letters* was published in the United States in 1901.

[5] Reggie Fane and Algernon are school friends in *Reginald's Flogging*.

[6] Published in 1870 and subtitled *Revelations of the School and Bedroom. By an Expert.* The anonymous author was St George Henry Stock.

TO JOHN DRINKWATER

Trinity College | Cambridge
14 April 1917

Dear Mr Drinkwater,

I am much obliged by the gift of your book,[1] which I value both for itself and for your kindness in sending it.

I am yours very truly
A. E. Housman.

Marquette University MS (Elizabeth Whitcomb Houghton Collection, series 5, box 4).

TO GRANT RICHARDS

I ought before now to have thanked you and Mrs Richards for the photographs.[1] I think I can just make out myself in the marine landscape with figures.

Yrs.
A. E. H.

27 May 1917.   Trin. Coll. Camb.

LC-GR MS: p.c. addressed 'Grant Richards Esq. | Bigfrith | Cookham Dean | Berkshire'. LC-GR t.s. Richards, 157 (excerpt).

TO GRANT RICHARDS

[Trinity College Cambridge]

Yes.

A. E. H.
2 June 1917

BMC MS: AEH's note on letter from Richards of 1 June 1917 asking 'Shall I give this man the usual permission?' LC-GR t.s.

---

[1] *Tides: A Book of Poems* (1917). The inscribed copy is at BMC.

[1] 'Some photographs of himself that my wife had taken': Richards, 157. One of them is reproduced in Richards opposite p. 152 (Richards, 161 n.). See AEH to GR, 11 Oct. 1918.

TO GRANT RICHARDS

Trinity College, Cambridge
20 June 1917

My dear Richards,

Vaughan Williams did have an interview with me six years or more ago, and induced me by appeals ad misericordiam[1] to let him print words on the programme of a concert for which he had already made arrangements; but the permission applied to that concert only. I knew what the results would be, and told him so.

Yours sincerely
A. E. Housman.

LC-GR t.s. Richards, 157–8; Maas, 152.

TO ALICE ROTHENSTEIN

Trinity College | Cambridge
9 Aug. 1917

Dear Mrs Rothenstein,

It is very good of you to write and enquire after me, and if I were to be in Gloucestershire I would certainly come and see you, but that is not likely to happen at present, and before long I am hoping to get <the> to France, where I have not been for two years and a half, much to the detriment of my health and spirits. I hope that you and William and all the family are as flourishing as is consistent with being fed on war-bread.

Yours sincerely
A. E. Housman.

Harvard bMS Eng 1148 (740) 36. Maas, 152.

TO GRANT RICHARDS

Trinity College | Cambridge
22 Aug. 1917

My dear Richards,

Symondsbury[1] was the village I spoke of, but I have never been inside it, and have only seen the beauty of its knolls and trees from the top of a neighbouring hill. It is two miles from the sea, and not in sight of it, as the

[1] 'To pity'.

[1] Dorset village. 'Housman's uncle, J. B. Housman, held his first curacy at Symondsbury, and married one of the rector's daughters': Richards, 158 n.

high hill and cliff of Eype, which you see from Lyme, intervene. When you do get to the beach, I expect it is chiefly pebbles. I know nothing about lodgings, and I don't think there can be much of an inn.

Abbotsbury[2] is not a bad place for downs and open country, but as for bathing—! it is on the Chesil Bank, where death is certain owing to the currents and desirable owing to the stones.

The War Office does not view with favour my proposed escape to France, so I shall start at the beginning of next month on a tour to Rochester, Canterbury, Chichester, Winchester and Salisbury. When I am turning home I will write to you, and if you then wish me to come to Bigfrith I shall be very pleased. I hope you are all well.

Yours sincerely
A. E. Housman.

LC-GR MS. LC-GR t.s. Richards, 158 (nearly complete); Maas, 152–3.

TO MARTIN SECKER

Trinity College | Cambridge
8 Oct. 1917

Dear Mr Secker,
Richards tells me to send you this,[1] which I do with much pleasure.

Yours very truly
A. E. Housman.

BMC MS. Tipped-in in Martin Secker's presentation copy of Grant Richards, Housman *1897–1936 (1941).*

TO GRANT RICHARDS

Trinity College | Cambridge
14 Oct. 1917

My dear Richards,
I have sent the book to Secker, and called on Mr Withers,[1] who seems an agreeable man.

[2] Dorset village.

[1] A signed copy of *ASL*: Richards, 158.

[1] Dr Percy Withers: see List of Recipients. Withers, an admirer of *ASL*, going to Cambridge on war work, had asked GR for a letter of introduction to AEH: Richards, 158.

The young friend who was educated at Oundle has been staying with me, and says it is probably the best equipped school in England for engineering.[2]

Yours sincerely
A. E. Housman.

LC-GR t.s. Richards, 158 (excerpt).

TO MESSRS GRANT RICHARDS LTD

Trinity College | Cambridge
3 Nov. 1917

Dear Sirs,

I do not allow my verses to be printed on concert programmes.

Yours faithfully
A. E. Housman.

LC-GR t.s.

TO S. M. ELLIS

Trinity College, Cambridge
7 Nov. 1917

Dear Sir,

It is more than twenty years since I was last photographed,[1] so that the portrait, even if I had no objection to sending it, would not be very like.

I am yours very truly
A. E. Housman

Yale MS. Envelope addressed to 'S. M. Ellis Esq. | 16 Defoe Avenue | Kew | Surrey'.

---

[2]   Frederick William Sanderson (1857–1922) as headmaster (1892–1922) introduced an elaborate building programme and established eminent departments of science and engineering.

[1]   In 1894: Naiditch (2005), 13.

TO F. J. H. JENKINSON

Trinity College
7 Nov. 1917

My dear Jenkinson,

I am not quite sure if you are the right person to write to, nor who is chairman of the Library Extension Subsyndicate; but anyhow I shall probably not be coming to the meeting to-morrow, as I am nursing a cold.

Yours
A. E. Housman.

CUL Add. MS 4251/691. Maas, 153.

TO GRANT RICHARDS

Trinity College | Cambridge
16 Nov. 1917

My dear Richards,

Thanks for both your notes. Ehrmanns[1] sent me their lists, and I ordered three sorts (including some dry Tokay,[2] as I remembered a very agreeable wine you used to have); and for two of the three they sent me what I had not ordered.

Yrs
A. E. Housman.

LC-GR MS. LC-GR t.s. Richards, 159 (incomplete).

TO WILBUR CROSS

Trinity College | Cambridge | England
18 Nov. 1917

Dear Sir,

I am obliged by your letter,[1] but I neither have any poem which I wish to publish nor am likely to write one at any early date.[2]

I am yours very truly
A. E. Housman.

Yale MS. Maas, 153.

---

[1] Wine merchants.   [2] Hungarian white wine, normally intensely sweet.

[1] Of 29 Oct. 1917 (Yale MS).

[2] Cross (editor of *The Yale Review*): 'I am most anxious to have something from you for a coming number. Have you not a war poem which you would care to send me?'

TO J. W. MACKAIL

Trinity College | Cambridge
11 Dec. 1917

Dear Mackail,

I am very glad to have your paper on Horace.[1] I thought your chapter on him in your *Latin Literature*[2] one of the best, and this is a worthy continuation.

Yours very truly
A. E. Housman.

TCC MS R.1.92.2. Maas, 153–4.

TO CHARLES SAYLE

Trinity College
14 Dec. 1917

My dear Sayle,

It was in a review by Parry of Hodgkin's life in a recent number of the *Cambridge Review.*[1] Mrs Creighton, poor thing, had printed *Juveni patiem,*[2] which has to be emended *Inveni portum,* and is the opening of an epigram quoted at the end of *Gil Blas,*[3] book IX. But in this form I don't think it is classical, and some attribute it to Ianus Pannonius saec. XV. The Greek original is anth. Pal. IX 49: the ancient Latin version, found more than once in inscriptions (C. I. L. VI 11743, anth. epigr. Buech. 1498, carm.

[1] Read to the Classical Association during the war. Repr. as 'Poetry and Life: The Odes of Horace' as part of the Proceedings of the Fourteenth General Meeting, Friday, 5 Jan. 1917, in *Proceedings of the Classical Association,* 14 (Jan. 1917), 87–101, and as ch. 8 ('The Odes of Horace') of Mackail's *Classical Studies* (1925), 139–58.

[2] Published in 1895. 'Horace': part 2, ch. 1 (pp. 106–19).

[1] Reginald St John Parry reviewed Louise Creighton's *Life and Letters of Thomas Hodgkin* (1917) in the *Cambridge Review,* 39. 965 (6 Dec. 1917), 176–7. He acknowledged AEH for supplying the reference to *Gil Blas.*

[2] On p. 202.

[3] Picaresque novel (1715–35) by Alain-René Lesage (1668–1747). 'Inveni portum: Spes et Fortuna, valete. | Sat me lusistis. Ludite nunc alios' ('I have found the haven: Hope and Fortune, farewell. You have trifled enough with me. Trifle with others now').

Lat. epigr. Engstroem 324), is

> evasi, effugi. Spes et Fortuna valete.
> nil mihi vobiscum est, ludificate alios.[4]

There is also a translation by Grotius.[5]

Yours very truly
A. E. Housman.

Lilly MSS 1. 1. 3. Maas, 412.

---

[4] 'I have come through, escaped. Hope and Fortune, farewell. I have no more to do with you; trifle with others.'
[5] In *Anthologia Graeca cum versione Latina Hugonis Grotii* (1795).

1918

TO DR PERCY WITHERS

Trinity College
18 Jan. 1918.

I will walk with you to the Navarros'[1] door on Sunday: I shall not cross the threshold myself, but I am not going to keep you out of Paradise.

Yrs.
A. E. Housman.

SCO MS: p.c. addressed 'Dr Withers | 35 Trumpington Street' and marked 'Local' by AEH. Maas, 154.

TO H. F. NEWALL

Trinity College
7 Feb. 1918

My dear Newall,

I told you a lie across the table last night, for the Burman who collected the anthology was the nephew of Bentley's Burman.[1] They were both christened Pieter.

The ancient Copernicus whose name I could not remember was Aristarchus of Samos, 3rd cent. B.C. The Farnese globe,[2] judging from the places in which it puts the equinoctial points, is near the same date.

circle is one of those English words (like *salt*) on which you men of science have laid hands and wrested \them/ out of their original meanings. The

---

[1] José María de Navarro (d. 1979). Admitted to TCC, 1915; Senior Scholar, 1920, the year when he took a starred first in the English Tripos. Fellow of TCC, 1923–9 (the first Catholic to attain such a distinction), and University Lecturer in Archaeology, 1926–56.

[1] Dutch philologist Pieter Burman I (1668–1741) supported Richard Bentley (1662–1742) in his controversy with Swiss Arminian and biblical scholar Jean Le Clerc (1657–1736), and published Bentley's *Emendationes in Menandri et Philemonis reliquias, ex nupera editione Joannis Clerici* under Bentley's pseudonym 'Phileleutherus Lipsiensis' in 1710. (Bentley had written an appendix of critical notes to an edn. of Cicero's *Tusculan Disputations* by Cambridge scholar John Davies in 1709, and Le Clerc had disparaged the notes in a review called *Bibliothèque Choisie*. In annoyance, Bentley produced 323 emendations to Le Clerc's subsequent edn. of the fragments of Menander and Philemon, restoring them metrically and demonstrating Le Clerc's incompetence.) Pieter Burman I's nephew, Pieter Burman II, lived from 1714 to 1778.

[2] The oldest celestial globe in existence; now in the Muzeo Nazionale Archeologico.

Latins called the zodiac and even the milky way a *circulus*; and Gray calls the hoop which he trundled at Eton a *circle*,³ though it must have had three dimensions.

Yours sincerely
A. E. Housman.

Yale MS. Maas, 412–13.

TO GRANT RICHARDS

Trinity College | Cambridge
28 Feb. 1918

My dear Richards,

Bon voyage, and also thanks for *Noel*,¹ though I have only found time to read a few pages yet.

Yours sincerely
A. E. Housman.

LC-GR MS. LC-GR t.s. Richards, 160 (excerpt).

TO MARY WITHERS

Trinity College
10 March 1918

Dear Mrs Withers,

Porters so seldom bring one things on Sundays that I am even more overwhelmed than I otherwise should be by your kindness in enriching me with blackberry jelly from your end of the town, where the grocers still have jams. I have been enjoined this evening not to write you a charming letter, so I will put a firm constraint on myself and abstain from doing so; but I am tempted to be very charming indeed.

I am yours sincerely
A. E. Housman.

SCO MS. Maas, 154.

---

³ *Ode on a Distant Prospect of Eton College*, 29: 'To chase the rolling circle's speed'.

¹ Gilbert Cannan's *Noel: An Epic in Seven Cantos* (1918), published in 1917 with the subtitle *An Epic in Ten Cantos*. Both versions were published by GR.

TO GRANT RICHARDS

Trinity College | Cambridge
19 April 1918

My dear Richards,

Messrs Winthrop Rogers Ld.[1] may publish the two songs as they wish.

It was kind of you to write to me from Nice: I did not answer, because I had nothing particular to say. I hope Mrs Richards is now well, and that you both enjoyed your outing as much as circumstance permitted.

Yours sincerely
A. E. Housman.

LC-GR t.s. Richards, 160 (excerpt).

TO STEPHEN GASELEE

Trinity College | Cambridge
7 May 1918

Dear Gaselee,

I shall be delighted to dine with you on Whit-Sunday. I was just on the point of writing to you about translations of Petronius, which I happen to be wanting to consult, and cannot find many within my reach. Burnaby, Wilson & Co.,[1] Lowe,[2] Ryan,[3] Heseltine,[4] Friedlaender,[5] and the French of 1694[6] are all I can get at either in the University or the College library or on my own shelves, for the University copy of Bohn[7] is out, as I suppose it always is. Jackson[8] possesses a copy, and also one of Addison,[9] but cannot lay hands on either. No doubt you have quite a number, and perhaps sometime you would let me have a look at them. It is only one passage that I am concerned with.[10]

---

[1] London music publishers.

[1] The second English translation, by William Burnaby, Mr Wilson, Mr Blount, Mr Thomas Brown, Captain Ayloff, *et al.* (1708).

[2] W. D. Lowe, 1905.

[3] *Petronius (Trimalchio's Banquet)*, with introduction by Michael J. Ryan (1905). AEH owned a copy: Naiditch (2003), 137.

[4] Michael Heseltine's Loeb edn., 1912.

[5] Ludwig Friedländer, 1891.

[6] By François Nodot.

[7] Ed. W. K. Kelly, 1848.

[8] Henry Jackson. See List of Recipients.

[9] Joseph Addison, 1736.

[10] 41.6–8. Cf. *CR* 32 (1918), 164 (*Classical Papers*, 962–3).

Perhaps you know that we have in the College library a MS translation, 18th century apparently, based on Burnaby[11] and not so good in diction, but more understanding and helpful in the passage I consulted it for.

Yours sincerely
A. E. Housman.

CUL MS CCC.12.34.

TO JOHN DRINKWATER

Trinity College
10 May 1918

Dear Mr Drinkwater,

Sir Arthur Quiller-Couch tells me that you are to be here for a day or two, and I hope that if you have time you will come and see me on Saturday or Sunday. I am pretty sure to be in from 11 to 1 and from 4 to 7, and if you came at 4. 30 or thereabouts I could offer you such tea as the times admit.

I am yours very truly
A. E. Housman.

Marquette University MS (Elizabeth Whitcomb Houghton Collection, series 5, box 4).

TO HENRY BROADBENT

I overlooked the passage in the *Anthology*, but it was afterwards adduced by an Austrian scholar, K. Prinz. There is a παρὰ τὴν ἱστορίαν in Cic. ad Att. XIII 10 1.

A. E. H.

Trin. Coll. Camb. 4 June 1918.

TCC Add. MS c. 112[8]: p.c. addressed 'H. Broadbent Esq. | Willowbrook End | Eton | Bucks.'

TO GRANT RICHARDS

Trinity College | Cambridge
6 June 1918

My dear Richards,

The working classes at any rate can well afford to pay 1/6, though I don't know if 5000 of them will want to.[1]

---

[11] The first English translation, by William Burnaby, 1694.

[1] He had been warned by GR that the price of *ASL* must be increased to 1/6 owing to the cost of labour and material: Richards, 160.

I am not likely to come to town, so far as I can see.

P. Withers, who is back again here, was asking after you the other day.

Yours sincerely
A. E. Housman.

LC-GR t.s. Richards, 160 (incomplete and dated as 4 June).

TO GRANT RICHARDS

Trinity College | Cambridge
14 June 1918

My dear Richards,

I suppose I must follow the example of the anonymous great poet (very likely Alfred Noyes)[1] and relax the rule, in order that the poem may be read by blind soldiers.[2]

Yours sincerely
A. E. Housman.

LC-GR t.s. Richards, 160.

TO ALICE ROTHENSTEIN

Trinity College | Cambridge
6 July 1918

Dear Mrs Rothenstein,

It is probable,—do not be agitated,—that I shall be coming to Woodchester or Amberley towards the end of August; and then you may be sure that I shall walk over to see you. Thank you all the same for your kindness in asking me to Oakridge, and also for amiable messages which I have received from our friend Dr Withers.

I have been glad to see in the papers and hear privately of the success of W's exhibition in London.[1]

I am yours sincerely
A. E. Housman.

Harvard bMS Eng 1148 (740) 37. Maas, 155.

[1] 1880–1958. Poet, novelist, and playwright, who gradually became blind, 1945–58.

[2] AEH is allowing one poem from *ASL* to be printed in a Braille anthology: Richards, 160.

[1] 'Of drawings of the fighting in Flanders. The exhibition, at the Goupil Gallery, was opened by H. A. L. Fisher, the President of the Board of Education, on 25 April 1918': Maas, 155.

TO M. R. JAMES

Trinity College
31 July 1918

My dear James,

Though I am sorry on account of Cambridge and myself, I hope and believe that your choice is for your own happiness and I wish you prosperity and contentment in all your doings.[1] You will be now in a snowstorm of congratulations or expostulations, so do not take any notice of this.

Yours sincerely
A. E. Housman.

CUL Add MS 7481/H128.

TO ALICE ROTHENSTEIN

Trinity College | Cambridge
22 Aug. 1918

Dear Mrs Rothenstein,

Alas, my plans for coming to Gloucestershire are upset. At the hotel at Amberley, where I had meant to stay, they are full till the end of September, which is too late. For me the cloud has a silver lining, as I escape the horrors which now encompass travelling: for you, of course, the gloom is unmitigated.

I have met M. André Gide,[1] who had a letter[2] from W., and I shall see him again if he does not shortly go off to France, as he threatens.

I wish W. good luck on the lines of communication.[3]

Yours sincerely
A. E. Housman.

Harvard bMS Eng 1148 (740) 38. Maas, 155–6.

[1] James was leaving Cambridge, where he was Provost of King's College, upon his election as Provost of Eton.

[1] The French novelist, essayist, critic, and playwright (1869–1951) was in Cambridge from 27 June to the end of September 1918. In the preface to his edition of *Anthologie de la Poésie Française* (Éditions Gallimard, 1949; repr. 1983), 7–8, Gide recalls meeting AEH at a ceremonial lunch in Cambridge in 1917 (in fact, 1918): AEH provocatively alleged that though between Villon and Baudelaire there was much French verse that had spirit, eloquence, virulence, and pathos, there was none that was poetry.

[2] Of introduction.

[3] After visiting Belgium (1916) and France (1917, 1918) as official war artist, Rothenstein ended up lecturing to Australian Education Officers at Cheshunt College, Cambridge, on town-planning, the museum of the future, and the decoration of buildings.

TO SYDNEY COCKERELL

Trinity College
9 Sept. 1918

Dear Cockerell,

I return with many thanks Ben Jonson's[1] book, done up safely I hope, and the poems of Charlotte Mew,[2] which have much that is good in them, only, as female poets are apt to be, <do>, she is too literary, and puts in ornament which does not suit the supposed speakers. I think the short piece on p. 27[3] is the best.

Yours sincerely
A. E. Housman.

MS inspected at Sotheby's, 4 Nov. 2001. Excerpt quoted in Sotheby's catalogue, The Library of Frederick B. Adams, Jr, Part 1: English & American Literature *(6 Nov. 2001), 34.*

TO PROFESSOR D'ARCY THOMPSON

[Trinity College | Cambridge]

I tried *uolumina* in I 416, but as it appeared to involve mauling the rest of the verse I judged that it was wrong: Garrod had the same notion and did maul the rest of the verse to carry it out.[1]

I cannot make out how your reading of I 311 would continue; and remember that *niue* is merely an insertion of mine.

I am writing in the country without books.

A. E. Housman.

18 Sept. 1918

Texas MS.

TO MARTIN SECKER

Trinity College | Cambridge
29 Sept. 1918.

Dear Mr Secker,

Many thanks to you for sending me the anonymous book on Women,[1] which is acute and entertaining to read and flatters some of my own

[1] Poet and dramatist (1572–1637). Cockerell previously owned a book bearing Jonson's signature, but gave it to Swinburne (d. 1909) and received a MS of Swinburne's in return: *Cockerell* by Wilfrid Blunt (1965), 101.

[2] *The Farmer's Bride* (1916).   [3] *À Quoi Bon Dire.*

[1] Manilius, 1. 416: *squamea dispositis imitatur tergora flammis.* Garrod proposed *squamea dispositis imitate uolumina flammis* in a review of AEH's and Breiter's edns. in *CQ* 2. 2 (1908), 129. In his apparatus to book 1 (1903), AEH recorded: '*tergora* Bentleius; *lumina* libri ridicule'.

[1] *Women,* by the novelist Frank Swinnerton (1884–1982), published by Secker.

prejudices; though it contains so many general propositions that it must contain a good deal which is not quite true.

I am yours very truly
A. E. Housman.

Lilly MSS 2. Maas, 156.

TO GRANT RICHARDS

Trinity College | Cambridge
11 Oct. 1918

My dear Richards,

I shall be very pleased to come to you[1] on the 25th, when your woodlands ought to be looking very well. I was in Gloucestershire most of September, and saw the Rothensteins. From the fragments of your autobiography which I see in the weekly press I gather that you too have had a holiday or holidays.[2]

My kind regards to Mrs Richards, who owes me a photograph of young pigs.[3]

Yours sincerely
A. E. Housman.

LC-GR MS. LC-GR t.s. Richards, 160–1; Maas, 156.

TO GRANT RICHARDS

Trinity College, Cambridge
23 Oct. 1918

My dear Richards,

I shall be delighted to lunch with you on Friday. I ought to arrive in town about 11. 30: I will then go and deposit my bag at Paddington, and come on to you some time before 1.

---

[1] To Bigfrith, Cookham Dean, Richards's house.
[2] A reference to GR's regular advertisements in the *TLS*, in some of which he announced his whereabouts and activities. In no. 863 (1 Aug. 1918), 359, he describes two 'wonderful inns' he has found in Wales (the George near Bangor and the St David's Hotel at Hariech); in no. 868 (5 Sept. 1918), 415, he states that he writes 'within the sound of sea waves'.
[3] 'Housman had on his Cornish holiday been photographed with a litter of young pigs by my wife in the neighbourhood of Zennor': Richards, 161 n. See AEH to GR, 27 May 1917.

I shall be interested to meet Squire,[1] some of whose poems I have read, and whose paper[2] I take in.

Yours sincerely
A. E. Housman.

PM MS. LC-GR t.s. Richards, 161 (excerpt).

TO MARIA RICHARDS

Trinity College | Cambridge
14 Nov. 1918

Dear Mrs Richards,

I am very sorry to hear of Grant's relapse.[1] I had gathered from the weekly bulletin in the *Times Supplement* that he was all right again;[2] and I hope now it will not be long before he is well. <again>. I have escaped hitherto, and I have not heard that Mr Squire has been attacked; and I hope that you will not catch it from the patient.

Yours sincerely
A. E. Housman.

BMC MS. LC-GR t.s. Richards, 161 (nearly complete).

TO GRANT RICHARDS

Trinity College | Cambridge
25 Nov. 1918

My dear Richards,

Yours is a terrible long illness, but I am glad that you seem to be fairly comfortable.

I have sent to your office a list of 8 mistakes in the 8vo edition, probably all taken over from 1916. The smaller editions (except the cursed 'Lesser Classics')[1] have a purer text, with only one error I think; but this reappears in the last issue (for which by the way I ought to have begun by thanking you): p. 5 (only the 5 is invisible), last line but two, there should be a colon after *town*.[2]

Yours sincerely
A. E. Housman

LC-GR t.s. Richards, 161; Maas, 157.

[1] J. C. Squire: see List of Recipients.

[2] *The New Statesman*, of which Squire was literary editor from its foundation in 1913 till 1919.

[1] GR had gone down with influenza a month before during AEH's visit to Bigfrith, and the illness had developed into pleurisy and then pneumonia: Richards, 161.

[2] In his personal advertisement in the *TLS* 876 (31 Oct. 1918), 523, he announced 'I write this in bed'. In the absence of any more announcements of illness, AEH had surmised his recovery.

[1] 1904.   [2] At the end of l. 26 of *The Recruit* (*ASL* III).

TO EDMUND GOSSE

Trinity College | Cambridge
29 Dec. 1918

My dear Gosse,

I send these notes on Swinburne's letters[1] in hopes that they may be of use for the next edition.

Vol. I

p. 162. Read '*as* Knox'.

171. *a* and *w* should be the Greek letters alpha and omega.

209. 'no person, may worship' would be a less puzzling punctuation: whether Swinburne's, I don't know.

212. 'as to *his* dealings of my own': *his* wants altering or removing.

260. *The Last Oracle* appeared in *Belgravia,* and as early as 1876 if the date of letter CXXXV is right.[2]

282. Read '*m*'est parvenu'.

Vol. II

p. 25. Veuillot's name is misprinted.

36. Read 'En *plein* été' and '*Ton* adorable'.

120. Read '*stray* squibs'.

126. Read 'damning *blot*'.

145. The League cannot have been the Primrose League.[3] Swinburne's verses were against the House of Lords, which was withstanding Gladstone's attempt to lower the franchise without a redistribution of seats.

183. Read '*such* pleasure'.

186. Read 'Sandys' '.

214. Read 'Etonie'.

An explanation of Vol. I letter CV would be welcome, if it could be given without causing pain in Buckingham Palace. Does it refer to the French play about Queen Victoria's foster-sister, of which I have heard fragments from you and others?[4]

---

[1] Ed. Gosse and T. J. Wise (1918).

[2] Swinburne's *The Last Oracle (A.D. 361)* appeared in *Belgravia: An Illustrated London Magazine,* 29 (May 1876), 329–32.

[3] Victorian Conservative organization, founded in 1883, to enable the Conservatives to adapt to the extension of democracy.

[4] It does. The *Daily News* had compared the potential illegitimate son of George IV to 'La Princess KITTY in an unacted French melodrama by a living English poet'. This is *La Soeur de La Reine,* Swinburne's private pastiche of Hugo's *L'Homme Qui Rit,* which presents Queen Victoria as a nymphomaniac with a twin sister, Kitty, who has been brought up as a prostitute in order to keep her safe from the throne. Swinburne to Thomas Purnell, 20 Feb. 1875: 'The return of Dr. Kenealy for Stoke has at last given me courage to make public as much as I dare

Thank you for collecting and editing the letters, and best wishes for the New Year to you and Mrs Gosse.

        Yours sincerely
        A. E. Housman.

TCC MS Y.10.143. Maas, 157–8.

TO ROBERT BRIDGES

        Trinity College | Cambridge
        30 Dec. 1918

My dear Bridges,

I must send you my thanks for the poems of G. M. Hopkins.[1] I value the book as your gift, and also for some good condensed lines and an engaging attitude of mind which now and again shines through. But the faults which you very fairly and judicially set forth thrust themselves more upon my notice; and also another. Sprung Rhythm,[2] as he calls it in his sober and sensible preface, is just as easy to write as other forms of verse; and many a humble scribbler of words for music-hall songs has written it well. But he does not: he does not make it audible; he puts light syllables in the stress and heavy syllables in the slack, and has to be helped out with typographical signs explaining that things are to be understood as being what in fact they are not.[3] Also the English language is a thing which I respect very much, and I resent even the violence Keats did to it; and here is a lesser than Keats doing much more. Moreover his early poems are the promise of something better, if less original; and originality is not

of the case of that Royal Claimant yesterday mentioned in the *Daily News*. I have *every* reason to believe ... that the rightful Queen of England is at this moment a prisoner in Newgate.' The surviving fragments of Swinburne's play (acts II and IV) were first published in *New Writings by Swinburne: or miscellanea nova et curiosa, being a Medley of Poems, Critical Essays, Hoaxes and Burlesques,* ed. Cecil Y. Lang (1964), 103–18.

[1] Ed. Bridges (1918). Hopkins died in 1889, and Bridges' edn. of 750 copies brought his poetry to prominence. AEH rendered Bridges' dedication to Hopkins's mother into Latin. Bridges to AEH, 25 May 1918 (Bodleian MS, Dep. Bridges 110. 97): 'What I want is something of this sort | To Kate | this late (public) recognition of the genius | of her beloved son the poet | on her 98th year | a tribute of long friendship | dedicates R B | which I don't offer "for translation", but that you may see the conditions.' Randall McLeod notes that the dedication appeared again at the front of the 2nd edn., that it was placed well into the vol. in the 3rd and 4th, and that it does not appear thereafter: 'Gerard Hopkins and the Shapes of his Sonnets', *Voice, Text, Hypertext: Emerging Practices in Textual Studies,* ed. Raimonda Modiano, Leroy F. Searle, and Peter Shillingsburg (2004), 291.

[2] Accentual metre, with feet made up of a stressed syllable and a varying number of unstressed ones, which Hopkins revived.

[3] Hopkins frequently marked heavy stresses with diacritics.

nearly so good as goodness, even when it is good. His manner strikes me as deliberately adopted to compensate by strangeness for the lack of pure merit, like the manner which Carlyle took up after he was thirty. Well, the paper warns me I must not run on, and perhaps you will not think this is a very grateful letter.

I am yours sincerely
A. E. Housman.

Bodleian MS, Dep. Bridges 110. 101–2. Maas, 158–9.

1919

TO H. A. HOLLOND

[Trinity College
1919]

Dear Hollond,

I am very much obliged to you for taking the trouble to write to me about the Russell business.[1] Russell is a great loss to the College, not merely for his eminence and celebrity, but as an agreeable and even charming person to meet; on the question of conscription I agreed with him at the time,[2] though I now see I was wrong, and I did not feel sure that the action of the Council was wise, though his behaviour was that of a bad citizen. So far therefore I am nearly neutral: what prevents me from signing your letter is Russell's taking his name off the books of the College. After that piece of petulance he ought not even to want to come back. I cannot imagine myself doing so; and my standard of conduct is so very low that I feel I have a right to condemn those who do not come up to it.

I am writing this, not to argufy, but only in acknowledgement of your civility in writing to me. I hope I shall not be able to discover 'conscious effort' in the amiability of yourself or Hardy[3] when I happen to sit next to you in the future. I am afraid however that if Russell did return he would meet with rudeness from some Fellows of the College, as I know he did before he left. This ought not to be, but the world is as God made it.

---

[1] In 1916, following Russell's conviction under the Defence of the Realm Act, the Council of TCC deprived him of the lectureship in Logic and the Principles of Mathematics to which he had been appointed in 1910. Twenty-two Fellows of TCC expressed dissatisfaction with the action at the time, and in 1919 Hollond drafted a letter to the Master of TCC, which twenty-eight Fellows signed and another five supported, requesting Russell's reinstatement, which followed.

[2] Hardy (55 n.): 'Housman's attitude to the war had been "orthodox" throughout. He may have thought at one time that conscription was not necessary on military grounds, but that question was quite irrelevant to the controversy, and I do not know that Russell had ever expressed an opinion about it.'

[3] G[odfrey] H[arold] Hardy (1877–1947), Fellow of TCC since 1900; FRS, 1910; Cayley Lecturer in Mathematics, Cambridge, 1914; Savilian Professor of Geometry, Oxford, 1920; Sadleirian Professor of Pure Mathematics, Cambridge, 1931–42.

Your party has a clear majority, and you ought, quite apart from this question, to vote yourself on to the Council as opportunities arise.⁴ There is not nearly enough young blood in it.

Yours sincerely
A. E. Housman.

Text based on that in G. H. Hardy, Bertrand Russell and Trinity *(1942), 54–5. Repr. in T. E. B. Howarth,* Cambridge Between Two Wars *(1978) with 'on' for 'in' at the close.*

TO EDMUND GOSSE

Trinity College | Cambridge
20 Jan. 1919

My dear Gosse,

I return with gratitude a memoir¹ which I have read with a great deal of pleasure, not only for the interest of the facts, which are pretty much what I had surmised, but also, if it is not impertinent to say so, for the wholesome air of good sense with which you have surrounded them, and the ease with which you have done it.

The Menken interlude² I partly knew through Bywater. If that lady had left an account of her various and eminent partners, it would be better reading than *Infelicia*,³ though I am afraid her tolerance of Swinburne shows that she did not properly appreciate the Benicia Boy.⁴

---

⁴ The Council had five *ex officio* members and eight elective members. There were already two Russell supporters on the Council who had signed Hollond's letter, and two new members were to be elected every year. By filling vacancies with Russell supporters, a majority would eventually be secured.

¹ Gosse's account, omitted from the 1917 biography, of Swinburne's addiction to flagellation and alcohol. Other recipients of the privately circulated typescript were Max Beerbohm, A. C. Bradley, Walter Raleigh, and William Michael Rossetti. It was first printed as an appendix to *The Swinburne Letters,* ed. Cecil Lang, 6 (1962), 233–48.

² Adah Isaacs Menken (1835–68), a much-married American circus performer, was given ten pounds by D. G. Rossetti to seduce Swinburne (and seduce him away from flagellation). Repeated attempts over a six-week period proved unsuccessful. She returned the money, saying that she had not been able to bring Swinburne 'up to scratch' or to make him understand that 'biting's no use': Jean Overton Fuller, *Swinburne: A Critical Biography* (1968), 163. Menken was a long-time close associate of Georges Sand.

³ A volume of her poems (1868). Most of them are concerned with painful, unrequited love for men.

⁴ The professional name of the Irish-American John Carmel Heenan (1833–73), a black-smith from Benicia, California, who became a prize-fighter in New York. He was American heavyweight champion (i.e. of the US and Canada) under bareknuckle rules in 1860. He married Menken in 1859 but stayed with her for only a few months. It transpired later that she was not divorced from her first husband, Alexander Isaac Menken. Heenan was a gambler and a drinker, and Menken claimed he was violent and inattentive: see *The Naked Lady: or Storm over Adah* by Bernard Falk (1934).

The Eton anecdote on p. 19 is perplexing,[5] because Etonians tell me that the only person privileged to flog is the headmaster.[6]

It is curious that though Sade is the author who most inflamed Swinburne, and though Swinburne's writings are full of sadism properly so called, his own propensities were those of Rousseau and Sacher-Masoch.[7] It is true that these are cheaper to indulge, but that does not seem to have been the reason.

Was *Charenton*[8] published? From the *Letters* (which are not in my hands at this moment) it seemed that Lord Houghton[9] had mentioned it in his review of *Atalanta in Calydon*,[10] which however is not the case.

Judging from dates, drink had a great deal to do with his best poetry, though the poetry declined before the drinking stopped. The history of the Mohammedan world confirms Horace's opinion of the connexion between the two;[11] and if American poetry were worth anything I should weep, as now I do not, at the sight of America going bone-dry.[12]

Can you tell me anything about *Quagg* and *Grace Walkers*[13] mentioned in connexion with Sala[14] on p. 16 of vol. I of the *Letters*? If, as I gather, they occur in some book which appealed to Swinburne's sense of humour,

[5] Swinburne's account, from a letter of *c.*10 Feb. 1863, of being allowed by his tutor (probably James Leigh Joynes) to bathe his face in eau-de-cologne before being beaten with the birch: 'he meant to stimulate and excite the senses by that preliminary pleasure so as to inflict the acuter pain afterwards on their awakened and intensified susceptibility.'

[6] They are right.

[7] i.e. he derived sexual pleasure from receiving pain (masochism) rather than from inflicting it (sadism).

[8] *Charenton en 1810*, a poem in French alexandrines by Swinburne which he dated 'Dimanche, 27 Octobre, 1861'. In it the Marquis de Sade appears to the author, a young man of twenty-four. Charenton was the asylum in which the Marquis died. The poem was first published by James Pope-Hennessy in *Monckton Milnes, the Flight of Youth 1851–1855* (1951), 257–9. Gosse had mistakenly printed '*Charenton*' instead of '*Antitheism*' in letter XVI.

[9] Richard Monckton Milnes (1809–85), politician and writer; created first Baron Houghton, 1863. His library at Fryston, Yorkshire, contained a large collection of erotica and scatological literature, and he introduced Swinburne to the works of the Marquis de Sade.

[10] In the *Edinburgh Review*, 249 (July 1865), 202–16.

[11] *Epistles*, 1. 19. 2–3: 'nulla placere diu nec vivere carmina possunt, quae scribuntur aquae potoribus' ('no poems can please long, nor live, which are written by water-drinkers').

[12] The Prohibition Amendment was ratified in the United States on 29 Jan. 1919 and went into effect one year later. On 28 Oct. 1919 the National Prohibition Act (or 'Volstead Act') was enacted, providing enforcement guidelines for of the manufacture and sale of alcohol for popular consumption.

[13] In *Colonel Quagg's Conversion*, a story in *Household Words*, 249 (30 Dec. 1854), 459–65, which Swinburne mentions several times in his letters, the blacksmith Colonel Goliah Washington Quagg flogs with an oiled leather strap any member of a Massachusetts sect called the Grace-Walking Brethren who happens to pass his smithy. He is then soundly beaten by the bare fists of Brother Zephaniah Stockdolloger, a former prize-fighter, and subsequently joins the sect.

[14] Popular journalist George Augustus Sala (1828–96). Swinburne 'spoke with high regard of G. A. Sala's talents as a writer': Lord Ronald Carver, *My Reminiscences* (1883), 2. 290. 'For

it might be worth looking up. If on the other hand they belong to the 'Mysteries of Verbena Lodge',[15] mysteries let them remain.

I am yours sincerely
A. E. Housman.

BL MS Ashley 5753, fos. 72–3. Maas, 159–60.

TO GRANT RICHARDS

Trinity College | Cambridge
27 Jan. 1919

My dear Richards,

I shall be in London, fulfilling various engagements, on Thursday, and could call on you about 12 if you would like me to. But I have nothing particular to say to you, and I don't wish to interfere with your serious pursuits.

The paper I got from Bedford Square[1] is a very daunting document, and I don't see how I can come to France with you in March.

Yours sincerely
A. E. Housman.

PM MS. LC-GR t.s. Richards, 162.

TO STEPHEN GASELEE

Trinity College | Cambridge
29 Jan. 1919

Dear Gaselee,

I shall be very pleased to dine with you in Hall on Sunday, though it would only show a proper abhorrence of perfidy if I refused to see any more of you, as you have not kept the promise you made more than once of letting me know when you were here and coming to dine with me.

Yours sincerely
A. E. Housman.

UCLA MS S/C 100/72.

Sala's work he always professed a tremendous admiration': Clara Watts-Dunton, *The Home Life of Swinburne* (1922), 130.

[15] According to Gosse's memoir, the 'mysterious house in St John's Wood where two golden-haired and rouge-cheeked ladies received, in luxuriously furnished rooms, gentlemen whom they consented to chastise for large sums'. Swinburne became a regular visitor in the mid-1860s, and stopped going in 1869.

[1] The French Consulate General.

TO GRANT RICHARDS

[Trinity College | Cambridge
8 February 1919

My dear Richards,

Have you] ever heard of Mitchell Kennerley?[1] I gather he is an American publisher who publishes *A Shropshire Lad*. If so, I should rather like a copy of his edition, if you can get hold of one for me.

[Yours sincerely
A. E. Housman.]

Text based on that in Richards, 162.

TO MARGUERITE WILKINSON

Trinity College | Cambridge | England
8 Feb. 1919

Dear Mrs Wilkinson,

For many years past I have been refusing to English anthologists permission to include poems from *A Shropshire Lad* in their collections, and telling them that this is my rule. I therefore cannot break the rule now in favour of your book,[1] if, as I understand you to say, it will be published in England as well as America. If it appeared in America alone, it would be different, as my book is not copyright in the United States, and I neither have nor wish to have any say in the matter.

I am yours sincerely
A. E. Housman.

Northwestern University (Charles Deering McCormick Library) MS.

---

[1] 'He was the American publisher to whom I had sold several hundred copies of one of my early printings of the book, a publisher who had, at the beginning of his career, worked in John Lane's office in London, an Englishman, a friend of mine, the first publisher in New York to put money into John Masefield and D. H. Lawrence, and who made a small fortune out of Victoria Cross': Richards, 162.

[1] No such book seems to have been published.

TO GRANT RICHARDS

[Trinity College | Cambridge
13 Feb. 1919

My dear Richards,]

I am much obliged by your letter of the 11th which gives me all the information I require. I do not want a copy of Mr Mitchell Kennerley's edition.

[Yours sincerely
A. E. Housman.]

Text based on that in Richards, 163.

TO GRANT RICHARDS

Trinity College | Cambridge
1 March 1919

My dear Richards,

It is exceedingly good of you to interest yourself in my behalf and write to me in such detail, but I don't much think I shall take advantage of it at present, or before June, as I hear appalling accounts of the prices of everything in Paris, and even accommodation seems to be scarce. I hope you and Mrs Richards are having good weather at Nice and enjoying yourselves as much as I did when I was there with you. Please remember me to Belfort Bax.

Yours sincerely
A. E. Housman.

LC-GR MS. Richards, 163; Maas, 160.

TO DR PERCY WITHERS

Trinity College | Cambridge
5 March 1919

My dear Withers,

The vaunt of Archimedes, 'give me where to stand, and I move the world' is quoted by the geometer Pappus (VIII 1060) as δός μοι ποῦ στῶ καὶ κινῶ τὴν γῆν, by the Aristotelian commentator Simplicius (Physic. VII 250^a) as δός μοι πᾶ βῶ καὶ κινῶ τὰν γᾶν, which, being Doric, is more likely to be what Archimedes said: the only difference in sense is that στῶ means 'stand' and βῶ 'set foot'.

I cannot call to mind at this moment a verse to suit your purpose, but if any occurs to me I will let you know.

I am a very bad correspondent, or I should have thanked you before now for your letter of a fortnight ago. I hope you and Mrs Withers are both well and enjoying your home. Cambridge already has half its regular number of undergraduates, and Whewell's Court and various other places are filled up with young naval officers.

Yours sincerely
A. E. Housman.

SCO MS. Maas, 413.

TO MESSRS GRANT RICHARDS LTD

Trinity College | Cambridge
14 March 1919

Dear Sirs,
The same answer should be made to Mrs Hillman as to the other American lady about whom I wrote yesterday.

Yours faithfully
A. E. Housman.

Messrs Grant Richards Ltd.
LC-GR t.s.

TO GRANT RICHARDS

Trinity College | Cambridge
8 April 1919

My dear Richards,
I shall be delighted to come to Bigfrith on the 25th and also to have the pleasure of entertaining you at lunch on that day. I hope you and Mrs Richards are very much set up by Geneva &c.

Yours sincerely
A. E. Housman.

LC-GR MS. LC-GR t.s.

TO J. S. PHILLIMORE

Trinity College | Cambridge
17 April 1919

Dear Phillimore,

pediculosi got into the text in the 16th century and stuck there more than 300 years, the creature being notoriously hard to dislodge: Schneidewin[1] added *non uis* IX 7 4 and XI 108 4 *salue* to prevent it from feeling lonely, but these soon dropped off.

The vocative is longer postponed after the first address in III 46 and several other epigrams.

I must thank you for sending me a copy lately of your civilities to the worthy Hartman.[2]

Yours very truly
A. E. Housman.

Private MS.

TO PROFESSOR D'ARCY THOMPSON

[Trinity College | Cambridge
17 April 1919]

The only example of *excetra* I have noted which is not in the dictionaries or in Goetz's thes. gloss. emend. is Ampelius lib. memor. 2. 4 "hydram Lernaeam quam nos *excetram* (Salmasius, *exertam* MS) dicimus".

A. E. Housman.
Trin. Coll. Camb. 17 April 1919

St Andrews MS 23591: p.c. addressed 'Professor Darcy[1] *W. Thompson | The University | Dundee' and redirected to 44 South Street, St Andrews.*

TO MARIA RICHARDS

Trinity College | Cambridge
28 April 1919

Dear Mrs Richards,

As I did not catch my first train at Liverpool Street, the daffodil was rather languid when it reached Cambridge, but is now reviving in water. In the crowd at Praed Street I was not able to take a proper farewell of

[1] F. G. Schneidewin in his 1842 edn. of Martial.
[2] Professor Jacobus Johannes Hartman of Leiden (1851–1924).

[1] For 'D'Arcy'.

Grant when I got into the train, so please make my apologies to him; and remember that I shall hope to see both of you here in the last week of May or the first of June.

Yours sincerely
A. E. Housman.

BMC MS. Richards, 163 (nearly complete).

TO GRANT RICHARDS

Trinity College | Cambridge
5 May 1919

My dear Richards,

I think that in writing to Mrs Richards I mentioned the first week of June as one in which you might find it pleasant to be here. I must now warn you against it, for there will not be a bed to be had in the place. The rowing authorities have stupidly put the races earlier than usual, at a time in the term when men have not finished their examinations and begun to go down; so there is much trouble ahead for this already congested town and university.

Yours sincerely
A. E. Housman.

LC-GR MS. Richards, 163; Maas, 161.

TO CHARLES SAYLE

[Trinity College]

Corp. inscr. Lat. VI 11743 = Buech. carm. epigr. 1498.
Mélanges d'hist. et d'archéol. de l'école Francaise de Rome 1905 p. 72 = Engstroem carm. Lat. epigr. 324.

A. E. H.
7 May 1919.

Lilly MSS 1. 1. 3: p.c. addressed 'C. E. Sayle Esq. | University Library' and marked 'Local' by AEH.

TO GRANT RICHARDS

Trinity College | Cambridge
15 May 1919

My dear Richards,

The dinner of the inter-University club "The Arcades"[1] is to take place at Oxford on the 31st, so I shall then be there, but I hope you will not be much put out by coming here on the 24th instead. I hope you will both lunch in my rooms on the Saturday and Sunday, and of course I should like you to dine in hall on Saturday, if Mrs Richards will not cry her eyes out at being deserted. I do not admire that demoralising animal the horse as much as you do, so I shall let you do your gloating at Newmarket[2] alone. Will you let me know exactly what time to expect you on Saturday? Perhaps I could get Quiller-Couch to meet you at lunch.

The best inn here on the whole is the University Arms, and the most pleasantly situated: its drawback is that it is more than half-a-mile from the College, nearly half-way to the station. The Bull is nearly central and stands on the best street in the town,[3] but it is dingy, and the food not very good, at least when I tried it last. The best for food is the Lion, which also is central, but stands on a narrow and busy street. A smaller inn, the Blue Boar, close to Trinity, is well spoken of.

The place is looking beautiful at present, and I hope this weather will hold. I am reading Wilfrid Blunt[4] with a good deal of interest.

With kind regards to Mrs Richards

I am yours sincerely
A. E. Housman.

LC-GR MS. Richards, 164 (almost complete); Maas, 161.

---

[1] Dining club, founded in 1919. See Naiditch (1988), 59 n. 22–4, for further information.

[2] GR (164) thinks he suggested that AEH should meet him overnight at Newmarket racecourse, where he had secured, through William Allison, a Balliol man and 'The Special Commissioner' of *The Sportsman*, the privilege of seeing the horses at exercise in the morning: Richards, 164.

[3] Trumpington Street leading on to King's Parade.

[4] Blunt's *My Diaries: Being A Personal Narrative of Events 1888–1914* (1919). In an entry recording a visit from AEH in 1911, Blunt expresses admiration for *ASL*, and a liking for AEH in spite of his prim donnishness, silences, and apparent lack of strong opinions. The index gives Laurence Housman as author of *ASL*.

TO SIEGFRIED SASSOON

Trinity College | Cambridge
23 May 1919

Dear Sir,

I shall be happy to take part in the tribute to Mr Hardy.[1]

I am yours very faithfully

A. E. Housman.

Huntington MS HM 39057.

TO J. W. MACKAIL

Trinity College | Cambridge
23 May 1919

Dear Mackail,

I cannot help being touched and flattered by your anxiety to make me publish, and I am grateful to you for sending me Mrs Meynell's volume,[1] though I had already seen it. But my unwillingness remains, because it is not due to any doubt of the possibility of deluding the public, by printing and binding and so on, into the belief that it is getting its money's worth, but to my own notions of what is proper. However, I shall be contributing a new piece shortly to a MS anthology which is being got up,[2] and in due season I will send you this drop of water to moisten your parched tongue.[3]

Yours sincerely
A. E. Housman.

Fitzwilliam MS Autogr. 3/1-1946. Maas, 162.

---

[1] *A Tribute to Thomas Hardy O.M.*, to which AEH contributed *Oh stay at home, my lad, and plough* (*LP* XXXVIII).

[1] *A Father of Women and Other Poems* (1917).

[2] See the previous letter.

[3] Luke 16: 24 (the rich man in hell): 'send Lazarus, that he may dip the tip of his finger in water, and cool my tongue; for I am tormented in this flame'.

TO GRANT RICHARDS

Trinity College | Cambridge
6 June 1919.

My dear Richards,

Mr Armstrong[1] may have what he wants.

It is extremely good of you to have taken so much trouble to get me *The Young Visiters*,[2] which I have begun to read, and have come to a delicious passage about a Sinister Son of Queen Victoria's.[3] Also I am glad to have Oldmeadow's article, which I had missed.

Yours sincerely
A. E. Housman.

On the 11th I am going away, probably for a month. I shall not try to get abroad till late in August.

LC-GR MS. Richards, 165 (incomplete).

TO MESSRS GRANT RICHARDS LTD

Lansdown Grove Hotel | Bath
18 June 1919

Dear Sirs,

Mr Sheridan can publish the songs as he desires.

Yours faithfully
A. E. Housman.

BMC MS.

TO HENRY JACKSON

[Trinity College
14 July 1919]

The present year, in which your eightieth birthday has been followed by your retirement from the office of Vice-Master, affords the Fellows of your College a suitable opportunity of expressing in symbol their affection for yourself and their sense of the services to the foundation which received you more than sixty years ago.

---

[1] Thomas H. W. Armstrong included a setting of *ASL* XL (*Into my heart an air that kills*) in his *Five Short Songs* (1920).

[2] *The Young Visiters; or, Mr Salteena's Plan* (1919), by the nine-year-old Daisy Ashford.

[3] The Prince of Wales, whom Mr Salteena meets in ch. 6.

We therefore ask you to accept from us,[1] as some token of these feelings, a copy of a vessel from which your most industrious predecessor in the Chair of Greek[2] is thought to have derived a solace not unknown or unwelcome to its present occupant; and we trust that the figure of Porson's tobacco-jar may often meet your eyes, and bring us before your mind, in moments tranquillised by its contents.

Our tribute carries with it the personal affection of friends and the gratitude of a community. From the day when first you were elected a Fellow of the College, no measure has been undertaken for the promotion of its welfare or the increase of its efficiency which has not been furthered by your zeal or due to your initiative. In Trinity, in Cambridge, in the whole academic world and far beyond it, you have earned a name on the lips of men and a place in their hearts to which few or none in the present or the past can make pretension. And this eminence you owe not only or chiefly to the fame of your learning and the influence of your teaching, nor even to that abounding and proverbial hospitality which for many a long year has made your rooms the hearthstone of the Society[3] and a guesthouse in Cambridge for pilgrims from the ends of the earth, but to the broad and true humanity of your nature, endearing you alike to old and young, responsive to all varieties of character or pursuit, and remote from nothing that concerns mankind.[4] The College which you have served and adorned so long, proud as it is of your intellect and attainments, and grateful for your devotion, is happy above all that in possessing you it possesses one of the great English worthies.

TCC Add. MS c. 32.49–54. The address and date, the salutation 'Dear Jackson', and the subscription 'We are | Your affectionate friends' are in another hand. Privately printed by CUP (1919), then in R. St John Parry, Henry Jackson (1926), 115. Maas, 162–3.

[1] AEH prepared the letter for signature by the Master and Fellows of TCC. See AEH to R. St John Parry, 3 Jan. 1920, on the pains it cost him.

[2] Richard Porson (1759–1808). Educated at TCC, 1778–81; MA, 1785; Regius Professor of Greek, 1792–1808. Publications include edns. of Euripides' *Hecuba* (1797, 1802), *Orestes* (1798), *Phoenissae* (1799), and *Medea* (1801), his second edn. of *Hecuba* being famous for a supplement to the preface in which he outlines rules of iambic and trochaic verse. AEH held Porson in very high regard as a scholar: see his review of Bywater's *Four centuries of Greek Learning in England* (1920) in *CR* 34 (1920), 110, repr. in *Selected Prose*, 120–3, and in *Classical Papers*, 1004–6.

[3] Of the Masters and Fellows of TCC.

[4] Terence, *Heauton Timorumenos*, 77: *Homo sum; humani nil a me alienum puto* ('I am a man, I count nothing human foreign to me').

TO MARIA RICHARDS

Trinity College | Cambridge
15 July 1919

Dear Mrs Richards,

On returning here after a month's holiday I found awaiting me the screens which you have been kind enough to make for my reading-lamp and candles. They beautify my surroundings very much, and I am very grateful to you for your skill and amiability.

I hope you and Grant are well.

Yours sincerely
A. E. Housman.

BMC MS. Richards, 165; Maas, 163 (nearly complete).

TO GRANT RICHARDS

[Trinity College | Cambridge
21 July 1919

My dear Richards

...] I am afraid we are not likely to travel together nor even to meet. I took a month's change at midsummer, which I was much in need of, and now I have settled down to work: and also I rather think that August heat in France might put my health out of order again. So I am thinking of starting on Aug. 28 or perhaps Sept. 2.

As it appears that a military permit is still required for Paris I should be glad if you could tell me whether your friend is still in power and prepared to make things easy for me. Moreover I am not clear whether, after leaving Paris for the South, one can re-enter it without further trouble.

Most likely I shall not stay long at Brive or any other place, but motor about. After my sacrifices for my country during the war[1] I am beginning to spend money on myself instead of saving it up for the Welsh miners.[2]

Please keep me informed of your plans, and let me know when you come back, as I ought to have the text and notes of Manilius IV ready before I go, and they may as well be printing while I am away.

I hope you will all enjoy yourselves.

[Yours sincerely
A. E. Housman.]

Richards, 165. Maas, 163–4.

---

[1] LH, *Memoir*, 106: 'At the beginning of the War he sent the Chancellor a donation of several hundred pounds'.

[2] Who were threatening a strike in protest at new income tax regulations.

TO GRANT RICHARDS

[Trinity College | Cambridge
23 July 1919

My dear Richards,]
    Thanks for your note.

As the post now goes to Germany, will you please send copies of my Manilius book III to the six addresses enclosed? Though I observe that one is in Austria, which probably is still out of bounds.

[Yours sincerely
A. E. Housman.]

Richards, 166.

TO J. C. SQUIRE

Trinity College | Cambridge
20 Aug. 1919.

Dear Mr Squire,
    I wish well to your enterprise,[1] and I am sensible of the compliment you pay me, but all the same I am keeping my few poems in the desk for the present, and I don't think I am likely to publish anything in periodicals unless I should happen to be inspired by current events.

I am yours sincerely
A. E. Housman.

BMC MS.

TO GRANT RICHARDS

Trinity College | Cambridge
21 Aug. 1919

My dear Richards,
    You are my guardian angel. I enclose my passport, which I only received yesterday, together with <an> \two/ extra photographs (as Cook[1] says that is the proper number) and postal order for 8/-, in order that you may try to get me the French visa. The day I intend to cross

---

[1] In 1919 Squire founded, and began work as editor of, the monthly literary periodical *The London Mercury.*

[1] Thomas Cook & Sons, tour operators.

is Sept. 2. I am glad you are back safe and I hope you enjoyed yourself all right.

Yours sincerely
A. E. Housman.

LC-GR MS. Richards, 166.

TO GRANT RICHARDS

[Trinity College | Cambridge
24 August 1919

My dear Richards,]
Your office has very kindly and dexterously secured me the French visa, but unluckily it is for Boulogne, whereas I am going by Dieppe. I ought to have mentioned this particular, but I did not think of it. I do not know if the Consulate is like Pontius Pilate and refuses to alter what it has written;[1] but in the hope that this is not so I am again enclosing the passport, if I can ask you to try to get it amended. As this is Sunday and there are no postal orders about, I enclose a 10/- note, in case it is wanted.

I shall have to come to town some day this week; and if there is any day (other than Saturday) on which you could lunch with me at the Café Royal, I wish you would let me know what day it is, and would also engage a table there in my name.

[Yours sincerely
A. E. Housman.]

Richards, 166; Maas, 164.

TO GRANT RICHARDS

Trinity College | Cambridge
25 Aug. 1919

My dear Richards,
Not knowing you were in Cornwall, I wrote to you yesterday to ask you to lunch with me in town some day this week; but that must be for another time.

There was nothing in my former letter that it was necessary for you to see. I said that you were my guardian angel, which I may now repeat. Your

---

[1] John 19: 22: 'Pilate answered, What I have written I have written.'

information will be useful to me whether I am obliged to go by Boulogne, or whether I go by Dieppe as I had intended. The passport has been visé for the former route, and I don't know if that can be altered, though I have sent it back to you at your office on the chance. I have engaged a room at the Terminus Hotel St Lazare.

The text and notes of Manilius IV will be ready for printing by the end of this week. Shall I send them to your office?

I hope you and your family have enjoyed and are enjoying yourselves.

Yours sincerely
A. E. Housman.

LC-GR MS. Richards, 166–7.

TO SIR CHARLES WALSTON

Trinity College | Cambridge
27 Aug. 1919

My dear Walston,

I am afraid I shall not be able even to look at your poems before I go, as I am occupied not only with preparing for the journey but with finishing a book which I want to send to the printers before leaving England.

I will therefore leave them for you at our Porter's Lodge, unless you think they will be safe in my desk till I come back,—before the end of September.

I am yours sincerely
A. E. Housman.

Private MS.

TO GRANT RICHARDS

Trinity College | Cambridge
29 Aug. 1919

My dear Richards,

I have sent Manilius IV to your Office. I leave here on Monday morning, and down to the next Sunday I expect to be at Hotel[1] Terminus St Lazare; after that, letters addressed to me at Cambridge will be forwarded from time to time.

I am going by Dieppe because the hotel is at the Paris station of that line. Besides, I crossed with you from Folkestone to Dieppe without

---

[1] For 'Hôtel'.

discomfort,—though that may have been due to your magic presence. The visa has been put right.

It would certainly be very agreeable to stay a couple of nights at Bigfrith on my way home, if nothing intervenes. I expect to come back about the 25th.

Yours sincerely
A. E. Housman.

This vol. of Manilius, apart from the rise in prices, is likely to be more expensive than I or II (let alone III, which was short), because it contains a larger proportion of notes, which I suppose are the most expensive part.

LC-GR MS. Richards, 167; Maas, 164–5.

TO GRANT RICHARDS

[Brive
14 September 1919

My dear Richards,]

If you do not intervene to prevent it, what will happen is this. On Wednesday the 24th I shall arrive at Bigfrith some time in the afternoon, in a motor which will deposit me with a small bag, containing little except a clean shirt, and will take my larger luggage on to Cambridge, and there you will have me for two nights.

I am returning to Paris, Hôtel Terminus St Lazare, on Thursday the 18th. There I shall be till Tuesday the 23rd, when I shall cross, and sleep at Newhaven. I should like to hear from you as soon as I reach Paris, because I shall have to write to Cambridge about the motor.

The passage of the Channel was as good as could be.

[Yours sincerely
A. E. Housman.]

Richards, 167; Maas, 165.

TO GRANT RICHARDS

Hôtel Terminus
19 Sept. 1919

My dear Richards,

This is a great pleasure, apart from its unexpectedness.[1] It will be no good looking for me here this evening, and I am also engaged to-morrow evening and Monday evening: otherwise I have no tie. Usually I leave the hotel not long after 9 <p> \a/.m., and tomorrow I will look you up at the Normandy soon after that time, unless I hear from you to the contrary.

Yours sincerely
A. E. Housman.

LC-GR MS. Richards, 168; Maas, 165.

TO GRANT RICHARDS

Trinity College | Cambridge
27 Sept. 1919

My dear Richards,

I enclose cheque for £100. Whether I shall post this letter to-day is uncertain, as I had better wait to see what effect the strike has on the post.[1] My *New Statesman* arrived this morning as usual.

I began to read *Antonio*[2] in the train and found it quite interesting.

I hope neither you nor Mrs Richards are suffering much from the cold you caught from me, which lies heavy on my conscience, as I do not like to return evil for so much kindness.

Yours sincerely
A. E. Housman.

LC-GR MS. Richards, 168 (incomplete); Maas, 165–6.

[1] GR unexpectedly had business in Paris: Richards, 167–8.

[1] A railway strike from 26 Sept. to 5 Oct. caused the suspension of the parcel post.

[2] Novel by Ernest Oldmeadow, 1914. It deals with Portugal and the wine trade.

TO JACQUELINE T. TROTTER

Trinity College | Cambridge
27 Sept. 1919

Dear Madam,

I have been abroad all the month and unable to answer your letter before. I now return the copy of the poem,[1] corrected, and I am happy to allow you to reprint it.[2] No other permission is required.

The poem appeared in the *Times* of October 31, 1917, the third anniversary of the battle of Ypres.[3]

I am yours truly
A. E. Housman.

Miss Trotter.

The King's School Canterbury MS.

TO ELIZABETH OPPENHEIM

Trinity College
8 Oct. 1919

Dear Mrs Oppenheim,

I have heard with great regret of the illness and death of Professor Oppenheim,[1] and I beg you to accept my sincere sympathy both with you and with your daughter in your great loss. I am afraid this is one of the calamities which we owe to the war, which from the very first was a great grief and shock to your husband, as I could easily see when he spoke to me about it.[2]

I am yours sincerely
A. E. Housman.

Copy of the MS kindly provided for inspection by Charles Cox Rare Books, 12 Jan. 2006.

---

[1] *Epitaph on an Army of Mercenaries* (later *LP* XXXVII).

[2] In her anthology *Valour and Vision: Poems of the War 1914–1918* (1920), where it was printed correctly.

[3] Below a leading article entitled 'The Anniversary of Ypres'.

[1] See List of Recipients. He died the day before at home in Cambridge.

[2] Professor Oppenheim was German, but he had resided in England since 1895, taken British citizenship in 1900, married an English wife, and supported the British war effort. In *The Times*, 19 May 1915, he denounced the German attack on Belgium as 'the greatest international crime since Napoleon I'.

TO GRANT RICHARDS

[Trinity College | Cambridge
9 Oct 1919

My dear Richards,]

I have not finished Proust's book,[1] but I have read enough to form the opinion that an English translation would not sell,[2] and, apart from that, could not be really satisfactory, as the merit of the French is in great part a matter of diction and vocabulary. Moreover, the 2nd section of the book, in which I am now rather stuck, is not at all equal to the first. The 2nd volume, I am told, is not good.

[Yours sincerely
A. E. Housman.]

Text based on that in Richards, 168; Maas, 166.

TO THOMAS HARDY

Trinity College | Cambridge
17 Oct. 1919

Dear Mr Hardy,

As you deny us the light of your countenance, your handwriting is more welcome than ever; and it is kind of you to let me know that you liked my poem.[1] It is one which has not been published, as I thought was only proper. I was glad to hear a good account of you not long ago from S. <G>C. Cockerell.

Your College,[2] as perhaps you know, is lamenting not only your absence but that of its Master,[3] who has been kept away more than two years by obstinate depression of spirits, and is a great loss to Cambridge.

---

[1] *A La Recherche Du Temps Perdu* by Marcel Proust (1871–1922). It was published in seven sections, 1913–27. Section 1, *Du Côté De Chez Swann* (*Swann's Way*) was reissued in one vol. (1917), then in two (1919); section 2, *A L'ombre Des Jeunes Filles en Fleurs* (*Within A Budding Grove*), was published in one vol. in 1918. There was an English translation by C. K. Scott-Moncrieff and Stephen Hudson, *Remembrance Of Things Past*, 1922–31.
[2] GR's view (Richards, 168) that 'experience would ... lead the one or two publishers who tried translations of Proust on the English public ... to endorse Housman's opinion' is puzzling in view of the success of the Scott-Moncrieff/Hudson translation published by Chatto and Windus.

[1] See AEH to Sassoon, 23 May 1919, and note.
[2] Magdalene College, Cambridge, to which Hardy was admitted as Honorary Fellow in Nov. 1913 following Cambridge's award of the Honorary D.Litt. in June 1913. AEH was present as a guest when Hardy was admitted as Honorary Fellow.
[3] A. C. Benson. See List of Recipients.

Please give my kind regards to Mrs Hardy, whom I had the pleasure of meeting once at C. W. Moule's,[4] and believe me always sincerely yours

A. E. Housman.

Dorset County Museum MS.

TO M. R. JAMES

Trinity College | Cambridge
27 Oct. 1919

My dear James,

I am no good for any of your enquiries. As to *Menestrates*, I can only wonder whether he had got hold of some MS (of Ovid?) in which this appeared as a corruption of *Menoetiades*,[1] who is the only eminent person with a similar name whom I can think of.

I don't know what the Rifle Brigade have done with their number, which used to be the 96th, if I remember.[2] I suppose the traitor Haldane[3] took it away, to enfeeble the spirit of the British Army. *Legio Principis Consortis propria*[4] is a possibility, but you had better try it on an individual before you fling it at the brigade. I am delighted to hear what the Latin for a rifle is:[5] the Latin for gunpowder I learnt from Newton's *Principia*,[6] and now what I chiefly want to know is the Latin for a Tank.

Yours sincerely
A. E. Housman.

CUL Add. MS 7481/H129.

[4] Charles Walter Moule (1834–1921), Tutor at Corpus Christi College, Cambridge, 1879–92, and Librarian, 1895–1913, was one of Hardy's oldest friends.

[1] i.e. 'son of Menoetius', Patroclus, mentioned in Ovid, *Heroides*, 1. 17. James was evidently wondering, even five years after publishing his edn., about the Menestrates paired with Hannibal as a great man of old by Walter Map, *De nugis curialium*, Distinctio 5, ch. 1. In the re-edition by C. N. L. Brooke and R. A. B. Mynors (Oxford 1983), xxxv f., the name is taken to be fictitious.

[2] It was the 95th Regiment of Foot that became in 1916 the Rifle Brigade, and the change had nothing to do with Haldane.

[3] Richard Burdon, first Viscount Haldane (1856–1928). As Secretary for War (1905–12) in Asquith's Liberal government he introduced reforms of the army, among which were the formation of the militia into a special reserve, the creation of the Officers' Training Corps, and the improvement of medical and nursing services under the Territorial system. After being created viscount (1911) and becoming Lord Chancellor (1912), he returned to the War Office in 1914, but public suspicions over his liking for Germany and German philosophy eventually led to his dismissal in 1915.

[4] 'The Prince Consort's Own Brigade'. In 1862, the year after the death of Albert, the Prince Consort, the Rifle Brigade became 'The Prince Consort's Own Rifle Brigade'. Albert had been Colonel-in-Chief of the Rifle Brigade since 1852.

[5] scopletum striatum.

[6] pulvis tormentarius. In Defintions, V, in the 1713 edn. of *Principia Mathematica*, Newton speaks of a lead weight 'vi pulveris tormentarii projectus'. AEH makes reference to the *Principia* in the Cambridge Inaugural Lecture of 1911: Ricks (1988), 304.

TO GRANT RICHARDS

Trinity College | Cambridge
28 Oct. 1919

My dear Richards,

I do not feel very like coming to Newmarket,[1] and I ought to attend a meeting on Thursday afternoon for which 4. 18 would be too late. Moreover I do not think I gave the 'promise' you speak of, unless I was more drunk than I remember being.

As you are returning the same day, I suppose it is no use offering you any hospitality, and I am afraid I could not find you a bed in College at short notice in our present state of over-population; but if you stayed the night in the town I should be very glad to have you as my guest at dinner.

In any case I hope that Newmarket will yield what you want from it.[2]

Yours sincerely
A. E. Housman.

PM MS. LC-GR t.s. Richards, 169.

TO GRANT RICHARDS

Trinity College | Cambridge
7 Nov. 1919

My dear Richards,

If you give me Simon's book[1] it will be very good of you. I enclose the poem.[2] The poems were not supposed to be *addressed* to Hardy, only specimens of our stuff, published or unpublished.

Yours sincerely
A. E. Housman.

LC-GR MS. Richards, 169; Mass, 166.

[1] 'To a race-meeting': Richards, 169.
[2] 'I myself was going with a view to getting material for a novel, *Double Life*': Richards, 169.

[1] André Simon, *Wine and Spirits: The Connoisseur's Textbook* (1919).
[2] See AEH to Sassoon, 23 May 1919, and note.

TO H. W. GARROD

Trinity College | Cambridge
26 Nov. 1919

Dear Mr Garrod,

I am grateful for the gift of your interesting and spirited book of poems,[1] and I am glad that the locust and the rest of the Lord's great army have not eaten all the last four years.[2] I hope too that you will not perish untimely by the fury of undergraduates.[3]

Yours very truly
A. E. Housman.

SJCO MS, Sparrow Collection. Envelope addressed 'H. W. Garrod Esq. C.B.E. | Merton College | Oxford'. Maas, 167.

TO GRANT RICHARDS

[Trinity College | Cambridge
30 November 1919

My dear Richards,]

I had thought of 6/- net as the price for Manilius IV. Of course the increase in the cost of production is greater than that, but I have always sold at less than cost price, so it does not make the difference between profit and loss.

This reminds me that it is just 3 months since I sent you the manuscript, and I wonder when the printers are going to start upon it.

Thanks for the book on wines:[1] but mortal passions have invaded the sacred precincts of the cellar to such an extent that he knows of no German or Hungarian wine[2] and does know of stuff from Australia and California.

[Yours sincerely
A. E. Housman.]

Richards, 169–70, Maas, 167.

[1] *Worms and Epitaphs* (1919). The *Epilogue* (pp. 53–5), praises *ASL*: 'No one else of modern men | Moved us much, save now and then | We met a wandering Shropshire Lad | Three parts melancholy mad: | But ah! how sweet of what he sang | Here and there the music rang!'

[2] Joel 2: 25: 'And I will restore to you the years that the locust hath eaten, the cankerworm, and the caterpiller, and the palmerworm, my great army which I sent among you'.

[3] *Intruders*, a poem in the book, expresses resentment at current undergraduates taking the places of those killed in the war: 'I hate your steps upon the stair, | Your vacant voices on the air. | Who asked you to come back at all, | Or why should bayonet and ball | Be kind to skins like yours, and then | Put out the lives of better men?'

[1] See AEH to GR, 7 Nov. 1919, and note.

[2] Richards, 170 n., blames the publisher (Gerald Duckworth) rather than the author (André Simon) for the omissions.

TO J. S. PHILLIMORE

Trinity College | Cambridge
30 Nov. 1919

Dear Phillimore,

I am very much in your debt for the gift of your address,[1] and am glad that I did not miss it by not hearing it delivered. It contains a great deal of truth well and tellingly said, together with some things which I do not assent to. <Some of> <y>Your strictures on German scholarship[2] <seem to> have \something of/ the intemperate zeal of the convert, like attacks on the Church of Rome by runaway monks. I should say that for the last 100 years \individual/ German scholars have been the superiors in genius \<and tact>/ as well as learning \<and industry>/ of all scholars outside Germany except Madvig and Cobet;[3] and that the \herd or group/ vices of the German school which you particularly reprehend took their rise from Sedan,[4] \<which drew Germanic editing [?] >/ and may be expected to decline after this second and greater Jena:[5] though indeed they have already been declining since the <opening> \early years/ of the century. There are some of your examples which do not at all convince me: for instance on p. 19 the required jingle is not procured unless the locative *Romai* was a trisyllable.[6] I thought pp. 7–8 very good and salutary.[7]

Yours sincerely
A. E. Housman.

TCC Add. MS c. 112[9]: ink, corrected in ink and pencil. Gow, 31 n. (excerpt); Maas, 167–8.

[1] 'The Revival of Criticism', delivered to the Classical Association at Oxford, 17 May 1919, and published in 1919 by B. H. Blackwell. AEH is praised three times in it (6, 27, 31).

[2] In particular, the 'effort to disestablish chance, reducing everything to mechanics', 'fatuity', and reading only themselves and shamelessly appropriating the ideas of others without acknowledgement (5, 6).

[3] Dutch editor and grammarian (1813–89).

[4] The Battle of Sedan, fought on 1 Sept. 1870, resulted in victory for King William I of Prussia over the French, and led to the end of the French Empire and the establishment of the Third Republic. Phillimore claimed (4) that 'Every sort of prestige radiates from victory; the battle of Sedan sold the Teubners'.

[5] i.e. the First World War. Napoleon Bonaparte defeated the Prussians in the Battle of Jena, 14 Oct. 1806.

[6] In *Fato fiunt Metelli consules Romai*, proposed by Phillimore as a replacement for *Fato Metelli Romae fiunt consules*, on grounds that 'It carries away a senarius and substitutes a Saturnian; it gives a verse which jingles exactly with the retort (surely a point in parody) and offers a characteristic alliteration and grouping of words.' The point is that *ai* is an archaic spelling for classical *ae*, but in the dative and the locative still represents a diphthong, whereas in the genitive the old writers know a disyllabic form (still occasionally used by Virgil) in which *a* and *i* are two separate long vowels.

[7] On a 'disintegration of criticism ... during the last century'.

TO GRANT RICHARDS

[Trinity College | Cambridge
2 December 1919

My dear Richards,]

No; Manilius I, II, III and Juvenal should be sold at the old price.[1]

If it is now possible to improve the binding of Manil. III and make it correspond with I and II, that should be done.

The blind may have *A Shropshire Lad* in Braille.

[Yours sincerely
A. E. Housman.]

Richards, 170.

TO LAURENCE HOUSMAN

Trinity College | Cambridge
4 Dec. 1919

My dear Laurence,

I have not thanked you as I should for the trilogy[1] you sent me on Nov. 17, but I have not been able to read it through at leisure till lately. You do not need to be told that there is a good deal to admire in it; and there are passages, such as the last four lines,[2] which I like very much. But as to the style in general I cannot do better than copy out a couple of sentences from a review of mine:[3] "In the sixties it seemed indeed as if there had arisen a band of writers to launch poetry on a new career; but time showed that they were cruising in a backwater, not finding a channel for the main stream, and in twenty years all heart had gone out of the enterprise. The fashions of that interlude are already so antique that Mr Gilbert Murray can adopt them for his rendering of Euripides; and there they now receive academic approbation, which is the second death."[4] As to the moral rules incumbent on gods and men, they alter as time goes on, but do not improve, though each age in succession thinks its own rules right. My own sense of

[1] 'In answer to a suggestion of mine that his earlier Latin books should have a shilling or so added to their price so that all would cost the same': Richards, 170.

[1] *The Wheel: A Dramatic Trilogy* (1919).

[2] 'Yonder, to cover mine eyes, | Grass grows, and the green leaves wave: | And the gold of the sun lies there, | All bright and at rest.'

[3] Of vols. XIII and XIV of *The Cambridge History of English Literature* in *The Cambridge Review*, 38. 954 (23 May 1917), 358–60. *Selected Prose*, 114–20; Ricks (1988), 319–24.

[4] Murray's translations were done in 1902, 1905, 1906, 1910, 1913, and 1915, and enjoyed considerable theatrical success. 'The second death': Rev. 2: 11, 20: 6, 14, 21: 8.

propriety however is not so much offended by anything you have taken from the ancient story as by your scuttling Alcestis at Scapa Flow on p. 74.[5]

I hear from Kate that you are leaving for America on the 30th, and I wish you a pleasant and prosperous tour. If they pay you in dollars you ought to come back rich.

Your affectionate brother
A. E. Housman.

BMC MS. Memoir, 176–7; Maas, 168.

?TO LOUIS UNTERMEYER

Trinity College | Cambridge | England
8 Dec. 1919

My dear Sir,

I take it very kindly of you that you should write to me about my books, especially as there are not very many who find pleasure, as you do, both in my poems and in my editions of the classics. If you are good enough to send me the work on Horace of which you speak,[1] I shall be glad and grateful.

I am yours very truly
A. E. Housman.

Princeton MS (Gen. MSS. Misc.). Maas, 169.

TO GRANT RICHARDS

[Trinity College | Cambridge
10 December 1919

My dear Richards,]

I suppose I ought to congratulate you on having at last sold off your pet edition.[1] So far as I remember, the text was correct.[2]

[Yours sincerely
A. E. Housman.]

Richards, 170.

---

[5] In Part 3. On 21 June 1919, the German high seas fleet had been scuttled at the naval base of Scapa Flow in the Orkneys.

[1] Ably identified by Maas, 169 n., as Untermeyer's *Including Horace* (1919), which in turn prompted his identification of the probable recipient of the letter.

[1] Of *ASL* (1908), with illustrations by William Hyde.

[2] In fact, in a copy now in Lilly (PR 4809.H15 S5 1908), which bears AEH's signature on the title-page, he removed a comma after 'stay' in *ASL* XIX 10.

TO GRANT RICHARDS

[Trinity College | Cambridge
16 December 1919

My dear Richards,]

This is molestation and persecution. You sent me the proofs to correct when the edition was preparing,[1] and when you do that there are practically no errors. I am too full at this moment of more interesting work to waste my time trying to find mistakes where none are likely to be. Besides, I have a copy of the edition, probably more than one.

If you do not like illustrations, why did you print this edition? It was all your doing, none of mine; and I thought the public quite right in not buying it.

[Yours sincerely
A. E. Housman.]

Richards, 170; Maas, 169.

TO MARIA RICHARDS

Trinity College | Cambridge
21 Dec. 1919

Dear Mrs Richards,

Many thanks for your gift of walnuts and deliciously scented apples. I am glad to see that your garden has prospered and that the children of the neighbourhood have not taken all the fruit. We are looking forward to the winter without much fear, as the Government has just allowed the Colleges quite a good coal ration. Tell Grant that I am eating and drinking a great deal, as there are many Feasts of one sort and another.

Yours sincerely
A. E. Housman.

BMC MS. Richards, 170–1; Maas, 169 (both nearly complete; neither with the exact date).

---

[1] GR was reprinting the 1908 illustrated edn. of *ASL*, originally issued in 2,000 copies. 'It had been designed as a gift-book edition and appeared just in time for the Christmas season. But it had little success as a gift-book': Richards, 84–5. For AEH's correction of the proofs, see the letter to GR, 27 June 1908; for his dislike of the edn., see the letter to GR, 8 Nov. 1908.

1920

TO GRANT RICHARDS

[Trinity College | Cambridge
2 January 1920

My dear Richards,]

The instalment of Manilius which I received yesterday consisted of 8 slips; but with them came not only the corresponding 46 pages of MS, but also 10 more pages of MS with no slips to correspond. So now I expect there will be a long pause, and when the printers are asked about it they will say they are held up by having unfortunately mislaid pp. 47–56 of the author's MS. Or possibly there are 2 slips more which they have omitted to send.

As to your note about the binding, that does not matter very much, but I hope the sort of paper on which the book is printed is still to be had.

A happy new year to you and all your family.

[Yours sincerely
A. E. Housman.]

Richards, 172.

TO REGINALD ST JOHN PARRY

Trinity College
3 Jan. 1920

My dear Parry,

I must begin with grateful acknowledgement to you and my other friends, because I could not read your letter without feelings which had some pure pleasure in them; but this was swallowed up in surprise, and surprise itself was engulfed in horror.

Not if the stipend were £150,000 instead of £150 would I be Public Orator.[1] I could not discharge the duties of the office without abandoning

---

[1] Naiditch (2005), 25–6, stresses that, contrary to common belief, AEH declined to stand for the post: he did not decline it. See AEH to Cornford, 3 May 1920. Sir John Sandys (1844–1922), Greek scholar and Fellow of St John's College, held the post from 1876 until his retirement in 1919, delivering in that time some 700 speeches presenting eminent men for honorary degrees at Cambridge. His successor was T. R. Glover (see List of Recipients), who served until 1939.

all other duties and bidding farewell to such peace of mind as I possess. You none of you have any notion what a slow and barren mind I have, nor what a trouble composition is to me (in prose, I mean: poetry is either easy or impossible). When the job is done, it may have a certain amount of form and finish and perhaps a false air of ease; but there is an awful history behind it. The letter to Jackson last year[2] laid waste three whole mornings: the first, I sat staring in front of me and wishing for death; the second, I wrote down disjointed phrases and sentences which looked loathsome; the third, after a night in which I suppose my subliminal self had been busy, I had some relief in fitting them together and finding they could be improved into something respectable. I can stand this once in a way; but to be doing it often, and have it always hanging over one, and in connexion with subjects much less congenial than Jackson, I could not bear.

The University has been very good to me, and has given me a post in which I have duties which are not disagreeable, and opportunity for studies which I enjoy, and in which I can hope to do the University credit; and I should not really be doing it a good turn if I sacrificed that work, as I must, to the performance, even if more efficient than mine would be, of the duties of the Orator.

Do not think this an unkind reply to a kind letter. I have also written to Jackson, as an interview would be useless, and distressing to both of us.

Yours sincerely
A. E. Housman.

TCC Add. MS c. 112[10]. Memoir, 109–10; Maas, 170.

TO MESSRS GRANT RICHARDS LTD

Trinity College | Cambridge
10 Jan. 1920

Dear Sirs,

Messrs Boosey are at liberty to publish Mr Manson's settings of "the three poems they mention".[1]

Yours faithfully
A. E. Housman.

Messrs Grant Richards Ld.
LC-GR MS. LC-GR t.s.

---

[2] 14 July 1919.

[1] Settings of *When I came last to Ludlow, Loveliest of trees,* and *Think no more, lad* by Willie [Braithwaite] Manson (1896–1916) were published in 1920, though they had first been performed on 26 July 1917 at London's Steinway Hall. See Peter Downes, 'Willie B. Manson and *A Shropshire Lad*', *HSJ* 30 (2004), 135–41.

TO DR PERCY WITHERS

Trinity College | Cambridge
18 Jan. 1920

My dear Withers,

I was very glad to hear from you at Christmas, and had intended to reply at the New Year, but I suppose the free luncheon of boar's head &c. which prevails in this College from Yule to Epiphany made me sleepy. Perhaps the new University Commission[1] will put a stop to it.

I was in the Cotswolds for a fortnight at midsummer, but no nearer to you than Stroud. September I spent in France, partly in Paris but mostly at Brive in the Limousin, a very beautiful neighbourhood, with some nice though not large Romanesque churches about. I found a proprietor of a garage who was a great connoisseur of the local scenery and delighted to take me by the best routes to the best spots; and the weather was just right for motoring and too hot for anything else.

I am glad to hear we may expect to see you here again some day. At present in term-time the place is very crowded, and in college the undergraduates are packed two or even three in a box.

Last year I think I wrote two poems,[2] which is more than the average, but not much towards a new volume.

My kind regards to Mrs Withers. I hope you will both enjoy yourselves in Italy; but as there is said to be no coal in that country you had better not start too soon.

Yours sincerely
A. E. Housman.

SCO MS. Withers, 47 (excerpt); Maas, 170–1.

[1] Set up in 1919 to investigate the organization of the universities and their allocation of public funds. The report (1922) brought no substantial change.

[2] Drafts of *Epitaph on an Army of Mercenaries*, written in Sept. 1917 and published in *The Times* on 31 Oct. 1917, are recorded by LH as being on pp. 92–3 of *Nbk C* (*Memoir*, 269) and *Oh, were he and I together* (*AP* II) on pp. 94–5. (The MS of pages 93 and 94 was sold at Sotheby's, London, on 27 May 2004: see Archie Burnett, 'Fastidious Housman', *TLS*, 25 June 2004, 13. AEH told Cockerell that *LP* XV (*Eight O' Clock*) dated from 1921 (*TLS*, 7 Nov. 1936; Richards, 437), and substantial evidence of the drafts LH records on *Nbk C* 96–9 does survive, though there are some problems with his pagination or his record of contents. AEH's statements to Withers and to Cockerell are therefore at odds with each other, and as the first date written by him in *Nbk D* is '30 March 1922' on p. 15, it is not possible to identify the 'two poems' he thought he had written in 1919.

TO GRANT RICHARDS

Trinity College | Cambridge
21 Jan. 1920

My dear Richards,

The translation[1] is literal, as he claims for it, except where it is a mis-translation, as it now and then is; and it is not affected or pretentious. But it is a very commonplace affair, and both the diction and the verse are poor.

Yours sincerely
A. E. Housman.

LC-GR t.s. Richards, 172; Maas, 171.

TO AN UNKNOWN CORRESPONDENT

Trinity College | Cambridge | England
22 Jan. 1920

My dear Sir,

Let me thank you very sincerely for your second gift, which also contains interesting matter, though, as you say, it is a slighter work than Miss Goad's.[1]

I am yours very truly
A. E. Housman.

Yale MS.

TO HENRY FESTING JONES

Trinity College | Cambridge
1 Feb. 1920

Dear Mr Festing Jones,

I shall be delighted if you will dine with me in Hall on Sunday the 15th. On Sundays we have more company than on other days, and generally a better dinner. We dine at 8 and do not dress. It would be well if you would come about 10 minutes before the time to my rooms, which are distant from the Hall: they are over the Sidney Street entrance of Whewell's Court.

I am yours sincerely
A. E. Housman.

Wellesley MS. Tipped-in on inner lining leaf of front cover of complimentary copy of the first edition of LP *(1922) sent by AEH to Henry Festing Jones.*

[1] Unpublished, of poems from *ASL* into French: Richards, 172.

[1] *Horace in the Literature of the Eighteenth Century* by Caroline [Mabel] Goad, *Yale Studies in English*, 58 (1918), which is 646 pages long.

TO A. S. F. GOW

Trinity College | Cambridge
11 Feb. 1920

Dear Gow,

Some scholars are under the impression that Lachmann investigated the frequency of elisions in which the elided syllable ends in *m* and is immediately preceded by a long vowel or diphthong, such as Verg. Aen. V 328 *Ledaeam Hermionen*. He did not; but one might think he ought to have done so in his note on Lucr. III 374, because one would hardly suppose these elisions to be less harsh than those which he there discusses. I have sometimes thought of seeing about it, and perhaps it might be worth your while.

Or you might take I. Hilberg's *Gesetze des Wortstellung im Pentamenter des Ovid*[1] and try how far they apply to the pentameters of other poets, if true.

Or the employment, in Attic tragedy for instance, of forms mostly used for metrical convenience, in places where metre does not require them: e.g. λαός in Eur. frag. 21 1 (Nauck ed. 2^2). Elmsley[3] would have to be consulted.

The seal looks like Boreas flying off with Orithyia; but what is she doing with a lyre?

Yours sincerely
A. E. Housman.

TCC Add. MS c. 112^{11}. Maas, 413–14.

TO A. S. F. GOW

Trinity College | Cambridge
15 Feb. 1920

Dear Gow,

I have filled in the form and will give it to Deighton and Bell.[1]

As to the spondee in the 4th foot, I examined the usage of Propertius in *Journ. Phil.* vol. XXI pp. 150 sq., and Meineke has some remarks on Horace's in his 2nd edition[2] (I have not got the 1st) pp. XXIII sq. I do not think a full collection would lead to anything definite: it is quite clear that

---

[1] Leipzig, 1894. AEH owned a copy: Naiditch (2003), 132.
[2] AEH owned a copy of *Euripidis tragœdiae ex recensione Augusti Nauckii editio tertia uolumen I (–II)* (1876): Naiditch (2002), 61.
[3] Peter Elmsley (1774–1825), whose edns. of Euripides and Sophocles were published in 1821 and 1826 respectively, in addition to his edns. of individual plays.

[1] Cambridge booksellers.   [2] Published in 1854; first edn., 1834.

there was no hard and fast rule, and Cortius[3] made a fool of himself in trying to rob Lucan of variety in the matter.

Yours sincerely
A. E. Housman.

TCC Add. MS c. 112¹². Maas, 414.

TO HENRY FESTING JONES

Trinity College
18 Feb. 1920

Dear Jones,

I return herewith the note-book,[1] in which I have found other unpublished matter worth reading besides the Pauli story,[2] which still remains mysterious.

I suppose you do not know anything about the Mr Griffin who was Pauli's executor. I know, or did know, a man of that name who is a barrister; and I am wondering if I could get any information from that side.

I hope you enjoyed your stay in Cambridge and will soon come again.

Yours very truly
A. E. Housman.

Wellesley MS.

TO ALICE ROTHENSTEIN

Trinity College | Cambridge
21 Feb. 1920

Dear Mrs Rothenstein,

The celestial globe arrived yesterday, and seems to have stood the journey pretty well. I am very grateful for it, and I am now completely equipped for dealing with the 5th book of Manilius, for which I required it: I am now just finishing the 4th.

---

[3] Gottlieb Cortius (1698–1731), whose edn. of Lucan was published in 1726. The point is the Imperial poets' preference for the rhythm *Troiae qui* over the Republican poets' *qui Troiae*. The work of collecting examples and exceptions was done by Friedrich Marx, *Molossische und bakcheische Wortformen in der Verskunst der Griechen und Römer* (Leipzig 1922). Respect for Marx and disrespect for Cortius may be found in AEH's Lucan, xxxii and n.

[1] Almost certainly of Jones's friend the writer and artist Samuel Butler.

[2] Charles Paine Pauli (d. 1897) was a charming rogue whom Butler met in New Zealand. He returned to England at the same time as Butler did, and Butler gave him financial support, discovering only at Pauli's funeral that others had been doing the same.

If you are going to settle at another spot, I hope you will let me know where it is, and I will try not to miss you if I find myself near it.

I daresay you have been as much amused as I was by the life-like portrait of William in Max Beerbohm's last book.[1] He is more successful with the pen than with the pencil in depicting this model.

With the kindest regards to both of you, I am

Yours sincerely
A. E. Housman.

Harvard bMS Eng 1148 (740) 39. Maas, 171–2.

TO J. W. MACKAIL

Trinity College | Cambridge
28 Feb. 1920

Dear Mackail,

I agree that χειρὶ παχείη is not parallel to *ingenti manu* nor τρήρωνα πέλειαν to *uolucrem columbam*, but I do think that XI 556 *dextra ingenti* is parallel to the one and Soph. Ai. 140 πτηνῆσ πελείασ to the other. *ingenti* no doubt is tumid, but in reading Virgil I often cry 'Out, hyperbolical fiend! how vexest thou this man!';[1] and *uolucrem* is useless, but if epic poets are debarred from useless epithets they will never fill their 12 or 24 or 48 books. The magnitude of Serestus' ship is not much to the point, so long as the mast itself was tall, which we are told in 489.

From what I see in the papers, you are to be congratulated on your son's connexion with *The Dynasts* at Oxford.[2]

Yours sincerely
A. E. Housman.

TCC MS R.1.92.3. Hawkins (1958), 187; Maas, 414–15.

---

[1] *Seven Men* (1919), in which Rothenstein is a prominent character in the story *Enoch Soames*. For Beerbohm, see List of Recipients.

[1] *Twelfth Night*, 4. 2. 26.

[2] 'Denis Mackail designed the scenery for the production which opened on 10 February 1920': Maas, 415 n.

TO GRANT RICHARDS

Trinity College | Cambridge
3 March 1920

My dear Richards,

It is a fortnight since I have received any proofs of Manilius IV, though you told me that the printers promised you to send the whole book in proof at the beginning of December.

Yours sincerely
A. E. Housman.

LC-GR t.s. Richards, 172

TO GRANT RICHARDS

Trinity College | Cambridge
19 March 1920

My dear Richards,

Thanks for sending me Mr Armstrong's music,[1] and his civil letter, which I return.

I am sorry you found Italy so bad: some one, I forget who, told me the passport was the only trouble and things were all right when you got there.

I hope you were not too early for the celebrated plenty of rare flowers in Capri. When I was there it was autumn and they were all gone to seed. I stayed at the Hotel Eden at Anacapri, and found it quite satisfactory; but you probably stuck to the lower town at this season.

In a day or two I will send the corrected proofs of the text and notes of Manilius IV, and those of the preface shortly after.

Yours sincerely
A. E. Housman.

LC-GR MS. LC-GR t.s. Richards, 172–3 (incomplete); Maas, 172.

TO GRANT RICHARDS

Trinity College | Cambridge
21 March 1920.

My dear Richards,

I enclose corrected proofs of the entire text and notes of Manilius IV: I shall be obliged if you will acknowledge receipt. The preface shall follow in a few days.

[1] See AEH to GR, 6 June 1919, and n. 1.

In making additions and subtractions I have taken considerable pains to bring the added or subtracted matter to such measurement that no rearrangement of lines, or only the very slightest, will be needed in the surrounding parts. It might be well to call the attention of the printers to this, that they may not hastily make more change than is necessary.

I think I had better see a revise of the notes before they and the text are made up into pages together.

Yours sincerely
A. E. Housman.

LC-GR MS. LC-GR t.s. Richards, 173.

TO A. S. F. GOW

Trinity College | Cambridge
29 March 1920

Dear Gow,

I suppose you would not like to be Professor of Latin at Liverpool?[1] because I think it possible you might be. They have so bad a field that they are making enquiries everywhere: Postgate wrote to me; Harold Butler has also been asked if he can recommend anyone. Although it is not the ideal situation for you, I would rather see you that than a schoolmaster; but you may not agree.

Yours sincerely
A. E. Housman.

TCC Add. MS c. 112¹³. Maas, 172–3.

TO ROBERT BRIDGES

Trinity College | Cambridge
9 April 1920

My dear Bridges,

It is good of you to send me your new volume,[1] and of course I am glad to have it, though I do not expect to be always reading it and carrying it in my head like the first four books of the *Shorter Poems*.[2] You have been

---

[1] The chair became vacant when Postgate retired later in the year. His successor was D. A. Slater.

[1] *October and Other Poems.*

[2] Published in 1873, 1879, 1884, and 1890. AEH owned a copy of the 4th edn. (1894), now in TCC. Several echoes and parallels in AEH's poetry are noted in *Poems* (1997), 321, 325, 332, 352, 408, 415, 430.

spinning down the ringing grooves of change[3] while I have been standing at gaze like Joshua's moon in Ajalon,[4] and the pieces I like best are those which remind me of old times, *Poor Child* and *Fortunatus nimium.*

I am yours sincerely
A. E. Housman.

Bodleian MS, Dep. Bridges 110. 103. Maas, 173.

TO GRANT RICHARDS

Trinity College | Cambridge
13 April 1920

My dear Richards,

By all means. The date which probably would suit me best is May 14, but either April 30 or May 7 would do if they are more convenient to you.

Yours sincerely
A. E. Housman.

LC-GR MS. LC-GR t.s.

TO WILLIAM ROTHENSTEIN

Trinity College | Cambridge
13 April 1920

My dear Rothenstein,

I am sorry if it upsets your arrangements, but I am not going to write literary criticism for you or anyone else; and moreover I should feel awkward and embarrassed in writing about Hardy under his nose.[1] I do not mean that it would violate any principles or general notions which I may happen to have, but it would distress my sensations, which I believe are in some respects morbid.

I sympathise with your feelings about leaving Oakridge, but Campden Hill, I always used to think, must be the best spot inside London to live in.

[3] Tennyson, *Locksley Hall*, 182: 'Let the great world spin for ever down the ringing grooves of change.'

[4] *Locksley Hall*, 180: 'stand at gaze like Joshua's moon in Ajalon!', referring to Joshua 10: 12–13.

[1] Rothenstein had asked AEH for a short piece to accompany his drawing of Hardy in *Twenty-Four Portraits* (1920).

Give my kindest regards to Mrs Rothenstein. I hope I shall see you when you are in Cambridge. I suppose, as your stay is so short, it is no use asking you to any meal here?

Yours sincerely
A. E. Housman

Harvard bMS Eng 1148 (740) 40. Maas, 173.

TO GRANT RICHARDS

Trinity College | Cambridge
14 April 1920

My dear Richards,

I enclose corrected revise of the notes to Manilius IV.

These may now be made up into pages with the text. In doing this, care should be taken that every note *begins* on the page containing the line of text to which it refers. This is not absolutely necessary provided that the page containing the line of text and the page containing the beginning of the note are pages both of which lie before the readers' eyes at the same time; but every effort should be made to avoid having the line of text on one side of a leaf and the beginning of the note on the other.

The preface also may now be put into pages; and I enclose the MS of a page to face the first page of text and notes. I think it ought to be possible to print this so that the word INTERPOLATOR comes out more clearly than it does in some copies of books II and III.

Yours sincerely
A. E. Housman.

LC-GR MS. LC-GR t.s. Richards, 173.

TO W. H. D. ROUSE

Trinity College
16 April 1920

Dear Dr Rouse,

I do not remember rearranging Lucr. II 453–5,[1] but I take verse 453 to mean that you can scoop up poppy-seed in your hand as easily as water. This is the proper meaning of *haurire*, as may be seen from Ouid. met. <VII> VI 347 "ut *hauriret* gelidos *potura* liquores" or IV 740 "manus

---

[1] Nor had he, though some editors had done. He did, however, favour transposing 456–63 to follow 477: *JP* 25 (1897), 233 (*Classical Papers*, 428).

hausta uictrices abluit unda"; and so you have XIII 425 sq. "cineres *hausit*" and 526 "peregrinae *haustas harenae*". *namque* indicates an argument from analogy: you see the effect of the roundness of the seeds, and you can infer the effect of the roundness of atoms, and presume that shape in the atoms of fluids.

> I am yours very truly
> A. E. Housman.

Private MS.

TO AN UNKNOWN CORRESPONDENT

> Trinity College | Cambridge
> 16 April 1920

Dear Sir,

A good number of the poems have been set to music by various composers, but I do not remember the details.

> I am yours faithfully
> A. E. Housman.

University of San Francisco MS.

TO KATHARINE SYMONS

> Trinity College | Cambridge
> 27 April 1920

My dear Kate,

I enclose the account of A. J. Macleane[1] in our Book of Admissions, which is not renowned for accuracy. 'Pensioner' means Commoner; 'Fellow-Commoner' was a purchasable status, now extinct, but held by Arthur Balfour[2] in his time, which entitled one to dine at High Table with the Fellows.

Macleane was 4th Classic in the Tripos of 1845. Together with George Long he was general editor of a series of classical authors for school and college called *Bibliotheca Classica*, which faithfully represented the low ebb of scholarship in England in the middle of the 19th century. The Horace

---

[1] The Revd A[rthur] J[ohn] Macleane (1813–58). He was admitted to TCC as a Pensioner at the age of 28. He was Principal of Brighton College, 1848–53, and Rector of Charcombe in Somerset and Headmaster of King Edward's School, Bath, 1853–8.

[2] Arthur James Balfour (1848–1930), British Prime Minister, 1902–5. He studied philosophy at TCC, 1866–9, and was elected to a fellowship in 1878.

and the Juvenal and the Persius he edited himself.[3] His learning was
small, and so was his modesty, but he had common sense, and some of
his impudence was sprightly. He sent his son to Shrewsbury, and there
is a story of Kennedy[4] putting him on to construe and asking 'where did
you get that translation from?' 'From my father's edition, sir' said the
youth. Kennedy said nothing, and the lesson proceeded; but after the class
had been dismissed some one happened to go into the study, and found
Kennedy sitting with his head on his hands and groaning to himself 'Poor
boy! poor boy! I couldn't tell him his father was no scholar'.

Aunt Kate would have been 96 next month.[5] When you say 'no doubt
she will be buried by Uncle Basil' no doubt that is true in one sense,
but it gave me a momentary shock. I expect that much of the bother
about the funeral <will> would be taken over by her step-daughter Alice
Huntingdon and her family.

I hope that the meeting which was to provide for your declining years at
the national expense went off all right. I have written a poem suited to
your infant mind[6] on the paper enclosed.

Love to Clemence.

Your affectionate brother
A. E. Housman.

Private MS.

---

[3] Macleane's edn. of Horace appeared in 1853, that of Juvenal and Persius in 1857. Revised edns. were subsequently produced by Long.

[4] Benjamin Hall Kennedy (1804–89), Fellow and Lecturer in Classics, St John's College, Cambridge, 1828; Headmaster of Shrewsbury School, 1836–66; Regius Professor of Greek at Cambridge and Canon of Ely Cathedral, 1867. Partly from funds collected at his retirement at Shrewsbury, the chair of Latin was founded at Cambridge to which AEH was elected in 1911. Later in 1911, the title of the position became 'The Kennedy Professorship of Latin'. See Naiditch (1995), 27–8.

[5] 'Death of Aunt Kate April 1920 aged 95': note in KES's hand written on the MS.

[6] Identified by KES on the MS as *Amelia mixed the mustard*: see *Poems* (1997), 250. If, as looks to be the case, the poem was sent to KES for the first time with this letter, then its date is over twenty years later than was previously thought: see *Poems* (1997), 535–6. The form of the capital 'A' in the text reproduced in facsimile in *Recollections*, 26, would not rule out this later date.

TO F. M. CORNFORD

Trinity College
3 May 1920

Dear Cornford,

After declining to stand for the Oratorship I suppose I shall make myself unpopular if I refuse the next request which is made me, so I will try to write something for Frazer.[1] But oh, why was I born? This is a rhetorical question, and does not expect an answer.

Yours sincerely
A. E. Housman

BL Add. MS 54827, fo. 96. Ackerman (1974), 359.

TO DR PERCY WITHERS

Trinity College | Cambridge
4 May 1920

My dear Withers,

I have decorated your infatuated purchase with my signature and the shortest of my unpublished poems:[1] unpublished, though I also wrote it for Meynell[2] in a book belonging to one of his daughters. I should have thought, though, that this would detract from the value of the book for a true bibliophile; but no doubt this is already a spoilt copy, the leaves having been cut.

I think you have found a house in a good part of the world.[3] I motored through Aynho last year, but I do not remember it distinctly, though I remember Deddington. My Oxford walks did not bring me nearer than Bicester. One great charm of all the parts of Oxfordshire I know is the wide horizon you command even from a slight elevation.

Sciatica is one of the few ailments I sympathise with, as I used to have it myself, no doubt in a mild form, twenty years ago, till I learnt to change my things when I had got into a sweat. Cancer is worse, they say, and being shot through the palm of the hand makes one scream louder.

---

[1] The address of Apr. 1921: *Selected Prose*, 163–4.

[1] AEH wrote out *LP* XXVII (*The sigh that heaves the grasses*) and signed it 'A. E. Housman' on the flyleaf of Withers's copy of the first edn. of *ASL*, now in SCO.

[2] Wilfrid Meynell (1852–1948), journalist and poet, and husband of the poet Alice Meynell (1847–1922).

[3] Souldern Court in the village of Souldern, north of Bicester, Oxfordshire. See Robin Shaw, *Housman's Places* (1995), 55–6.

No doubt you know that Rothenstein also has deserted Gloucestershire, owing, he says, to the ambitions of his children.

I spent three weeks of last September in France, most of it in beautiful country in the Limousin, where I had not been before. Things were cheap, and they were yearning for the return of the English tourist.

My kind regards to Mrs Withers.

Yours sincerely
A. E. Housman.

SCO MS. Maas, 174.

TO GRANT RICHARDS

Trinity College | Cambridge
10 May 1920

My dear Richards,

On Friday I shall be lecturing till 12, but I can reach Liverpool Street either at 2. 21 or at 5. 15. Perhaps th<at>e latter would be too late to catch you at Paddington.

The bad weather of these last weeks has kept back the trees so perhaps the hawthorn will not be over in Berkshire.

It is nearly a month since I saw any proofs of Manilius IV.

Yours sincerely
A. E. Housman.

LC-GR MS. LC-GR t.s. Richards, 174 (excerpt).

TO GRANT RICHARDS

Trinity College | Cambridge
12 May 1920

My dear Richards,

I shall be very glad to stay till Tuesday morning.

As you give me the choice, I will come by the second[x] train and be at Paddington for the 6. 50.

Yours sincerely
A. E. Housman.

[x] To be exact, I shall \perhaps <probably>/ come by a third train, which gets to Liverpool Street at 6. 10[.]

LC-GR MS. LC-GR t.s.

TO MARTIN SECKER

Trinity College | Cambridge
18 May 1920

Dear Mr Secker,

It is exceedingly good of you to give me the book which Richards handed me yesterday,[1] and if it is half as good as *South Wind*[2] I have a great treat in store.

I am yours very truly
A. E. Housman.

PM MS MA 2808 R.V. Autographs Misc. English.

TO GRANT RICHARDS

Trinity College | Cambridge
24 May 1920

My dear Richards,

I enclose the MS of the Index to Manilius IV and of a page to be inserted before it. This completes the book.

But I am perplexed and disquieted by certain phenomena in the paged proofs of the text and notes. New errors have been introduced in places which were previously correct. Two of these (p. 3 l. 4 of notes and p. 113 l. 18 of notes) have been put right again by the proof-reader; but I have noticed others (p. 114 line 5 from bottom, *61* for *861*; line 2 from bottom, Vrigo for Virgo), and I do not know how many more there may be. As for preventing letters at the beginning and end of lines from getting out of their place, it seems a hopeless business: as fast as they are put straight in one place they fly crooked in another.

Yours sincerely
A. E. Housman.

LC-GR MS. LC-GR t.s. Richards, 174; Maas, 174–5.

---

[1] Probably *They Went*, a novel, published in 1920, by Norman Douglas (1868–1922).
[2] Novel by Douglas, published by Secker in 1917.

TO GRANT RICHARDS

Trinity College | Cambridge
26 May 1920

My dear Richards,

Thanks for your note. Send Dr Kroll[1] the copy of Manilius III which he wants.

Yours sincerely
A. E. Housman.

LC-GR MS. LC-GR t.s.

TO GRANT RICHARDS

Trinity College | Cambridge
1 July 1920

My dear Richards,

Your rather immoral but very readable novel[1] reached me at a crisis which made me particularly grateful, for there was a great dearth of literature around me and I had been reduced to *Agatha's Husband*[2] by the authoress of *John Halifax, Gentleman*. Both Agatha's and Olivia's husbands had rather odious wives, and your heroine would have incurred the ruin she deserved if God had been her creator instead of you. I did not think the Monte Carlo part so good as the rest. Your knowledge of the turf and everything connected with it fills me with admiration and horror. I believe however that you have confused the persons of Mr Backhouse and Mr Eaton. The latter (p. 85) "was the racecourse member of the firm", so I do not see why the firm should tell the lie you make them tell on p. 113, and I think it was probably Mr Eaton whom Olivia met at Kempton Park[3] on p. 127. How did Mr Eaton on p. 249 form an opinion on Brocklesby's possibilities at Liverpool, a city to which you never sent the horse?[4] That both Mr Eaton and his clerk were christened Alfred may be a compliment to me or merely a coincidence. I cannot square

---

[1] Wilhelm Kroll (1869–1939), editor of *Paulys real-encyclopädie der classischen Altertumswissenschaft*, which began publication in 1894.

[1] *Double Life* (1920).

[2] Published in 1853. The anonymous author was Dinah Maria Mulock.   [3] Racecourse.

[4] GR retorted that the 'racing army' goes from London to Lincoln and thence to Liverpool before returning to London, and that therefore he was being very exact when he spoke of the bookmaker having come back from Liverpool impressed by Brocklesby's abilities: to AEH, 5 July 1920 (BMC MS).

Olivia's arithmetic on p. 91 with the facts (if facts they are) recounted on p. 90.[5]

I enclose the final proofs of Manilius IV, in which there are three corrections to be made. These have been held up for a fortnight because they were sent to Cambridge and not to me in Gloucestershire, whence I returned yesterday. Now will begin the delays of binding, on which you are always descanting in the *Times Literary Supplement*.[6]

I may attempt Paris by the aeroplane route in September, so any information about it which you may possess or acquire would be welcome; also about passports.

Yours sincerely
A. E. Housman.

Lilly MSS 2. LC-GR MS (copy in GR's handwriting). Maas, 175.

TO GRANT RICHARDS

Trinity College | Cambridge
14 July 1920

My dear Richards,

Many thanks for your enclosures. As you are generously disposed to give me a copy of Saintsbury's cellar book,[1] I certainly shall be grateful for it.

Yours sincerely
A. E. Housman.

Lilly MSS 1. 1. 3. LC-GR t.s. Richards, 174 (nearly complete).

---

[5] GR defended the arithmetic as correct: Olivia won £50, which, after deducting the £45 she had lost during the week, left her £5 to the good: to AEH, 5 July 1920 (BMC MS).

[6] In his weekly advertisements. *TLS* 963 (1 July 1920), 421, contained an announcement that R. W. Postgate's *The Bolshevik Theory*, due to be published on 22 June 1920, 'was unavoidably postponed'.

[1] George Saintsbury, *Notes On A Cellar-Book* (Macmillan & Co., 1920). AEH's copy is in Lilly: Naiditch, *HSJ* 31 (2005), 154.

TO THOMAS MOULT

Trinity College | Cambridge
21 July 1920

My dear Sir,

I am naturally flattered by the handsome compliment which you and your contributors have paid me, and I am pleased and grateful to receive a gift so full of interest and merit.[1] I beg also to thank you personally for the kindness of your note, and I am

Yours very truly
A. E. Housman.

Thomas Moult Esq.

Brotherton MS (Moult Correspondence).

TO KATHARINE SYMONS

Trinity College | Cambridge
21 July 1920

My dear Kate,

I enclose the Provost of Eton's[1] answer to your enquiries. The change from A. M. and A. B.[2] to M. A. and B. A. signifies, at least in the Universities, that English was superseding Latin in formal writing and speaking,—such as statutes and notices; and it took place early in the 19th century.

Your affectionate brother
A. E. Housman.

King Edward's School, Bath, MS.

TO KATHARINE SYMONS

Trinity College | Cambridge
26 July 1920

My dear Kate,

Christ Church seems to have been the name conferred on the cathedral when it became a cathedral in 1546. To this day Christ Church is not strictly a college: its official description is 'The Dean and Chapter of the

[1] Probably a copy of *Georgian Poetry 1918–1919* (1920), of which Moult was editor.

[1] M. R. James: see List of Recipients.

[2] 'artium magister' and 'artium baccalaureus' (in Latin word order), for 'Master of Arts' and 'Bachelor of Arts'.

Cathedral Church of Christ in Oxford of the foundation of King Henry the Eighth'. They call themselves 'the House'.

I forgot to say that where Magdalene now stands in Cambridge there was formerly a Benedictine Hostel, with separate buildings or staircases for the different monasteries,—Crowland[1] etc.

I am glad that Denis[2] is D. P. H.,[3] but I rejoice on trust, as I don't know what it means,—Devastator of Public Health, or Dispenser of Pharmaceutical Horrors.

Your affectionate brother
A. E. Housman.

Private MS. Maas, 176.

TO GRANT RICHARDS

Trinity College | Cambridge
12 Aug. 1920

My dear Richards,

Thanks, if you would answer such letters for me it would save some little trouble. But I seem to remember that on one occasion in the past you mixed up my benevolence to composers with my hard-heartedness to anthologists, so that a poem of mine was published in one collection on your permission when I had refused mine to the editors of others, who had applied to me.

Yours sincerely
A. E. Housman.

LC-GR t.s. Maas, 176.

TO GRANT RICHARDS

Trinity College | Cambridge
15 Aug. 1920

My dear Richards,

I am very grateful for the leaflets. I am most attracted by the Aircraft Transport people because theirs is more explicit, and by mentioning a charge for 'Passengers' Excess Baggage' they give me hope of disappointing

---

[1] *Historia Crowlandensis* (1413), a source of information about medieval monasteries.

[2] KES's second son, Arthur Denis Symons (1891–1951).

[3] Doctor of Public Health.

your malevolent expectations about difficulty arising from the weight of my bag. You should not always insist on carrying it.

Do you still possess backstairs influence at the French consulate? Last year you relieved me of the trouble of having to appear in person to get my visa, and I don't yet know if Cook & Son can.

Yours sincerely
A. E. Housman.

LC-GR MS. LC-GR t.s. Richards, 175; Maas, 176–7.

TO GRANT RICHARDS

Trinity College | Cambridge
17 Aug. 1920

My dear Richards,

Cook professes himself able to get me a Visa, so I will not trespass on your kindness. The Visa of last year was for 2 months.

My inclination to go by the Air Express is confirmed by the crash they had yesterday, which will make them careful in the immediate future.[1] Their cars start from your neighbourhood, the Victory Hotel, Leicester Square; so I shall try to get a bed there for the night, unless you warn me against it.

Yours sincerely
A. E. Housman.

LC-GR MS. LC-GR t.s. Richards, 175; Maas, 177.

---

[1] AEH made his first flight on 9 Sept. 1920: see AEH to GR on that date. Jeremy Bourne, 'Housman in the Air', *HSJ* 23 (1997), 43, notes that crashes were frequent at the time. Graves, 158, records that 'one pilot's total of forced landings climbed to seventeen during the first few years of passenger flights'.

TO GRANT RICHARDS

Trinity College | Cambridge
21 Aug. 1920

My dear Richards,

Revenge is a valuable passion, and the only sure pillar on which justice rests, so I do not want to hinder your pursuit of Constable if it can be conducted without making me seem to be the pursuer. But have you also a vendetta against James Agate?[1] From reading your serial in the *Literary Supplement* I supposed that he was one of your pets.[2]

I shall stay at the Victory Hotel on the night of Wednesday Sept. 8, and I shall be delighted if you will dine with me that evening. As I shall have no dress clothes, but only a dark grey or brown suit, you had better select, from your superior knowledge of London, the best restaurant where that costume would not be conspicuous. Not that I really much mind public reprobation if you do not.

Yours sincerely
A. E. Housman.

LC-GR MS. LC-GR t.s. Richards, 177; Maas, 177–8.

TO KATHARINE SYMONS

[Trinity College | Cambridge
Before 3 Sept. 1920][1]

[…] Library to have the two books sent to Bath. Of course they may be out.

I return Jerry's letters with many thanks. They are very full and interesting, and he seems to be beginning well.[2]

Your affectionate brother
A. E. Housman.

Housman Society MS: fragment.

---

[1] Messrs Constable and Company's publication, *L[ines] Of C[ommunication]* (1917), being the letters of a temporary officer in the army service corps, Captain James E. Agate (1877–1946), contained on p. 1, as an epigraph to the first chapter ('Joining Up'), an unauthorized printing of *ASL* XXV (*On the idle hill of summer*). See AEH to GR, 13 Jan. 1917.

[2] GR's advertisement in the *TLS* 970 (19 Aug. 1920), 533, countered the claim in the *Athenaeum* that 'no first novel of literary merit can hope to sell more than a thousand' with the example of Agate's *Responsibility*: 'It was a first novel; it had literary merit … and it did sell—oh! very many more than a thousand.'

[1] Dated according to the next letter, in which AEH tells KES that the two library books had arrived back.

[2] Her youngest son began work in the Indian Civil Service in 1920.

TO KATHARINE SYMONS

Trinity College | Cambridge
3 Sept. 1920

My dear Kate,

I return the document[1] with my signature. I made you a present of the two dishes, and I have no business to take any credit with R. E. and M. Symons[2] for your thoughtfulness on their behalf.

The two books arrived in time. The Library[3] now closes for three weeks or so, but after that there is no reason why you should not have again the book which is not at Bath.

They tell me here that the right thing to do with railway stock and shares is to stick to them; but I shiver when I look forward to the additional trouble of filling up my Income Tax return.

I shall leave here on the 8th and return not later than the 18th.

When I was at Monmouth I did not succeed in finding all the beauty you speak of; but I was there less than a week, and was walking to distant places like Raglan and Chepstow and Speech House.

I am glad for the sake of both of you to hear about the school. Do you remember Mr J. C. Whall who was an assistant master at Bromsgrove?[4] I see he died the other day.

Your affectionate brother
A. E. Housman.

TCC Add. MS c. 50³. Maas, 178.

[1] A Record Office note of Chancery Proceedings *c.*1440 in which the Petitioner is 'Richard Houseman'.

[2] KES's grandsons Robert Edward and Michael, both born in 1920, the latter on 10 August.

[3] The London Library. AEH sponsored KES as a ticket-holder.

[4] An obituary appeared in *The Times*, 1 Sept. 1920, 13b. The Revd John Clephane Whall was Assistant Master at Surrey County School before moving to Bromsgrove in 1874, where he was appointed Assistant Master at The Grammar School of King Edward VI. He subsequently became Warden of Christ's College, Hobart, Tasmania; Master of the Lower School, Queen Elizabeth's School, Ipswich; Chief Inspector of Religious Education in the Diocese of Worcester, 1891–1906; Vicar at Montgomery; and Vicar of Hopesay, Salop, 1914–20.

TO RIDGELY TORRENCE

Trinity College | Cambridge | England
5 Sept. 1920

Dear Sir,

I am obliged by your letter, but I hope you will not mind if I make the same reply which I have made to editors in this country,—that I do not care to publish verse in periodicals unless it is concerned with current events.

I am yours very truly
A. E. Housman.

Ridgely Torrence Esq.

Princeton MS (Frederick Ridgely Torrence Collection, II. 41, folder 7).

TO GRANT RICHARDS

Trinity College | Cambridge
5 Sept. 1920

My dear Richards,

7. 30 at the Café Royal on Wednesday. Perhaps you and Charles[1] would come and find me about 5 minutes earlier in the lounge of the Victory Hotel (are you sleeping there?)

About the probable date of publication of Manilius IV, the probable strike in the binding trade, the inevitable shipwreck of the vessel which conveys it from Glasgow to London, we can talk when we meet; but I want to put in writing for your convenience that on its publication I think it ought to be advertised once at least both in the *Classical Review* and the *Classical Quarterly*, as the other day I discovered that a scholar here, and a friend of mine, did not know that book III had yet appeared.

Suppose I produced a new volume of poetry,[2] in what part of the year ought it to be published, and how long would it take after the MS left my hands?

Yours sincerely
A. E. Housman.

LC-GR t.s. Richards, 178 (incomplete); Maas, 178–9.

---

[1] GR had been invited by AEH to dinner on 8 Sept., and, that being the birthday of his son Charles, GR had asked if he might bring him along: Richards, 177.

[2] AEH's first hint of what would be *LP*.

TO GRANT RICHARDS

8 Sept. Hôtel Continental<e>.
Safely arrived: you also I hope.

A. E. H.

LC-GR MS: p.c. addressed 'M Grant Richards | British Hotel | Gorey | Jersey' and redirected to Cookham Dean, Berkshire.

TO GRANT RICHARDS

All right[1]

A. E. Housman

9 Sept. 1920

LC-GR MS: p.c addressed 'Grant Richards | 8 St Martin's Street | Leicester Square | Londres (W. C. 2) | Angleterre'. LC-GR t.s. Richards, 179; Maas, 179.

TO GRANT RICHARDS

HÔTEL CONTINENTAL | 3, RUE CASTIGLIONE | PARIS
13 Sept. 1920

My dear Richards,

I have decided to come home on Friday morning, and this, if I remember your plans correctly, will prevent me from having the pleasure of meeting you here.

At this instant I am suffering much from indigestion, whether chiefly due to myself or to Montagne,[1] Traiteur,[2] I do not know.

Yours sincerely
A. E. Housman

LC-GR MS. LC-GR t.s. Richards, 179.

---

[1] AEH is reassuring GR of his safe arrival in Paris after his first flight: Richards, 178–9. Jeremy Bourne, 'Housman in the Air', *HSJ* 23 (1997), 42, notes that the first flight across the English Channel had been Blériot's on 25 July 1909, and that the first attempt at setting up an organized transport company for the route had been made in 1919. Bourne judges AEH to be 'remarkably courageous' in choosing to fly.

[1] The restaurant of Prosper Montagné in Paris.   [2] 'Restaurateur'.

TO GRANT RICHARDS

Room 386. | HÔTEL CONTINENTAL | 3, RUE CASTIGLIONE | PARIS
16 Sept. 1920

My dear Richards,

I am very glad we can meet after all.

At 2. 30 a newly married couple are going to make a short call on me here, but otherwise I am not engaged in the afternoon. I will come to the Normandy at 1 o' clock and wait a little: if you find this letter without me, that will mean that I have gone for my lunch. I shall be in this hotel at 3 o' clock, but do not think this an engagement.

I could dine with you if you are willing to dine early and lightly: that is to say, I shall dine lightly; there is no reason why you should. I should have to leave you soon after 8. 30, but the nearer I was to a station on the Vincennes-Maillot line of the Metropolitain, the longer I could sit at table. If we dont[1] meet at 3, I shall be here from 6 to 7. 15.

Yours sincerely
A. E. Housman.

LC-GR t.s. Richards, 179–80.

TO LAURENCE HOUSMAN

Trinity College | Cambridge
21 Sept. 1920

My dear Laurence,

That is all right. I hope that by fair means and foul together you despoiled America of a great deal of its appreciated coinage.[1]

I have just flown to Paris and back, and I am never going by any other route, until they build the Channel Tunnel, which I will give a trial, if it is much cheaper.

Love to Clemence: I hope Bath did her good.

Your affectionate brother
A. E. Housman.

BMC MS. Memoir, *177–8 (nearly complete).*

---

[1] For 'don't'.

[1] LH left England on 30 Dec. 1919 for a twelve-week visit, his second, to the United States. His ostensible purpose was to advocate a League of Nations, but he spent much of the time giving readings from his plays: *The Unexpected Years* (1937), 318, 320.

TO GRANT RICHARDS

Trinity College | Cambridge
21 Sept. 1920

My dear Richards,

I enclose cheque for £80.

Also, on the next leaf, two additions to the lists I sent you yesterday.

Please send me 4 copies.

Yours sincerely
A. E. Housman

Grant Richards Esq.

LC-GR MS. LC-GR t.s.

TO GRANT RICHARDS

[Trinity College | Cambridge]

No copy of Manilius IV is to be sent to the *Classical Quarterly*, which does not review books.

Again the label on the back has been stuck on upside-down, as in the first copies of book III four years ago.

A. E. Housman.
22 Sept. 1920

LC-GR MS: p.c. addressed 'Grant Richards Esq. | 8 St Martin's Street | Leicester Square |
W. C. 2.' LC-GR t.s. Richards, 180 (incomplete); Maas, 179.

TO GRANT RICHARDS

Trinity College | Cambridge
28 Sept. 1920

My dear Richards,

Oh, damn the *Bookman*.[1] The author wrote to me some months ago, asking for private particulars, and I thought that my reply had chilled him off. I have not been photographed, I think, since 1894: that was the year when I was beginning to write *A Shropshire Lad*, and if for that reason they would care to have it, I could send you one, as I do not want to seem churlish. As to Rothenstein, his portraits are of 15 years ago, and one of them, the one he shows in exhibitions, is a venomous libel, to which he

---

[1] *The Bookman* had asked GR for a photograph or other portrait of AEH to reproduce. In no. 350 (Nov. 1920), 71–2, was an article on AEH by John Freeman. It was illustrated by photographs by Van der Weyde (1894), E. O. Hoppé (1911), and GR (1916).

adds fresh strokes whenever he feels nasty. This is full face; the other one, more side face, he reserves for his private delectation.

Now I think of it, I was photographed by Oppé,[2] also about 15 years ago, and I think I rather lately received a copy for the first time; but I do not know what I have done with it.

Yours sincerely
A. E. Housman.

LC-GR t.s. (with 'reverses' corrected to 'reserves', and other minor corrections). Richards, 180; Maas, 179–80.

TO GRANT RICHARDS

Trinity College | Cambridge
30 Sept. 1920

My dear Richards,
    The signed copy is for you,[1] the other for the *Bookman*.

Yours sincerely
A. E. Housman.

LC-GR MS. LC-GR t.s. Richards, 180.

TO KATHARINE SYMONS

Trinity College | Cambridge
3 Oct. 1920

My dear Kate,
    Well, I flew there and back all right, and am never going by any other route in future. Surrey from overhead is delightful, Kent and France less interesting, the Channel disappointing, because on both days there was too much mist to let both shores be seen [at] once. It was rather windy, and the machine sometimes imitated a ship at sea (though that is due to differing densities of atmosphere and not to wind) but not in a very life-like manner. Members of your unhappy sex were sick, however. The noise is great, and I alighted rather deaf, not having stuffed my ears with the cotton-wool provided. Nor did I put on the life-belt which they oblige one to take. To avoid crossing the 60 miles of sea which a straight flight would involve, they go from Croydon to Hythe, Hythe to Boulogne, Boulogne to Paris. You are in the air $2\frac{1}{2}$ hours: from Leicester Square to your hotel in

---

[2] For 'Hoppé'.

[1] Of the photograph of AEH by Van der Weyde from 1894.

Paris you take little more than 4; though on the return journey we were 2 hours late in starting because the machine required repairs, having been damaged on the previous day by a passenger who butted his head through the window to be sick. My chief trouble is that what I now want is no longer a motor and a chauffeur but an aeroplane and a tame pilot, which I suppose are more expensive. The weather in France was beautiful, though I read of storms in London. Unfortunately I got poisoned at a restaurant and was out of action for the best part of two days. Pray why should the manager of W. H. Smith's establishment in Paris want to know if you are my sister?[1] It was not me he asked, but Grant Richards; and twice.

Love to all[.]

Your affectionate brother
A. E. Housman.

Lilly MSS 2, with the corner bearing 'at' torn off. Memoir, 147–8 (nearly complete); Maas, 180.

TO GRANT RICHARDS

Trinity College | Cambridge
12 Oct. 1920

My dear Richards,

Certainly I should be delighted to come to you for a week-end in November; but I delayed answering because on one week-end in that month, I am not sure which, there is a dinner at Oxford of an inter-University Club to which I belong,[1] and I tried to find out the date from the secretary. He however is in Hungary; and, as I think the Oxford dinner is on the 13th, I should like to fix the 19th for coming to you. But it is no good hoping to lunch with you that day, as on Fridays I am lecturing till noon.

I wrote to Clemence about the wood-engraving, but she has not answered yet.

As I have not received the labels for Manilius IV I suppose it is not yet published.

Yours sincerely
A. E. Housman.

LC-GR MS. LC-GR t.s.

[1] 'Answer: W. H. S.'s manager came from Bath, and knew I was the sister of *Laurence Housman*': KES's handwritten note in her copy of LH's *Memoir*, inspected at Sotheby's, 4 Nov. 2001.

[1] The Arcades.

TO F. M. CORNFORD

Trinity College
14 Oct. 1920

Dear Cornford,

I send you this draft of an address to Frazer because I despair of making it better by keeping it longer. It seems to me not only too ornate, as some of Frazer's own writing is, but also stilted, which Frazer's writing is not. Perhaps you and Giles[1] can improve it, or create something better of your own.

Yours sincerely
A. E. Housman.

BL Add. MS 58427, fos. 97–8. Ackerman (1974), 359. Envelope addressed 'F. M. Cornford Esq. | Conduit Head | Madingley Road' and marked 'Local' by AEH. Enclosed is a draft in ink on two lined foolscap sheets of the address to Sir James Frazer, for which see Selected Prose, *163–4. The only difference from the text finally printed in 1921 is that the last paragraph is not a separate paragraph.*

TO DR G. C. WILLIAMSON

Trinity College | Cambridge
24 Oct. 1920

Dear Dr Williamson,

I am sorry that your earlier letter failed to reach me, probably when I was abroad last month. Certainly I have all the will in the world to do honour to Keats, whom I *admire*, in the strict sense of the word, more than any other poet; but unfortunately I am not able to write poetry (nor even prose that is worth writing) at will; and it would be no good my making you any promise. If anything should soon come into my head, I would send it you;[1] but it is very unlikely.

I am yours very truly
A. E. Housman.

Dr G. C. Williamson.

Princeton MS (Keats Memorial Volume II: Letters Gen. MSS [bound] Am 21565). Envelope addressed 'Dr Williamson | Burgh House | Well Walk | Hampstead | N. W. 3.'

[1] Identified by Ackerman, loc. cit., as 'Peter Giles (1860–1935), classical scholar, Master of Emmanuel College, and member of the Organizing Committee for the Frazer fund'. Giles was elected Reader in Comparative Philology at Cambridge, 1891, and served as Master of Emmanuel, 1911–35, and as Vice-Chancellor, 1919–21. His only book was a *Short Manual of Comparative Philology for the Use of Classical Students* (1895).

[1] For *The John Keats Memorial Volume* which Williamson (1858–1942) edited in 1921.

TO GRANT RICHARDS

Trinity College | Cambridge
28 Oct. 1920

My dear Richards,

I enclose cheque for £31. 15. 10, and return Maclehose's[1] invoice.

When exactly was the book published, and were the copies from the author sent out simultaneously? I ask because one unlucky fellow appears to have bought one before mine reached him. Perhaps he was premature, and ordered one.

Yours sincerely
A. E. Housman.

LC-GR MS. LC-GR t.s.

TO A. F. SCHOLFIELD

Trinity College
6 Nov. 1920

Dear Scholfield,

I have the Lucretius,[1] and it is not worth having: The Persius,[2] from what I know of Cartault, would be much the same; and no edition of a Greek author produced in France can be fit for exportation. The editions of Cicero,[3] when they appear, might be worth getting; and also any book, if there were any, edited by Havet[4] or Lejay.[5]

Yours sincerely
A. E. Housman.

TCC Add. MS c. 80²⁰. Maas, 181.

TO GRANT RICHARDS

[Cambridge]
19 Nov. 1920

Missed train will try meet you at Paddington

Housman

LC-GR t.s. Telegram addressed to 'Grant Richards | 8 St Martin's Street | Leicester Sq | Ldn.'.

---

[1] For 'MacLehose'.

[1] Ed. Alfred Ernout (b. 1879), in the 'collection Budé' of classical authors (1920). Naiditch (2003), 125, gives full details. Scholfield, as Librarian of TCC, had asked advice on purchases.

[2] Ed. Augustin Cartault (1847–1922), 1920.

[3] In the *Collections des Universités de France*, beginning in 1921.

[4] Louis Havet (1849–1925). He published an edn. of the *Phaedrus* (1895) and *Notes Critiques sur Properce* (1916). AEH owned a copy of the former: Naiditch (2003), 138.

[5] Paul Lejay (1861–1920). He published an edn. of Horace (1903) and vols. on Virgil (1921).

TO D. S. ROBERTSON

Trinity College
8 Dec. 1920

Dear Robertson,

I enclose the three essays for the Members' Prize.[1]

I have marked such misprints and false accents as I have noticed, and have also marked or indicated a good many other mistakes.

I was wrong when I told you that the bad handwriting would disqualify the written essay: I had wandered into the regulations about the Hare Prize[2] on the same page.

Perhaps you will let me know, verbally or otherwise, that you have received the essays.

Yours sincerely
A. E. Housman.

Private MS.

TO GRANT RICHARDS

Trinity College | Cambridge
12 Dec. 1920

My dear Richards,

I enclose a cheque for £500,[1] which my bank-book seems to be capable of standing; not more I am afraid, for I have other friends who are in difficulties. But I hope this will be some good. I am not losing any interest, as I always keep in my current account enough money to flee the country with.

I am glad to hear good news of Gioia,[2] and I hope this last expert is right.

What do you know of the genesis of the enclosed press-cutting?

Will you send me one copy of the illustrated edition of *A Shropshire Lad*?

Yours sincerely
A. E. Housman

---

[1] The Members' Classical Prize, either for a thesis submitted in Part II of the Classical Tripos or for an M.Phil. thesis.

[2] For a Ph.D. dissertation.

[1] GR's publishing business was in financial difficulties. See AEH to GR, 27 Oct. 1921, and n. 1.

[2] GR's daughter.

I observe that your pet bruiser has beaten Beckett. It appears that he does something wrong with his elbow,[3] which I hope he has not taught to Charles.[4]

BMC MS.

TO GRANT RICHARDS

Trinity College | Cambridge
20 Dec. 1920

My dear Richards,

I return Lovat Frazer's designs[1] most of which I do not like at all, though the landscapes are generally pleasing. The trouble with book-illustrators, as with composers who set poems to music, is not merely that they are completely wrapped up in their own art and their precious selves, and regard the author merely as a peg to hang things on, but that they seem to have less than the ordinary human allowance of sense and feeling. To transpose into the 18th century a book which begins with Queen Victoria's jubilee[2] is the act of a rhinoceros. I should look a fool if I allowed the book to appear with these decorations.

This reminds me. I am told that composers in some cases have mutilated my poems,—that Vaughan Williams cut two verses out of *Is my team ploughing* (I wonder how he would like me to cut two bars out of his music),[3] and that a lady whose name I forget has set one verse of *The New Mistress*, omitting the others.[4] So I am afraid I must ask you, when giving consent to composers, to exact the condition that these pranks are not to be played.

[3] The British boxer Joe Beckett was knocked out in the second round by Frank Moran of Pittsburgh in a fight at the Albert Hall, London. In *The Times*, 11 Dec. 1920, Beckett is criticized for not using his superior speed to advantage; Morgan for using the 'Mary Ann' punch ('The referee ... had to warn Morgan for a second time against making use of his elbow').

[4] GR's son.

[1] Joseph Thorp had suggested to GR that the painter, illustrator, and decorator Claud Lovat Fraser (1890–1921) should make a set of illustrations to *ASL*: Richards, 180–1. They were published in 1924 under the auspices of the First Edition Club as *Sixty-three Unpublished Designs*. AEH writes 'Frazer' for 'Fraser'.

[2] The first poem in *ASL* is '*1887*'.

[3] In Vaughan Williams's song cycle *On Wenlock Edge*, originally performed on 26 January 1909, the third song, *Is my team ploughing* (*ASL* XXVII), at some point in its performance history came to lack stanzas 3 and 4, and the first line of the final stanza was represented as 'Yes, lad, Yes, lad, I lie easy'. The prefatory quatrain was also omitted from 'Clun' (*ASL* L).

[4] Christabel Marillier, *A Farewell* (published by J. Curwen & Sons Ltd., 1920). The setting also repeated the last line of the first stanza.

Mr Cecil Roberts[5] must be an angelic character, if he persists in being civil to you after a quarrel. I was not annoyed by the paragraph,[6] for undeserved renown is what I chiefly prize. I am much more celebrated in Cambridge for having flown to France and back last September than for anything else I have done.

I don't think Machen[7] ought to drink port on the top of burgundy.

Yours sincerely
A. E. Housman.

[Enclosure]

1.

X Poem on March illustrated by tree in full leaf

IV Early morning light very good

XX What on earth is this? I recognise a water-lily, but nothing else.

XLI Not an illustration

XLVIII Not an illustration; and no illustration is possible.

XL Good in itself, but not distant enough to be an illustration.

XXXVIII Very good

XXXII No illustration: none possible.

XLV Pretty but hardly appropriate

2.

XVIII Lunatic at large.

XXIV No illustration

LI Fancy selecting a *mutilated* statue!

XXXIX Hybrid between broom and hawthorn, I suppose: much unlike either.

II What a cherry-tree!

LII The poem is about black poplars growing by pools and whispering at night when there is no wind. The illustration displays Lombardy poplars in broad day and a furious gale: no water anywhere about, except suspended as vapour in a cloud.

3.

XXXVII One of my friends at farm-work, keeping my head from harm by wearing enormous boots.

---

[5] Cecil [Edric Mornington] Roberts (1892–1976), prolific miscellaneous writer, and at this time editor of *The Nottingham Journal and Express*.

[6] 'Mr Housman has just published, with his friend Grant Richards, another book of his edition of Manilius. The Professor is less known than the poet of "The Shropshire Lad", and still less known is the Mr Housman the gourmet, to whom I believe such a skilled epicure as Mr Grant Richards gives first place': *The Nottinghamshire Journal and Express*, 2 Dec. 1920.

[7] Arthur Machen (1863–1947), novelist and translator, to whom GR was both friend and publisher. See AEH to GR, 3 Apr. 1922.

XLII Good
XLIII Good enough
XXI Bredon Hillock
XXII The soldier was not so much astonished and horrified as all that.
XIII How like an artist to think that the speaker is a woman!
XVII What a weed! No wonder he was unfortunate in love.

4.

XLIX Satyr dressed up as John Bull: allegory, I suppose: quite inappropriate.
L Good
LV Good in itself
XI A broad joke
XXX Poem contrasting the passions of youth and the unwholesome excitement of adultery with the quiet and indifference of death, illustrated by figure of obese old man: possibly the injured husband.
LXIII Pretty, but because I call them stars he makes them bells.
IX Fancy stringing *two* chaps to the gallows!
XXVI What an aspen!

State University of New York at Buffalo MS (for the letter alone). LC-GR t.s. Richards, 181–3 (incomplete); Maas, 181–2 (without enclosure).

TO MILDRED PLATT

Trinity College | Cambridge
23 Dec. 1920

Dear Mrs Platt,

I shall be delighted to dine and stay the night on Monday Jan. 3. The 31st Dec. is excluded because I and other choice spirits here always see the New Year in on oysters and stout, to do what we can for the cause of human progress and the improvement of the world.

I congratulate you on having managed to live with Platt so long.[1] This is a compliment of the season.

Yours sincerely
A. E. Housman.

UCL MS Add. 165. Maas, 182.

[1] 35 years.

TO DR PERCY WITHERS

Trinity College | Cambridge
28 Dec. 1920

My dear Withers,

You certainly have had plenty of troubles, but I hope you are now happily at the end of them,—except that the shocking convulsion in your cellar must be permanent in its effects. Yours must be a pleasant part of the country, though in my Oxford days I never walked nearer it than Bicester. I am here for Christmas as usual, my own family having an aversion for Christmas gatherings and Trinity College very much the reverse. I am afraid we shall not have our new and much superior Combination Room ready for you by the spring, as a builders' strike and other things have delayed operations. The wall at the dais end of the Hall was found to have stood 300 years on no foundation supporting a weight of 60 tons: it might have fallen on us any day as we sat at meat, but contented itself with merely cracking.

A happy new year to both of you, and many of them.

Yours sincerely
A. E. Housman.

SCO MS. Maas, 183.

TO WILLIAM ROTHENSTEIN

Trinity College | Cambridge
28 Dec. 1920

My dear Rothenstein,

I am very grateful for the proof,[1] especially as the portrait is not in the eminent artist's most virulent vein.

I very seldom find myself in London, but when next I do I will try to find you out in your eligible quarter of the town.

My kindest regards to Mrs Rothenstein, and a happy new year to all of you, not even excluding the ambitious children who have uprooted you from Oakridge.[2]

Yours sincerely
A. E. Housman.

Harvard bMS Eng 1148 (740) 41. Maas. 182–3.

---

[1] Of Rothenstein's 1915 portrait of AEH in his *Twenty-Four Portraits* (1920).

[2] Iles Farm, Far Oakridge, Gloucestershire, where the Rothensteins lived from 1912 until moving to Campden Hill, London, in 1920. Their children, according to Rothenstein, *Men and Memories*, 2. 364, 'missed the companionship of others of their own age' and 'were pining for concerts and plays'.

1921

TO DR W. H. D. ROUSE

Trinity College
2 Jan. 1921

Dear Dr Rouse,[1]

In Lucr. III 83 I think your *hic … hic*, which Heinze[2] and Merrill[3] assign to one Bergson,[4] may quite well be right; but I do not see anything wrong with Munro's reading. *hunc … hunc* divide up the *homines* of the verse which he inserts, and may get support of one kind from Verg. georg. II 505–12 and of another from Aen. X 9 sq.[5]

IV 418–9 is a passage I have often broken my head over without avail. The lections of the MSS are as you say: *caelum ut* A, *caelum* B, *corpora* AB. *caeli ut* (with other changes) was proposed by Bergk,[6] and Giussani[7] adopts it without other changes. I only feel clear that *mirande* was not Latin in the time of Lucretius, if it ever was, and that *caelum* cannot be right in *both* verses. Also I do not think he would say *mirando caelo*. What I should expect is something like 'et *mole* ut uideare uidere | corpora *miranda*'.[8]

I am yours very truly
A. E. Housman.

Trinity College, Dublin, MS 2287. Maas, 415.

---

[1] Rouse's edn. of Lucretius was published in the Loeb Classical Library in 1924.
[2] Richard Heinze's edn. of book 3 of Lucretius (Leipzig, 1897), of which AEH owned a copy: Naiditch (2003), 125.
[3] W. A. Merrill's edn. (1907), of which AEH owned a copy: Naiditch (2003), 125.
[4] French philosopher Henri Bergson (1859–1941) early in his career (1884) published an edn. of extracts from Lucretius with a critical study of the text and the poet's philosophy.
[5] Rouse printed *hunc … hunc*.
[6] Wilhelm Theodor Bergk (1812–81), among his proposed emendations to Lucretius (1895).
[7] Carlo Giussani in his edn. (1896–8), of which AEH owned a copy: Naiditch (2003), 125.
[8] Rouse printed *nubila despicere et caeli ut videare videre | corpora mirande sub terras abdita caelo* ('so that you seem to look down upon the clouds and to see the heavenly bodies after a wonderful fashion buried in a heaven below the earth').

TO GRANT RICHARDS

[Trinity College | Cambridge
5 January 1921

My dear Richards,]

'My new book' does not exist, and possibly never may. Neither your traveller nor anybody else must be told that it is even contemplated. What I asked you[1] was a question inspired by an unusually bright and sanguine mood, which has not at present been justified.

I saw E. B. Osborn's remarks,[2] but they did not alter my opinion of him.

[Yours sincerely
A. E. Housman.]

Grant Richards, Author Hunting *(1932), 268; Richards, 184; Maas, 183.*

TO GRANT RICHARDS

Trinity College | Cambridge
25 Feb. 1921

My dear Richards,

I wish you would send me Grant Allen's *Umbrian Towns*[1] and *Smaller Tuscan Towns*[2] as I expect to be going there these holidays.

Yours sincerely
A. E. Housman.

LC-GR MS. Richards, 184 (excerpt).

---

[1] See AEH to GR, 5 Sept. 1920.

[2] 'E[dward] B[olland] Osborn, author and journalist (1867–1938). In a review of Harold Monro's *Some Contemporary Poets* (1920) in *The Morning Post*, 46355 (17 Dec. 1920), 4, he wrote of AEH's 'smooth, shining tabloids of sentimentality' as 'an antidote to the bulky pomposity of late Victorianism'.

[1] *The Umbrian Towns*, by J. W. and A. M. Cruickshank (Grant Richards Ltd, 1901; 2nd edn., 1912), in the 'Grant Allen's Historical Guides' series.

[2] *The Smaller Tuscan Towns*, by the same authors and in the same series from the same publisher.

TO GRANT RICHARDS

Trinity College, Cambridge
28 Feb. 1921

Many thanks for the Grant Allen guides, which are more elaborate than
I knew.

Yrs
A. E. Housman.

*LC-GR MS: p.c. addressed 'Grant Richards Esq. | 8 St Martin's Street | Leicester Square |
W. C. 2.' Richards, 185 (excerpt).*

TO MESSRS GRANT RICHARDS LTD

Trinity College | Cambridge
17 March 1921

Dear Sirs,
 Mr Ireland[1] may set to music all the poems he wishes, but he must not
print No. 50 as a motto; \nor No. 40, which is what he means./ I return
his letter.

Yours faithfully
A. E. Housman.

LC-GR MS. Richards, 185 (incomplete and wrongly dated 2 March).

TO MESSRS GRANT RICHARDS LTD

Trinity College | Cambridge
20 March 1921

Dear Sirs,
 I do not want revenue from gramophone and mechanical rights, and
Mr Ireland is welcome to as much of it as his publisher will let him have. I
hope it may be sufficient to console him for not being allowed to print the
poem he wants.

Yours faithfully
A. E. Housman.

Messrs Grant Richards Ld.

PM MS. LC-GR t.s. Richards, 185; Maas, 184.

[1] John Ireland (1879–1962) published a setting of the last three stanzas of *ASL* X (*March*) in
1917 and of **XXXIX** (*'Tis time, I think, by Wenlock town*) in 1919. In 1921 he published *The Land of
Lost Content. Six Poems by A. E. Housman.*

TO D. A. WINSTANLEY

Trinity College
29 April 1921

Dear Winstanley,

I enclose my essays at inscriptions for Prior[1] and Sedley Taylor.[2] Their form is dictated by the necessity of putting the names in the nominative case; for neither Taylor nor Sedley is declinable, and the question of the declinability of Prior would excite acrimonious controversy.

To prevent the engraver from introducing J or U I have copied them out in proper script; but I know that my labour will be lost,[3] as it was in the case of the late Master's inscription.

Yours sincerely
A. E. Housman.

TCC Add. MS Letters b. 1^{26}. Maas, 185.

TO J. F. DUFF

Trinity College
30 April 1921

Dear Mr Duff,

I should be pleased to come to the meeting of your society[1] on Monday May 9th, and I suggest the *Moselle* of Ausonius if you think it suited.

I am yours sincerely
A. E. Housman.

TCC Add. MS a. 393/1.

[1] Joseph Prior (1834–1918), Fellow of TCC, 1860–1918.
[2] 1834–1920. Fellow of TCC, 1861–9, and resident in TCC thereafter.
[3] The inscriptions (for memorials in the college chapel) were in fact done correctly. See AEH to GR, 12 Oct. 1902, n. 4.

[1] Classical Reading Society.

TO AN UNKNOWN CORRESPONDENT

Trinity College | Cambridge
10 May 1921

Dear Sir,

I am obliged and flattered by your letter, but I do not wish to see the Fragment[1] separately published, nor, incidentally, to break the tender heart of Mr Grant Richards, which would be one consequence of my doing as you kindly suggest.

I am yours very truly
A. E. Housman.

Private MS.

TO GRANT RICHARDS

Trinity College | Cambridge
18 May 1921

My dear Richards,

The number of the Dutch *Museum*, containing a review of Manilius IV, which you have just sent me,—was it sent to you spontaneously by the publisher (as I rather gather from the word *Bewijsnummer* stamped upon it), or was it procured for you by some agency which you employ to collect reviews? And do the publishers of *Museum* generally send you a copy when it contains a review of a book published by you? (But I suppose it seldom does, being a classical periodical).

Yours sincerely
A. E. Housman.

LC-GR MS. Richards, 185.

TO DR PERCY WITHERS

Trinity College | Cambridge
1 June 1921

My dear Withers,

Next Tuesday, the 7th, I am motoring to Stroud; and as you lie on my way I was wondering if I might drop in on you for lunch and renew acquaintance with you and Mrs Withers after what seems a rather long

---

[1] *Fragment of a Greek Tragedy* (first published in 1883), or *Fragment of a Didactic Poem on Latin Grammar* (first published in 1899). A version of the former was printed in the *Trinity Magazine* in 1921, with acknowledgement of the *Cornhill Magazine* printing of 1901 but with a slightly different text: see *Poems* (1997), 531.

interval. I should arrive some time between 12 and 1. I suppose there is some place near where the chauffeur could stable his steed. I hope you are both well and still contented with your home.

Yours sincerely
A. E. Housman.

SCO MS. Withers, 49 (excerpt); Maas, 185.

TO MESSRS GRANT RICHARDS LTD

6 June 1921
Trinity College | Cambridge

Dear Sirs,
    Dr Ley[1] may publish his settings.

Yours faithfully
A. E. Housman.

Messrs Grant Richards Ld.

LC-GR MS.

TO GRANT RICHARDS

Trinity College | Cambridge
28 June 1921

My dear Richards,
    I am motoring to Eton on Saturday, and as you are, so to speak, in the neighbourhood, and spend that day at home, I was wondering if I might drop in for lunch, as I am not wanted at Eton before tea-time.
    I wrote you a letter more than a month ago, with questions about foreign reviews of my Manilius, to which you have not condescended to reply.[1]
    My kind regards to Mrs Richards.

Yours sincerely
A. E. Housman.

LC-GR MS. Richards, 185; Maas, 185–6.

---

[1] Henry George Ley (1887–1962), English organist and composer; appointed organist of Christ Church, Oxford, whilst an undergraduate, 1909; Director of Music at Eton, 1926. His settings of *ASL* XXXVI (*White in the moon the long road lies*) and LII (*Far in a western brookland*) were published in 1921.

[1] See AEH to GR, 18 May 1921.

TO ROBERT BRIDGES

Trinity College | Cambridge
29 June 1921

My dear Bridges,

I was in the country when I got your letter, and as my memory did not contain all the words of *Orpheus with his lute*[1] I put off answering till I returned here.

The translation of this piece seems to me graceful and easy, and there is nothing against it except that *eo* in the sense of *there* has no authority which can be trusted. If what he wrote is *ea*, that would be defensible (= along his route), though *ibi* would be more correct.

Tell me where[2] is not so good: without the English I could not have found out what the last five lines meant; and there are also faulty details.

I am yours very truly
A. E. Housman.

Bodleian MS, Dep. Bridges 110. 106–7.

TO J. D. DUFF

Trinity College
30 June 1921

Dear Duff,

I have looked at Lucr. I 657 and I think it ridiculous that the subject of the verbs *cernunt, fugitant, metuunt, amittunt, cernunt, credunt, reparcent*, should be the title of a book, the alternative title of a book, and the title of two other books,—the history of Herodotus and the epistles of Aeschines. The subject must be the same as the subject of *faciant* 655, namely *qui materiem rerum esse putarunt ignem*.

It is a further absurdity of Ernout's[1] to fancy that the names Μοῦσαι and περὶ φύσεως were given to Heraclitus himself.

Yours sincerely
A. E. Housman.

TCC Add. MS c. 196¹. Maas, 415–16.

---

[1] *All is True* (or *Henry VIII*), 3. 1. 3, by Shakespeare and John Fletcher.
[2] The song *Tell me where is Fancy bred: The Merchant of Venice*, 3. 2. 63.

[1] In his edn. of Lucretius (1920).

TO GRANT RICHARDS

Trinity College | Cambridge
14 July 1921

My dear Richards,

I am afraid that the reason why you do not answer my letters is that you feel awkward because you said that you would be able to repay my loan by April.[1] But I never imagined that you would: I knew your sanguine temperament (due, in Herbert French's[2] opinion, to an over-generous diet) far too well; and I write now to prevent you from afflicting yourself unnecessarily. I am not suffering any inconvenience, and the money would only be lying at the bank in my current account.

Yours sincerely
A. E. Housman.

BMC MS.

TO GRANT RICHARDS

Trinity College | Cambridge
21 July 1921

My dear Richards,

I am very sorry to hear the tale of all your unmerited troubles; though 'lassitude and inertia'[1] are my normal condition, especially in this weather. I hope you will not worry yourself about anything connected with me.

I have been away from Cambridge a great deal since the beginning of June, and I now am settling down to work. I am obliged to be here at the beginning of August for a meeting of the Classical Association, damn it: I am not a member, but they have chosen to meet here, and Americans are coming, and I am the only classical professor \of Cambridge/ who is able to deliver an address.[2] If I go away later in the month it will be to meet some of my family at Monmouth. I intend to go to Paris for a week about September 10, and if that is about the time when you would be going to fetch Mrs Richards back, of course I should like to go with you.

[1] See AEH to GR, 12 Dec. 1920.   [2] Author Herbert [Stanley] French (1875–1951).

[1] Standard medical phraseology.
[2] AEH read *The Application of Thought to Textual Criticism* to the Classical Association at Cambridge on 4 Aug. 1921.

I would not insist on your flying, as I could face land and sea with you for courier.

Yours sincerely
A. E. Housman.

Thanks for the information about *Museum*.[3]

LC-GR MS. Richards, 185–6 (nearly complete); Maas, 186.

TO A. S. F. GOW

[Trinity College
5 Aug. 1921]

Belger's *Moriz Haupt* p. 126. But what he said was that he would write *Constantinopolitanus* for *o*.[1]

A. E. H.

With TCC Add. MS c. 112[56].

TO F. W. HALL

Trinity College | Cambridge
10 Aug. 1921

Dear Mr Hall,
    If there is yet time, I should be obliged if the following correction could be made in my paper on Lucan VII 460–465.[1]
    On the second page the name Lemaire occurs twice: it ought in both places to be Weber.

I am yours very truly
A. E. Housman.

BMC MS.

---

[3] See AEH to GR, 18 May and 28 June 1921.

[1] A reference to the statement made by Moriz Haupt in opposition to the strictly palaeographical method of emendation, which AEH the previous day quoted in *The Application of Thought to Textual Criticism*: 'If the sense requires it, I am prepared to write *Constantinopolitanus* where the MSS. have the monosyllabic interjection *o*': *Selected Prose*, 141; Ricks (1988), 333.

[1] *CQ* 15 (Oct. 1921), 172–4: *Classical Papers*, 1043–5.

TO GRANT RICHARDS

KING'S HEAD HOTEL, | MONMOUTH.
21 Aug. 1921

My dear Richards,

My present intention is to fly to Paris on Sept. 8 and stay there a week. But if you are thinking of going there at anything like the same date, I would rather travel with you, even if you went by land and water instead of air, if it were agreeable to you. I shall not begin taking steps to secure passage by aeroplane till I return to Cambridge, which will be on next Friday. I hope your health is all right or improving.

Yours sincerely
A. E. Housman.

LC-GR MS. Richards, 186.

TO GRANT RICHARDS

Trinity College | Cambridge
26 Aug. 1921

My dear Richards,

Thanks for you letter, which I have just found here; but you do not say whether, on the 8th or 9th Sept., you would or would not travel by air. My intention is to go to Paris, and I not only must notify the Air Service people in good time but also must send some short notice to my friends and acquaintances there. I mean to stay \there/ a week, and I have taken so much holiday and done so little work in this vacation that I do not think I shall prolong the time. St Malo would be interesting, but too far; Boulogne not interesting, nor probably Dieppe. My kind regards to Mrs Richards.

Yours sincerely
A. E. Housman.

LC-GR MS. Richards, 186.

TO GRANT RICHARDS

Trinity College | Cambridge
1 Sept. 1921

My dear Richards,

As I did not hear from you by Tuesday evening I wrote and secured passage to Paris by the Messageries Aeriennes on the morning of the 8th. I wrote you a letter last Friday to the Hôtel Normandy, which apparently you did not get, to say that Paris was my only objective and that I had already taken more than my due of holiday in the country, so that St. Malo etc. would not suit me; and this naturally applies to Jersey. I am sorry it could not be managed, and I hope you will get a holiday which will do you good.

Yours sincerely
A. E. Housman.

I expect to be at the Hôtel Continental, and stay a week.

LC-GR MS. Richards, 186–7.

TO GRANT RICHARDS

Trinity College | Cambridge
16 Sept 1921

My dear Richards,

I suppose you are back from Jersey. In the first place I must thank you for *Tahiti*,[1] which in my postcard I forgot to do. Secondly, Winstanley,[2] whom you have met here, and I are coming to London some day next week, *not Friday*, to see Max Beerbohm's things at the Leicester Gallery[3] and lunch at the Café Royal[x] [←xat 1 o' clock]; and I wish you would join us, at least at lunch, and let me know in good time what day will suit you best.

Yours sincerely
A. E. Housman.

PM MS. LC-GR t.s. Richards, 187; Maas, 186.

TO GRANT RICHARDS

[Trinity College | Cambridge
27 September 1921

My dear Richards,]

Tell him that the wish to include a glimpse of my personality in a literary article is low, unworthy, and American. Tell him that some men are more interesting than their books but my book is more interesting than its man.[1] Tell him that Frank Harris found me rude and Wilfrid Blunt found me

---

[1] By 'Tihoti' (George Calderon), an account, written 1913–15, of Calderon's visit to Tahiti in 1906. It was left unfinished when Calderon was killed at Gallipoli.

[2] See List of Recipients.

[3] An exhibition of his caricatures opened on 11 May 1921.

[1] Cf. Dr Johnson, *The Plan of a Dictionary of the English Language*: 'my book is more learned than its author'. (I owe this parallel to Christopher Ricks.)

dull.[2] Tell him anything else that you think will put him off. Of course if he did nevertheless persist in coming to see me I should not turn him out, as I only do that to newspaper reporters.

> [Yours sincerely
> A. E. Housman.]

Richards, 187; Maas, 187.

TO CHARLES SAYLE

> Trinity College
> 11 Oct. 1921

My dear Sayle,

Many thanks for your letter. I cannot let you be my host, as you kindly offer; but when I know more exactly than I yet do about my engagements in the neighbourhood of Nov. 14 I will write again.[1]

> Yours sincerely
> A. E. Housman.

Lilly MSS 1. 1. 3.

TO GRANT RICHARDS

> Trinity College | Cambridge
> 18 Oct. 1921

My dear Richards,

Come to lunch at 1. 30 by all means to-morrow.

> Yours sincerely
> A. E. Housman.

LC-GR MS.

TO GRANT RICHARDS

> Trinity College | Cambridge
> 20 Oct. 1921

My dear Richards,

I wish I could be of real help to you in your troubles, which I am very sorry to hear of; but the worst of it is that you are not the only one of my friends who is in want of money. Besides your £500[1] I have lent £600 to

---

[2] See AEH to GR, 15 May 1919 n. 3.

[1] Sayle had invited AEH to the annual dinner of Oxford men at Cambridge on 14 Nov.

[1] See AEH to GR, 12 Dec. 1920.

others, £300 of which I do not expect to see again (and I do not mind if it is the same with your £500), and the last loan I was obliged to restrict and make it less than was asked. I possess much less than you probably suppose. As I have nobody dependent on me I have always spent nearly up to my income; and at this moment my wealth consists of about £300 in the bank, and £1500 in investments which would fetch much less if realized, and the dividends from which do not pay my income-tax. Therefore, in view of my means and of other claims on them which may arise, I am not properly able to lend you even the least which you think enough for your immediate needs; and, being despondent by temperament as you are sanguine, I do not believe that it really would be enough. Even if your calculations are right, accidents will happen, like your ill-health earlier in the year. Naturally your troubles make me unhappy, and I hope you will not increase them by vexing yourself about repaying the £500. I shall never think of it.

Yours sincerely
A. E. Housman.

BMC MS.

TO GRANT RICHARDS

Trinity College | Cambridge
27 Oct. 1921

My dear Richards,

I had one of my loans repaid yesterday, so I can send what you want, and I enclose two \(2)/ cheques for £125. 0. 0. each. I am glad things are going better.[1]

The walnuts are being eaten in Combination Room,[2] and I must thank you also for the works of Willy-Collette,[3] though I have not yet found time to start demoralizing myself with them.

Yours sincerely
A. E. Housman.

BMC MS.

[1] AEH is being very generous. When GR's business was in difficulties in 1920, he lent him £500, and transformed the loan into a gift before now advancing him another £250. See AEH to GR, 12 Dec. 1920 and 14 July 1921. In 1932 GR sent AEH a copy of George Bernard Shaw's *Three Plays for Puritans: The Devil's Disciple, Caesar and Cleopatra, & Captain Brassbound's Conversion*, which he had published in 1901 and Shaw had autographed on 27 March 1929, in an attempt to compensate for AEH's large losses. It was appraised as having a market value of £250. See Naiditch (2005), 27–8, for further information.

[2] The senior common room at TCC.

[3] Henri Gauthier-Villars (1859–1931), husband of French author Sidonie-Gabrielle Colette (1873–1954), published in 1900–3 the four 'Claudine' novels, reminiscences of an uninhibited young woman, under his pen-name 'Willy'.

TO DR PERCY WITHERS

Trinity College | Cambridge
30 Oct. 1921

My dear Withers,

It is very kind of you to ask me, and I know that if I came I should enjoy myself; but I do not see the chance of getting away this term, which is full of continuous engagements to an extent which I cannot remember the like of. These engagements, I ought in honesty to confess, are many of them convivial, but not all: for instance next week is full of prelections by candidates (10 in number) for the professorship of Greek, some of which I want to hear and one of which I must.[1]

This extraordinary autumn is at last beginning to put on colour, about a month late.

Coming back from Stroud I was arrested by the beauty of the church at Bloxham, and so made the acquaintance of the Vicar (or Rector), who directed me to Adderbury and King's Sutton. It was a great treasure-trove, as I had never heard of this group, though it appears that they are celebrated.

My kind regards to Mrs Withers. I am really sorry not to be able to take advantage of your invitation.

Yours sincerely
A. E. Housman.

SCO MS. Maas, 187.

TO CHARLES SAYLE

Trinity College
3 Nov. 1921

My dear Sayle,

I will come to the Oxford dinner on the 14th and I enclose Postal Order for 8/-[.]

Yours sincerely
A. E. Housman.

CUL Add. MS 2588/321.

---

[1] AEH's friend and former colleague Arthur Platt was a candidate for the Regius Professorship left vacant by the death of Henry Jackson. A. C. Pearson was appointed. See AEH to Pearson, 16 Nov. 1921.

TO CHARLES SAYLE

Trinity College
9 Nov. 1921

My dear Sayle,

It may be vanity, but I believe myself to be more capable of uttering one word and adding nothing than either the late Mr Gladstone[1] or the present Sir John Sandys.[2] But I rather gather that 'Oxford' is to be prefaced by other words, which is not so much in my true vein: still, I suppose I could say something.[3]

Yours sincerely
A. E. Housman.

Lilly MSS 1. 1. 3. Maas, 188.

TO DR G. C. WILLIAMSON

Trinity College | Cambridge
11 Nov. 1921

Dear Dr Williamson,

It was not pressure of duties which prevented me from sending you a contribution last year,[1] but torpor of the inventive faculty; and this, I regret to say, persists.

I am yours very truly
A. E. Housman.

Princeton MS (Keats Memorial Volume II: Letters Gen. MSS [bound] Am 21565). Envelope addressed 'Dr Williamson | Burgh House | Well Walk | Hampstead | N. W. 3'.

[1] 1809–98. British Prime Minister.
[2] John [Edwin] Sandys (1844–1922). Fellow of St John's College, Cambridge (1867–1907), Tutor (1870–1900), and Public Orator at Cambridge (1876–1919); knighted, 1911; author of *A History of Classical Scholarship* (1903–8) and numerous works on classical oratory.
[3] Sayle had asked AEH to propose the toast of Oxford at the annual dinner of Oxford men at Cambridge on 14 Nov.
[1] See AEH to Williamson, 24 Oct. 1920.

TO GRANT RICHARDS

Trinity College | Cambridge
11 Nov. 1921

My dear Richards,

I will not under any circumstances allow a portrait of me to appear in an "authorised edition". Mrs Asquith[1] and Lord Alfred Douglas[2] can do such things if they like.

The municipal hospitality of Ventimiglia must have made me very drunk, for I forget the whole affair.[3] My recollection is that you and I climbed in mist or drizzle a hill with a castle on it, that we lunched at a restaurant where you after much palaver induced the proprietor to furnish us with a viand which I did not much admire, small envelopes of paste enclosing mincemeat,[4] and that we walked through the town and under some trees by the shore to a rough stone breakwater. But I suppose I dreamt all this while I was under the table.

Yours sincerely
A. E. Housman.

LC-GR MS. LC-GR t.s. Richards, 135 (incomplete); Maas, 188.

TO PROFESSOR A. C. PEARSON

Trinity College | Cambridge
16 Nov. 1921

Dear Professor Pearson,

I congratulate you very sincerely on your election.[1] As Platt was after all a candidate, my sentiments were divided, and my joy is not unalloyed; but I told those electors who consulted me that I was glad it was they and not <me> \I/ who had to choose between you, and that they would be very wrong if they chose any of the other eight. The chief danger was that

---

[1] Margot (1864–1945), second wife of statesman Herbert Henry Asquith (1852–1928), published in 1920 an autobiography that contained as a frontispiece a photographic portrait of her in a turban reading.

[2] Lord Alfred [Bruce] Douglas (1870–1945) customarily included portraits of himself in his books. *The Collected Poems of Lord Alfred Douglas* (1919) had a photographic portrait by W. Ramsford as a frontispiece.

[3] According to Belfort Bax's recollection of GR's and AEH's report of the event, an official reception for AEH during his visit in 1915: Richards, 132–5. GR had appealed to AEH for confirmation that the story was not true.

[4] Ravioli.

[1] As Regius Professor of Greek at Cambridge.

some of them had a passion for youth, or comparative youth; but merit
has gained the day against it.

Yours very truly

A. E. Housman.

KCC MS Misc. 34/31. Maas, 189.

TO HARRIET MONROE

Trinity College | Cambridge | England
30 Nov. 1921

Dear Madam,

I do not think I have ever sent unpublished poems to Mr Witter Bynner:[1]
I have sent him a few which have appeared in English papers or journals,
and one or more of these have reappeared in American publications.

I am flattered by your request, but I have no poems by me which I wish
to see in print. I thank you much for the two numbers of *Poetry* which you
have been kind enough to send me.

I am yours sincerely

A. E. Housman.

*University of Chicago MS. Envelope addressed 'Mrs Harriet Monroe | Editor of Poetry | 543 Cass
Street | Chicago, Ill. | U. S. A.' Maas, 189.*

TO SIR HERBERT WARREN

Trinity College | Cambridge
6 Dec. 1921

My dear Warren,

I have been a long time without thanking you for your lecture on Virgil,[1]
for I see that your accompanying note was about the candidates for our
Greek chair. So in thanking you I will say that I think the right man was
chosen, as Platt, whom I should put beside him, did not really want to
leave London.

[1] In fact, he sent Bynner *The sigh that heaves the grasses* (later *LP* XXVII) with a letter of 12
Oct. 1913.

[1] *Virgil in Relation to the Place of Rome in the History of Civilization: A Lecture Given to Oxford University
Extension Students by Sir Herbert Warren, K. V. C. O., in August mdccccxxi* (1921).

Your brother[2] has built us a new Combination Room with which everyone is pleased and which we are to handsel[3] on Christmas Day.

Yours sincerely
A. E. Housman.

BMC MS. Tipped-in on fly-leaf of copy of LP *(1922) which contains the slip 'With the author's compliments'.*

TO HENRY FESTING JONES

Trinity College | Cambridge
6 Dec. 1921

Dear Jones,

I thought I had a lot of copies knocking about, but it took some little time to rout out a decent specimen, and now I am belated, as your book[1] came this morning. I can see that I shall greatly enjoy reading it, and I wish that I on my part could have sent you something new.

I am yours sincerely
A. E. Housman.

CUL MS, Keynes I. i. 43, in ASL *(1907).*

TO MARIA RICHARDS

Trinity College | Cambridge
10 Dec. 1921

Dear Mrs Grant Richards,

Many thanks for your kind invitation,[1] which I am delighted to accept. If I may come to you on Friday the 23rd and stay till the Tuesday, that will suit me excellently. I hope to find you all well.

Yours sincerely
A. E. Housman.

BMC MS. Richards, 187.

[2] Edward Prioleau Warren (1856–1937), who specialized in domestic and collegiate architecture.

[3] Inaugurate the use of. Cf. *ASL* L 16: 'handselled them long before'.

[1] *Mount Eryx and Other Diversions of Travel* (1921).

[1] For Christmas.

TO SYDNEY COCKERELL

Trinity College
16 Dec. 1921

My dear Cockerell,

This[1] is so very precious that I return it instantly, after showing it to Winstanley, who shared my curiosity about Miss Cornforth.[2] I am very grateful for the sight of it. It will often flash upon that inward eye which is the bliss of solitude.[3]

Yours very truly
A. E. Housman.

Princeton MS (Gen. MSS. Misc.). Maas, 190.

TO GRANT RICHARDS

Trinity College | Cambridge
1<7>6 Dec. 1921

My dear Richards,

It is very kind of you to ask me to stay longer, and I should not be averse from meeting Robert Lynd;[1] but it would upset arrangements which I have made, and would consequently interfere with my comfort, to which I am much attached; so I will pray you to have me excused.

On Friday I would travel with you to Cookham, if that would suit you.

Yours sincerely
A. E. Housman.

LC-GR MS. Richards, 188; Maas, 189.

---

[1] 'A photograph of Rossetti with his brother W. M. R., Swinburne and Fanny Cornforth': Cockerell's note written on the MS. 'W. M. R.' is William Michael Rossetti.

[2] Fanny Cornforth (1824–1906)—real name Sarah Cox—became Rossetti's model in 1858 and his mistress and housekeeper in 1862. Nicknamed 'The Elephant', she antagonized his family and friends by her coarseness and quarrelled with them when he died. Mention of her was substantially edited out of memoirs of Rossetti for over sixty years after his death.

[3] Wordsworth, *I wandered lonely as a cloud*, 21–2: 'They flash upon that inward eye | Which is the bliss of solitude'.

[1] Robert [Wilson] Lynd (1879–1949). Journalist and essayist; contributor to the *Daily News*, 1908–47. A collection of his articles, *The Pleasures of Ignorance*, was published by GR in 1921. On AEH's death, he paid tribute in the *Daily Chronicle*: 'In his use of his simple materials ... he was profoundly original. He ordered his unambitious words with the skill of an epigrammatist and, though the music of his verse was an echo from the past, he contrived by his genius to impose it on his generation as a personal music expressive of a personal vision of life' (quoted in Richards, 290).

TO GRANT RICHARDS

Trinity College | Cambridge
19 Dec. 1921

My dear Richards,

Very well, 5. 45 on Friday at Paddington. I had decided on general grounds of propriety to bring a dress suit. I ought to have thanked you before for Norman Douglas's book.[1]

Yours
A. E. Housman.

LC-GR MS. Richards, 188 (excerpts).

TO MARIA RICHARDS

Trinity College | Cambridge
28 Dec. 1921

Dear Mrs Grant Richards,

There is nothing in to-day's *Times* about the great Cookham and Maidenhead match,[1] but I hope you had the pleasure of watching a glorious victory, and that Charles and Geoffrey particularly distinguished themselves.[2] I got safely home, very much the better for my Christmas under your roof. A happy new year from

Yours sincerely
A. E. Housman.

BMC MS. Richards, 190 (nearly complete).

TO PROFESSOR D'ARCY THOMPSON

Trinity College | Cambridge
31 Dec. 1921

Dear Thompson,

This is to thank you heartily for your Christmas present, which I have read with the greatest enjoyment, and to wish you a happy New Year.

Yours sincerely
A. E. Housman.

St Andrews MS 23592.

---

[1] *Alone* (1921), a memoir of travels during the Great War.

[1] A local rugby match.

[2] The Richards's son Charles, recently a naval cadet, was instrumental in setting up a Cookham rugby club: Richards, 190. Geoffrey was the Richards's younger son.

1922

TO MAJOR HENRY CHOLMONDELEY JACKSON

Trinity College | Cambridge
4 Jan. 1922

Dear Colonel[1] Jackson,

I know from experience that the paper of this edition[2] does not take ink well, so I have copied the poem[3] on a separate sheet.

I am yours sincerely
A. E. Housman.

TCC Add. MS 167, with the volume designated C. 13. 74. UCL has a photograph, Lilly MSS 2. 1. 10 is a t.s. copy.

TO A. S. F. GOW

Trinity College | Cambridge
7 Jan. 1922

Dear Gow,

There is a short and rather good book on Rossetti by Joseph Knight,[1] who knew him well, and I suppose the diffuse and solemn William Michael[2] would yield you something; but lives of Meredith are no use. W. B. Scott[3] is more promising; but most of the amusing tales about the menagerie[4] probably do not exist in print.

Yours sincerely
A. E. Housman.

TCC Add. MS c. 112[14]. Maas, 190.

[1] For 'Major',
[2] The 1st edn. of *ASL* (1896), a copy of which was put into the Trinity Book Club in 1897 at the request of Henry Jackson and bought by him at the subsequent sale for 1s.
[3] *Loveliest of trees, the cherry now* (*ASL* II).

[1] *Life of Dante Gabriel Rossetti* (1887).
[2] *Rossetti Papers, 1862–1870*, ed. William Michael Rossetti (1903).
[3] *Autobiographical Notes of the Life of William Bell Scott ... and notices of his artistic and poetic circle of friends, 1830 to 1882*, ed. W. Minto (1892).
[4] 'The eccentrics in Rossetti's circle' (Maas, 190), but Naiditch (1995), 162, thinks 'perhaps only the zoo'. Either is possible. Rossetti shared Tudor House, 16 Cheyne Walk, Chelsea, with his brother William Michael Rossetti, Swinburne, Meredith, and the painter Frederick Sandys,

TO A. S. F. GOW

Trinity College | Cambridge
22 Feb. 1922

Dear Gow,

Ovid does not in point of fact use *nescĭŏ* except in *nescioquis*, but it cannot be supposed that he would feel any scruple, when Catullus had already used it 85 2, and he himself \has/ *conferŏ* ex Pont. I 1 25 and *oderŏ* amor. III 11 35.

I may be in Eton at the end of term, as that Minotaur (or Μινώκριος[1] rather) the Essay Society is bleating for a new victim.

Yours sincerely
A. E. Housman.

TCC Add. MS c. 112¹⁵. Maas, 416.

TO A. F. SCHOLFIELD

Trinity College
25 Feb. 1922

Dear Scholfield,

This gentleman[1] is hoping to pay his railway fare to Italy by selling some of the few copies remaining of this book;[2] he has also bought a copy of my Manilius and presumably thereby impaired his fortune: therefore I am to suggest to the College Library that it should purchase a copy of his work. He will send one on approval if you should wish it.

Yours sincerely
A. E. Housman.

TCC Add. MS c. 80²¹. Maas, 190–1.

---

and the household was notorious for its drunkenness, fights, parties, and indiscreet love-affairs. However, Rossetti kept a menagerie of exotic and rare birds and animals. Knight, 95, tells 'the only surviving story presenting Rossetti in a light absolutely comical': it involves a zebu which 'by super-bovine exertion ... tore up by the roots the tree to which it was attached, and chased its tormentor round the garden'. E. R. and J. Pennell, *The Life of James McNeill Whistler*, 5th edn. (1911), 80, cited by Naiditch, tell of a bull of Bashan charging at Rossetti, and of a wombat, thought lost, being discovered dead in a cigar box. Evelyn Waugh, *Rossetti: His Life and Works*, 2nd edn. (1975), 117, lists the animals in the household.

[1] 'The ram' was the nickname of A[llan] B[eville] Ramsay (1872–1955), Assistant Master at Eton, 1895–1925, and host to the Essay Society. He was Master of Magdalene College, Cambridge, 1925–47. For another metaphorical Minotaur, see *Selected Prose*, 154.

[1] R. T. Günther.
[2] *Pausilypon.* Author and work are identified in Naiditch (1995), 162.

TO DR PERCY WITHERS

Trinity College | Cambridge
3 March 1922

My dear Withers,

I am very sorry to hear that you are ill,[1] especially with one of those abominable maladies which require one to govern one's appetites. I hope you may succeed in nipping it in the bud by dint of your abstinence. I for my part am not more gouty than usual, and expecting to eat a particularly good dinner this evening. I did get your Christmas letter, which I ought no doubt to have answered; but letters which do not ask questions very often go without answers from me. I do not go abroad in the winter, and I only spent just Christmas itself in Berkshire, where the carol-singers walked off with a bottle of champagne which had been put out of doors to cool. My host thereupon wrote to the vicar of the parish; but as they were not choir-boys he disclaimed all responsibility for their morals.

It would be a great pleasure to me to come and see you some time in May or thereabouts, when your country and garden are likely to be near their best. If you had the storms of rain that we had the day before yesterday, it must have done something towards replenishing your watersprings.

No, no more poetry, or at least nothing to speak of.

My kind regards to Mrs Withers.

Yours sincerely
A. E. Housman.

It is a fearful thing to be
    The Pope.
That cross will not be laid on me,
    I hope.
A righteous God would not permit
    It.
The Pope himself must often say,

---

[1] Withers, 11–12: 'Not illness merely, but physical disabilities and cares generally, light or heavy, real or threatened, won his immediate interest and solicitude, and however diffident the inquiries he made, there was no doubting their absolute sincerity: he genuinely wished to know as one confident of the sympathy he had to give, and desired to give.' The correspondence with Withers, and Withers's own reminiscences, bear this out.

After the labours of the day,
"It is a fearful thing to be
   Me."[2]

SCO MS. TCC MS a. 71^{151} is a copy. Withers, 66, quotes the poem and one sentence.

TO AN UNKNOWN CORRESPONDENT

Trinity College | Cambridge | England
8 March 1922

Dear Sir,

The Press of this University proposed to Jackson in the last year of his life that his scattered papers should be collected and reprinted. He was pleased by the proposal, but he wished to make changes and additions, which were prevented first by the state of his health and then by his death. The Press, after consulting those members of the University who are most interested in Greek philosophy, has decided not to proceed with the design. The reasons given are that the collection would not possess unity or completeness, and that the papers themselves are readily accessible. This of course is truer of England than of Norway; and I am sorry that your wish is not likely to be gratified. It is possible that a memoir may some day be published,[1] but I do not think it has yet been taken in hand. I thank you for the interest which you take in the matter, and it would have given pleasure to Jackson.

I am yours very truly
A. E. Housman.

Columbia MS, Housman Box. Maas, 191.

TO ANDREW BENNETT

15 March 1922

I must begin by expressing my high sense of the honour which the Senatus Academicus of the University of St Andrews have designed to confer upon me, and my gratitude to them for their proposal; and I must then beg them to forgive me if I ask leave to decline it, as I have declined

[2] Benedict XV died on 22 Jan. 1922, and Pius XI was elected his successor on 6 Feb. See *Poems* (1997), 514, 523, 561, for disrespectful remarks by AEH about Catholicism.

[1] *Henry Jackson, O. M.* by R. St John Parry (1926) contained a memoir, a list of books dedicated to Jackson, a bibliography of his writings, *obiter scripta* (mostly letters), two lectures, and a sermon, but none of Jackson's substantial papers.

similar honours which other Universities have with similar kindness been prepared to bestow. The reasons which render me unwilling to receive such distinctions would be tedious to enumerate, and some of them might not be easy to express; but they are in my judgment <sufficient> decisive. There is no need to assure you that they do not include any lack of veneration for your ancient and famous University, any failure to understand the dignity conferred by its degrees, or any indifference to the goodwill and generosity of the Senatus Academicus in my regard; and I trust that I am showing more respect for St Andrews in writing thus, than if I put forward the excuse of inability to be present at the appointed date.

I am, dear Sir,

Yours faithfully
A. E. Housman.

Lilly MSS 1. 1. 3 (draft).

TO JEAN-LOUIS PERRET

[*c*.27 Mar. 1922]

I wish I could make some return for your amiable letter by giving you counsel of any value or utility.[1] But the tradition of Juvenal's MSS is so blended and erased that no classification, in the full sense of the word, can be hoped for. It is however interesting to note the occurrence of good and rare lections in MSS which are not on the whole good and <which> some of which are quite late; and I suggest that you might find it worth while to read \and compare/ if you have not done so already, the account of the Dresden MSS of Juvenal given in Rhein. Mus. LX pp. 202 sq.

I am afraid I can hardly expect you to find many MSS in Finland,[2] but I hope <you> \it/ will prove agreeable in other respects.

TCC MS with Adv. c. 20. 32: draft in pencil replying to Perret's letter of 24 Mar. 1922.

[1] Perret's doctoral thesis was on the MSS of Juvenal and was published as *La Transmission du texte de Juvénal* (Helsinki, 1927).

[2] Where he was going after his time in Florence.

TO SYDNEY COCKERELL

Trinity College
3 April 1922

Dear Cockerell,

Heffer[1] sent Hardy's poems all right, and at odd times I have been reading and marking them.[2] When you require them I can finish the job with little delay. At this moment I am rather full of my own affairs.[3]

Yours sincerely
A. E. Housman.

Fitzwilliam MS 64-1950. Maas, 192.

TO GRANT RICHARDS

Trinity College | Cambridge
3 April 1922

My dear Richards,

Thanks to you, I believe I possess Machen's[1] complete works. He is always interesting (except in the *Evening News*) and to some extent good. Mixing up religion and sexuality is not a thing I am fond of, and in this book[2] the Welsh element rather annoys me. The imitation of Rabelais is very clever.

I knew already, having been told, that it is wrong to have one's wine brought in a cradle, and now I know further that it is wrong to decant it; so in future I shall just have the cork drawn, and suck the liquid out of the bottle through a tube.

Yours sincerely
A. E. Housman.

Lilly MSS 1. 1. 3. Richards, 191; Maas, 191.

[1] Cambridge bookseller.

[2] Apparently for a projected selection (never published) from Hardy's *Collected Poems* (1919). See letter of 1 May 1922.

[3] During April, in at least 85 pages of his fourth notebook ('D'), AEH wrote 4 poems and most of another 2, and brought to completion at least 10, perhaps as many as 17, others. See *Poems* (1997), Introduction, lvii.

[1] Welsh writer Arthur Llewellyn Jones Machen (1863–1947), who contributed to the London *Evening Standard* from 1910. His fiction and verse were strongly influenced by Welsh folklore and the supernatural, and he was a member of the magical Order of the Golden Dawn. His novels include *The Great God Pan* (1894), *The Three Impostors* (1895), and *The Hill of Dreams* (1907). The latter was published by GR, as were two or three other works of his.

[2] *The Secret Glory* (1922).

TO GRANT RICHARDS

Trinity College | Cambridge
9 April 1922

My dear Richards,

It is now practically certain that I shall have a volume of poems ready for the autumn;[1] so I wish you would take what steps are necessary as soon as they are necessary. But do not mention it to anyone until you are obliged to mention it.

Perhaps you can tell me what my legal position is as regards a poem which I contributed in 1899 to the *Academy*.[2] They sent me a cheque, but I returned it: I don't know if that makes any difference.

Yours sincerely
A. E. Housman.

Lilly MSS 1. 1. 3. Richards, 191; Maas, 192.

TO GRANT RICHARDS

Trinity College | Cambridge
18 April 1922

My dear Richards,

Thanks for your reply. The book will probably be rather shorter than *A Shropshire Lad*; and it had better have a wider page, or smaller print, or both, as there are more poems in it which have long lines.

I desire particularly that the price should be moderate.

As to America, I much prefer that they should wait.

What is the *latest* date for sending you the complete manuscript?

Yours sincerely
A. E. Housman.

Lilly MSS 1. 1. 3. Richards, 191–2; Maas, 192–3.

---

[1] AEH's first definite mention to GR of *LP*, published on 19 Oct. 1922. He had hinted at it in a letter of 5 Sept. 1920 and denied its existence in another of 5 Jan. 1921.

[2] *Illic Jacet* (*LP* IV), published in *The Academy*, 58. 1451 (24 Feb. 1900), 169, and signed 'A. E. Housman'.

TO J. B. PRIESTLEY

Trinity College
19 April 1922.

Dear Mr Priestley,

I am much obliged by your kindness in sending me your *Brief Diversions*.[1] Some of the parodies and other verses I had read with great interest and pleasure in the *Cambridge Review*.[2]

I am yours very truly
A. E. Housman.

Texas MS. Maas, 193.

TO GRANT RICHARDS

Trinity College | Cambridge
22 April 1922

My dear Richards,

The end of September, as far as I can judge, would suit me quite well for publication. The size of page should at any rate not be more than in the Riccardi edition,[1] if so much. The poems should not be run on, as originally in *A Shropshire Lad*, but each should start on a fresh page.

If, as I rather gather from what you say, printers no longer print from MS, then I should be obliged if you did the type-writing,[2] though it will not be more legible than the hand I write literature in.

The Oxford dictionary defines *reach* as 'to stretch out continuously, to extend', and quotes 'how high reacheth the house' (1526) and 'the portico reaches along the whole front' (16<7>87). Perhaps your friends are baffled by the subjunctive mood, and think it ought to be *reaches*;[3] but see Psalm 138. 6 '*Though* the Lord *be* high, yet hath he respect unto the lowly'.

---

[1] *Brief Diversions: being Tales, Travesties, and Epigrams* (1922). It contains a parody of AEH, a 'Dedication for the "Shropshire Lad" ' entitled *To All the Gravediggers Between Ludlow Town and Hughley*. AEH's (unannotated) copy is now at BMC: Naiditch, *HSJ* 31 (2005), 173.

[2] Nearly all the pieces in the volume appeared in this journal. Priestley had in 1919 gone up to Trinity Hall, Cambridge, to read English and History (later switching to History and Political Science), and he was still in Cambridge when *Brief Diversions* was published.

[1] Of *ASL*, published in 1914.

[2] A t.s. copy of AEH's handwritten MS was prepared for the printers of the Riverside Press by GR's secretary Pauline Hemmerde: Richards, 197.

[3] In *ASL* XXXVI 10: 'And straight though reach the track'.

When you next print *A Shropshire Lad* I want to make 2 alterations.[4]

Yours sincerely
A. E. Housman.

Lilly MSS 1. 1. 3. Grant Richards, Author Hunting *(1932), 268–9. Maas, 193.*

TO D. B. HARDEN

Trinity College
24 April 1922

Dear Mr Harden,

It is only a year since I last had the pleasure of attending a meeting of the Classical Reading Society.[1] Spare me a little that I may recover my strength.[2] Social intercourse with human beings, however agreeable, is exhausting, and I cannot make a habit of it. Perhaps ten years hence, if the world lasts.

Yours sincerely
A. E. Housman.

TCC Add. MS a. 393/2. Envelope addressed 'D. B. Harden Esq. | Trinity College.' Note added at lower corner: "A.E.H. to be asked again <Easter> Lent Term | 1932".

TO DR PERCY WITHERS

Trinity College | Cambridge
22 April 1922

My dear Withers,

I could come to you on Saturday May 13 and stay till the Tuesday, and if that suits you it will delight me. I should be interested and pleased to meet Gordon Bottomley.[1] Most likely I should motor from Bletchley, and should not need to stable my steed. My kind regards to Mrs Withers.

Yours sincerely
A. E. Housman.

SCO MS.

[4] 'Loose' for 'Thick' in XXXVIII, and 'no more remembered' for 'long since forgotten' in LII. The changes, which he told to GR in person, were meant to appear in an issue simultaneous with *LP* (published on 19 Oct. 1922), but by GR's fault they did not appear until Nov. 1922. See AEH to Sparrow, 19 June 1934, and Richards, 264–5.

[1] See AEH to Duff, 30 Apr. 1921.

[2] Ps. 39: 13: 'O spare me, that I may recover strength, before I go hence, and be no more.'

[1] 1874–1948. Poet and dramatist. He published *The Mickle Drede and Other Verses* in 1896, and his work was included in Edward Marsh's first vol. of *Georgian Poetry* in 1912. His plays include *The Crier by Night* (1902), *King Lear's Wife* (performed in 1915; published in 1920), and *Gruach* (1921).

TO JOHN DRINKWATER

Trinity College | Cambridge
26 April 1922

Dear Mr Drinkwater,

A silly review in to-day's *Times*[1] reminds me that I never thanked you—or at least I think I did not, and indeed I usually put off writing letters till they do not get written at all—for giving me your *Seeds of Time*[2] when you were last in Cambridge. I particularly admired the \<second\> \third/ poem.[3]

I am yours very truly
A. E. Housman.

Marquette University MS (Elizabeth Whitcomb Houghton Collection, series 5, box 4). Maas, 194.

TO GRANT RICHARDS

Trinity College | Cambridge
30 April 1922

My dear Richards,

The specimen page looks all right to my untutored eye.

I am sorry that all my week-ends are occupied, either here or elsewhere, for the next month or so; and even this late spring will not delay your cherry blossom till June.

Yours sincerely
A. E. Housman.

Lilly MSS 1. 1. 3. Richards, 192–3 (excerpts).

---

[1] The review, of Drinkwater's *Selected Poems*, denounced him for plagiarism from *ASL*. AEH told Withers with 'anger and annoyance' that it was 'grossly unfair, the charge spitefully exaggerated—the work of jealousy' (Withers, 42).
[2] Published in 1921.   [3] *A Lesson to my Ghost.*

TO SYDNEY COCKERELL

Trinity College | Cambridge
1 May 1922

Dear Cockerell,

I return Hardy's poems, and in the table of contents I have marked those I like best. Longer lines mean that I feel sure those poems ought to be included in a selection.[1]

Yours sincerely
A. E. Housman.

Princeton MS (Gen. MSS. Misc.). Maas, 194.

TO GRANT RICHARDS

Trinity College | Cambridge
9 May 1922.

My dear Richards,

There is no leakage:[1] what has happened is merely that John o' London casually wrote a paragraph, completely false, about the early adventures of *A Shropshire Lad*,[2] and this reminded a man whom I knew here as Lieut. Lee, and who now seems to have a job on the *Weekly Despatch*, that I had let him have a poem for the *Blunderbuss* which he was editing.[3]

The only person besides you whom I have told is sure to be equally trustworthy, and is not in touch with journalists.

---

[1] See the letter of 3 Apr. 1922. Naiditch, *HSJ* 26 (2000), 108, notes that the copy of Hardy marked up by AEH now appears to be lost.

[1] Of the contents of *LP* in advance of publication.

[2] *John O' London's Weekly*, 6 May 1922: 'When, in 1896, Mr A. E. Housman sent the manuscript of *A Shropshire Lad* to a London publisher, it was accepted forthwith. In the letter of acceptance was a query as to when a second book of verse might be expected. Mr Housman replied: "As it has taken me twenty years to write this volume, maybe after twenty years more I'll send you another." '

[3] 'Argonaut' in his column 'Books and their Writers' (*The Weekly Dispatch*, 7 May 1922) recalls printing *As I gird on for fighting* (*LP* II) in *The Blunderbuss*, the Book of the 5th Officer Cadet Battalion, TCC, which he edited, and reprints the poem, which originally appeared above AEH's signature on p. 36 of vol. 3 (Mar. 1917) of the magazine. The poem was also reprinted in *The Trinity Magazine*, 2. 5 (Nov. 1920), 4.

The photograph is Oppé's, about 15 years ago I should think.[4] It appeared in the *British Weekly* in an article which you had more to do with than I.[5]

Yours sincerely
A. E. Housman.

Lilly MSS 1. 1. 3. Grant Richards, Author Hunting *(1932), 270; Richards, 193; Maas, 194–5.*

TO KATHARINE SYMONS

Trinity College | Cambridge
12 May 1922

My dear Kate,

I do not think that the rules of the London Library are to be taken very seriously. I never paid a fine in my life, and once when I kept a book three years it provoked no more than a mild remonstrance.

I fell into conversation the other day with a great though very Protestant medievalist,[1] and I enclose his rather illegible letter, which probably is not much to your purpose. Gasquet's book[2] is said to be rather dishonest in its suppressions. If one of your authorities is a book on Bath Abbey by one Hunt,[3] be warned that his preface betrays great ignorance, or what specialists regard as such.

To prefer Sussex to Monmouth is a sign of some refinement of taste. I think that very likely in late July or August I might come down your way. I think of going to Paris for a week at the beginning of June, and then staying here.

Thanks for the learned *Edwardian*,[4] which I return, as I seem to remember you are not rich in copies. I also return Jerry's letter, interesting as usual. His present companion is a new character to me.

---

[4] AEH gets both the name of the photographer and the date wrong. The photograph by E. O. Hoppé dates from 1911: Naiditch (2005), 163.

[5] A supplement to *The British Weekly*, 51. 1310 (7 Dec. 1911) contained numerous photographic portraits, some of literary figures, but AEH's is not among them.

[1] George Gordon Coulton (1858–1947), Lecturer in Medieval History, and author of such works as *Christ, St Francis, and To-day* (1919), *The Roman Catholic Church and the Bible: Some Historical Notes* (1921), and *Infant Perdition in the Middle Ages* (1922).

[2] Francis Aidan, Cardinal Gasquet (1846–1929), *Monastic Life in the Middle Ages, with a Note on Great Britain and the Holy See, 1792–1806* (1922).

[3] William Hunt, *An Account of the Priory of St Peter and St Paul, Bath* (1893).

[4] Magazine of King Edward's School, Bath, where Kate's husband was headmaster until 1921.

Another book by Laurence,[5] rather well reviewed. I hope Edward is quite recovered from his illness.

> Your affectionate brother
> A. E. Housman.

City of Bath Municipal Libraries MS. Maas, 195.

TO MARY WITHERS

> Trinity College | Cambridge
> 17 May 1922

Dear Mrs Withers,

We made a capital run to Bletchley in little more than 50 minutes, with the sun lighting the landscape and green leaves just as it should. To-day it rains in Cambridge, and appropriate gloom surrounds my emotions of regret, and of envy for Mr and Mrs Bottomley.[1]

> Yours sincerely
> A. E. Housman.

SCO MS.

TO GRANT RICHARDS

> Trinity College | Cambridge
> 22 May 1922

My dear Richards,

I am very much touched by your solicitude for the corruption of my mind, and I eagerly expect the new Proust.[1] I rather gather from your epistle to the world last Thursday[2] that your Mr Ronald Firbank[3] is a bit in the same line. I never heard of Jean Coctreau,[4] but I do know something of the Paris *bains de vapeur* (or *vapeurs* as Mr van Vechten[5] says).

[5] *Little Plays of St Francis.*

[1] See AEH to Withers, 22 Apr. 1922.

[1] Probably vol. 2 of *Le Côté des Gueramantes* (1921).

[2] GR's advertisement in the *TLS* 1061, 18 May 1922, 322.

[3] 1886–1926. Homosexual, a flamboyant aesthete, and an habitué of the Café Royal, he was known for his novels *Vainglory* (1915), *Caprice* (1917), and *Valmouth* (1919), and a short story *Santal* (1919), which were innovative in style. GR published his *Flower Beneath the Foot* in 1923.

[4] French writer, film actor and director Jean Cocteau (1889–1963). AEH gets his name wrong.

[5] American author Carl Van Vechten (1880–1964), from whose article on Firbank GR's advertisement quotes. In it Firbank is characterized as 'Aretino in Piccadilly. Jean Cocteau at the Savoy. The Oxford tradition with a dash of the Paris *bains de vapeurs* [*sic*]'.

I am flying to Paris (though not necessarily to these haunts of vice) on June 1 and I shall sleep in London the night before, Hotel Victoria, Northumberland Avenue; so perhaps we might manage to dine together.

Yours sincerely
A. E. Housman.

LC-GR MS. Richards, 193; Maas, 196.

TO DR PERCY WITHERS

Trinity College | Cambridge
23 May 1922

My dear Withers,

The marmalade has just arrived quite safe, and two pots when I only hoped for one; and I am very grateful both to you and Mrs Withers for your respective shares in the gift. It is a great pity that you should be laid up, and very nice of you to lay it on Bridges[1] and not on your entertainment of me.

Yours sincerely
A. E. Housman.

SCO MS. Maas, 196.

TO GRANT RICHARDS

Trinity College | Cambridge
25 May 1922

My dear Richards,

It is possible that I might be back from Paris on June 9, but not at all sure, and I might find myself hampered if I made any promise, so I had better regretfully decline.

Would you see about engaging a table at Verrey's at 7. 30 on the 31st. I have hardly ever been there, but I suppose it is a place where one dines in comfort without dressing: anyhow I shall have no dress things with me.

I am not at all likely to burst in on you at Oundle.[1]

Yours sincerely
A. E. Housman.

LC-GR MS. Richards, 194.

---

[1] Robert Bridges.

[1] 'A school of which he vaguely approved and where I had a son, Geoffrey': Richards, 194.

TO GRANT RICHARDS

Trinity College | Cambridge
26 May 1922

My dear Richards,

Many thanks for Proust. The 3 volumes are the right ones, though the numeration outside is absurdly stupid. I am keeping them to read in France.

Yours sincerely
A. E. Housman.

LC-GR MS. Richards, 194 (incomplete).

TO GAILLARD LAPSLEY

Trinity College
27 May 1922

Dear Lapsley,

I shall be very glad to come to-morrow at 1. 15.

Yours sincerely
A. E. Housman.

Brown University MS.

TO KATHARINE SYMONS

Trinity College | Cambridge
30 May 1922

My dear Kate,

I am just off to France for a week or so, so I send back Jerry's letters. The book you speak of, Wilkins (David), *Concilia*, is in the London Library but is in Latin.[1]

Your affectionate brother
A. E. Housman.

BMC MS.

---

[1] *Concilia Magnae Britanniae et Hiberniae, a synodo Verolamiensi, A.D. 446 ad Londinensem, A.D. 1717* (1737).

TO ALICE C. COOPER

Trinity College | Cambridge
31 May 1922

Dear Miss Cooper,

For many years I have been refusing English anthologists permission to print poems from *A Shropshire Lad*; but the book is not copyright in America, and my consent is not required.

I am yours very truly
A. E. Housman.

UCLA MS S/C 739/1. Envelope addressed 'Miss Alice C. Cooper | University High School | Oakland | California | U. S. A.'

TO LADY ANDERSON

Paris
3 June 1922

Dear Lady Anderson,

When these honours fall to my friends and acquaintances, I always write to congratulate their wives, if I have the pleasure of knowing them, because they are the persons who take most pleasure in the affair; and so I send these felicitations to you in particular, though I do not altogether exclude Sir Hugh.[1]

Yours sincerely
A. E. Housman.

CUL Add. MS 7649/46.

TO MARIA RICHARDS

Trinity College | Cambridge
12 June 1922

Dear Mrs Richards,

I am afraid I was even duller than usual, for I was not very well when I came to you; but I hope you will be pleased to hear that I think my stay at Bigfrith has set me right again.

Yours sincerely
A. E. Housman.

BMC MS. Richards, 194 (nearly complete).

[1] Sir Hugh Kerr Anderson (1865–1928). See List of Recipients.

TO DR PERCY WITHERS

Trinity College | Cambridge
12 June 1922

My dear Withers,

I am concerned to hear about your health, and I hope you will soon find relief, whichever way the doctors may decide.

The photograph[1] is not quite true to my own notion of my gentleness and sweetness of nature, but neither perhaps is my external appearance.

I am just back from France and have broached the first jar of marmalade, which inspires me with respect as well as gratitude towards Mrs Withers.

Yours sincerely
A. E. Housman.

SCO MS. Maas, 196–7.

TO GRANT RICHARDS

Trinity College | Cambridge
15 June 1922

My dear Richards,

I cannot arrange the order of the poems satisfactorily until I know for certain which I shall include and which omit; and on that point, as I told you, I want to consult one or two people.[1] Therefore I want the poems printed first simply according to the various metres they are written in, not at all as they will afterwards stand. Will the transpositions \<and>/ <omissions>, <and possibly insertions> which will then have to be made before the book arrives at its proper form be very expensive? If so, perhaps type-writing had better be used, but I do not like it, as it makes things look repulsive.

Yours sincerely
A. E. Housman.

PM MS. LC-GR t.s. Richards, 194–5; Maas, 197 (both nearly complete).

[1] Taken in May 1922, and reproduced opposite the title-page in Withers.
[1] W. P. Ker, J. W. Mackail, and a third, unnamed adviser.

TO GRANT RICHARDS

Trinity College | Cambridge
15 June 1922

My dear Richards,

I do not believe that *A Shropshire Lad* could be well translated into French, and I should not be able to judge whether the translation was even as good as it might be.

I return Charles's[1] post-card. As it comes from University College, I think I can guess who has been indiscreet.

Yours sincerely
A. E. Housman.

PM MS. Richards, 194 (nearly complete).

TO GRANT RICHARDS

17 June 1922

Ulysses received, also Firbank.[1] Thanks for both.

A. E. Housman.

PM MS. LC-GR t.s: p.c. addressed 'Grant Richards Esq. | 8 St Martin's Street | Leicester Square | W. C. 2'.

TO GRANT RICHARDS

Trinity College | Cambridge
19 June 1922

My dear Richards,

Herewith the manuscript, 50 pages.[1] Please acknowledge receipt. After all, I do not think much transposition will be required.

You must not do what you spoke of doing, preserve a copy of the book in its present state, as I value the opinion of posterity too much. When it is printed, let *two* copies be sent to me at first, for correction. It will save the

[1] 'My son's': Richards, 194.

[1] 'James Joyce's *Ulysses*, which he thought he might like to read, and ... some of the books of Ronald Firbank': Richards, 195. *Ulysses* was published in Paris in Feb. 1922 in an edn. of 1,000 numbered copies. Foreign edns. were banned in the United States until 1933, and in England until 1936, when the first English edn. appeared. On Firbank, see AEH to GR, 22 May 1922, n. 3.

[1] In fact, 51: AEH had numbered two pages '47', and '48' survives. See *Poems* (1997), Introduction, xxxiii, xxxiv.

printers trouble if you tell them that they had better not try to improve my spelling and punctuation.

Yours sincerely
A. E. Housman.

PM MS. LC-GR t.s. Richards, 195; Maas, 197.

TO A. S. F. GOW

Trinity College | Cambridge
20 June 1922

Dear Gow,

Many thanks: these Persons of Quality drink from a Hippocrene or Onocrene of their own.[1]

I shall be here till the end of July, I expect. I hope we shall see you as usual when your term is over.

Yours
A. E. Housman.

TCC Add. MS c. 112[16]. Maas, 197–8.

TO GRANT RICHARDS

I am returning *Ulysses*, which I have scrambled and waded through, and found one or two half-pages amusing. Firbank also is very unrewarding hitherto. But I am grateful to you all the same.

A. E. H.
24 June 1922

Trin. Coll. Camb.

Yale MS (MS Vault. Joyce, series 1, box 4, folder 5): p. c. addressed 'Grant Richards Esq. | 8 St Martin's Street | Leicester Square | W. C. 2.' Richards, 197.

---

[1] Hippocrene ('horse-fountain', because thought to have been produced by a stamp of the hoof of the winged horse Pegasus) was a spring, sacred to the Muses, on Mt. Helicon. Its waters were thought to inspire with poetry those who drank them. Onocrene, by analogy, would be an ass-fountain.

TO J. W. MACKAIL

Trinity College | Cambridge
26 June 1922

Secret as the grave.

Dear Mackail,

I am bringing out a volume of poems this autumn: will you do me the kindness to look through them first? They are neither long nor many.

Yours sincerely
A. E. Housman.

Fitzwilliam MS Autogr. 3/2–1946. Maas, 198.

TO GRANT RICHARDS

Trinity College | Cambridge
8 July 1922

My dear Richards,

I do not know what penalty the *Tatler* people have laid themselves open to,[1] and anyhow I should think they had better be left alone. I am told that Vaughan Williams has mutilated another poem just as badly, to suit his precious music.[2] Probably the sort of people who read the *Tatler* would not realise that anything was missing, or prefer the full text if they had it.

The poem in italics is to stand facing p. 1,[3] so I do not think the print is too small.

Yours sincerely
A. E. Housman.

Lilly MSS 1. 1. 3. Richards, 197; Maas, 198.

TO GRANT RICHARDS

Trinity College | Cambridge
10 July 1922

My dear Richards,
I enclose:
Proofs corrected

---

[1] By printing without permission part of *Bredon Hill* (*ASL* XXI), illustrated by Percy Home, on 5 July.
[2] See AEH to GR, 20 Dec. 1920.   [3] The prefatory poem, *We'll to the woods no more.*

One MS piece for insertion[1]

Directions for rearrangement.

When all this has been done please send me 4 copies.[2] It is not yet to be put into regular pages.

Remember that there is to be a vine-leaf at the end of each poem,[3] except the introductory piece in italics.

Yours sincerely
A. E. Housman.

Lilly MSS 1. 1. 3. Richards, 198.

TO MARIA RICHARDS

Trinity College | Cambridge
10 July 1922

Dear Mrs Richards,

Thanks for the photographs. Though I do not forgive you for taking them, I am bound to say that your camera is not such a venomous caricaturist as some that I have met.

Yours sincerely
A. E. Housman.

BMC MS. Envelope addressed 'Mrs Grant Richards | Bigfrith | Cookham Dean | Berks.' Richards, 197–8 (nearly complete).

TO GRANT RICHARDS

Trinity College | Cambridge
12 July 1922

My dear Richards,

I am no judge of this sort of thing, but there is nothing in the design which I much object to, except the portrait of a tramp sucking a stick.

Yours sincerely
A. E. Housman.

Lilly MSS 1. 1. 3. Richards, 198; Maas, 198.

[1] XXII, *The sloe was lost in flower*: see *Poems* (1997), Introduction, xxxiii.
[2] One for himself, and one for each of his three advisers.
[3] As in the 1st, 2nd, and 4th edns. of *ASL*.

TO THEODORE SPICER-SIMSON

Trinity College | Cambridge
17 July 1922

Dear Sir,

I am not qualified to judge your medallions as works of art, but they please me, and Mr Hardy's portrait is certainly a good likeness.[1] As you are kind enough to propose a portrait of me, I shall be very willing to sit to you, if it can be arranged; only it unfortunately happens that I shall be away from Cambridge from the 21st to the 24th.

I am yours very truly
A. E. Housman.

Princeton MS: Gen. MSS. Bound (oversize), Spicer-Simson Am 17277, p. 83. Maas, 199.

TO J. W. MACKAIL

Trinity College | Cambridge
18 July 1922

Dear Mackail,

Thanks for *The Dead Sanctuary*,[1] which I have read with mild pleasure and disapproval. It is quite a wrong sort of thing, as wrong as *The Revolt of Islam*,[2] and there is something of silliness in expending so much adornment on a quite arbitrary fiction, which does not seem to have even the bad excuse of allegory; and it very seldom rises, as it does at the end of the 56th stanza,[3] into anything really poetical. And yet it is somehow winning and likeable, and it is quite free from vice and sham.[4]

Thanks also for consenting to look through my proofs, which I enclose. I want you to note anything that strikes you as falling below my average,

[1] Spicer-Simson did a medallion of Thomas Hardy in 1921.

[1] By J. B. Trinick, with an introductory note by Mackail (OUP, 1922). Trinick was born and brought up in Melbourne, served in France in the Australian Imperial Forces, and later became a practising craftsman in stained glass.

[2] By Shelley, 1818.

[3] Yet once again there lay betwixt mine eyes, | Her lips—a moment ere there came the slow, | Hushed, broken murmur of their words, 'O friend, | 'Sleep well—sleep well—', uttered in weary wise. | Then, answering her softly, 'Thou also— | 'May that be with thee, that my soul would spend | 'Its very life to bring to thee,' I said— | 'Oh, rest indeed—my soul's one friend.' Her brow | Made stillness for my lips, ere it was laid | Gently upon my breast. And as the deep, | Last breath of dying day, at evening's end, | So did she sigh but once and fall asleep.

[4] Mackail's judgement was: 'throughout, in the whole treatment as in the metrical handling, we shall not be mistaken in recognizing the hand of a competent artist, who knows how to use his medium, who can preserve clarity of drawing and harmony of colouring, and whose attained faculty, both in design and execution, holds out promise of higher fulfilment' (vi–vii).

or as open to exception for any other reason. The piece I myself am most in doubt about is the longest;[5] and I fear that is not its worst fault. You need not be afraid of stifling a masterpiece through a temporary aberration of judgment, as I am consulting one or two other people, and shall not give effect to a single opinion unless it coincides with my own private suspicions.

Yours sincerely
A. E. Housman.

Fitzwilliam MS Autogr. 3/3-1946. Maas, 199.

TO GRANT RICHARDS

I asked for 4 copies of proofs,[1] but have only received 2.

A. E. Housman.
18 July 1922

Trin. Coll. Camb.

Lilly MSS 1. 1. 3: p.c. addressed 'Grant Richards Esq. | 8 St Martin's Street | Leicester Square | W. C. 2.' Richards, 198.

TO THEODORE SPICER-SIMSON

K, Whewell's Court | Trinity College | Cambridge
19 July 1922

Dear Sir,
    I shall be pleased to see you here any time before 1 o' clock to-morrow.

I am yours very truly
A. E. Housman.

BMC MS. Envelope addressed 'T. Spicer Simson Esq. | 55ª Sloane Square | S. W. 1.', with the hyphen in the surname omitted.

TO WALTER DE LA MARE

Trinity College | Cambridge
20 July 1922

My dear Sir,
    The statements I have made to other anthologists in refusing to let them include poems from *A Shropshire Lad* prevent me, much to my regret, from

---

[5] *Hell Gate* (*LP* XXXI).

[1] See the letter to GR, 10 July 1922.

giving permission to you or to anyone,[1] though it would be a pleasure to me to serve you in any way.

I hope to make your personal acquaintance when you are here for the Clark lectures.[2]

I am yours very truly
A. E. Housman.

Bodleian MS: Walter de la Mare Uncatalogued Collection.

TO J. W. MACKAIL

Trinity College | Cambridge
25 July 1922

Dear Mackail,

I thought that p. 27 and 50 and perhaps 33 were rather thin, and I shall probably take them out, though another counsellor is very strong for 27.[1] 15 is not much in itself, and I only put it in for variety, as I did No. XX in *A Shropshire Lad.*[2] 57 I have no particular admiration for, though I like bits of it.[3] 39 I think good, and 10 does not dissatisfy me; but I believe I am too fond of the Laura Matilda stanza,[4] which I think the most beautiful and the most difficult in English.

On p. 5[5] 'home' and 'native land' signify 'the sea where they fished for you and me'.

25 dissatisfies me too, but not quite in the same way. The first and last stanzas came into my head; the middle ones are composed. I think the last stanza really requires that the poem should have five stanzas.

---

[1] de la Mare's anthology *Come Hither: A Collection of Rhymes & Poems for the Young of all Ages* was published in 1923.

[2] In Michaelmas Term, 1922. He gave six lectures, on 'the status of fiction', 'the medium of prose', 'the material of fiction', 'its relation to life', ' a comparison', and 'portrayal of character'. In a 1952 letter to M. Morant, de la Mare recalls that AEH attended one of the lectures 'and with a dry little smile remarked: "You seem to have caught the knack" ': cited in *Imagination of the Heart: the Life of Walter de la Mare* by Theresa Whistler (1993), 327.

[1] It is not possible to identify all the poems. The pages were page-proofs, but not the final page-proofs, than which they were larger; the order of pages may not have corresponded in every case to the final order; and poems were selected provisionally at this stage.

[2] *Oh fair enough are sky and plain.*

[3] There survive only pages 57 and 58 bearing *Smooth between sea and land*, which was not included in *LP*, but later printed as *MP* XLV.

[4] *LP* VIII (*Soldier from the wars returning*) is in this verse form, and may have been on p. 10. AEH used the stanza for *ASL* I and XXXV, and for *AP* I, and the metre for *MP* XLVI. See also AEH to Bridges, 19 Dec. 1925. 'Laura Matilda' was the pseudonym of Horace and James Smith when they used the stanza for *Drury's Dirge* in *Rejected Addresses* (1812).

[5] Bearing *LP* I (*The West*).

36. 'you do lie'[6] is not really for metre's sake, but an imitation, false I daresay, of the ballads which I do imitate.

About *Hell Gate*[7] my troubles were, first, that the whole thing is on the edge of the absurd: if it does not topple over, that is well so far. Secondly, as you perceive, the texture of the diction, especially in the parts which I had to compose, is not what it should be, and I rather despair of mending it. It would not do simply to omit the passages you mention: I should have to put something in their place, and it probably would be nothing better. As to three consecutive initial *and*'s, that occurs in the *L'Allegro* of my great exemplar;[8] and Shelley in *The Invitation* and again in *Ariel to Miranda* has five.[9] On p. 43 I think the repetition has a certain value; on p. 42 it is mitigated by the intervention of a full stop, and offends the eye more than the ear.

46. I must confess I do not know what lines 3 and 4[10] mean. I find that I originally wrote 'forest hut', which may be better.

I wish you would turn an unfriendly eye on p. 29. I stuck it in to keep apart two poems which should not come together. The first two lines are as good as need be; but is not the idea of the poem trite and banal, and the execution too neat and too near to smartness?

Please keep the proofs for the present, if you will allow me to worry you again, as perhaps I may want to when W. P. Ker comes back from the Alps, on whose summits he is now pirouetting. Meanwhile thanks for what you have already done.

Yours sincerely
A. E. Housman.

Exception is taken, as I foresaw it would be, to 'spruce'[11] on p. 44. I think it is the right word, and helps, like 'finery of fire',[12] to keep the piece from being too solemn; and moreover Milton talks about 'the spruce and jocund Spring'.[13] The alternative is 'brave', which I like less, partly

---

[6] 'In the land where you do lie': *LP* XXVI 6.   [7] *LP* XXXI..

[8] 'And the milkmaid singeth blithe, | And the mower whets his scythe, | And every shepherd tells his tale': Milton, *L'Allegro*, 65–7.

[9] *To Jane: The Invitation*, 13–17: 'And smiled upon the silent sea, | And bade the frozen streams be free, | And waked to music all their fountains, | And breathed upon the frozen mountains, | And like a prophetess of May ... '; *With a Guitar; To Jane* (which starts 'Ariel to Miranda:—'), 49–53: 'And dreaming, some of Autumn past, | And some of Spring approaching fast, | And some of April buds and showers, | And some of songs in July bowers, | And all of love; and so this tree,—'.

[10] Of *LP* XXXIII, published as 'And about the forest hut | Blows the roaring wood of dreams'. The first and second drafts and the MS sent to the publisher had 'hunter's' for 'forest'.

[11] In l. 99 of *Hell Gate*: 'As in all his spruce attire'.   [12] 'In his finery of fire' (l. 40).

[13] *Comus*, 985.

because it has the same vowel-sound as 'failed' in the next line.[14] What do you think?

Fitzwilliam MS Autogr. 3/4–1946. Maas, 200–1.

TO THEODORE SPICER-SIMSON

Trinity College | Cambridge
26 July 1922

Dear Mr Spicer Simson,[1]
 Next Monday and Tuesday will suit me quite well.

I am yours very truly
A. E. Housman.

Colby College MS.

TO GRANT RICHARDS

Trinity College | Cambridge
26 July 1922

My dear Richards,
 The correction of proofs will be held up for three weeks or so by the absence of W. P. Ker in Switzerland; so I write on details which I want to be clear about.
 What is the exact height of a page available for containing printed matter? The p. 22 which I enclose is a specimen of the largest number of verses, composing one poem, which now stand on one page. Would the addition of the vine-leaf at the end exceed the measure, or involve diminishing the spaces between verse and verse?[1] Would the further prefixing of a number or a title do so?
 The p. 2 which I enclose will probably be p. 1. That being so, does the poem begin too high up, and will one verse or more have to go over the page?
 I ask these questions because I want to be able to map out exactly what page each poem or part of a poem will stand on.[2]

---

[14] 'Failed the everlasting fire'.

[1] AEH omits the hyphen in the surname.

[1] See AEH to GR, 10 July 1922, and n. 3.

[2] In the 1st edn. of *ASL*, the poems were printed continuously. In *LP*, at AEH's request, each poem began on a fresh page: AEH to GR, 22 Apr. 1922.

What is the proper procedure about the agreement? Does your solicitor draw it up and send it to my solicitor; or do you draw it up and I submit it to some Society for the Protection of Authors against Publishers?

Thanks for Story's book on Paris restaurants,[3] which I have not yet had time to look at properly: I see a fair sprinkling of names unknown to me.

Yours sincerely
A. E. Housman.

Lilly MSS 1. 1. 3. Richards, 198–9; Maas, 201.

TO J. D. DUFF

Trinity College
27 July 1922

Dear Duff,

μοῦσαι in Plat. Soph. p. 242 D is a generic term: Ἰάδες μοῦσαι is *the literary Ephesian* and Σικελαὶ μοῦσαι is *the literary Agrigentine*, and Clement copies the phrase. The result of considering these passages is that I do not believe Μοῦσαι really was the title of anything which Heraclitus wrote, and when Diog. Laert. gives it as an alternative to περὶ φύσεως he is merely misunderstanding Plato's phrase. And this is the opinion of Wellmann in Pauly-Wissowa VIII i. p. 505.

Yours sincerely
A. E. Housman.

TCC Add. MS c. 196². Maas, 416.

TO A. B. RAMSAY

[Trinity College
3 Aug. 1922]

Multa decem lustris addantur lustra precantur Arietis Housmanus Gouius Harrisonus[1]

TCC MS: Ernest Harrison's Commonplace Book, fo. 9ʳ.

---

[3] Sommerville Story, *Paris à la Carte: Where the Frenchman Dines and How* (1922).

[1] A greeting to A. B. Ramsay ('The Ram') on his fiftieth birthday from Housman, Gow, and Harrison: 'Housman, Gow, and Harrison pray that fifty more years be added to the fifty of the Ram.' The greeting is an elegiac couplet, the second verse beginning at 'Arietis' (scanned as a dactyl). The arrangement of names, with Housman first, is the only one that will make metre. Ernest Harrison (1877–1943) had been a Fellow of TCC since 1900. By 1932 AEH was using the form 'Housmannus': *Manilius*, editio minor, p. viii n.1.

TO GRANT RICHARDS

Angel Hotel | Midhurst
24 Aug. 1922

My dear Richards,

I enclose corrected proofs, which can now be put into book form, as there will be little further change.

Silence may now be broken, as I am safely away from Cambridge and out of humanity's reach. When you make the announcement in print I shall have to censure your fanfares. I should think the first had better be something quite short, such as—

'I shall publish on —— the only book of poetry written by Mr A. E. Housman since the appearance of *A Shropshire Lad* twenty-six years ago.'

or perhaps better simply—

—'Mr A. E. Housman's second volume of poetry'.[1]

I shall be here, as I told you, till the 5th Sept., and then I shall be going into Gloucestershire for a week, not returning through London; so I shall be glad if you can pay me a day's visit here as you say.

Yours sincerely
A. E. Housman.

The printers, as usual, when making corrections, seize the opportunity of introducing new errors.

Lilly MSS 1. 1. 3. Richards, 199; Maas, 201–2.

TO MR SMITH

Trinity College | Cambridge | England
26 Aug. 1922

Dear Mr Smith,

You have my permission to publish your setting of *With rue my heart is laden*. I am obliged to you for offering to submit the music to my approval; but my taste in music is not good enough to constitute me a judge.

I am yours very truly
A. E. Housman.

BMC MS.

---

[1] GR's announcement in the *TLS* a month later stated simply: 'Early in October I shall publish a new book by A. E. Housman. It will be entitled *Last Poems* (5/-)'.

TO GRANT RICHARDS

From the 5th to the 12th my address will be
    c/ Mrs Yorke
    Selsley Road
    N. Woodchester
    Stroud.
So far as I know at present, I shall be glad to see you at Cambridge on the 14th.
1 Sept. 1922   A. E. Housman.

LC-GR MS: p.c. addressed 'Grant Richards Esq. | Torcross Hotel | Kingsbridge | Devon'. Richards, 200 (nearly complete).

TO L. W. PAYNE

Trinity College | Cambridge | England
14 Sept. 1922

Dear Mr Payne,

    I have so long made it a rule to refuse English anthologists permission to reprint poems of mine that I cannot now give permission to anyone. But my permission is not required in America, where the poems are not copyright.[1]

I am yours sincerely
A. E. Housman.

Texas MS. Maas, 202–3.

TO THEODORE SPICER-SIMSON

Trinity College | Cambridge
14 Sept. 1922

Dear Mr Spicer Simson, [1]

    I am very grateful for your gift of the medallion[2] which I find awaiting me here on my return from a month's absence.

---

[1] Payne sought permission to include poems in *Selections from English Literature*, edited by himself and Nina Hill (1922).

[1] As before, AEH omits the hyphen from the surname.

[2] The medallion portrait of AEH is reproduced opposite p. 178 of LH's *Memoir* (and the artist's name is mutilated). See AEH to Spicer-Simson, 17 July 1922.

Neither Thompson[3] nor Rutherford[4] seems to be in residence here at present, but when they come back I will not fail to show them the portrait and excite their envy.

I am yours sincerely
A. E. Housman.

Princeton MS: Gen. MSS. Bound (oversize), Spicer-Simson Am 17277, p. 83. Maas, 202.

TO GRANT RICHARDS

Trinity College | Cambridge
16 Sept. 1922

My dear Richards,

Here are the 33 persons to whom I want copies to be sent from me.[1]

Thanks for Sacheverell Sitwell.[2]

My wrapper should be as simple as possible: just white paper and letterpress.

Yours sincerely
A. E. Housman.

PM MS. LC-GR t.s. Richards, 200–1 (excerpts).

TO GRANT RICHARDS

Trinity College | Cambridge
20 Sept. 1922

My dear Richards,

I return the agreement signed; also the wrapper, which does not cause me any special disgust, as most wrappers do.

Yours sincerely
A. E. Housman.

Lilly MSS 1. 1. 3. Richards, 201.

---

[3] For 'Thomson'. See List of Recipients.   [4] See List of Recipients.

[1] SIU MS VFM 1082 lists the following, almost all with their addresses: Miss [Clemence] Housman, Laurence Housman, Mrs Symons [i.e. KES], 'Fräulein Sophia Becker', Miss [Edith] Wise, Mrs [John] Maycock, A. W. Pollard, The Revd Canon Watson, D.D., The President of Magdalen College, Oxford [i.e. Sir Herbert Warren], T. C. Snow, Professor Gilbert Murray, Sir James Frazer, J. D. Duff, The Master, Magdalene College, Cambridge [i.e. A. C. Benson], Herbert Millington, Ralph Thicknesse, Mrs [Ralph] Thicknesse, William Rothenstein, Dr [Percy] Withers, Thomas Hardy, O.M., Witter Bynner, J. W. Mackail, Arthur Platt, W. P. Ker, H. Festing Jones, Signore H[oratio] Brown, Robert Bridges, D.Litt., John Masefield, Edmund Gosse, C.B., Sir William Watson, Signore H[erbert] Trench, John Drinkwater, and Mrs H. G. Woods.

[2] Very probably Sitwell's *The One Hundred and One Harlequins*, published by GR in 1922.

TO GRANT RICHARDS

Well then, if you are a man of your word, send me the *Weekly Westminster Gazette*.[1]

A. E. Housman.
Trinity College

21 Sept. 1922
Cambridge

LC-GR MS: p.c. addressed 'Grant Richards Esq. | 8 St Martin's Street | Leicester Square | W. C. 2.' Richards, 201.

TO GRANT RICHARDS

Trinity College | Cambridge
23 Sept. 1922

My dear Richards,
    This seems all right.
    Thanks for the *Westminster*.
    Remember that I have not yet seen the final proofs of the book.

Yours sincerely
A. E. Housman.

PM MS. LC-GR t.s. Richards, 201 (excerpt).

TO GRANT RICHARDS

Trinity College | Cambridge
26 Sept. 1922

My dear Richards,
    Please look at what I have written on pages 55 and 79.[1]

Yours sincerely
A. E. Housman.

Lilly MSS 1. 1. 3. Richards, 201.

[1] See AEH to KES, 26 Mar. 1923. Richards, 201 n., finds the two letters difficult to reconcile. He sent the periodical to AEH: see the next letter.

[1] On p. 55, referring to the spacing between stanzas of poem XXIX, AEH complained 'Too much white. Why not bring first stanza lower? or space the lines as on p. 75'; on p. 79 he asked ' "The End", as in Shropshire Lad?'

TO DR PERCY WITHERS

Trinity College | Cambridge
30 Sept. 1922

My dear Withers,

I enclose the reply I got from the *custos hortorum*[1] at St John's[2] when I wrote about the alleged distribution of surplus Alpines at this season; and I hope that, operation or no operation, you will be in case to do as he proposes in the spring. I wish you had a better account to give of yourself, and I am sorry there seems to be no chance of seeing you here this term. As to seeing you at Souldern, I am afraid there is not much chance of that either, and, considering the effect I have on your health, it is better so. The book of poems is even smaller than *A. S. L.*, so do not promise yourself repletion. My kind regards to Mrs Withers.

Yours sincerely
A. E. Housman.

SCO MS. Withers, 47 (excerpt); Maas, 203.

TO GRANT RICHARDS

[Trinity College | Cambridge
3 October 1922

My dear Richards,]

You must not print editions of *A Shropshire Lad* without letting me see the proofs. I have just been looking through the editions of 1918 and 1921, and in both I find the same set of blunders in punctuation and ordering of lines, some of which I have corrected again and again, and the filthy beasts of printers for ever introduce them anew.

[Yours sincerely
A. E. Housman.]

Richards, 201; Maas, 203.

[1] Keeper of the Gardens.
[2] SJCO has a rock garden which is famous for its rare plants. It was formed in the NW corner of the inner grove in the early years of the twentieth century by the Bursar, Henry Jardine Bidder (1847–1923), with the assistance of the botanist R. J. Farrer.

TO THE RIVERSIDE PRESS LTD

Trinity College | Cambridge
6 Oct. 1922

Dear Sirs,

I return the three specimens. I do not like the red, and I agree with Mr Richards that the dark blue[1] is on the whole the best.

I am yours faithfully
A. E. Housman.

Lilly MSS 1. 1. 3. Richards, 201.

TO GRANT RICHARDS

Trinity College | Cambridge
9 Oct. 1922

My dear Richards,

As to your kind invitation to me to dine with you, the 19th would not be an available date, and a Monday or Wednesday would probably be best.

Yours sincerely
A. E. Housman.

LC-GR MS. Richards, 201 (nearly complete).

TO GRANT RICHARDS

Trinity College | Cambridge
11 Oct. 1922

My dear Richards,

No, don't send Mr Bert Thomas a photograph.[1]

One or two of his cariacatures[2] which I have seen I thought not bad.

Yours sincerely
A. E. Housman.

LC-GR MS. Richards, 201; Maas, 203.

---

[1] Cloth binding, used for *LP*.

[1] Bert Thomas (1883–1966), famous for his cartoons of the First World War, and a regular contributor to *Punch*, had asked GR for a photograph of AEH to help him with a caricature, which appeared in *Punch* on 25 Oct. 1922, six days after the publication of *LP*. It is reproduced in Richards opposite p. 202. See AEH to KES, 29 Dec. 1922.

[2] For 'caricatures'.

TO GRANT RICHARDS

Trinity College | Cambridge
12 Oct. 1922

My dear Richards,

1. I knew the printers would do something, and I only wondered what it would be. On p. 52[1] they have removed a comma from the end of the first line and a semi-colon from the end of the second.

2. Remember that I am not P. B. Mais,[2] and do not quote reviews in your weekly epistle, when reviews begin to appear. Brag about the sale as much as you like.

3. Please add to the list of those who are to have copies from the author sent them:[3]

W. T. Vesey Esq.[4]
Caius College
Cambridge.

Yours sincerely
A. E. Housman.

Lilly MSS 1. 1. 3. Richards, 202; Maas, 204.

TO GRANT RICHARDS

No, don't put in an errata slip. The blunder will probably enhance the value of the 1st edition in the eyes of bibliophiles, an idiotic class.

Yrs
A. E. Housman.

14 Oct. 1922 Trin. Coll. Camb.

Lilly MSS 1. 1: p.c. addressed 'Grant Richards Esq. | 8 St Martin's Street | Leicester Square | W. C. 2.' Richards, 202; Maas, 204.

---

[1] In *The half-moon westers low, my love* (*LP* XXVI).

[2] S[tuart] P[etre] B[rodie] Mais (1885–1975), prolific novelist, journalist, and writer on travel and the countryside. Most of his books were published by Richards.

[3] See AEH to GR, 16 Sept. 1922, and note.

[4] William Trevor Lendrum (1854–1935), who assumed the name Vesey in 1917. Fellow of Gonville and Caius College since 1890, and an authority on Pindar. Maas, 204 n., notes that AEH contributed to his obituary in *The Caian*, 43 (1935). On AEH and Vessey, see Naiditch (1995), 37–9.

TO GRANT RICHARDS

Trinity College | Cambridge
18 Oct. 1922

My dear Richards,

I return the printers' letter. Printers seem to regard this sort of error as the act of God: I remember the same thing in several places in the Juvenal.

I do not require any copies beyond the six I have.

What the *Times*[1] has done is what the *Standard* did in the case of Lord Beaconsfield's *Endymion*;[2] and in some way which I do not understand it was supposed to have injured the sale.

Yours sincerely
A. E. Housman.

Lilly MSS 1. 1. 3. Richards, 202; Maas, 204.

TO MOSES JACKSON

Trinity College | Cambridge
19 Oct. 1922

My dear Mo,

I have been putting off writing so as to be able to send you this precious book,[1] published to-day. The cheerful and exhilarating tone of my verse is so notorious that I feel sure it will do you more good than the doctors;[2] though you do not know, and there are no means of driving the knowledge into your thick head, what a bloody good poet I am.[3] In order to intimidate you and repress your insolence I am enclosing the review and the leader which the *Times* devoted to the subject.[4] I may also inform you that the copy of the 1st edition of my other immortal work which I gave you is now

---

[1] A premature review of *LP* appeared in *The Times*, 17 Oct. 1922, 8.

[2] Novel, published in 1880, a year before Disraeli's death.

[1] *LP.*   [2] Jackson was ill, and died from stomach cancer on 14 Jan. 1923.

[3] E. W. Watson, a contemporary in Oxford days, told Gow in a letter of 25 May 1936 that Jackson was 'a perfect Philistine ... a vigorous rowing man, quite unliterary and outspoken in his want of any such interest': TCC Add. MS a. 71[169]; Page, 41. Jackson's son, G. C. A. Jackson, is quoted in George L. Watson, *A. E. Housman: A Divided Life* (1957), 160, as saying that 'My father jokingly always professed to have a contempt for Housman's poems'. This may explain the heading of AEH's dedicatory poem in the Manilius I: *sodali meo M. I. Iackson harum litterarum contemptori*.

[4] *The Times*, 17 Oct. 1922, carried a review and a leading article (entitled *Ave Atque Vale*) on pp. 8 and 13 respectively.

worth £8 or more if you have kept it at all clean;[5] and that the average annual sale is over 3000 copies. That is largely due to the war, because so many soldiers, including at least one V. C., carried it in their pockets, and thus others got to know of it and bought it when they came home. But it does not seem to stop bullets as the Bible does when carried in the pocket, so I have been disappointed of that advertisement, probably through the jealousy of the Holy Ghost. Of this new book there were printed 4000 copies for a 1st edition, which were all ordered by the booksellers before publication, so there is already a 2nd edition in the press. It is now 11 o'clock in the morning, and I hear that the Cambridge shops are sold out. Please to realise therefore, with fear and respect, that I am an eminent bloke; though I would much rather have followed you round the world and blacked your boots.[6]

In June I flew over to Paris for a week as usual, and late in the summer I spent a month at Midhurst in about the best part of Surrey, between the chalk downs and the Haslemere type of country. I motored through Godalming: Witley Common has been rather devastated by the Canadian camp there.[7]

Gerald[8] writes to me now and then, and seems to be a wonder in the way of industry and determination; both Oscar and Rupert[9] evidently think a lot of him.

[5] AEH had presented an inscribed copy of the first edn. of *ASL* to Jackson on publication in 1896. It was sold at Sotheby's on 6 Nov. 2001 for £48,500, as Naiditch (2005), 140, notes. Cf. *ASL* XXXIV 7: 'She will not be sick to see me if I only keep it clean'.

[6] Cf. Tennyson, *Lancelot and Elaine*, 934: 'To serve you, and to follow you through the world'. The unique notebook draft of *ASL* IX (*On moonlit heath and lonesome bank*) contains the variant reading at ll. 23–4: 'In shoes I'd liefer black than most | That walk upon the land'. Cf. other references to boot-blacking: Swinburne, *The Sisters*, 2. 1. 139–41: 'REGINALD I'd like to black his boots. MABEL You weren't his fag, | Were you?'; Oscar Wilde in a letter to Leonard Smithers, 11 Dec. 1897: 'Ask for dear Robbie [Ross], if he will kindly send me out a pair of his oldest boots I will blacken them with pleasure'.

[7] In Jan. 1915 a camp for training Canadian soldiers before they were sent to France was created at Witley Common near Godalming, Surrey. It was occupied 1916–Sept. 1919 and used afterwards as a demobilization camp. 30,000–50,000 soldiers passed through. Local traders built wooden shops with tin roofs and the place was nicknamed 'Tin Town'.

[8] Gerald C. A. Jackson. See List of Recipients.

[9] Oscar Adalbert Edmund Jackson (1895–c.1973) and Rupert W. P. Jackson (b. 1890), Jackson's third and eldest sons respectively: Naiditch (1995), 143.

My very kind regards to Mrs Jackson.

Yours very truly
A. E. Housman.

MS inspected at Sotheby's, 4 Nov. 2001. T.s. copy, with some errors of transcription, in SJCO, Sparrow Collection. Two sides reproduced in reduced photographic facsimile, and excerpts quoted, in Sotheby's catalogue, The Library of Frederick B. Adams, Jr, Part 1: English & American Literature *(6 Nov. 2001), 33. Shortly afterwards, the photograph was reproduced a second time between pp. 56 and 57 of* HSJ *(2001).*

TO JOHN DRINKWATER

Trinity College | Cambridge
22 Oct. 1922

My dear Mr Drinkwater,

I have written your name and mine in the book[1] with great pleasure, and I thank you much for the gift of your own volume of poems,[2] among which I think perhaps I like the two sonnets best.[3]

I am yours very truly
A. E. Housman.

I have corrected the errors of the press on p. 52.[4]

Marquette University MS (Elizabeth Whitcomb Houghton Collection, series 5, box 4). Maas, 205.

TO PROFESSOR GILBERT MURRAY

Trinity College | Cambridge
25 Oct. 1922

My dear Murray,

I seem to be esteemed on Boar's Hill,[1] which is satisfactory. I am not conscious of having been influenced by writing verse in Greek and Latin, and I think we have models enough in English. The new-fangled verse you speak of hardly comes to my ears (I suppose you move in the midst of

[1] *LP*, a copy of which AEH had sent through the Richards Press Ltd: AEH to GR, 16 Sept. 1922, n. 1; Drinkwater to AEH, 20 Oct. 1922 (BMC MS).

[2] *Preludes 1921–1922* (1922).

[3] *Prelude* and *Interlude* (on pp. 9, 62).

[4] See AEH to GR, 12 Oct. 1922.

[1] For 'Boars Hill', just outside Oxford. Murray and his family moved to their house 'Yatscombe' there in 1919, and Robert Bridges and John Masefield were neighbours. Bridges had written a letter of warm appreciation for *LP* to AEH on 19 Oct. 1922 (SJCO MS).

some of its authors); but I have been admiring Blunden[2] for some time. He describes too much; but when one can describe so well, the temptation must be great.

Yours sincerely
A. E. Housman.

Bodleian MSS Gilbert Murray, 45. 206–7. Maas, 205.

TO EDMUND GOSSE

Trinity College | Cambridge
25 Oct. 1922

My dear Gosse,

I thought you were very nice about me in the *Sunday Times*,[1] and I have copied out a poem[2] for you as you wish. It is one of those which I did not put into the book; for I know you bibliophiles, and your passion for l'inédit irrespective of merit.

Please thank Mrs Gosse for her kind remembrances, which are reciprocal.

Yours sincerely
A. E. Housman.

BL MS Ashley B. 903, fos. 44–5. Maas, 205–6.

TO GRANT RICHARDS

Thanks. The press-cutting agency sends me, with due delay, more notices than I want to see.

What guarantee have I that all these editions of yours are being printed correctly?

A. E. Housman.
Trin. Coll. Camb.

26 Oct. 1922.

LC-GR MS: p.c. addressed 'Grant Richards Esq.| 8 St Martin's Street | Leicester Square | W. C. 2.' Richards, 204; Maas, 206.

---

[2] Edmund [Charles] Blunden (1896–1974), author at this time of *The Waggoner and other poems* (1920) and *The Shepherd* (1922).

[1] Gosse's review of *LP* appeared on p. 6 of *The Sunday Times*, 22 Oct. 1922. It is reprinted in Gosse's *More Books on the Table* (1923), 21–6.

[2] *Tarry, delight; so seldom met* (*MP* XV). In a letter of 18 Oct. 1922 (LC-AEH MS) Gosse had asked AEH to copy out a poem to go with similar gifts received from Tennyson, Swinburne, Patmore, and Hardy.

TO P. P. STEVENS

Trinity College | Cambridge
27 Oct. 1922

Dear Stevens,

Certainly not. I have only two spare copies, and they are for the good and pure. The most shocking things about you "devotees of editions" are the shamelessness with which you avow your vice and the calm stupidity with which you stab the vanity of authors. How do you suppose we feel when we hear all this fuss about the difference between a first edition and a tenth? The only merits of any edition are correctness and legibility. This astounds you; and when I tell you that the first edition contained an error which was corrected in the second, you will be ready to tear your hair.

I told the publishers to send a copy on publication to one of your fellow devotees, who insincerely pretends, like you, to be interested in my poetry. When he got it, he could not wait to read it, he despatched it to me by the next post for my autograph. I am really glad when I hear that knavish booksellers are practising extortion on fellows of your sort, and demanding sums which range from 7/6 to a guinea, according as the customer looks a lesser or a greater fool.

However, in consideration of the Tankard,[1] and your share in my education, I am prepared to autograph a copy of the second edition, if you like to buy one; but as it has the proper number of stops on p. 52, you may think 5/- too high a price.

How are you earning your bread? Honestly, I hope.

Yours sincerely
A. E. Housman.

Text from a t.s. (Lilly MSS 3. 1. 10) made by John Carter from the autograph MS, which was sold at Sotheby's on 17 Dec. 1946. Maas, 206–7.

[1] A silver loving-cup presented to AEH by his students from the previous nineteen years when he left UCL in 1911 for Cambridge. It was inscribed with a quotation from *ASL* LXII 21–2: 'Malt does more than Milton can to justify God's ways to man': R. W. Chambers, *Man's Unconquerable Mind* (1939), 380.

TO E. V. LUCAS

Trinity College | Cambridge
28 Oct. 1922

Dear Lucas,

I am honoured by the request of the English Association, but I must ask to be excused. While I was at University College I was in a measure compelled to read things to the Literary Society now and then;[1] but I am escaped even as a bird out of the snare of the fowler,[2] and I shall never do it again. To prepare a paper would be endless labour and anxiety, and the result nothing in which I could take pride; for I am only a connoisseur and do not mistake myself for a critic. Thanks for your letter all the same.

I am yours sincerely
A. E. Housman.

Private MS.

TO GRANT RICHARDS

Trinity College | Cambridge
29 Oct. 1922

My dear Richards,

I return the proofs of the small edition of *A Shropshire Lad*, which seem to need no corrections beyond those which have been marked.

I have found no errors yet in the second impression of *Last Poems*, but it seems to me that the stanza on p. 56 ought to be leaded, or whatever you call it, in the same way as the two stanzas on p. 55.[1]

Yours sincerely
A. E. Housman.

Lilly MSS 1. 1. 3. Richards, 204–5.

---

[1] Naiditch (1988), 144, affirms that AEH gave five or six lectures to the Literary Society at UCL: on Matthew Arnold, the Spasmodic School, Erasmus Darwin, Robert Burns, Tennyson, and (perhaps) Swinburne. Naiditch (1988), 142–51, gives a full account of AEH's relations with the Society.

[2] Ps. 124: 7: 'Our soul is escaped as a bird out of the snare of the fowlers'.

[1] No change was made to the layout of the page.

TO MARIA RICHARDS

Trinity College | Cambridge
29 Oct. 1922

Dear Mrs Richards,

A heavy case has arrived, and I have had it opened and have come to the top layer, but have not eaten my way further down at present.[1] I write now to thank you, before I make myself ill. It seems that your garden has been doing its duty this year.

Yours sincerely
A. E. Housman.

BMC MS. Richards, 204 (nearly complete).

TO STEPHEN GASELEE

Trinity College
30 Oct. 1922

Dear Gaselee,

I should be delighted to dine with you at Magdalene on Saturday Nov. 11 at 7. 45. I think you don't dress on weekdays.

The epitaph[1] was reprinted in an anthology of War poems called *Valour and Vision* by Jacqueline T. Trotter (1920),[2] and also, with 5 emendations by the University Press, in *Cambridge Readings in Literature* book V (1918).[3] I think too that I gave permission in some other case or cases; and it must also have been printed in weeklies where it was turned into Greek and Latin and Hebrew. I wrote it in September 1917.[4]

The caucus has gone wrong.

Yours sincerely
A. E. Housman.

I have just remembered that the *Times* itself reprinted it in an article on a later 31st of October[.]

BMC MS.

---

[1] Mrs Richards had sent him a box of walnuts from their garden: Richards, 204

[1] *Epitaph on an Army of Mercenaries* (*LP* XXXVII).

[2] *Valour and Vision: Poems of the War 1914–1918*, ed. Jacqueline T. Trotter (1920), 117.

[3] There were four: 'heaven' and 'earth's' (twice) began with capitals, and there was no space between 'foundations' and 'fled'. The editor was George Sampson, and the poem appeared on p. 286.

[4] LH, *Memoir*, 269, records 'rough draft, and second draft corrected' on *Nbk* C 92–3. The MS of the second draft was sold at Sotheby's on 27 May 2004. See Archie Burnett, 'Fastidious Housman', *TLS*, 25 June 2004, 13. The poem was published in *The Times*, 31 Oct. 1917, 7, beneath a leading article entitled 'The Anniversary of Ypres', and signed 'A. E. Housman'.

TO GRANT RICHARDS

31 Oct. 1922

I have noted some more corrections. Perhaps that on p. 59 may not be feasible.

A. E. Housman.

Lilly MSS 1. 1. 3. Richards, 205.

TO GRANT RICHARDS

1 Nov. 1922

American agreement enclosed signed.

A. E. Housman.

Grant Richards Esq.

Trinity College Cambridge

LC-GR MS.

TO HORATIO F. BROWN

Trinity College | Cambridge
3 Nov. 1922

My dear Brown,

Your queries[1] do you credit on the whole. XL is entirely of last April,[2] and XXII except the first two lines;[3] and most of the others \which you name/ finished then, though conceived and partly executed earlier or even much earlier (IX for instance).[4] But XII and XLI are quite old,[5] XXV

---

[1] About composition dates of poems in *LP*.

[2] The two drafts date from 10–30 Apr. 1922.

[3] 'Finished April, 1922': AEH to Cockerell (*TLS*, 7 Nov. 1936; Richards, 437). The surviving draft dates from 10–30 Apr. 1922, and no earlier draft of ll. 1–2 survives. The fair copy was written Apr.–10 July 1922, possibly after 19 June.

[4] What LH, *Memoir*, 264, describes as 'fragments' and a 'rough draft of first verse' date respectively from Oct.–Dec. 1895 and Dec. 1895–24 Feb. 1900. The second and third drafts date from 30 Mar.–10 Apr. 1922.

[5] Of the drafts of XII, the first dates from Aug.–Dec. 1894, the second from 30 Mar.–10 Apr. 1922, and the third from before 19 June 1922. Of the drafts of XLI, the first dates from Dec. 1895–24 Feb. 1900, the second and third from *c.*1900–7 June 1902 (the third probably after 30 Oct. 1901), and the fourth from *c.*1900–Sept. 1917 (possibly *c.*1900–5, but not Oct. 1910–Oct. 1912).

was published in 1903,[6] and III was actually printed in *A Shropshire Lad* but removed before publication in consequence of other changes.[7]

The book is selling at such a rate that I am afraid I cannot be such a very good poet after all.

Yours sincerely
A. E. Housman.

CUL Add. MS 8534/2. Published by Maas in HSJ *2 (1975), 35.*

TO GRANT RICHARDS

[Trinity College | Cambridge
3 Nov. 1922

My dear Richards,]
Do *not* at present put in hand the new edition of *A Shropshire Lad* which you speak of.

[Yours sincerely
A. E. Housman.]

Richards, 205.

TO GRANT RICHARDS

[Trinity College | Cambridge
8 Nov. 1922

My dear Richards,]
I would rather there were no one but you and Mrs Richards.[1]

[Yours sincerely
A. E. Housman.]

Text based on that in Richards, 204.

[6] On p. 39 of vol. 1 of *The Venture*, ed. LH and W. Somerset Maugham.

[7] The first draft dates from Aug.–Dec. 1894, the second from 10 Aug.–30 Sept. 1895. In the sheets of page proofs that survive (Lilly) it is printed as poem XLIII, and cancelled by AEH.

[1] At the dinner to celebrate the publication of *LP*.

TO MARIA RICHARDS

Trinity College | Cambridge
10 Nov. 1922

Dear Mrs Richards,

I hope to see you and your frock on Monday, but I am sorry I shall not be able to plunder your Christmas tree.[1] We have a regular feast here, which last year I deserted for you, but this year I am expecting a guest of my own. Many thanks all the same.

Yours sincerely
A. E. Housman.

BMC MS. Envelope addressed 'Mrs Grant Richards | Bigfrith | Cookham Dean | Berks.' Richards, 205 (nearly complete).

TO GRANT RICHARDS

I shall reach town (Great Northern Hotel) at 6 p.m. on Monday, and I can stay till 11. 50 a.m. on Tuesday, so we can arrange to meet some time that morning.

A. E. H.

12 Nov. 1922   Trin. Coll. Camb.

LC-GR MS: p.c. addressed 'Grant Richards Esq.| 8 St Martin's Street | Leicester Square | W. C. 2.'

TO SYDNEY COCKERELL

Trinity College
17 Nov. 1922

Dear Cockerell,

As I still cannot lay my hands on the *Shropshire Lad* MS,[1] and as you are more ardent for possession than the College Library, I send the MS of *Last Poems*. Half-a-dozen pieces are missing.[2] The MS, as you will see, did

---

[1] On 9 Nov., before AEH dined on 13 Nov. at the Carlton restaurant with GR and his wife to celebrate the publication of *LP*, Mrs Richards invited him to come to their home at Bigfrith for Christmas: Richards, 204, 205.

[1] See AEH to Adams, 3 Mar. 1926, and AEH to Martin, 20 Nov. 1933

[2] The MS of *LP* sent to GR for printing contained *Smooth between sea and land* (*MP* XLV), *The stars have not dealt me the worst they could do* (*AP* XVII), *Oh were he and I together* (*AP* II), XV (*Eight O'Clock*), XVIII (*The rain, it streams on stone and hillock*), and one other poem on a single sheet. See *Poems* (1997), Introduction, xxxii, xxxv.

not go to the printers, but a type-written copy was made in the publisher's office.[3]

Yours sincerely
A. E. Housman.

Fitzwilliam MS, Gen. Ser. 539-1964. Maas, 207.

TO AN UNKNOWN CORRESPONDENT

Trinity College | Cambridge
28 Nov. 1922

Dear Sir,

The only uncollected poem of mine that I can think of is a parody of Greek tragedy in the *Cornhill* for April 1901.[1]

I am yours faithfully
A. E. Housman.

BMC MS.

TO GRANT RICHARDS

[Trinity College | Cambridge
30 Nov. 1922

My dear Richards,]

Mr Vickers can have what he wants, and any of his countrymen. I am told that Americans are human beings, though appearances are against them.

[Yours sincerely
A. E. Housman.]

Richards, 205.

---

[3] See AEH to GR, 22 Apr. 1922, n. 2.

[1] *Fragment of a Greek Tragedy* appeared in *The Cornhill Magazine*, NS 10 (Apr. 1901), 443–5. This was the third printing: see *Poems* (1997), 531–2.

TO LAURENCE HOUSMAN

Trinity College | Cambridge
5 Dec. 1922

My dear Laurence,

Thanks for *Dethronements*,[1] though I do not think it one of your good books, nothing like so good as *Angels and Ministers*.[2] I do not believe that any of the people resembled or resemble your figures; and in the second dialogue the falsification of history is quite awful.

On p. 48 there is a misprint, *make* for *may*, and on p. 61, *Collins*. I gather from p. 19 that you are one of the many people who think that Morley[3] wrote a book in favour of compromise: else I don't understand "And yet".[4]

I liked the remark about America on p. 71.[5]

Your affectionate brother
A. E. Housman.

Lilly MSS 2. Memoir, 178, where the letter is cut and misleadingly merged with another of 11 Dec.; Maas, 207.

TO LAURENCE HOUSMAN

Trinity College | Cambridge
11 Dec. 1922

My dear Laurence,

To represent Chamberlain as an injured man, and Balfour as a man who injured him, is like saying that Christ crucified Pontius Pilate. 'The downfall of the Man of Business' (p. 6)[1] was caused by eating, drinking, and smoking immoderately, and taking aperients instead of exercise. From the election of 1905 he came back in much better plight than Balfour, and was in a position to patronise him by finding him a seat. What Balfour did in his premiership was to prevent Chamberlain from quite ruining the party. Outside Parliament, Chamberlain was much the stronger of the two: everything in

[1] *Dethronements: Imaginary Portraits of Political Characters, Done in Dialogue* (1922).
[2] Published in 1921.
[3] John, Viscount Morley of Blackburn (1838–1923), statesman and man of letters.
[4] Morley opposes compromise throughout his *On Compromise* (1874). LH has Parnell say 'Morley's an authority on compromise. And yet I like him'.
[5] 'In the distance an occasional blare of brass and the beat of drums ... the kind of noise which America knows how to make; a sound of triumph insistent and strained, having in it no beauty and no joy.'

[1] The second dialogue in LH's *Dethronements*, 'The Man of Business', is between Joseph Chamberlain and a distinguished visitor.

Unionism which was vulgar and sordid and greedy looked to him as its leader. When he started his precious tariff-reform, a thing which he had not intellect enough to comprehend, Balfour could not oppose him, especially as Free Trade was not the fetish to him that it is to Liberals: what he did was to temporise, and hold together, at the cost of much humiliation to himself and damage to his position, the party which Chamberlain would have torn asunder and led two thirds of it down a blind alley into a pit. His reward was to be driven from the leadership a few years later by those two thirds.

Page 64. The only occasion when Churchill came down to fight in the Central division of Birmingham was in 1885, before a Unionist party existed. In 1889, when Bright died, he did not come down, and the reason was Chamberlain, who was not going to have another cock crowing on his dunghill. On April 2, when the writ was moved, Hartington came to Churchill and said that Chamberlain was furious and in a state of extreme irritation. The question was decided straight away by a meeting of Chamberlain, Hartington, and Hicks Beach, Churchill having declared that he would accept their decision. That Balfour, who was then Chief Secretary for Ireland, had even an opportunity of hearing about it before it was settled is hardly possible. He was afterwards sent down to Birmingham to pacify the Conservatives there and persuade them to vote for Chamberlain's nominee; so I think your report of Chamberlain's remarks on the subject makes him out a very impudent dog.

Your affectionate brother (though I have received a press-cutting which authoritatively states that we are not brothers).

A. E. Housman.

BMC MS. Memoir, *178–9, where it is presented as the continuation of the first paragraph of the letter of 5 Dec. 1922. Maas, 208, separates the letter off properly, but gives it the imprecise date 'circa 7 December 1922'.*

TO DOUGLAS GOLDRING

Trinity College | Cambridge
15 Dec. 1922

Dear Sir,

I am much obliged by your kindness in sending me your book on Flecker,[1] which is interesting as a record and contains, if I may say so, discriminating criticism.

---

[1] *James Elroy Flecker: An Appreciation, with some biographical notes* (1922).

I shall be pleased to see you when you are in Cambridge.

> I am yours very truly
> A. E. Housman.

BMC MS. Envelope addressed 'Douglas Goldring Esq. | 19 Taviton Street | Gordon Square | W. C. 1'.

TO SIR JAMES BARRIE

> Trinity College | Cambridge
> 18 Dec. 1922

Dear Sir James Barrie,

It is kind of you to write as you do,[1] and I on my part was very grateful to Whibley[2] for bringing us together, as he had long promised he would.

> I am yours sincerely
> A. E. Housman.

PM MS MA 3568 R. V. Autographs Misc. English.

TO DR PERCY WITHERS

> Trinity College | Cambridge
> 22 Dec. 1922

My dear Withers,

Your generous enthusiasm is very nice, but I have not myself felt more than a faint pleasure in the success of the book, which is not really a matter of much importance. I was pleased by letters I had from Masefield and others.

Lewis,[1] as perhaps you know, had a long and severe illness this year; and although he is now quite chirpy, I think he is rather shaken. His pronunciation is less distinct, and he is less regular in coming to Combination Room.

---

[1] Barrie wrote on 15 Dec. 1922: 'Dear Mr Houseman [*sic*], Though I have made such poor use of my opportunity, owing to my being an uncommon dreary character, to meet you last night was a great thing to me. That was mainly what I journeyed to Cambridge for with Charles Whibley's kindly help, and I am very glad I went. My admiration for your poems passes words. Yours sincerely J. M. Barrie'. The letter was printed in Scribner's cat. 110 (1936), no. 1233A, where it is described as a 'letter, so often misquoted': on which, see Naiditch (2005), 26–7.

[2] Leonard Whibley (1863–1941). Fellow of Pembroke College, Cambridge, 1889–1941; University Lecturer in Ancient History, 1899–1910; published *Companion to Greek Studies* (1905), and, with P. J. Toynbee, an edn. of the letters of Thomas Gray (3 vols., 1935).

[1] William James Lewis (1847–1926), Professor of Mineralogy at Cambridge since 1881.

You do not say anything about your own health, nor whether you have had or are going to have an operation. I hope silence means that things are not going badly.

With kind regards to Mrs Withers

I am yours sincerely

A. E. Housman.

I met the Rector (or Vicar) of Croughton[2] at Eton some months ago.

SCO MS. Withers, 47 (excerpt); Maas, 209.

TO JOHN DRINKWATER

Trinity College | Cambridge
25 Dec. 1922

My dear Mr Drinkwater,

There are only two complete translations of Horace's odes which I have done more than glance at, and of those I think Conington's[1] better, though less showy, than Theodore Martin's:[2] closer to the sense, and nearer, though of course not near enough, to Horace's manner. The most poetical versions of Horace which I have come across are Calverley's in his *Verses and Translations*,[3] and they are as close as Conington's; but they are too Tennysonian to be very Horatian.

I am yours sincerely
A. E. Housman.

Conington's translations of Horace's satires and epistles[4] are among the best verse translations in English.

Marquette University MS (Elizabeth Whitcomb Houghton Collection, series 5, box 4). Maas, 209.

[2] Identified by Maas, 209, as the Revd John Willis Price (1872–1940): 'novelist and writer of verse; Vicar of Croughton, 1912–1940'.

[1] *The Odes and Carmen Saeculare of Horace*, translated into English verse by John Conington (1863). Conington (1825–69), was the first Corpus Christi Professor of Latin at Oxford, 1854–69, and known chiefly as a Virgil scholar.

[2] *The Odes of Horace*, translated into English verse, with a life and notes, by Theodore Martin (1860). Martin (1816–1909) was an eminent man of letters. He published translations of Catullus (1861), Dante's *Vita Nuova* (1862), Goethe's *Faust* (1865–6), and Heine (1878), among others; collaborated with William Aytoun on *Bon Gaultier Ballads* (1845, etc.); and prepared a life of the Prince Consort for Queen Victoria (5 vols., 1875–80). He was knighted in 1880.

[3] *Verses and Translations*, by C. S. C. [Charles Stuart Calverley] (1862, etc.) Calverley (1831–84) was elected Fellow of Christ's College, Cambridge, in 1857, and called to the Bar in 1865. He published a translation of Theocritus (1869), but is best remembered for his light verse and parodies, which include *Fly Leaves* (1872, and subsequent edns.).

[4] *The Satires, Epistles and Ars Poetica of Horace*, translated into English verse by J. Conington (1870).

TO GRANT RICHARDS

[Trinity College | Cambridge
28 Dec. 1922

My dear Richards,]

The wine has arrived, and I am very grateful.[1] There is a great amateur of sherry in this college, with whom I must sample it.

I am prepared to receive royalty from America for the sale of *A Shropshire Lad*. I suppose it will be the same as for *Last Poems*.

In the copies of the small *Shropshire Lad* which you sent me a few weeks ago the corrections I gave you have not been made. Is that the case with all the 5000 (or whatever it was) which you had printed lately?

A happy new year to you and yours.

[Yours sincerely
A. E. Housman.]

Richards, 206; Maas, 210.

TO KATHARINE SYMONS

Trinity College | Cambridge
29 Dec. 1922

My dear Kate,

I hope your lumbago has gone or is going, and that you and Edward <als[o]> are about to begin a happy new year. I return Jerry's letter, and am glad of his success: also the *Edwardian*[1] (for which also thanks) as I believe you are short of copies.

The artist in *Punch* is one Bert Thomas. He asked Grant Richards for a photograph, which I would not send,[2] and I think he had to depend on one of Rothenstein's drawings of me.

Janet's nephew is to go to Worcester Grammar school: so Rosalie told me in a letter which I forwarded to Basil, as she appeared to intend.

---

[1] 'We sent him some sherry as a Christmas present—sherry from John Fothergill's cellar at The Spreadeagle at Thame': Richards, 205.

[1] The magazine of King Edward's School, Bath, where KES's husband Edward was headmaster.

[2] See AEH to GR, 11 Oct. 1922, and n. 1.

The notice of Mr Millington in the *Times*,[3] which I thought good, though it left out some points, was by Paul Roberts, now Vice-Provost of Worcester College.[4]

I am well, except that I am eating and drinking too much.

Your affectionate brother

A. E. Housman.

Private MS; Richards, 202 (excerpt).

[3] The unsigned obituary of Herbert Millington: *The Times*, 21 Dec. 1922, 12.
[4] Paul E. Roberts (1873–1949), Tutor in Modern History.

1923

TO GRANT RICHARDS

I suppose the Braille people[1] may do *Last Poems* as they did the other book. The blind want cheering up.

Yours
A. E. Housman.
Trin. Coll. Camb.

10 Jan 1923.

Lilly MSS 1. 1. 4: p.c. addressed 'Grant Richards Esq. | 8 St Martin's Street | Leicester Square | W. C. 2'. Richards, 207; Maas, 210.

TO F. W. HALL

I have told Arnold that I can send him six or eight pages about the middle of February.[1]

A. E. H.
Trin. Coll. Camb.

15 Jan. 1923

Lilly MSS 1. 1. 4: p.c. addressed 'F. W. Hall, Esq. | St John's College | Oxford'. Maas, 210.

TO A. W. POLLARD

Trinity College | Cambridge
17 Jan. 1923

My dear Pollard,

Jackson[1] died peacefully on Sunday night in hospital at Vancouver, where he had gone to be treated for anaemia, with which he had been ailing for some years. I had a letter from him on New Year's Day, which he ended by saying 'goodbye'. Now I can die myself: I could not have

---

[1] The National Institute for the Blind.

[1] Edward [Vernon] Arnold (1857–1926), Professor of Latin at the University College of North Wales, was co-editor with Hall of *CQ*. It looks as though Hall had heard AEH read a paper and asked him to send it to *CQ*, and that Arnold rejected it (AEH to Hackforth, 12 Mar. 1931 and note). The only article by AEH in *CQ* in 1923 or subsequent years is 'Dorotheus Once More', *CQ* 17. 1, and it occupies only two pages of print (53–4).

[1] Moses Jackson: see List of Recipients.

borne to leave him behind me in a world where anything might happen
to him.

Yours sincerely
A. E. Housman.

Private MS.

TO GRANT RICHARDS

[Trinity College | Cambridge
18 January 1923

My dear Richards,]
Did you succeed in finding out Witter Bynner's address and send him a
copy of *Last Poems*?[1] I have a letter from him which reads as if he had not
received one.[2]

I am told that the Brighter London Society[3] are printing Lovat Fraser's
illustrations to *A Shropshire Lad*[4] on calendar covers.

[Yours sincerely
A. E. Housman.]

Richards, 207.

TO W. H. SHEWRING

Trinity College | Cambridge
18 Jan. 1923

Dear Mr Shewring,
The *Fragment of a Greek Tragedy* was published in *Cornhill* in 1901, I think;
at any rate in one of the early years of the century.[1]

I am yours very truly
A. E. Housman.

*SJCO MS, Sparrow Collection. Tipped-in on the flyleaf of the 1914 Riccardi Press edn. of ASL
(paper copy no. 800), with envelope addressed 'W. H. Shewring Esq. | 7 Birchwood Road |
St Anne's Park | Bristol' tipped-in on front inside cover.*

[1] See AEH to GR, 16 Sept. 1922, n. 1.
[2] GR duly wrote to Bynner on 24 Jan. 1923. Richards, 207: 'he did receive his copy all right,
but … he was a man who moved about a great deal'.
[3] *The Times*, 18 Jan. 1922: 'A society, as announced yesterday in *The Times*, has now been
formed to make London a more cheerful and a more beautiful place. It is called the Brighter
London Society … It is, however, concerned with more than the beauty of the Metropolis. It
aims at creating within it more of the holiday atmosphere that may be found in the big cities on
the Continent.'
[4] See AEH to GR, 20 Dec. 1920.

[1] It appeared in *The Cornhill Magazine*, NS 10 (Apr. 1901), 443–5, having first been published
in *The Bromsgrovian*, NS 2. 5 (8 June 1883), 107–9. See *Poems* (1997), 531–2.

TO KATHARINE SYMONS

Trinity College | Cambridge
18 Jan. 1923

My dear Kate,

They have sent me these, which had better be in your possession. I am ordering the Catalogue to be sent to you: if it does not arrive in a few days, scream.

Your affectionate brother
A. E. Housman.

BCD: The Journal of the Book Club of Detroit, *3. 1 (Spring 1978), 22.*

TO PROFESSOR KARL BREUL

Trinity College
25 Jan. 1923

Dear Professor Breul,

I shall be delighted to be your guest at King's on Feb. 13 at 8 o' clock.

Yours sincerely
A. E. Housman.

BMC MS.

TO GRANT RICHARDS

Trinity College | Cambridge
2 Feb. 1923

My dear Richards,

Lord Henry Bentinck[1] can have what he wants.

I have heard from Witter Bynner that he has received his copy.

Yours sincerely
A. E. Housman.

LC-GR MS.

---

[1] Lord Henry Cavendish-Bentinck (1863–1931).

TO PROFESSOR O. L. RICHMOND

Trinity College | Cambridge
6 Feb. 1923

Dear Richmond,

I am really grateful to you and Grierson[1] for your kind intentions, and to you for your very pretty letter, and I do not lack veneration for the University of Edinburgh nor appreciation of the honour which her degrees confer; but it is an old resolve of mine, the reasons for which it would be tedious and in some respects difficult to set forth, not to accept such compliments from any quarter. I am also obliged to you for giving me private warning; for when matters have been allowed to go as far as the academical senate it causes one a good deal of embarrassment.

Yours sincerely
A. E. Housman.

Private MS.

TO WITTER BYNNER

Trinity College | Cambridge | England
6 Feb. 1923

Dear Witter Bynner,

You sent me your *Canticle of Pan*,[1] and I ought to have thanked you for it if I did not; but I am afraid you are not the only person who has reason to complain of my ungracious silence. The fact is that I have a strong tendency to postpone writing all letters; and so it often happens that they do not get written at all, because I have gradually come to fancy that I have written them because I ought to have written them.

Thanks for what you say about my last volume.[2] The sale is larger than I expected, though I expected a larger sale than the publishers and booksellers did.[3]

I am yours sincerely
A. E. Housman.

Harvard MS Eng 1071 (17). Bynner/Haber (1957), 21–2; Maas, 211.

[1] Herbert [John Clifford] Grierson (1866–1960), Regius Professor of Rhetoric and English Literature at Edinburgh University, 1915–35.

[1] *The Canticle of Pan And Other Poems* (1920).

[2] *LP*, published on 19 Oct. 1922.

[3] Discouraged by booksellers, GR decided to print 4,000, not 5,000, copies. AEH had advised 10,000. By the end of 1922, 21,000 had been printed. See Richards, 200.

TO MESSRS GRANT RICHARDS LTD

If I did lay it down (which I do not remember) that composers were not to give titles of their own to my poems, they have broken the rule often before now, and it is no good adhering to it.

A. E. Housman

14 Feb. 1923   Trin. Coll. Camb.

LC-GR MS: p.c. addressed 'Messrs Grant Richards Ld. | 8 St Martin's Street | Leicester Square | W. C. 2.' Richards, 207; Maas, 211.

TO PERCY SIMPSON

Trinity College | Cambridge
24 Feb. 1923

Dear Sir,

I do not now clearly remember what proposals I made for restoring Jonson's verses,[1] but I remember that I was not at all satisfied with them; and therefore, though of course you are at liberty to use any suggestions which will fit in with your own reconstruction, I would rather that my name were not mentioned.

What you say about the construction sounds as if it were right, but I have not the context in my memory.

I am yours very truly
A. E. Housman.

Yale MS (Percy Simpson Papers, Osb MSS 8).

TO E. M. FORSTER

Trinity College | Cambridge
25 Feb. 1923

Dear Mr Forster,

It is very kind of you to write, and I value what you say. I remember meeting you, and the circumstances; and so perhaps this letter may find you even though you withold[1] your address.[2]

I am yours very truly
A. E. Housman.

KCC MS (EMF Library), tipped-in in Forster's copy of LP *(2nd impression, Oct. 1922).*

---

[1] Simpson and his wife Evelyn were completing work on the Oxford edn. (11 vols., 1925–52), begun by C. H. Herford, of the works of Ben Jonson.

[1] For 'withhold'.

[2] Forster had written on 22 Feb. 1923 (BMC MS) to express 'thankfulness from the bottom of my heart' for AEH's poetry and 'the wish that you may be happy'. The meeting between

TO PERCY SIMPSON

circularem is not 'convincing' to me in default of a context. I could not ascertain that *philtram* really was capable of meaning headgear; but perhaps you have.

A. E. Housman.

2 March 1923   Trin. Coll. Camb.

Yale MS (Percy Simpson Papers, Osb MSS 8): p.c. addressed to 'Percy Simpson Esq. |
Oriel College | Oxford'.

TO ERNEST HARRISON

Trinity College
26 March 1923

Dear Harrison,

uersant in Iuu. VI O 18 is not the word for turning in a particular direction: that would be *uertunt: animum uersant* would naturally mean the same as Hor. serm. I 8 19 *uersant ... humanos animos*. Nor ought *magistris* to stray outside the clause in which *discunt* is. But, quite apart from these two points, I do not see how anyone could guess that the sense of the words is what R.[1] says it is. 'Heavy irony' is litotes, and 'characteristically' and 'Juvenalian' are libel.

You have spotted two of the metrical points in the *C. R.*:[2] the others are these.

p. 12[a]. It would not be a Sophoclean elision[3] unless the preceding syllable were long; it would not even be possible; because, until one foot is full, nothing can overflow into the next.

p. 13[b]. Do you know of any place where the first vowel of Ἰόνιος is short?

Forster and AEH had taken place in the company of G. Lowes Dickinson and Roger Fry at Harry Norton's house in Cambridge. Forster had withheld his address to preclude a reply. He wrote to AEH on 28 Mar. 1928 (BMC MS): 'I don't know whether there is such a thing as impersonal affection, but the words best express the feeling I have had towards you, through your poems, for the last thirty years, and I ask you to pardon this expression of it.'

[1] A note on the MS states that 'P. 1 refers to a note on Juvenal by D. S. R.' Naiditch (1995), 163, readily identifies D. S. Robertson. The note was not published, either in *CR* or *CQ*.

[2] In Harrison's article, 'Aristophanes, *Frogs*, 1203', *CR* 37. 1/2 (Feb.–Mar. 1923), 10–14.

[3] Between lines in Greek iambics, to avoid a final tribrach.

p. 16ᵃ. Ag. 239 has no\<t\> 'metrical flaw' except in the imagination of the ignorant and immodest Agar,[4] and similar folk.

Yours sincerely
A. E. Housman.

TCC Add. MS c. 112¹⁷. Maas, 417.

TO KATHARINE SYMONS

Trinity College | Cambridge
26 March 1923

My dear Kate,

Thanks for your letter on my birthday with its enclosures. I may as well sit down at once and answer it, not being much good for anything else. For the last three weeks I have been about as ill as I ever have been in the course of a fairly healthy life with boils on the neck and a carbuncle on the back; though I daresay poor Basil has often been worse. The doctor says I am better today, and I think perhaps I am.

It is very pleasant to see how happy and active Jerry is: he seems to have found his vocation. I don't exactly know what his office is,[1] nor whereabouts he is in the large province of Bengal: not far from Calcutta apparently.

I had meant to spend this vacation in interesting work: now, as soon as I can get out, I shall probably have to waste the rest of it at the seaside.

I receive, though I do not wish to, the *Weekly Westminster*[2] in which my verses are translated. The prize copy of Greek elegiacs had a false quantity in the second line: I did not read on to see if there were more.

Your affectionate brother
A. E. Housman.

Lilly MSS 2. 1. Memoir, 148; Maas, 211–12.

---

[4] T. L. Agar, 'Suggestions on the *Agamemnon* of Aeschylus', *CR* 37. 1/2 (Feb.–Mar. 1923), 16–18.

[1] In 1920, Kate's son 'Jerry' had begun a career in the Indian Civil Service that was to last twenty-five years. In 1931 he was made Secretary to the Bengal Board of Revenue; in 1934, Secretary to the Governor of Bengal. For further information, see Jo Hunt's obituary tribute: *HSJ* 12 (1986), 1–8.

[2] Cf. AEH to GR, 20 Sept. 1922.

TO KATHARINE SYMONS

23 April 1923
SANDRINGHAM HOTEL. | HUNSTANTON-ON-SEA, | NORFOLK.

My dear Kate,

I am better, and have been staying here since the 19th; to-morrow I go back. Thanks for your instalment of history: it is now at Cambridge, but I will send it back.

Your affectionate brother
A. E. Housman.

TCC Add. MS c. 50⁴.

TO AN UNKNOWN CORRESPONDENT

Trinity College | Cambridge | England
28 April 1923

Dear Sir,

I have been unwell for many weeks, and my letter-writing is much behind-hand; so in thanking you for your kindness in sending me your Greek versions I must apologise for not having thanked you before.

I am yours truly
A. E. Housman.

Text as printed in Waiting for Godot Books, *cat. 35 (Feb. 1996), no. 619.*

TO PRINCESS MARIE LOUISE VICTORIA

Trinity College | Cambridge
1 May 1923

Madam,

I willingly give my permission for the printing of the poems which I selected in *The Book of the Dolls' House Library.*[1]

I am, Madam,

Your Highness's obedient servant
A. E. Housman.

Private MS.

---

[1] See the next letter.

TO GRANT RICHARDS

Trinity College| Cambridge
4 May 1923

My dear Richards,

I wish, if you can, you would stop the *Westminster*[1] (Saturday) setting poems of mine to be turned into Greek and Latin. They will soon have reprinted the whole volume. What makes it worse is that they award prizes to copies containing false quantities.

My old, dear, and intimate friend Princess Marie Louise, who is furnishing the Queen's doll's-house,[2] asked me some months ago to let 12 poems of mine be copied small to form one volume in the library; and I selected the 12 shortest and simplest and least likely to fatigue the attention of dolls or members of the illustrious House of Hanover. Now she says that there is to be printed a book describing or reproducing the contents of this library, and asks me to allow these poems to be included in it; and I have consented. So do not send a solicitor's letter to the Queen (for the book is to be hers) when it appears. The issue is to be 2000 copies in this country and 500 for America, and the Queen is to do what she likes with the proceeds. As I say, the poems are my shortest, and the 12 together are 96 lines.

I have to thank you for sending me several things, including Mrs Taylor's book on the renascence,[3] which I find I can read, though what she writes is not prose. I think her verse is better, though it has not much beyond mere gorgeousness.

I have been ill for two months, worse than I ever was in my life (though that may not be saying much), with carbuncles, which I never had before and do not want to have again. At last I am better, but it has ruined my Easter holiday.

Yours sincerely
A. E. Housman.

PM MS. LC-GR t.s. Richards, 207–8; Maas, 212 (both incomplete).

[1] See AEH to GR, 23 Sept. 1922.

[2] Designed by Sir Edward Lutyens and decorated by Philip Connard, A. R. A., and now exhibited at Windsor Castle. E. V. Lucas advised on the choice of books for the library. Apart from AEH's, each book contained a specially commissioned story. Maas, 212, notes that only Bernard Shaw refused to oblige.

[3] *Aspects of the Italian Renaissance* by Rachel Annand Taylor. Published by GR in 1923. Richards, 208 n.: 'It was Dr. Gilbert Murray who first drew Housman's attention to Mrs. Taylor's work—to her poetry rather than her prose, which had not then been published. She was a warm admirer of Housman's work.'

TO HETTIE GRAY BAKER

Trinity College | Cambridge | England
9 May 1993

Dear Miss Baker,

I wish I could return your kindness, but I have no bookplate of my own. I have written my name on one of yours as you request, and enclose it.

I am yours very truly
A. E. Housman.

Private MS. One of her bookplates bears the signature 'A. E. Housman.'

TO DR PERCY WITHERS

Trinity College | Cambridge
16 May 1923

My dear Withers,

For nearly three months I have been ill, not on a scale which would inspire your respect, but enough to make me very angry and disgusted, and in fact worse than I ever was in my life. It has been a succession of carbuncles, which I thought had ended a week ago, but it had not. At present I am not in a case to accept hospitality, and, in particular, your cellar would be almost as bad for me as for you. I had thought of proposing to call on you when I motor into Gloucestershire on June 4, but it is now settled that I shall go by another route. When I come back, about June 20, it appears that you will not be at home; so I cannot hope for anything nearer than July<.>, \as I don't want to leave Cambridge again till the vacation term begins./

When I saw the invention of Insulin[1] I thought of you, and I expected to hear that you were cured already. I hope you will be soon; and then we will try if our Audit ale[2] can make you ill again. I doubt its power, for it is not as good as it was before the war.

How about your book?[3]

My kind regards to Mrs Withers and many thanks to both of you for the kindness of your invitation.

Yours sincerely
A. E. Housman.

SCO MS. Maas, 213.

[1] Anti-diabetic hormone obtained by Canadian surgeon and physiologist Frederick G. Banting and C. H. Best, who first successfully treated a human being in Jan. 1922.
[2] Strong ale supplied to TCC by E. Lacon and Company. The audit was the annual check of the college's finances, and TCC celebrated the occasion with a feast: see Naiditch (2005), 25.
[3] *Friends in Solitude* (1923).

TO A. S. F. GOW

Trinity College | Cambridge
21 May 1923

Dear Gow,

Yes, I shall be grateful for your spare Porson.[1] I hope I am getting better.

Yours sincerely
A. E. Housman.

TCC Add. MS c. 112[18].

TO DR P. H. COWELL

Trinity College | Cambridge
22 May 1923

Dear Sir,

I believe that your Office kindly allows its assistants to undertake for private payment astronomical calculations for those who cannot easily perform them themselves, and I should be very grateful if I could thus be supplied with answers to the questions which I have set out on the next page.[1]

I am yours faithfully
A. E. Housman.

Dr Cowell
    Superintendent Nautical Almanac Office
        At the date
            XVI kal. Febr. A.U.C. 705
            = 15 Jan. 49 B.C.,
which, according to most chronologers, corresponds, in the reformed calendar, to
            28 Nov. <48> \50/ B.C.,
when the sun had lately entered Sagittarius:

in what degrees of what zodiacal signs were *Saturn, Jupiter, Mars,* and *Venus* situated?

Was *Mercury* \either/ stationary or retrograde? If not, what are the nearest dates, before and after, at which he was stationary? And how

---

[1] Probably one of his edns. of Euripides.

[1] Cowell wrote five letters to AEH in 1923 (SJCO MSS). His help is acknowledged in AEH's edition of Lucan (1926), 326.

long does he usually remain stationary? and at what intervals does he become so?

Private MS. On the last page, 'either' and the final question are in pencil.

TO MARIA RICHARDS

Trinity College | Cambridge
31 May 1923

Dear Mrs Richards,
    I hope to get to Bigfrith by 1 o' clock on Saturday.

Yours sincerely
A. E. Housman.

BMC MS. Richards, 208 (nearly complete).

TO F. W. HALL

Trinity College | Cambridge
22 June 1923

Dear Hall,
    I am sorry if I have kept you waiting, but I have been three weeks in the country.

Yours sincerely
A. E. Housman

Private MS.

TO ROBERT BRIDGES

Trinity College | Cambridge
2 July 1923

My dear Bridges,
    Thanks for the enquiries, and also for what you say of my poems. The title of the next volume will be *Posthumous Poems* or *Chansons d'Outre-tombe*.[1]

    Before the end of the month I hope to go abroad: till then I am here, as I do not think myself quite well enough to stay with people, and I am taking periodical inoculations; but <I think> I should be quite able to look after you properly if you could find time to stay as my guest in Trinity, and we should all be pleased and honoured. I expect to be back again before

[1] '*Songs from beyond the Tomb*', by analogy with Chateaubriand's *Mémoires d'Outre-tombe* (1849–50).

the end of August, and by then I ought to be quite well. There is nothing now to prevent me from running over to Oxford for the day, except on a Thursday, if you could not find time to come here.

Yours sincerely
A. E. Housman.

Bodleian MS, Dep. Bridges 110. 108–9. Maas, 213–14.

TO ROBERT BRIDGES

Trinity College | Cambridge
5 July 1923

My dear Bridges,

I am not likely to go abroad before the 31st,—if then; for they are making such a fuss about my passport that I apprehend war with France is imminent; so there would be plenty of time for you to favour me with a visit here. If you have not yet slept in our Guest Room, emblazoned by Sir William Harcourt[1] with the emblems of his descent from the Plantagenets, I think you ought. But if not, I certainly should be pleased to pay you a visit in September.

Yours sincerely
A. E. Housman.

Bodleian MS, Dep. Bridges 110. 110. Maas, 214.

TO GRANT RICHARDS

Trinity College | Cambridge
24 July 1923

My dear Richards,

This proceeding of the *Weekly Scotsman*, with its mutilation and misprint, is intolerable.[1]

As to the *Westminster*, it did, to my surprise, set a piece from *A Shropshire Lad* for translation a few weeks ago; and I thought perhaps your embargo had been confined to the other book. But I am told by those who read the paper that the translations have never appeared; so I suppose you have terrorized it somehow.

---

[1] 1827–1904. Son of William Vernon Harcourt and descended from the twelfth-century Robert de Harcourt, whose wife was a cousin of Adela of Louvain, second wife of King Henry I. Statesman; elected Honorary Fellow of TCC in 1904.

[1] On 21 July it printed *The Deserter* (*LP* XIII). There was no apology.

I shall cross to Paris on the 31st by the Handley Page[2] from Croydon at 4. 30. I shall stay at the Continental for about 3 days, and then, I think, go by train to Le Mans and engage a car there, which will be cheaper than in Paris. My idea is to follow the south coast[3] and come back by the north. Thanks for all your maps, books and other aids.

If we are in Paris together, I probably should not be free in the evenings but should be during the day. I am afraid I cannot come up to town this week. The Poet Laureate is paying me a visit on Thursday.

I suppose I gave Christabel Marillier permission,[4] but I forget, and it does not matter. Boosey[5] have suddenly enriched me with £6 for gramophone rights, Vaughan Williams I think.[6]

Your not sending me a cheque is not inconvenient to me but it is demoralising for you, especially as you ought to be wallowing in wealth from the enhanced sale of *A Shropshire Lad*. The American advance you obviously should have sent straight on to me.

I read through the *Bookman* you sent me a week or two ago, and it may have improved my mind, but I did not make out why you sent it.[7]

I hope you will keep your end up with Frank Harris.

Yours sincerely
A. E. Housman.

LC-GR t.s. Richards, 208–9; Maas, 214–15 (both incomplete). Excerpt from autograph MS reproduced in facsimile in Verlyn Klinkenborg, British Literary Manuscripts. Series II: from 1800 to 1914. Catalogue. *(1981), opposite p. 112.*

TO KATHARINE SYMONS

Hôtel Continental | Paris
18 Aug. 1923

My dear Kate,

Your letter reached me here yesterday on my return from a motor tour of a fortnight in Britanny.[1] The weather has been most obsequious; blazing hot all the time while motor-travel could temper it, and turning

---

[2] Aircraft. One crashed at Boulogne in 1920, and there would be other crashes: two in the English Channel (1926, 1929), one at Abbeville (1928).

[3] Of Brittany.

[4] For her setting of *Loveliest of trees* (*ASL* II), published in 1923.

[5] Messrs Boosey & Hawkes, music publishers.

[6] Gervase Elwes's fine recording in March 1917 of Vaughan Williams's song cycle *On Wenlock Edge* greatly increased the cycle's popularity: Banfield (1985), 236.

[7] In 'Two New Composers', *The Bookman*, 381 (June 1923), 170–1, Watson Lyle reviewed settings by C. W. Orr of *ASL* XXXIX ('*Tis time, I think, by Wenlock town*), II (*Loveliest of trees*), XLVII (*The Carpenter's Son*), and VI (*When the lad for longing sighs*).

[1] For 'Brittany'.

cool now that heat would be a nuisance. Britanny is much less wild than I supposed, and much like parts of England, the neighbourhood of Midhurst for instance, though not so hilly. The churches and cathedrals are better than I had any idea of, and extraordinarily numerous. You would be more interested in the varieties of the female head-dress, which is different for every district. Finisterre is an impressive headland, and provided a fine sunset, and also a Scotch mist. The coast scenery in general is extraordinarily superior to the English in its mixture of land and water, and the islands and rocks. Carnac is almost as unimpressive as Stonehenge.

Together with your letter I have one from some photographers, who say that they are taking, 'for press purposes', photographs of ladies and gentlemen who are in the habit of flying between London and Paris, and they want to take mine, as <that> they 'understand that I have also had that distinction'. I was delayed a day because the weather of July 31 was too dangerous for the aeroplane to start; but on August 1 I had the best voyage I have ever had. We crossed <that> the Channel 7000 feet high, higher than the piles of clouds which lay over both shores, and both coasts were visible at once, which I have not found before.

I am better, but not well. I spent the first half of June at Woodchester, and went over to Cheltenham to see J. R. Polson,[2] whom I had not met for 30 years, and who seems very well and flourishing. I expect to return to Cambridge on the 28th. Love to all on the premises.

Your affectionate brother
A. E. Housman.

TCC Add. MS 50[5–7]. *Envelope addressed 'Mrs Symons | 61 Prior Park Road | Bath | Angleterre'. Memoir, 149–50 (incomplete); Maas, 215.*

TO HERBERT THRING

Trinity College | Cambridge
10 Sept. 1923

Dear Sir,

I am obliged by your letter of the 6th inst. with its enclosures, and I enclose an application for membership of the Society of Authors.

As regards the British Broadcasting Company, if what they want to broadcast are readings from my poems, I refuse my consent. In respect of

---

[2] James Ronald Polson (b. 1859), was AEH's contemporary at The Grammar School of King Edward VI, Bromsgrove, which he attended 1870–8. He studied medicine at Queen's College, Birmingham, and practised as a doctor in Worcester.

musical settings I should not interfere nor exact any payment, but leave
the decision in the hands of the composers.

I am yours faithfully
A. E. Housman.

The Secretary
  The Society of Authors
BMC MS.

TO HERBERT THRING

Trinity College | Cambridge
18 Sept. 1923

Dear Sir,

  I am flattered by the infatuation of the British Broadcasting Co., but I
cannot entertain their proposal.

Yours faithfully
A. E. Housman.

BMC MS.

TO GEORGE SUTCLIFFE

Trinity College | Cambridge
20 Sept. 1923

Dear Sir,

  If you will be good enough to send the book here I shall be pleased to
sign it.

I am yours faithfully
A. E. Housman.

BMC MS. Envelope addressed 'G. Sutcliffe Esq. | 1 Poland Street | Oxford Street | W. 1'.

TO GRANT RICHARDS

Trinity College | Cambridge
23 Sept. 1923

My dear Richards,

  I have seen a reply which your firm sent to Longmans when they asked
if they might include two pieces from *Last Poems* in Bridges' selection of
poetry for schools.[1] It is quite the sort of answer which I should wish you

---

[1] *The Chilswell Book of English Poetry* compiled and annotated for the use of schools by Robert
Bridges, Poet Laureate (published in 1924 by Longmans, Green & Company). It contained *ASL*
XXXVII, XXXI, and XL, and *LP* XXXII and III.

to write, though in point of fact I do not unconditionally prohibit the use of *Last Poems* as I do of *A Shropshire Lad*; <and> but I have given Bridges my permission to include the two poems in question.[2]

I had better also tell you that I believe that he, (being Poet Laureate, and an unscrupulous character, and apparently such an admirer of my verse that he thinks its presence or absence will make all the difference to his book), intends to include three poems from *A Shropshire Lad*, though I have not given him my permission, because he thinks he has reason to think that I shall not prosecute him. Well, I shall not; and you will please turn a blind eye too.

Yours sincerely
A. E. Housman.

PM MS MA 3570 R.V. Autographs Misc. English. Envelope addressed 'Grant Richards Esq. | 8 St Martin's Street | Leicester Square | W. C. 2.' Richards, 53; Maas, 216.

TO GEORGE SUTCLIFFE

Trinity College | Cambridge
24 Sept. 1923

Dear Sir,

I return the book with my signature added, and with my compliments on its elegance.

I am yours faithfully
A. E. Housman.

BMC MS. Envelope addressed 'George Sutcliffe Esq. | 1 Poland Street | Oxford Street | W. 1'.

TO DR PERCY WITHERS

Trinity College | Cambridge
7 Oct. 1923

My dear Withers,

I was glad to receive your letter and the gift of your book,[1] with which I will make more acquaintance when I have finished reading *Main Street*,[2] which I am doing at the request of an American, and find that it takes some time. I was hoping that you would carry out your threat of coming here

---

[2] Acknowledged by Bridges in a letter to AEH, 25 Sept. 1923: *The Selected Letters of Robert Bridges*, ed. Donald E. Stanford, 2 (1984), 811–12. AEH's letter is missing.

[1] See AEH to Withers, 16 May 1923, n. 3.

[2] Novel by Sinclair Lewis, published in 1920.

this term and sampling our port, which at present is 1900 and very good. Although it seems that this is not to be, I am glad that you are progressing, and that Insulin is not a fraud.[3]

I am not well yet, though nearly so, I hope; but I hoped that at the beginning of August, and went abroad, and was attacked anew the very first day. However, I had what was on the whole a good time touring about Britanny[4] in a motor, which mitigated what would otherwise have been the excessive heat. I found the country less wild than I expected, the stonehenges no more impressive than I expected, but the churches and cathedrals better than I had ever supposed to exist in that corner of France. Just at this moment I have sciatica in a mild form.

Palgrave had to do without Swinburne,[5] so I think Binyon can afford to do without me.[6]

My kind regards to Mrs Withers.

Yours sincerely
A. E. Housman.

It is kind of you to invite me, but with two maladies on me I am likely to be staying at home most of this term.

SCO MS.

TO MR CASTELLO

Trinity College | Cambridge
9 Oct. 1923

Dear Castello,

I return the book embellished with my signature. The omission of a comma and a semicolon which you note on p. 52[1] constitute the chief merit of this edition in the eyes of bibliophiles. One can no more keep printers in order than Job could bind the sweet influences of the Pleiades.[2]

I am yours sincerely
A. E. Housman.

University of North Carolina MS.

---

[3] See AEH to Withers, 16 May 1923, n. 1.   [4] For 'Brittany'.

[5] F. T. Palgrave's anthology *The Golden Treasury* (1861; 2nd series, 1897) contained no work by Swinburne. See *The Swinburne Letters*, ed. Cecil Y. Lang, 6 (1962), 103 n.

[6] *The Golden Treasury of Modern Lyrics*, ed. Laurence Binyon (1924) contained no work by AEH.

[1] Of the first edn. of *LP*.

[2] Job 38: 31: 'Canst thou bind the sweet influences of Pleiades?'

TO KATHARINE SYMONS

Trinity College | Cambridge
15 Oct. 1923

My dear Kate,

One of these enclosures concerns you; the other, though I do not suppose it refers to our family, you might perhaps send on to the genealogical cousin whose Christian name I forget.

I hope I am now about right again, and I hope you and yours are well.

Your affectionate brother
A. E. Housman.

TCC Add. MS c. 50[8].

TO A. S. F. GOW

Thanks; but it is a mere reprint of the Aldine.[1] The ed. princeps[2] which I am after fetched £60 the last time it was up at auction.

Yours
A. E. Housman.

Yes, I think I am fairly right at last.
17 Oct. 1923   Trin. Coll. Camb.

TCC Add. MS c. 112[19]: p.c. addressed 'Andrew Gow Esq. | 2 Common Lane | Eton'.

TO A. S. F. GOW

Trinity College | Cambridge
21 Oct. 1923

Dear Gow,

Regiomontanus' is the edition I want, and I did authorise Sotheby's[1] to bid for me up to £40 (the highest price it had yet fetched) on the occasion when it was bought for £60; but that was rather an act of extravagance on my part, as I can really get all I want out of it by paying a visit to the British Museum when I am about to produce a volume. Books that I want more, if you should happen to see them, are on the opposite page; I should be ready to pay any price which is likely to be asked for them. Do not

---

[1] Edn. of Manilius.   [2] Regiomontanus (*c.*1472): see the next letter.

[1] London auctioneers.

bother to keep a look out for them: it is very kind of you to make the offer you do.

Yours sincerely
A. E. Housman.

Manilius, Scaliger ed. 1600
” E. Burton ed. 1783
” T. Creech transl. 1697 or 1700
Paulus Alexandrinus, Witebergae, 1586
Salmasius, *de annis climactericis*, 1648
Procli in Ptolemaei Quadripartitum enarrationes, accedunt Porphyrii introductio etc.,
Basileae, 1559. [The full title is longer.][2]

TCC Add. MS c. 112²⁰. Maas, 417–18. The square brackets round the last sentence are AEH's.
Envelope addressed 'Andrew Gow Esq. | 2 Common Lane | Eton'.

TO H. W. GARROD

TRINITY COLLEGE, | CAMBRIDGE.
2 Nov. 1923

Dear Mr Garrod,
   Many thanks for the gift of your Wordsworth,[1] which I am reading with great interest and finding in it many things which I did not know.

I am yours very truly
A. E. Housman.

SJCO MS, Sparrow Collection. Envelope addressed 'H. W. Garrod Esq. C.B.E. | Merton
College | Oxford'.

TO PROFESSOR KARL BREUL

Trinity College
2 Nov. 1923

Dear Professor Breul,
   It will give me great pleasure to dine with you at the King's Audit on Nov. 15 at 8 o' clock.
   Will you give me the further pleasure of dining with me at the same hour at our Audit feast on Thursday Dec. 6?

Yours sincerely
A. E. Housman.

BMC MS.

[2] AEH acquired Scaliger's edn. and Creech's translation: Naiditch (2003), 126, 128.
[1] *Wordsworth: Lectures and Essays* (1923).

TO E. V. LUCAS

Trinity College | Cambridge
3 Nov. 1923

Dear Lucas,

Thanks for your letter, which is the second I owe to the poet in the *Times*, whom I judge from his versification to be a very gallant soldier.[1]

Yours sincerely
A. E. Housman.

Berg MS. Tipped in on end-paper of copy of Introductory Lecture *(1937 reprint) which bears Lucas's signature. Maas, 216.*

TO F. C. OWLETT

Trinity College | Cambridge
15 Nov. 1923

Dear Mr Owlett,

I thank you for the magazine and article which you have sent me. When you find yourself in Cambridge I shall be pleased to see you; and if you send me a copy of *A Shropshire Lad* I shall be pleased to sign it.

I am yours very truly
A. E. Housman.

BMC MS.

TO F. C. OWLETT

Trinity College | Cambridge
29 Nov. 1923

Dear Mr Owlett,

I am going to Oxford to-morrow, and I am afraid that on Tuesday I may not be back in time to have the pleasure of seeing you.

I think that there is a gallery at the Union[1] from which non-members can hear the debates.

I am yours very truly
A. E. Housman.

Eton MS: with ASL (1903) inscribed 'A. E. Housman | 19 Nov. 1923' on the half-title. Envelope addressed 'F. C. Owlett Esq. | 82 West Hill | Sydenham | S. E. 20'.

[1] On p. 17 of *The Times*, 1 Nov. 1923, appeared *An Armistice Day Anthem* by the Master of the Temple, the Revd William Henry Draper, MA. Its scansion leaves much to be desired.

[1] The Oxford Union Debating Society.

TO A. S. F. GOW

No reference is required. It was not I who wrote about the passage in *C. R.*, but a plagiarist knowing of my emendation and suppressing my name.

A. E. H.

14 Dec. 1923   Trin. Coll. Camb.

TCC Add. MS c. 112²¹ : p.c. addressed 'Andrew Gow Esq. | 2 Common Lane | Eton | Bucks.'

TO SIR CHARLES WALSTON

Trinity College | Cambridge
23 Dec. 1923

My dear Walston,

Thanks for your letter and its enclosure; but the pride and ample pinion of the Theban eagle[1] are not more out of my reach than his readiness and fluency.

Yours sincerely
A. E. Housman.

Private MS.

TO DR PERCY WITHERS

Trinity College | Cambridge
28 Dec. 1923

My dear Withers,

I am glad that Insulin has behaved well and not failed as these new infallible remedies do fail on occasion. I am sorry that it has not yet brought you to the level of drinking audit ale, because this year's brew is quite good: last year's was a powerful explosive, and filled our cellars with the shards of bottles till we sent it back to its brewer,[1] for use in case Yarmouth were bombarded again;[2] but there its strength ended, and you could probably have drunk it with impunity.

---

[1] Pindar. Thomas Gray, *The Progress of Poesy. A Pindaric Ode*, 114–17: 'Though he inherit | Nor the pride nor ample pinion, | That the Theban eagle bear | Sailing with supreme dominion | Through the azure deep of air.'

[1] See AEH to Withers, 16 May 1923, n. 2.

[2] A minor bombardment of Yarmouth was carried out by a Zeppelin in Jan. 1915, a major one by German cruisers in 1916.

I return you all good wishes for the new year, and I hope there may be nothing to prevent me from availing myself of your kind invitation in the warm months.

I was pleased to see a very favourable review of your book[3] not long ago in one of the weeklies.

There is nothing the matter with me except too much alcohol and too little exercise, as usual in the winter.

With kind regards to Mrs Withers I am yours sincerely

A. E. Housman.

SCO MS. Withers, 75 (excerpt); Maas, 216–17.

[3] See AEH to Withers, 16 May 1923, n. 3.

1924

TO KATHARINE SYMONS

Trinity College | Cambridge
3 Jan. 1924

My dear Kate,

This post-card comes in the nick of time to make me answer your letter. I am quite well now, except for a slight goutiness; but that is chronic, my friends, so do not grieve for me.[1] I have been here since I came back from Britanny[2] at the end of August, except that a month ago I went to Oxford to read a paper and stayed a week-end with the Poet Laureate[3] on the top of Boar's[4] Hill there. He is an amazing old man: at 79 he gets up at 5 in the morning, lights his own fire and makes his coffee, and does a lot of work before breakfast. He has a large number of correct opinions, and is delighted when he finds that I have them too, and shakes hands with me when I say that the *Nuns' Priest's Tale*[5] is Chaucer's best poem, and that civilisation without slavery is impossible.

I am very sorry to hear of the break in Jerry's[6] career, which seemed to be proceeding so famously; and it is a pity that the wretched country of India should be deprived of his services. I do not yet know how much Denis[7] was fined at Cambridge over the motor-car affair.

I am glad you and Edward are so comfortable. I like the notion of coming to Bath some time this year. I believe the Pump-room hotel, which used to be a good one, is opened again; and that, I suppose, is not so very far from you.

Your affectionate brother
A. E. Housman.

TCC Add. MS c. 50[9–10]. *Envelope addressed 'Mrs Symons | 61 Prior Park Road | Bath'. T.s. extract, Lilly MSS 1. 1. 10. Memoir, 150 (incomplete); Maas, 217.*

[1] ' "Do not repine, my friends," said Mr Pecksniff, tenderly. "Do not weep for me. It is chronic." ': Dickens, *Martin Chuzzlewit*, ch. 9, following a drunken Sunday dinner at Todgers's.
[2] For 'Brittany'.   [3] Robert Bridges.   [4] For 'Boars'.
[5] For '*Nun's Priest's Tale*'.
[6] Her youngest son 'Jerry' was on his first leave from civil service work in India, and AEH entertained him as his guest at TCC: see *HSJ* 7 (1981), 7, 9.
[7] Her second son, Arthur Denis Symons: see List of Recipients.

TO A. S. F. GOW

Trin. Coll. Camb.
9 Jan. 1924

Dear Gow,

I am glad you are to be here at the end of next week. I am writing because you are lodged in the inner Guest Room, and I want to entertain the Family[1] at dinner in the outer room on Friday Jan. 18, which I cannot do without your permission, for which I hereby sue. Will you yourself make one of the party? unless you prefer to dine in Hall. It is at 8 o' clock.

Yours sincerely
A. E. Housman.

I am writing with a sprained wrist.

TCC Add. MS c. 112²². Maas, 218.

TO H. F. B. BRETT-SMITH[1]

Trinity College | Cambridge
11 Jan. 1924

My dear Sir,

I am obliged by your note and also by your poem. I would have written before if I had not sprained my wrist.

I am yours very truly
A. E. Housman.

MS inspected at Sotheby's, London, 23 May 2004. Envelope addressed 'H. F. B. Brett-Smith Esq. | Grantley Dene | Boscombe | Hants.'

[1] Exclusive dining-club of resident Cambridge graduates, limited to twelve persons, which met on alternate Fridays in term-time. Members took turns to give a dinner. AEH, a connoisseur of food and wine, was elected a member in May 1919, and left the contents of his wine cellar to it in his will. Gow was not a member at this time, but became one later. Membership included A. C. Benson, R. V. Laurence, S. C. Roberts, and Sir J. J. Thomson, who notes in his *Recollections and Reflections* (1936), 314–15, 316, that AEH was 'very seldom absent' from the dinners and that 'the dinners which he gave as a member ... had, like everything he did, the air of distinction'. See S. C. Roberts, *The Family* (1967) for further information.

[1] Oxford don notable principally for initiating, 1910–20, a collection of Restoration plays and dramatic literature.

TO GRANT RICHARDS

Trinity College | Cambridge
12 Jan. 1924

My dear Richards,

I am going to write to Henry Holt & Co. to tell them to send my royalties direct to me in future.[1]

Yours sincerely
A. E. Housman.

BMC MS. Envelope addressed 'Grant Richards Esq. | 8 St Martin's Street | Leicester Square | W. C. 2', and marked 'Private'.

TO PROFESSOR J. S. PHILLIMORE

The month was April, the year 1901 or thereabouts. It[1] was first published in a school magazine in 1884.

Yrs
A. E. Housman.
Trin. Coll. Camb.

7 Feb. 1924.

Private MS: p.c. addressed 'Professor J. S. Phillimore | The University | Glasgow'.

TO ARTHUR ST JOHN ADCOCK

Trinity College | Cambridge
9 Feb. 1924

Dear Sir,

For many years I have been refusing permission to print poems from *A Shropshire Lad* in anthologies, and I am sorry that I cannot make an exception in your case.

I am yours faithfully
A. E. Housman.

A. St John Adcock Esq.

BMC MS.

[1] Late in 1923 or early in 1924, Richards had failed to send American royalties to AEH, and this letter marks a change in their relationship: Naiditch (2005), 28, notes that from now until 30 Sept. 1924 'no letter from Housman to Richards himself is known; Housman's letters are only to the firm'.

[1] AEH's parody *Fragment of a Greek Tragedy*, which was in fact first published in *The Bromsgrovian*, NS 2.5 (8 June 1883), 107–9. Among reprintings was that in *The Cornhill Magazine*, NS 10 (April 1901), 443–5. See *Poems* (1997), 531–2.

TO ARTHUR ST JOHN ADCOCK

Trinity College | Cambridge
12 Feb. 1924

Dear Sir,

You are at liberty to print in your anthology[1] one poem from my *Last Poems*.

I am yours faithfully
A. E. Housman.

A. St John Adcock Esq.
BMC MS.

TO GEORGE ROSTREVOR HAMILTON

Trinity College | Cambridge
12 Feb. 1924

Dear Sir,

You are at liberty to include in your anthology my *Epitaph on an Army of Mercenaries*, but for many years I have been refusing permission to reprint poems from *A Shropshire Lad*.

I am yours faithfully
A. E. Housman.

G. Rostrevor Esq.
Bodleian MS Eng. lett. c. 272, fo. 34.

TO A. S. F. GOW

Trinity College | Cambridge
16 Feb. 1924

Dear Gow,

I am very much obliged to you for your present of Creech's Manilius,—the 1st edition too.[1] The copies in the University Library require the Librarian's signature to be taken out.

Several of Ellis's[2] books have wandered to me through second-hand booksellers.

---

[1] *The Bookman Treasury of Living Poets* (1926). It contained *Sinner's Rue* (*LP* XXX).

[1] 1697 verse translation by Thomas Creech (1659–1700).

[2] Robinson Ellis. See List of Recipients.

I have a sprained wrist, in spite of which I hope to shake hands with you on March 2.

Yours sincerely
A. E. Housman.

SJCO MS, with The Five Books of M. Manilius *(1697)*.

TO A. S. F. GOW

[Trinity College]

Frontinus de aquis 13 *anno post urbem conditam octingentesimo Kalendis Augustis*
The formula in inscriptions is

P. R. C. ANN.

anno urbis conditae is chiefly Pliny.

A. E. H.
2 March 1924

Waseda MS, Gow e 64–1 (Gow P3/1), with Kühner, Ausf. Gram. *1 (Han. 1912), 838–9.*

TO LILY THICKNESSE

[Trinity College | Cambridge]
10 March 1924

Dear Mrs Thicknesse,

Last year a French school-ma'm wrote to me wanting to translate *A Shropshire Lad* and asking what share of the proceeds I should expect. I replied that I should take nothing; but then mine is a character of unusual and almost disagreeable nobility.

Yours sincerely
A. E. Housman.

Memoir, 206; Maas, 218.

TO MESSRS GRANT RICHARDS LTD

Trinity College | Cambridge
14 March 1924

Dear Sirs,

I have never laid down any general rule against the inclusion of poems from *Last Poems* in anthologies.

The rule regarding *A Shropshire Lad* still holds good. It is true that the Poet Laureate has printed three poems from it in his recent anthology,[1] but he does not pretend that I gave him permission to do so.

I am yours faithfully
A. E. Housman.

LC-GR t.s. Richards, 211; Maas, 218.

TO F. C. OWLETT

Trinity College | Cambridge
18 March 1924

Dear Mr Owlett,

Gilbert Murray introduced me some 12 years ago to Mrs Taylor's[1] poems, and I admired the beauty and richness of their ornament. I do not put her first among living women poets in this country: I will not provoke your wrath and scorn by saying whom I do; especially as you have on your side 'names from which there would be no appeal'. But there are no such names really: contemporary criticism is always fallible: think of Lamb and Shelley. It is very unreasonable for people to be depressed by unfavourable reviews: they should say to themselves 'do I write better than Wordsworth and Shelley and Keats? am I worse treated than they were?'

I am yours very truly
A. E. Housman.

Princeton MS (Robert H. Taylor Collection). White (1950), 405; Maas, 219.

[1] See AEH to GR, 23 Sept. 1923, and note. In *The Chilswell Book of English Poetry* (1924) Bridges makes acknowledgement of 'the living authors who have allowed their poems to be printed' and thanks them 'individually for their generosity'; but he mentions neither AEH nor GR.

[1] Rachel Annand Taylor: see AEH to Murray, 9 Dec. 1909, n. 1.

TO SYDNEY COCKERELL

Trinity College | Cambridge
24 April 1924

My dear Cockerell,

Thanks for Middleton Murray's[1] article, returned herewith, which is worth reading; but he pauses over the silliest and most disgusting thing, the representation of Hardy as conceited and arrogant.[2]

Yours sincerely
A. E. Housman.

Princeton MS (Gen. MSS. Misc.).

TO THE EDITOR OF *THE TIMES*

[Trinity College | Cambridge
Before 8 May 1924]

KEATS, "THE FALL OF HYPERION," I., 97.

Sir,—This poem was not printed in Keats's lifetime, and his manuscript has been lost; but in the copy made under the direction of Woodhouse[1] lines 97–101 of the first canto run as follows:—

> When in mid-way the sickening east wind
> Shifts sudden to the south, the small warm rain
> Melts out the frozen incense from all flowers,
> And fills the air with so much pleasant health
> That even the dying man forgets his shroud.

When an east wind shifts to the south, whether "in mid-way," whatever that may be taken to mean, or "in mid-day," as Lord Houghton printed,[2] the result which is here described does not necessarily nor even usually

---

[1] For 'Murry's'.

[2] John Middleton Murry in 'Wrap me up in my Aubusson Carpet', *The Adelphi*, 1. 11 (Apr. 1924), 951–8, attacks the writings of George Moore, berating him in particular for his envy of Hardy. Moore claimed that Hardy, with false pride, would like to sit next to Shakespeare and Aeschylus in the next world.

[1] Richard Woodhouse (1788–1834). 'A nearly lifelong friend and legal and literary adviser to Keats's publishers Talyor and Hessey, [he] made or directed various clerks in making no fewer than 182 of the surviving transcripts of Keats's poems, and he was undoubtedly responsible for others that are now lost': *The Poems of John Keats*, ed. Jack Stillinger (1978), 748.

[2] Richard Monckton Milnes, first Baron Houghton (1809–85), educated at TCC, and friend of Tennyson, Hallam and Thackeray; established the Philobiblon Society, 1853; created baron, 1863. He published 'Another Version of Keats's "Hyperion"' in *Biographical and Historical Miscellanies of the Philobiblon Society*, 3 (1856–7; date on spine, 1857), and edns. of Keats's poetry in 1854, 1871, 1876, and 1883.

follow. In order that rain may melt out incense from flowers, both flowers and incense must be there; and this condition is not fulfilled in any month between the autumnal and the vernal equinox. Such flowers as bloom in that half of the year are mostly scentless.

Keats wrote "in mid-May,"[3] as in the Ode to a Nightingale he wrote "mid-May's eldest child"; and for confirmation the next lines are these:—

> Even so that lofty sacrificial fire,
> Sending forth Maian incense, spread around
> Forgetfulness of everything[4] but bliss.

A.E.H.

TLS, *8 May 1924, 286; Maas, 219–20.*

TO D. S. ROBERTSON

Trinity College
22 May 1924

Dear Robertson,

It is very good of you to send me your papers on the MSS of Apuleius. I had skimmed them in the *C. Q.*[1] and have now looked at them more attentively, and I find your argument both successful and interesting.

I was wrong when I told you that the bad handwriting would disqualify the written essay: I had wandered into the regulations about the Hare Prize[2] on the same page.

Perhaps you will let me know, verbally or otherwise, that you have received the essays.

Yours sincerely
A. E. Housman.

Private MS.

[3] AEH was the first to propose the emendation.

[4] Strictly, 'every thing'. AEH is using Milnes's 1857 reading.

[1] 'The Manuscripts on the *Metamorphoses* of Apuleius. I', *CQ* 18. 1 (Jan. 1924), 27–42, and 'The Manuscripts on the *Metamorphoses* of Apuleius. II', *CQ* 18. 2 (Apr. 1924), 85–99.

[2] Awarded annually at Cambridge University for a dissertation on a subject, proposed by the candidate and approved by the Faculty Board of Classics, which falls within the scope of the Faculty of Classics.

TO THEODORE SPICER-SIMSON

Trinity College | Cambridge
27 May 1924.

Dear Mr Spicer-Simson,

I am glad to hear from you and it is kind of you to let me know of your return. I am going to France next week, but expect to be back before June 20, and I shall then be spending most of my time here till August, so that if you come to Cambridge before you leave the country you would probably find me here and I should be greatly pleased to see you.

I am yours sincerely
A. E. Housman.

Princeton MS: Gen. MSS. Bound (oversize), Spicer-Simson Am 17277, p. 85.

TO DR PERCY WITHERS

Trinity College | Cambridge
27 May 1924

My dear Withers,

I am going to France next week, but I expect to be back by June 20, and at any date in the month after that I should be free and joyful to come and stay a day or two.

I am sorry you do not speak as if you were quite well yet. Ravenna, Perugia, and Siena are places I have not seen, and people who find out that, always assure me that they are the best in Italy.

My kind regards to Mrs Withers: your successful daughter[1] I do not think I have met, but still I congratulate her.

Yours sincerely
A. E. Housman.

SCO MS. Withers, 83 (excerpt).

TO MESSRS HENRY HOLT & CO

Trinity College | Cambridge | England
2 June 1924

Dear Sirs,

I wrote to you last January requesting that, in the future, payments due from you to me should be made direct and not through Messrs Grant Richards Ltd.[1]

---

[1] Audrey, who had been accepted to read Philosophy, Politics, and Economics at Somerville College, Oxford. See List of Recipients.

[1] See AEH to GR, 12 Jan. 1924.

By the terms of our agreement settlements of accounts up to each January and July are to be had on the 25th day of April and October respectively subsequent.

A payment made by you to me on April 25 would in the natural course of things have reached me before now, and I therefore infer that none was made and that none was due, there having been no sale of my *Last Poems* in America between July 1923 and January '24. I shall be obliged if you will inform me whether I am right.

Yours faithfully
A. E. Housman.

Messrs Henry Holt & Co.
Princeton MS (Henry Holt Papers, 58).

TO MARY WITHERS

Trinity College | Cambridge
27 June 1924

Dear Mrs Withers,

I am safely returned from a delightful stay, and I hope that you are not suffering from your strenuous afternoon.

It was a great pleasure to me to find your husband so far on the way to recovery.

Yours sincerely
A. E. Housman.

SCO MS.

TO MESSRS GRANT RICHARDS LTD

Trinity College | Cambridge
2 July 1924

Dear Sirs,

Mr Ramsay is at liberty to print the two poems with his Latin verses, but not to substitute a new title for *Epitaph on an Army of Mercenaries.*

Yours faithfully
A. E. Housman.

LC-GR MS. LC-GR t.s. Richards, 211.

TO IVOR GURNEY

<ETON COLLEGE, | WINDSOR,> \ Trinity College | Cambridge
22 July 1924

Dear Sir,

You have my permission to publish your settings, with the words, of the eight poems included in your Song Cycle *The Western Playland*,[1] and also of any others, with the restriction that no omission of lines must be made in any poem.[2]

I have always refused to allow the printing of the words of poems in concert programmes, and to this prohibition I must adhere.

I am yours very truly
A. E. Housman.

Gloucester Library MS.

TO EDMUND GOSSE

Trinity College | Cambridge
24 July 1924

My dear Gosse,

It would be kind of you if in some odd moment<s> you would look through these translations and say what you think of them. They are by a Dane in America, H. Troller Steenstrŭp who wants to translate my poems and says that perhaps I am acquainted with Mr Edmund Gosse, who is excellently well versed in Danish, and might induce him to compare the original with the translations to decide if he is qualified for the work.[1]

I assure you that my request is not prompted by rancour at receiving this morning a circular from you asking for a contribution to the W. P. Ker Memorial, when I had sent one more than a week ago. I daresay you thought it insufficient, or perhaps it was embezzled by Gregory Foster,[2] who signed the receipt.

---

[1] *The Western Playland (and of Sorrow)*, a song cycle for baritone voice, string quartet, and piano (composed 1919; published 1926). It consisted of *Reveille* (*ASL* IV), *Loveliest of Trees* (*ASL* II), *Golden Friends* (*ASL* LIV), *Twice a Week* (*ASL* XVII), *The Aspens* (*ASL* XXVI), *Is my team ploughing?* (*ASL* XXVII), *The Far Country* (*ASL* XL), and *March* (*ASL* X). Gurney had set other poems by AEH to music in *Ludlow and Teme* (1919).

[2] This was observed. Apart from the addition of titles to six poems, there were alterations such as 'through' for 'thorough' in XVII 1 and 'in clover clad' for 'with clover clad' in XXVI 19.

[1] The translation was never published.   [2] See List of Recipients

Please give my kind regards to Mrs Gosse. I see that Philip[3] has been writing a successful book.[4]

Yours sincerely

A. E. Housman.

BL MS Ashley B. 903, fos. 47–8. Maas, 220–1.

TO C. A. ALINGTON

Trinity College | Cambridge

24 July 1924

My dear Headmaster,

In consequence of your flattering request I have been looking at my verses,[1] and I think them so much inferior to the *Loves of the Triangles* that I am not willing to have them published. Do not tell me that there is much more vanity than modesty in this, because I know it already.

I am yours sincerely

A. E. Housman.

TCC Add. MS c. 112[23]. Gow, 22 n. (excerpt); Maas, 220.

TO KATHARINE SYMONS

Trinity College | Cambridge

30 July 1924

My dear Kate,

Thanks for your letter. I think of coming to Bath on Monday Aug. 18 and staying for 3 weeks. As you kindly offer to see about rooms, I shall be glad if you will. I think you said that the hotel made out of the old Bath College would be the nearest to you, and the situation at any rate is pleasant. But I shall want a sitting room as well as a bed-room, and it must

---

[3] Philip Gosse: see List of Recipients.   [4] *The Pirates' Who's Who* (1924).

[1] Beginning 'See on the cliff fair Adjectiva stand': *Poems* (1997), 265–7. AEH included them in a paper on Erasmus Darwin (1731–1802) which he read to the UCL Literary Society before the close of the term in Mar. 1899. He gave the paper again, on 29 Nov. 1907 at UCL and at Eton in 1922: Naiditch (1988), 147. *The Loves of the Triangles*, by George Canning and others, is a parody principally of *The Loves of the Plants* (1789), the second part of Darwin's *The Botanic Garden*, and was published in *The Anti-Jacobin* (16 and 23 Apr. and 7 May 1798). AEH's verses were published in *The University College Gazette*, 2. 20 (2 Feb. 1899), 34, and Naiditch (1988), 147, notes that the issue in fact contains references to events of 3 and 14 Mar. AEH refused publication similarly to E. V. Lucas, and to Geoffrey Tillotson in 1935: Tillotson, *Essays in Criticism and Research* (1942), 159. See the letter to G. M. Trevelyan, 18 Oct. 1929.

depend on whether they can furnish that.[1] I am not sure if lodgings might not be better than an hotel, and I suppose they might be got even nearer to you. I do not limit you to any particular price, and I am prepared to go even to the Empire (or Imperial) if necessary.

I hope by now you are both, or all, safe home from Wales, and the better for your holiday. I have managed to get sciatica, but it is passing away.

Your affectionate brother
A. E. Housman.

TCC Add. MS c. 50[11–12]. Envelope addressed 'Mrs Symons | 61 Prior Park Road | Bath'. Maas, 221.

TO WITTER BYNNER

Trinity College | Cambridge | England
6 Aug. 1924

Dear Witter Bynner,

Many thanks for your friendly letter and flattering poem.[1] I cannot write sonnets myself, but I suppose the next best thing is to be the cause of sonnets.

Yours very truly
A. E. Housman.

Harvard MS Eng 1071/18. Bynner/Haber (1957), 23; Maas, 221.

---

[1] AEH stayed at the Spa Hotel, Bath, 'for a change of air while he finished some writing on which he was engaged. A writing-room was provided for him with a pleasant outlook that pleased him well and did him good': *More Memories of A.E.H.* by Mrs E. W. Symons (1936), 4.

[1] Published in *The New Republic*, 2 July 1924; *To A. E. Housman*: While Shropshire rises, lyrical and sweet, | Lived in and loved in, more than merely read, | A rainfall on the gable overhead | Becomes your rhythm. In the hollow street, | Alternate passers-by and lulls repeat | Your changes. I can hear the happy tread | Of lovers, and the silence of the dead, | Motionless under newer lovers' feet. | So subtile, deep and true you consecrate | Your song, decking with laurel and with bay | The deathful face of youth, that Shropshire hills, | When I am ageing and the hour is late, | Will shine again with dawn and hush my clay | And quit me clean of these maturing ills.

TO ROBERT BRIDGES

The Spa Hotel | Bath
27 Aug. 1924

My dear Bridges,

I am glad you are safe home from America,[1] where I hope you have lit a candle or sown seed. They are terribly docile, but have not much earth, so it is apt to wither away.[2]

I am here till Sept. 8, when I shall greedily be returning to urgent and agreeable work. But as you are kind enough to ask me, will you put me up for that night? It is half way home and will be a pleasant halt. I could get to you before 1 o' clock, and should be moving on about 2 o' clock on the next day. Do not get up a dinner party for me, because I have no proper clothes.

My kind regards to Mrs Bridges.

Yours sincerely
A. E. Housman.

Bodleian MS, Dep. Bridges 110. 117–18. Maas, 221–2.

TO ALICE ROTHENSTEIN

The Spa Hotel | Bath
2 Sept. 1924

Dear Mrs Rothenstein,

It is very good of you to write to me, and I am glad to see that you are at Oakridge again, which I know you like better than London. But I am afraid there is no chance of my seeing you there this year. I am now at the end of my holidays; in a few days I shall be going to Robert Bridges at Oxford, and thence back to Cambridge and my proper pursuits. I have not been at Woodchester this year, except for one afternoon. My June holiday I took in France, at the time of the Presidential election, when I hoped to witness a French revolution; but on the crucial day it rained continuously and damped their spirits.[1] I am sorry your daughter's health

[1] Where he had been a visiting lecturer at the University of Michigan, Ann Arbor, for three months from 22 Mar. 1924. He received honorary degrees at Michigan and Harvard.

[2] Mark 4: 5–6 (the parable of the sower): 'And some fell on stony ground, where it had not much earth and … because it had no root, it withered away.'

[1] The Radicals and Socialists who held the balance of power following the parliamentary elections of May 1924 refused to take office under the presidency of Alexandre Millerand. He resigned, and on 13 June the National Assembly elected Gaston Doumergue as his successor.

is such a trouble.[2] I have no doubt William will bring home some grave and weighty studies of Alps and Swiss peasants rendered invisible by rain. There has been a good deal of invisibility in England for the last month, but I hope you are well and none the worse for it.

Yours sincerely
A. E. Housman.

Harvard bMS Eng 1148 (740) 42.

TO MESSRS GRANT RICHARDS LTD

Trinity College | Cambridge
15 Sept 1924

Mr Williams may be allowed to use the poem as he wants to.

A. E. Housman.

LC-GR MS. LC-GR t.s.

TO J. B. PRIESTLEY

Trinity College | Cambridge
18 Sept. 1924

Dear Sir,

I am much obliged by your kindness in sending me your book,[1] parts of which I had read with pleasure in periodicals.

I can easily swallow all the flatteries brewed by you and F. L. Lucas;[2] but I wish people would not call me a Stoic.[3] I am a Cyrenaic;[4] and

[2] The Rothensteins' eldest daughter Rachel suffered from a chronic illness. In the summer of 1923 and again early in 1926 her father took her to Leysin and Rapallo for sun and warmth: Rothenstein, *Since Fifty: Men and Memories, 1922–1938* (1940), 27, 48.

[1] *Figures in Modern Literature* (1924), a collection of essays on nine authors, including AEH, repr. from *The London Mercury*. For the 1922 essay on AEH, see *Critical Heritage*, 136–53.

[2] 1894–1967. Essayist and critic. Fellow of KCC, 1920–67. He published an essay on AEH, 'Few, but Roses', in *New Statesman and Nation*, 23 (20 Oct. 1923) 45–7; repr. in *Dial*, 71 (Sept. 1924), 201–8, in Lucas's *Authors Dead and Living* (1926), and in *Critical Heritage*, 178–86.

[3] Priestley had described him as 'a Stoic, but one not disdainful, in some moods, of the opposite camp', and noted that his mood could harden into 'Senecan despair'. Lucas quoted from Matthew Arnold's *To a Gipsy Child by the Sea-shore*: 'Is the calm thine of stoic souls, who weigh | Life well, and find it wanting, nor deplore'. Stoicism was a school of philosophy founded at Athens *c*.300 BC. It advocated living in harmony with Nature (or divine reason), which controls everything, and maintained that everything else, including death, is indifferent.

[4] A follower of the school of philosophy probably founded (at Cyrene) by the grandson of the pupil of Socrates, Aristippus. Its doctrines were that immediate pleasure is the only end of action, but that pleasures must be carefully selected so as not to prove painful; that knowledge is based on sensation; and that the present moment is the only reality.

for the Stoics, except as systematisers of knowledge in succession to the Peripatetics,[5] I have a great dislike and contempt.

I am yours faithfully
A. E. Housman

Texas MS. Maas, 222.

TO THE EDITOR OF *THE TIMES*

Sir,—In to-day's *Illustrated London News* there are reproduced in facsimile the four lines which Dr. Max Funke says that Dr. di Martino-Fusco allowed him to copy from the MS. shown to him. When a few slight and necessary corrections have been made, they will run as follows:—

Ubi multitudo hominum insperata occurrit audire Gallum de sancti Martini virtutibus locuturum.

This reference to Dr. di Martino's patron saint cannot plausibly be assigned even to the prophetic books of Livy. The Provost of Eton[1] may know where the words come from—I do not; but clearly they are an abridgment of what Sulpicius Severus relates in his Dialogus II. (III.), 1, 5:—

Quid, inquam, tam subito et *insperati* tam ex diversis regionibus tam mane *concurritis*? Nos, inquiunt, hesterno cognovimus *Gallum* istum per totum diem *Martini* narrasse virtutes, et reliqua in hodiernum diem, quia nox oppresserat, distulisse: propterea maturavimus frequens auditorium facere de tanta materia *locuturo*.

German scholars, who have had the facsimile before them ever since September 12, must have found out this more than a week ago.

Yours faithfully,
A. E. HOUSMAN.

Trinity College, Cambridge, Sept. 20.

The Times, 22 Sept. 1924, where the letter appeared under the heading 'NOT LIVY'. Maas, 418. Misdated '1923' in Classical Papers, 1266.

TO THE EDITOR OF *THE TIMES*

Sir,—I can now complete the identification of the supposed excerpt from Livy. In Vol. XXXII. of the "Mémoires de l'Institut National de France (Académie des Inscriptions)," at the end of a paper (pp. 29–56)

---

[5] The Aristotelian school of philosophy at Athens.

[1] M. R. James: see List of Recipients.

read in 1884 by Léopold Delisle, there is printed a facsimile (Plate III.) of a page from a manuscript now at Quedlinburg, but written early in the ninth century in St. Martin's own abbey at Tours. There may be seen the four lines transcribed by Dr. Funke: the hand is very similar, the divisions identical, the text a trifle more correct. They constitute the first item in a table of contents prefixed to the dialogue of Sulpicius, which I quoted in my former letter.[1]

Yours faithfully,

A. E. HOUSMAN.

Trinity College, Cambridge, Sept. 22.

The Times, 24 Sept. 1924, 13, where the letter appeared under the heading 'NOT LIVY.'. Maas, 419. Misdated '1923' in Classical Papers, *1266.*

TO ROBERT BRIDGES

Trinity College | Cambridge
25 Sept. 1924

My dear Bridges,

I adjure you not to waste your time on Manilius.[1] He writes on astronomy and astrology without knowing either. My interest in him is purely technical. His best poetry you will find in I 483–531, where he appeals to the regularity of the heavenly motions as evidence of the divinity and eternity of the universe. He has nothing else so good, and little that is nearly so good.

Yours sincerely
A. E. Housman.

Bodleian MS, Dep. Bridges 110. 115–16. Maas, 222.

TO GRANT RICHARDS

Trinity College | Cambridge
1 Oct. 1924

My dear Richards,

The publishers of Lovat Fraser's drawings should not be allowed to print lines as legends, but I do not suppose they will want to: they will number the drawings as the poems are numbered, and their inappropriateness would only be emphasised by quotation.

[1] The identification was also made by F. W. Hall in *The Times* on 24 Sept. 1924.

[1] Bridges had written three days before to say that he had been persuaded to get a copy of AEH's Manilius. He had enjoyed the prefatory matter and had been assured that the notes would carry him through the text (TCC MS, with Adv. d. 20. 11).

There is no occasion for writing to the papers. I do not want to say anything against the drawings, which are probably all right as works of art, and some of which seemed pretty even to me.

As matters stand, it would cause me embarrassment to stay or dine with you.[1]

Yours sincerely
A. E. Housman.

BMC MS.

TO JOHN SPARROW

Trinity College | Cambridge
3 Oct. 1924

Dear Sir,

Judging from the context I should say that seeing the record cut is one of the unpleasant things which the athlete escapes by dying young; and this may help to determine the meaning.[1]

I am yours very truly
A. E. Housman.

SJCO MS, Sparrow Collection. Envelope addressed 'John Sparrow Esq. | The College | Winchester'. Maas, 223.

TO GRANT RICHARDS

Trinity College | Cambridge
5 Oct. 1924

My dear Richards,

Certainly I will not have the two books published in one volume;[1] and as this is what the Florence Press asks, the answer is simply no.

Yours sincerely
A. E. Housman.

LC-GR t.s. Richards, 211; Maas, 223.

[1] See AEH to GR, 12 Jan. 1924, and note.

[1] *ASL* XIX, *To an Athlete Dying Young*, 13–14: 'Eyes the shady night has shut | Cannot see the record cut'. On 'cut', see the letter to Martin, 22 Mar. 1936.

[1] AEH remained firm on this issue: see letters of 4 Jan. 1925 to Henry Holt & Co and to GR; of 2 Feb. 1925 to Henry Holt & Co; of 9 Feb. 1925 to Rudge; of 1 Feb. 1929 to Finberg; of 12 Apr. 1931 to Bynner; and of 26 Sept. 1934 to Martin.

TO A. C. PEARSON

Trinity College
12 Oct. 1924

My dear Pearson,

I am very grateful for the gift of your Sophocles.[1] To what you say in your note I must reply that if your judgment is not worth more than mine you ought not to be editing Sophocles nor sitting in the Greek chair. From turning over your pages I should say that it is rather about Nauck's conjectures than mine that I should differ from you. The two first places I look at to form an opinion of an editor are O.T. 597 and 795, and I give you a good mark at the one and a bad one at the other. Your own emendations, some of which are very neat, I have already seen, or most of them. I might be tempted to a good deal of discussion but that I must really stick to my desk and finish my Lucan. One observation: O. C. 1212 πάρεκ was proposed before Verrall by Badham,[2] *Euthydemus* p. 93.

If this is the end of the Oxford series, I think it comes to a very distinguished close.

Yours sincerely
A. E. Housman.

KCC MS Misc. 34/31. Maas, 419. A facsimile of part of the letter, with a transcription in which 'judgment' is rendered as 'judgement', appears as no. 65 in Modern Literary Manuscripts from King's College. Cambridge: an Exhibition in Memory of A. N. L. Munby *(Fitzwilliam Museum, Cambridge, 1976).*

TO J. N. KEYNES

Trinity College
28 Oct. 1924

My dear Registrary,

I gather from this gentleman's attempt at translation that by *education* he means not the process but that which it confers; so perhaps his two sentences may be rendered as over the page.

I strongly hold the opinion that the Public Orator is the proper person to molest on such occasions, though possibly he may not.

Yours sincerely
A. E. Housman.

---

[1] *Sophoclis fabulae* (Oxford 1924).

[2] Charles Badham (1813–84), Professor of Classics and Logic in the University of Sydney (1867–84), published an edn. of Plato's *Euthydemus and Laches* in 1865.

1.

Nulla sine moribus doctrina, or *nihil doctrina sine moribus proficit.*

2.

Non discendi sed agendi causa vivimus (or *vivitur*). (*Finis vitae,* though correct, would be ambiguous).

TCC Add. MS c. 112²⁴. Maas, 420.

TO GRANT RICHARDS

[Trinity College | Cambridge
3 Nov. 1924

My dear Richards,]

The misprints are all copied from a publication of the Cambridge University Press.[1]

Thanks for *The Thirteenth Caesar,*[2] though I am finding it dull. On the other hand I have just tried the first bottle of the Fernando VII sherry from Thame[3] and found it excellent.

[Yours sincerely
A. E. Housman.]

Richards, 211.

TO F. M. CORNFORD

Trinity College
7 November 1924

Dear Cornford,

I am ready to sign your report, but my recollection is that we were appointed to suggest forms of declaration[1] not merely for Scholars but Fellows and the Master. If I am right, and if you agree with me that the existing declarations do not want altering, would you add a paragraph to say so?

Yours sincerely
A. E. Housman.

BL Add. MS 58427, fos. 102–3.

---

[1] 'Obscure' (Richards, 211). See AEH to Hamilton, 15 Apr. 1925.

[2] *The Thirteenth Caesar, and other poems* by Sacheverell Sitwell, published by GR in 1924.

[3] See AEH to GR, 28 Dec. 1922, and n. 1, and also AEH to GR 22 June 1927 and 14 Dec. 1931.

[1] Oaths, in Latin, sworn by the Master, Fellows, and Scholars on being admitted to TCC.

TO MESSRS MACMILLAN & CO

Trinity College | Cambridge
16 Nov. 1924

Dear Sirs,

In the last twenty years I have produced several editions of Latin classics, which are printed at my expense, offered to the public at less than cost price, and sold for me by a publisher on commission.

I am just completing an edition of Lucan, which I wish to produce in the same way. The printers of my last three books, Messrs Robert Maclehose[1] & Co. of the Glasgow University Press, are prepared to undertake the work; and Mr Charles Whibley[2] has suggested to me that you may be willing to act as publishers for me on the usual terms, and to be the channel of my communications with the printers. As in 1895 you refused to publish another book of mine, *A Shropshire Lad*, under similar conditions, I did not think this likely; but he assures me that you are now less haughty.[3]

If so, I will send you the text and notes, which are already complete and constitute the bulk of the work, that you may transmit them to Messrs Maclehose and obtain an estimate of the cost.

I am yours faithfully
A. E. Housman.

Messrs Macmillan & Co.

BL Add. MS. 55274, fos. 145–6. T.s. copy, Lilly MSS 3. 1. 10. Letters to Macmillan, ed. Simon Nowell-Smith (1967), 242; Maas, 223–4.

TO KATHARINE SYMONS

Trinity College | Cambridge
23 Dec. 1924

My dear Kate,

I enclose, with all its mysterious contents, an envelope which I have received this morning. I suppose you sent your priceless extracts inside the books when you returned it to the Library.

A merry Christmas to both of you, much though you dislike the festival.

Your affectionate brother
A. E. Housman.

TCC Add. MS c. 50^13.

---

[1] For 'MacLehose'.
[2] Essayist, critic, and journalist (1859–1930).
[3] The Lucan was published by Basil Blackwell in 1926.

TO PEARCE HIGGINS

Trinity College
28 Dec. 1924

Dear Mr Pearce Higgins,

The poems which seem to me to stand out as particularly good are *The Eternal City* and *Love's Loneliness,* of which I like the latter better, and indeed very much. This preference is perhaps partly due to its not being a sonnet. The sonnet is a form of verse which is oftener a substitute than a vehicle for poetry; and though you write it with ease and accomplishment, and have many good lines, I do not think it altogether a good sign that you should be so ready to use it. Moreover the ability to make sonnets even as well as you do is not in our time rare. 'Everyone writes so well nowadays' said Tennyson;[1] and the average of proficiency has risen since then. Blank verse is a much tougher job, and there I think you do not succeed. The Masque is drawn out thin, and the plot I find not only slight but rather irritating in its artificial delays. The anapaests of *Necessity* are very untidy, and the lines are of three different lengths.

You will not expect minute criticisms; but to take *Charge*, which is among the best pieces, the 3rd line is weak and the 11th is from William Watson.

I demurred when your father[2] asked me to look through your poems, because I am always afraid of hurting young poets' feelings, and one of them once wrote back to say that he had put his verses in the fire; but your father assured me that you would not mind, and that my criticisms would probably be less hostile than his own, so I hope no bones are broken.

I was sorry to miss seeing more of you on Christmas day, but I had a guest of my own to look after.

You must delete Aegisthus' appalling suggestion about Hecuba,[3] who was 80 if she was a day.

I am yours very truly
A. E. Housman.

Private MS. T.s. copy in SJCO MS 341. Graves, 239 (excerpts).

[1] Not quite. *William Allingham: A Diary 1824–1889*, ed. H. Allingham and D. Radford (1907), 18 Feb. 1867 (reporting Tennyson on Queen Victoria): ' "She was praising my poetry: I said "Every one writes verses now. I daresay Your Majesty does." ' I owe this source to Christopher Ricks.

[2] Alexander Pearce Higgins (1865–1935). BA and LLB, Cambridge, 1891; LLD, 1904; Whewell Professor of International Law, London University, 1919–23; KC, 1919; Whewell Professor of International Law, Cambridge, 1923–35; Hon. Fellow of Downing College, 1923; Fellow of TCC, 1926; FBA, 1928.

[3] In Greek myth, Aegisthus was the son of Thyestes and his daughter Pelopia, and lover of Clytemnestra, whom he helped kill Agamemnon and his concubine Cassandra, daughter of Priam and Hecuba.

TO DR PERCY WITHERS

Trinity College | Cambridge
31 Dec. 1924

My dear Withers,

I am glad to have what I suppose is tolerably good news of your health, and to receive your Christmas reproaches. It is true that I do not write to you, but then there are few people to whom I do, and never willingly. You write with ease, elegance, and evident enjoyment, whereas I hate it. Like Miss Squeers, I am screaming out loud all the time I write, which takes off my attention rather and I hope will excuse mistakes.[1]

I will remember you at midnight, when I shall be drinking to absent friends in stout and oysters, which are very salubrious and which I take medicinally to neutralise the excesses of Christmas. When you give Mrs Winslow's soothing syrup to a baby, 'the little darling wakes up as bright as a button';[2] and so do I on New Year's day.

The Poet Laureate's joke was made subsequently but independently by a scholar here in the form 'all my eye and Beatus Martinus'.[3]

I was in Paris in June at the Presidential Election, when the French Revolution which I had hoped to witness was spoilt by the rain, and at Bath in August, where the rain would have spoilt an English Revolution had Bath been never so Bolshevik. George Saintsbury[4] lives there now, and <its> is to be recognised, I hear, by the shabbiness of his clothes and especially of his top-hat, which nevertheless, when rain comes on, he protects with oil-cloth.

My kind regards to Mrs Withers, and a happy New Year to both of you.

Yours sincerely
A. E. Housman.

SCO MS. Withers, 73 (excerpt); Maas, 224.

---

[1] 'I am screaming out loud all the time I write and so is my brother which takes off my attention rather and I hope will excuse mistakes': Fanny Squeers in Dickens's *Nicholas Nickelby*, ch. 15.

[2] AEH mentions the children's medicine in *The shades of night were falling fast*, 7: see *Poems* (1997), 210. See also letters of 31 Dec. 1926 to Withers and 30 Dec. 1929 to Jeannie Housman. Naiditch (2005), 6, notes advertisements for the syrup, which was first marketed in 1849, in the *Illustrated London News*, 19 Nov. and 24 Dec. 1898, and in the '*Bromsgrove Messenger*', 21 June 1873. Another appears in the same newspaper below the first printing of AEH's poem *The Death of Socrates*, 1 Aug. 1874, with the assurance that 'the little cherub awakes "as bright as a button"'. Naiditch also notes that the syrup contained morphine.

[3] See letters to the editor of *The Times*, 22 and 24 Sept. 1924. 'All my eye and Betty Martin' is slang for 'nonsense'.

[4] George Edward Bateman Saintsbury (1845–1933). Literary critic, historian, and authority on wine. Regius Professor of Rhetoric and English Literature at Edinburgh, 1895–1915; FBA, 1911.

1925

TO SIR JAMES G. FRAZER

Trinity College
1 Jan. 1925

My dear Optime Maxime,[1]
(for I have looked it out in Cagnat's *Épigraphie Latine*[2] and find that this is what it means): my best congratulations to you on your birthday present, and many happy returns of the day.

Tell Lady Frazer that I think even she must be enjoying a brief moment of contentment.

Yours sincerely
A. E. Housman.

TCC MS Frazer 4[72].

TO SIR ERNEST RUTHERFORD

Trinity College
1 Jan. 1925

Dear Rutherford,
This is a sad day for poor old England, and will put new and unnecessary pep into the All Blacks;[1] but I am afraid there was no avoiding it. When Geikie's death left an O.M. vacant,[2] everybody expected it would be yours, and if a Trinity prime minister[3] had failed to do his duty he would have been unpopular in Trinity. Long may you live to enjoy your honour.

Yours sincerely
A. E. Housman.

CUL Add. MS 7653/H187.

---

[1] 'Best and Greatest', as in the cult title for Jupiter: *Oxford Latin Dictionary*, optimus 7.

[2] René Louis Victor Cagnat, *Cours Élémentaire de L'Épigraphie Latine* (Paris, 1885). AEH owned a copy of the 1898 edn.: Naiditch (2004), 149.

[1] The national rugby team of New Zealand, Rutherford's native country.

[2] Sir Archibald Geikie (1835–1924), Murchison Professor of Geology and Mineralogy at Edinburgh, 1871–81, was knighted in 1891 and awarded the OM in 1913.

[3] Stanley Baldwin (1867–1947). Educated at Harrow and at TCC (third class in history, 1888). Prime Minister, 1923–4, 1924–9, 1935–7.

TO MESSRS HENRY HOLT & CO

Trinity College | Cambridge | England
4 Jan. 1925

Dear Sirs,

I have received a press-cutting from the *New York Times* of 7 Dec. 1924 which reads as follows:

'A. E. Housman's *A Shropshire Lad* and *Last Poems* have recently been published by Henry Holt & Co. in a limp leather edition, so that it is now possible to buy the complete works of this poet in a uniform de luxe edition.'

I beg that you will inform me without delay whether this statement is true.[1]

I am yours faithfully
A. E. Housman.

Messrs Henry Holt & Co.

Princeton MS (Henry Holt Archives).

TO GRANT RICHARDS

Trinity College | Cambridge
4 Jan. 1925

My dear Richards,

I am obliged to write to you about the following matter, because I do not know how I stand.

I have received a press-cutting from America which says that Henry Holt & Co have published *A Shropshire Lad* and *Last Poems* together in one volume.[1] I have written to ask them if this is true: if it is, I shall take *Last Poems* away from them, supposing that I can. But I find that in my agreement with them there is no clause empowering me to withdraw from them my license to publish, as there is in my agreement with you. Before I go to a solicitor, perhaps you can give me a notion of what my rights are.

---

[1] It was; but, as Richards, 212, points out, the two vols. were boxed, not bound, together. The format was also adopted in the edn. of 1929 from the Alcuin Press, who deliberately also issued a few copies bound together: Naiditch (2005), 98. On AEH's opposition to a single vol., see the letter to GR, 5 Oct. 1924, and note.

[1] AEH's misunderstanding. See the note on the previous letter.

Thanks for your novel,[2] though neither it nor any of them are as good as *Caviare.*[3]

I enclose the *menus regionales*[4] which you wished to have returned, and I do not wonder, as they make one's mouth water.

Yours sincerely
A. E. Housman.

Can I make them destroy the combined book?

LC-GR t.s. Richards, 212; Maas, 225.

TO HERBERT THRING

Trinity College | Cambridge
12 Jan. 1925

Dear Sir,

My subscription to the Society of Authors does not, I presume, entitle me to ask for your official assistance in the following matter; but if you would consent to act as my solicitor, or recommend to me some other solicitor competent to deal with the case, I should be grateful.

My book *Last Poems* is copyrighted in the United States and published there by Messrs Henry Holt and Co of 19 West 44th Street, New York. I learn that they have lately issued, in a single volume, these poems together with the contents of another book of mine, which is not copyrighted in the United States, *A Shropshire Lad.* This they have done without asking my leave, and against my desire. I wish therefore, if I can, to do two things: to make them withdraw this volume, and to transfer *Last Poems* to another American publisher.

I do not send you my agreement with Messrs Holt (which does not seem to contain anything exactly bearing on the case) till I have your reply.

I am yours faithfully
A. E. Housman.

Text based on that in Maas, 225–6, which was based on the MS once in the possession of the Society of Authors and now missing.

---

[2] *Every Wife: An Amusement* (1924). 'His opinion ... I expected, for he had been lukewarm about its predecessors': Richards, 213.

[3] Published in 1917.

[4] For '*régionales*'. 'The menus which were issued in connexion with the Section Gastronomique Régionaliste of the Paris Salon d'Automne, 1924: they were the *Menus des Journées Régionales*, a series of luncheons and dinners which visitors to the Salon could eat on certain fixed days, drinking with them the wines of the districts chosen. Housman from his various French journeys already knew most of the dishes': Richards, 213.

TO HERBERT THRING

Trinity College | Cambridge
16 Jan. 1925

Dear Sir,

I beg to acknowledge the return of the publisher's agreement which I sent you; and beyond that I have only to thank you for your opinion and excuse myself for troubling you.

I am yours truly
A. E. Housman.

Text based on that in Maas, 226, which was based on the MS once in the possession of the Society of Authors and now missing.

TO ERNEST HARRISON

[Trinity College
*c.*16/17 Jan. 1925]

I do not \<know> \think/ that the Greeks imagined that the acronychal rising of a star was particularly bright, and if they did they were of course quite wrong. But a star is brighter \<on> \near/ the horizon than when it is higher, and I should say \that/ this is why παμφαίνων is used in Hes. op. 567 \Hom. Il. 5. 6./, and that πρῶτον signifies simply emergence into sight \(προλιπὼν ῥόον Ὠκεανοῖο)/ and does not conflict with the fact that an ἐπιτολὴ ἑσπερία is, \<in fact> \<from another point of view>/ a last and not a first appearance.[1]

BMC MS. Draft in ink written on verso of Harrison's note, dated 16 Jan. 1925. Maas, 420.

TO MESSRS HENRY HOLT & CO

Trinity College | Cambridge | England
2 Feb. 1925

Dear Sirs,

I am much obliged by your letter of the 16th Jan. and by the books you have been kind enough to send me, from which I see that the press-cutting gave me a false alarm. I have no objection at all to the issue of the two books as companion volumes (which seem to me, though I am no judge,

---

[1] Harrison had asked on behalf of his co-editor of the *CR*, W. M. Calder, whether Hesiod, *Works and Days*, 567, meant 'shining for the first time in full radiance rises for the last time', i.e. whether the Greeks thought that the acronychal rising of a star is the brightest.

to be very pretty): what I should have objected to, and have not allowed in England, is the combination of the two sets of poems in a single volume.

If you reprint *A Shropshire Lad* I should be obliged if you would make two alterations which have been made in England since 1922:—[1]

No. XXXVIII line 10
for 'Thick' read 'Loose'.

No. LII line 9
for 'long since forgotten' read 'no more remembered'.

I am yours very truly
A. E. Housman.

In No. XXXIV line 3 there ought to be no inverted comma.[2] The inverted comma in line 1 is right. Printers cannot understand this.

Messrs Henry Holt & Co.

Princeton MS (Henry Holt Archives).

TO MESSRS GRANT RICHARDS LTD

Trinity College | Cambridge
2 Feb. 1925

Dear Sirs,

I wish you would rap these people over the knuckles.[1]

Yours faithfully
A. E. Housman.

BMC MS. Tipped-in in Martin Secker's presentation copy of Grant Richards, Housman 1897–1936 *(1941).*

TO F. W. HALL

Trinity College | Cambridge
3 Feb. 1925

Dear Hall,

I am quite willing that my name should appear in the appeal for subscriptions towards Cave's portrait,[1] and I enclose cheque for five guineas. I am to meet him next week for the first time.

[1] See AEH to GR, 22 Apr. 1922, and notes.
[2] In *The New Mistress*, after '*you are not wanted here.*' There should be no inverted comma because the entire poem, including the quotation in ll. 1–3, is supposedly uttered by the soldier, and the inverted commas should be closed only at the end.

[1] 'Response to application to Richards press for use of a poem': note written on the MS in an unidentified hand.

[1] Of SJCO, where AEH, like Cave, had been an undergraduate. On George Cave, see List of Recipients.

I am busy finishing off my Lucan, and also writing a review,[2] a job which I always regret undertaking, as it always absorbs a disproportionate amount of time, because I am so fearfully conscientious. When it is completed, if it ever is, I ought to turn to at Manilius V, or the unfinished window in Aladdin's tower unfinished will remain.[3]

Yours sincerely
A. E. Housman.

Lilly MSS 1. 1. 4. Maas, 226.

TO W. E. RUDGE

Trinity College | Cambridge | England
9 Feb. 1925

Dear Sir,

I am obliged and flattered by your letter of Jan. 22.

I am personally willing that you should publish, as you wish, an edition of *A Shropshire Lad* or *Last Poems* or both, provided that the two are not included in one volume.[1]

As to *A Shropshire Lad* you do not need my consent, as it is not copyright in America.

As to *Last Poems*, I suppose it would be proper to consult my American publishers, Messrs Henry Holt & Co.

I must make it a condition, in the case of *Last Poems*, that the proofs are sent to me for correction; and though I have no right to make conditions in the case of *A Shropshire Lad*, I shall be obliged if you will follow the same course, as the last American edition I saw was full of errors.

I am yours very truly
A. E. Housman.

As you are good enough to offer me a copy of Mr Spicer-Simson's book,[2] I should be very glad to have it.

Lilly MSS 2. 1. Maas, 227.

---

[2] Of A. C. Pearson's edn. of Sophocles in *CR* 39 (1925), 76–80 (*Classical Papers*, 1093–8). AEH praised the edn. as 'much the best critical edition of Sophocles now in existence; the most complete and the most judicious', but the review was largely taken up with detailed criticisms.

[3] In *The Arabian Nights*, Aladdin's belvedere, built by the genie of the lamp, had twenty-four windows set in frames of precious stones, 'and one window remained unfinished at the requirement of Aladdin that the Sultan might prove him impotent to complete it'.

[1] See AEH to GR, 5 Oct. 1924, and note.

[2] *Men of Letters of the British Isles: Portrait Medallions from Life* (1924). AEH's copy is now at BMC.

TO J. W. MACKAIL

Trinity College | Cambridge
22 Feb. 1925

Dear Mackail,

With *optandum*[1] you require something like *quicquam*, which Estaço[2] obtained by writing *dicere quid*. With *optandam* of course you can supply *uitam* from *uita*; but yet the MS reading is *optandus*. Because Catullus once elides *que* at the end of a verse it cannot safely be inferred that he would elide anything else. I have seen nothing better than Munro's *magis aeuom | optandum hac uita*,[3] though it is not all the heart could desire.

Yours sincerely
A. E. Housman.

TCC MS R.1.92.4. Maas, 420–1.

TO SIR JOSEPH J. THOMSON

Trinity College
22 Feb. 1925

My dear Master,[1]

I take up my pen in a rather sorrowful mood because I recognise the compliment implied in the Council's offer of the Clark Lectureship, and am grateful for their friendliness and for yours, and therefore I cannot help feeling ungracious in making the answer which nevertheless is the only answer possible.

I do regard myself as a connoisseur; I think I can tell good from bad in literature. But literary criticism, referring opinions to principles and setting them forth so as to command assent, is a high and rare accomplishment and quite beyond me. I remember Walter Raleigh's Clark lecture[2] on Landor:[3] it was unpretending, and not adorned or even polished, but I was thinking all the while that I could never have hit the nail on the head like that. And not only have I no talent for producing the genuine article, but no taste or inclination for producing a substitute. If I devoted a whole year (and it would not take less) to the composition of six lectures on literature,

[1] In Catullus 107. 8.
[2] Achilles Statius (1524–81), whose edn. of Catullus was published in 1566.
[3] H. A. J. Munro's proposal appeared in *The Journal of Philology*, 9. 8 (1880), 185.

[1] Thomson was Master of TCC.
[2] On 3 June 1911, the last in the series *Prose Writers of the Romantic Revival* by Sir Walter Raleigh (1861–1922).
[3] Poet and essayist Walter Savage Landor (1775–1864).

the result would be nothing which could give me, I do not say satisfaction, but consolation for the wasted time; and the year would be one of anxiety and depression, the more vexatious because it would be subtracted from those minute and pedantic studies in which I am fitted to excel and which give me pleasure.

I am sorry if this explanation is tedious, but I would rather be tedious than seem thankless and churlish.

I am yours sincerely
A. E. Housman.

TCC Add. MS Letters c. 1[193]*; also TCC Add. MS c. 112*[25] *(t.s. copy). Gow, 20–1 (incomplete); Maas, 227–8.*

TO GRANT RICHARDS

[Trinity College | Cambridge
3 March 1925

My dear Richards,]
   I have not read this through, but I have dipped into it, and it will not do. It is sometimes surprisingly close to the original, but at other times the formal French phrases crop up; and my verse really will not go into French verse. The worst is that he sometimes does not understand the English: for instance in VIII "a love to keep you clean" is translated "amour, qui garde propre ta maison".[1]

[Yours sincerely
A. E. Housman.]

Richards, 213; Maas, 228.

TO H. B. PETTITT

Trinity College | Cambridge
12 March 1925

Dear Mr Pettitt,
   If you like to send me the books I shall be pleased to sign them.

Yours very truly
A. E. Housman.

Colby College MS. Envelope addressed 'H. B. Pettitt Esq. | Cupola House | Paglesham | Rochford | Essex'.

---

[1] The translation was not published.

TO KATHARINE SYMONS

Trinity College | Cambridge
14 March 1925

My dear Kate,

I was very sorry to have your news of Jerry's misfortunes. I suppose he is now back, and you have seen him, and I hope that the voyage and absence from India has already done him good. I should have written to you before, but I am so languid with a month of bronchitis that I neglect most things, correspondence especially. I have gone on lecturing, which I daresay did me no good; and now that term is over matters may mend.

The Eton Librarian I suppose was Mr Broadbent,[1] whom I have often met. When he and the Earl of Oxford & Asquith[2] were undergraduates together they were supposed to be about equally able; but it was a great mistake. He is rather a figure of fun, with the largest and most bloodshot eyes I ever saw, and produces Greek and Latin verses which should be pointed but are not.

Love to all.

Your affectionate brother
A. E. Housman.

Lilly MSS 2. 1. Maas, 228–9.

TO UNIVERSITY COLLEGE, LONDON, APPOINTMENTS COMMITTEE

Trinity College | Cambridge
15 March 1925

Mr Lawrence Solomon was my assistant for some ten years when I was Professor of Latin in University College, London, having entire charge of the lowest class and taking part of the work of the highest. He was an excellent colleague and a most efficient teacher; and I was particularly grateful to him for succeeding, where I always failed, in making the students write decent Latin prose.

A. E. Housman.

T.s. copy in UCL Applications Greek 1925.

---

[1] Henry Broadbent (1852–1935). Fellow of Exeter College, Oxford, 1874; Assistant Master at Eton, 1876; Librarian, 1920.
[2] The statesman Herbert Asquith was created Earl of Oxford and Asquith in 1925.

TO GRANT RICHARDS

25 March 1925

Look at this.[1]

A. E. H.

BMC MS.

TO A. S. F. GOW

Trinity College | Cambridge
26 March 1925

Dear Gow,

If anyone knows what Catull. 104 4 means, I do not; and the commentators are no good. But I see no reason to think it corrupt.

I wish you would make a correction on my p. xv: the date of Creech's translation[1] should be 1697: 1700 was the second edition.

No, I am not well, though in my case it is bronchial tubes and not a leg.

Yours sincerely
A. E. Housman.

TCC Add. MS c. 112²⁶. Maas, 421.

TO GRANT RICHARDS

[Trinity College | Cambridge
31 March 1925

My dear Richards,]

If you think you can bully the malefactors into sending 5 guineas each to the Literary Fund, do so by all means.

[Yours sincerely
A. E. Housman.]

Richards, 213.

---

[1] Note on the MS in Richards's hand: 'Reynolds's Newspaper'.
[1] Of Manilius.

TO WITTER BYNNER

Trinity College | Cambridge | England
15 April 1925

My dear Witter Bynner,

There is no need for you to apologise, but writing an introduction[1] is what I would not do for anyone, or rather, it would be more accurate to say, I could not. I am sorry that the publishers attach so much weight to such a thing.

I hope you are well and flourishing. New Mexico must be one of the more romantic of the States.

I am yours sincerely
A. E. Housman.

Harvard MS Eng 1071/19. Envelope addressed 'Witter Bynner Esq. | Box 1061 | Santa Fe | New Mexico | U. S. A.'. Bynner/Haber (1957), 24; Maas, 229.

TO GEORGE ROSTREVOR HAMILTON

Trinity College | Cambridge
15 April 1925

Dear Sir,

In my *Epitaph on an Army of Mercenaries* as printed in your book *The Soul of Wit* five alterations have been made, one of which is quite ruinous; and I shall not allow its inclusion in an American edition unless it is corrected.

I am yours faithfully
A. E. Housman.

G. Rostrevor Hamilton Esq.

Bodleian MS Eng. lett. c. 272, fo. 36.

---

[1] To Bynner's *Caravan* (1925). 'He had been emboldened to ask for the introduction after hearing from Louis Ledoux that Housman told him he thought as highly of Bynner's verse as of any other American poet's': Bynner/Haber (1957), 24 n., where it is also noted that AEH's seven-page preface to *Nine Essays* by Arthur Platt (1927) is the only introduction to another person's work that AEH ever wrote.

TO GEORGE ROSTREVOR HAMILTON

Trinity College | Cambridge
18 April 1925

Dear Sir,

If my *Epitaph on an Army of Mercenaries* is printed as it stands in my book and not in the publication of the Cambridge University Press from which you took it, I make no objection to its inclusion in your American edition. It is copyright in the United States, and the publishers are Henry Holt & Co, New York.

I am yours faithfully
A. E. Housman.

G. Rostrevor Hamilton Esq.

Bodleian MS Eng. lett. c. 272, fos. 38   9.

TO AN UNKNOWN CORRESPONDENT

Trinity College | Cambridge
22 May 1925

Dear Sir,

The first edition of *A Shropshire Lad* was 500 copies.

Yours very truly
A. E. Housman.

Lilly MSS 1. 1. 4.

TO DR PERCY WITHERS

Trinity College | Cambridge
26 May 1925

My dear Withers,

I am sorry to hear no better account of your health, though glad that your tour was a success. As to your kind invitation, June I am spending in Gloucestershire; but if you could have me to lunch on my way there, on Tuesday the 2nd, that would be very delightful.

Death and marriage are raging through this College with such fury that I ought to be grateful for having escaped both.

My kind regards to Mrs Withers.

Yours sincerely
A. E. Housman.

SCO MS. Withers, 75 (extract); Maas, 229, misdated 29 May.

TO RIDGELY TORRENCE

Trinity College | Cambridge | England
1 June 1925

Dear Sir,

I return you many thanks for the gift of your *Hesperides*,[1] which I have read with admiration for its poetic impulse and for the accomplishment of much of its verse. It has also more substance than most modern poetry.

I am yours very truly
A. E. Housman.

Princeton MS (Frederick Ridgely Torrence Collection, II. 41, folder 7). Envelope addressed 'Ridgely Torrence Esq. | c/ The Macmillan Company | 64 Fifth Avenue | New York | U. S. A.', and redirected to 107 Waverly Place.

TO MARGARET WOODS

Trinity College | Cambridge
24 June 1925

Dear Mrs Woods,

I am sorry for this delay in answering your letter, which has been caused by my absence from Cambridge. On the line which you suggest I should propose the inscription

BREVEM LVCEM EXTINCTAM
EXCIPIAT FOVEATQVE AETERNA.[1]

I have written it in capitals as it should be written, and I hope the stonecutter will not defile it with the letter U, which is not a capital.

I am very glad to be of any service, and I hope that you are well.

Yours sincerely
A. E. Housman.

BMC MS.

[1] Published in 1925.

[1] 'May the eternal light take in and watch over the brief light that has gone out'.

TO A. S. F. GOW

Trinity College | Cambridge
27 June 1925

Dear Gow,

I understand that the Council will shortly invite you to return to the College and offer you a post on the teaching staff, and I earnestly hope that you will accept it. I have always gone about saying that you ought never to have been allowed to leave Cambridge, and I am delighted at the chance of getting you back.[1] I know of course that you have been successful in your present profession, and I suppose that you are on the eve of having a house, which means what may be called opulence; but it will never allow you the leisure which you ought to have if you are to lay out your talents properly and enter into the joy of the Lord.[2] Eton no doubt is a very pleasant society, but Cambridge is not bad, even after our lamentable loss of Benson.[3] If you resent all this as impertinent interference, I am quite prepared to support that.

Yours sincerely
A. E. Housman.

TCC Add. MS c. 112²⁷. Maas, 229–30.

TO PROFESSOR FRANCIS H. FOBES

Trinity College | Cambridge | England
27 June 1925

My dear Sir,

I am much obliged by your kindness in sending me the *Fragment of a Greek Tragedy*.[1] I am no judge of typography, but I suppose yours to be in the best tradition.

Yours very truly
A. E. Housman.

Johns Hopkins University MS, L. L. Mackall Papers 35 (t.s. copy). Cited in letter from Fobes to Mackall, 21 September 1936.

---

[1] Gow returned to TCC in 1925, having left to be an Assistant Master at Eton in 1914.
[2] Matt. 25: 21, 23: 'enter thou into the joy of thy lord'.
[3] A. C. Benson, Master of Magdalene College since 1915, died in 1925.

[1] Professor Fobes had produced a private reprinting at the Snail's Pace Press, Amherst, Massachusetts, in 1925.

TO THE EDITORS OF *THE CLASSICAL REVIEW*

[Trinity College | Cambridge
Summer 1925]

Sirs,

No, it would not be helpful. If Professor Mair asks such questions and makes such statements after reading what I wrote, he would still ask and make them after reading what I do not intend to write.[1]

I am conscious that this is the tone which would be adopted by some scholars, whom I could name, if they knew that they were wrong and did not want to confess it; but it ought to be understood by this time that I am not of that brood.

A. E. Housman.

CR *39. 7/8 (Nov.–Dec. 1925), 214.*

TO KATHARINE SYMONS

Trinity College | Cambridge
5 July 1925

My dear Kate,

I can easily spare you £200, and I enclose a cheque for the amount. I rejoice with you over Denis's success, and heartily congratulate him on it, as it seems very creditable to him. I am glad too to have such good news of Jerry's health.

My three weeks at Woodchester consisted of quite perfect weather; only motoring home in a cold wind has given me rather a cold in one eye, not so bad as last year. The Wises do not seem to alter. The younger of the two Trollopes[1] whom you met there last year has been at death's door with eczema, and having recovered appears to be going off her head. I shall probably go to France towards the end of August.

Love to all your circle.

Your affectionate brother
A. E. Housman.

Private MS.

---

[1] A. W. Mair, whose letter preceded AEH's on pp. 213–14 of the same issue, questioned the reading of Sophocles, *Oedipus Tyrannus*, 794–6, that AEH had proposed in a review of A. C. Pearson's edition in *CR* 39.2/3 (May–June 1925), 76–80: '... one cannot argue with a mere dogmatic assertion. It would be helpful if Professor Housman would (1) translate the passage with the reading τεκμαρούμενος, (2) explain why either of Jebb's renderings is inadmissible, (3) suggest a reason for the supposed corruption, and (4) tell us how he knows that the words found in Libianus are the very words of Sophocles.'

[1] Neighbours of the Wise family at Woodchester.

TO DANFORD BARNEY

Trinity College | Cambridge | England
21 July 1925

Dear Mr Barney,

I am obliged and flattered by your letter, but it is out of the question for me to promise contributions to your journal or any other.

I am yours very truly
A. E. Housman.

Yale MS (Za Barney 6). Envelope addressed 'Mr Danford Barney | 58 West 49ᵗʰ Street | New York | N. Y. | U. S. A.', and redirected to York Harbor, Maine.

TO EUGEN MILLINGTON-DRAKE

Trinity College | Cambridge
1 Aug. 1925

Dear Mr Millington-Drake,

I have signed the volume[1] and returned it to Best & Co.

I remember with great affection and gratitude one who had half your name, Herbert Millington, my old headmaster at Bromsgrove.

I am yours very truly
A. E. Housman.

Eton MS.

TO GRANT RICHARDS

Trinity College | Cambridge
7 Aug. 1925

My dear Richards,

It[1] was not 'originally published at 5s.' but at 2/6; even the 2ⁿᵈ edition, though much inferior, was only 3/6.

I have just been stopped in the street by an American lady who was yearning for the last work of your Mr Mais in the window of a shop whose door was locked. She seemed to want me to break the glass for her, but I persuaded her that there were other shops in the town.

Yours sincerely
A. E. Housman.

PM MS. LC-GR t.s. Richards, 213–14; Maas, 230.

[1] A copy of *LP* for a collection of books relating to World War I (the Macnaughton Library), which was given to Eton in 1938.

[1] *ASL.*

TO LAURENCE HOUSMAN

Trinity College | Cambridge
18 Aug. 1925

My dear Laurence,

On the 27th I am going abroad for about a month, leaving behind me a nearly completed and in great part printed edition of Lucan with Basil Blackwell of Oxford. If the French kill me with one of these lethal railways of theirs, J. D. Duff of this college is to be asked to finish it and see it through the press.

Love to Clemence: I hope you are both flourishing.

Your affectionate brother
A. E. Housman.

It occurs to me that I ought also to tell you something which my executors should know. Grant Richards has not paid me a penny of royalties on *Last Poems*, and has intercepted the first year's royalties from the American publishers. He also owes me £750 which I lent him four or five years ago.

BMC MS. Memoir, *179–80; Maas, 230 (both incomplete).*

TO MARY CLARE RYAN

Trinity College | Cambridge
19 Aug. 1925

Dear Mrs Ryan,

I am sorry to have to say that I possess no *ex libris plate*;[1] and indeed I am not a person of culture, and treat my books badly.

I am yours very truly
A. E. Housman.

BMC MS. Envelope addressed 'Mrs Mary Clare Ryan | 1151 North Hew Hampshire | Los Angeles | Calif. | U. S. A.'

---

[1] 'Plate' should be in roman, but AEH underlines it as well as '*ex libris*'.

TO MESSRS GRANT RICHARDS LTD

Trinity College | Cambridge
21 Aug. 1925

Dear Sirs,

Composers may be allowed to set poems from *Last Poems* as well as from *A Shropshire Lad* without fee; but in both cases it should be stipulated that only *entire* poems are to be set, with no omissions.

Yours faithfully
A. E. Housman.

PM MS. LC-GR t.s. Richards, 214.

TO J. D. DUFF

Trinity College | Cambridge
26 Aug. 1925

Dear Duff,

To-morrow I am going to France, and as I cannot fly to every spot I wish to reach I shall probably perish in a railway accident; in which event you will receive a request from my executors that you would be so good as to finish off my Lucan; and I hope you will not refuse. The text, notes, and appendix are in print and corrected; the MS of the preface is in the printers' hands; I enclose the table of MSS and the title-page; and nothing remains to be done but the index, which I cannot compile till the book is in pages. This of course is a nasty job, and when the engine is on the top of me I shall console myself with the thought that I have escaped it.

I hear from Hicks[1] that you have been reading that neglected poet Silius, whom his contemporaries would have done well to imitate, at least in straightforwardness. I hope you are having other enjoyments.

Yours sincerely
A. E. Housman.

TCC Add. MS a. 225⁸⁹⁽²⁾.

---

[1] Robert Drew Hicks (1850–1929), Fellow of TCC since 1876.

TO LAURENCE HOUSMAN

Paris, 19 Sept. 1925

My dear Laurence,

The parody of me is the best I have seen, and indeed the only good one.[1]

I don't know if Hugh Lunn is the author of *The Harrovians*:[2] if so, I am told that I once sat next to him at a feast at Jesus College, and that he was drunk, and afterwards acknowledged the fact and expressed regret for his forward behaviour; but I suppose I was drunk too, for I remember neither it nor him.

Your affectionate brother
A. E. Housman.

BMC MS. Memoir, *180 (first sentence only).*

TO H. E. BUTLER

Trinity College | Cambridge
2 Oct. 1925

Dear Butler,

I cannot possibly decline the kind and flattering invitation of the Professors' Dining Club,[1] and the 16th will suit me quite well.

I am yours very truly
A. E. Housman.

SJCO MS 305. Maas, 231.

TO GRANT RICHARDS

Trinity College | Cambridge
6 Oct. 1925

My dear Richards,

Thanks for your offer, but I have so little room for the books I already possess that I am very chary of acquiring more; and your father's studies and mine did not lie much along the same lines; and in view of my age I am rather narrowing my reading than widening it.

---

[1] Parody by Hugh Kingsmill [Lunn] (1889–1949), beginning 'What, still alive at twenty-two, | A clean, upstanding chap like you?' It is printed in *Memoir*, 180, and in Richards, 345.

[2] The author of *The Harrovians* (1913) was in fact Kingsmill's younger brother, skiing pioneer Arnold [Henry Moore] Lunn (1888–1974), who was educated at Harrow and at Balliol College, Oxford.

[1] At UCL.

At Pau there is a very good bourgeois restaurant called, I think, *Dupon, successeur Rolland,* in the *place du Casino,* nowhere near the present Casino. *Truite à l'Americaine* (with écrévisses) is the best thing I came across.

Yours sincerely
A. E. Housman.

Somebody, I hope it was not you, told me that the local dish of Carcasonne was something called *Soufassou,* but on the spot they denied all knowledge of it and wanted to make me eat *cassoulet* instead, which is a plat of Toulouse, hardly deserving its reputation. I twice fed on the *isard,* the chamois of the Pyrenees; not very good.

LC-GR MS. Richards, 214–15.

TO H. E. BUTLER

It is very good of you to offer to put me up on the 16th and I shall gladly avail myself of your kindness.

Yours
A. E. Housman.

7 Oct. 1925   Trin. Coll. Camb.

SJCO MS 305: p.c. addressed 'Professor H. E. Butler | University College | London W. C.'

TO MRS H. E. BUTLER

Trinity College | Cambridge
17 Oct. 1925

Dear Mrs Butler,

Enfeebled though I am by the jolting of the Great Eastern Railway, I must write a line to thank you for your hospitality and say how much I enjoyed my stay. I hope your youngest son brought the first day of his second year to a happy close.

Yours sincerely
A. E. Housman.

SJCO MS 305. Maas, 231.

TO R. Y. LOGAN

Trinity College
1 Nov. 1925

Dear Mr Logan,

Mr W. R. M. Lamb, 51 Church Road, Richmond, Surrey, is willing to review Dr Butler's life for you.[1] You should tell him what length you want the review to be.

I am yours very truly
A. E. Housman.

Private MS. Tipped-in in Logan's copy of 1st edn. of LP *(1922).*

TO A. S. F. GOW

Trinity College
5 Nov. 1925

Dear Gow,

ἑσπερίοις in Theocr. VII 53 means *vespertinal,* and he neglects to say whether it is the vespertinal rising or setting that he means; Horace carm. III 1 28 *orientis Haedi* neglects to say whether he means the vespertinal or the matutinal rising; Virgil Aen. IX 668 *pluuialibus Haedis* neglects both. But all three mean the same, the vespertinal rising of the Kids about the autumnal equinox, which was or was supposed to be stormy. I say 'about', because the actual time differed with the latitude and with the progress of centuries; and moreover there is ambiguity even in the terms ἐπιτολή and δύσις themselves, as they may be either ἀληθιναί or φαινομέναι, a distinction concerning which you have no lust to hear nor I to tell.

Verse 54 signifies the *beginning* of the matutinal setting of Orion, early in November, when the sea was becoming unfit for navigation. It is equivalent to the setting of the Pliades.

Yours sincerely
A. E. Housman.

TCC Add. MS c. 201[77].

---

[1] For *The Trinity Magazine,* of which Logan was editor. Lamb wrote to him at the address 'C. Great Court | Trinity College | Cambridge' on 5 Nov. 1925 agreeing to do the review.

TO AN UNKNOWN CORRESPONDENT

Trinity College | Cambridge
7 Nov. 1925

Dear Sir,

I am obliged and flattered by your proposal; but *A Shropshire Lad* has been reprinted in a form which I presume to be suitable for collectors by the Riccardi Press, and that is a sufficient concession to a class of people who do not seem to me to deserve encouragement.

I am yours faithfully
A. E. Housman.

BMC MS. Reproduced in reduced facsimile in Christie's New York catalogue, 22 Nov. 1985, above item 55.

TO MESSRS GRANT RICHARDS LTD

Trinity College | Cambridge
8 Nov. 1925

Dear Sirs,

I should be obliged if you could tell me how many copies of my edition of Juvenal remain unsold.[1]

Yours faithfully
A. E. Housman.

BMC MS.

TO AN UNKNOWN CORRESPONDENT

Trinity College | Cambridge
11 Nov. 1925

Dear Sir,

The Professorship of Latin[1] was founded in 1869 in honour of B. H. Kennedy, sometime headmaster of Shrewsbury School and afterwards Regius Professor of Greek, the fund being chiefly subscribed by his friends and former pupils.

I am yours very truly
A. E. Housman.

BMC MS.

---

[1] 47.

[1] Which AEH held at Cambridge.

TO T. R. GLOVER

Trinity College
26 Nov. 1925

Dear Glover,

1. The next meeting of the Examiners for the University Scholarships etc. will be in my rooms on Dec. 14 at 2. 30. I understand that the Vice-Chancellor's clerk forgot to send you notice of the first meeting.

2. In your absence I made notes of the proceedings. Would you wish me to send them to you or to enter them in the Minute Book myself?

3. Can you give me the reference to a correspondence, which I think you initiated, about the line on Benjamin Franklin, *eripuit fulmenque Ioui sceptrumque tyrannis?*[1] I thought it was in the *Cambridge Review*, but have failed to find it there.

Yours very truly
A. E. Housman

CUL Add. MS 7874[50].

TO T. R. GLOVER

Trinity College
28 Nov. 1925

Dear Glover,

I am returning herewith the University Scholarships minute-book and the documents which Charlesworth[1] handed to me along with it. Thanks for the information about the Franklin verse.

Yours sincerely
A. E. Housman.

CUL Add. MS 7874[51].

[1] The French economist and statesman Anne-Robert-Jacques Turgot (1727–81), Franklin's friend and occasional rival for the affections of Madame Helvétius, wrote the famous epigram about him: *eripuit cœlo fulmen sceptrumque tyrannis* ('he snatched lightning from the sky and the sceptre from tyrants').

[1] Martin Percival Charlesworth (1895–1950). Cambridge classical scholar. First classes in both parts of the Classical Tripos, 1920–1; BA, 1921. Fellow of St John's College, Cambridge, 1923. University Lecturer in Classics, 1926–31, and Laurence Reader in Classics (for Ancient History), 1931–50. He was the author of *Trade Routes and Commerce of the Roman Empire* (1924), and editor of the *Cambridge Ancient History*, vols. 7–12 (1928–39).

TO A. S. F. GOW

Trinity College | Cambridge
30 Nov. 1925

Dear Gow,

Thanks for your instructive memorandum. Genders over the leaf.

Yours
A. E. Housman.

Lucr. VI 28	recta … cursu
736	albos … ningues
806	terra … ipso
820	quodam … parte
Manil. II 715	sua … corpore
III 20	magno … classe
56	summo … ratione
174	praedicta … ordine
IV 257	iuncta … pisce
Pers. VI 40	crassa … unguine
Mart. IX 67 1	toto … nocte.

I omit examples like Manil. III 195 *materno … aluo*, where the vowel is the same.

TCC. Add. MS c. 112²⁸.

TO MESSRS GRANT RICHARDS LTD

Trinity College | Cambridge
30 Nov. 1925

Dear Sirs,

The 5th book of my Manilius is not likely to be published before 1929.

Yours faithfully
A. E. Housman.

PM MS. LC-GR t.s. Richards, 215.

TO GRANT RICHARDS

Trinity College | Cambridge
3 Dec. 1925

My dear Richards,

Mr W. L. Williams[1] may have *In the morning* for use in his *First Steps to Parnassus.*[2]

Yours sincerely
A. E. Housman.

LC-GR MS.

TO LAURENCE HOUSMAN

[Trinity College | Cambridge]
8 Dec. 1925

My dear Laurence,

An American named Keating wrote to me the other day and said he had bought a signed copy of *A Shropshire Lad* for £80. I suppose this is one of your commercial successes.

Your affectionate brother
A. E. Housman.

Memoir, *180.*

TO ROBERT BRIDGES

Trinity College | Cambridge
18 Dec. 1925

My dear Bridges,

I am very grateful for your kindness in sending me your new poems[1] to cheer my Christmas. Though some of them were not new to me, or not quite; and I was amused to read in verse on pp. 69–72[2] what I had heard from your lips in prose.

---

[1] [William] Emrys Williams (1896–1977). Staff Tutor in Literature, Extra-Mural Department, London University, 1928; Secretary, British Institute of Adult Education, 1934–40. Publications include *The Craft of Literature* (1925) and *Plain Prose: The Elements of a Serviceable Style* (1928). AEH gets his middle initial wrong.

[2] Published in 1926.

[1] *New Poems* (1925).

[2] The bizarrely comic narrative poem *A Dream*, in which St Peter at the entry-court of heaven refuses admission to heaven, on the grounds that everything has changed since they 'took in a batch of those French poets'.

Along with your novelties I am glad to see you using the old and beautiful stanza, now unjustly despised because so often ill managed, of XVIII, which ought not to be left to Laura Matilda.[3] You will probably condemn my judgment if I say that what most affects me is the last verse[4] on p. 63.

My kind regards to Mrs Bridges, and all wishes for a happy Christmas.

Yours sincerely

A. E. Housman.

Bodleian MS, Dep. Bridges 8. 39–40. Maas, 231.

TO KATHARINE SYMONS

Trinity College | Cambridge

22 Dec. 1925

My dear Kate,

There is not the least hurry about repaying me the £200.[1] You are at liberty to look upon me as one of the ancient Gauls, who were quite willing to lend money on a promise to pay it back in the next world; such was their belief in the immortality of the soul, until Christianity undermined it.

I am very glad to hear good news of Jerry's health. Your last letter but one was written before he had seen his Board and been pronounced well. I myself am all right, and am staying here for the vacation, as I almost always do.

Thanks for your article: the account of the Scotch grammarian is very interesting.

There is a great Cambridge book by the late John Venn[2] corresponding to *Alumni Oxonienses*, the name of which I will put into this letter before I close it; but I am not sure if it is exactly what you want.

---

[3] Poem XIV (*To His Excellency*): 'One of all our brave commanders, | Near of kin and dear my friend, | Led his men in France and Flanders, | From the first brush to the end.' 'Laura Matilda' was the pseudonym of Horace and James Smith when they used the stanza for *Drury's Dirge* in their *Rejected Addresses* (1812): for further information, see D. M. Low and George de Fraine, *N&Q* 197 (1952), 547–8, and R. L. Moreton, ibid. 569. AEH used the stanza for *ASL* IV, XXXV, *LP* VIII, and *AP* I, and the metre for *MP* XLVI. See AEH to Mackail, 25 July 1922.

[4] Of *The Sleeping Mansion*: 'But I long since had left it; | what fortune now befalls | finds me in other meadows | by other trees and walls.'

[1] See AEH to KES, 5 July 1925.

[2] 1834–1924. Cambridge logician and mathematician; Fellow of Gonville and Caius College, 1857–1923.

This is the only *winter* I have known since the February of 1895. I laugh at young folk who think they had winters in 1900 or 1916 or such dates.

Happy Christmas to both of you, much though you dislike it.

> Your affectionate brother
> A. E. Housman.

Alumni Cantabrigienses.[3]

Private MS. The title of Venn's book is added in pencil.

TO DR PERCY WITHERS

> Trinity College | Cambridge
> 25 Dec. 1925

My dear Withers,

I am very sorry to hear of your breaking down after you had been enjoying yourself so much in Italy, and I hope the gradual improvement you report will go steadily on. Lewis lately got <pneumonia> \pleurisy/ and was carried off by his doctor to the <hospital> \nursing home/, but there is <no bad> \quite good/ news of him, and he may manage to beat, as he is determined, the longevity of his predecessors in the Chair.[1] I am well enough: I believe I answered your letter in September and told you I had been in the Pyrenees. I have a book just coming out,[2] but it is one of my serious works, and you will not want to read it; nor will any mad American millionaire pay £80 for it, as one did the other day for an autographed first edition of *A Shropshire Lad.*[3] My brother, who has commercial talents, had bought the last six copies in 1898 and got me to sign them. I hope you will be consoled for the stiff price which, I gathered, you paid for your own copy.

I close this letter in order to go and dress for our domestic Feast, and as I guzzle and guttle I shall wish that you were here and had not taken leave of these agreeable vices.

With kind regards to Mrs Withers I am yours sincerely

> A. E. Housman.

SCO MS. Maas, 232.

---

[3] 2 vols. (1922–54), Part 1 (1922) covering the earliest times to 1751.

[1] William James Lewis (1847–1926), had been Professor of Mineralogy at Cambridge since 1881. See AEH to Withers, 22 Dec. 1922. One predecessor, William Hallowes Miller (1801–80), was Professor of Mineralogy at Cambridge for forty-eight years.

[2] His edn. of Lucan (1926)

[3] See AEH to LH, 8 Dec. 1925.

TO HENRY FESTING JONES

Trinity College | Cambridge
29 Dec. 1925

Dear Festing-Jones,[1]

A happy new year to you, and thanks for *Little Blue Book* No. 306.[2] The text does not seem to be so corrupt as it sometimes is in American editions.

Yours sincerely
A. E. Housman.

Wellesley MS. Tipped-in in Jones's complimentary copy of the first edition of LP *(1922).*

TO LAURENCE HOUSMAN

Trinity College | Cambridge
29 Dec. 1925

My dear Laurence,

Thanks for your Christmas present.[1] I like *Blind Man's Buff* the best of the stories. *Farvingdon* I read when it came out, perhaps in Quilter's magazine.[2]

At our last Feast I had the new Dean of Westminster[3] next me, and he said he had long been wanting to thank me for the amusement he had derived from my writings, especially about Queen Victoria and her Ministers. So if I bring you money, you bring me fame.

Now that Hagley[4] is burnt down it is curious to think that I never saw it; though it cannot have been much to see.[5]

A happy new year to both of you.

Your affectionate brother
A. E. Housman.

Somerset County Library, Street, MS (copy at BMC). Clemens (1936), 4 (incomplete); Maas, 232–3, with 'Hughley' for 'Hagley'.

[1] AEH inserts a hyphen in the name.
[2] An edn. of *ASL* by Emanuel Haldeman-Julius (1889–1951).

[1] His book *Odd Pairs: A Book of Tales* (1925).
[2] AEH is mistaken. *The Universal Review* (1888–90), ed. Harry Quilter, in 1890 contained three contributions from LH, but not *The Defence of Farvingdon*, which he wrote in 1895.
[3] The Very Revd William Foxley Norris (1859–1937).
[4] The eighteenth-century house Hagley Hall, Hagley, Worcestershire, was heavily damaged by fire on Christmas Eve, 1925.
[5] It was, and is.

1926

TO KATHARINE SYMONS

Trinity College | Cambridge
15 Jan. 1926

My dear Kate,

I am obliged to write to you, as otherwise you may be perplexed by communications from the London Library. I am taking steps to have you made a life member; but as you cannot be elected before Feb. 8 (if then), the Librarian suggests sending you a receipt 'subject to the Committee's Approval' which will entitle you to full privileges and enable you to make use of the Library at once in your own right. Finally you will have to sign a form. Make hay while the sun shines, for perhaps the Committee will not approve of you.[1]

Your affectionate brother
A. E. Housman.

TCC Add. MS c. 50[14–17]. Envelope addressed 'Mrs Symons | 61 Prior Park Road | Bath' and postmarked 18 Jan. Memoir, 79; Maas, 233.

TO REGINALD ST JOHN PARRY

Trinity College
17 Jan. 1926

My dear <Laurence> \Parry/, (please forgive)

There is at least one address of Platt's, besides the Prelection,[1] which well deserves to be published:[2] a most interesting and entertaining discourse on Aristotle, delivered on some public occasion at University College.[3] If Mrs Platt has not the manuscript, it is probably in the possession of the secretarial department or the Union Society.

---

[1] They did approve, and upon payment of a fee of £25. 4s. she became a life member.

[1] On chs. 45–8 of Plato's *Phaedo*. Delivered at Cambridge in 1921 when Platt was a candidate for the Professorship of Greek.

[2] In *Nine Essays by Arthur Platt*, published by Cambridge University Press in 1927.

[3] 'Science and Arts among the Ancients', delivered at the Opening of Session at UCL, Oct. 1899.

His other remains are likely to be papers read to the students' Literary Society, some of which I heard, and they were very good to listen to. How they would look in print I do not feel quite sure; but they were full of good stuff, apart from the fun.

I should not enjoy writing an introduction, but I would do it for his sake, and in the interests of scholarship and literature.[4]

Yours sincerely
A. E. Housman.

CUL Add. MS. 7735[1]. Maas, 233.

TO J. D. DUFF

Trinity College
21 Jan. 1926

Dear Duff,

This is an advance copy. The copy which you should receive from the publisher in a week or so you might send to me in exchange.

Yours sincerely
A. E. Housman.

SJCO MS, Sparrow Collection. Tipped-in on the flyleaf of a copy of Housman's 1926 edn. of Lucan, which bears the inscription 'J. D. Duff from A. E. Housman' on the half-title.

---

[4] AEH did write an affectionate biographical preface to the vol., repr. in *Selected Prose*, 154–60, and in Ricks (1988), 344–8.

TO S. C. ROBERTS

Trinity College | Cambridge
22 Jan. 1926

Dear Mr Roberts,

About a week ago I heard from the Vice-Master of this college[1] that the Press was thinking of printing Platt's prelection and perhaps some more of his remains; and he asked me some questions, which I answered. Yesterday I had a letter from Mrs Platt to say that she was having some of <the> his MSS typed and proposed to send them \(in that form)/ to me; and I told her that they should go to you. But this morning Edward Platt[2] sends me the MS of the prelection, which I now hold at your disposal. It has not been typed.

Yours very truly
A. E. Housman.

CUL Add. MS 7735². Maas, 234.

TO T. R. GLOVER

Trinity College
22 Jan. 1926

Dear Glover,

I enclose, for your minute-book, notes of to-day's meeting of the Examiners for the University Scholarships.

Yours sincerely
A. E. Housman.

Private MS.

---

[1] Reginald St John Parry.   [2] The Platts' son.

TO A. D. NOCK

Trinity College | Cambridge | England
27 Jan. 1926

Dear Nock,

To say seriously that the stars follow the moon's course is of course absurd, as they move in the opposite direction;[1] so I surmise that this is an ornate expression of Genesis I 16,[2] that the Moon is confused with Night (they both ride in a coach and pair) as in Ovid fast. VI 235 and Luc. I 218, and that then one may compare Eur. Ion 1151 ἄστρα δ' ὠμάρτει θεᾷ, Theocr. II 166, Tibull. II i 87 sq.

Yours sincerely
A. E. Housman.

If the moon's δρόμος is her visible motion from her rising in the east to her setting in the west, the herd of stars may seem to be following a great leader, if the observer is not sharp enough to notice that they are always overtaking her.

The Harvard Theological Review, *45. 1 (Jan. 1952), [1]; Maas, 421.*

TO GRANT RICHARDS

Trinity College | Cambridge
28 Jan. 1926

My dear Richards,

The Headmaster of Winchester can have **XXXVI** from *Last Poems*, and if he wants a title he can call it *Revolution*,[1] which may be of use, as most readers do not seem to see that it is a parable.

I hope your negotiations may turn out as you hope, but you are apt to be sanguine.

Yours sincerely
A. E. Housman.

LC-GR MS. Richards, 215 (incomplete); Maas, 234.

---

[1] Nock had asked AEH the meaning of τὰ ἄστρα τῷ τῆς σελήνης ἀκολουθοῦντα δρόμῳ ('the stars as they follow the course of the moon') in the *Epistle to Diognetus*, 7. 2.

[2] 'And God made two great lights; the greater light to rule the day, and the lesser light to rule the night: he made the stars also'.

[1] The poem appeared with the title on page 63 of the *Winchester College. Sixth Book. Lines Book* (P. and G. Wells, Winchester, 1926). This, the first addition of the title, was the only change (apart from the correction of two misprints) that AEH made to the text of *LP*. See AEH to the Richards Press Ltd., 17 May 1928, where he asks for the title to be added in a reprint of *LP*.

TO WITTER BYNNER

Trinity College | Cambridge | England
31 Jan. 1926

Dear Witter Bynner,

Many thanks for your remembrance of me and your lively and various book.[1] I think perhaps *A Song of the Winds*[2] was what I liked best.

Yours sincerely
A. E. Housman

Harvard MS Eng 1071/20. Envelope addressed 'Mr Witter Bynner | c/ Mr Alfred A. Knopf | Publishers | New York | U. S. A.' and redirected to 50 W. 45th Street. Bynner/Haber (1957), 25.

TO GRANT RICHARDS

Trinity College | Cambridge
3 Feb. 1926

My dear Richards,

A Shropshire Lad is still prohibited to anthologists. What you probably have in mind is that the Poet Laureate, having ascertained that I should not prosecute him, put three poems from it into his selection for schools.[1]

Yours sincerely
A. E. Housman.

Stanford University MS (Cecil H. Green Library). Scribner's cat. 132 (1946) prints a facsimile. Richards, 215–16.

[1] *Caravan* (1925).
[2] I used to go on windy days | Where many birds were light along the sea, | And light as wings down watery ways | The winds were wandering free | That blew the nights and blew the days, | And blew the clouds and ships and birds and me. || Lost are the early winds that caught me, | Low are the winds that used to blow so high; | Leaving the calm that bitter years have taught me; | Only the peace remains that comes to men who die ... | Joy was an early wind and wonder, | Love was a wind that lifted me on wings; | Far is the rim they all have drifted under: | Faint is their melody that wanders back and sings: || I used to go on windy days | Where many birds were light along the sea, | And light as wings down watery ways | The winds are wandering free | That blew the nights and blew the days, | And blew the clouds and ships, and the birds and me.
[1] See AEH to GR, 23 Sept. 1923, and n. 1.

TO LILLY FRAZER

Trinity College | Cambridge
26 Feb. 1926

Dear Lady Frazer,

Thanks for your card; but I am told that if I show myself at the Queens'
Society[1] they will worry me to read them a paper myself. They must be
quite impudent enough, for I do not suppose that Sir James volunteered
his. Besides, an undergraduate went into Heffer's[2] the other day and asked
when my Posthumous Poems would be published; so, as I am a *sexagenarius*,
I am afraid of becoming an *Argeus*, and I especially avoid Queens', because
they have a *pons sublicius*.[3]

Yours sincerely
A. E. Housman.

BMC MS. Maas, 234–5 (incomplete).

TO H. M. ADAMS[1]

Trinity College
3 March 1926

Dear Adams,

I enclose the MS of *A Shropshire Lad*. XXXV is missing, and after XXXVI
the numeration differs a good deal from the final order, because while the
book was printing I took out five pieces and put in the three now numbered
XXXIV, XXXVII, and XLI, which are together at the end.[2]

Yours sincerely
A. E. Housman.

*TCC MS R. 1.31. Lilly MSS 2. 1. 10 (t.s. copy). The Manuscript Poems of A. E.
Housman, ed. Tom Burns Haber (1955), 120–1; Maas, 235.*

---

[1] At Queens' College, Cambridge. The Society invited senior members of the university to
speak on their research or on a topic of general interest in which they were expert.

[2] Cambridge booksellers.

[3] The Argei were effigies of twenty-seven men made of rushes which were cast by Vestal
Virgins from the Sublician Bridge into the Tiber. They are mentioned in Ovid's *Fasti*, 5. 621–34,
and Frazer gives an account in his five-vol. edn. (1929), 4. 73. One theory of the origin of the
practice was that in ancient times men over sixty years of age (called 'Depontani') were thrown
from the bridge into the river. There has been a bridge crossing the river from the President's
Lodge of Queens' College since 1749.

[1] Librarian of TCC, 1924–57.

[2] For an account of the changes in the Trinity MS, see *Poems* (1997), Introduction, xx–xxiii,
supplemented by Naiditch (1995), 92–3, and Naiditch (2005), 70.

TO HENRY FESTING JONES

Trinity College
11 March 1926

Dear Jones,

The sentence is explanatory of κατὰ τρόπον, 'in their proper order'. The moon is in the first and lowest of the eight concentric spheres, the sun in the fourth, the fixed stars in the eighth and outermost. Scaliger's *ipso ambitu* means 'the actual circumference' of the universe, which is what the eighth sphere is. τὰ κοῖλα means the concavity of the inmost sphere, by which we are surrounded.

Yours sincerely
A. E. Housman.

TCC Add. MS Letters c. 1[189].

TO GAILLARD LAPSLEY

Trinity College
14 March 1926

Dear Lapsley,

I am very grateful for the glimpse.

Yours
A. E. H.

Yale MS.

TO A. S. F. GOW

Trinity College
18 March 1926

Dear Gow,

The only additions which I can think of are on the next leaf.[1] But 'Notes on the text of the ᾽Αθηναίων πολιτεία' should be subtracted: there is only one, extracted from a private letter, and it was made simultaneously by others. And the notes on Apoll. Sid. are on his prose, and so belong rather to *Miscellanea* than to *Poetae minores*.

Yours sincerely
A. E. Housman.

---

[1] Gow had begun in 1925 to prepare the list of AEH's publications that would eventually appear in Gow, 65–137. See AEH to Gow, 4 June 1926.

J. P. X pp. 187–196 *Horatiana.*
Athenaeum, May 1899, letter on the new fragment of Juvenal.
Academy 1891, two letters on the *Antiope* of Euripides.
Times Literary Supplement 1924, letter on Keats' *Fall of Hyperion.*
Proceedings of the Classical Association vol. XVIII (Aug. 1921) pp. 67–84 *On the Application of Thought to Textual Criticism.*
Introductory Lecture, Univ. Coll. Lond. Oct. 3 1892.

TCC Add. MS c. 112²⁹.

TO A. S. F. GOW

[Trinity College | Cambridge]
Further addenda
Berl. Phil. Woch. 1910 p. 476, Αἴτια Καλλιμάχου.
Berl. Phil. Woch. 1912 p. 1490 (signed J. N. Madvig† and transcribed from Madvig opusc. ed. 2 p. 735 n. 2).
C. R. 1916 p. 128 (signed D. Erasmus).
Will the line stretch out to the crack of doom?[1]

A. E. H.
19 March 1926

TCC Add. MS c. 112³⁰.

TO AN UNKNOWN CORRESPONDENT

Trinity College | Cambridge
6 April 1926

Dear Sir,

My poems are not arranged in order of date in either volume. *Hell Gate* was finished in April 1922 by the filling up of gaps, but it was conceived and partly written in 1906 or a little later.[1]

I have some times thought of attaching the dates to the poems, so far as I can remember them.

I am yours faithfully
A. E. Housman.

Private MS.

---

[1] *Macbeth*, 4. 1. 133.

[1] 'Begun 1905', AEH told Cockerell in 1936 (Richards, 437). LH, *Memoir*, 269, records only 'five lines' on *Nbk C* 81, which is the first (and the only pre-1922) trace of the poem, and it could belong to 1905 or 1906. No MS has been found of this first draft. The evidence of the *Nbks* is that the second and third drafts date from 30 Mar.–10 Apr. 1922, and that the fourth draft is dated 10 Apr. 1922 by AEH on the last page.

TO THE EARL OF OXFORD AND ASQUITH

Trinity College | Cambridge
22 April 1926

Dear Lord Oxford,

I am much obliged by your kindness in sending me your address on Scaliger,[1] a short report of which I had been interested to read in the papers.

One statement which both you and Sandys[2] have made in reliance upon Mark Pattison,[3] that Scaliger in the Manilius of 1579 passed from textual criticism to chronology, is not true. There is hardly a word about chronology in the book, which is in fact his greatest work in textual criticism; and this study continued to occupy him long after the *Emendatio temporum* of 1583, for the second edition of Manilius in 1600, when he had at last got hold of a good manuscript, was much enlarged and in great part rewritten. Pattison had never read the book; he was a spectator of all time and all existence,[4] and the contemplation of that repulsive scene is fatal to accurate learning.[5]

I am yours very truly
A. E. Housman.

Bodleian MS Asquith 35, fo. 192. Maas, 236.

TO DR PERCY WITHERS

Trinity College | Cambridge
23 April 1926

My dear Withers,

I was just thinking of writing to you about Lewis's[1] death. He left Cambridge only about a fortnight or three weeks before, and seemed in his usual health, but for the last twelvemonth he had been aging, and his

---

[1] *Scaliger*, Asquith's Presidential Address to the Scottish Classical Association, delivered at Edinburgh, 20 Mar. 1926.

[2] Sir John Sandys, *A History of Classical Scholarship* (1903–8), 2. 202.

[3] 1813–84. Rector of Lincoln College, Oxford, 1861–84. In his review of Jacob Bernays' 1855 biography of Scaliger, which appeared in the *Quarterly Review*, 108 (1860), 34–81, and was reprinted in his *Essays* (1889), 132–95, Pattison states that Scaliger's Manilius 'was, in fact, but an introduction to a comprehensive chronological system which he brought out in 1583 in his De Emendatione' (*Essays*, 162). Scaliger's *De emendatione temporum* revolutionized received ideas about ancient chronology.

[4] As Plato required the philosopher to be: *The Republic*, 6. 486 (Jowett translation).

[5] 'An echo of Scaliger's remark on Pliny (quoted by Asquith): "Fere omnia tractavit: nil exacte" ['He dealt with nearly everything: nothing precisely']': Maas, 236 n. Plato thought that the philosopher who considered all time and all existence could not 'think much of human life'.

[1] W. J. Lewis.

articulation had grown very indistinct. At Godalming, where he was staying with his sister, he had an attack of what the doctors called false angina pectoris, but he had got better, and on the morning of the day when he died he wrote a letter; in the afternoon he went to his bedroom to sleep, and was found dead. The cause of death was given as a clot in the lungs. He was buried from Oriel, and our Vice-Master[2] went over to represent the College: the other Lewis[3] and Hicks were also there.

You do not give definite information about your own health, but I hope no news is good news. I expect to be away for the first half of June, and again for about a month from July 26; but outside those periods I know of nothing to keep me from your arms. I remember no spring so early as this, not even 1893.

With kind regards to Mrs Withers I am

Yours sincerely
A. E. Housman.

SCO MS. Maas, 236–7.

TO A. F. SCHOLFIELD

Trinity College
8 May 1926

Dear Scholfield,

Mattaire's[1] *Opera et fragmenta ueterum poetarum Latinorum*, 1713, though obsolete, is a book which a University Library ought to have, and I have sometimes wanted to consult it.

The ed. princeps of Manilius (Regiomontanus') is interesting to scholars as well as bibliophiles, for its merit and authorship, and Jenkinson,[2] when I was trying to buy a copy for myself, offered to buy one for the Library out of some fund which he said was available; but I did not feel justified in taking advantage of that, and the copy I was after sold for £60.

Yours sincerely
A. E. Housman.

TCC Add. MS c. 112[1]. Maas, 237.

[2] Reginald St John Parry.
[3] 'Thomas Crompton Lewis (1851–1929); Fellow of TCC, 1877; employed in the Indian Education Service, 1881–1906; thereafter lived in Cambridge and served on the Board of Indian Civil Service Studies': Maas, 237 n.

[1] For 'Maittaire's'.   [2] F. H. Jenkinson: see List of Recipients.

TO THE DIRECTOR, STUDENTS' ROOM, BRITISH MUSEUM

Trinity College | Cambridge
27 May 1926

Dear Sir,

I shall be obliged if you can renew the enclosed ticket.

Yours faithfully
A. E. Housman

BL Add. MS 45982 W, fo. 95. Envelope (fo. 96) addressed 'The Director | Students' Room | Department of MSS | British Museum | London W. C.'

TO WALTER ASHBURNER

Trinity College | Cambridge
1 June 1926

My dear Ashburner,

I am glad to hear there is a chance of your coming to England this year, and I hope I may see you. Next week I shall be nearer to you than I have been for a long time, as I shall be in Venice from the 7th to the 10th to see my gondolier, who is dying, or thinks so.[1] I don't know if I shall catch Horatio.[2]

Your industry is laudable, and I suppose it is high time that Malalas[3] was edited again. My note about the mandarins is not from any poetic source—I cannot now remember whether it was a traveller or a French encyclopedia—and any traces of metre must be my own native wood-notes wild.[4] Everybody who opens the book lights first upon that passage, and tells all his acquaintance.

---

[1] This was to be AEH's last visit to Venice, and the last time he saw his gondolier Andrea: see the letter to KES, 23 June 1926, and *MP* XLIV 21–2 (written 10–30 Apr. 1922): 'Andrea, fare you well; | Venice, farewell to thee'. Andrea died in 1930: AEH to KES, 11 Dec. 1930. Withers, 79: 'while he [Andrea] lived Housman wrote to him, and in turn received reports of his condition ... Housman told me when he died, and told me with considerable acerbity, how the relatives were pestering him to continue his gratuities, and copiously lying. The pleas were at first fawning, then suddenly passed to anger and vituperation. He too was angry, and I think very sore that a benefaction that had proved so useful to the recipient, so pleasant to himself to make, should end in mendacity and squabbling.'

[2] Horatio Brown: see List of Recipients.

[3] John Malalas (*c.*491–578), author of Syrian origin whose *Chronographia* is a compilation of history from the creation to his own times.

[4] Milton, *L'Allegro*, 134: 'his native wood-notes wild'. AEH's note on Lucan 8. 402 ends *Sinarum proceres accipimus quinas feminas simul inire, pene et ambarum manuum pedumque pollicibus* ('We are told that the Chinese mandarins had five women at a time, with their penis, their thumbs, and their big toes'). Evidently someone had observed that *Sinarum proceres* made the first half of a hexameter.

I was sorry to see the death of dear old Rotton.[5] I had seen nothing of him since I came here in 1911, but I heard from Godalming that he was not quite master of his household.

Guy le Strange[6] seems very well and lively.

I am yours sincerely

A. E. Housman.

NLS MS 20369, fos. 281–2. Ashburner/Bell (1976), 19.

TO D. S. MACCOLL

Trinity College | Cambridge

2 June 1926

My dear MacColl,

My name may be added to an appeal to the Prime Minister asking for an inquiry into the bridge question generally, including Charing Cross, before Waterloo Bridge is condemned.[1] My own admiration for Waterloo Bridge, as for other buildings of that age and style, is temperate, but I perceive that it is esteemed by competent judges.

Yours sincerely

A. E. Housman.

Glasgow University MS (MacColl Collection H386).

[5] Sir John Rotton, who died on 9 Apr. 1926 at the age of 88. He was a member of the Council of UCL (1869–1906) and Vice-president of the Senate (1878, 1882). He served as legal assistant to the Medical Department of the Local Government Board (1869–76), becoming its Legal Adviser (1883). He was knighted in 1899.

[6] 1854–1933, Orientalist. After his wife's death in 1907 he settled in Cambridge, becoming a member of Pembroke College. By 1912 he was almost totally blind. Publications include *Palestine under the Moslems* (1890), *Baghdad under the Abasssid Caliphate* (1900), and *The Lands of the Eastern Caliphate* (1905).

[1] Waterloo Bridge in London, designed by John Rennie, was opened on 6 June 1817 to commemorate the Duke of Wellington's victory in the second battle of Waterloo. In 1923 two of its piers settled alarmingly and a temporary bridge was built alongside. After a long controversy whether to restore or to reconstruct, the bridge was demolished in 1936 and a new bridge was built, 1937–42.

TO KATHARINE SYMONS

Trinity College | Cambridge
2 June 1926

My dear Kate,

I should write to tell you that I am going abroad on Saturday for a fortnight or three weeks: first on a short visit to Venice, where my poor gondolier[1] says he is dying and wants to see me again, and then to Paris.

Laurence was here a month ago and seemed well and thriving, as I hope are you and Edward.

Your affectionate brother
A. E. Housman.

TCC Add. MS c. 50[18]. Memoir, *150 (incomplete); Maas, 237.*

TO A. S. F. GOW

Trinity College
4 June 1926

Dear Gow,

I am very much taken aback, and my feelings are mixed; but, however deeply I may deplore the misdirection of so much industry, it is impossible not to be touched and pleased by the proof of so much kindness and friendliness, and I thank you for it.[1]

Yours sincerely
A. E. Housman.

TCC Add. MS c. 112[31]. *Gow, 55 (excerpt); Maas, 238.*

[1] See AEH to Ashburner, 1 June 1926, n. 1.

[1] Gow, vi: 'In the year 1925 Housman allowed me to collect from parcels in his rooms such offprints of his articles as were still available. They numbered nearly a hundred, and tempted me to compile a complete list. This list Housman himself revised, and the resulting typescript proved useful, so that in the following year, partly for that reason and partly as a compliment to Housman, three friends, Mr E. Harrison, Professor D. S. Robertson, and Mr A. F. Scholfield, joined me in printing a hundred copies of it.' A corrected, rearranged, revised, and updated list forms the second part of Gow's 1936 memoir of AEH.

TO A. F. SCHOLFIELD

Trinity College
5 June 1926

Dear Scholfield,

I take a double pleasure in the gift I received yesterday from you and Gow and others, because it evinces both friendly feelings and a scholarly interest in the infinitely little.

Yours
A. E. Housman.

TCC Add. MS c. 112². Maas, 238.

TO D. S. ROBERTSON

Trinity College
5 June 1926

Dear Robertson,

I am necessarily very grateful for what I received yesterday from you and your amiable associates, and no such words as περιεργία[1] or ματαιοπονία[2] shall escape from my pen.

Yours
A. E. Housman.

Private MS.

TO KATHARINE SYMONS

Trinity College | Cambridge
23 June 1926

My dear Kate,

I got back safe yesterday, after three days' beautiful weather in Venice and a very dull time in Paris till just the last. My gondolier was looking pretty well, as warmth suits him, but he is quite unable to row and gets out of breath if he goes up many stairs. He is being sent by the municipal authorities for another three months' treatment in hospital, as they still find bacilli in his blood, and I suppose he will go steadily down hill.[1] I was surprised to find what pleasure it gave me to be in Venice again. It was like coming home, when sounds and smells which one had forgotten

---

[1] Meddling in others' affairs.   [2] Labour in vain.
[1] See AEH to Ashburner, 1 June 1926, n. 1.

steal upon one's senses; and certainly there is no place like it in the world: everything there is better in reality than in memory. I first saw it on a romantic evening after sunset in 1900,[2] and I left it on a sunshiny morning, and I shall not go there again.

I enclose a notice about the Woodchester pavement,[3] which you may wish to see. I shall be there from July 31 to August 7.

I did not know of our grandfather's[4] christening feat. It must have been just when he was leaving Stroud for Woodchester, and I suppose he wanted to clear things up.

Your affectionate brother
A. E. Housman.

TCC Add. MS c. 50[19-21]. Envelope addressed 'Mrs Symons | 61 Prior Park Road | Bath'.
Memoir, 151 (incomplete); Maas, 238–9.

TO SYDNEY COCKERELL

Trinity College
24 June 1926

Dear Cockerell,

Many thanks for your gift of Bridges' handwriting book.[1] The most magnificent specimen, to my thinking, is Nairne's;[2] the ugliest, with nothing but legibility to commend or excuse it, 33.[3] When we do lose Bridges, it will be some small consolation that we shall hear no more of his swan-geese. I don't see that S. Butler had any title to inclusion except as brother-in-law.[4] \(really something less)./ On the other hand Elizabeth

---

[2] See AEH to Lucy Housman, 15 Oct. 1900.

[3] A spectacular Roman mosaic pavement of the hall of a villa, discovered in the churchyard. It was opened up in 1880, 1890, and 1926 (and subsequently), and consisted of a square of nearly 49 feet surrounded by a strip of red brick tesserae and bordered with a wide labyrinth fretted pattern. See AEH to KES, 14 Nov. 1926.

[4] The Revd John Williams (1779–1857), who became Rector of Woodchester in 1834.

[1] *English Handwriting.* Roger Fry and E. A. Lowe were responsible for the first collection of 34 facsimiles (1926), Bridges and Alfred J. Fairbank for a further collection of 31 (1927). There are copies in the National Art Library of the Victoria and Albert Museum, London.

[2] Alexander Nairne (1863–1936). Theologian; Canon of St George's Chapel, Windsor, 1921–36; Regius Professor of Divinity at Cambridge, 1922–32; author of *The Faith of the Old Testament* (1914). The handwriting sample is from an 1883 letter to Bridges.

[3] An extract from a letter written by Gerard M. Hopkins to Richard Watson Dixon in 1886.

[4] Samuel Butler (1835–1902). Bridges' elder brother George (1836–60) was married to Harriet Fanny Butler (1834–1918), Butler's sister.

Daryush[5] is a credit to both of her parents, and I hope she is now out of jail.[6]

I have not succeeded in finding the feline element in 13.[7]

> Yours sincerely
> A. E. Housman.

BMC MS.

TO F. W. HALL

> Trinity College | Cambridge
> 2 July 1926

My dear Hall,

I am very much complimented by the wish of the College to have a drawing of me, and I gratefully accept the proposal that I should sit to Mr Dodd.[1] I expect to be here from the 11th to the 24th of the month.

> I am yours sincerely
> A. E. Housman.

SJCO MS, Sparrow Collection.

TO DR PERCY WITHERS

> Trinity College | Cambridge
> 7 July 1926

My dear Withers,

I am very much grieved to hear that you are laid up, and I suffer on both sides of my nature, the altruistic and the egotistic. I hope it is not very serious and will not last long. My gondolier, who had summoned me to his death-bed, was quite revived by the summer weather: pray follow his example.

> Yours sincerely
> A. E. Housman.

SCO MS. Maas, 239.

---

[5] 1887–1977. Daughter of Robert Bridges. Her poems appeared in *Charitessi 1911* (1912), and in her own collections *Verses* (1930) and *Verses, Third Book* (1933). In 1923 she married Ali Akbar Daryush, a government official in Persia, where she lived till her return to England in 1927.

[6] Apparently a jocular reference to purdah (whereby women were excluded from public view).

[7] A letter written by Cockerell to Mrs Bridges in 1925.

[1] Francis Dodd (1874–1949), commissioned in 1926 by SJCO to make a portrait drawing of AEH. It is reproduced opposite the title-page of Gow. Dodd executed portraits of naval and military commanders (1914–18), which are now in the Imperial War Museum. He exhibited at the Royal Academy from 1923. ARA, 1927; RA, 1935.

TO S. C. ROBERTS

Trinity College
17 July 1926

Dear Roberts

(for members of the Family need not throw one another's titles in their teeth): if you were able to come to tea on Tuesday the 20th, that would suit me well.

Yours sincerely
A. E. Housman.

Photograph in Maas, after p. 202.

TO A. F. SCHOLFIELD

Trinity College
21 July 1926

Dear Scholfield,

It appears that the Library has a rule by which no more than 5 books can be had out for a person in statu pupillari. I do not know if this is ever widened, but, if so, it might properly be done for W. H. Semple, a research student in St John's College, who is studying Apollinaris Sidonius under my direction and finds that 5 books are not enough to work with and that the books he wants are not to be found elsewhere than in the Library. He is a graduate of Belfast, and has acted for three years as assistant to the Professors of Latin and of English there.

Yours sincerely
A. E. Housman.

TCC Add. MS c. 112³. Maas, 239.

TO A. F. SCHOLFIELD

Trinity College
21 July 1926

The name of the author is one I do not know, and I do not gather from the title that it has to do with antiquity in particular; but the subject is of interest and the price small, so that I should think it might be bought.[1]

A. E. Housman.

TCC Add. MS c. 112⁴.

[1] A note written on the MS, apparently in Scholfield's hand, refers to R. O. Frick, *Le Peuple et La Prévision du Temps* (Basel, 1926).

TO J. W. MACKAIL

coniux is rather commoner in inscriptions, but *coniunx* occurs earlier, and is rather commoner in the earliest MSS; Priscian and the other grammarians generally inculcate *coniunx*, though they mention the other.

A. E. H.

24 July 1926 Trin. Coll. Camb.

TCC MS R.1.92: p.c. addressed 'Dr J. W. Mackail | 6 Pembroke Gardens | Kensington | W. 8'.
Maas, 422.

TO AN UNKNOWN CORRESPONDENT

Trinity College | Cambridge
25 July 1926

Dear Sir,

I do not feel able to refuse your request, and I have copied and signed two poems. If I do not say that I hope this will do the good you expect, it is because I have one thing in common with Keats and am incapable of hope.[1]

Yours very truly
A. E. Housman.

Newcastle MS. G. B. A. Fletcher, Durham University Journal, 38 (1946), 93; Maas, 240.

TO A. S. F. GOW

Lower House | Tardebigge | Bromsgrove
[26 July–3 Aug. 1926]

Dear Gow,

I accede to the kind and flattering request of the Memorials Committee. I shall be back on the 21st and shall then be continuously at home. Mr Gleadowe[1] had better not write to me before, as for the last week of my absence I shall have no fixed address.

Yours sincerely
A. E. Housman.

TCC Add. MS a. 232³⁰⁽¹⁾. '[1926]' pencilled on MS. The date is narrowed down by P. G. Naiditch in HSJ 20 (1994), 40.

---

[1] Keats to Mrs Samuel Brawne, 24 Oct. 1820: 'if ever there was a person born without the faculty of hoping I am he.'

[1] Reginald [Morier York] Gleadowe (1888–1944), Slade Professor of Fine Art at Oxford, 1928–33, had been commissioned by TCC to do a portrait of AEH.

TO A. F. SCHOLFIELD

Thanks to you and the Syndicate for your action in the matter of W. H. Semple.

A. E. Housman.

21 Aug. 1926 Trin. Coll. Camb.

TCC Add. MS c. 112⁵: p.c. addressed 'The Librarian | University Library' and marked 'Local' by AEH.

TO F. W. HALL

Trinity College | Cambridge
21 Sept. 1926

My dear Hall,

Many thanks for the photographs. I much prefer Dodd[1] to Rothenstein, who never gets a likeness of anyone, being presumably too great an artist.

I enclose the list of Adversaria. Some years ago your Librarian, Stevenson[2] I think it was, asked me for copies of the Adversaria themselves. The offprints were then in packages on a top shelf, and I had not the courage to tackle them; but Gow has sorted them out, and I now have a set, not complete however, which I mean to send when I have found time to correct misprints and such things.

Yours sincerely
A. E. Housman.

SJCO MS, Sparrow Collection. Maas, 240.

TO DR PERCY WITHERS

Trinity College | Cambridge
21 Sept. 1926

My dear Withers,

This is very good and delightful news about your health, and apparently the consequence of shingles!

> Ye fearful saints, fresh courage take:
> The clouds ye so much dread
> Are big with mercy, and shall break
> In blessings on your head.[1]

---

[1] See AEH to Hall, 2 July 1926.

[2] William Henry Stevenson (1858–1924), Fellow and Librarian of SJCO, 1904–24.

[1] Verse 3 of William Cowper's hymn *God moves in a mysterious way.*

I hope Sussex and Kent will give the finishing touches. Do not miss Boxgrove,[2] four miles from Chichester, with its black marble.

I have seen some good ones too: Coventry for the first time, Southwell, Newark, and Tideswell. I have been spending a month in Gloucestershire and Worcestershire, winding up with a motor-tour through Derbyshire, which was new to me. Consequently I have had my full allowance of running about, and am now settled down to work in this quietest of Cambridge months; so that I shall put off availing myself of your kind invitation. The peaches in the bowling-green are ripe, and a good crop, as they generally are; and the younger fellows of the College, in spite of their aversion from port, stay after dinner to eat them in the Combination Room.

Now that Lewis is gone, I don't know whom to send you news of. I think that the Master of Magdalene,[3] though his home is Croughton and I believe he is there now, is not an acquaintance of yours, though quite a desirable one.

My kind regards to Mrs Withers.

Yours sincerely
A. E. Housman.

SCO MS. Withers, 12 (excerpt); Maas, 240–1.

TO MRS BLINKHORN

Trinity College | Cambridge
22 Sept. 1926

Dear Mrs Blinkhorn,
I am obliged and flattered by your letter, but I lecture only under compulsion, and for literary criticism I have neither talent nor inclination, so that I hope you will not mind my declining your kind invitation as I have declined others.

I am yours very truly
A. E. Housman.

BMC MS.

---

[2] Church. AEH and Withers shared an interest in church architecture: Withers, 84–93.
[3] A. B. Ramsay.

TO PROFESSOR EDUARD FRAENKEL

[Trinity College | Cambridge]

Eduardo Fraenkelo s.d. A. E. Housman.

accepi, uir doctissime, beneuole <scr[iptam]> missam censuram tuam nec minus beneuole scriptam. laudes nimias esse intellego, partim etiam falsas, nam quod in IX 766 extat scripsisse Lucanum nec dixi nec credo. reprehensionum, qui hominibus insitus est amor sui, ne unam quidem iustam esse agnosco, nisi quod recte interpungis IX 491; omninoque uos censores in eo errare soletis quod uobis me magis circumspecti uidemini, estis autem multo minus. occurrit exemplum in ipso limine positum; ego enim id, quod tu p. 501 refutandum sumis, non dixi, sed, quid dicerem, accurate definiui praemissis uerbis 'Of these manuscripts',[1] quos quinque numero inter se comparare, nulla ceterorum ratione habita, instituebam. item quae p. 504 de 'Housm. S XVIII' scripsisti non scripsisses[2] nisi paginae XVII oblitus esses. sed haec ne longius excurrant subsistam, si prius gratum donum pensare conatus ero admonitione. igitur cauendum est ne nunc odio liborum[3] MZ non minus peccetur quam antea amore; sunt enim nullis secundi. multum mali feci cum Manilii Gemblacensem interpolatum esse ostendi coram hominibus qui Charybdin uitare non possent nisi ita ut ad Scyllam[4] confugerent.   Oct. I an. 1926.

TCC MS, with Adv. c. 20. 25.

Adam Gitner has provided the following translation: 'A. E. Housman greets Eduard Fraenkel. I received, most learned colleague, the review you kindly sent and no less kindly wrote. I understand your praise to be excessive and indeed partly false, for what stands in 9. 766 I neither said nor believe Lucan wrote. Of your criticisms (as self-love is innate to men) I do not acknowledge even one as just, except that you rightly punctuate 9. 491. You critics are altogether in the habit of mistakenly supposing yourselves more prudent than I am, but you are much less so. An example occurs at the very beginning, for I did not say what you undertake on p. 501 to refute; what I said I carefully defined in the prefatory words 'Of these manuscripts', which manuscripts, five in number, I set out to collate, no account being taken of the others. Likewise what you wrote on

---

[1] AEH quotes the phrase from the introduction to his edn. of Lucan (1926), vii. Fraenkel's review of the Lucan appeared in *Gnomon*, 2. 9 (Sept. 1926), 497–532. It is reprinted in his *Kleine Beiträge Zur Klassischen Philologie* (1964), 2.

[2] For 'scripsisses'.   [3] For 'librorum'.

[4] In Greek myth, Scylla was a man-eating monster who lived in a cave in the straits of Messina between Sicily and Italy, with the whirlpool of Charybdis opposite. To be between Scylla and Charybdis is to be faced with two equally dangerous courses of action.

p. 504 about 'Housman S XVIII' you would not have written unless you had forgotten p. XVII. However, I shall cease lest the matter run out at length, if I first repay the nice gift with an admonishment. Accordingly, one must now beware of going wrong from the hatred of manuscripts MZ no less than previously from the love of them; they are inferior to none. I did a great harm when I showed that the Gemblancensis manuscript of Manilius had been interpolated in the presence of men who could not avoid Charybdis but by flying to Scylla.   October 1, 1926.'

TO PROFESSOR D'ARCY THOMPSON

Trinity College | Cambridge
7 Oct. 1926

My dear D'Arcy Thompson,

It is very kind of you to send me your forthcoming note on *Merops*,[1] as well as the article on *Ciris*, which naturally I read when it came out.[2] I do not think it likely that Seruius or Donatus, whichever one calls him, would have commented as he does on *apiastrae* if he had already written *apiarios*. Moreover as *barbaros* is both in Seruius and in 'Probus' it must be as old as 400 A. D. or thereabouts, and such a corruption, if it is one, is not likely to be so old. I do not see why the Italian rustics should not have called these birds *barbari*, savages, Huns, for devouring the industrious, chaste, and lucrative bee.

Yours sincerely
A. E. Housman.

St Andrews MS 23594.

---

[1] 'Merops Aliaeque Volucres', *CQ* 20. 3/4 (July–Oct. 1926), 191–2.
[2] In *CQ* 19. 3/4 (July–Oct. 1925), 155–8.

TO F. W. HALL

Trinity College | Cambridge
12 Oct. 1926

Dear Hall,

Very many thanks for the new photograph,[1] which is even better than the old.

We have just elected two Fellows, a classic[2] and a mathematician,[3] as in the good old days.

Yours sincerely
A. E. Housman.

Texas MS. Maas, 241.

TO LILLY FRAZER

Trinity College | Cambridge
12 Oct. 1926

Dear Lady Frazer,

Many thanks for your kind effort on behalf of my proper feeding.[1] You look very benign in the picture, and I hope the interior corresponds, and that you and Sir James are well.

Yours sincerely
A. E. Housman.

TCC MS Frazer 18⁹².

---

[1] Of the portrait by Dodd.

[2] R[obert] M[antle] Rattenbury (1901–70). Admitted to TCC as Entrance Exhibitioner, 1920; awarded first class in each part of Classical Tripos, 1921, 1923; BA, 1923; Lecturer in Classics at Cambridge, 1932–52.

[3] L[lewellyn] H[illeth] Thomas. (1903–92). Admitted to TCC as Entrance Scholar, 1921; Senior Scholar, 1922; awarded first class in each part of Mathematical Tripos, 1922, 1924; Smith's Prizeman, 1926; Ph.D., 1927.

[1] At the Frazers' house in Queen Anne's Mansions, St James' Park, London, S. W. 1 (BL Add. MS 55142, fo. 70).

TO S. C. ROBERTS

Trinity College | Cambridge
14 Oct. 1926

Dear Roberts,

A report of mine, some twenty years ago, decided the Syndics[1] not to accept a treatise of Richmond's[2] on the pagination of the archetype of Catullus' MSS;[3] and, as A. W. Ward,[4] who was his grandmother or some such relation, had gone and told him that I was the referee, he knew to whom he was indebted. He bore me no ill will, and has an almost embarrassing respect for me; and I am not willing to risk the chance of doing him another ill turn. He is an active and competent chaser and collator of MSS, but I seldom agree with his criticism or interpretation. That should not count against him, as I should have to say the same of several scholars whose works are printed by University Presses, and they would naturally say the same of me.

If it is not impertinent, I suggest that H. E. Butler might be asked for his opinion. I daresay the Syndics, or some of them, know enough about the passions which seethe in the world of classical scholarship to understand that there is one person to whom the work should not be submitted.[5]

I asked the Syndics through their Secretary that my former report, which was very elaborate, might be returned to me, if that were legitimate: as it did not come, I suppose it was not.

Yours sincerely
A. E. Housman.

Text based on that in Maas, 241–2, which was based on a MS in private hands that is now missing.

[1] Since 1698, a committee deputed to make publishing decisions at Cambridge University Press.

[2] O. L. Richmond: see List of Recipients.

[3] The treatise on Catullus remained unpublished. Cambridge University Press published his edn. of Propertius in 1928.

[4] Adolphus William Ward (1837–1924), Master of Peterhouse, Cambridge, 1900–24; editor-in-chief of *The Cambridge Modern History*, 1901–12, and co-editor, with Alfred Rayney Waller, of *The Cambridge History of English Literature*, 1907–16; President of the British Academy, 1911–13; knighted, 1913. Ward was chairman of the Syndics, 1905–19.

[5] Identified by Maas, 242 n., as J. S. Phillimore. See List of Recipients.

TO A. C. PEARSON

Trinity College
14 Oct. 1926

Dear Pearson,

Is it good Greek to say τοῖν δυοῖν Κάστωρ μὲν ἱππεὺς ἦν, Πολυδεύκης δὲ πύκτης, or τῶν Ἀθηναίων Θεμιστοκλῆς ... Περικλῆς ... Ἀλκιβιάδης? The corresponding genitive, without *alter ... alter* or the like, is good Latin, though apparently not Ciceronian.

Hunt[1] has just sent me some new Callimachus from the next Oxyrhynchus volume,[2] and I am making a manful pretence of knowing the language; but you see I require your assistance.

Yours sincerely
A. E. Housman.

KCC MS Misc. 34/31. Maas, 422.

TO A. C. PEARSON

Trinity College
15 Oct. 1926

Dear Pearson,

The particular case is this. Callimachus, descanting on his favourite theme that small things are often better than great ones, has a couplet which I have filled up thus: [τοῖν δὲ] δ[υ]οῖν, Μίμνερμοσ ὅτι γλυκὺσ ἄ[μμε τὸ μεῖον] [βιβλίον] ἡ μεγάλη δ᾽οὐκ ἐδίδαξε γύνη, 'we have learnt the sweetness of Mimnermus from the smaller of his two books, not from the portly Nanno':[1] that he did write two is stated by Porphyrion at Hor. epist. II 2 101. Now in an ill-written and ill-preserved scholium there are traces of the name of the other book, and it may turn out to be μέλισσαι. It therefore occurs to me that he may have written, more smartly, ἄ[μμε τὸ μικρὸν θηρίον] (see Theocr. XIX 5 sq, τυτθὸν θηρίον ἐντὶ μέλισσα), and, though I feel inside me that the genitive is right enough, I have no <good> \quite/ parallel passage.

---

[1] A. S. Hunt (1871–1934), Fellow of Queen's College, Oxford, and Professor of Papyrology, 1913–34.

[2] Part XVII of *The Oxyrhynchus Papyri* (1927), which contained a fragment from the prologue to the *Aetia*.

[1] Hunt chose to leave the missing words blank, though he thanks AEH in his preface for 'several illuminating suggestions'.

Thanks for your letter. The number of good Greek scholars whom I have deceived into thinking that I know Greek is mounting up, and I add your scalp to Platt's and Headlam's.[2]

Yours sincerely
A. E. Housman.

KCC MS Misc. 34/31. Maas, 422–3. The square brackets in the text are AEH's.

TO S. C. ROBERTS

Trinity College
18 Oct. 1926

Dear Roberts,

I return the eight papers by Platt, in which I have made a few small corrections. The Prelection[1] you will probably soon receive from Harrison[2] or Parry.[3]

Yours sincerely
A. E. Housman.

CUL Add. MS 7735³.

TO F. W. HALL

Trinity College | Cambridge
20 Oct. 1926

Dear Hall,

I still have by me the famous bone of contention.[1] When the Board of Management offered to have it inserted, I declined, because I thought it would be humiliating to Arnold; but that obstacle no longer exists. Its length, 20 foolscap pages of my handwriting, may be greater than what you are in want of.

Yours sincerely
A. E. Housman.

Lilly MSS 1. 1. 4. Maas, 242.

[2] See AEH to Postgate, 22 Feb. 1908, and n. 1.

[1] Public lecture delivered in 1921 by Platt as a candidate for the Regius Professorship of Greek at Cambridge.

[2] Ernest Harrison.   [3] Reginald St John Parry.

[1] See AEH to Hall, 15 Jan. 1923, and note.

TO GRANT RICHARDS

Trinity College | Cambridge
21 Oct. 1926

My dear Richards,

I think I ought to be included among your creditors.[1] It is all very well to say that I shall not lose the £750 if you can help it, but it may easily turn out that you can't help it.

I am glad to hear of Geoffrey's[2] success.

Yours sincerely
A. E. Housman

BMC MS.

TO GRANT RICHARDS

Trinity College | Cambridge
21 Oct. 1926

My dear Richards,

Do what you like about the "Curwen Editions" and *When I was one-and-twenty*, provided that I am not required to sign an agreement. These musical people are more plague than profit.[1]

Yours sincerely
A. E. Housman.

PM MS. LC-GR t.s. Richards, 216 (nearly complete).

TO GRANT RICHARDS

Trinity College | Cambridge
21 Oct. 1926

My dear Richards,

I do not want to take the books away from your firm.[1] The *vis inertiae*,[2] no longer regarded as a true cause in the physical world, governs me all the same.

[1] Richards had gone bankrupt again. Though AEH was owed £1014. 11. 8 for sales and royalties on *LP* and the edns. of Juvenal and Manilius, and he took legal action to protect his interests, there is no evidence of personal animus towards Richards for failure to pay unpaid royalties: J. D. Tunnicliffe and M. Buncombe, 'A. E. Housman and the Failure of Grant Richards Limited in 1926', *HSJ* 11 (1985), 101–6; Naiditch (2005), 27–8. Tunnicliffe and Buncombe, 102, point out that AEH's annual stipend as Professor of Latin was £1,000 at the time.

[2] The Richards's son.

[1] This concerns 'a request for permission to make a gramophone record': Richards, 216.

[1] According to Richards, 216, AEH is 'writing in the expectation that I was on the verge of new financial difficulties'.

[2] Force of inertia.

I expected something of this sort, because it was hinted by a publisher who wrote to me a few weeks ago asking for *A Shropshire Lad*.

Yours sincerely
A. E. Housman.

PM MS. LC-GR t.s. Richards, 216; Maas, 242 (both incomplete).

TO F. W. HALL

Trinity College | Cambridge
24 Oct. 1926

Dear Hall,

I enclose the MS. I am sorry you are quitting the *C. Q.*, but I should think you must now be very tired.[1]

Yours sincerely
A. E. Housman.

Lilly MSS 1. 1.

TO GRANT RICHARDS

Trinity College | Cambridge
28 Oct. 1926

Leave out.

A. E. Housman.

Lilly MSS 2. 1: p.c. addressed 'Grant Richards Esq. | 8 St Martin's Street | Leicester Square | W. C. 2.'

TO AN UNKNOWN CORRESPONDENT

Trinity College | Cambridge
28 Oct. 1926

Dear Sir,

If you like to send me the first edition of *Last Poems* I will write my name in it; but I warn you that I shall also insert the two missing stops on page 52 and thereby, I imagine, destroy its value for bibliophiles.

I am yours faithfully
A. E. Housman.

BMC MS. Note on MS indicates its removal from a copy of LP *(1922) bearing AEH's signature on the half-title and his corrections on p. 52.*

---

[1] Hall had been co-editor of *CQ* since 1911, and stayed on till 1930.

TO S. C. ROBERTS

Trinity College
29 Oct. 1926

Dear Roberts,

Your order for Platt's *Essays* is logical in itself, but in some cases it visibly conflicts with the order in which they were composed. In particular, *FitzGerald*, which is the earliest of all, ought not to come after *Cervantes* nor near *Cervantes*, because in *FitzGerald* he speaks of himself as knowing hardly any Spanish, whereas when he wrote *Cervantes* he knew it quite well.

Plato on the Immortality of the Soul (a title which will have to be altered) rightly stands last, and I should like to put first *Arts and Science among the Ancients*, which is the most carefully written and was delivered before a large public; then between them the Literary Society essays, whose chronology I roughly know, in an order nearly that of their date, which can best be managed by sandwiching ancient and modern subjects. I give the list over the page.

Yours sincerely
A. E. Housman.

1. Arts & Science among the Ancients.
2. FitzGerald.
3. Lucian.
4. La Rochefoucauld.
5. Aristophanes.
6. Cervantes.
7. Julian.
8. Poetry and Science.
9. Plato on the Immortality of the Soul.[1]

CUL Add. MS 7735⁴. Maas, 243.

---

[1] In a letter to Roberts of 1 Mar. 1927, AEH requested that 3 and 5 be reversed. With this exception, the order proposed here was adopted.

TO EDWIN MARKHAM

Trinity College | Cambridge | England
31 Oct. 1926

Dear Mr Markham,

The poems which you wish to include in your anthology[1] seem to be from *A Shropshire Lad*, which is not copyright in the United States of America, so that I have no right either to withhold my consent or to give it.

I am yours sincerely
A. E. Housman.

Kent State University MS.

TO GRANT RICHARDS

Trinity College | Cambridge
4 Nov. 1926

My dear Richards,

Heinemann write to me saying that they are thinking of taking over your assets and asking particularly for *A Shropshire Lad*. Before I answer them I should like to have anything you may wish to say on the subject.

Yours sincerely
A. E. Housman.

PM MS. LC-GR t.s. Richards, 216 (nearly complete).

TO GRANT RICHARDS

Trinity College | Cambridge
6 Nov. 1926

My dear Richards,

I do not understand this, for I did not seek to withdraw any permission. They can make their record if they like: all I want is not to have to write letters.

Yours sincerely
A. E. Housman.

PM MS. LC-GR t.s.

[1] *The Book of Poetry, collected from the whole field of British and American Poetry*, ed. Edwin Markham, 7 (1926) included seven poems from *ASL*, three from *LP*, and a chorus from *Fragment of a Greek Tragedy*.

TO MESSRS GRANT RICHARDS LTD

[Trinity College | Cambridge
6 Nov. 1926]

ˣYes, it is.[1] A. E. H. Especially as he says *re* when he means *about*.[2]

PM MS. LC-GR t.s. Note written at the foot of a letter to AEH from Thomas Keighley of Ashton-under-Lyne. Richards, 216.

TO WALTER ASHBURNER

K Whewell's Court | Trinity College
12 Nov. 1926

My dear Ashburner,

I am rejoiced to hear from le Strange that you will dine with me on Sunday. You will be in good time if you come to my rooms at 7. 50. On issuing from your hotel, turn to the right and follow the main street for rather more than half a mile, till you have passed Sidney and have Jesus Lane on your right and the tower which I inhabit on your left.

1896 port, which I gather you do not despise, will be offered to you, and the sherry and Madeira are not beneath notice.

Yours sincerely
A. E. Housman.

NLS MS 20369, fos. 283 – 4. Ashburner / Bell (1976), 20.

TO KATHARINE SYMONS

Trinity College | Cambridge
14 Nov. 1926

My dear Kate,

I knew it was a long time since I had written to you, but did not realise how long, and fancied that I wrote when I came back here at the end of August. The week at Woodchester was fine: the pavement,[1] which I had seen the last time it was opened, 35 years ago, attracted great numbers and was kept open for a second week. I was dragged in to make speeches

---

[1] The answer to Keighley's question 'Is this decision irrevocable?' Permission had been refused to print the words of Vaughan Williams's *On Wenlock Edge* song cycle in the programme of a concert at Stockport.

[2] Keighley : 'In reply to my enquiry re printing the words in the concert programme … ' He had used the same expression in a previous letter to Richards.

[1] See AEH to KES, 23 June 1926, and note.

explaining it, as there were few local orators to do so, and the visitors were very ignorant and very grateful. I had pleasant motor journeys from Bromsgrove and back by different routes. Basil was not well enough to come with me. The two stays at Tardebigge were quiet and agreeable. Then I spent the inside of a week motoring about Derbyshire, which was new to me, and in parts very picturesque indeed, especially Dove-dale, of which I walked the best ten miles. September I passed here in pleasant and peaceful work.

Your house looks nice and I am glad you are so content with it. Laurence was here in the summer, to arrange for performing his plays here this term; but as I have heard no more about it I suppose it fell through. We have good store of coal in the college, which we eke out with wood, and I am not stinted.

I am glad your sons are going on well, and I hope your husband is. Send the *Shropshire Lad* for signature by all means: I am used to it.

Your affectionate brother
A. E. Housman.

TCC Add. MS c. 50²²⁻³. Envelope addressed 'Mrs Symons | 61 Prior Park Road | Bath'. T.s. extract, Lilly MSS 3. 1. 10. Maas, 243–4.

TO GRANT RICHARDS

Trinity College | Cambridge
14 Nov. 1926

My dear Richards,

I have been told that the scheme for the carrying on of your business by the creditors has fallen through,[1] and therefore I suppose I shall have to close with one of the offers made by publishers for *A Shropshire Lad* and *Last Poems*.

Yours sincerely
A. E. Housman.

PM MS. LC-GR t.s. Richards, 216 (excerpt).

---

[1] This proved not to be the case, and GR told AEH so in a letter of 15 Nov. 1926 (PM t.s.).

TO H. E. BUTLER

Trinity College | Cambridge
21 Nov. 1926

Dear Butler,

The University Press here is bringing out a collection of Platt's papers, and I have undertaken to write a preface; and, for purposes of plagiarism, I want to get hold of your obituary in the *Times*[1] and Chambers' in the *College Magazine*.[2] If you have them and would lend them to me, I would return them faithfully. I feel sure that I really have them myself, but if so I cannot lay my hands on them. If you have not the *Times* notice, could you give me the date? That wretched publication *Whitaker's Almanac*[3] does not.

Yours sincerely
A. E. Housman.

SJCO MS 305. Maas, 244.

TO H. E. BUTLER

Trinity College | Cambridge
24 Nov. 1926

Dear Butler,

Many thanks for the obituary notice: as you call it a copy I infer that I may keep it, and will do so unless you reclaim it.

Do by all means send me the sonnets etc. which you mention.

Yours sincerely
A. E. Housman.

SJCO MS 305.

---

[1] On 17 Mar. 1925, 17.

[2] R. W. Chambers's note on Platt appeared in *The University College Magazine*, 3. 5 (June 1925), 258–60. In the biographical preface to *Nine Essays* by Arthur Platt (1927), AEH quoted Chambers's account of the giraffe at London Zoo rubbing its head on Platt's bald head, and adapted a passage from Lawrence Solomon's memoir of Platt in the *University College Magazine* 3. 6 (June 1925), 260, as Naiditch (1995), 128, shows.

[3] For '*Almanack*'.

TO GRANT RICHARDS

Trinity College | Cambridge
30 Nov. 1926

My dear Richards,

Thanks for your letter; but I don't think it has anything to do with Messrs Few & Wild,[1] or any bearing on my presentation of my claims against the Company, which I made at the request of Sir Maxwell Hicks.[2]

Yours sincerely
A. E. Housman.

PM MS. LC-GR t.s.

TO MESSRS GEORGE ALLEN & UNWIN LTD

Trinity College | Cambridge
8 Dec. 1926

Dear Sirs,

I am obliged and flattered by your letter of the 6th;[1] but one of the publishers who have written to me about the future of my two books is a young man personally known to friends of mine, and whom I should like to help; and my inclination is to transfer them to him.

I am yours faithfully
A. E. Housman.

Messrs George Allen & Unwin Ld.

Reading MS (Allen & Unwin Archive 14/3)

TO S. C. ROBERTS

Trinity College
12 December 1926

Dear Roberts,

I enclose the preface I promised for Platt's book, and also, what is more valuable, a list which I have compiled of his writings.

---

[1] J. E. Few and A. H. Wild, Cambridge solicitors, who had represented AEH's interests by writing on 26 Sept. to Hicks pointing out that AEH was owed £1014. 11. 8 up to 6 Sept. 1926 and another £5. 12. 3 up to 31 Oct.: LC-GR1 MS. Hicks confirmed the figures, and said he had paid the £5. 12. 3 on 8 November: J. D. Tunnicliffe and M. Buncombe, 'A. E. Housman and the Failure of Grant Richards Limited in 1926': *HSJ* 11 (1985), 103. AEH was never paid the much larger sum.

[2] Receiver and Manager in respect of Richards's business.

[1] Expressing a desire to take over publication of *ASL* and *LP*, and offering advance payment for the privilege.

Is there to be a portrait? It would be a great addition, and there is an excellent photograph.[1]

I feel sure that it will be necessary for me to see the proofs of Platt's essays.

Yours sincerely
A. E. Housman.

CUL Add. MS 7735⁵. Maas, 244–5.

TO S. C. ROBERTS

Trinity College
14 Dec. 1926

Dear Roberts,

I have Platt's photograph, but in a large size: if that makes no difference to the reproducer I can send it. I enclose what appeared in the *University College Magazine.*[1]

Yours sincerely
A. E. Housman.

CUL Add. MS 7735⁶.

TO GRANT RICHARDS

Trinity College | Cambridge
17 Dec. 1926

My dear Richards,

I suppose the new arrangement[1] is satisfactory to you, and if so I am glad of it; and for my own part it is a relief not to have the bother of making new arrangements. But when the arrangements are complete I am going to exact royalties on *A Shropshire Lad* for the future as well as on the other book.

Yours sincerely
A. E. Housman.

PM MS. LC-GR t.s. Richards, 217; Maas, 245.

---

[1] The volume included a photograph.

[1] See AEH to Butler, 21 Nov. 1926, n. 2.

[1] For the carrying on of Richards's business.

TO SIR FREDERICK MACMILLAN

Trinity College | Cambridge
27 Dec. 1926

Dear Sir Frederick Macmillan,

I am much obliged by your amiable letter.[1] The Lucan however was published last January, and is now nearly sold out, which testifies to such efficiency in the publisher as even you could hardly surpass.

I am yours sincerely
A. E. Housman.

BL Add. MS. 55275, fos. 218–19. T.s copy, Lilly MSS 3. 1. 10. Letters to Macmillan, *ed. Simon Nowell-Smith (1967), 243; Maas, 245.*

TO S. C. ROBERTS

Trinity College
31 Dec. 1926

Dear Roberts,

Thanks for the return of the photograph. I think there should be nothing under the portrait but 'Arthur Platt'.[1]

Yours sincerely
A. E. Housman.

CUL Add. MS 7735[7].

TO DR PERCY WITHERS

My new edition of Lucan sells just twice as fast as *A Shropshire Lad* did.

Trinity College | Cambridge
31 Dec. 1926

My dear Withers,

I am very glad to have such good news of your health, though I wish the good were nearer to best than it is; and I shall look forward to seeing you here when you pass through to Norfolk in the spring. My own health

---

[1] Following AEH's proposal that Macmillan act as publisher of his edn. of Lucan (AEH to Messrs Macmillan and Company, 16 Nov. 1924), and Macmillan's refusal three days later, Sir Frederick Macmillan wrote to AEH on 22 Dec. 1926 offering to publish the edn. after all: 'I remember thinking at the time that this was possibly a case in which it would be wise to relax our rule, but I expect that what decided us not to do so was a phrase in your letter describing us as "haughty"—an adjective that seemed then, as it still does, singularly inappropriate … It may be that it is too late, but this letter will at all events convince you that the quality of humility has not been omitted from our composition' (*Letters to Macmillan*, 243).

[1] The words (in capitals) were printed under the photograph of Platt in *Nine Essays*.

is good, but for the excess in eating and drinking which attends this sacred season. To-night however I am going to take my medicine, which will consist in 3 dozen oysters and as many more as I can get, with stout in proportion; after which (as it says in the advertisements of Mrs Winslow's soothing syrup) the little darling wakes up as bright as a button.[1]

Now that Lewis is gone, I don't know if there is any one in Cambridge of whom I ought to send you news. Mr de Navarro, as I daresay you know, has been having neurasthenia, for which I prescribed Bynogen,[2] and his son bought him a bottle, with what result I do not know.

My kind regards to Mrs Withers, and good wishes for the New Year to her and you and all your household.

Yours sincerely
A. E. Housman.

SCO MS. Withers, 76 (excerpt).

[1] See AEH to Withers, 31 Dec. 1924.
[2] Nerve food for convalescents and invalids.